THE LETTERS OF
ERNEST HEMINGWAY
VOLUME 1
1907–1922

With the first publication, in this edition, of all the surviving letters of Ernest Hemingway (1899–1961), readers will for the first time be able to follow the thoughts, ideas, and actions of one of the great literary figures of the twentieth century in his own words. This first volume encompasses his youth, his experience in World War I, and his arrival in Paris. The letters reveal a more complex person than Hemingway's tough-guy public persona would suggest: devoted son, affectionate brother, infatuated lover, adoring husband, spirited friend, and disciplined writer. Unguarded and never intended for publication, the letters record experiences that inspired his art, afford insight into his creative process, and express his candid assessments of his own work and that of his contemporaries. The letters present immediate accounts of events and relationships that profoundly shaped his life and work. A detailed introduction, notes, chronology, illustrations, and index are included.

Hear some of the gulls

Walloon Lake, Mich.

"WINDEMERE"

Dear papa
today I mama and the rest of us took a walk.
We walked to the school House.
Marcelline ran on ahead.
Wile we stopt at Clouses.
I in a lille wile she came back.
She soid that in the Wood Shed of the
School house there was a porcupine.
So we went up there and looked in the door,
the porcupine was asleep.
I went in and gave I a wack with the axx.
Then I caue I anthor and another.
Then I crald in the Wood.
Wean to Mr Cloas and he got his gan and
Shot it,

Ernest Hemingway to Clarence Hemingway, postmarked 23 July [1909] from Walloon Lake, Michigan. Ernest Hemingway Collection, John F. Kennedy Presidential Library.

THE LETTERS OF
ERNEST HEMINGWAY

VOLUME 1
1907–1922

EDITED BY

Sandra Spanier

and

Robert W. Trogdon

VOLUME ASSOCIATE EDITORS

Albert J. DeFazio III

Miriam B. Mandel

Kenneth B. Panda

VOLUME ADVISORY EDITOR

J. Gerald Kennedy

CAMBRIDGE
UNIVERSITY PRESS

CAMBRIDGE UNIVERSITY PRESS
Cambridge, New York, Melbourne, Madrid, Cape Town,
Singapore, São Paulo, Delhi, Tokyo, Mexico City

Cambridge University Press
The Edinburgh Building, Cambridge CB2 8RU, UK

Published in the United States of America by Cambridge University Press, New York

www.cambridge.org
Information on this title: www.cambridge.org/9780521897334

First published 2011

Printed in the United States of America

A catalogue record for this publication is available from the British Library

ISBN 978-0-521-89733-4 Hardback

CONTENTS

PLATES

MAPS

GENERAL EDITOR'S INTRODUCTION TO THE EDITION

Sandra Spanier

On 1 July 1925, Ernest Hemingway wrote exuberantly to his friend F. Scott Fitzgerald from the Spanish mountain village of Burguete: "We are going in to Pamplona tomorrow. Been trout fishing here. How are you? And how is Zelda?" "God it has been wonderful country," he exclaimed, then remembered his audience: "But you hate country. All right omit description of country." Hemingway wondered what would be Scott's idea of heaven and declared, "To me heaven would be a big bull ring with me holding two barrera seats and a trout stream outside that no one else was allowed to fish in and two lovely houses in the town; one where I would have my wife and children and be monogamous and love them truly and well and the other where I would have my nine beautiful mistresses on 9 different floors." He urged Fitzgerald to write to him at the Hotel Quintana in Pamplona: "Or dont you like to write letters. I do because it's such a swell way to keep from working and yet feel you've done something."[1]

Hemingway always distinguished between letter writing and writing that counts, but this letter only goes to show the enormous interest and vitality of his correspondence. That next week in Pamplona, with his wife Hadley and a coterie of fellow expatriate friends from Paris, he plunged into the noisy nonstop public celebration of the annual fiesta of San Fermín and privately faced the real-life conflict between rectitude and desire that he had described to Fitzgerald in jest. By the end of the month, he was already well into the first draft of what would become *The Sun Also Rises*, the 1926 novel that would launch his career and forever transform a provincial Spanish town into an international literary mecca. Although he was a confident and ambitious writer from the start, even the young Hemingway could not have dreamed that in the ensuing decades and into the next century, pilgrims by the tens of thousands would descend upon Pamplona the second week of each July to revel in the streets, drink red wine from goatskin *botas*, and run with the bulls—drawn largely by the force of his imagination.

In a 1950 letter to Fitzgerald's biographer, Hemingway recalled Ford Madox Ford's advice that "a man should always write a letter thinking of how it would read to posterity." He remarked, "This made such a bad impression on me that I burned every letter in the flat includeing Ford's." He continued:

> Should you save the hulls a .50 cal shucks out for posterity? Save them. o.k. But they should be written or fired not for posterity but for the day and the hour and posterity will always look after herself. . . . I write letters because it is fun to get letters back. But not for posterity. What the hell is posterity anyway? It sounds as though it meant you were on your ass.[2]

Unguarded and never intended for publication, Hemingway's letters constitute his autobiography in the continuous present tense. They enrich our understanding of his creative processes, offer insider insights into the twentieth-century literary scene, and document the making and marketing of an American icon. They track his moods and movements, capture his emotions in the heat of the moment, and reveal a personality far more complex and nuanced than many might expect from his sometimes one-dimensional public persona. At times he would vent his anger in a letter and then not send it—usually wisely. He could be tender, boorish, vulnerable, critical, and self-critical, and he could be wickedly funny. However casually or hastily fired off, each letter records with immediate intensity the experiences and impressions of the day and hour: much of it raw material later to be transformed, by the alchemy that Hemingway the artist brought to bear, into some of the most enduring works of literature in the English language.

Few writers' lives have been as closely examined as Hemingway's, both as he lived it and in the decades after his death. Since the publication in 1969 of Carlos Baker's authorized biography, *Ernest Hemingway: A Life Story*, at least six additional biographies have appeared, Michael S. Reynolds's richly textured study running to five volumes. Counting memoirs by family members and friends, pictorial volumes, collections of his conversations and conversations about him, and books focusing on his relationships with particular people or places, the volumes devoted to Hemingway's life number in the dozens. As Reynolds observed, "A biographer connects up the dots to draw the picture just as we did as children. First, of course, he must find the dots of data, leaving as little space between them as possible."[3] The unpublished letters hold untold thousands of new details to enhance the picture. The author's son Patrick Hemingway has said in support of the present edition, "Ernest Hemingway was a prodigious letter writer. His correspondence has been the principal source for his biographers, none of whom to date have succeeded in presenting the man as vividly as he does himself in his letters."[4]

The letters represent the last great unexplored frontier of Hemingway studies. And because Hemingway was always, as Edmund Wilson pointed out as early as the 1930s, a "gauge of morale," a barometer of his times, interest in his letters is more than biographical.[5] Hemingway's first widely read book—a groundbreaking modernist experiment in English prose published in Paris in 1924 and expanded into his first trade collection of short fiction in 1925—was famously titled *In Our Time*. His work perennially reflected the temper of his times. In *The Sun Also Rises* he captured the postwar malaise of the so-called "Lost Generation"; in *A Farewell to Arms* (1929), the World War I experiences that precipitated that mood of disillusionment and dislocation; in *To Have and Have Not* (1937), the inequities and anxieties of the Great Depression; in *For Whom the Bell Tolls* (1940), the complicated tragedy of the Spanish Civil War; and in *The Old Man and the Sea* (1952), the dignity and grace of a Cuban fisherman battling brute natural forces while dreaming of Joe DiMaggio. Hemingway was always of the moment, and in both substance and style, his work stands as a chronicle of the twentieth century.

Among modern writers the breadth of Hemingway's appeal is remarkable, if not unique, transcending political divisions and national borders. At a low point of relations between the United States and Cuba, a month after his suicide and just four months after the Bay of Pigs invasion, it was with the personal cooperation of both Presidents John F. Kennedy and Fidel Castro that Hemingway's widow, Mary, traveled to Cuba in August 1961 and removed a small boatload of papers and belongings from their Havana bank vault and from Finca Vigía, Hemingway's home from 1939 until shortly before his death. Those papers—letters, notes, manuscripts, fragments, galley proofs, and other documents—now form the core of the Ernest Hemingway Collection at the John F. Kennedy Presidential Library in Boston, the world's largest Hemingway archive. The Finca itself, where Hemingway spent half of his writing life and where he received the international press when awarded the 1954 Nobel Prize for Literature, is now the Museo Hemingway, dedicated in 1962 as a national museum of Cuba. Four decades later, Hemingway again served as a bridge between the estranged nations, as an unprecedented cooperative agreement between the Cuban National Council of Cultural Patrimony and the U.S.–based Social Science Research Council provided for the conservation and preservation of the thousands of pages of his papers remaining at Finca Vigía, the originals to stay in the collection of the Museo, with copies to be deposited at the Kennedy Library. In November 2002, Fidel Castro appeared at the Finca to add his signature to the agreement in a poolside ceremony witnessed by a crush of journalists and reported in the international news media. The 2009 opening of the Finca papers to researchers, both by the Museo Hemingway and by the Kennedy Library, once more attracted international attention.

A roster of Hemingway's correspondents reads like a twentieth-century *Who's Who*: Ezra Pound, Gertrude Stein, Sherwood Anderson, F. Scott Fitzgerald, Gerald and Sara Murphy, John Dos Passos, Archibald MacLeish, Janet Flanner, Charles

Scribner (three generations of them), Maxwell Perkins, Pablo Picasso, Ingrid Bergman, Gary Cooper, and Marlene Dietrich, to name a few of the luminaries. He also corresponded copiously with family members, including his parents and grandparents, five siblings, four wives, three sons, and numerous in-laws, and with friends scattered across continents. Even after attaining global celebrity, he responded conscientiously and generously to students and strangers who wrote to express their admiration, ask questions, and seek advice or autographs.

On his desk in the library at Finca Vigía sits a rubber stamp that reads, "I never write letters. Ernest Hemingway." Perhaps he had it made to ease the burden of correspondence, perhaps someone gave it to him as a joke, but if he ever actually used the stamp in place of writing a letter, the evidence has yet to be found. As Carlos Baker put it, "All his life after adolescence Hemingway was a confirmed, habitual, and even compulsive correspondent for whom communication was a constant necessity."[6]

Letter writing was a habit that Hemingway's parents fostered in their children from an early age. What might be considered the earliest surviving "Hemingway letter," dated 26 December 1903 and addressed to "My own dear Ma Ma," enumerates the Christmas gifts he received from members of the family and from Santa Claus. Written and signed "Your son Ernest" in his father's hand, it bears the scribbles of the three-and-a-half year old "author."[7] When the teenage Ernest went away—whether to canoe the Illinois River with a high school friend in April 1917, or to tend the family farm in northern Michigan during the summer of 1919—his father sent along pre-addressed stamped postcards, by which his son could and did keep in touch. Correspondence was a habit that Hemingway felt important to instill in his own sons, from whom, when they were apart, he expected regular letters, and to whom he would express his pleasure or disappointment regarding their spelling, grammar, and penmanship. Some of Hemingway's earliest letters are marked with circled dots, signifying "tooseys" or "toosies," the family term for kisses. That, too, was a custom he shared with his sons. Even into their adulthood, Hemingway would end his letters to them with whimsical drawings bearing such captions as "Finca kuss" or "mango kuss" in letters from Cuba or, when writing from Africa, a "LARGE (Dark Continent) kuss." Patrick Hemingway had not realized that this was a family tradition predating his own generation until at the age of seventy-eight he was shown a 1912 letter from Ernest to his father, Dr. Clarence Hemingway, and immediately recognized the circled dots as symbols for kisses.[8]

Throughout his life, Hemingway thrived on the contact of letters and constantly urged family and friends to write. "Screed me and tell me all your troubles," he wrote in his characteristic slang to his sister Ursula in 1919. "Screed a man," he implored his friend Howell Jenkins in 1922. "Slip me the dirt in its totality," he

wrote conspiratorially in November 1925 to his sister Madelaine ("Sunny"), referring to other siblings by nicknames: "I've heard nothing but the official versions for
a hell of a long time. Those kind of bulletins are as dry as official communiques of
the reparation commission. Let me have the frigid on the paternal, maternal,
Masween, Carol, Liecester, misspelled, Ura and all. Write again and slip me the
frigid."[9]

While eagerly soliciting letters from others, he often apologized for the quality of
his own. In December 1925 he wrote to *This Quarter* editors Ernest Walsh and
Ethel Moorhead from the village in the Austrian Tyrol where he and his wife
Hadley were spending their second winter: "Write me here. Letters are tremendous
events in Schruns. I can write a better letter when I've one to answer."[10] To
Archibald MacLeish he sent a similar plea: "It is Sunday today so there isn't any
mail. And by the way if you ever write letters for god's sake write to us down here.
We have a swell time but letters are terribly exciting things in Schruns . . . Write me
a letter. I wont turn out such a dull mess as this again. Tell me all the dirt. We miss
Scandal very much here."[11]

As much as he loved to get letters, he often procrastinated in writing them. He
variously viewed correspondence as a diversion, a lifeline, an exasperating obligation, and, at worst, a peril to his work. Less than two months after he arrived in
Paris, pursuing his vocation as a writer of fiction while making a living as a reporter
for the *Toronto Star*, he wrote to his mother on 15 February 1922: "I am sorry to
write such dull letters, but I get such full expression in my articles and the other
work I am doing that I am quite pumped out and exhausted from a writing stand
point and so my letters are very commonplace. If I wrote nothing but letters all of
that would go into them."

In March 1923, en route from Italy via Paris to Germany to cover the French
occupation of the Ruhr, he reported to his father that he had been thirty-eight
hours on the train and in the past year had logged nearly 10,000 miles by rail.
Affectionately and apologetically he added, "I hope you have some good fishing
this spring. I appreciate your letters so much and am dreadfully sorry I dont write
more but when you make a living writing it is hard to write letters."[12]

It would be a recurring theme. In November 1952, enmeshed in settling the
estates of his mother and his second wife, Pauline, both of whom had died the year
before, he wrote in exhaustion to Scribner's editor Wallace Meyer:

> I want to get the hell away from here and from the daily destruction of
> correspondance. That doesn't mean that I do not want to hear from you
> when there is anything I should know. I can dictate in an hour what will
> keep two stenographers busy all day. But writing letters by hand in the
> mornings, when he should work or exercise, is the quickest way for a
> writer to destroy himself that I know.[13]

Two years later in a letter to Charles Scribner, Jr., he sent his best regards to Meyer: "He knows that when I don't write I am not being snotty or touchy. It is the logistics of work. If you are writing well there is no thing left in you to write letters with."[14]

Hemingway once described his letters as "often libellous, always indiscreet, often obscene and many of them could make great trouble."[15] His letters are written in a range of voices, varying according to mood and occasion and calibrated to each audience with perfect pitch. "What he wrote is always performance," Patrick Hemingway said of his father's letters. "Of course, a person is always writing to a person. They're always taking a tone with that person, but isn't that the way we behave with people? I'm sure he didn't behave with Charles Scribner, the old man, the way he behaved with me."

When what he wrote privately ended up in the public print, Hemingway was not pleased. After he was wounded as an eighteen-year-old volunteer ambulance driver in Italy in World War I, he was agitated to discover that two of his letters home had appeared in the local Oak Park, Illinois, newspaper, courtesy of his proud father. "Now Kid who in hell is giving all my letters out for publication?" he asked his sister Marcelline in a letter of 23 November 1918. "When I write home to the family I don't write to the Chicago Herald Examiner or anybody else—but to the family. Somebody has a lot of gall publishing them and it will look like I'm trying to pull hero stuff. Gee I was sore when I heard they were using my stuff in Oak Leaves. Pop must have Mal di Testa."

Even as he sought and was gratified by popular and critical attention to his work and would become the most public of writers, he closely guarded his privacy. On 12 October 1929, just fifteen days after the publication of *A Farewell to Arms*, he happily reported to his mother: "I have not yet heard how the book is going but hear it has had very good reviews and Scribners cable 'splendid press. prospects bright.'" But, he cautioned, "If anyone ever wants to interview you about me please tell them that you know I dislike any personal publicity and have promised me not to even answer questions about me. Don't ever give out <u>anything</u>. Just say your sorry but you cant. Scribners have the same instructions. If I'm to write at <u>all</u> I have to keep my private life out."[16] It would be a lifelong struggle. His letters of the 1950s reflect his deep ambivalence and wariness about the growing interest of biographers and scholars, including Charles Fenton, Carlos Baker, and Philip Young, whose attentions he found worrisome and intrusive, even as he engaged in correspondence with them.

As early as 1930, Hemingway letters were on the market as collectors' items—a development he found discomfiting. A group of nine letters he wrote to Ernest Walsh was touted in the March 1930 catalog of the Ulysses Book Shop in London as "a complete revelation of the man as he really is."[17] Maxwell Perkins informed

Hemingway on 8 April that Scribner's rare books department had purchased the letters to get them out of circulation, and he offered to destroy them or return them to Hemingway unread. Hemingway responded: "It certainly is a crappy business to find your own personal letters up for sale—am going to quit writing letters."[18] He did not, and as the decades passed, his letters only increased in interest and value. In July 1952 he wrote to Meyer, Perkins's successor, asking if the head of Scribner's rare books department had recently bought any letters he had written. If so, Hemingway wrote, "I would like a list of the purchases he made in order that I may be relieved of some correspondents."[19]

Two months before his fifty-ninth birthday, Hemingway typed out a directive, sealed it in an envelope marked "Important / To be opened in case of my Death," and placed it in the safe at the Finca. Dated 20 May 1958, the note reads: "To my Executors: It is my wish that none of the letters written by me during my lifetime shall be published. Accordingly, I hereby request and direct you not to publish, or consent to the publication by others, of any such letters."[20]

Following his death in 1961, nearly two decades passed before Mary Hemingway, as his literary executor, decided to authorize the compilation of a volume of his selected letters. Scribner's 1981 publication of *Ernest Hemingway: Selected Letters, 1917–1961*, edited by Carlos Baker, was a landmark literary event, heralded, amid other publicity, by an illustrated cover spread in the 15 February 1981 *New York Times Magazine*.

As Baker notes in his introduction to *Selected Letters*, Hemingway did, in fact, consent during his lifetime to the publication of a few of his letters or extracts from them. These included three abridged letters in Edmund Wilson's *The Shores of Light* (1952), four letters in Donald Gallup's *The Flowers of Friendship: Letters Written to Gertrude Stein* (1953), and one to the chief librarian of the Oak Park Public Library on the occasion of the library's fiftieth anniversary, published in the 15 February 1954 *Library Journal*. (Hemingway had missed the celebration dinner but wrote on 10 June 1953 to say, "I was at sea ... or I would have sent you a message telling you how much I owe to the Library and how much it has meant to me all my life." He enclosed a $100 check to cover any costs of making and distributing copies of his message and added, "If you find that I owe any fines or dues you can apply it against them."[21]) A few of Hemingway's letters to his German and Italian publishers, Ernst Rowohlt and Arnoldo Mondadori, also appeared in print: one (in English) in *Rowohlts Rotblonder Roman* (1947) and three (translated into Italian) in *Il Cinquantennio Editoriale di Arnoldo Mondadori, 1907–1957* (1957). And Hemingway permitted Arthur Mizener to quote from his letters to F. Scott Fitzgerald in *The Far Side of Paradise*, the 1949 biography of his old friend.

Hemingway wrote some letters expressly for publication, including letters to editors or columnists of various magazines and newspapers, answers to questionnaires, blurbs to promote the books of other writers, and the occasional commercial product endorsement.[22] He may, however, have regretted his endorsement of Ballantine Ale after a two-page advertisement appeared in the 5 November 1951 issue of *Life* magazine, featuring a facsimile of his letter on his stationery headed "FINCA VIGIA, SAN FRANCISCO DE PAULA, CUBA." After *The Old Man and the Sea* was published complete in *Life* (1 September 1952), he "got smacked with 3800 letters." "An awful lot of them got through straight here due to the Ballantine ad which published my address," he reported to a friend in November 1952. "I answered one whole school at Louisville Ky. and am going to answer another whole school," he claimed. But, he said, "I am a writer and not an homme des lettres. So I am going to drift now and not have an address for a while so my conscience won't bother me about answering kids (all of whom I will answer until I have to cast off) and I want to write again and not write letters."[23]

Despite Hemingway's 1958 directive, after his death additional letters appeared in print, in part or in full, including two to Sylvia Beach (both in English and in French translation) in *Mercure de France* (1963); seven to Milton Wolff, last commander of the Abraham Lincoln Battalion in the Spanish Civil War, in *American Dialog* (1964); and four, quoted in Italian in *Epoca* (1965), to Adriana Ivancich, the aristocratic young Venetian with whom he became infatuated in 1948 and upon whom he modeled the character Renata in *Across the River and into the Trees* (1950). When Mary Hemingway publicly objected to what she felt was A. E. Hotchner's extensive unauthorized use of Hemingway's letters in his 1966 book *Papa Hemingway: A Personal Memoir*, Philip Young, a professor at The Pennsylvania State University, took up her side with an exposé in the August 1966 *Atlantic Monthly* called "On Dismembering Hemingway."[24] Although Mary lost the case in court, "in the face of a common enemy Mary and I became friendly," Young recalled.[25] She subsequently invited him, along with Charles W. Mann, Chief of Rare Books and Special Collections at The Pennsylvania State University Libraries, to catalog her late husband's papers. At the time, the papers—gathered from Cuba, their house in Ketchum, Idaho, the back room of Sloppy Joe's bar in Key West, and elsewhere—were stored in her New York City bank vault and in shopping bags in her apartment closet. Young and Mann's 1969 volume, *The Hemingway Manuscripts: An Inventory*, was the first public accounting of the 19,500 pages that Mary would donate to the Kennedy Library and that would become accessible to scholars with the 1980 opening of its Hemingway Collection.

Audre Hanneman's landmark 1967 volume, *Ernest Hemingway: A Comprehensive Bibliography*, included entries for 110 Hemingway letters partially quoted in print or published in full. Her 1975 supplementary volume listed 122 more. Many had appeared as extracts or facsimiles of letters in sale catalogs and dealer listings.

Hemingway at Auction, 1930–1973, compiled by Matthew J. Bruccoli and C. E. Frazer Clark, Jr., reproduced pages from sixty auction and fifty-five dealer catalogs describing Hemingway books, manuscripts, and letters that had been offered for sale. "Most remarkable in recent years has been an almost magisterial series of sales of letters in which Hemingway the old battler scores in the same league with such older pros as Goethe," wrote Charles W. Mann in his introduction to that 1973 volume. He marveled that auction sales of Hemingway books, letters, and manuscripts to date had totaled $130,342.75: "One would like to hear Ernest Hemingway's reaction to it," he remarked. While to the present-day reader the sum may sound quaint (a single 1925 letter from Hemingway to Ezra Pound sold at Christie's in London for £78,000 in 2007, equivalent at the time to more than $157,000), Mann cited it as evidence that reports of the decline of Hemingway's reputation were greatly exaggerated. But what Mann found most intriguing was the glimpse that these catalogs and advertisements provided of Hemingway's correspondence: "Finally, Hemingway with his guard down in his letters remains a startling, aggressive, compelling writer. As we will never read his collected letters, these pages will remain the only medium through which, however fragmentarily, we can still occasionally hear his voice".[26]

The intensity of scholarly interest in Hemingway's correspondence (and attendant frustration at its inaccessibility) before the publication of Baker's selected edition is evident in E. R. Hagemann's 1978 "Preliminary Report on the State of Ernest Hemingway's Correspondence." Taking into account the sixty-eight extracts from Hemingway's letters to Mary Hemingway in her 1976 memoir, *How It Was*, Hagemann counted approximately 83,000 words "in the public print." Compiling "Hemingway epistolary wordage" was painstaking and tedious work, he said, "but what has been revealed up to now demands an even greater effort. This is not a demand for literary gossip or prurience; it is a demand for literary history. But there it is! Hemingway's note of 20 May 1958. Never has a dead man's hand lain heavier on academic excellence."[27]

It was in May 1979 that Mary Hemingway and her attorney, Alfred Rice, in consultation with Charles Scribner, Jr., decided to publish a volume of Hemingway's letters. "There can be no question about the wisdom and rightness of the decision," Baker remarked.[28] On the publication of his father's letters in light of the 1958 directive, Patrick Hemingway commented, "If you don't want them published, burn them. That's the only way you're going to prevent it. It's like a great heap of cellulose, you know. It's going to burn."

Since the 1981 publication of *Selected Letters*, two additional volumes focusing on Hemingway's letters have appeared, each representing both sides of his correspondence with one person: *The Only Thing That Counts: The Ernest Hemingway/ Maxwell Perkins Correspondence, 1925–1947*, edited by Matthew J. Bruccoli with

Robert W. Trogdon (1996); and *Dear Papa, Dear Hotch: The Correspondence of Ernest Hemingway and A. E. Hotchner* edited by Albert J. DeFazio III (2005). Baker's edition includes 581 letters, reproduced in their entirety. The Bruccoli– Trogdon volume includes 130 letters from Hemingway to Perkins (of the 472 extant in the Scribner's archives at Princeton University Library), some previously published by Baker and many abridged for length considerations. DeFazio's volume includes 161 letters exchanged between Hemingway and Hotchner from 1948 to 1961, eighty of them written by Hemingway.

Other clusters of Hemingway letters, some previously published, have appeared in books including *Hemingway in Cuba*, by Norberto Fuentes (1984); *Hemingway in Love and War*, edited by Henry S. Villard and James Nagel (1989); and *Letters from the Lost Generation: Gerald and Sara Murphy and Friends*, edited by Linda Patterson Miller (1991; expanded edn., 2002). The published memoirs of Hemingway's siblings also include some of his letters. Quotations from them appear in Madelaine Hemingway Miller's *Ernie: Hemingway's Sister "Sunny" Remembers* (1975; rpt. 1999), and selections of complete letters are featured in the revised editions of *My Brother, Ernest Hemingway* by Leicester Hemingway (1961; rev. edn., 1996) and *At the Hemingways* by Marcelline Hemingway Sanford (1962; rev. edn., 1999). *Running with the Bulls: My Years with the Hemingways* (2004) by Valerie Hemingway (née Danby-Smith), who served as his secretary and married his son Gregory after Hemingway's death, includes an October 1959 letter she received from Hemingway. And *Strange Tribe: A Family Memoir* (2007) by Gregory's son John Hemingway includes extracts of correspondence between his father and grandfather. A few additional extracts or letters, representing Hemingway's correspondence with Jane Mason (Havana friend, perhaps lover, of the 1930s), Lillian Ross, and Ezra Pound, have appeared in magazine pieces.[29] Scattered extracts and facsimile reproductions of letters have continued to appear in auction catalogs and dealer listings over the years.

While these publications testify to the interest in and value of the letters (and their perennial marketability as collectibles), together they account for only a fraction of Hemingway's more than 6,000 surviving letters, underscoring the need for a comprehensive scholarly edition. The Kennedy Library holds more than 2,500 outgoing Hemingway letters, and Princeton University Library holds approximately 1,400 (among the papers of Sylvia Beach, F. Scott Fitzgerald, Patrick Hemingway, Carlos Baker, and others, in addition to the Scribner's archive). The rest are scattered in scores of additional institutional repositories and private collections around the world. Among repositories with significant holdings are the Library of Congress, New York Public Library, Newberry Library, the Harry Ransom Center at the University of Texas, and the libraries of Yale, Pennsylvania State, Indiana, and Central Michigan Universities, Knox

College, Colby College, and the Universities of Chicago, Delaware, North Carolina, Tulsa, Wisconsin-Milwaukee, Maryland, South Carolina, Virginia, and Reading (England).

The Cambridge Edition of *The Letters of Ernest Hemingway* brings together for the first time as many of the author's surviving letters as can be located, approximately 85 percent of them never before published. The edition is authorized by the Ernest Hemingway Foundation and the Hemingway Foreign Rights Trust, holders, respectively, of the U.S. and international copyrights to the letters. This collection will provide scholars and general readers alike with ready access to the entire corpus of Hemingway's extant letters, those that previously have appeared in print as well as the thousands new to publication. The edition is planned for publication in more than a dozen volumes, with letters organized chronologically by date of composition. The edition includes only letters written by Hemingway, but the incoming letters of his many correspondents will inform editorial commentary throughout.

Because Hemingway did not routinely keep copies of his letters and because they are so widely dispersed, locating the letters has been a massive undertaking, requiring resourceful archival research and grassroots detective work. In addition to procuring copies of letters from the dozens of institutional archives known to hold Hemingway correspondence, we also sent blind-search letters of inquiry to more than 500 other libraries and institutional repositories in the United States and abroad. The edition has benefited from the generosity and interest of scores of scholars, archivists, aficionados, book and autograph specialists, collectors, and surviving correspondents and their descendants, including members of Hemingway's extended family, who have provided valuable information or shared copies of letters. Our transcriptions have been meticulously compared against the original documents on site visits whenever possible.

Since the launching of the edition project was publicly announced in the spring of 2002, it has attracted considerable attention, not only in scholarly circles, but in the news media, nationally and internationally. As a result of this widespread publicity, as well as our own queries, published in such venues as the *Times Literary Supplement* and the *New York Review of Books*, dozens of people around the globe have contacted us to share information or copies of letters in their possession. To cite just a few examples, Walter Houk, the widower of Hemingway's part-time secretary in the late 1940s and early 1950s (otherwise employed by the U.S. Embassy in Havana), has shared copies of her transcriptions of 120 letters that Hemingway dictated into a wire recorder, as well as letters that Hemingway wrote to her, reporting domestic details and discussing his work in progress. John Robben, of Greenwich, Connecticut, sent copies of three letters that Hemingway wrote to him in the early 1950s in response to a critique he had written for his college newspaper of the newly published *The Old Man and the Sea*. He was astonished that the great writer would take the time to respond to "a 21-year-old college student who had the temerity to critique his work," evidence, he says, that Hemingway was "a caring and understanding person."[30] We also were contacted by a relative of Roy Marsh, who piloted the plane that crashed in Africa on 23 January 1954 with Ernest and Mary aboard and who also was a passenger with them on the rescue plane that crashed the following day. Living in retirement in the Seychelles islands, Captain Marsh sent scanned copies of his letters via electronic mail.

To date we have gathered copies of Hemingway letters from nearly 250 sources in the United States and abroad, including more than 65 libraries and institutional repositories, and more than 175 dealers, private collectors, and Hemingway correspondents. We will continue to pursue extant letters for the duration of the edition project. The final volume will feature a section of "Additional Letters," to include those that come to light after publication of the volumes in which they would have appeared in chronological sequence.

It is the particular wish of Patrick Hemingway that this be a complete collection of his father's letters, rather than a selected edition. "I think the real interest from writers' letters is all of them," he has said. "Let the cards fall where they may. People can make up their own minds." We aim for this edition to be as inclusive as possible, comprising all of Hemingway's outgoing correspondence that we can locate, including postcards, cables, identifiable drafts and fragments, in-house missives, and letters he completed but put away unsent. Yet even in a "complete edition," some editorial judgment regarding selection is required—especially given Hemingway's celebrity, which has made a collector's item of nearly anything he signed, from checks to bar coasters, and given his own tendency to save nearly every scrap of paper he handled, including bills and grocery lists. We do not as a rule include book inscriptions, except those that the editors consider substantive or of particular interest. For the most part only one authorial copy of each letter exists; thus we have faced few problematic issues of textual history and textual variants. When such issues do arise, they are addressed in the notes that follow each letter.

Letters are transcribed whole and uncut whenever possible. When letters are known only through facsimiles or extracts appearing in auction catalogs or dealer listings, we publish whatever portions are available, citing their source. Such extracts typically reflect the most substantive and interesting aspects of letters, and while they are no substitute for the original documents, they can serve as place markers in the sequence of letters until such time as complete originals may become available.

For the preservation of Hemingway's earliest letters, we can be grateful to his mother, Grace Hall Hemingway, who meticulously maintained volumes of scrapbooks for each of her six children, pasting in correspondence as well as photographs, locks of hair, a swatch of fabric from a christening gown, crayon drawings, baby teeth, program booklets for concerts and Sunday School pageants and high school dances, and other memorabilia of their young lives. The five volumes she compiled for Ernest date from his birth through high school graduation, and another volume that she prepared for his grandparents covers his World War I experience. Perhaps it was the value his family placed on the well-documented life that fostered Hemingway's tendency to maintain a paper trail of his own. Like many writers, he saved drafts, manuscripts, and galley proofs of his published work, manuscripts of work in progress, and carbon copies of some business letters. But over the decades and through multiple moves, he also preserved drafts and false starts of letters, completed letters that in the morning light he thought better of mailing (sometimes scrawling "Unsent" across a dated envelope), and sliced-off outtakes of letters he scissor-edited before sending.

Fortunately, too, for this edition, Hemingway was famous enough at an early enough age that many of his correspondents beyond his family saved his letters. And beginning in the 1920s, many recipients of his letters were sufficiently well known themselves that their own correspondence has been preserved in archival collections.

We are aware, of course, that some of Hemingway's correspondence simply does not survive, whether by accident or intent, for personal or political reasons. For example, the bulk of Hemingway's letters to Juanito Quintana, proprietor of his favorite hotel in Pamplona and friend since the 1920s, were lost (along with the hotel) in the Spanish Civil War. Five surviving letters, written in Spanish in the 1950s, are held in the collections of the Princeton University Library.[31] Sadly for scholarship, if understandably from the recipients' perspective, among the letters known to be lost are those he wrote to some of the most important women in his life. In late 1918 and early 1919 he carried on an intense correspondence with Agnes von Kurowsky, the nurse with whom he fell in love at the American Red Cross hospital in Milan and who served as a prototype for the character Catherine Barkley in *A Farewell to Arms*. "I got a whole bushel of letters from you today, in fact haven't been able to read them all, yet. You shouldn't write so often," Agnes wrote to him on 1 March 1919. The next week she broke the news to him in a "Dear Ernie" letter that she was engaged to marry another man.[32] Domenico Caracciolo, a dashing Italian artillery officer and heir to a dukedom, jealously forced her to burn all of Hemingway's letters, before his family objected to the notion of his marrying a common American and the romance ended.

Hemingway's courtship correspondence with his first wife, Hadley Richardson, was even more intense, judging from the tone and volume of the surviving letters she wrote to him: nearly 200, totaling more than 1,500 pages, between November

1920 and their marriage on 3 September 1921. In 1942, fifteen years after leaving her to marry Pauline Pfeiffer, he reminisced fondly and nostalgically to Hadley, "I sometimes think that I wrote you so many letters to St. Louis from Chicago at one time that it crippled me as a letter writer for life. Like a pitcher with a dead arm."[33] Characteristically, Hemingway kept her letters all his life. His widow Mary returned them to Hadley after his death, and after Hadley's death in 1979, her son John found them in a shoe box in her Florida apartment. The vast majority of Hemingway's letters to Hadley, however, do not survive. As her biographer Gioia Diliberto reports, "Hadley burned them one day after their marriage collapsed, one of the few outward signs of her rage and sorrow."[34]

Nor do many of the letters survive that Hemingway wrote to Pauline, whom he divorced in 1940 to marry Martha Gellhorn. After Pauline died suddenly and unexpectedly in 1951, her twenty-four-year-old son Patrick received a call from her executor, saying she had left instructions that all of her correspondence was to be burned. "So, unlike some of these people, at least she was logical," Patrick recalled. "She didn't want her correspondence to be immortalized. That was the way to deal with it. And he was shocked. I was shocked. He said, 'Pat, if you want to go in and look through it, if you think that anything shouldn't be burned . . .' And I said, 'She said burn it. Burn it.'" The letters were destroyed in accordance with her wishes.

Hemingway claimed to have rewritten the ending of *A Farewell to Arms* thirty-nine times before he was satisfied. Surviving manuscripts prove he was not exaggerating: the Kennedy Library has cataloged forty-one variants in its collection. In contrast to the painstaking craftsmanship of his published work, his letter-writing style was spontaneous and informal. In 1952 he wrote to his editor:

> It could be argued that I have no right to speak of English Prose since I mis-spell and make errors of grammar in letters. But this usually happens because my head races far ahead of my hands on the type-writer, my typewriter sometimes sticks and over-runs and my time in this life is so short that it is not worthwhile to look up the proper spelling of a word in the dictionary when writing a letter. The spelling and construction of my letters is careless rather than ignorant. I try to avoid the level on which I write seriously when I write a letter. Otherwise each letter would take all day. As it is too many take much too much time that should go into writing.[35]

Of the relationship between his father's letters and his writing for publication, Patrick Hemingway commented, "I don't think they interfered much with his writing. I think it was just another part of his brain, and I don't think he ever mulled over them or tried to reach his idea of perfection with them. He just wrote them. But he was engaged with the person he was writing to." In the *New York*

Times Magazine piece that allowed the first public glimpse of Hemingway's letters shortly before the release of *Selected Letters* in April 1981, James Atlas also remarked on the difference between Hemingway's professional and personal writing, expressing surprise "that such a hoarder of words as Ernest Hemingway should have been so garrulous in his letters": "After a day that produced perhaps 500 words, he might turn out a 3,000-word letter the same evening. And where in his work he labored to be as tight-lipped as possible, to intimate rather than describe emotion, in his correspondence he was profligate, expansive, anecdotal."[36]

Lively, colorful, and idiosyncratic, Hemingway's letters present numerous challenges to the reader (and transcriber) not privy to the experiences, in-jokes, and private lingos that he shared with his various correspondents. He conferred upon family and friends a sometimes bewildering array of nicknames, in many cases more than one per person.[37] Hemingway variously addressed his sister Marcelline as "Marce," "Mash," "Masween," "Ivory," "Old Ivory," and "Antique Ivory." Hadley was "Hash," "Bones," "Binney," "Feather Cat," "Miss Katherine Cat," "Wickey," and "Poo." Conversely, a single nickname might apply to different persons: "Kitten" was a term of endearment not only for Hadley, his first wife, but for Mary, his last. Sometimes he and someone close to him affectionately shared a nickname, as when he addressed a letter to Martha Gellhorn as "Dearest Beloved Bongy" and signed it "Bongy." In his youth he and his friend Bill Smith had done the same, writing to each other as "Bird," "Boid," or (in a Latin variation on the theme) "Avis." Hemingway's sons John, Patrick, and Gregory were almost always "Bumby," "Mouse," and "Gigi."

Hemingway signed off his letters with multiple variants on his own name. Before he became "Papa," in early letters he was not only "Ernie," but "Oin," "Oinbones," "Miller" (his middle name), "Old Brute" (sometimes shortened to "O. B." or amplified to "Antique Brutality"), and "Wemedge." His high school nickname "Hemingstein" morphed to "Stein" or "Steen," and sometimes a sketch of a foam-topped beer stein served as his only signature. From here the private patois spun on, as rainbow trout became "rainsteins" and the Dilworths (the Horton Bay family who ran the local blacksmith shop, chicken dinner establishment, and guest houses) became the "Dillsteins" and even "Stilldeins."

The linguistic acrobatics that marked much of his correspondence with Ezra Pound, the master of modernist innovation, were already evident in Hemingway's much earlier letters to the friends of his youth in Oak Park and up in Michigan. Suffering a head cold in mid-March 1916, he apologized to his friend Emily Goetzmann for the lateness of his letter in prose mimicking his nasal congestion (throwing in an allusion to a popular poem for good measure): "On pended gknees I peg your bardun vor the ladness of this legger. Bud a gombination of monthly examinachugs and Bad goldt are my eggscuse, or to quote 'them immortal lines,' the brooks are ruggig–also my gnose." To Bill Smith he wrote on 28 April 1921, "Laid non hearage from you to some form of displeasure with the enditer and so after a time stopped screedage." His slang is fluid, with some words changing meaning with the context, and occasionally it is nearly impenetrable. As a rule, we leave it to readers to experience Hemingway's language on their own as he wrote it, without editorial intervention or attempts at explication.

In transcribing the letters, we have made every effort to preserve verbatim "Hemingway's endearing or exasperating idiosyncrasies" of mechanics and style, as Baker put it.[38] These include his well-known habit of retaining the silent "e" in such word forms as "loveing," "haveing," or "unbelieveable," and the invented "Hemingway Choctaw talk," stripped of articles and connectives, that Lillian Ross captured in her famous (or infamous) 13 May 1950 *New Yorker* profile of the writer. The letters exhibit Hemingway's often exuberant love of language, as he plays with such phonetically spelled and humorously conflated inventions as "Yarrup" (for Europe), "genuwind," "eggzact," "langwiges," "Alum Mattress" (for alma mater), and "Christnose" (as in "CHRISTNOSE IVE BEEN INFLUENCED BY EVERY GOOD WRITER IVE EVER READ BUT OUT OF IT WE COME, IF WEVE GOT ANYTHING, HARD AND CLEAR WITH OUR OWN STUFF," from a typewritten 1925 letter to composer George Antheil).[39]

Hemingway employed languages other than English in his letters as well, with varying degrees of expertise. Some letters of his teenage years are peppered with fractured high school Latin. Throughout his life he inserted into his correspondence a variety of words and phrases of other languages as he encountered and acquired them: Italian, French, German, Spanish, and Swahili, in some of which he eventually became fluent, if not always achieving grammatical perfection. Even when using English words, he sometimes adopted the syntax of another language: a linguistic cross-over that he also experimented with in his published works, as when he evokes the inflections of Spanish dialog in *For Whom the Bell Tolls*. In an 18 November 1918 letter written from the American Red Cross hospital in Milan on stationery with the letterhead "Croce Rossa Americana," he refers to a "cross red nurse"—imitating the grammar of Italian, while playing on the meaning of the words in English. From the Finca in 1942 he wrote to Martha Gellhorn with pleasure and pride in her skill as a writer after reading her *Collier's* magazine account of a rugged Caribbean "cruise" she made on a thirty-foot potato boat in hurricane season in order to report on German submarine activity in those waters. In his praise, he mixes Spanish syntax with his own "Choctaw talk," declaring, "Ni Joyce ni nobody any better ear than my Bong has now."[40]

When not taking deliberate liberties with the English language or experimenting in another, Hemingway generally was a sound speller, and his handwritten letters exhibit few errors, apart from occasional slips of the pen. But his typewritten letters often are riddled with mechanical errors that he did not bother to correct. As one example, he often did not depress the shift key sufficiently, resulting in oddities like "I8ve" instead of "I've," or causing only a portion of an uppercase letter to appear, suspended above the line. When he mistyped a word or phrase, rather than stop to erase and retype it accurately, he typically would type a string of x's through the mistake and continue on, or sometimes simply retype his correction or revision over the original attempt with more forceful keystrokes. "This typeing is a little woosy, but the light is bad and I am trying to make speed," he explained in a 17 December 1917 letter to his parents, in which a number of sentences end not with a period, but with the symbol "¾".

The condition of his typewriter was frequent cause for colorful comment. "Calamity has in the language of the Michigese Moss Back 'Laid hold of' the typer," he reported in a handwritten letter from northern Michigan to an unidentified friend in late September 1919. "It just let off a series of jarring whirrs like an annoyed rattler and quit frigidly. The main spring I imagine." In a letter of 10 January 1921 to his mother he wrote, "Love to you, pardon the rotten typer—it's a new one and stiff as a frozen whisker." To his friend Kate Smith he explained in a letter of 27 January 1922 from Paris, "Don'yt get to thinking I can't spell, I can' but this is an accursed French typer and the key board is rotten to work." "THIS MILL IS DIRTY AND ONLY FUNCTIONS IN THE UPPER REGISTER," he wrote to *Little Review* editor Jane Heap in 1925, "SO IF I NEED THE EMPHASIS USUALLY GIVEN BY CAPITAL LETTERS I WILL INSERT SOME PROFANE PHRASE OR VULGAR EJACULATION LIKE SAY HORSESHIT FOR EXAMPLE."[41]

To silently correct spelling and punctuation or to regularize capitalization in the letters would strip them of their personality and present a falsely prettified and homogenized view of the letters his correspondents received. Such tidying up also would render meaningless Hemingway's own spontaneous "meta-commentary" on the imperfections of his letters ("Excuse the bum spelling and typographicals," he wrote to his father on 2 May 1922), as when he took a phonetic stab at writing words in a foreign language or a proper name and followed it with a disclaimer such as "Spelling very doubtful." And it would render invisible Hemingway's comical manipulations of people's names, as when he addressed Sylvia Beach as "Dear Seelviah," or Ezra Pound as "Dear Uzra," or referred to poet and publisher Robert McAlmon as "MuckAlmun."[42]

Yet in attempting to preserve the strong idiosyncratic flavors of Hemingway's epistles, we do not want to give readers what one scholarly editor termed "literary dyspepsia."[43] So as not to tax the reader's patience or ability to focus on the sense of the letters, we have regularized the placement of such elements as dateline, inside address, salutation, closing, signature, and postscripts. We also normalize Hemingway's often erratic spacing and paragraph indention. For example, frequently he would type a space both before and after punctuation marks or hit the space bar two or three times between words, creating a visual quirkiness that we do not attempt to reproduce in print. We are mindful that no published transcription of a typed or handwritten letter can ever fully capture its appearance on the page. This is not a facsimile edition, and for those wishing to study in depth the physical characteristics of a letter, no printed rendition can substitute for an examination of the original.

In order to avoid what Lewis Mumford termed the "barbed wire" entanglements of too many editorial marks,[44] we rely primarily on notes, rather than more intrusive symbols within the text, to supply necessary contextual information, translations of foreign words and passages, and first-mention identifications of people in each volume. Annotations appear as endnotes immediately following each letter.

In addition to an introduction discussing Hemingway's life, work, and correspondence of the period represented, each volume includes a brief chronology of events in Hemingway's life and career during that span of years, a note outlining editorial policies, a roster of correspondents represented in that volume, a selection of illustrations, and relevant maps. The back matter of each volume includes a calendar of letters, an index of recipients, and a general index to the volume. The final volume will contain a comprehensive index to the complete edition.

A more detailed description of editorial practices and procedures appears in the Note on the Text. Our aim is to produce an edition that is at once satisfying to the scholar and inviting to the general reader.

Publication of Hemingway's collected letters will be a crucial step forward for the study of American literature and literary modernism. Hemingway has had an indelible impact on English prose—and on the popular imagination. Nearly every book he wrote since 1925 remains in print. He has had an uncommonly prolific posthumous career. Dozens of previously unpublished or uncollected stories, articles, and poems have appeared in new collections of his work. And several major new books have been published since his death, edited from manuscripts he left behind in varying stages of completion. These include *A Moveable Feast* (1964), *Islands in the Stream* (1970), *The Garden of Eden* (1986) , and two editions of his "Africa book": *True at First Light* (1999), edited by Patrick Hemingway, and a complete unabridged edition, *Under Kilimanjaro* (2005), edited by Robert W. Lewis and Robert E. Fleming. *A Moveable Feast: The Restored Edition*, edited by the author's grandson Seán Hemingway, was published in 2009.

Ernest Hemingway is arguably the most widely recognized and influential of all American writers. More than a half century after his death, interest in his life and work is seemingly insatiable, his iconic stature unshakable, his celebrity still global. Serious writers and readers must come to terms with his artistic legacy. Few writers' letters can rival his in importance and interest—both for scholars of modern literature and for the reading public.

Hemingway's letters present fresh and immediate accounts of events and relationships that profoundly shaped his life and work. "We go to the front tomorrow," the eighteen-year-old volunteer ambulance driver wrote home on a picture postcard from Milan on 9 June 1918. A month later he would be wounded seriously in a mortar explosion and hospitalized in Milan, where he would fall in love: experiences that fueled his fiction, from "A Very Short Story" (a version of which first appeared in his 1924 *in our time*) to *A Farewell to Arms*. On 14 February 1922, newly arrived in Paris and about to take his place among the expatriate writers and artists of the Left Bank, he wrote to his mother back in Oak Park: "Paris is so very beautiful that it satisfies something in you that is always hungry in America." "Gertrude Stein who wrote Three Lives and a number of other good things was here to dinner last night and stayed till mid-night," he reported. "She is about 55 I guess and very large and nice. She is very keen about my poetry." He continued, "Friday we are going to tea at Ezra Pounds. He has asked me to do an article on the present literary state of America for the Little Review." Hemingway's description of Pamplona's fiesta of San Fermín in a July 1924 letter to his mother is particularly striking, considering that his own novel, published two years later, would forever alter the scene: "It is a purely Spanish festa high up in the capital of Navarre and there are practically no foreigners altho people come from all over Spain for it."[45]

Hemingway's letters express and provoke the gamut of human emotions. They are by turns—and sometimes simultaneously—entertaining, informative, poignant, silly, wrenching, depressing, outrageous. Surprising to some readers will be the extent to which the letters contradict the common image of Hemingway the solitary artist, adventurer, and tough guy, unencumbered by if not estranged from his family. To be sure, the family relationships were complicated and at times contentious, but despite the strains, the ties did bind. The letters show Hemingway's less familiar but no less honest faces: as loving husband, as proud father, as playful and devoted brother, and as affectionate and ever-dutiful son. They reveal other less familiar facets of the writer as well: Hemingway the political observer, the natural historian, the astute businessman, the infatuated lover, the instigator and organizer of festivities, and the everyday Hemingway. Even when writing about the least literary of subjects—financial transactions, brands of motor oil, the necessity of car insurance, varieties of avocados and mangoes growing at the Finca, what provisions to take on a hunting trip or aboard his beloved boat *Pilar*, the logistics of his children's travels, remodeling plans and roof repairs—he was rarely dull. His briefest cables capture his inimitable voice: "SUGGEST YOU UPSTICK BOOK ASSWARDS," he wrote in December 1922 to his employer, Frank Mason, who had suggested that his expense reports did not match the accounting books.

Hemingway was famously competitive about his writing. "You should always write your best against dead writers," he advised William Faulkner in a 1947 letter, "and beat them one by one."[46] To Charles Scribner in 1949 he confessed, "Am a man without any ambition, except to be champion of the world."[47] He told Lillian Ross: "I started out very quiet and I beat Mr. Turgenev. Then I trained hard and I beat Mr. de Maupassant. I've fought two draws with Mr. Stendhal, and I think I had an edge in the last one. But nobody's going to get me in any ring with Mr. Tolstoy unless I'm crazy or I keep getting better."[48] Yet Hemingway did not view his correspondence as art (even if it was always performance) and regarded it lightly. He did not recognize the letter as one of his own richest and strongest genres.

In "Old Newsman Writes: A Letter from Cuba," published in *Esquire* in 1934, Hemingway declared:

> All good books are alike in that they are truer than if they had really happened and after you are finished reading one you will feel that all that happened to you and afterwards it all belongs to you; the good and the bad, the ecstasy, the remorse and sorrow, the people and the places and how the weather was. If you can get so that you can give that to people, then you are a writer.[49]

While he always drew a clear distinction between the importance of letter writing and "real" writing, the same standards of judgment can be brought favorably to bear on his own letters, written without thought of their lasting power, or self-consciousness of their testimony to his prowess as a writer. Each letter is a snapshot capturing the news of the day and mood of the hour. Together they form a vast album, a detailed and candid record not only of his own extraordinarily eventful, complicated, and accomplished life, but of the places and times in which he lived and on which he made his mark. Ernest Hemingway's collected letters constitute a rich self-portrait of the artist and a vivid eyewitness chronicle of the twentieth century.

NOTES

1 EH to F. Scott Fitzgerald, 1 July 1925 (PUL; *SL*, 165–66). A key to abbreviations and short titles used in this volume follows the Note on the Text. Unless otherwise cited, all letters quoted in this introduction are included in this volume.
2 EH to Arthur Mizener, 12 May 1950 (UMD; *SL*, 695).
3 Michael S. Reynolds, *Hemingway: The Paris Years* (Oxford, Basil Blackwell, 1989), 356.

4 Patrick Hemingway letter, "To Whom It May Concern," 12 October 2004 (in the archives of the Hemingway Letters Project, The Pennsylvania State University).

5 Edmund Wilson, "Ernest Hemingway: Bourdon Gauge of Morale," *Atlantic Monthly* 164 (July 1939): 36–46.

6 *Ernest Hemingway: Selected Letters, 1917–1961*, ed. Carlos Baker (New York: Scribner's, 1981), ix.

7 The letter is in the collection of the Harry Ransom Humanities Research Center at the University of Texas.

8 Interview with Sandra Spanier, Boston, Massachusetts, 2 April 2007. All subsequent quotations from Patrick Hemingway are from this interview.

9 EH to Ursula Hemingway, [c. 17 September 1919]; EH to Howell Jenkins, 8 January [1922]; EH to Madelaine Hemingway, [24 November 1925] (PSU).

10 EH to Ernest Walsh and Ethel Moorhead, [c. 27 December 1925] (JFK).

11 EH to Archibald MacLeish, [c. 20 December 1925] (Library of Congress; *SL*, 179).

12 EH to Clarence Hemingway, 26 March 1923 (JFK).

13 EH to Wallace Meyer, 28 November 1952 (PUL).

14 EH to Charles Scribner, Jr., 7 August 1954 (PUL).

15 EH to Wallace Meyer, 21 February 1952 (PUL; *SL*, 750).

16 EH to Grace Hall Hemingway, 12 October 1929 (PSU).

17 *Hemingway at Auction, 1930–1973*, ed. Matthew J. Bruccoli and C. E. Frazer Clark, Jr. (Detroit: Gale Research Co., 1973), 235.

18 EH to Maxwell Perkins, [c. 11 April 1930] (PUL; *TOTTC*, 143).

19 EH to Wallace Meyer, 29 July 1952 (PUL).

20 EH to "my Executors," typescript of statement, 20 May 1958 (JFK).

21 EH to Frederick Wezeman, 10 June 1953 (OPPL).

22 These are collected in *Hemingway and the Mechanism of Fame: Statements, Public Letters, Introductions, Forewords, Prefaces, Blurbs, Reviews, and Endorsements*, ed. Matthew J. Bruccoli and Judith S. Baughman (Columbia: University of South Carolina Press, 2006).

23 EH to Daniel Longwell, 5 November 1952 (Columbia). EH's letter thanking twenty-three junior high school students in Louisville, Kentucky, for their letter about *The Old Man and the Sea* was quoted in *Time*, 2 March 1953, 33.

24 The piece was published as "I Dismember Papa" in Philip Young, *Three Bags Full: Essays in American Fiction* (New York: Harcourt Brace, 1967), 55–67.

25 Philip Young, "Hemingway's Manuscripts: The Vault Reconsidered," in *American Fiction, American Myth: Essays by Philip Young*, ed. David Morrell and Sandra Spanier (University Park: The Pennsylvania State University Press, 2000), 120.

26 Bruccoli and Frazer Clark, Jr., *Hemingway at Auction*, vii, xi.

27 In *Literary Research Newsletter* 3, no. 4 (1978): 163–72; 165.

28 *Selected Letters*, xxiii.

29 Alane Salierno Mason, "To Love and Love Not," *Vanity Fair*, July 1999, 108–18ff.; Lillian Ross, "Hemingway Told Me Things," *New Yorker*, 24 May 1999, 70–73; Matthew J. Bruccoli, ed., "'Yr Letters Are Life Preservers': The Correspondence of Ernest Hemingway and Ezra Pound," *Paris Review* 163 (Fall 2003): 96–129.

30 John Robben to Sandra Spanier, 10 May 2002 (Hemingway Letters Project archives).

31 Carlos Baker, "Letters from Hemingway," *Princeton University Library Chronicle* 24 (Winter 1963): 101–7.

32 Henry S. Villard and James Nagel, eds., *Hemingway in Love and War: The Lost Diary of Agnes von Kurowsky, Her Letters, and Correspondence of Ernest Hemingway* (Boston: Northeastern University Press, 1989), 162.

33 EH to Hadley Mowrer, 23 July 1942 (PUL); quoted in Gioia Diliberto, *Hadley* (New York: Ticknor and Fields, 1992), xiii.

34 Diliberto, *Hadley*, xii.

35   EH to Wallace Meyer, 28 November 1952 (PUL).
36   James Atlas, "The Private Hemingway," *New York Times Magazine*, 15 February 1981, 23.
37   Kenneth B. Panda notes Hemingway's penchant for slang and nicknames, in the introduction to "Ernest Hemingway: Letters, 1908–1925" (doctoral dissertation, University of Delaware, 2002).
38   *Selected Letters*, xxv.
39   EH to George Antheil, [c. January 1925] (Columbia).
40   EH to Martha Gellhorn, 19 September [1942] (JFK).
41   EH to Jane Heap, [5 April 1925] (University of Wisconsin-Milwaukee).
42   EH to Sylvia Beach, [6 November 1923] (PUL; *SL*, 97–99); EH to Ezra Pound, [c. 10 April 1925] (Yale). EH refers to "MuckAlmun" in this letter to Pound.
43   Frederick Karl, "General Editor's Introduction," *The Collected Letters of Joseph Conrad* (Cambridge: Cambridge University Press, 1983), vol. 1, xlv.
44   Lewis Mumford, "Emerson Behind Barbed Wire," *New York Review of Books*, 18 January 1968, 3–5, 23.
45   EH to Grace Hall Hemingway, 18 July 1924 (PSU).
46   EH to William Faulkner, 23 July 1947 (JFK; *SL*, 624).
47   EH to Charles Scribner, 1 September 1949 (PUL).
48   Lillian Ross, *Portrait of Hemingway* (New York: Modern Library, 1999), 19.
49   "Old Newsman Writes: A Letter from Cuba," *Esquire*, December 1934 (*BL*, 184).

ADDITIONAL WORKS CITED

Bruccoli, Matthew J., ed., with Robert W. Trogdon. *The Only Thing That Counts: The Ernest Hemingway–Maxwell Perkins Correspondence*. New York: Scribner's, 1996.

"Dear Seelviah . . ." *Mercure de France*, August–September 1963, 105–10. (Letters to Sylvia Beach)

DeFazio, Albert J. III, ed. *Dear Papa, Dear Hotch: The Correspondence of Ernest Hemingway and A. E. Hotchner*. Columbia: University of Missouri Press, 2005.

Fuentes, Norberto. *Hemingway in Cuba*. Translated by Consuelo E. Corwin. Secaucus, New Jersey: Lyle Stuart, 1984.

Gallup, Donald, ed. *The Flowers of Friendship: Letters Written to Gertrude Stein*. New York: Knopf, 1953.

Hagemann, E. R. "Preliminary Report on the State of Ernest Hemingway's Correspondence." *Literary Research Newsletter* 3, no. 4 (1978): 163–72.

Hemingway, Ernest. *A Moveable Feast: The Restored Edition*. With a foreword by Patrick Hemingway; edited and with an introduction by Seán Hemingway. New York: Scribner's, 2009.

Hemingway, John. *Strange Tribe: A Family Memoir*. Guilford, Connecticut: Lyons Press, 2007.

Hemingway, Mary. *How It Was*. New York: Knopf, 1976.

Hemingway, Valerie. *Running with the Bulls: My Years with the Hemingways*. New York: Random House, 2004.

Il Cinquantennio Editoriale di Arnoldo Mondadori, 1907–1957. Verona, Italy: Mondadori, 1957. (Letters to Arnoldo Mondadori)

"La Renata di Hemingway sono io." *Epoca* 60 (25 July 1965), 72–75. (Letters to Adriana Ivancich)

Miller, Linda Patterson, ed. *Letters from the Lost Generation: Gerald and Sara Murphy and Friends*. Expanded edn. Gainesville: University Press of Florida, 2002.

Mizener, Arthur. *The Far Side of Paradise: A Biography of F. Scott Fitzgerald*. New York: Avon, 1949.

Mumford, Lewis. "Emerson Behind Barbed Wire." *New York Review of Books*, 18 January 1968, 3–5, 23.

Rowohlts Rotblonder Roman. Hamburg, Germany: Rohwohlt, 1947, 44. (Letters to Ernst Rowohlt)

"Unpublished Letters of Ernest Hemingway." *American Dialog* 1, no. 2 (October–November 1964): 11–13. (Letters to Milton Wolff)

Wilson, Edmund. *The Shores of Light: A Literary Chronicle of the Twenties and Thirties*. New York: Vintage Books, 1952.

ACKNOWLEDGMENTS

The Cambridge Edition of *The Letters of Ernest Hemingway* owes its existence to the authorization and kind cooperation of the Ernest Hemingway Foundation and the Hemingway Foreign Rights Trust, which hold, respectively, the U.S. and international copyrights to the letters. It was Patrick Hemingway who originally conceived of a complete scholarly edition of his father's letters, and he has been most generous and supportive of this effort, meeting with the general editor on several occasions and graciously answering questions, identifying references, and sharing stories that illuminate the letters.

The Hemingway Letters Project is supported in part by a Scholarly Editions Grant from the National Endowment for the Humanities. We are honored to have been designated a *We, the People* project, "a special recognition by the NEH for model projects that advance the study, teaching, and understanding of American history and culture." (Any views, findings, or conclusions expressed in this publication do not necessarily represent those of the National Endowment for the Humanities.)

We deeply appreciate the generosity of those organizations and endowments that have supported the Project through grants and gifts: AT&T Mobility, the Heinz Endowments, the Michigan Hemingway Society, the Dr. Bernard S. and Ann Re Oldsey Endowment for the Study of American Literature in the College of the Liberal Arts at The Pennsylvania State University, and the Xerox Corporation, which has contributed copying, printing, faxing, and scanning equipment as well as a DocuShare database management system that has been customized for our needs. We are grateful, too, to individual donors, including Ralph and Alex Barrocas, Linda Messer Ganz, Eric V. Gearhart, Walter Goldstein, Gary Gray and Kathleen O'Toole, Harold Hein, Bill and Honey Jaffe, Ira B. Kristel, Mary Ann O'Brian Malkin, Randall Miller, Barbara Palmer, Graham B. Spanier, David A. Westover III, and Mark Weyermuller.

For fellowships and grants to support travel to archives and other research activities by Project scholars, we also wish to thank the Bibliographical Society (U.K.), the Bibliographical Society of America, the Idaho Humanities Council, and the John F. Kennedy Presidential Library.

The Pennsylvania State University has provided indispensable institutional support and an ideal home for the Project from its inception in 2002. We are particularly grateful to the following for their sponsorship and commitment: Dean Susan Welch and Associate Deans Raymond E. Lombra, Jack Selzer, and Denise Solomon, College of the Liberal Arts; Dean Emeritus Nancy Eaton and Dean Barbara Dewey, University Libraries; Rodney Erickson, Office of the Provost; Eva Pell and Henry Foley, Office of the Vice President for Research; Marie Secor, Robert Caserio, and Robin Schulze, Heads of the Department of English; and Laura Knoppers, Marica Tacconi, and Michael Bérubé, Directors of the Institute for Arts and Humanities.

Penn State's Office of Development and Alumni Relations has provided valuable assistance in securing external philanthropic funding; Rodney Kirsch, Peter Weiler, Joanne Cahill, and Rebecca Mills have been instrumental in these efforts. Others to whom we owe thanks include Ron Huss, Mark Righter, and the Intellectual Property Office; Bill Mahon, Cynthia Hall, and Cyndee Graves in University Relations; Trish Alexander, Shane Freehauf, Mary Kay Hort, Mark Luellen, Michael Renne, Cathy A. Thompson, and Sandra Wingard in the College of the Liberal Arts; Robert Edwards, Elizabeth Jenkins, and Mark Morrisson in the English Department's Graduate Studies Program, as well as Amy Barone, Sharissa Feasler, Laurie Johnson, Kim Keller, Charlie Reese, Michael Riden, Wendy Shaffer, and Peg Yetter in the Department of English; Roger Downs and Deryck Holdsworth of the Department of Geography; and cartographer Erin Greb and the Peter R. Gould Center for Geography Education and Outreach.

We wish also to acknowledge support provided to volume I co-editor Robert W. Trogdon by Kent State University, with particular thanks to Ronald Corthell, Chair of the Department of English, and Timothy Moerland, Dean, College of Arts and Sciences. Boise State University and Illinois State University have provided much appreciated support to scholars working on later volumes of the edition.

From the start the Hemingway Letters Project has benefited immensely from the sound guidance and strong support of our Editorial Advisory Board, whose members have given generously and tirelessly of their time and expertise. Headed by Linda Patterson Miller, the advisors include Jackson R. Bryer, Scott Donaldson, James Meredith, Linda Wagner-Martin, and James L. W. West III. They deserve special recognition for their exceptional commitment and active involvement, including advising in the establishment of editorial policies and reading the manuscript of this volume at several stages. The edition is much the stronger for their contributions.

Project Associate Editor LaVerne Kennevan Maginnis has served with dedication and professionalism on a daily basis in myriad ways, and the Project is most fortunate to have the benefit of her editorial and organizational expertise.

In addition to those named on the title page of this volume, others serving on editorial teams of later volumes and as consulting scholars to the Project merit grateful acknowledgment: Edward Burns, Rose Marie Burwell, Stacey Guill, Hilary K. Justice, Ellen Andrews Knodt, Mark Ott, Gladys Rodriguez Ferrero, Chtiliana Stoilova Rousseva, Rena M. Sanderson, Rodger L. Tarr, and Lisa Tyler. We owe special thanks to Professors Knodt and Sanderson for their contributions in the preparation of volume 1.

We are deeply indebted to the dozens of libraries, museums, and institutional archives that have supplied copies of letters in their collections and assisted in research for the edition.

The John F. Kennedy Presidential Library, the world's largest repository of Hemingway papers, has been particularly generous in its support of the Project, donating copies of its entire holdings of more than 2,500 outgoing letters, providing a number of images for illustrations free of charge, and responding tirelessly to our requests and queries. Special thanks are due to Director Thomas J. Putnam; past Director Deborah Leff; Hemingway Collection Curator Susan Wrynn; retired Chief Archivist Allan Goodrich and his successor, Karen Adler Abramson; James Roth; Stephen Plotkin; Amy Macdonald; Megan Desnoyers; James B. Hill, Laurie Austin, and Maryrose Grossman of Photo Archives; and interns Shanti Freundlich, Becky Robbins, Samuel Smallidge, Marti Verso, and Diana Wakimoto.

We also gratefully acknowledge the outstanding support of the Pennsylvania State University Libraries, with warmest thanks to William L. Joyce, Head of Special Collections; Sandra Stelts, Curator of Rare Books and Manuscripts; and William S. Brockman, Paterno Family Librarian for Literature. Mark Saussure, Steven Baylis, Shane Markley, and Peggy Myers of Digital Libraries Technologies have provided indispensable technical and database management support. We also wish to thank Timothy R. Babcock, Sandra Ball, Shirley Davis, Catherine Grigor, Susan Hamburger, Catherine Hanhauser, Sally Kalin, Amy Yancey, and Stelts/ Filippelli Intern Buthainah Al Thowaini.

For supplying copies of letters in their collections and granting permission for their publication in volume 1 of *The Letters of Ernest Hemingway*, we acknowledge the following libraries and archives, with special thanks to the librarians, curators, and staff members named here for their kind assistance: Brown University Library; Clarke Historical Library, Central Michigan University—Frank J. Boles; Lewis Galantière Papers, Rare Book and Manuscript Library, Columbia University— Bernard Crystal, Susan G. Hamson, Jennifer B. Lee; Lilly Library, Indiana University—Directors Breon Mitchell and Saundra Taylor, and Rebecca Cape, Zachary Downey, and Gabriel Swift; Ernest Hemingway Collection at the John F. Kennedy Presidential Library and Museum; Special Collections and Archives, Knox College Library—Carley Robison, Kay Vander Meulen, and Mary

McAndrew; Richard John Levy and Sally Waldman Sweet Collection, Manuscripts and Archives Division, The New York Public Library, Astor, Lenox and Tilden Foundations—Thomas G. Lannon; The Newberry Library, Chicago—John H. Brady, Martha Briggs, JoEllen Dickie, Alison Hinderliter, and John Powell; North Central Michigan College Library—Eunice Teel; Oak Park Public Library— Leigh Gavin and William Jerousek; Petoskey District Library—Andrew Cherven; Manuscripts Division, Department of Rare Books and Special Collections, Princeton University Library—Don C. Skemer, Curator of Manuscripts, and Charles E. Greene, AnnaLee Pauls, Ben Primer, and Margaret Sherry Rich; Department of Special Collections and University Archives, Stanford University Libraries—Margaret J. Kimball, Sean Quimby, and Mattie Taormina; Special Collections Research Center, University of Chicago Library—Julia Gardner, Daniel Meyer, Reina Williams; Hemingway Collection, Special Collections, University of Maryland Libraries—Beth Alvarez; Harry Ransom Humanities Research Center, University of Texas at Austin—Richard Workman, Lea K. Cline, Nick Homenda, Francisca Folch, Elspeth Healey, Caitlin Murray; Department of Special Collections, McFarlin Library, University of Tulsa—Marc Carlson; Special Collections, University of Virginia Library—Christian Dupont, Margaret D. Hrabe, Edward F. Gaynor, Heather Riser, and Robin D. Wear; Yale Collection of American Literature, Beinecke Rare Book and Manuscript Library— Frank M. Turner, Director; Nancy Kuhl, Curator, Collection of American Literature; and Heather Dean, Diane Ducharme, Stephen C. Jones, Laurie Klein, Susan Klein, Ngadi W. Kponou, John Monahan, Karen Nangle, Natalia Sciarini, Adrienne Sharpe, and Graham Sherriff.

The many additional libraries and archives whose contributions of materials and assistance pertain primarily to later volumes of the edition will be acknowledged there.

The following manuscript specialists and dealers have been most helpful in a variety of ways, including supplying sale catalogs and information about their offerings, forwarding queries to owners, sharing copies of letters, and otherwise assisting in our research: Bart Auerbach; David and Natalie Bauman, Ernest Hilbert, Bauman Rare Books; Patrick McGrath, Christie's New York; Steve Verkman, Clean Sweep Auctions; David Bloom, Freeman's Auctions; Thomas A. Goldwasser; Glenn Horowitz Bookseller, Inc.; George R. Minkoff; David Meeker, Nick Adams Rare Books; Kenneth W. Rendell Gallery; Selby Kiffer, Sotheby's New York; and Swann Galleries.

We are extremely grateful to a number of individuals for their generosity in sharing copies or transcriptions of letters with the Project: Nick Angell, Charles Bednar, Edwin McHaney Bennett, Ricardo Bernhard, Edward Brown, Benjamin Bruce, Annette Campbell-White, Herbert S. Channick, Andrew Cohen, Joseph J. Creely, Jr.,

Page Dougherty Delano, Wesley J. Dilworth, Roger DiSilvestro, Fraser Drew, T. Mike Fletcher, Peggy Fox, Arthur T. Garrity, Mark Godburn, Hank Gorrell, Jr., Edgar Grissom, Mina Hemingway, Patrick and Carol Hemingway, Dan Hodges, Walter Houk, Ellen Andrews Knodt, Genevieve Kurek, Elizabeth Gardner Lombardi, Ernest H. Mainland, Lou Mandler, Loretta Valtz Mannucci, Roy Marsh, Robert and Susan Metzger, Ulrich Mosch, Maurice F. and Marcia Neville, Frederick W. Nolan, Sarah Parry, Arne Herlov Petersen, Paul Quintanilla, John Robben, Dan Rosenbaum, James and Marian Sanford, John E. Sanford, Michael Schnack and family, Dorothy Shaw, Paul Sorrentino, Charles Strauss, Mel Yoken, Mark and Rhonda Zieman, Edward L. Ziff, and Daniel Zirilli. We are grateful, too, to those donors of letters who wish to remain anonymous.

In order to ensure accuracy in the transcriptions and annotations of letters that Hemingway wrote from a range of locales and employing various languages, we have called upon the local expertise and language skills of a number of willing volunteers. The following deserve special thanks for the information and insights they have provided.

For information concerning Hemingway's hometown of Oak Park, Illinois, Kathryn J. Atwood, Barbara Ballinger, Virginia Cassin, Dan Fang, Grant Gerlich, Redd Griffin, Katie Simpson, and the Ernest Hemingway Foundation of Oak Park; William Jerousek and Leigh Gavin, Oak Park Public Library; Donald Vogel, Oak Park and River Forest High School; and Blaise Dierks, Hadley Ford, and Michael McKee of the River Forest Public Library.

For details relevant to Hemingway's 1910 visit to Nantucket, Susan F. Beegel.

For Michigan people and places, Janice Byrne, Michael Federspiel, Jack Jobst, Ken Marek, Charlotte Ponder, Frederick J. Svoboda; Ann Wright, Otsego County Historical Society; and Ray Argetsinger, Gary and Maxine Argetsinger, Wesley J. Dilworth, and Bob and Judy Sumner, descendants of those in Horton Bay who knew the Hemingway family.

For Kansas City, Steve Paul.

For St. Louis and other Missouri connections, Catey Terry, Doris Mayuiers, and Steve Weinberg, University of Missouri; Deborah E. Cribbs, St. Louis Mercantile Library; and Harry Charles and Dan Lilienkamp, St. Louis County Library.

For Key West, Brewster Chamberlin, Key West Arts and Historical Society; and Tom Hambright, Monroe County Library.

For Hemingway's high school Latin, Paul B. Harvey, Jr.

For Hemingway's Italian, Mark Cirino, Sherry Roush, and Marica Tacconi.

For French language and Parisian references, Edouard Cuilhé, Michel and Marie-Isabelle Cuilhé, and J. Gerald Kennedy.

For Spanish language and references to Spain and bullfighting, Miriam B. Mandel.

And for German language and references to Germany, Switzerland, and Austria, Thomas Austenfeld and Rena M. Sanderson.

For providing information and assisting the Project in various other ways, we also wish to thank the following: Norman Aberle, Frank Aldrich, Robert Baldwin, Jonathan Bank, A. Scott Berg, James Brasch, Carlene Brennan, Silvio Calabi, Maureen Carr, Suzanne Clark, Peter Coveney, Gioia Diliberto, Quentin Fehr, Ande Flavelle, Thomas P. Fuller, William Gallagher, Matthew Ginn, Cheryl Glenn, Lavinia Graecen, Kathryn Grossman, Sue Hart, John Harwood, Hilary Hemingway, John Hemingway, Sean and Colette Hemingway, Valerie Hemingway, Paul Hendrickson, Donald Junkins, Mary Kiffer, John King, Jobst Knigge, Linda Lapides, Douglas LaPrade, David Lethbridge, Richard Liebman, Gaille Marsh, Laurence W. Mazzeno, David Morrell, John Mulholland, Robert M. Myers and sons Bruce and David Myers, James Nagel, Robert Nau, David Nuffer, Sean O'Rourke, Claudia Pennington, Stéphanie Perrais, Andrea Perez, Bruno Riviere, DeWitt Sage, Patrick Scott, Charles Scribner III, Pat Shipman, Gail Sinclair, Tom Stillitano, Neil Tristram, Alan Walker, Emily Wallace, and William B. Watson.

A milestone for Hemingway studies and an important benefit for this edition as we strive for completeness has been the preservation of Hemingway's letters and other documents at Finca Vigía, his longtime home outside Havana, and the 2009 opening of these materials to researchers by both the Museo Hemingway in Cuba and the Kennedy Library in Boston. For their parts in this effort, the following deserve recognition: in Cuba, Dra. Margarita Ruíz Brandi, President, Consejo Nacional de Patrimonio Cultural (National Council of Cultural Patrimony); her predecessor, Dra. Marta Arjona; Gladys Rodríguez Ferrero; Ada Rosa Alfonso Rosales, Isbel Ferreiro Garit, and the staff of the Museo Hemingway; in the United States, Congressman Jim McGovern, Jenny and Frank Phillips, Mary-Jo Adams, Thomas D. Herman, Consuelo Isaacson, Martin Peterson, Bob Vila, and the Finca Vigía Foundation; Stanley Katz, Social Science Research Council; and Ann Russell and Walter Newman, Northeast Document Conservation Center. For various help in our research of Hemingway's life in Cuba we also are grateful to Ana Elena de Arazoza, Enrique Cirules, Esperanza García Fernández, Oscar Blas Fernández, Raul and Rita Villarreal, and René Villarreal.

Those who have served as graduate research assistants at Penn State deserve much appreciation for their dedication and diligence and their many valuable contributions to the edition: Lauren Christensen, Geffrey Davis, Michael DuBose, Charles Ebersole, Jeffrey Gonzalez, Janet Holtman, Verna Kale, Julius Lobo, Stefani Marciante, Susan Martin, and Katie Owens-Murphy.

We appreciate, too, the fine work of these undergraduate assistants at the Project center: Kyle Bohunicky, Alicia Brennan, Claudia Caracci, Mark Celeste, Jennifer Cihonski, Bekah Dickstein, Lauren Eckenroth, David Eggert, Lauren Finnegan, John Gorman, Catherine Grabenhorst, Samantha Guss, John Haefele, Jabari Hall, Matthew Hook, Juliet Howard, Robert Huber, Matthew Inman, Lindsay Keiter, Allison Kuchta, Katherine Leiden, Carolyn Maginnis, John Malone, Ashlee Mayo, Andrew Mihailoff, Ashley Miller, Letitia Montgomery, Bryon Moser, Kooshan Nayerahmadi, Alice Portalatin, Megan Shawver, Aline Smith, Kelly Snyder, Brian Tkaczyk, Kevin Todorow, Michelle Vincent, and Danielle Zahoran.

For their excellent service to the Project in various other capacities we thank Linnet Brooks, Elizabeth Knepp, Richard Stutz, JoAnn Wilson, and Shannon Whitlock.

We also wish to recognize those based at the following universities for their contributions: Boise State University graduate assistants Lauren Allan, Nicole Christianson, Marek Markowski, Christy C. Vance, and Kristin W. Whiting; Illinois State University graduate assistant Catherine Ratliff; and at Kent State University, Catherine Tisch, administrative assistant for the Institute for Bibliography and Editing, and graduate assistants Jennifer Beno, Jennifer Butto, Benjamin Gundy, Rebecca Johnson, Chad Junkins, Jacqueline Krah, Adam McKee, Rachel Nordhoff, Joanna Orcutt, Garth Sabo, Christa Testa, and Simone West.

We are most grateful to our publisher, Cambridge University Press, for its commitment to producing this comprehensive scholarly edition. We wish to express our particular thanks for the vision and support of publisher Linda Bree and the expert assistance of Maartje Scheltens. We also wish to thank the following for their roles in the preparation and publication of this volume: in the United Kingdom, Elizabeth Davey and Audrey Cotterell, and in New York, Liza Murphy, Melissanne Scheld, and Michael Duncan. We owe thanks, too, to Chip Kidd.

Finally, we are deeply grateful for the interest and support of other colleagues, family members, and friends too numerous to name, but who, we trust, know of our appreciation. The list of those to whom we owe thanks inevitably will grow much longer as publication of the edition proceeds, and we will continue to acknowledge our accumulating debts of gratitude in subsequent volumes.

SANDRA SPANIER

NOTE ON THE TEXT

RULES OF TRANSCRIPTION

As a rule, the text is transcribed exactly as it appears in Hemingway's hand or typewriting, in order to preserve the flavor of the letter—whether casual, hurried, harried, inventive, or playful (as when he writes "goils" instead of "girls," refers to his cats as "kotsies," remarks "we cant stahnd it," or exclaims "Goturletter thanks!"). When his handwriting is ambiguous, we have given him the benefit of the doubt and transcribed words and punctuation in their correct form. Special challenges of transcription are treated as follows:

Spelling
- When a typed character is incomplete, distorted, or visible only as an impression on the paper (whether due to a weak keystroke, type in need of cleaning, or a worn-out ink ribbon) but nevertheless is discernible (as ultimately determined in the field checking of the original document), the intended character is supplied without editorial comment.
- When a blank space suggests that an intended letter in a word is missing but no physical trace of a keystroke exists on the manuscript page, or when Hemingway types a word off the edge of the paper, the conjectured missing letter or portion of the word is supplied in square brackets: e.g., "the[y] are trying," or "meningiti[s] epidemic."
- Similarly, when a word is incomplete due to an obvious oversight or a slip of the pen or pencil, and the editors deem it advisable for clarity's sake, we supply missing letters in square brackets: e.g., "I[t] makes no difference."
- Because typewriter keyboards varied over time and from one country to another and did not always include a key for every character Hemingway wished to write, he necessarily improvised: e.g., for the numeral one he often typed a capital letter "I," and for an exclamation point, he would backspace to type a single quotation mark above a period. We have not attempted to reproduce those improvisations or conventions of the day but have silently supplied characters that Hemingway would have typed himself had his keyboard allowed.

- We have not attempted to reproduce in print the appearance of mechanical malfunctions. For example, when jammed typewriter keys cause two letters to appear superimposed in a single letter space, such errors are silently corrected, the letters transcribed without comment in the sequence that makes sense.
- Hemingway's occasionally uncrossed t's and undotted i's appear correctly without editorial comment.

Capitalization

As a rule, Hemingway's usage is preserved exactly. However, while his handwriting is generally open and legible, his uppercase and lowercase letters are sometimes indistinguishable. (The letters "a" and "g," for example, almost always take the form of the lowercase, with capital letters often differentiated only by their size relative to other letters.) In ambiguous cases, we have silently followed correct usage in the context of the sentence.

Punctuation

Whether Hemingway is writing by hand or on a typewriter, there is no apparent pattern to his use or omission of apostrophes, and in handwritten letters he frequently marks the end of a sentence with a dash rather than a period. Hemingway's often erratic punctuation—or lack thereof—has been strictly preserved, except in the following instances:

- In handwritten letters Hemingway sometimes marked the end of a declarative sentence with a small "x" (likely a carryover from his early habits as a newspaper reporter), a wavy flourish, or another mark difficult to render in print. Rather than attempting to reproduce these markings, we have normalized them without comment as periods.
- Hemingway sometimes wrote parentheses as vertical or slanted lines; these have been normalized as curved parentheses.
- Hemingway often neglected to put a period at the end of a paragraph's last sentence (as indicated by indentation of the following line) or at the end of a sentence enclosed in parentheses. Other sentences simply run together. To routinely insert ending punctuation for the sake of grammatical correctness would alter the letters' pace and tone: masking Hemingway's carelessness or breathlessness, erasing both the inadvertent charm of some childhood letters and his intentional wordplay, and imposing an arbitrary logic or false clarity on some ambiguously worded passages. Generally we do not supply missing full stops, except when the editors deem it necessary for clarity or when Hemingway's intention seems obvious: e.g., as indicated by extra spacing after

a word and capitalization of the following word to mark the beginning of a new sentence. In such cases, we supply a period within square brackets.

- Whenever the editors have supplied punctuation for clarity's sake, those punctuation marks are enclosed within square brackets: e.g., as when Hemingway neglected to use commas to separate proper names in a list.

Cancellations and corrections

Hemingway rarely bothered to erase errors or false starts in his letters, typically canceling or correcting written material either by drawing a line through it or typing over it. Usually his intent is clear, and we have not reproduced every cancellation and correction. However, when deleted or altered material is legible and the editors deem it of significance or interest, a cancellation or correction may be retained in place, with a line drawn through the text that Hemingway canceled, as the reader would have encountered it in the letter.

When he typed over his misstrikes with more forceful keystrokes so that his intended phrasing appears in darker type, we present only his corrected version. When he canceled words and phrases by backspacing and typing over them (usually with strings of the letter "x"), he occasionally missed a letter at the beginning or end of the canceled material; we do not reproduce stray characters that he obviously intended to cancel. Nor do we transcribe stray characters and false starts that he simply neglected to cancel: e.g., a portion of a word typed off the right margin of the page, followed by the complete word on the following line.

Interlineations, marginalia, and other markings

Hemingway's insertions, whether they appear as interlineations or marginalia, have been transferred into the text at a point that, in the editors' judgment, most accurately reflects his intended placement. However, when the insertion would render a sentence or passage confusing if simply transcribed at the indicated point without comment, we enclose the inserted material within square brackets and provide a brief editorial explanation in italics: e.g. [*EH insertion*:]. When the intended position of any material is questionable or an insertion merits editorial comment, the situation is addressed in a note.

When Hemingway's markings indicate that the order of letters, words, or phrases should be transposed, we have done so without comment. When he uses ditto marks to indicate repetition of a word or phrase appearing on a previous line of the original text, we have supplied that word or phrase within square brackets at the indicated place: e.g., "Did you write the Steins? [*ditto marks*: Did you write the] Ford Maddox Fords."

Whenever possible, Hemingway's occasional sketches or drawings are reproduced as they appear in the text of the letter. Otherwise, brief descriptions are provided in square brackets where such graphic elements appear in the text: e.g. [*drawing of a sleeping cat*], and any commentary that the editors deem necessary is supplied in a note.

Other markings in the text that are difficult to render in print, such as stray doodles or flourishes underneath the letter date or signature, are not noted unless the editors deem them to be of particular interest. We do not transcribe Hemingway's page numbering.

Indentation and spacing

In both handwritten and typewritten letters, Hemingway's indications of paragraph breaks are irregular or non-existent. Sometimes, instead of indenting, he signaled a paragraph break by starting a new page, leaving a gap between lines, or ending the previous sentence in midline. The editors have indicated new paragraphs by regular indentation of the first line.

In typewritten letters, Hemingway's spacing is erratic. Frequently he hit the space bar both before and after punctuation marks or several times between words, and extraneous blank spaces occasionally appear in the middle of a word. The spacing around punctuation marks and between words has been normalized, and extraneous blank spaces appearing within words have been silently eliminated.

However, when Hemingway ran words together with no space between, they are transcribed exactly as they appear, as it is often impossible to determine whether he did this accidentally or intentionally for effect. Run-together words also may indicate a mood of haste or excitement that would be lost to readers if conventional spacing were editorially inserted.

Compound words

Transcriptions follow Hemingway's treatment of compound words exactly, with no attempt made to impose consistency or to correct or standardize hyphenation or spacing: e.g., there is no apparent pattern to his usage of such compounds as "good-bye," "goodbye," and "good bye," or "someone" vs. "some one."

In handwritten letters, Hemingway's "y" is often followed by a space that might or might not mark a gap between words: e.g., it is sometimes difficult to tell if he intended to write "anyway" or "any way." When Hemingway's handwriting is ambiguous, we transcribe the word as it would be used correctly in that sentence.

Underlined words

Words underlined by Hemingway are underlined in the transcriptions; the double, triple, and quadruple underlining he occasionally employed also is indicated in order to capture his emphasis or exuberance.

Missing portions of text
Square brackets are used to indicate illegible, damaged, or missing text at the point of occurrence, with a description of the manuscript's condition in italics: e.g., [*illegible*], [*MS torn*], [*MS razor-cut by censor*]. Any conjectured reconstruction of missing text is supplied in roman type within square brackets.

Date and place of writing
The date and place of origin (often a specific return address) as supplied by Hemingway in the text of his letters are transcribed exactly as he wrote them; however, we have standardized the line placement of these elements so they appear flush to the right margin. The use of letterhead is indicated in the source note following the complete text of a letter, and letterhead address information also is recorded there rather than transcribed as part of the text of the letter.

Valediction and signature
Hemingway's valediction and signature are transcribed as he wrote them, whether on one line or two, but their position on the page is standardized so that they appear flush to the right margin.

Postscripts
Regardless of where a postscript appears in the manuscript (in a margin, at the top or bottom of a letter, or on the back of a letter's final page), it is transcribed as a new paragraph following the signature, reflecting the probable order of composition.

Joint letters
Letters that Hemingway wrote with another person or to which he adds a post-script are presented in their entirety so as to preserve the context of his portion, with the point at which one writer takes over from another indicated in brackets: e.g., [*EH begins:*] or [*Hadley begins:*]. Where one writer inserts a brief remark into the text of another, the point of interjection as well as the remark itself are indicated in brackets: e.g., [*EH interjects*: I doubt this.].

Foreign languages
Any portion of a letter written in a language other than English is transcribed exactly as Hemingway wrote it, with no attempt to correct errors or to supply any missing diacritical marks.

When a word, phrase, sentence, or passage within a letter is in a foreign language, a translation is supplied in a note preceded, when deemed necessary for clarity, by the correct spelling or diacritical form of a word. Translations are not supplied for words or phrases presumably familiar to most readers: e.g., *adios, au revoir.* When Hemingway wrote an entire letter in another language, the transcription of the original text is followed by an English translation in square brackets.

We have not attempted in our translations to replicate Hemingway's foreign-language grammatical errors: e.g., in conjugation of verbs and in gender agreement of nouns and adjectives. Rather, we provide a translation that conveys the sense of the message, while briefly noting the presence and nature of such errors. Similarly, we do not attempt to replicate the exact syntax and mechanics (e.g., capitalization and punctuation) of Hemingway's use of a foreign language, but rather aim in our English translation to convey the style and tone of his usage, whether formal or colloquial.

EDITORIAL APPARATUS

Heading
Each letter is preceded by a heading indicating the recipient and date of the letter, with any portion supplied by the editors enclosed in square brackets.

Source note
A bibliographical note immediately following each letter provides information about the source text upon which the transcription is based, including the location and form of the original letter. Abbreviations used are described in the list of Abbreviations and Short Titles in the front matter of each volume. Information appears in this order:

(1) Symbols indicate the location and form of the original letter. For example, "JFK, TLS" indicates a typed letter signed that is located in the collections of the John F. Kennedy Library. When the original letter cannot be located and the transcription derives from another source (e.g., a photocopy, a recipient's transcription, a secretary's transcription of dictation, an auction catalog, or another publication), that source is indicated. When Hemingway closed a letter with a "mark" instead of writing his name (as when he drew a beer stein to signify his nickname "Stein," short for "Hemingstein"), we have considered the letter to be signed, describing it, for example, as "TLS" rather than "TL."

(2) The use of letterhead stationery is noted and the address information supplied. Additional letterhead elements tangential to the study of Hemingway (e.g., an advertising slogan, description of a hotel's facilities, proprietor's name, phone number) are not generally recorded. However, in the rare cases when Hemingway provides commentary on these elements, the situation is

described in a note. If the text is from a picture postcard, a brief description is provided: e.g., A Postcard S, verso: Sun Valley Lodge, Idaho.

(3) Surviving postmark information is supplied. When a postmark stamp is incomplete or illegible, portions of place names or dates supplied by the editors are enclosed in square brackets: e.g., SCH[RUN]S. When the original letter cannot be consulted and postmark information derives from another source (e.g., a description in an auction catalog), we enclose that information in square brackets.

Endnotes

Annotations appear as endnotes following each letter. In notes Ernest Hemingway is referred to as EH. Initials are not used for any other persons, but editors frequently use the short names that Hemingway would have used: e.g., Hadley for his first wife, Elizabeth Hadley Richardson Hemingway; or Buck Lanham for his friend General Charles T. Lanham. Recipients of letters included in a given volume are identified in the Roster of Correspondents in the back matter of that volume. Other people are identified in endnotes at first mention. There necessarily may be some duplication and cross-referencing as we aim to make the volumes useful to readers, not all of whom will read the letters strictly chronologically within a given volume or across the edition.

In determining which references merit annotation, we have been mindful of the international audience for the edition and, in consultation with the publisher, have provided notes for some references likely to be familiar to U.S. readers: e.g., Karo syrup, Old Faithful geyser. We do not generally attempt to explicate EH's inventive expressions, private slang, and other wordplay, leaving it to readers to experience and interpret his language as he wrote it.

The editors have made every effort to identify EH's references to people, places, events, publications, and artistic works. However, the identities of some are inevitably lost to history. When a note is not provided at the first mention of a reference, the reader can assume that it remains unidentified.

SANDRA SPANIER

ABBREVIATIONS AND SHORT TITLES

Stanford	Department of Special Collections and University Archives, Stanford University Libraries; Stanford, California
UChicago	Special Collections Research Center, University of Chicago; Chicago, Illinois
UMD	Special Collections, University of Maryland Libraries; College Park, Maryland
UT	Harry Ransom Humanities Research Center, The University of Texas at Austin; Austin, Texas
UTulsa	Department of Special Collections, McFarlin Library, University of Tulsa; Tulsa, Oklahoma
UVA	Special Collections, University of Virginia Library; Charlottesville, Virginia
Yale	Yale Collection of American Literature, Beinecke Rare Book and Manuscript Library, Yale University; New Haven, Connecticut
Zieman	Mark and Rhonda Zieman Collection

FORMS OF CORRESPONDENCE

The following abbreviations are used in combination to describe the form of the original source text (e.g., ALS for autograph letter signed, TLS for typed letter signed, ACD autograph cable draft, TLcc for typed letter carbon copy, phJFK for a photocopy at the John F. Kennedy Library):

A	Autograph
C	Cable
cc	Carbon copy
D	Draft
Frag	Fragment
L	Letter
N	Note
ph	Photocopy
S	Signed
T	Typed

Other Abbreviations

b.	born
c.	circa
d.	died
m.	married
OPRFHS	Oak Park and River Forest High School; Oak Park, Illinois

PUBLISHED WORKS

Works by Ernest Hemingway

The following abbreviations and short titles for Hemingway's works are employed throughout the edition; not all of them appear in the present volume. First U.S. editions are cited, unless otherwise noted.

ARIT   *Across the River and into the Trees.* New York: Scribner's, 1950.

BL   *By-line Ernest Hemingway: Selected Articles and Dispatches of Four Decades.* Edited by William White. New York: Scribner's, 1967.

CSS   *The Complete Short Stories of Ernest Hemingway: The Finca Vigía Edition.* New York: Scribner's, 1987.

DLT   *Dateline: Toronto: The Complete "Toronto Star" Dispatches, 1920–1924.* Edited by William White. New York: Scribner's, 1985.

DIA   *Death in the Afternoon.* New York: Scribner's, 1932.

DS   *The Dangerous Summer.* New York: Scribner's, 1985.

FC   *The Fifth Column and the First Forty-nine Stories.* New York: Scribner's, 1938.

FTA   *A Farewell to Arms.* New York: Scribner's, 1929.

FWBT   *For Whom the Bell Tolls.* New York: Scribner's, 1940.

GOE   *The Garden of Eden.* New York: Scribner's, 1986.

GHOA   *Green Hills of Africa.* New York: Scribner's, 1935.

iot   *in our time.* Paris: Three Mountains Press, 1924.

IOT   *In Our Time.* New York: Boni and Liveright, 1925. Rev. edn. New York: Scribner's, 1930.

IIS   *Islands in the Stream.* New York: Scribner's, 1970.

MAW   *Men at War.* New York: Crown Publishers, 1942.

MF   *A Moveable Feast.* New York: Scribner's, 1964.

MF-RE   *A Moveable Feast: The Restored Edition.* Edited by Seán Hemingway. New York: Scribner's, 2009.

MWW   *Men Without Women.* New York: Scribner's, 1927.

NAS   *The Nick Adams Stories.* New York: Scribner's, 1972.

OMS   *The Old Man and the Sea.* New York: Scribner's, 1952.

Poems   *Complete Poems.* Edited, with an Introduction and Notes by Nicholas Gerogiannis. Rev. edn. Lincoln: University of Nebraska Press, 1992.

SAR   *The Sun Also Rises.* New York: Scribner's, 1926.

SL   *Ernest Hemingway: Selected Letters, 1917–1961.* Edited by Carlos Baker. New York: Scribner's, 1981.

SS   *The Short Stories of Ernest Hemingway*. New York: Scribner's, 1954.

TAFL   *True at First Light*. Edited by Patrick Hemingway. New York: Scribner's, 1999.

THHN   *To Have and Have Not*. New York: Scribner's, 1937.

TOS   *The Torrents of Spring*. New York: Scribner's, 1926.

TOTTC   *The Only Thing That Counts: The Ernest Hemingway–Maxwell Perkins Correspondence, 1925–1947*. Edited by Matthew J. Bruccoli with Robert W. Trogdon. New York: Scribner's, 1996.

TSTP   *Three Stories and Ten Poems*. Paris: Contact Editions, 1923.

UK   *Under Kilimanjaro*. Edited by Robert W. Lewis and Robert E. Fleming. Kent, Ohio: Kent State University Press, 2005.

WTN   *Winner Take Nothing*. New York: Scribner's, 1933.

Reference works frequently cited in this volume

Baker *Life*	Baker, Carlos. *Ernest Hemingway: A Life Story*. New York: Scribner's, 1969.
Bakewell	Bakewell, Charles M. *The Story of the American Red Cross in Italy*. New York: Macmillan, 1920.
Bruccoli *Apprenticeship*	Bruccoli, Matthew J., ed. *Ernest Hemingway's Apprenticeship: Oak Park 1916–1917*. Washington, D.C.: Microcard Editions, National Cash Register, 1971.
Bruccoli *Cub*	Bruccoli, Matthew J., ed. *Ernest Hemingway, Cub Reporter: "Kansas City Star" Stories*. Pittsburgh: University of Pittsburgh Press, 1970.
Diliberto	Diliberto, Gioia. *Hadley*. New York: Ticknor and Fields, 1992.
Fenton	Fenton, Charles. *The Apprenticeship of Ernest Hemingway: The Early Years*. New York: Farrar, Straus and Young, 1954.
Griffin	Griffin, Peter. *Along with Youth: Hemingway: The Early Years*. New York: Oxford University Press, 1985.
Hanneman	Hanneman, Audre. *Ernest Hemingway: A Comprehensive Bibliography*. Princeton, New Jersey: Princeton University Press, 1967.
Hanneman2	Hanneman, Audre. *Supplement to Ernest Hemingway: A Comprehensive Bibliography*. Princeton, New Jersey: Princeton University Press, 1975.

P. Hemingway   Hemingway, Patricia S. *The Hemingways: Past and Present and Allied Families*. Rev. edn. Baltimore: Gateway Press, Inc., 1988.

M. Miller   Miller, Madelaine Hemingway. *Ernie: Hemingway's Sister "Sunny" Remembers*. New York: Crown Publishers, 1975.

Ohle   Ohle, William H. *How It Was in Horton Bay, Charlevoix County, Michigan*. Boyne City, Michigan: William H. Ohle, 1989.

Reynolds *PY*   Reynolds, Michael S. *Hemingway: The Paris Years*. Oxford: Basil Blackwell, 1989.

Reynolds *YH*   Reynolds, Michael S. *The Young Hemingway*. Oxford: Basil Blackwell, 1986.

Sanford   Sanford, Marcelline Hemingway. *At the Hemingways: With Fifty Years of Correspondence Between Ernest and Marcelline Hemingway*. Moscow: University of Idaho Press, 1999.

Smith   Smith, Paul. *A Reader's Guide to the Short Stories of Ernest Hemingway*. Boston: G. K. Hall, 1989.

Villard and Nagel   Villard, Henry S., and James Nagel, eds. *Hemingway in Love and War: The Lost Diary of Agnes von Kurowsky, Her Letters, and Correspondence of Ernest Hemingway*. Boston: Northeastern University Press, 1989.

FOREWORD TO
THE VOLUME

Linda Patterson Miller

Ernest Hemingway the writer changed the way people saw and thought about their world. But even as his works continue to command scholarly attention and global acclaim, the interplay between his artistry and the life that shaped it remains only half understood. A fuller understanding is needed, and the complete letters of Ernest Hemingway, which promise to challenge shop-worn myths and assumptions about Hemingway and his transformative art, will help make that possible.

This initial volume provides an epistolary portrait of Hemingway becoming Hemingway. It brings together the letters he wrote from his youthful days in his native Oak Park through his first year in Paris in 1922, and in so doing traces his apprenticeship as a writer. In correspondence with family and friends—from his time in Kansas City with the *Kansas City Star*, to his wounding and convalescence in Italy during World War I, to his return to the camping and fishing of northern Michigan where he had spent his boyhood summers, to his first adventures in the City of Light—Hemingway was foregrounding the experiences and describing the places that would figure in his earliest and perhaps best stories. The fresh voice that emerges in these letters is that of the young Hemingway, an ambitious hard-working youth but not yet a legend, not yet Papa.

Hemingway did not become an established writer until after 1922 (he was still essentially unpublished except for his newspaper pieces), but his early letters reveal that he was very much aware of himself as a writer in the making. After working as a cub reporter at the *Kansas City Star* for six months, Hemingway wrote his father on 16 April 1918 to express his understanding that professional newspaper writing demanded immediacy and precision, along with endurance. He was "bushed! . . . mentally and physically," he told his father, from months of "[h]aving to write a half column story with every name, address and initial verified and remembering to use good style, perfect style in fact, an get all the facts and in the correct order, make it have snap and wallop" and "see it all in your minds eye," while "a boy snatches the pages from your machine as fast as you write them."

Already Hemingway was learning to capture moments that flash to life on the page. A number of such flashpoints occur in his letters, particularly when he reflects on earlier times. Thus in a letter of 20 May 1921 to his sister Marcelline, Hemingway described his recent return from a "swell party" in Chicago with his Oak Park friend Issy Simmons on an evening when the spring air reminded him of his childhood: "It was a glorious night. We'd come out of some place where we'd been waltzing and into the outer air and it would be warm and almost tropical with a big moon over the tops of the houses. Kind of a warm softness in the air, same way it used to be when we were kids and we'd roller skate or play run sheep run with the Luckocks and Charlotte Bruce."

Such recaptured moments intermingle with Hemingway's day-to-day thoughts and encounters in his letters. He wrote qualitatively different letters to each family member and close friend, creating parallel yet divergent narrative lines even when writing to more than one of them on the same day about the same matters. Each letter has its own pitch of voice and slant of light; it tells its own story. When read chronologically and collectively, this multiplicity of perspectives suggests the contrapuntal resonance and emotional discord inherent in the modernist art Hemingway would begin to absorb once he arrived in Paris in late 1921.

The letters in this volume gauge the emotional compass of Hemingway's coming of age as he confronted his rapidly changing world firsthand. Sometimes the letters seem self-absorbed and boastful, not unusual for someone so young, but often they are humorous, exuberant, honest, and engaging. They reveal as well Hemingway's emerging and maturing style, including his eye for specific detail and his rejection of platitudes, pretense, and the language of abstraction.

The letters testify to two basic shaping influences of Hemingway's early years on his psyche and his art: his middle-class upbringing and his World War I experiences. Those accustomed to believing that Hemingway resented his Oak Park roots, and that he had a difficult relationship with his family, may be surprised by the number of tender, considerate letters he wrote to his parents and siblings. Their tone, complexity, and textual richness show that Hemingway's family meant a great deal to him and that his relationships with them over time should not be oversimplified.

Hemingway's exposure to war and its relationship to his writing deserve to be reexamined in the light of his wartime correspondence—much of it to his family, and including several previously unpublished letters. It has become a critical commonplace that his wounding as an American Red Cross ambulance driver in World War I scarred him psychologically and led him to create emotionally damaged heroes attempting to live in a troubled world through the code of grace under pressure. Yet Hemingway's letters underscore how little he saw of actual battle, and how he was inclined to romanticize his wartime feats. During his convalescence in Milan between July and December 1918, he wrote his family often, sometimes in back-to-back letters that collectively capture the rhythm of his mood swings. In these letters home, we see his thinking evolve from the gee-whiz tone of an eighteen-year-old with the sense of war as a grand adventure—"Oh, Boy!!! I'm glad I'm in it," he wrote a friend c. 9 June 1918—to the more philosophical reflections of a wounded "soldier" who lived to tell his story.

On 14 July 1918 Hemingway's friend Ted Brumback wrote to Clarence and Grace Hemingway about the details of their son's wounding six days earlier. Brumback emphasized Hemingway's bravery in going directly to the front to deliver cigarettes and chocolates to the troops, and his gallantry under fire when, despite serious injuries to his own legs, he carried a wounded Italian soldier to safety. In a postscript to this letter, Hemingway downplayed these actions, assuring his parents, "I am all O.K. and . . . I'm not near so much of a hell roarer as Brummy makes me out." In a follow-up letter home written on 21 July, his nineteenth birthday, he turned his attention to detailing the physical landscape of the Italian front, where he had picked up "a wonderful lot of souvenirs" shortly before his wounding. The letter was more inventory than introspection, until its ending: "I was all through the big battle and have Austrian carbines and ammunition, German and Austrian medals, officers automatic pistols, Boche helmets[,] about a dozen Bayonets, star shell pistols and knives and almost everything you can think of. The only limit to the amount of souvenirs I could have is what I could carry for there were so many dead Austrians and prisoners the ground was almost black with them." The specificity of detail and cataloging, culminating in stark and unsettling understatement, hints at Hemingway's future writing style and foreshadows later war stories such as "A Way You'll Never Be," in which he evokes the physical and psychological aftermath of battle. In that story, Nick Adams tries to suppress a mounting hysteria over what he had seen on the battlefield, where you could tell "what had happened by the position of the dead." [1]

After initially downplaying the account of his wounding, Hemingway elaborated more in the weeks that followed. As he regained his physical strength, he began to face the reality of his experience more directly. The violence of the war could not be overstated, he wrote his family on 18 August 1918. "When a shell makes a direct hit in a group where you're standing . . . your pals get spattered all over you. Spattered is literal." Hemingway then vividly described the immediate aftermath of his own wounding when he "lay for two hours in a stable, with the roof shot off, waiting for an ambulance" that would take him to a dressing station, all the while hearing the shelling "still pretty thick" in the background and the "big 250s and 350's going over head for Austria with a noise like a railway train." The suggested trauma of that night anticipates that of Nick Adams in "Now I Lay Me." Nick lies in a shed exposed to the night air and listening "to the silk-worms eating" as he tries to avoid sleep, believing that "if I ever shut my eyes in the dark and let myself go, my soul would go out of my body." [2]

Subsequent letters during the fall of 1918, however, document Hemingway's attempts to detach himself from the war and his own near-death experience by philosophizing about his invulnerability and the grandeur of the cause. "Dying is a very simple thing," he wrote his family on 18 October. "I've looked at death, and really I know. If I should have died it would hve been very easy for me. Quite the easiest thing I ever did . . . And how much better to die in all the happy period of undissillusioned youth, to go out in a blaze of light, than to have your body worn out and old and illusions shattered."

In terms of Hemingway's disillusionment, some have argued that his coming of age occurred not by being wounded in war but by being wounded in love after he returned to America. The letters that he wrote in the months following his early 1919 homecoming in Oak Park, chiefly to his new wartime friends, shed new light on this issue. While he was hospitalized in Milan, Hemingway had fallen in love with an American nurse, Agnes von Kurowsky. When he returned to the States, it was understood that she would follow him and they would be married. Then, on 30 March 1919, he received a devastating letter from Agnes breaking off the relationship. She felt a fondness for him "more as a mother than as a sweetheart," Agnes wrote, and she expected "to be married soon" to an Italian officer.[3] On the very day that Hemingway received her letter, he wrote Bill Horne, a friend from the ambulance corps, to communicate his shock and sorrow. "I can't write it honest to Gawd," Hemingway began. "It has hit me so sudden. So I'll tell you everything I know first." After chatting for a couple of paragraphs, he continued, "Now having failed miserably at being facetious I'll tell you the sad truth which . . . culminated with a letter from Ag this morning. She doesn't love me Bill. She takes it all back . . . Oh Bill I can't kid about it and I can't be bitter because I'm just smashed by it."

Yet that smash-up may well have left him less distraught or emotionally damaged than most commentators have maintained. Less than a month later, in a long letter to Jim Gamble written between 18 and 27 April, Hemingway was able to rationalize that he felt liberated by Agnes's rejection. "All entangling alliances ceased about a month ago and I know now I am most damnably lucky . . . I did love the girl, though I know now that the paucity of Americans doubtless had a great deal to do with it. And now it's over I'm glad . . . I'm now free to do whatever I want. Go whereever I want and have all the time in the world to develop into some kind of a writer."

For nearly three years between his return to America in early 1919 and his embarkation for Paris in late 1921, though, Hemingway remained rooted in and around Chicago, with one brief stay in Canada and occasional sojourns to his boyhood haunts in northern Michigan, the country of his heart. His letters of this period, most often written to friends from the war, underscore the powerful pull northern Michigan had on him and the significant role that his youth there would play in inspiring the Nick Adams stories of *In Our Time* (1925).

Hemingway promoted the "beautiful country" of northern Michigan as he organized camping and fishing excursions there for his male companions. In his letter of 18 and 27 April 1919, for instance, he urged Gamble to join him and other friends for "[a]bsolutely the best trout fishing in the country." As Hemingway described the "manner of the fishing" for trout, he wrote how they would "paddle over across the bay and stop at this old lumber dock. Just level with the water." From there they would "run out about four or five lines into the channel" and eventually, at least by nightfall, hook "a big rainbow [that] shoots up into the air. And then the fight."

This letter is just one of several that, taken together, convey a sense of innocence lost to the passage of time and evoke a lyricism reminiscent of Mark Twain's *Adventures of Huckleberry Finn* (1884), a book Hemingway admired as the beginning of "all modern American literature." [4] Huck describes the easy-going camaraderie of life on the water as he and the runaway slave Jim "kind of lazy along and by and by lazy off to sleep" on the Mississippi River.[5] Similarly, in his April 1919 letter to Gamble, Hemingway spoke of northern Michigan as "a great place to laze around and swim and fish when you want to. And the best place in the world to do nothing." They'd set out their lines. "Then if it is night we have a camp fire on the point and sit around and yarn and smoke or if it is daytime we loaf around and read and await results."

Gertrude Stein labeled the postwar generation the "Lost Generation," but Hemingway believed that he and his comrades were not so much lost in the world as the pristine countryside was becoming lost to them. His 1919–1921 letters show him seeking to recapture the last good country that he would eventually re-envision for Nick Adams's postwar restoration in "Big Two-Hearted River." As he wrote Bill Horne on 25 March 1920, "Words can't describe the Fishing in the Black, Pidgeon and Big Sturgeon Rivers" where "We camp at the Black way out on the barrens and you won't see a house or a soul. Nothing but the Pine Barrens with great wide sweep and ridges of pine trees rising up like islands." In "Big Two-Hearted River," Nick stops to rest within such an "island of pine trees" where "the trunks of the trees went straight up or slanted toward each other" before he hiked a bit farther to set up camp "in the good place ... in his home where he had made it." [6]

Wonderful as northern Michigan might be, Hemingway could only reclaim that territory in his writing after moving abroad in late 1921. His postwar letters from the United States reveal his yearning to cut free from America by returning to live and write in Europe. As early as 3 March 1919, he began articulating his ambivalence about his homeland. "I'm patriotic and willing to die for this great and glorious nation," he wrote Gamble. "But I hate like the deuce to live in it." By the time he and his wife Hadley, newly married, moved to Paris, he expressed his feelings more forcefully. "There's no living in the States," he wrote Kate Smith on 27 January 1922. What was "the use of trying to live in such a goddam place as America when there is Paris and Switzerland and Italy"? Hemingway had been exploring Switzerland for ten days when he sent that letter to Kate, his friend from summers at Michigan's Horton Bay: "here is country that has the bay lashed to the mast. Enormous forests, good trout streams, wonderful roads, and thousands of places to go." Still, he was already "a little lonesome for Paris" and eager to get back there. "This town of Paris bites into a man's blood."

During 1922 Hemingway also visited Italy, Germany, and the French country-side, and his letters reveal his passion for the new locales even as they lament the time he had to devote to his newspaper articles. "This goddam newspaper stuff is gradually ruining me," he confessed to Sherwood Anderson on 9 March 1922. He hoped "to cut it all loose pretty soon" so as to become a writer only, working out of his home base in Paris.

Hemingway had arrived there in late December 1921 armed with letters of introduction from Anderson to leading figures in the literary community, and with a determination to make his mark as a serious writer. The Paris he encountered was a strange new world unfettered by American expectations and swirling with artistic turbulence. Hemingway's first letters from Paris teem with the intensity of the city that was to nurture and shape his emerging identity as a pioneer of modern American prose. Shortly after his arrival, he wrote Anderson and his wife, Tennessee, in a letter of c. 23 December 1921, that he and Hadley were sitting in the heart of Paris, "outside the Dome Cafe, oposite the Rotunde that's being redecorated, warmed up against one of those charcoal brazziers." The weather was "damned cold outside," Hemingway declared, but "the brazier makes it so warm and we drink rum punch, hot, and the rhum enters into us like the Holy Spirit." He and Hadley had "been walking the streets, day and night, arm through arm, peering into courts and stopping in front of little shop windows. The pastry'll kill Bones even-tually I'm afraid. She's a hound for it." His account of those first days in Paris is reminiscent of Benjamin Franklin's entrance into the heart of Philadelphia, another young man resolutely determined to make his way in the world, carrying "three great Puffy Rolls" purchased from a local baker.[7] Hemingway and Hadley, like Franklin, watched in wonder as the great city blossomed before them.

The Hemingways settled into an apartment at 74, rue du Cardinal Lemoine, where they soon played host to Gertrude Stein and Alice B. Toklas. On 14 February Hemingway wrote approvingly of Stein in a letter to his mother, adding that "We know a good batch of people now in Paris and if we allowed it would have all our time taken up socially." Equipped with considerable charm and an abundance of talent, Hemingway was quickly accepted by the literati of Paris, including Stein and Ezra Pound, and just as quickly Paris became home to him. In late January, he reported to his family that Hadley "has a piano and we have all our pictures up on the walls and an open fire place and a peach of a kitchen and a dining room and big bed room and dressing room and plenty of space." Their apartment, he added, was "on top of a high hill in the very oldest part of Paris."

This elevated perspective—the sense of being on high and looking out and beyond his immediate surroundings—pervades the early letters in this volume. Before he went off to war in Europe, he wrote his family from New York City on 14 May 1918 that he had gone "up in the top of the Woolworth Tower 796 feet—62 stories high" from where he "could see the camouflajed boats going in and out of the harbor and see way up the East river to Hell's Gate." Writing to his mother from Italy on 29 July 1918, he stated proudly that he had "glimpsed the making of large gobs of history during the Great Battle of the Piave, and have been all along the Front From the mountains to the Sea." Back in Chicago in 1921, Hemingway wrote to his sister Marcelline on 20 May describing his "new Domocile" as "a wonder—much larger than the old one—and with an elevator and a view from my front window looking down over the queer angled roofs of the old houses on Rush street down to the big mountain of the Wrigley building, green of the new grass along the street and trees coming out." Above and beyond the hilltop Paris apartment, Hemingway sought out the greater heights of Switzerland, "a swell place" he implicitly compared to the environs of Walloon Lake in Michigan. Hemingway painted the scene in his letter to Marcelline c. 25 January 1922. He and Hadley would "ride up the mountin in a fine little train like the Peto-Walloon dummy, climbing, winding, climbing, winding, till we get way to hell and gone above everything where the train stops and you get into another one that runs on cog wheels to the top tip of the mt," from where, below, a whole world glistened in white-washed promise.

The letters in this volume show Hemingway striving toward artistic recognition, and conclude by foretelling his successful trajectory as a writer, despite the famous loss in late 1922 of all of his apprenticeship writing in the theft of a suitcase at the Gare de Lyon. Accounts differ regarding the particulars of this incident, but the horrible reality was that when Ernest met Hadley at the train station in Lausanne, the suitcase in which she had packed all of his extant writing was gone.

Surprisingly, Hemingway made no reference to the lost manuscripts in any located surviving letters immediately following this incident. Several weeks later, though, he did write Ezra Pound about it. "I suppose you heard bout the loss of my Juvenilia? . . . All that remains of my complete works are three pencil drafts of a bum poem which was later scrapped, some correspondence between John McClure and me, and some journalistic carbons." He suspected that Pound would probably say "'Good' etc." yet warned him: "Don't say it to me. I aint yet reached that mood. I worked 3 years on the damn stuff." [8] In *A Moveable Feast*, Hemingway recalled a conversation he had about the missing typescripts with Edward O'Brien, editor of the annual *Best Short Stories* anthologies. O'Brien was distressed to hear the news, and Hemingway kept reassuring him "not to feel so bad. It was probably good for me to lose early work and I told him all that stuff you feed the troops. I was going to start writing stories again I said and, as I said it, only trying to lie so that he would not feel so bad, I knew that it was true." [9]

Hemingway's relative silence in his letters about his devastating loss perhaps spoke to his newfound belief regarding omission in modernist art. As he later expressed it in conjunction with writing the first story that followed this incident, "Out of Season," "You could omit anything if you knew that you omitted and the omitted part would strengthen the story and make people feel something more than they understood." [10] The next year would see the publication of his first book, *Three Stories and Ten Poems*, containing that new story along with what remained of his pre-theft writings. In early 1924, back in Paris after a brief hiatus in Toronto for the birth of his son in October 1923, Hemingway started over. One lesson he had learned from his youthful years was that you had to get over the worst of it— the wounding in the war, the rejection by Agnes, the theft of the suitcase—and keep working. He would draw upon his losses as he went back to his typewriter and began to craft minimalist yet layered stories that cut to the quick. Refining experience through the fire of memory, he transmuted into art the childhood and coming of age that these letters graphically depict as he lived it. Read in concert with the stories, the letters illuminate the genesis of Hemingway's earliest and most iconic prose. They reveal the artist in the making and the boy becoming a man.

NOTES

1 *The Complete Short Stories of Ernest Hemingway: The Finca Vigía Edition* (New York: Scribner's, 1987), 306.

2 *Ibid.*, 276.

3 Henry S. Villard and James Nagel, eds., *Hemingway in Love and War: The Lost Diary of Agnes von Kurowsky, Her Letters, and Correspondence of Ernest Hemingway* (Boston: Northeastern University Press, 1989), 163–64.

4 Ernest Hemingway, *Green Hills of Africa* (New York: Scribner's, 1935), 22.

5 Mark Twain, *Adventures of Huckleberry Finn*, ed. Victor Fischer and Lin Salamo (Berkeley: University of California Press, 2003), 157.

6 Hemingway, *Complete Short Stories*, 166–67.

7 *Benjamin Franklin's Autobiography: An Authoritative Text*, ed. J. A. Leo Lemay and Paul M. Zall (New York: Norton, 1986), 20.

8 *Ernest Hemingway: Selected Letters, 1917–1961*, ed. Carlos Baker (New York: Scribner's 1981), 77.

9 Ernest Hemingway, *A Moveable Feast* (New York: Scribner's, 1964), 74–75.

10 *Ibid.*, 75.

INTRODUCTION TO
THE VOLUME

Robert W. Trogdon

While the structure and path of a writer's creative life defy easy categorization, especially a life as complex as Ernest Hemingway's, the letters in this volume illustrate four major periods in his development: his childhood in Oak Park and in Michigan; his young adulthood in Kansas City as a cub reporter and in Italy as an ambulance driver; the postwar interlude in Michigan and Chicago from 1919 to 1921 as he strove to become a professional author; and the beginning of his true literary apprenticeship during his first year in Paris in 1922. His correspondence maps the changes in his circumstances and personality through these periods and offers fresh insights into his craft and relationships. Perhaps the most important letters are those to his family, for they give us a more nuanced view of his relationship with them than has any other account to date. Of the 264 letters collected in this volume, more than half were written to members of his family: sometimes to a grandparent or a sister (especially Marcelline, older by fifteen months), but most often to his parents (addressed to them either separately or in a joint letter). Most of the remaining letters went to Michigan friends, including Bill Smith and Grace Quinlan, or to his friends from the war, including Bill Horne, Howell Jenkins, and Jim Gamble. Taken together, these early letters underscore the importance Hemingway placed on the people and places of his youth and the impact they had in shaping his sense of self and stoking his creative imagination.

Ernest Hemingway's formative years were spent in the American Midwest. The second child and first son of Clarence Hemingway, a physician in Oak Park, and Grace Hall Hemingway, a music instructor, he was born on 21 July 1899 and came of age with the twentieth century. A prosperous suburb of Chicago, the village of Oak Park maintained a rural aspect during his childhood. Dr. Hemingway kept a horse and buggy for making rounds during the first decade of the century, eventually replacing them with a Ford Model T when Ernest was a teenager, and the family maintained a coop for eggs and chickens. The young Hemingway could hunt on a game farm within easy walking distance of the family home. During the summers, the family moved to Windemere, their cottage on Walloon Lake in northern Michigan. While Ernest spent part of his time there swimming and fishing, when he was a teenager he also worked at nearby Longfield Farm (purchased by his family in 1905), haying and harvesting the apples and potato crops in late summer and early fall.

Hemingway's earliest letters reflect the typical interests of a boy with his background. He was an ardent baseball fan, especially of the Chicago Cubs and White Sox and the New York Giants, and wrote to order posters of his favorite players. Reflecting his father's love of the outdoors and the study of nature, he filled his letters with reports on fishing and observations of wildlife. On Nantucket Island with his mother Grace in 1910, he wrote his father asking for advice on the possible purchase of an albatross foot for the Oak Park Agassiz Club. As a teenager, he exchanged notes with classmates to plan camping and canoe trips, including one across Ontario, a trip he did not make. His high school letters are full of comments and jokes about his classmates and teachers, with remarks about schoolwork and extracurricular activities (including playing the cello in the school orchestra) and expressions of enthusiasm for fishing and hunting. Even when he was bad, Hemingway proved to be a dutiful son. In his letter of 31 July 1915 to his mother, written after he had killed a blue heron illegally and taken refuge at his Uncle George Hemingway's summer home in Ironton, Michigan, he outlined what he had done to provide for his family before fleeing from the game warden. But the teenage Hemingway's letters also frequently refer to reading and writing. He sprinkled them with quotations from Rudyard Kipling and recommendations of poets and novelists he thought his friends should read. When away from Oak Park, he frequently asked his family to send him issues of local papers as well as the *Chicago Tribune*. Although he wrote about the merits of various colleges and universities, after his senior year it was apparent that Hemingway was destined to be a newspaper reporter, and his English teacher Fannie Biggs wrote to Chicago papers in an attempt to help her pupil land a job.

No Chicago newspaper hired the new Oak Park high school graduate, but the *Kansas City Star* did. In October 1917, the cub reporter started work there while living with his Uncle Tyler and Aunt Arabell Hemingway. Before long, however, he moved in with Carl Edgar, a friend who summered in Horton Bay, and began living a life unimagined by his parents. While he wrote them most often about the long hours on the job—enclosing clippings of stories he had written—he was writing his sister Marcelline (then a freshman at Oberlin College) that he was going to vaudeville and burlesque shows, boasting that he could distinguish different types of wine with his eyes closed. He also confided to her that he carried a pistol as he made his rounds on the "short-stop run": the 15th Street police station, Union Station, and General Hospital. While he may have been exaggerating for his sister's benefit, Hemingway seemed to revel in his newfound independence and in being treated as an adult by the other employees of the *Star*.

Judging by the clippings that accompanied some of his letters to his parents, Hemingway's early assignments resulted in short items of fewer than ten lines, though he likely contributed material for longer pieces. As he gained experience, his stories earned more space. He interviewed the Chicago Cubs' Grover Cleveland Alexander when "the world's greatest pitcher" passed through town en route to California. He covered a political corruption case involving the city hospital and a strike by laundry workers. He turned out articles on the local war effort, and he helped to rewrite wire reports about the German offensive in France in March 1918.

Hemingway also enlisted in the Missouri Home Guard (soon to become part of the Missouri National Guard), no doubt in response to the entry of the United States into the Great War in April of 1917. He would have been unable to enlist in the U.S. Army or the other armed services without his parents' permission until he turned nineteen on 21 July 1918. In addition, his poor eyesight made it unlikely that he would be drafted. Still, within a month of arriving in Kansas City, Hemingway was writing home about his desire to enlist in one service or another, as so many young men were eager to do. As he told Marcelline in a letter of 6 November 1917, "I will go not because of any love of gold braid glory etc. but because I couldnt face any body after the war and not have been in it." When Ted Brumback, a fellow reporter for the *Star* and veteran ambulance driver on the Western Front, suggested they enlist in the American Red Cross—which took men unfit for duty with the military—Hemingway signed up and then told his parents. After a last fishing trip to Michigan (cut short when his orders arrived to report for duty) and a week and a half in New York City, he shipped out for Europe in May of 1918.

After a brief stopover in Paris, Hemingway arrived in Milan during the first week in June, and on 10 June he reported to the Red Cross Ambulance Service Section Four at Schio. While the war on the Italian Front did not match the magnitude of destruction and devastation experienced on the Western Front in France and Belgium, it nevertheless crippled Italy. During the Battle of Caporetto in October 1917, the Italian army lost 300,000 men, 270,000 of them taken as prisoners of war. Although the army established a strong defensive line on the Piave River, it was incapable of launching an offensive against Austria-Hungary without assistance from its British and French allies. Hemingway's education in the horrors of modern war began immediately upon his arrival in Milan, when he and other members of his unit helped dispose of the bodies of workers following an explosion at a munitions factory; he recounted the experience in a postcard to the *Kansas City Star* and, fourteen years later, in *Death in the Afternoon* (1932).

With little to do in his sector of the front (the last Austro-Hungarian offensive on the Italian front took place 15–22 June), Hemingway volunteered to run a rolling canteen near Fossalta on the Piave, where the action was more intense. On the night of 8 July he was severely wounded by an Austrian trench mortar shell. Transferred to the American Red Cross Hospital, he spent the summer and fall in Milan recovering from the more than 200 wounds to his legs—a time that would be significant for both personal and literary reasons. It was during his convalescence that Hemingway met Eric Edward "Chink" Dorman-Smith, a British army officer. The two would become especially close after Ernest and his wife, Hadley, moved to Europe a few years later. Of greater literary importance was Hemingway's meeting Agnes von Kurowsky, an American nurse seven years his senior. Soon after they met, he was writing to his family that he was in love with her. Agnes was an attractive and outgoing young woman, and Hemingway had a propensity for falling in love. One of his complaints about work at the *Star*, as he told his mother in a letter of 21 November 1917, was that he was working so hard that he had not seen any girls, adding, "that is a hard predicament for guy that has been in love with someone ever since he can remember." Agnes may not have been the first of the many women with whom the young Hemingway fell in love, but their relationship provided him with the inspiration for "A Very Short Story" and for the love story in *A Farewell to Arms* (1929), which he began writing nearly ten years after his wounding. His letters during this period reveal many similarities between the novel's protagonist, Frederic Henry, and Hemingway himself, including a prolonged hospitalization in Milan, a trip to Stresa, a friendship with an elderly diplomat, and a desire to visit the Abruzzi to hunt. Hemingway also returned to the front after recuperating from his wounds, as did the invented Frederic Henry; in a letter to his family of 1 November 1918 he reported that he was at the front for the final Italian offensive and assisted in the evacuation of the wounded before succumbing (like his character) to jaundice.

The war introduced the young Hemingway to the harsher realities of human existence. He saw the effects of modern weapons on human flesh and witnessed death both in the trenches and in the hospital. In letters to his parents, however, he maintained a patriotic attitude that mirrored much of the propaganda of the time. His wounding did not make him a hero, he wrote them on 18 October 1918:

> There are no heroes in this war. We all offer our bodies and only a few are chosen, but it shouldnt reflect any special credit on those that are chosen . . . And the real heroes are the parents . . . When a mother brings a son into the world she must know that some day the son will die. And the mother of a son that has died for his country should be theproude[s]t woman in the world, and the happiest.

Only after witnessing the political machinations of the victorious Allies in the 1920s would Hemingway become disillusioned with what Woodrow Wilson had called "the War to End All Wars."

Hemingway returned to Oak Park in January of 1919 a very different man from the one who had left for Kansas City in October of 1917. His time with the *Kansas City Star* and with the American Red Cross in Italy had fundamentally altered his attitudes and perspectives. Moving back into the family home after a year and a half on his own proved especially difficult. Hemingway tried to make the best of the situation until the end of May, concealing from his teetotaling parents the liquor he kept in a false bookcase. His family wanted him to go to college, and toward the end of May, en route to northern Michigan, he visited a friend at the University of Michigan in Ann Arbor. But Hemingway had already decided on the course of his future. On 3 March 1919, he wrote to James Gamble, his commanding officer when he operated the rolling canteen, that he had "written some darn good things . . . And am starting a campaign against your Philedelphia Journal the Sat. Eve. Post. I sent them the first story Monday last." Although the *Saturday Evening Post* would never publish a Hemingway story, and none of the stories that he wrote during the next two years—stories such as "The Mercenaries," "The Ash Heel's Tendon," and "Crossroads"—would be published in his lifetime, this postwar period marked the beginning of Hemingway's career as a writer of fiction.

The time between his return to America in early 1919 and his return to Europe in December 1921 was the third phase of a literary apprenticeship that began at Oak Park High School, continued with the *Kansas City Star*, and would conclude in Paris under the tutelage of Ezra Pound and Gertrude Stein. What Hemingway wrote at this time was unexceptional, consisting mainly of formulaic adventure stories that he thought fit the magazine markets of the time, but he was perfecting his craft by working at it. And he was storing up memories to use in the fiction that he would write in Paris a few years later. Much as he mined his childhood experiences for "Indian Camp" and "The Doctor and the Doctor's Wife," he transformed his fishing trips with Bill Smith and others and his relationships with Kate Smith and Marjorie Bump during the summers of 1919 and 1920 into the subject matter of "Big Two-Hearted River," "Summer People," "The End of Something," and "The Three-Day Blow." "The End of Something" records the break-up of characters Nick and Marge after they have fished in the same place and using the same method as Hemingway described in a 27 April 1919 letter to Gamble. The story also hints at the strains in Hemingway's relationship with the real Marjorie Bump when Nick, angling for a fish but also angling for a fight, tells Marjorie, "You know everything. That's the trouble. You know you do." [1]

Hemingway's April 1921 break-up letter to Marjorie that he drafted but may not have sent echoes this motif as he recounts all he has taught her and then concludes,

"I wasn't so bad for you—Except as Bill always said— But I won't repeat that because I never agreed with him." In "The Three-Day Blow," the follow-up story to "The End of Something," Nick and his friend Bill get drunk together, whereupon Bill finally pronounces that Nick was very wise to "bust off that Marge business," primarily because Nick would have married her and thus "would have had to marry the whole family."[2] Additional letters between Hemingway and his Michigan friends allow further insight into Hemingway's ultimately strained relationship with Marjorie and the way that his summers in Michigan after the war inspired his early fiction. As Hemingway expressed it to Marjorie, "Was going to write you a sarcastic letter—but don't feel like it now. Got started remembering that summer of 1919— It was idyllic—perfect as some days in Spring are and mountain valleys you pass on puffing trains—and other impermanent things."

While Hemingway was making an independent life for himself in northern Michigan in 1919 and 1920—and enjoying his idyllic freedom there—he could not separate himself wholly from family issues. During the first summer after the war he was his father's on-site advocate against his mother's plan to build a cottage for herself at Longfield. On 9 June 1919 he urged his father to "Stand By Your Guns!" in his fight with Grace—a fight the two men lost. Spending most of his time at Bill Smith's or on extended camping trips, Hemingway apparently saw little of his parents that summer. When the rest of the family returned to Oak Park, Ernest did too, but he returned to Michigan the following week to spend the rest of the year, staying first with the Dilworths in Horton Bay before moving to Eva Potter's boarding house at 602 State Street in Petoskey.

For the first four months of 1920, he was in Toronto, serving as a companion to Ralph Connable, the son of Ralph and Harriet Connable. (Hemingway and Harriet Connable met when he spoke about his wartime experiences to the Ladies' Aid Society at the Petoskey Public Library.) While in Toronto, Hemingway began freelancing for the *Toronto Star*. But the lure of northern Michigan drew him back in the summer of 1920. This time marked a turning point in Hemingway's relationship with his parents, both of whom were becoming increasingly irritated with their son's behavior. Although living at the family's Windemere cottage, he provided little help to his mother in the management of his siblings and the upkeep of the property. When, at midnight on 27 July, Hemingway slipped out to go on a picnic with his younger sisters Ursula and Sunny and five friends—an escapade that created a stir with a neighbor who awakened at 3 a.m. to find her children and their guests missing—Grace wrote him a furious letter in which she told him that he had overdrawn on the account of his mother's love.[3] Hemingway moved out of Windemere and never lived with his family again.

The next phase of Hemingway's life centered in Chicago, where he moved that fall in an attempt to improve his job prospects. Living first with Bill Horne, with whom he had served in the Red Cross, and later with Y. K. and Doodles Smith (Bill Smith's brother and his common-law wife), he attempted to carve out a life of his own. Without his family's financial support, he had to concentrate on making a living for himself. While the letters suggest that he may have worked on some advertising projects, his main source of income came from writing for and editing the *Co-operative Commonwealth*, the magazine of the Co-operative Society of America. His fiction stayed on the back burner, but this time in Chicago was significant for two reasons. Through Y. K. Smith, Hemingway met members of the Chicago literary world, specifically Carl Sandburg and Sherwood Anderson, both of whom were frequent visitors to Smith's apartment. (Anderson and Smith had worked together at the Taylor-Critchfield advertising firm.) Anderson, whose *Winesburg, Ohio* had been published in 1919, encouraged Hemingway's fiction writing and urged him to settle in Paris rather than return to Italy. When Hemingway arrived in Paris in December 1921, he carried with him letters of introduction from Anderson to Gertrude Stein, Ezra Pound, and others in the city's thriving expatriate literary community.

It was also in Chicago, in October of 1920, that Hemingway met Elizabeth Hadley Richardson. A native of St. Louis and friend of Kate Smith, she was a tall redhead with bobbed hair, eight years older than the twenty-one-year-old Hemingway. The two began an intense courtship, most of which was carried out through correspondence. (Unfortunately, very few letters from Ernest to Hadley of this period survive: after their divorce, she destroyed his courting letters to her.) Hadley was cultured, well-read, and a talented pianist, enjoying her first taste of freedom and happiness since her mother's death the previous month following a long illness. Ernest, though young, had already experienced much and was confident of his future. Within six weeks of their first meeting, they were talking about marriage, and the couple were wed on 3 September 1921 in Horton Bay. After a brief residence in Chicago, they decamped in December for Paris. Ernest had a dream job, serving as a feature-writing correspondent for the *Toronto Star*, with all of Europe as his beat. And in Paris he found an environment that facilitated his fiction writing as well.

Hemingway arrived in Paris on 20 December 1921 to begin the last and most important period of his apprenticeship. Although Hemingway's expatriate years in Paris during the 1920s have been thoroughly researched and written about, the letters in this volume add new details to his earliest encounter with the city. Writers, composers, and painters were moving to France in good part because of the extremely favorable exchange rate. One of the earliest articles in the *Toronto Star Weekly* from their newest European correspondent proclaimed that "A

Canadian with One Thousand a Year Can Live Very Comfortably in Paris" (4 February 1922).[4] The Hemingways, bolstered by an income of $3,000 a year from Hadley's trust fund, did indeed live comfortably and could afford to travel in France, Germany, Switzerland, Austria, and Italy, which they began to do within weeks after they first arrived in Paris.

Paris was a more open and permissive society, offering American artists a milieu in which their art and their style of living would not be judged by the puritanical standards then prevalent in the United States. In Paris, Sylvia Beach, owner of the Left Bank bookstore Shakespeare and Company, could freely publish James Joyce's *Ulysses* in 1922. The previous year, Margaret Anderson and Jane Heap serialized portions of the novel in the *Little Review* (which was then based in America), and were charged and convicted by a New York City jury of publishing an obscene work. (Joyce's novel would be banned in the United States until 1933.) French society was more tolerant than American society in other ways as well. While the United States was embarking on what would be the failed experiment of Prohibition, all forms of alcohol were readily available in France, as Hemingway cheerfully noted in some of his letters. Many of Hemingway's new acquaintances and mentors (including Robert McAlmon, Beach, and Stein) were bisexual or homosexual. Another friend and mentor, Ezra Pound, enjoyed a seemingly happy marriage yet was known to have several mistresses. Many of the night clubs in the city featured African-American musicians who were introducing many of their white compatriots along with the French to jazz. Paris in the 1920s was the place where the modern world was made.

At first, Hemingway mocked his fellow expatriates, as he did in "The Mecca of Fakers Is French Capital," published in the *Toronto Daily Star* on 25 March 1922.[5] But soon he became an enthusiastic participant in this new world. He continued to work for the *Toronto Star*, but also spent precious hours writing fiction and—in that brief period—poetry as well. At Shakespeare and Company, Hemingway discovered nineteenth-century French and Russian literature and the works of his contemporaries. In Pound and Stein, he found mentors to further his education. These letters reveal that Hemingway would meet Stein as early as February 1922, and they also demonstrate how quickly his relationship with Pound intensified throughout the year. Pound, who was working on *The Cantos*, had a particular talent for discovering and advising other writers. He used his contacts to influence magazines and presses to publish the work of the young Hemingway. Without Pound's influence, his work might not have eventually appeared in *Poetry*, the *Little Review*, or the *Transatlantic Review*. Gertrude Stein was just as important as Pound to Hemingway's development, albeit in a different way. Best known at the time as the author of *Three Lives* (1909), Stein introduced the young American to modern art, particularly the works of Paul Cézanne and Pablo Picasso that were on display in her home at 27, rue de Fleurus. While Pound opened doors to publishers, Stein offered critiques on his writing, doled out over tea while Hadley conversed with Stein's companion, Alice B. Toklas. And Stein sparked Hemingway's interest in bullfighting, an interest that would become a lifelong obsession and the subject of much of his writing. These letters from 1922 underscore how Hemingway's early friendships with Stein and particularly Pound were instrumental in forming the mature writer that emerged from his Paris apprenticeship.

Still, during his first year in Paris, Hemingway's primary focus was journalism. While many of his stories for the *Toronto Star* were feature articles, he also reported the hard news stories on the political and social upheaval that followed the Great War. He spent most of April 1922 at the Genoa Economic Conference in Italy, where he met fellow journalists Lincoln Steffens and Bill Bird. He was based in Constantinople for three weeks in October of the same year, covering the Greco-Turkish War. And at the end of the year he was in Switzerland, reporting on the Lausanne Peace Conference. That trip was most notable for the theft of a suitcase containing most of his fiction and poetry, which Hadley had left unattended at the Gare de Lyon as she was leaving Paris to join him—an incident that attained mythic proportions in his later years. Hemingway's newspaper assignments supplemented the income from Hadley's trust fund (and were further supplemented by the sale of some of his stories to competing news organizations). They also provided Hemingway with lessons in politics and war on an international scale.

Shortly after the loss of Hemingway's manuscripts, Hadley became pregnant. Fatherhood would mean a curtailment of Hemingway's freedom and, with the decision to return to Toronto in the fall of 1923 for the birth of their son, an end to the couple's first Paris sojourn.

Hemingway's letters in this volume show how the places of his youth and young adulthood would remain for him important touchstones. The stories of *In Our Time* (1925) repeatedly evoke the Michigan landscapes he had known around Walloon Lake, Petoskey, and the Upper Peninsula. In what would become his characteristic method of composition, Hemingway transformed his remembered experiences into fiction, sometimes explicitly but usually in more subtle ways. As he remarked in a 17 July 1923 letter to his friend Bill Horne, "We cant ever go back to old things or try and get the old kick out of something or find things the way we remembered them. We have them as we remember them and they are very fine and wonderful and we have to go on and have other things because the old things are nowhere except in our minds now."[6] The times and places that shaped Hemingway belonged to his past, but in his mind and through his craft he was able to recapture and recreate them, not only for himself but for his readers.

The letters in this volume document the change and development of Ernest Hemingway as both a man and a writer during the first twenty-three years of his life. Along the way they fill in many gaps in our knowledge of his life and craft, telling his story in a way that no biography or memoir can.

NOTES

1 *The Complete Short Stories of Ernest Hemingway: The Finca Vigía Edition* (New York: Scribner's, 1987), 81.
2 *Ibid.*, 90.
3 Michael S. Reynolds, *The Young Hemingway* (Oxford: Basil Blackwell, 1986), 136–38.
4 *Dateline: Toronto: The Complete "Toronto Star" Dispatches, 1920–1924*, ed. William White (New York: Scribner's 1985), 88–89.
5 *Ibid.*, 114–116.
6 EH to William D. Horne, Jr., 17 July 1923 (Newberry; *SL*, 85).

VOLUME 1 (1907–1922) CHRONOLOGY

9 April 1871	Clarence Edmonds Hemingway, Ernest Hemingway's father, is born in Oak Park, Illinois.
15 June 1872	Grace Hall, EH's mother, is born in Chicago.
1 October 1896	Clarence Hemingway and Grace Hall are married in Oak Park, Illinois, and move into the home of her father, Ernest Hall, at 439 North Oak Park Avenue—across the street from Clarence's parents, Anson and Adelaide Hemingway.
15 January 1898	Marcelline Hemingway, EH's sister, is born in Oak Park.
21 July 1899	Ernest Miller Hemingway is born in Oak Park.
c. 1 September 1899	Hemingway family travel to Windemere, their cottage on Walloon Lake, Michigan, where EH will spend part of every summer through 1917.
29 April 1902	Ursula Hemingway, EH's sister, is born in Oak Park.
28 November 1904	Madelaine Hemingway, EH's sister, is born in Oak Park.
10 May 1905	Ernest Hall dies.
c. September 1905	EH begins first grade.
1906	Grace Hall Hemingway builds house at 600 North Kenilworth Avenue, Oak Park, using the inheritance from her father.
August 1910	Grace takes EH to visit relatives in Nantucket, Massachusetts.

19 July 1911	Carol Hemingway, EH's sister, is born at Windemere.
September 1913	EH and Marcelline enter Oak Park and River Forest High School.
28 June 1914	Austria-Hungary's Archduke Franz Ferdinand and wife are assassinated in Sarajevo, Bosnia, precipitating the First World War.
28 July 1914	Austria-Hungary declares war on Serbia.
1–4 August 1914	Germany declares war on Russia, France, and Belgium and invades Belgium; Great Britain declares war on Germany. President Woodrow Wilson declares a policy of U.S. neutrality.
1 April 1915	Leicester Hemingway, EH's brother, is born in Oak Park while EH and friend Lewis Clarahan are on a spring vacation hiking trip to Lake Zurich, Illinois.
June 1915	EH, Clarahan, and friend Ray Ohlsen travel to Frankfort, Michigan, on the Lake Michigan steamer *Missouri*; EH and Clarahan hike from there to Walloon Lake.
September 1915	EH begins writing for *The Trapeze*, his high school newspaper.
February 1916	EH publishes his first short story, "The Judgment of Manitou," in the school literary magazine, *Tabula*.
June 1916	EH and Clarahan again travel by lake steamer to Frankfort, Michigan; after a hiking and fishing trip, EH goes on alone to Horton Bay, Michigan.
c. July 1916	EH meets Bill and Kate Smith at Horton Bay.
2–6 April 1917	EH and Ohlsen take a spring vacation canoe trip on the Illinois River and Illinois–Michigan Canal to Starved Rock State Park.
6 April 1917	The United States declares war on Germany and enters the First World War.
14 June 1917	EH and Marcelline graduate from high school.

June–September 1917	EH spends the summer and early fall in Michigan, working at the family's Longfield Farm.
c. 15 October 1917	EH begins work as a cub reporter for the *Kansas City Star*, staying at first with Uncle Tyler and Aunt Arabell Hemingway at 3629 Warwick Boulevard, Kansas City, Missouri.
19 October 1917	EH moves into nearby boarding house run by Gertrude Haynes at 3733 Warwick Boulevard, where many junior staffers from the *Star* stay.
5 November 1917	EH is enlisted in the Missouri Home Guard by this date.
c. 6 December 1917	EH moves into Carl Edgar's apartment at 3516 Agnes Avenue, Kansas City.
16 December 1917	"Kerensky, the Fighting Flea," the first article attributed to EH, appears in the *Kansas City Star*.
c. 2 March 1918	EH enlists in the American Red Cross Ambulance Service with his friend Ted Brumback.
30 April 1918	EH draws last paycheck from *Kansas City Star* and immediately boards train for a last fishing trip in Michigan with Carl Edgar, Charles Hopkins, and Bill Smith before leaving for war. He stays overnight in Oak Park.
13 May 1918	EH arrives in New York City for training with other Red Cross volunteers and meets up with Brumback; the volunteers are quartered at Hotel Earle on Washington Square.
18 May 1918	EH is in Red Cross Parade on Fifth Avenue. The parade is reviewed by President Wilson.
c. 23 May–c. 4 June 1918	EH sails from New York for France on the *Chicago*, landing in Bordeaux. He and his Red Cross comrades take a night train to Paris and spend a few days in the city before departing by train for Milan, Italy.
10 June 1918	EH leaves Milan for Schio, where he is assigned to the American Red Cross Ambulance Service, Section 4. He soon volunteers for canteen service closer to the front near the Piave River.

8 July 1918	While distributing cigarettes and candy to Italian troops at Fossalta on the Piave River, EH is wounded by an Austrian trench mortar and machine gun fire.
summer–fall 1918	EH recuperates at the American Red Cross Hospital in Milan. He falls in love with Agnes von Kurowsky, an American nurse. He also meets British officer Eric Edward ("Chink") Dorman-Smith.
24–30 September 1918	EH is on convalescent leave in Stresa, Italy.
24 October 1918	The Italian Army launches the final offensive of the war (the Battle of Vittorio Veneto). EH leaves the hospital that day to assist in the effort but by 1 November is back in the hospital with a case of jaundice.
4 November 1918	An armistice between the Italian and Austro-Hungarian forces goes into effect, ending fighting in the theater.
11 November 1918	Armistice is declared, effectively ending the First World War.
7–11 December 1918	Accompanied part way by Chink Dorman-Smith, EH travels via Padua and Torreglia to Treviso to visit Agnes, who is working there in a field hospital.
late December 1918	Between Christmas and New Year's Day, EH visits Jim Gamble in Taormina, Sicily.
4 January 1919	EH is discharged from the Red Cross and sails from Italy to the U.S. aboard the *Giuseppe Verdi*.
21 January 1919	EH arrives on crutches in New York and returns to Oak Park by train.
24 February 1919	EH sends his first story to the *Saturday Evening Post*, which rejects it and his subsequent submissions.
7 March 1919	Agnes breaks off relationship with EH via letter; he receives the news about 30 March.
late May–fall 1919	EH returns to Michigan for the summer and fall to fish and write; he also works at Longfield Farm.

	With varying groups of friends he takes several fishing and camping trips, including to the Black River and Pine Barrens (July and August) and to the Upper Peninsula of Michigan, near Seney (late August).
June 1919	Grace contracts to have a separate cottage built for herself across the lake from Windemere on Longfield Farm. Grace Cottage is completed on 26 July.
late October–December 1919	After a visit home to Oak Park, EH returns to Petoskey, rents a room at 602 State Street, and devotes himself to writing.
31 December 1919	EH returns to Oak Park for the holidays.
mid-January 1920	EH begins working as companion to Ralph Connable, Jr. , in Toronto where he also will write freelance articles for the *Toronto Star*.
14 February 1920	EH's first article (unsigned), "Circulating Pictures a New High-Art Idea in Toronto," appears in the *Toronto Star Weekly*.
mid-May 1920	EH returns to Oak Park; he leaves shortly thereafter for northern Michigan.
27 July 1920	EH is evicted from Windemere by Grace.
October 1920	EH moves to Chicago and rooms with Bill Horne at 1230 North State Street. He soon meets Hadley Richardson and Sherwood Anderson.
December 1920	EH begins writing and editing the *Co-operative Commonwealth*.
late December 1920	EH moves into Y. K. Smith's apartment at 63 East Division Street, Chicago.
May 1921	EH moves to Y. K. Smith's quarters at 100 East Chicago Avenue.
3 September 1921	EH and Hadley marry at Horton Bay, Michigan.
early October 1921	EH and Hadley move to 1239 North Dearborn Avenue in Chicago. The *Co-operative Commonwealth* folds.

29 October 1921	EH agrees to write for the *Toronto Star* as a European correspondent, paving the way for his move to Paris.
8 December 1921	EH and Hadley sail for France aboard the *Leopoldina.*
20 December 1921	After their ship docks at Le Havre, France, EH and Hadley take the night train to Paris and stay briefly at the Hotel Jacob on the Left Bank.
4 January 1922	EH meets Sylvia Beach, owner of the bookstore Shakespeare and Company.
9 January 1922	EH and Hadley move into a rented apartment at 74, rue du Cardinal Lemoine.
15 January 1922	EH and Hadley arrive in Switzerland, where they will vacation at Chamby-sur-Montreux.
2 February 1922	EH and Hadley return to Paris. That same day, Sylvia Beach receives the first two copies of James Joyce's *Ulysses.*
February 1922	EH meets Gertrude Stein and Ezra Pound.
6–27 April 1922	EH covers the Genoa Economic Conference for the *Toronto Star* and meets Lincoln Steffens and William Bird.
May 1922	EH's "A Divine Gesture," a fable written in Chicago in 1921, is published by the *Double Dealer.*
24 May 1922	EH and Hadley return to Chamby-sur-Montreux, Switzerland. With Chink Dorman-Smith, they will hike over the St. Bernard Pass into Italy.
11 June 1922	EH and Hadley tour Italy, including EH's old battle sites. EH writes "A Veteran Visits the Old Front" for the *Toronto Star.*
18 June 1922	EH and Hadley return to Paris.
summer 1922	Pound asks EH to contribute a volume for his "Inquest" series, to be published by Bill Bird's Three Mountains Press.

4 August–early September 1922	EH and Hadley fly to Strasbourg and join Bill and Sally Bird and Lewis Galantière and Dorothy Butler in the Black Forest.
early to mid-September 1922	EH and Hadley visit Chink Dorman-Smith in Cologne.
25 September–21 October 1922	EH travels from Paris (via Sofia, Bulgaria) to Constantinople to cover the Greco-Turkish War, arriving in Constantinople on 29 September and returning to Paris via Adrianople.
21 November 1922	EH arrives in Switzerland to cover the Lausanne Peace Conference.
2–3 December 1922	A suitcase containing nearly all of EH's manuscripts is stolen from Hadley at the Gare de Lyon, Paris, as she is en route to join him in Switzerland.
c. 15 December 1922	EH and Hadley leave Lausanne for Chamby, where Chink Dorman-Smith and other friends will join them for the holidays.

MAPS

Oak Park, Illinois

1 EH birthplace and maternal grandparents' home:
   439 North Oak Park Ave. (renumbered 339 in 1915)
2 Paternal grandparents' home: 444 North Oak Park Ave. (renumbered 400 in 1915)
3 EH boyhood home: 600 North Kenilworth Ave.
4 Oliver Wendell Holmes Elementary School
5 Oak Park-River Forest Township High School
6 Oak Park Public Library (Scoville Institute)

0   0.5 mi

Lake
Michigan   MICHIGAN
Oak Park
Chicago
ILLINOIS   INDIANA

1 Oak Park, Illinois, map distributed in the 1920s by Hemingway's Uncle George, a local realtor.

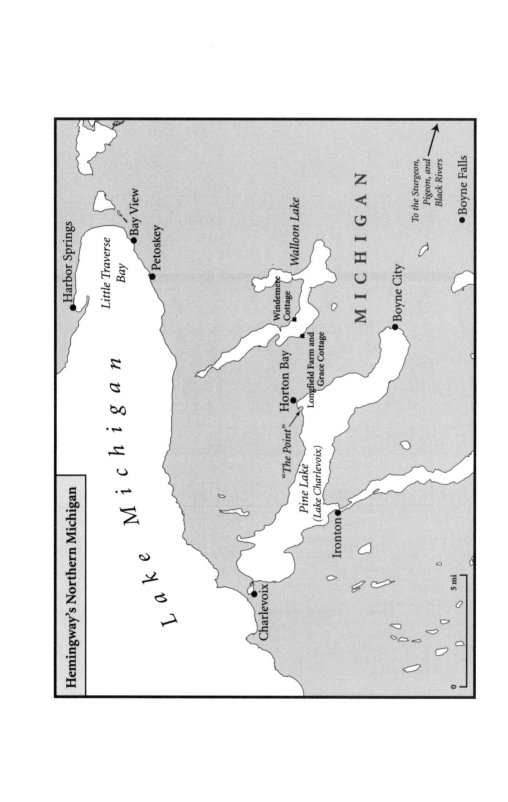

Hemingway's Northern Michigan

Harbor Springs

Little Traverse Bay

Bay View
Petoskey

Lake Michigan

Windemere Cottage

Walloon Lake

"The Point" Horton Bay

Longfield Farm and Grace Cottage

MICHIGAN

Boyne City

Pine Lake
(Lake Charlevoix)

Ironton

Charlevoix

To the Sturgeon,
Pigeon, and
Black Rivers

Boyne Falls

0   5 mi

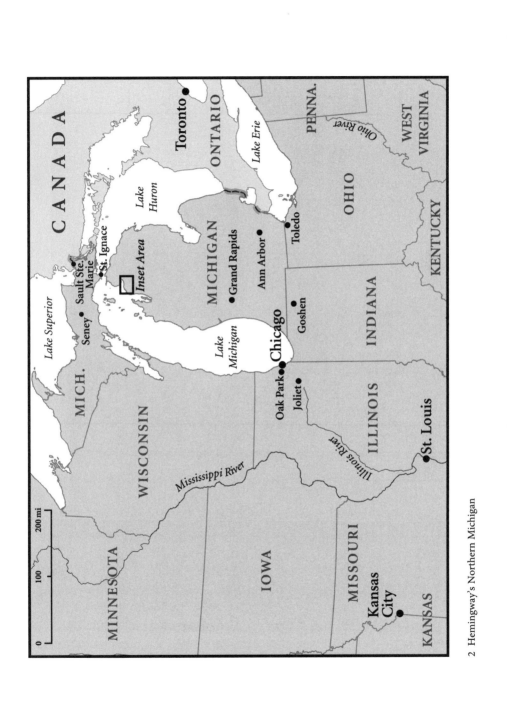

2 Hemingway's Northern Michigan

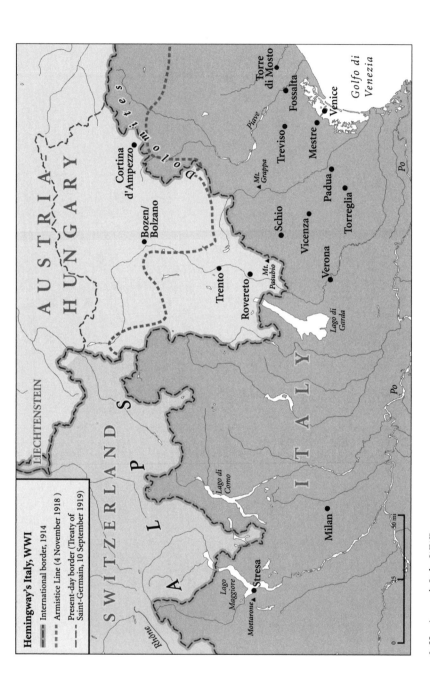

3 Hemingway's Italy, WWI.

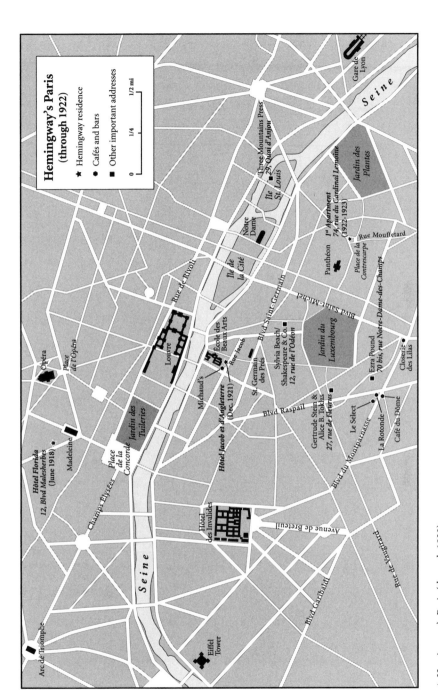

4 Hemingway's Paris (through 1922).

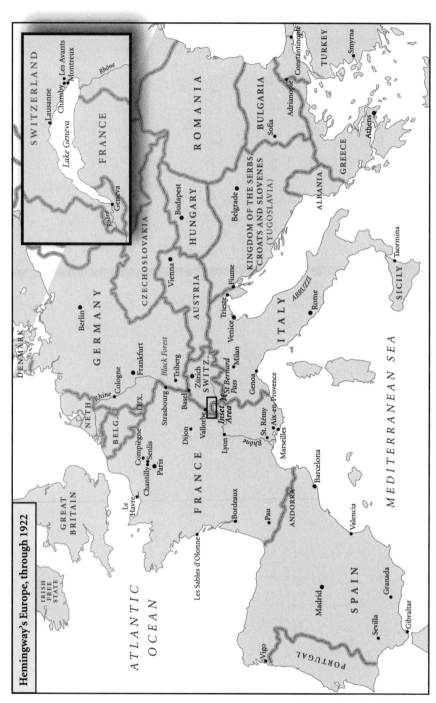

5 Hemingway's Europe (through 1922).

THE LETTERS
1907–1922

To Clarence Hemingway, [c. early July 1907]

Dear papa.

I saw a mother duck with seven little babies.

how big is my corn?

Ursula saw them first

We went strawberry piking and got enough to make three short-cakes.

Ernest Hemingway

Meeker, A Postcard S; letterhead: Walloon Lake, Mich. / "Windemere," with printed photograph of EH and his sisters Marcelline and Ursula as very young children.

The conjectured postcard date is based on Clarence's response in a letter from Oak Park, dated 8 July 1907: "I received your card and you and Ursula keep very quiet about the wild ducks, so when I come you two can go hunting ducks with me and we will have a glorious time" (JFK, Scrapbook III). Under his image in the printed photograph, EH wrote "Ernest" in pencil. Windemere was the Hemingways' summer cottage on the shore of Walloon Lake, Michigan. Another copy of this photograph is in EH's grandparents' scrapbook (JFK), labeled, "Ernest, 3 years, laughing at little sister Ursula."

To Clarence Hemingway, 28 September and 4 October 1908

Mon. Sep. 28, 1908

Dear papa—.

last night an inch of rain fell.

thank you very much for the postal card.

Oct 4 1909

I put sone fresh staw in flossys nest

All the squabs died

I went to gampas for dinner[1]

Your loving Son

Ernest M. Hemingway

Meeker, ALS; letterhead: CLARENCE E. HEMINGWAY, M.D. / 600 KENILWORTH AVENUE. / CORNER IOWA STREET / OAK PARK, ILL.

Grace noted on verso of the letter: "Keep for Ernest." Clarence was away from home in the summer and fall of 1908, taking a four-month course in obstetrics at the New York Lying-In Hospital (Baker *Life*, 10). EH misdated the second portion of the letter as 1909.

1 EH's paternal grandparents, Anson Tyler and Adelaide Edmonds Hemingway, lived a few blocks away in Oak Park.

To Clarence Hemingway, [19 October 1908]

Dear papa—.

last Friday in our equriam in School the water was all riley I looked in a clam that I had brought to scool from the river.[1]

Had shut down on one of our big Japinese fantail gold fishes tales

On Sat Mama and I went across the ford at the river It is very muche higher.

I got six clames in the river and some weat six feet tall.

Your loving son
Ernest M Hemingway

Stanford, ALS; letterhead: CLARENCE E. HEMINGWAY, M.D. / 600 KENILWORTH AVENUE. / CORNER IOWA STREET / OAK PARK, ILL.

Grace dated the letter, "Oct 19th.08." and enclosed it with her own letter to Clarence of the same date. Clarence was returning from New York via New Orleans, and Grace wrote that she hoped he was getting a good rest there (Stanford). He took a steamboat up the Mississippi River and arrived home in November (Baker *Life*, 10).

1 The Des Plaines River, about 2 miles west of the Hemingways' Oak Park home.

To Grace Hall Hemingway, 18 December 1908

Dear Mama—

I got your nice letter Aunt Laura was here for dinner:

I gave her a squirrel skin to give herald for Christmas.[1]

I have got all my Christmas presents bought.

Thank you for your nice letter.

Your loving son Ernest M. Hemingway.
Dec. 18 1908:
Oak Park

Schnack, ALS

1 Where Grace was traveling at the time is unknown, but Clarence also wrote to her on 18 December 1908, reporting that EH was very pleased with his letter from her and that "Aunt Laura Burr Gore" had come for dinner (UT). Alfred W. and Laura Burr Gore (both b. circa 1873) were family friends who lived in the Chicago area with their children, Harold (b. 1901) and Josephine (b. 1904). The Gores appear in several Hemingway family photographs taken at Windemere (PSU, Madelaine Hemingway Miller scrapbooks; M. Miller, 24).

To Marcelline Hemingway, 9 June [1909]

Wed June 9

Dear Marc.

Our room won in the field day against Miss Koontz room.

Al Bersham knocked two of Chandlers teeth out in a scrap and your dear gentle Miss hood had Mr. Smith hold him while she lickt him with a raw hide strap.[1]

Lovingly, Ernest

Cohen, ALS; postmark: OAK PARK / ILL., JUN 9 / 10-PM / 1909

Grace and Marcelline were spending the month of June visiting friends and relatives on the island of Nantucket, Massachusetts, a trip Grace intended to make with each of her children during his or her eleventh summer.

1 Marcelline recalled that she liked Miss Mary L. Hood, principal of the Oliver Wendell Holmes Elementary School in Oak Park, but "Obviously Ernie did not" (Sanford, 115). Flora Koontz and Warren R. Smith were teachers at the school.

To Grace Hall and Marcelline Hemingway, 9 June 1909

June 9 '09

Dear mama and Mash—

I helped papa clean out his closet and saw him send you group they are just fine. I got a lot of pictures for my map.

Thank you very much for the stamp you sent me. Marcellines mothers magazine came today with the Youths companion.[1]

I have been doing the dishes this week.

Lovingly Ernest.

UT, ALS

1 *The Mother's Magazine*, published monthly 1905–1920 by David C. Cook, Elgin, Illinois, and *Youth's Companion* (1827–1929), founded in Boston by Nathaniel Parker Willis (1806–1867) as a religious publication for children and acquired in 1857 by Daniel Sharp Ford (1822–1899). Ford transformed it into one of the most popular magazines in the United States, with a weekly circulation of more than a half million by the 1890s. An editorial piece in the 3 June 1909 issue of *Youth's Companion* described the magazine as "edited with a conscience," aiming "not merely to be entertaining, but to be beneficial" for the entire family (267).

To Grace Hall Hemingway, [c. 10 June 1909]

Dear mama—

Ruth just came home from the "Servant in the house."[1] "Ted" and "sonny" went to the "wee folks band" and "Ted" spoke her piese.[2]

Franklin and Jane have been here and papa gave Franklin a gun like mine only better.

They went to there summer home on lake Chautaqua in New York.[3]

"Bill" cant write just now but sends her best toosey this is it (B). (B) to (G).[4] will right later.

Lovingly Ernest H and Bill

P.S. Bill enjoid the play very mutch.

JFK, ALS; letterhead: CLARENCE E. HEMINGWAY, M.D. / 600 KENILWORTH AVENUE / CORNER IOWA STREET / OAK PARK, ILL.

The letter is laid into EH's scrapbook on the same page as a pasted-in envelope, postmarked 10 June, that contains the following letter to "mom and marse"; however, internal evidence dates this letter as 10 June, pointing to the likelihood that it was originally mailed in that envelope (JFK, Scrapbook IV).

1 *The Servant in the House*, a moral drama by Charles Rann Kennedy (1871–1950), opened at the Savoy Theatre in New York in 1908 and ran at the Bush Temple theater in Chicago 31 May–19 June 1909. Ruth Arnold, Grace's live-in voice student and household helper, wrote to Grace on 8 June 1909 that she would be seeing the play that Thursday, 10 June (UT).
2 Wee Folks' Bands were organized by the Woman's Board of Missions of the Interior, of the Congregational Church, to teach preschool-age children about missionary work around the world and to contribute funds for that work. (EH's name appeared on the roster of the Wee Folks' Band for the First Congregational Church of Oak Park in April 1901.) In her 8 June letter, Ruth told Grace that she was taking Ursula and Sunny to the church that afternoon to rehearse (probably for the annual June "Children's Day" program).

3 Franklin White Hemingway (1904–1984) and Jane Tyler Hemingway (1907–1965) were EH's first cousins, children of Clarence's brother Alfred Tyler Hemingway (1877–1922) and his wife, Fanny Arabell Hemingway (née White, 1876–1963), of Kansas City, Missouri. Aunt Arabell's parents, Arabell White (née Bowen) and John Barber White, a prominent Kansas City lumberman, were natives of Chautauqua County, New York. Their summer home was across the lake from the Chautauqua Institution (originally the Chautauqua Lake Sunday School Assembly), founded in 1874 as an educational experiment in vacation-time learning.

4 "Tooseys" or "toosies" was a family term for "kisses," usually represented by circles surrounding a dot or other symbol. "Bill" may be a nickname for Ruth Arnold, also known as "Boofie," "Bobs," or "Bobby" (Reynolds *YH*, 79, 105). In a 12 August 1909 letter to Grace at Walloon Lake, Ruth promised to be "'Billy' on the spot" when the Hemingway family returned home in September (UT).

To Grace Hall and Marcelline Hemingway, [c. 17 June 1909]

Dear mom and marse.—

I Passed to 6 grade so did marse.

Papa and I got some wild Roses and wild Strawberrys. Ursula passed too. the sundy School picknic is tomorow ST. Nicholos came and did not have marces thing in it about the bird.[1]

Emily Harding sent you a brass bowl for birthday[2]

We went to Forest Park and went down the Grand Canon it is just like the jiant coaster[3] Sunny and ted were very scared.[4]

Lovingly Ernest.

P.S. Pa gave me 5 Silver dollers for passing.

JFK, ALS; letterhead: CEH [Clarence Edmonds Hemingway]

Grace noted on verso of the letter: "Written to Mama at Nantucket June 17th '09 by Ernest Hemingway" (perhaps the date she received it). The letter is preserved in EH's scrapbook, folded and enclosed in an envelope addressed in EH's hand to "Mrs. CE Hemingway / Nantucket / Mass. / care of A. C. Ayers / 45 peral [Pearl] St." and postmarked Oak Park, 10 June 1909. On a postcard from Nantucket picturing a sperm whale hunt, Grace replied, "Hurrah for the 6th grader. Thanks for your nice letter" (JFK, Scrapbook IV).

1 *St. Nicholas: Illustrated Magazine for Boys and Girls*, published monthly in New York 1873–1943, first by Charles Scribner's Sons, and from 1881 by Century Company. A competitor of *Youth's Companion*, *St. Nicholas* was distinguished by its high-quality illustrations, articles, and fiction by leading writers, including Louisa May Alcott, Rudyard Kipling, and Mark Twain. Marcelline may have entered the magazine's monthly competition for best original

poems, stories, drawings, photographs, puzzles, and puzzle answers by its young readers. The May 1909 issue featured winning poems on the topic of "The Growing Year" and prose on the subject of "My Garden."

2 Grace would celebrate her thirty-seventh birthday on 15 June.

3 The popular Forest Park Amusement Park, in operation 1907–1922, was about a mile southwest of Oak Park in the neighboring suburb of Forest Park, Illinois. It boasted three roller coasters: the Giant Safety Coaster (then billed as the nation's highest), the Leap the Dip, and the Grand Canyon.

4 Nicknames for EH's sisters Madelaine and Ursula.

To Clarence Hemingway, [23 July 1909]

Dear papa

today Mama and the rest of us took a walk.

We walked to the school house.

Marcelline ran on ahead.

Wile we stopt at Clouse's.

In a little wile she came back.

She said that in the Wood Shed of the Scool house there was a porcupine.

So we went up there and looked in the door, the porcupine was aslleep.

I went in and gave I[t] a wack with the axx.

Then I cave I[t] anthor and another.

Then I crald in the wood.

Wrane to Mr Clous and he got his gun and Shot It.

Hear some of the quills.

JFK, AL; letterhead: Walloon Lake, Mich. / "WINDEMERE," with printed photograph of a very young EH and Marcelline splashing in lake next to a docked boat; postmark: [WALL]OON LAKE [MICH.], JUL / 23 / 9 AM

While the month and day appear in the postmark, the conjectured year of the letter is based on the young EH's account of the same incident in "An Adventure with a Porcupine." That story is bound with string into a one-page homemade "book," the paper cover of which bears the lettering "SPORTS-MAN / HASH EDITED / by E. M. and T. H." (probably "Ted Hemingway," nickname for Ursula) and is dated in EH's hand, "Oct. 10. 1909" (CMU). Another copy of the photograph printed on the stationery is found in EH's grandparents' scrapbook (JFK), where it is labeled, "Ernest 2 years / in swimming." The envelope, addressed to Dr. C. E. Hemingway in Oak Park, bears the handwritten notation "For Ernest."

To Ursula Hemingway and Ruth Arnold, [30 August 1910]

Dear Ted,

I am writing this on the train after we have left the Depot. Our trunk is on the train with us. We had breakfast this morning at Hoollsoats because the other restraunt had moved away.

Yours truly
Ernest H.

Dear Ruth,

There are only three people in our sleeper beside ourselves. We are now just coming in to Pullman Ill. We will have dinner on the dining car. I will write again when we get to Albany N.Y.[1]

Yours truly
Ernest.

IndU, A Postcard S; postmark: DETROIT & CHI / [R.P.O.],[2] AUG / 30 / 1910

The prepaid one-cent postal card is addressed to "Ursula Hemingway / Care of Dr. C. E. Hemingway, / Walloon Lake, Mich." (with Dr. Hemingway's name and address rubber-stamped on the card and Ursula's name handwritten by Grace).

1 In EH's scrapbook Grace wrote, "Mama and Ernest left 'Windemere' for Nantucket by way of Chicago Aug 29. We spent the month of Sept. 1910 on the island; boarding with S'annie Ayers" (JFK, Scrapbook IV). For details of the visit, see Susan F. Beegel, "The Young Boy and the Sea: Ernest Hemingway's Visit to Nantucket Island," *Historic Nantucket* 32, no. 3 (1985): 18–30. On the return trip, mother and son toured historical sites in and around Boston, as had Grace and Marcelline the previous summer (Baker *Life*, 11).
2 Railway Post Office, a U.S. postal station housed in a train car in which mail could be received and sorted en route.

To Clarence Hemingway, 10 September 1910

Sept. 10. 1910.

Dear Dad,

I went fishing by my self yesterday morning off the jettie. I caught 13 sea Trout. They are very gamy fish and fight like black bass. The four biggest ones supplied our table of six people. The meat tastes better than speckkled trout we think.

I am trying hard to get The Whittlesey $50 of ice cream.[1] I lost a big eel that a fisherman said would weigh four pounds.

I went to the Hutchinson's with mama while she practiced with Mrs. H, and played games with Katherine and Lucy.

I am going fishing this morning.

Your Loving Son
Ernest Hemingway

IndU, ALS; letterhead: house and garden scene with caption, "HOME, SWEET HOME, NANTUCKET, MASS."

1 Probably a reference to Walter Whittlesey, an Oak Park grocer. The Whittleseys belonged to the same church as the Hemingways, and their son Robert visited Windemere.

To Clarence Hemingway, [11 September 1910]

Dear Daddy,

Last night mother got Mrs Hutchinson to play for her and sang to the people at Sannie's[1] grandly. How is my weasel? I can get an albatross foot here for two dollars for the aggassiz.[2] Is it worth it?

Your Loving son Ernest H.

IndU, A Postcard S; postmark: NANTUCKET MASS, SEP 11 / 1230PM / 1910

In the upper right corner, Grace wrote "Sunday Morn." The prepaid one-cent postal card is rubber-stamped on the verso with the address, "C. E. Hemingway, M.D. / Kenilworth Ave. & Iowa St. / Oak Park, Illinois."

1 Probably a contraction of "Miss Annie," Annie Ayers, in whose guest house Grace and EH were boarding. Grace wrote this word in ink over EH's original attempt and added the question mark after "weasel" in the next sentence.
2 Clarence Hemingway founded the Oak Park chapter of the Agassiz Club, a nature study organization for children named after naturalist Louis Agassiz (1807–1873). In his response of 13 September 1910, Clarence cautioned his son to ask questions before buying the specimen. He also reported the results of an Agassiz election, in which he was chosen as president and EH as assistant curator of the club (JFK, Scrapbook IV).

To Marcelline Hemingway, 13 September 1910

Sep 13 1910

Dear titty mouchouse,

I went sailing up to Great Point,[1] which is fourteen miles. I[t] was fine and rough so we went out in the open ocean and shipped water grandly. I have bought a large sword fish sword for the agassiz of an old salt by the name of Judas.[2]

Mama and I went to the suffrage meeting, thru wich I slept soundly, and did not get to bed till ~~eleven~~ ten oclock.[3]

Today is Lucy's birthday. We are going to the historical society this afternoon and morning.[4]

Your loving brother
Ernest Hemingway.

UT, ALS; letterhead: house and garden scene with caption, "HOME, SWEET HOME, NANTUCKET, MASS."

1 Northernmost tip of Nantucket Island.
2 Possibly Judah Nickerson, a retired fisherman who passed the time telling tales on the docks and who had once caught an exceptionally large swordfish (Beegel, "The Young Boy and the Sea," 27).
3 Marcelline, who also attended these meetings with her mother, recalled that they were held in Annie Ayers's parlor (Sanford, 113).
4 EH and Grace likely were going to view a whaling exhibit of the Nantucket Historical Association (founded in 1894) at its Fair Street Museum.

To Charles C. Spink and Son, [c. 1912]

Mr. Chales C. Spink & Son
gentelmen—

Enclosed find $.35 for which send me the following baseball action pictures—

Mathewson—Mordecai Brown. Sam Crawford. Jas. P. Archer. Frank shulte. Owen Bush. Fred Snodgrass.[1]

Yours Truly
Ernest Hemingway
600 N. Kenilworth
Oak Park. Ill.

JFK, ALS

The conjectured letter date is based on advertisements in 1912 issues of the weekly *Sporting News* (1886–) for five-cent "action pictures" of baseball players, including the seven named in EH's letter. The newspaper was founded in St. Louis by Alfred Henry Spink (c. 1854–1928) to promote a variety of sports; after 1899, when his brother Charles Claude Spink took over as publisher, it focused exclusively on baseball. After Charles died in 1914, his son J. G. Taylor Spink (1888–1962) assumed editorship and continued in this post until his death.

1 New York Giants pitcher Christopher (Christy) Mathewson (1880–1925) and outfielder Fred Snodgrass (1887–1974); Chicago Cubs pitcher Mordecai "Three Finger" Brown (1876–1948), catcher James P. (Jimmy) Archer (1883–1958), and outfielder Frank "Wildfire" Schulte (1882–1949); Detroit Tigers outfielder Sam Crawford (1880–1968) and shortstop Owen "Donie" Bush (1887–1972).

To Clarence Hemingway, [c. second week of May 1912]

Pullman sleeper

Seven gabels[1]

Kenilworth

Ave.

Oak Park

Dear Daddy

I feel a lot better when all my work is done and my concience is clear.

I looked up in my baseball schedule and found that the New York giants play chicago cubs for the championship on Sat. May 11[2]

next Sat. we will have choir Rehearsal in the morning and the afternoon will be free.[3] The game starts at 3 o'clock.

Lets see if we can't go it will be a dandy game the last of the Series.

Yours

Lovingly

Ernie.

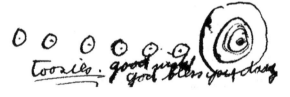

Sotheby's catalog, The Maurice F. Neville Collection Sale (Part I), New York, 13 April 2004, Lot 85 (illustrated), ALS

1 References to the railway sleeping car designed and manufactured by American industrialist George Pullman (1831–1897) and to the 1851 novel *The House of the Seven Gables* by Nathaniel Hawthorne (1804–1864).
2 The Cubs lost this home game at West Side Park by a score of 10–3. EH's reference to a championship is unclear; this was the second game of an early-season, three-game series (played on 10, 11, and 13 May) between the Giants and the Cubs, who finished third in the National League for the 1912 season.
3 EH sang in the children's choir of Oak Park's Third Congregational Church, where Grace Hemingway was choir director.

To Leicester and Nevada Butler Hall, 22 October 1912

Oct 22 1912

Dear Uncle Liester and Aunt Vada,—[1]

Daddy and mama said at supper that they had a wonderful surprise for us and we guessed and guessed but couldn't think what it was. I thot it was something to eat. Then mama read us your letter. Then I stood on my head on the chair and just yelled for joy. We all yelled exept mama, and papa and ruth. I want to thank you awful much for the lovely present.

Sunny said that she is going to buy a bycycle with her money. I dont know yet what I will do with mine. I am afraid I will wake up and find it a dream.

Your Loving Nephew—
Ernest Miller Hemingway

P.S. Mama said for me to tell you I am taking lessons on the cello. and will be able to play in the church orchestra by christmas

E.H.

Private Collection, ALS

1 Grace's brother and his wife lived in Bishop, California, where he practiced law. Marcelline recalled that when Uncle Leicester, a long-time bachelor, married Nevada, the family was delighted and curious to meet her. In 1918, when her husband went to serve in WWI, Nevada made her first trip East to meet her "new family" and charmed them all. Shortly after her visit to Oak Park and before Leicester returned from the war, she died in the influenza pandemic (Sanford, 173–78).

To Clarence Hemingway, 11 May 1913

My conduct at the Coloseum yesterday was bad and my conduct this morning in church was bad my conduct tomorrow will be good.

Ernest Hemingway

May 11, 1913

JFK, ANS

Grace wrote on the envelope, "To Daddy / 'Confession'" (JFK, Scrapbook IV). Along with other youth from the Third Congregational Church of Oak Park, EH, Marcelline, and Ursula participated in "The World in Chicago," a missionary exposition held 3 May–7 June 1913 at the Chicago Coliseum. The envelope and exhibition program are pasted into the album on facing pages. Underneath photographs of the costumed group, Grace noted that every Saturday afternoon they enacted a "Japanese Wedding," a scene in the Pageant of Women's Missions, in which EH played the part of "Go Between."

To Anson Hemingway, [c. 30 August 1913]

Dear Grandpa—.

Thank you very much for the ring toss for my birthday. I have caught 147 trout day before yesterday I caught one 11 in long. It is very windy and rainy now. Have just finished picking 3 ducks.

Ernest Hemingway

JFK, A Postcard S; postmark: WALLOON LAKE / [MICH.], AUG / 30 / 9 AM / 1913

This postcard is pasted into EH's grandparents' scrapbook on the same page as a postcard featuring a map of Charlevoix County, Michigan (JFK). The album page bears the hand-lettered caption, "Where Ernest spent his summers." Given that EH's birthday (21 July) was six weeks past and that he wrote the next two postcards to his parents in Michigan after returning to Oak Park but before his high school classes began on 2 September, this card may have been written somewhat earlier than the postmarked date of 30 August; perhaps it was mailed by a family member after EH left Michigan, or, as occasionally happened, the date on the postmark stamp was not accurate.

To Clarence and Grace Hall Hemingway, [c. late August 1913]

Dear Dad and Mother—,

arrived alwright fine weather but rough at night. Mr. and Mrs. Sampson,[1] met us at the dock. Thank you for the lunch and letter we are going over to the house now grandpa says to have you bring home the ring toss. The town is as hot as ____ Boyne city.

good by

Ernie

JFK, A Postcard S

Pasted onto the same scrapbook page as this postcard and the next is a letter dated 11 August 1913 to Grace from "Mother Hemingway" (EH's paternal grandmother), expressing pleasure that Ernest and Marcelline soon would be sleeping under her roof in Oak Park (JFK, Scrapbook IV). Grace wrote on the page, "Ernest and Marcelline, Ruth McCollum and Harold Sampson all went home on the [Lake Michigan steamship] 'Manitou' to start school on time." In 1913 classes at Oak Park and River Forest High School (hereinafter abbreviated as OPRFHS) began on Tuesday, 2 September, the day after Labor Day; grammar school, for younger children, opened on 8 September (as reported in the local newspaper, *Oak Leaves*, 23 and 30 August 1913).

1 Oak Park friend and neighbor Harold Sampson had spent the final weeks of August 1913 with EH in Michigan.

To Clarence Hemingway, [c. late August–1 September 1913]

Dear Dad—,

I went to High school this morn and got Program and book list. Our peaches are fine am going to pick them today and store in our cellar.

McAllister cut the lawn yesterday. Aunt Arabelly[1] comes to grandmas tomorrow. The trunks arrived allright. My night gown and my other clothes are in the long trunk I would like to have them <u>very</u> much

Lovingly

Ernie

JFK, A Postcard S; letterhead (rubber-stamped): A. T. Hemingway / 444 Oak Park Avenue / Oak Park, Ill.

A "High School Announcement" in the 23 August 1913 *Oak Leaves* reported that the principal's office at OPRFHS would be open the mornings of August 28–30 and 1 September, the day before classes started.

1 Arabell Hemingway, who lived in Kansas City.

To [Unknown], [c. June 1914]

To gum shoe Mac, Neither my principal, my adviser nor my friend, Ernest Hemingway.

Sotheby's catalog, Jonathan Goodwin Collection Sale (Part One), New York, 29 March 1977, Lot 123, Inscription

According to the Sotheby's catalog description, EH wrote this inscription on the dedication page of a copy of the 1914 *Senior Tabula*, the OPRFHS yearbook. At the time, he was in the freshman class. The yearbook's printed dedication reads, "To our adviser, principal and friend Marion Ross McDaniel we respectfully dedicate this book." McDaniel, the school's principal 1914–1939, was called "Gum-Shoe Mac" because he wore rubber-soled shoes and always appeared noiselessly (EH to Charles Fenton, 22 June 1952, JFK).

To Grace Hall Hemingway, 2 September 1914

Sept 2, '14

Dear Mother—,

The weather is awfuly rough here. Yesterday I caught 9 trout and Sam got 2 in Hortons creek.[1] This is the way they say one for the money two for the show in Boston. "One for the currency, two for the Exhibition, three for the preparation and four for the procedure. ["][2] Sam goes tomorrow night. I wrote you a postal card from Charlevoix but have not had any answer yet. We dug and sorted Fifty Bushel of spuds. The rye and clover on red top[3] has sprouted. Wish I was [nut ?]

Yur Lovin Sun

Ernest

[*On verso:*]
Bulletin.
Buchaanaland. Sep 15

Information has been recieved from unoficial sources to the effect that the Irish will be unable to participate in the yuropeon war owing to the recent Brick strike.[4]

JFK, ALS; letterhead: "Windemere" / Walloon Lake, Michigan

1 Harold Sampson visited EH in Michigan again that summer for a working vacation at Longfield Farm, a 40-acre property across Walloon Lake from Windemere, purchased by the Hemingways in 1905 and leased to tenant farmers, the Washburns (Sanford, 87–88). As a teenager, EH worked on the farm during summer holidays and frequently camped out there alone or with friends. Horton Creek runs through the village of Horton Bay, about 2 miles from the farm.
2 EH is poking fun at supposedly effete Bostonians by inflating the language of the saying, "One for the money, two for the show, three to get ready, and four to go." At the time, Grace was visiting Nantucket, Massachusetts.
3 The central hilltop at Longfield Farm was known as "Red Top Mountain" because of its reddish-colored grass (Sanford, 88).
4 Although his intent is not entirely clear, EH is alluding to recent events in the news, including the outbreak of the "European war" in early August 1914, and a brickmakers' strike in Chicago in the spring of 1914 known as the "Million Dollar a Day" strike, which brought building to a standstill for more than three months. Despite their conflict with the British, in September 1914 Irish nationalist leaders called for suspension of the struggle for Home Rule and pledged Irish support to Great Britain in the war against Germany. "Buchaanaland" may be EH's misspelling of Bechuanaland (later Botswana), a British protectorate in south central Africa, where forces of the Union of South Africa would clash with and ultimately conquer the forces of German Southwest Africa in 1914 and 1915.

To Grace Hall Hemingway, 8 September 1914

Sep 8 14

Dear Mother—,

I got your card thanks very much. Our Train was 2.25 minutes late!! so no school.

The Program is all changed around lunch at a different time and alot of other changes. There was a report circulated around that I was drowned and some of my pals thot I was a ghost. May I please have some long pants[.] Every other Boy in our class has them, Lewie Clarahan Ignatz smith and every other little shrimp.[1] My pants are so small every time I wiggle I think they are going to split. And I have about 8 or Ten inches of wrist below me cuffs thusly.

Please say I can have them long ones.

Your drowned son
Ernest Hemingway

R.S.V.P. P.D.Q.[2]
P.S.
My shirt buttons all fly off when I take a full Breath.

JFK, ALS

The letter is preserved in JFK, Scrapbook IV, in an envelope embossed with Clarence Hemingway's name and return address in Oak Park; on the envelope EH wrote "Irgunt" [Urgent], and Grace noted, "Received at Miss Ayers Sept 1914 in Nantucket." She also wrote in the scrapbook, "Ernest grew an inch a month this summer and became very strong and capable on the farm . . . He outgrew all his clothes. Came home to Oak Park Sept 8th and entered Sophomore year. Plays on light weight football Team and Cello in orchestra."
    In 1914 Oak Park schools opened on 8 September, the day after Labor Day (*Oak Leaves*, 5 September 1914).

1 Lewis Clarahan (1897–1994), a friend of EH whose family moved from Newton Highlands, Massachusetts, to Oak Park in 1911. He graduated from OPRFHS in 1915.
2 R.S.V.P.: *répondez s'il vous plaît*: please respond (French). P.D.Q.: "pretty damn quick."

To *Baseball Magazine*, 10 April [1915 or 1916]

April 10,
Base Ball Magazine
70 5th Ave.
New York

Gentlemen;
    Enclosed please find 2.50 $. for which send me the Base Ball Magazine for one year beginningwith the May number. Also the following art posters. Matty, Walsh, Tex Russel, Schulte, Archer, Marquard.[1]

With best wishes to your magazine
Ernest Hemingway[2]
600 N. Kenilworth ave.
Oak Park
Ill.

IndU, TLScc; letterhead: CLARENCE E. HEMINGWAY, M.D. / 600
KENILWORTH AVENUE / CORNER IOWA STREET / OAK PARK, ILL.

In both 1915 and 1916, *Baseball Magazine* (1908–1965) advertised the six posters that EH
requested in his letter. In this, his earliest known typewritten letter, EH crossed out his father's
name on the letterhead and wrote in his own.
1 New York Giants pitchers Christy "Matty" Mathewson and Richard "Rube" Marquard
(1886–1980); Chicago White Sox pitchers Ed Walsh (1881–1959) and Ewell Albert "Reb"
Russell (1889–1973); and Chicago Cubs outfielder Frank Schulte and catcher Jimmy Archer.
2 EH started to type his name, got as far as "ERn," then crossed that out and added in ink his
signature and address.

To Marcelline Hemingway, [5 May 1915]

You poor bonus caput[1] how in the name of all things just and unjust did
you get in the story club. If I couldn't write a better story than you I'd consign
myself to purgatory. Congratulations.

Thine eternally.

Ernestum

phJFK, ANS; letterhead: MEMORANDUM

At the bottom of the page in Grace's hand is the circled date, "May 5, / '15" along with the
notation, "To Marcelline from Ernest on hearing that she had 'made' the Story Club / 12 out of
100 candidates accepted." In another hand (likely Marcelline's) is the circled notation, "Crazy
Nuts!" Girls in their sophomore year were eligible to compete for membership in the OPRFHS
Story Club. Copies of all EH letters to Marcelline at the JFK were donated by her son John
E. Sanford.

1 Good head (Latin), perhaps intended ironically as "bone head."

To "Carissimus," 17 July 1915

July 17 1915

Carissimus— ;[1]

I got your catalogues thanks hellish much, Honest that _ _ _ _ _ _ _ _ _ _ _
of a _ _ _ _ _ _ _ of a Boat[2] of mine is-- . I use these dashes because I swore so
much this afternoon at the thing that It would Break my head wide open to
invent any more. The female that gave them all typhoid in the lunch room is
that old one that cut ice cream on the opposite side from where we always
ate.[3] My dad found it out. I have got some good news for you cuspidoriac. I
was reading Marcelline my sweet ??????? sister's mail as usual trying to find
out what the dames think of me when I saw a letter and I read it and it was
from your friend Dorothy Hollands.[4] I copped it and will enclose it in this
letter[.] Gosh but it is mushy. I tell you guy beware! All females are alike. She
wrote me a letter and I will send it to you too. Why dont you write to some
females? It is fun all you do is say "I am having a fine time. Do write and tell
me about all the news of Dear old Oak Park." You send this and get a sixteen
Page letter to laugh at. Try it my son. That is a peach of a porcupine I shot[.] I
skinned it! It took about half a day and the skin is about 1/4 of an inch thick.
I am tanning the skin. I saw those dear deer's the Buck and the doe. Gee but
the[y] can run! They go along in long jumps with their white tails sticking up.
Believe your Uncle Isadore their is going to Be venison in this camp some day
this summer! Not a dam soul knows they are there. I wrote dad and he said to
wait until he came up and then we would shoot the buck. His horns are in
velvet now. I shot 3 squirrels and a sapsucker yest. Gosh but it is lonesome
here. Dad and Lewy gone. Nobody to swear with[.] That boat is a helleritius.
Every once in a while when I am stuck out in the lake somebody will come by
and yell "What's the matter?" Boy you should here me then. I get off some
deuced eunique ones. Write me a long one. So long.

Ernie

Thanks awful much for those catalogues.

E.H.

JFK, ALS; letterhead: "Windemere" / Walloon Lake, Michigan, with printed
photograph of EH and Marcelline as toddlers in lake next to a docked boat

1 Dearest (Latin). This may be EH's classmate Ray Ohlsen, who in June 1915 accompanied him and Lewis (Lewy) Clarahan on the lake steamer *Missouri* as far as Frankfort, Michigan, on their trip north to Walloon Lake. EH and Clarahan walked the remaining distance of more than 100 miles via Traverse City and Charlevoix (Baker *Life*, 20).

2 Perhaps EH's birchbark canoe, of which he said, "Just as sturdy as a church, like hell. You have to part your hair in the middle to balance it" (M. Miller, 64).

3 The typhoid epidemic that swept through Oak Park in spring and summer 1915, afflicting at least forty people and claiming the life of high school teacher Vera Bleeker, was traced to Mary Burke, who worked in the school's lunch room (*Oak Leaves*, 3 July 1915, 1, and 10 July 1915, 1; *Chicago Daily Tribune*, 15 July 1915, 1). Earlier that year in New York, Mary Mallon (1869–1938), or "Typhoid Mary," also a cook and healthy carrier of the disease, had infected more than two dozen people, two of whom died.

4 A classmate of EH and Marcelline.

To Grace Hall Hemingway, 31 July 1915

July 31, 1915.

Dear Mother—,

I am at Uncle Georges at Ironton.[1] I came across the Lake last night with Bert van Houson dads trout fishing friend.[2] I killed the chicken and put it in the Barn in front of one of the horse stalls. I picked a half bushel basket of Beans and a half bushel basket of potatoes. The beans are in front of the icehouse and the potatoes in the milk house. I gave Warren[3] the key to the milkhouse the same key unlocks the ice house and the chicken coop. The chicken food is in the Barn. Arkensinger knows where every thing is and will be glad to get out ice for you.[4] Write me at R.F.D. no 2 East Jordan Mich. Wesley[5] says that Smith the Warden is a good friend of his and he will try to fix it up. I am going to work in the harvest field today with Uncle George.

Write me the particulars and how long I had better stay. Don't worry as the farm is in good shape.

Lovingly

Ernie

P.S. Arkensinger has a key to the milk house, ice house and Barn.

JFK, ALS; letterhead: GEO. R. HEMINGWAY / REAL ESTATE / 121 MARION ST. / OAK PARK, ILL.; postmark: IRONTON. / MICH., JUL / 31 / A.M. / 1915

1 Clarence's brother George R. Hemingway (1879–1953), a real estate agent in Oak Park, and his wife Anna (née Ratcliff, 1875–1957), had a summer home in Ironton, Michigan, where EH had taken refuge after shooting a blue heron during an outing on Walloon Lake with his sister Sunny. With the local game warden in pursuit, EH had hurried to Windemere to tell his mother, fled across the lake to Longfield Farm, then to the home of the Dilworth family in Horton Bay, and on to his Uncle George's place. He later turned himself in to the judge at Boyne City and paid a fifteen-dollar fine (Baker *Life*, 20–21). The incident is the basis of EH's final Nick Adams story, "The Last Good Country" (*NAS*), which he left unfinished.

2 Bert VanHoesen and his parents lived beyond the "Point" near Horton Bay on Pine Lake (renamed Lake Charlevoix in 1926); later he worked for the telephone company in Horton Bay (Ohle, 67).

3 Warren Ellsworth Sumner (1878–1947), born in Fenton, Michigan, came to the Horton Bay area at the age of ten and was a lifelong resident, raising five children with his wife Myra (née Lake). He owned the farm adjacent to Longfield Farm and did work for the Hemingways.

4 Probably James Ray (Ray J.) Argetsinger (1885–1966) of Boyne City, who worked as a hired hand on farms in the area.

5 Forrest Wesley Dilworth (1887–1950), son of James and Elizabeth Dilworth and EH's friend from early childhood.

To Clarence and Grace Hall Hemingway, [16 September 1915]

Dear Folks—;

Goturletter thanks! I am having hard work being a light weight but by eating a negative quantity of nothing I succeed. I am getting along alright in school[.] Got 100% on an ancient hist. t[e]st. Cicero is a pipe[.][1] I could write better stuff than he could with both hands tied behind me. Please bring home my photos' which are on the north end of the fire place in an envelope addressed To me[.] Please do this. Glad about spuds. What's the row with Singer?[2]

Ernie.

P.S. ~~I pawned my shoes to buy this card.~~

JFK, A Postcard S

The postcard is dated "Sept 16. '15" in Grace's hand and is preserved along with her annotation, "From Ernest in Oak Park to Father and Mother at Walloon Lake" (JFK, Scrapbook V).

1 Marcus Tullius Cicero (106–43 B.C.), Roman philosopher, orator, and statesman. EH uses the colloquialism "pipe" to mean something easily done, a cinch.

2 Probably Argetsinger.

To Ursula and Madelaine Hemingway, [16 September 1915]

Carus Yaps—;

That is great stuff about a window in Hem now I know where to spend next summers vacation.[1] Did Ana and Ruth put it in with a screw driver or knock it out with a grub maul. I hear Warren and his mules had a scrap and Arkensinger won. Eh wot? Can you picture your Uncle Oinutz living on 1/2 a lemon a day?[2] Some picture. So Long.

Butch.

PSU, A Postcard S; postmark: OAK PARK / ILL., SEP 16 / 10 PM / 1915

1 "Hem" is "Hemlock Park," the outhouse at Windemere. Sunny recalled that it was decorated with deer antlers and stocked with magazines and catalogues, and she described it as "a fine retreat when undesirable jobs were to be done" (M. Miller, 49).
2 Likely a reference to EH's effort to stay under the weight limit for the lightweight football team at OPRFHS by eating very little, as he mentioned in the previous letter.

To Susan Lowrey, [c. 1916]

Dear Sue—;

I think it's all straight in my dome now except what Hetty was being tried for. Who did she murder? Much obliged for writing it out you sure saved my life on this book.

Ernie

[*Lowrey responds:*]

Why, you see she didn't mean to murder her child but she was ashamed to go back to Mr. & Mrs. Poyser & thought maybe they wouldn't ever find it out. She left her child in the woods where it probably died of cold & exposure. You see that would be counted murder wouldn't it? Well, thats what they arrested her for & she was found guilty. The punishment was that she should be hung. C? But Arthur Donnithorne who had wronged her, repented & got her pardoned.

Now do you see?

OPPL, ANS

This note apparently was exchanged at school between EH and his classmate, who seems to be summarizing an assigned book that EH neglected to read. On the reverse side of the page, the note is twice addressed, first to "Sue" (whose name is crossed out) and then to "Ernie." The book is *Adam Bede* (1859) by English novelist George Eliot (née Mary Ann Evans, 1819–1880). The conjectured date of the note is based on the year EH is believed to have read the novel (Michael S. Reynolds, *Hemingway's Reading, 1901–1940: An Inventory* [Princeton, New Jersey: Princeton University Press, 1981], 120; item 800). School records show that both EH and Lowrey took English III and IV in their junior and senior years, which would place this note in either spring or fall 1916.

To [Unknown], [c. January 1916]

[*EH's friend:*] Great stuff I like to have another two weeks for vacation[.] We'll go to Zurich again won't we next April?[1] If we go Saturday Ill have to be at [dressing ?] at half past three we can make it easily after dinner run on the mountains and take pictures.

[*EH:*] W'ell go to Zurich all right. I know a new way to build a fire so that it reflects the heat right into the mouth of the tent and we'll be as warm as we want to it is like this

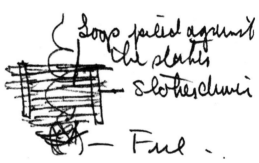

It reflects the heat right into the mouth of the tent.

Gosh but I wish we could bum down south. I've got a lot of folks down there.

[*EH's friend:*] We will have scribere litteris ad Edithior Est non dertex?[2]

[*EH:*] Eddy is having a swell time. The rector made him go to church the first day he was there. We will write a rough letter to him to keep his courage up est non verus.

[*EH's friend*:] Est verus[.]³ Where is Eddy at some Catholicismistic church school?

[*EH*:] Naw it is at Howe Indiana. It is an Episcopal school.⁴ How are your new classes. I finish my math—

[*EH's friend*:] ? What that mean for the [lark ?] tomorrow night. Then yo heave Ho and a bottle of Rum.⁵

[*EH*:] I finish my work. Tunique est ad mihi quam cuss words sunt ad Eddy Gale.⁶

[*EH's friend*:] Tomorrow I sit in seat 71 way over by [Goodwillie ?]. The note writing must come to an end eh Tunique? write it[.] Tomorrow I sit in seat 71 far away Then the note writing must come to an end eh Tunique.

[*EH*:] To an end it must come oh apple of my eye. For truly on that same day I myself sit in orchestra far far away from the preserver of my soul Tunique you have a friend Tunique preserved to you from all iniquity and sin. The name of that friend is Ernestum Tunique Sit. Est ille non verissimus⁷

[*EH's friend*:] rarissimum tunique sed the real sustainer of your sole soul est mihi ita est tunique ad mihi ita est [natibus ?] ad [Garborjor ?] can.⁸

UTulsa, AN

This note apparently was exchanged at school between EH and a friend. Written on twelve sequential pages of a notepad-style calendar, it starts on the page for "Saturday, January 1." On the page headed "Monday, January 3," EH circled the date and wrote, "School Begins."

1 Lake Zurich, Illinois, about 35 miles northwest of Oak Park. During spring vacation 1915, EH hiked there and back with Lewis Clarahan, returning on 3 April 1915, three days after the birth of EH's brother Leicester (JFK, Scrapbook V).

2 The banter of EH and his friend, mixing Latin and Latin-sounding words and phrases with private slang, defies exact translation or explication. The sentence probably means "We will have to write letters to Eddy" (the boy mentioned subsequently), with a possible pun on "Edithor," as in "letters to the editor." While *dertex* is not a Latin word, *dexter* means "right" (as opposed to "left"); "Est non dertex?" probably is intended to mean "Isn't that right?" although the correct word for "right" in this context would be *verus* ("true").

3 Is it not true? / It is true (Latin).

4 Howe Military School in Howe, Indiana, founded in 1884.

5 Apparent reference to the sailors' song that begins, "Fifteen men on a dead man's chest / Yo ho ho and a bottle of rum." It is quoted by Robert Louis Stevenson in his 1883 novel *Treasure Island*, which Marcelline recalled as one of the books that she and EH "devoured" in their youth (Sanford, 133).

6 "Tunique" is not a recognizable Latin word, and its meaning in the context of the letter appears to be fluid; it seems to be a private slang term, perhaps a nickname. The sentence roughly translates as "[Tunique] is to me as cuss words are to Eddy Gale."
7 Isn't that very true? (Latin)
8 Essentially, "The real sustainer of your sole soul is me."

To Emily Goetzmann, [c. 18 March 1916]

Oakus Parkibus—
III after the Ides of March
or is it the nones?[1]

Dear Emily—;

On pended gknees I peg your bardun vor the ladness of this legger. Bud a gombination of monthly examinachugs and Bad goldt are my eggscuse, or to quote "them immortal lines," the brooks are ruggig—also my gnose.[2]

Your friend Masefield is certainly good. As soon as I recieved your letter I went down to the library and got "The Story of a Round House". It is the light of Barnsness—really quite melior—in fact really optimus. Please notice the light and airy way in which I work little snatches of the classics into my conversation. But seriously Masefield is a whangdinger. I read all the ones you recommended and at the same time got another volume. Sea Ballads or some such name.[3] Hope you read Stalky and Co.[4] You'll like it.

For once, beside the usual merry bunk I have a little news. There is an epidemic of Scarlet Fever at school and they may have to close school! The household arts teacher came down with it and all the H.H.A. students are therefore quarantined[.][5] And I had a date with one of the H.H.A. girls. "Curses' on you Jack Dalton" he hissed thru his bent teeth. And lit another of his endless cigarettes.[6] Why in heavens name could it not have been my Cicero teacher?[7]

The other news is that Haasie recieved all A's on his report.[8] D'ont worry about corresponding me to death. It cawnt be did.

Another little item of information is that my beautiful Graeco Roman Etruscan Irish nose, or to use the Language of the Vulgar my pulchritudinous proboscis has wandered over on one side of my face as the result of a little boxing bout. However it has about got back to normal and people can now pass me on the street without emmitting loud coarse guffaws of touching mirth. As soon as my knose recovers I am billed to box Mr. Sexton. Marces' dear Ancient History teacher.

Since the last alteration of my well known countenance papá (accent on the last syllable) has frouned upon boxing. It came about in this wise.

Dad had been informed that no bodily harm could be done with the 8 oz. gloves and so he had consented to our using the music room. Attracted thither by the shouts of the Roman Mob he pushes open the door and beholds a slightly gory spectacle. My beeootiful nose was emulating Old Faithful Geyser my worthy opponent Mr. Townsend champion of River Forest was in a more or less recumbent position on the floor. Coxy the referee was counting 4-5-6-7-.[9] Did dad break-up that little social tea? Wow. Talk about the IV Phillipic. Dad certainly rose to the occassion in the oratory line. Demosthenes,—Cicero, Daniel Webster—didn't have anything on my worthy pater.[10] Anyway boxing is now frouned upon in this household.

I'm glad you have started on your opera. We have worked up the first three acts of Martha. It is certainly great music. Fairly easy to play too after ~~Mendahlsons'~~ Midsummer Nights Dream.[11] 54 More Days of School. 5 More days before Spring Vacation. I wish you luck with your opera.

Your Friend.

Ernest Hemingway.

Yale, ALS

1 In the ancient Roman calendar, the "Ides" was the fifteenth day of March, May, July, and October, and the thirteenth day of other months; the "Nones" was the ninth day before the Ides. Julius Caesar was murdered on the Ides of March.
2 Allusion to "Strawberries" by American poet Dora Read Goodale (1866–1953): "When the brooks are running over, / And the days are bright with song, / Then, from every nook and bower, / Peeps the dainty strawberry flower."
3 English poet, novelist, and playwright John Masefield (1878–1967). *The Story of a Round-House and Other Poems* (New York: Macmillan, 1912) contained his long narrative poem "Dauber," about the tribulations of the ship's painter, or dauber, on a voyage around Cape Horn. *Salt-Water Ballads*, his first published collection of poems (London: Grant Richards, 1902; New York: Macmillan, 1913), includes the popular "Sea-Fever." EH may be referring to the Barns Ness Lighthouse, constructed in 1901 on the Firth of Forth, near Dunbar on the eastern coast of Scotland. *Melior, optimus*: better, best (Latin).

4 An 1899 collection of short stories by English novelist and poet Rudyard Kipling (1865–1936) that recount the adventures of three schoolboys at an English boarding school.

5 EH's hometown newspaper, *Oak Leaves*, reported that fifty-five students were excused from the high school the previous day because household arts teacher Avis Sprague had scarlet fever ("Scarlet Fever at High School," 11 March 1916, 35).

6 *Curses! Jack Dalton* (1915) is a short animated film written and directed by Vincent Whitman.

7 EH's Latin teacher, Lucelle Cannon, who taught Latin and Greek at OPRFHS from 1907 to 1920.

8 Paul Haase, EH's high school classmate and hiking companion. In "Confessions," an essay he wrote in English class his senior year, EH claimed to have been put out of his freshman English class for "shooting craps" with Haase, and, during sophomore year, to have skipped class with him nine times without being caught. His teacher, Margaret Dixon, commented, "I detect in this interesting account your old love of making yourself appear much worse than you are" (Morris Buske, *Hemingway's Education, A Re-Examination: Oak Park High School and the Legacy of Principal Hanna* [Lewiston, New York: Edwin Mellen Press, 2007], 119–23).

9 In a scrapbook entry dated December 1915 through February 1916, Grace noted that after the fall football season, EH "had a spell of boxing enthusiasm, using the music room for a ring . . . But as the boxing began to degenerate into fighting, 'The House' objected and the 'Music Studio' was restored to its pristine purity after mopping up the blood." Among the participants were Phil White, Fred "Coxy" Wilcoxen, Harold "Sam" Sampson, Lewis Clarahan, and Jo Townsend (JFK, Scrapbook V). The Old Faithful geyser at Yellowstone National Park, Wyoming, erupts powerfully at frequent intervals.

10 Philippic, a denunciatory oration, named for the four speeches of Greek orator Demosthenes (384–322 B.C.) against Philip II of Macedon; Cicero adopted the term for his own fourteen speeches against Mark Antony in 44 B.C. Daniel Webster (1782–1852), American statesman and orator who served as U.S. congressman from New Hampshire, U.S. senator from Massachusetts, and secretary of state under three presidents.

11 EH played the cello in the high school orchestra for the 18 February 1916 senior class play, Shakespeare's *A Midsummer Night's Dream*, and for the 28 April 1916 Musical Club's production of *Martha: An Opera in Three Acts*, by Freidrich von Flotow (first performed in 1847). Grace preserved the programs of both performances (JFK, Scrapbook V). EH's cancellation of the word "Mendahlsons" suggests that the orchestra may have played the Overture to *A Midsummer Night's Dream* (1826) by Felix Mendelssohn (1809–1847), but the composer's name does not appear in the school program booklet.

To [Unknown], [c. Spring 1916 or 1917]

[*EH:*] Tonight maybe, any time we can get together. How about it? The river is good and high now. When shall we pull off our trip with A.D.V. and C.M.[1]

[*EH's friend:*] Come on over tonight and we'll start that Tabula Grind.

You write them sometime this week and we can pull it off next week— Tuesday or Wednesday. How about it?

UTulsa, AN

This note and the following one were written by EH and a friend and apparently passed between them in class. "Hemingway in high school" is written in another hand at the bottom of the page. Internal references point to either 1916 or 1917. Grace noted in EH's scrapbook that in April and May 1916, "Canoeing came into vogue. The 'Storm Class' Canoe and the Desplaines River furnishing the modus operandi" (JFK, Scrapbook V). EH contributed stories and poems to the *Tabula*, the OPRFHS literary magazine, between February 1916 and March 1917, and his humorous "Class Prophecy" appeared in the June 1917 *Senior Tabula* yearbook.

1 A.D.V., Annette DeVoe, class of 1918, served on the staff of the *Tabula*. C. M., probably Catherine M. Meyer (c. 1901–1930), also in the class of 1918; she lived at 601 North Kenilworth, across the street from the Hemingways.

To [Unknown], [c. Spring 1916]

[*EH:*] Were going on that Hudsons Bay trip I wrote to Ottawa last night for maps. How do you stand about going? If we get one more guy we will take 2 canoes.

[*EH's friend:*] I can go I guess. Where is it.

[*EH:*] Starting at the Soo—down Moose river to Hudsons Bay.[1] It will last a month and we will go as soon as school lets out. Lewy I and Charley Clarahan. It is about 400 miles down stream.

[*EH's friend:*] I don't know about next summer I may go to N.D.

[*EH:*] If either you or Haasy[2] cant go we will take just one canoe and us three go or maybe just Charlie and I.

It is classy thro forests all the way nifty rapids and long swift flowing stretches. The current of the river is about 4 miles per hour so with paddling you can go the heck of a ways in a day. When we get to Moose Factory (the name of the Fort at the Hudson Bay post) we will camp for a while and then go up with the summer supply bateaus.[3]

[*EH's friend:*] I mabe could go along in the latter part of July

[*EH:*] ~~That will be too late.~~

UTulsa, AN

1 "The Soo" refers to the Soo Locks, constructed in the nineteenth century between Sault St. Marie, Michigan, and Sault St. Marie, Ontario, to enable navigation between Lake

Superior and the other Great Lakes. The Moose River, in northeastern Ontario, empties into James Bay (on the southern end of Hudson Bay) near Moose Factory, the site of an eighteenth-century fort built by the Hudson Bay Company. EH's plans to canoe and camp across the Canadian province did not come to fruition.

2 Paul Haase.

3 *Bateaux*: boats (French).

To [Unknown], [c. Spring 1916]

[*EH:*] If we cant have a meeting at Haasies house we can have one at my house on Thursday night we'll get some cider etc. Est non optimus?[1] Can you get the prose? Did you pass the chemistry test.

[*EH's friend:*] I dont know about prose but I passed the chem test by 1

[*EH:*] Benē Benē.[2] I know a classy stunt. We will go out in our canoe and have a moonlight paddle some night this week.

JFK, AN

This and the following exchange between EH and a friend are preserved in JFK, Scrapbook V. The page on which they are pasted lies between pages holding the program of the musical *Martha*, dated 28 April 1916, and the program of the Junior–Senior Prom, 19 May 1916.

1 Isn't this best? (Latin).

2 *Bene bene*: good, good (Latin). EH's use of the macron (commonly printed in elementary Latin textbooks to mark long vowel sounds) is incorrect here.

To [Unknown], [c. Spring 1916]

Next spring vacation lets go to Lake Zurich again. And come home the way we did last time (Eh)! I can feel that turkey going down like hot pancakes right off the griddle. You can fry the [cowbirds ?]

JFK, AN

To Marcelline Hemingway, 20 June 1916

June 20 [*191*]6[1]

Dear Antique Ivory—;

Well old soak I suppose you have had quite the "Je su pas" time as it were. While commencement was going on Lew and I were fishing all night on a pool of the Rapid River 50 miles from no-where. Murmuring pines and hemlocks—black still pool—~~rush~~ roar of rapids around bend of river—devilish solem still—deuced poetic.[2]

When 9 Bells came I arose and gave a skinny wow-wow. Then I gave a masterly oration in my best English-French and Ojibway. Just when I had reached the part telling of my touching boyhood friendship with Mac,[3] Lew heaved a big rainbow out of the pool into my face. "Oh shut up", quoth he "Here's your diploma."

So having recieved my diploma I shook hands with all the balsams—bowed to my trout basket—kissed my fly rod and murmured, [X] ___ ___ ___ ___."

[X] deleted by censor.[4]

Then we had the alumni banquet. It was about 12.30 and I opened the sacred can of apricots that I had packed about 200 miles. You know you always carry something like that for anticipation. We ate the apricots and I made another speech which was spoiled by the log I was standing on rolling over. Lew didn't appreciate my oratory a bit and ate most of the apricots. Did you see France? Are my pictures any good?[5] I'll bet you have some rare time at Emily's. Did old Coxy come across with the necessa[r]y bid? I would wager a tuppence that Sammy looked foolish when he grasped his diploma in his hairy right mitt and stalked across the stage looking like a cross between Charlie Chaplain and Lord Kitchener.[6]

I caught so many trout that it was bushing. We got so that we would throw all back under about 9 inches. We gave several big ones away. Ivory dearest you should have seen the old brute doing a war dance in the costume of Adam eneveloped by a cloud of mosquitoes on top of a bluff about 300 feet high at night while my clothes were drying on a rack of cedar poles in the driving rain. One hand waved a shoe aloft the other helped me swear. The calm and quiet of the abysmal wilderness of the Boardman river were violated by the old Brute. Lew nearly died of Paroxysms. You see It was about Ten P.M. and It would have furnished quite a sensation to any one within a mile or so. I was singing Ban-Ban-Bay. Nuff sed. We didn't go anywhere but what the people asked us to come back and visit them again. Gosh but we made a lot of folks happy with giving them big fish. We gave an old couple

two great big suckers the first theye'd had in ten years and they darn near fell on my neck. I was glad they didn't because the old woman smoked a clay pipe and she might of busted it. Go to a lot of dances for me and eat some civilized food
  I suppose you saw Lewis. He would forget to tell you any of the interesting things tho—. Tell Emily for me that some time after she gets fairly graduated and every body else is dead and it is raining and she has absogoldarnlutely nothing else to do to write to me. You can tell her to[o] that I've got a picture to send to her after I hear that she is still alive. Bet you have some rough time without me to guide and protect you?

So Long

Yours Sin Seardly

O.B.[7]

Nutty P.S.
P.P.S
For John's sake write (Not Emily's John)[8]

PhJFK, ALS; letterhead: Pinehurst Cottage / CHARLEVOIX COUNTY / HORTON BAY, MICH.; postmark: BOYNE CITY MICH., JUN 24 / 5-PM / 1916

On envelope verso EH wrote, "From Rev. E. M. Hemingway. / Hellanback. / New Jersey." It is addressed to "Miss Marcelline Hemingway / 27 West Avenue South / LaCrosse / Wisconsin / 'Tender care / Miss Emily Goetzmann.'"

1 "191" is preprinted on the stationery; EH wrote in the "6."
2 As soon as the school year was over, EH and Lewis Clarahan left Oak Park on 10 June and took a steamer across Lake Michigan to Frankfort, Michigan, as they had the previous summer. From there they hiked south, fishing along the Manistee River to Bear Creek to the Boardman River, then caught the train northeast to Kalkaska and hiked to nearby Rapid River. After Clarahan returned home by train from Kalkaska, EH took a train from Mancelona to Petoskey and hiked to Horton Bay, where he stayed at the Dilworths' place (Baker *Life*, 24–25). EH alludes to "the murmuring pines and the hemlocks" in the opening lines of "Evangeline: A Tale of Acadie" (1847) by American poet Henry Wadsworth Longfellow (1807–1882).
3 Probably an ironic reference to OPRFHS principal Marion Ross McDaniel.
4 This line (the last on that page of the letter) is EH's own mock footnote to explain the blanks after the superscript "x" in the preceding sentence.
5 High school classmate Frances Coates. In May 1916, Marcelline wrote "A Sonnet / To 'Eoinbones,'" a teasing poem that reads in part, "He wonders if F Coates is looking his way / He straightens his tie, and heaves a great sigh / But oh how he jumps when sweet FC comes by!" (JFK, Scrapbook V). At the end of May 1916, EH, Marcelline, Harold Sampson, and Frances Coates took what Grace described in EH's scrapbook as "A beautiful canoe trip up The Desplaines river with supper on the Banks near the University Camp." The album includes two snapshots of the group on the river.

6 Tuppence, a British bronze coin worth twopence, or two pennies. Sammy, Harold Sampson. Charles Chaplin (1889–1977), silent-film actor and director best known for his character The Tramp, from the 1915 film of the same name. British Army officer Horatio Herbert Kitchener, Earl Kitchener of Khartoum (1850–1916), served as commander-in-chief of British forces in the Boer War, in India, and in Egypt, before being appointed Secretary of State for War in August 1914. WWI recruitment posters featured his image pointing at the viewer above the slogan "Your country needs YOU." He died on 5 June 1916, two weeks before EH wrote this letter, when the ship carrying him to Russia struck a German mine.

7 Short for "Old Brute," one of EH's nicknames.

8 Presumably a boyfriend of Emily Goetzmann. In a poem dated May 1916 and preserved in EH's scrapbook, Marcelline wrote: "Ernest dear / Please come here / Emily's voice from far & near / Can't you hear her calling, dear! / I'll kiss you again with Joy / Come to LaCrosse, my precious joy! / I've got lots of beauxs but I want a new toy! / Ernie come!" (JFK, Scrapbook V).

To Emily Goetzmann, 13 July [1916]

July 13 Thursday

Dear Emily—;

Marce says that the letter I wrote you may not reach you so here is another to make sure. This is a horrible stub pen but there is only one other in camp and it is worse so I hope you can translate these Higherowglifics—reformed spelling. (This is the other pen from now on.) We have been working hard on the farm haying and have got in about 8 tons of alfalfa and clover. I don't know whether you know an awful lot about hay so you are hereby informed that that is quite a lot for a junk of a place like ours.

Marce has been visiting over at Hortons Bay a Summer resort near here. There she met a Freshman at Illinois named Horace. The sweet lads sole interest is Mathematics and he believes fishing is an idle waste of time.

Can you concieve such a creature. Yes he wears amber coloured tortoise shell glasses. Yet the more or less sane sister of mine spent some time with him and says he is a nice boy. The marvel of the Feminine mind! How are you getting along on the Ranch? I'll bet you are having a stupendous time.

My old Ojibway Pal and woodcraft teacher Billy Gilbert was over to see me Sunday. Billy relapsed into a state of matrimony three years ago. The last time I saw him he was a part of the forest, one of the last of the old woods Indians.[1] Now he lives in a cabin and raises vegetables and cuts cord wood

"My Woman," said Bill, "she no like the woods." Do you remember this fragment from Kipling? It seems to apply to Billy.

"Through the nights when thou shalt lie
Prisoned from our mother sky,
Hearing us, thy loves, go by;
In the dawns when thou shalt wake
To the toil thou cans't not break
Heartsick for the Jungles sake."

The rest of it doesn't matter; that is the part that applies to Bill. You remember that piece don't you? It is what the animals say to Mowglie when he leaves the Jungle to be married.[2]

If the Lad Horace is what they turn out at Illinois Me for Cornell. Just think how pleased My family would be if they would civilize me and inculcate a taste for Math and a distaste for Fishing.[3]

Your sincere Friend
Ernest Hemingway.

JFK, ALS; letterhead: "Windemere" / Walloon Lake, Michigan; postmark: WALLOON LAKE / MICH., JUL / 15 / 8 AM / 1916

The envelope is addressed to "Miss Emily Goetsmann / 714 Pine Street / Helena, Montana." On it the post office stamped, "Not in Directory" and "No such street number."

1 The Ojibway (also known as the Chippewa) are a Native American tribe from the north central United States and southern Canada. The Gilbert family lived in an Indian lumber camp near Windemere Cottage, the setting of EH's short story "Indian Camp" (*IOT*); EH played with the Gilbert children and also knew the adults through his father, who often provided free medical care to the community (M. Miller, 25–26). Billy Gilbert and his wife figure by name in EH's unpublished "Crossroads: An Anthology" (Griffin, 126–27), and Billy would serve as the prototype for the amputee Indian war veteran in *TOS*.
2 EH accurately quotes from chapter 16 of *The Second Jungle Book* (1895) by Rudyard Kipling.
3 Marcelline recalled that in his senior year EH spoke of attending Cornell University, in Ithaca, New York, as well as the University of Illinois (Sanford, 149).

To F. Thessin, 30 January 1917

Oak Park Ill.
Janurary 30th' 1917

Mr. F. Thesin
Coach Culver Military Academy.[1]
Dear Mr. Thessin:

Your letter of the 25th at hand and we are much obliged for the details you have given. Would it be possible for our teams to meet on the 24th or have you that date filled? The 10th is a bit early to get our squad in shape but if you have that date closed, (the 24th) we would be willing to accept the 10th.

Thanking you again for the details and hoping to hear in the near future I am;

yours sincerely

Ernest M. Hemingway

Manager.[2]

JFK, TLS

1 College preparatory boarding school in Culver, Indiana, founded in 1894 by businessman Henry Harrison Culver (1840–1897) "for the purpose of thoroughly preparing young men for the best colleges, scientific schools and businesses of America."

2 EH was manager of the OPRFHS track team in his senior year. The team would lose to Culver in a meet in March and finish second to Culver in the Northwestern University National Interscholastic meet in April. EH would report on both events in pieces for the weekly high school newspaper, *Trapeze* ("Track Team Loses to Culver," 30 March 1917, and "Oak Park Second in Northwestern U / Culver Takes Meet," 20 April 1917; in Bruccoli *Apprenticeship*, 72–77).

To Al [Walker], [c. Spring 1917]

600 N. Kenilworth Ave.

Oak Park.

Ill.

Dear Al—; ! ? : *[1]

I've been busy as the immortal deuce therefor the absence of a letter from O.P. Say, old chap. If you are the Kabeza that designs Dort motor cars[2] kindly swallow sulphuric acid. In other words If you are the bloke that inflicts Dort motor cars on the long suffering public I beg that our Friendship may cease.

Did you make a few remarks about the indisposition of Oak Park Foot Ball Teams? Lean closer that I may spot you on the [pizzazd ?] or to use the vernacular bounce one on you cocabola.

Spring Brook sounds good to me! We sure will take some speckled beauts out of there next summer.[3] It is getting spring down here now. Yours sincerely is attempting to put the shot and the Base Ball teams are practising in the cage.

Wev'e got a boxing club down here now. I've put on enough weight so that I am in the 165 pound class now. Summary of Last two Months work.

KO's of Me   1

K'Os by Me   4

Decisions lost   2

Decisions won   6

We have six round bouts. I've got one on for Thursday night with a guy named Nellie Jenkins, who is about 6 feet 2 inches but skinny as a rail. I cant reach his jaw but will try and make his ribs sore. The K.O. you see against me is thus. A bunch of us fellows went down town to Gilmores gym, Sat. night on amateur night.[4] I went up against a guy named Tony Millichen who you may of heard of. We sparred for a minute and then I felt one of the fellows rubbing my face with a sponge full of ice water. I had a lump on my jaw the size of an egg. After that I will stay in my own class and no 200 pounders.

I wonder how Maurice Breen the W.K. B.S'er is?[5]

When are you coming up? What are you making? I hope to see you in about 3 months and a half more. Eh? I'll bet the trout dread our arrival. I've remembered buying Hooks[,] flies and I'm going to get a new rod. We're going to hike up take the Train to Marquette and Hike from there to Saint Ignace.[6] Peach of a trip. Wish you could Be along.

Write soon a long letter.

Your Friend,

Gus alias Ernest Hemingway

JFK, ALS

1 Most likely Al Walker (né George Alan Walker, b. 1898), EH's Michigan friend and fishing companion.

2 The Dort Motor Car Company of Flint, Michigan, founded by Joshua Dallas Dort, produced automobiles between 1915 and 1924. Al Walker and his family lived in Flint (Grace Cottage guest book, Mainland; 1920 U.S. Federal Census records).

3 Speckled beauties: light-colored, speckled trout.

4 "KO," a boxing term for "knockout." Harry Gilmore, a Canadian-born former lightweight bare-knuckle champion (b. 1854), moved to Chicago in 1888 and ran a boxing academy on East Adams Street in Chicago that was popular among professional and amateur boxers

(Harvey T. Woodruff, "Harry Gilmore, Who Battled in the Days of Skin Gloves," *Chicago Daily Tribune*, 26 July 1914, B3).
5 In EH's personal slang, "W.K." means "well known." "B.S'er" is short for "bullshitter."
6 The Grand Rapids and Indiana Railroad linked the Michigan Upper Peninsula towns of Marquette (on the shore of Lake Superior) and St. Ignace (at the southern tip of the peninsula on the Mackinac Straits). It would have been an ambitious hike of more than 150 miles, comparable to EH's long hikes from Frankfort to Walloon Lake in 1915 and 1916.

To Clarence Hemingway, [3 April 1917]

Dear Dad—
Am mailing this from Joliet at 4.10. Had a hard trip today from Lamont. Easy from now on. Have seen literally thousands of ducks and Mud hens. Are in Illinois-Michigan canal now. At Lockport are the I.N.G.[1] They passed us all night.

Much love
Ernie.

IndU, A Postcard S; postmark: JOLIET / ILL., APR 3 / 1917 / 8 PM

EH wrote on a prepaid one-cent postal card, rubber-stamped on the verso with the address, "C. E. Hemingway, M.D. / Kenilworth Ave. & Iowa St. / Oak Park, Illinois."

1 From 2 to 6 April, during spring vacation, EH and Ray Ohlsen made a canoe trip to Starved Rock State Park, near LaSalle, Illinois, about 95 miles southwest of Oak Park. They followed the Illinois–Michigan canal, opened in 1848 to link the Great Lakes to the Illinois and Mississippi rivers. A series of locks enabled boats to navigate the 140-foot drop in elevation between Lake Michigan and the Illinois River. The 96-mile canal passed through Lemont, Lockport, Joliet, Channahon, and several other towns before ending at LaSalle/Peru. With U.S. entry into WWI imminent (the nation declared war on Germany on 6 April), the Illinois National Guard (I.N.G.) were guarding the canal. Ohlsen wrote to his father that their second day had been a hard one and that he and EH had been stopped and searched by soldiers (Baker *Life*, 28).

To Clarence Hemingway, [5 April 1917]

Dear Dad—,
am writing from Chanahon a little village on the sleepy old canal—about 10:30. This morning the river was absolutely black with ducks blue bills, pin

tails and mallards. Weather is warm and are getting some good pictures. Fine eats. I. and M. Canal is very pretty and picturesque along here. We go into Illinois River this aft.[1] Have made about 50 miles. Many portages.

Ernie.

Swann Galleries catalog, New York, 8 June 2000, Lot 184 (illustrated), A Postcard S; postmark: [Channahon, 5 April 1917]

1 Channahon, about 10 miles southwest of Joliet, is at the confluence of the Des Plaines and Kankakee rivers, which meet to form the Illinois River.

To Fannie Biggs, [c. late June 1917]

Dear Miss Biggs—;

It is so lonesome up here that if I should see J. Carl Urbauer[1] I would fall on his neck and loan him half a buck instantaneously!

If it wasn't for the mosquitoes and the fish I would go absolutely bats. Mosquitoes are very companionable and I am trying to get a full chorus. I have captured a Soprano two bases a barytone and an alto and if a good tenor can be secured there will be complete harmony in the tent. The fish are running big. Saturday a 5 lb. Rainbow succumbed to the back to the land movement.[2] Before making the journey however he raised quite a fuss. It was 11.50 P.M. and I was alone and the moon forgot to shine, you oughta been there. But it is a good thing you weren't because all the time I had him on I was just wishing there was somebody there to swear at.

Probably you saw that story in the Trib about our scrap? Well with a few slight changes that was all straight stuff. Then did you see the story Thexton wrote about it for Oak Leaves?[3]

I wonder if he thot that because Jock and I were out of town that he could get away with stuff like that! My first act on returning to O.P. in Sept will be to slip Art what he has brung on himself.

Everything is about a month late up here.

About that scrap. You see Jock[,] Mussy and I thot we were being jumped by the Keystone Gang and we were fighting for our lives. None of us were hurt except Muss had a puffed eye. Jocks and my knuckles were cut split but we weren't marked. I wouldn't have missed it for 100 bucks and then that etc. of a Thexton took all the credit, made us appear to be liars, and wrote the false story for Oak Leaves. The Blight[4] being a gentleman did not mix in. If he had results might have been different. We didnt know who they were until we knocked one guy out with a club chasing thru the woods and I went to kick him in the face and it was F. Lee. Mussy had bit a big place in his arm during the first scrap while we were in our beds.

It really wasn't fair because they did not want to kill us but we thot that if we could kill a man it would cut down the odds. Gee you ought to have seen Jock fight!

Do you remember when I told you I'd rather have him with me in an emergency than anybody else? That was right. Mussy didn't come up to expectations—you see after our first scrap at the beds when they jumped us we chased after them thru the woods and when we found em Muss was not with us. After we had the second scrap in the woods we recognized 'em, it was pitch dark, and then the Blight quieted us down and came back to the fire. Mussy was sitting there. He said he thot he'd better protect the stuff.

When the story came out in the Trib the Jokers got kidded quite a lot and so they put that across in Oak Leaves. The worst part was the Trib man got the stuff from Cusack and Wright and they didn't know they were giving themselves away.

The Blight goes across pretty soon. He's written me. It looks serious to him now. "The tumult and the shouting dies etc."[5]

Yours.

Ern

JFK, ALS

1 School records show that Urbauer was a freshman at OPRFHS in 1916–1917 and dropped out in the middle of his sophomore year.
2 "Back to the land" was the slogan of a contemporary movement that encouraged city dwellers to move to the country, both to combat population loss and economic decline in rural areas and to promote wholesome agrarian values.
3 "Athletes Rout 'Scare Band' of Joker Friends: Humor Fades When Oak Parkers Tear Forth After Prowlers," by George Shaffer, *Chicago Daily Tribune*, 20 June 1917, 10. The story reports: "Ten Oak Park High school boys attempted to play a joke on Track Capt. Jack Pentecost, Track Manager Ernest Hemingway, and Morris Musselman, hero of the annual class play, at 2:30 a.m. Tuesday. They were nursing broken noses and black eyes yesterday

and vowing to go easier on the next chance for a good laugh." Arthur (Art) Thexton was a classmate of EH and a member of the gang that attacked him, "Jock" Pentecost, and "Mussy" Musselman. EH attributed to Thexton the unsigned article "Joke Is Warlike," which appeared in the 23 June 1917 *Oak Leaves*, 31. That account depicts EH as badly frightened and reports that he was rolled into the river to "cool off" after he gave one of the attackers a "sore nose." The pranksters included Franklin Lee, Thomas Cusak, and Clarence Wright, fellow seniors at OPRFHS.

4 Classmate Fred Wilcoxen.

5 Wilcoxen had joined the U.S. Army, eventually rising to the rank of sergeant in the tank service (Sanford, 286). The quotation is from the Rudyard Kipling poem, "Recessional" (1897).

To Grace Hall Hemingway, [3 August 1917]

Dear Mother—;

Dad and Ursula and Carol and Leicester are going in to Bay View this aft with Kenneth White and they will bring Marce home.[1] I've been on the farm every day since last Wednesday until today. Father is as cheerful as ever. I hope you get a good rest. The Kids were very glad to get the things you sent them.

It has cooled off here now and everything about the weather is nice except lack of rain. Our potatoe crop is drying down and the beans the same if it does not rain inside of about three days our potatoes will be just like last year. We have more hay up than last year and it is better stuff.

K. White has been here since Wednesday.

I hope to go fishing soon. Please don't burn any papers in my room or throw away anything that you don't like the looks of and I will do the same by you.[2]

Much Love
Ernie

JFK, ALS; letterhead: CLARENCE E. HEMINGWAY, M.D. / 600 KENILWORTH AVENUE. / CORNER IOWA STREET / OAK PARK, ILL.; postmark: BAYVIEW / MICH., AUG / 3 / 8PM / 1917

1 The cottage colony of Bay View, just north of Petoskey on Little Traverse Bay, was established in 1875 by the Methodist Church as the site of Chautauqua-style "Summer Assembly" programs. Trumbull White (1868–1941), originally from New York and former

editor of *Everybody's Magazine*, managed the 1917 program. His sons Kenneth and Owen were among EH and Marcelline's friends, and she spent July 1917 at Bay View as a guest of the family (Baker *Life*, 30; Sanford, 151–52).
2 In EH's 1927 story "Now I Lay Me" (*MWW*) Nick Adams's mother, cleaning house in her husband's absence, burns some of his treasured artifacts that she considers junk. In the manuscript of the story, EH inadvertently calls Nick "Ernie" (Smith, 173).

To Anson Hemingway, 6 August [1917]

Walloon

Aug 6.

Dear Grandfather—.

I have been wanting to write you to thank you for the birthday presents and papers but we have been putting in about 12 hours per day haying and working on the farm. We need a rain awfully bad as everything is drying up and we stand to lose our potatoe crop if it doesn't rain soon.

Uncle Geo. and family and Aunt G. and Uncle T. are coming over tomorrow to spend the day.[1] All our hay is in now and we can take things easier now. Dad's Ford is running fine now that the cylinders are clean and he wouldnt think of selling it.[2]

The other night I caught three rainbow trout that weighed 6 lb. 5½ lb and 3½ lb respectively also a two lb. brook trout in Hortons Bay. That is the largest catch of trout that has ever been made there.

I certainly appreciate your sending me the papers as we have nothing to read up here except the daily paper two days late.

I may stay up here thru October working for Dilworth as I am not going to the U of Illinois this fall. When I get home I am either going out to Uncle Leicesters or try and get a job with the Chicago Tribune.[3] By next year I ought to be fixed so I can go to school.

Much love to Grandma and yourself.

Ernest

JFK, ALS

1 EH's paternal uncles and aunt: George Roy, Grace Adelaide, and Alfred Tyler Hemingway.
2 In June 1917 Clarence Hemingway, with Grace, EH, and two-year-old Leicester, drove from Chicago to Walloon Lake in a Model T Ford touring car, a grueling five-day trip of more than

480 miles over primitive roads. The girls traveled by steamer as usual (Baker *Life*, 30; Sanford, 150).

3 In the 1917 *Senior Tabula*, EH had indicated that he would attend the University of Illinois. He was a regular reader of the *Tribune*.

To Clarence Hemingway, [c. 3 September 1917]

Monday 6 A.M.

Dear Dad—;

Last week I pulled beans for four days. Two for Wesley and two for Bill Smith in return for his helping me out at Lonfield. I will work today tomorrow and Wed. and then start home Thurs. Morning on the P.M. or G.R and I.[1] Did the bags and barrels arrive O.K?

We are having the equinoxials and you have to work between storms. Pulling beans is some hard job but I can pull about twice as many as Wesley.

In the rain the other day we went down to Charlevoix and caught a mess of the big perch that come in from Lake Mich. None under 1/4 lb and up to 1 lb. Bill S. and I caught 75 and sold 25 for 50¢ and split the rest to our families. It is stormy now and there maybe storms for a couple of weeks with nothing doing.

I'm glad you are having lots of business now.

Yours with love to all the gang.

Ernie

IndU, ALS

The date "Sept. 1917" is written in pencil in another hand below "Monday 6 A.M."

1 Pere Marquette or Grand Rapids and Indiana Railroad.

To Hemingway Family, 6 September 1917

Sept 6. [*191*]7[1]

Dear Folks—;

I'm sorry to hear you were so late getting in. GR and I is rapidly getting in the Pere Marquette class.[2] Everything is going good up here. (Rotten Pen)[3]

So far I have not fought with my employees. The last three days I have put in working for Wesley 10 hrs. Per. I have been weeding and thinning out carrots about 1/4 acre, on my hands and knees. There are callouses on my knees like a horse. Wesley seems well satisfied. Grub is very good. The first day I got here (Monday) Wes. was on a picnic and there was nothing doing in the labour line so I went fishing and got enough to last for some time. Al W. came over to go fishing with Bill G. and I went out with them.[4] We got 8 rainbow wt. 32 lbs. of which I got 5 and also caught on my fly rod a <u>Musky</u> that weighed 6 lbs. It jumped out of water about 8 times and acted very brutal. Bit me on the hand and tore the landing net. It is the first one caught here in three years. Aunty Beth gave me 18¢ per pound credit on my board bill for the fish she used.[5] So the wolf will not howl at the door for some time. I have been working hard and steady getting up at 5.30 and starting work at 6.30 and quitting at 6 P.M. so do not get the Idea that I have been fishing all the time just that once. Will get the barrells off just as soon as possible and send Bill of Lading to you. Sorry I wasn't there to see Harry Austin but he may call again sometime.[6]

Thanks very much for the papers. Cut the Line O'Type out of the Ed. Page of the Trib and send to me will you please?[7] Give my love to the gang.

Love to all of you
Ernie.

P.S.
Mrs. Dilworth sends you her love and will write Mother. She is going to have a red ✝ dinner here Monday night.[8]

IndU, ALS; letterhead: Pinehurst Cottage / CHARLEVOIX COUNTY / HORTON BAY, MICH.; postmark: BOYNE CITY, MICH., SEP 7 / 7-PM / 1917

On the letterhead, EH wrote quips in response to the printed text:

BROOK AND LAKE FISHING	[*EH:*]	You Bet
SPLENDID BATHING BEACH	[*EH:*]	<u>Very Cold</u>
RATES $1.50 PER DAY		
SPECIAL WEEKLY RATES	[*EH:*]	$5. Per

1 "191" is preprinted on the stationery; EH wrote in the "7."
2 In a letter to EH of 3 September, mailed together with a letter from Grace, Clarence reported that they had arrived home in Oak Park five hours late after a train journey plagued by delays (JFK). Petoskey was served from separate depots both by the Grand Rapids and Indiana

Railroad (since 1873) and by the Pere Marquette Railroad. Formed in 1900 in a merger of railroads, the Pere Marquette went bankrupt in spring 1917 and was reorganized in April.

3 There is a large ink blot on the page.

4 "Wes," Wesley Dilworth. "Al W.," Al Walker. Bill Grundy and his sisters, from Louisville, Kentucky, were among the friends Marcelline made that summer at Bay View and introduced to EH. In the manuscript of *SAR*, Bill Gorton was originally named "Bill Grundy."

5 The muskellunge, or musky, a large North American freshwater game fish of the pike family. Elizabeth Dilworth, proprietor of Pinehurst Cottage, bought fish from EH and applied the sum against his lodging expenses.

6 In her letter of 3 September, Grace wrote that Senator Harry Austin had called several times to see EH, having heard that he would be attending the University of Illinois and wanting EH to join his fraternity, of which he was the national president (JFK). An Oak Park native, Henry W. Austin (1864–1947) was a prominent businessman and civic leader, then serving as an Illinois state senator (1915–1922). As a student at Williams College (class of 1888), Austin belonged to the Alpha Delta Phi fraternity; he later served several terms as national president.

7 "A Line o' Type or Two," a popular humorous editorial column created by American journalist Bert Leston Taylor (1866–1921), ran in the *Chicago Daily Tribune* for nearly twenty years.

8 A dinner to benefit American Red Cross humanitarian efforts during the war.

To Clarence Hemingway, [11 September 1917]

Petoskey

5 P.M.

Tuesday

Dear Dad—;

Had a light attack of tonsilitis Thursday and Friday but gargled alcohol and water and peroxide and it cleared up in the throat. I was working all the time shovelling gravel and helping build road for Wes and cutting brush. Sat felt all right but pain in chest kept on working with pretty bad headache. Sunday I felt good but Monday morning had awful head ache on top of head in front. (Dont get excited) Went to bed Monday and head bad all night. Today my head was better and I came into Petoskey to see Doc Witter.[1] He said the toxin from the tonsilitis had given me the head ache and that my pulse was 120 but no fever. He said my heart was going a lot faster than it ought to and just a trifle irregular and gave me some stuff for my headache and some Argyrol for tonsils.[2] He said to take it easy and just loaf around for three or four days and I would be all right. I was very weak and the pounding on my head was kind of getting my goat but I will be all right now. I have written you everything there is so you wont be worried.

I walked down to the farm this morning and had Al Walker take me to the foot. Frost has not touched our crops and Warren says potatoes will be ready to dig the first of next week. Bad frosts but not hit us.

The other morning I went down early and caught a 7 lb. 9 oz. rainbow which they took in and put on exhibition at Bump and McCabes.[3] It is the biggest they have had there and the season ends in 4 days so they say I will probably get 1st prize ($5.00 worth of fishing tackle).

How is everybody at Home. I have been having a dandy time even tho sick and am getting swell eats. Mrs. Dilworth gave a big Dinner Last night for benefit of red cross and cleared $40 for them. I was sick thru it but picked and drew the majority of 25 springs chickens. Also shucked corn and helped otherwise.

All the Dilworths send you their kind regards also the two Bumps send their very coziest love to the kids.

Love to all
Ernie.

P.S. I got the tonsilitis thinning carrots in the rain Tues. and Wed. Thanks for the Papers. Will write Grampa. The weather is wonderful up here very clear last three days and cold nights. Th[r]ee frosts on low spots.

E.M.H.

Got 1.40 for Fish caught the other night for Dinner party 18¢ lb.

IndU, ALS; postmark: MACK. & RICH. / R.P.O., 11 / SEP / 1917

On envelope verso EH wrote, "P.S. Will write Ivory when I have More Pep."

1 Petoskey physician Frank C. Witter, whose office was at 322 1/2 East Mitchell Street.
2 Trademark name for a compound of silver and protein patented in 1908 by German chemist Hermann Hille and Philadelphia physician Albert Coombs Barnes (1872–1951) and widely used in the first half of the twentieth century as an antiseptic to treat mucous membrane infections.
3 Petoskey hardware store founded by George Bump and later run by his son Sidney S. Bump (1872–1911), father of EH's friends Marjorie and Georgianna Bump. It was named Bump and McCabe in 1909, when George W. McCabe became a partner in the business.

To Clarence Hemingway, 12 September [1917]

Wed 12 Sept

Dear Dad—;

Enclosed is Bill of Lading for BBls.[1] They went down on the Mo. today and ought to get to Chic. Friday.[2] I am going to start digging our stuff the first of next week. Spoke to Warren and he said they ought to be good by then. Did you get my letter from Petoskey? I am feeling good now but following Doc Witters instructions.

I got your letter this morning when I got back to the Bay. I will follow all your instructions about apples and potatoes.

Sure I miss Sunny and the Bipe House and all the rest of you but havent had any home sickness[3]

The young Bump kids are still here and will maybe stay a few days longer. Everybody else has went.

Much Love
Ernie.

Please Send me Chic. Tribs whenever you can.

IndU, ALS

1 Abbreviation for "barrels."
2 The lake steamer *Missouri* (owned and operated by the Northern Michigan Line) crossed Lake Michigan from Chicago to Harbor Springs, Michigan, on Little Traverse Bay across from Petoskey.
3 In his letter to EH of 8 September (JFK), Clarence wrote detailed instructions for shipping the apples and potatoes harvested from Longfield Farm and asked if EH was lonesome for Sunny and "Les." He added, "I send you Oak Leaves."

To Clarence and Grace Hall Hemingway, 14 September [1917]

Friday. Sept 14

Dear Dad—;

Here is the Bill of Lading that I thot I'd enclosed. Sorry it is delayed. All the stuff ought to be in good shape. We sent it by boat to Charlevoix.

Dear Mother—;

Thank you very much for the handkerchief and good letter. Everything is going good up here but today and yest. it stormed bad probably equinoxials. Im glad Urs has such a good bunch of Teachers. She ought to do hot dog stuff. Ask her for me if she didn't get the dramatic stuff in Boots from hearing it on Chrissie Youngs Victrola.[1] Dont ask her that unless she gets the big head but I've heard the same record.

Monday I start digging our spuds. Doc Whitters medicine has cleared up my head ache and I am feeling good. He sent his kind regards to Dad.

Much obliged for the clipping. Glad it begins to percolate. A ray of light in the Dark continent, So shines a good deed in this our naughty world etc.[2] There's hope for you yet Mother if you begin to understand Baseball. If a baby balls does a base cry?

It looks as tho Mr. And Mrs. Baby Dale Bumstead might have a hot time in the great Russian Empire. Probably there wont be any by the time they get there. They better stay in Honolulu and learn to dance the hula Huloo.[3]

Tell Pop I am going to bring him a birthday present so keep up hope.[4] Do you ever see any of the guys? Kiss Mr. Baldwin for me. Probably I will be home in time for the Worlds Series the middle of Oct.[5] ~~All the trees are turning red up here now~~.

All the birds are putting on their beautiful autumn foliage and the trees are gathering in twittering flocks ready for their flight to the glorious south land.

Give my kind regards to Anna Meyers wedding.[6]

With Love

Ernie

JFK, ALS; postmark: BOYNE CITY, MICH., SEP14 / 7-PM / 1917

On envelope verso EH wrote, "P.S. Please send me some stamps."

1 Ursula had just started high school; she and classmate Christine B. Young would graduate in 1921. In 1906 the Victor Talking Machine Company introduced the first "internal-horn phonograph" (with the amplifying horn inside the cabinet); "Victrola" became a generic term for a record player. Rudyard Kipling's poem "Boots" was narrated on a 1915 phonograph record by Taylor Holmes (1878–1959).
2 EH quotes from Shakespeare's *The Merchant of Venice*: "So shines a good deed in a naughty world" (5.1.91).

47

3 An article in the 18 August 1917 *Oak Leaves* reported that Mr. and Mrs. Dale Bumstead were en route to Russia, where they had been sent by his employer, the DuPont Powder Company, and expected to remain for three years. Their son, Dale, Jr. (a high school classmate of EH), would accompany them as far as Hawaii and then return to study at Cornell University ("A Mission in Russia," 11). EH is alluding to the volatile political situation in Russia: after the abdication of Czar Nicholas II in March 1917, months of conflict ensued between the Provisional Government and the radical Bolshevik party. The Bolsheviks, led by Vladimir Lenin (1870–1924), would seize power in the October Revolution of 1917.

4 Clarence had turned forty-six on 4 September.

5 Perhaps a joking reference to Whitford Baldwin, then a senior at OPRFHS. The 1917 World Series would run from 6 to 15 October, with the Chicago White Sox defeating the New York Giants, four games to two.

6 The 22 September 1917 *Oak Leaves* would report the marriage on 14 September of Anna Mary Meyer, daughter of Mr. and Mrs. John J. Meyer of 601 North Kenilworth, to Mason Osgood Tilden of Chicago. The wedding was held at the bride's home, across the street from the Hemingways. In her letter to EH of 17 September, responding to this one, Grace described the wedding as "very 'royal,'" with refreshments served in a 100-foot long tent on the lawn (JFK).

To Clarence Hemingway, [15 September 1917]

Dear Dad—;

Tell Mr. Julus Hall that I am interested and want to have an interview with him the first part of Oct.[1] I go to Walloon Sunday aft. and start digging Monday. Thanks for papers.

Ernie

IndU, A Postcard S; verso: PERE MARQUETTE PARK, PETOSKEY, MICHIGAN; postmark: BOYNE CITY, MICH., SEP15 / 7-PM / 1917

1 In the fall of 1917, EH's family and friends apparently were inquiring on his behalf concerning a position with a newspaper. JFK holds two letters to Fannie Biggs in answer to her queries about a job for her former pupil: from Walter Howry, managing editor of the *Chicago Examiner* (27 September 1917), and from Ed Beck, managing editor of the *Chicago Daily Tribune* (29 September 1917). Mr. Hall remains unidentified.

To Marcelline Hemingway, [15 September 1917]

WK Hell—;

This shows my room.[1] Fine time. Wish you could be here. Maybe you will sometime.

Aunt Grace[2]

Write me often. <u>Don't</u> join any fraternities. It's lonesome as hell.

Love and kisses,

[Drawing of a beer stein][3]

phJFK, A Postcard S; verso: PERE MARQUETTE PARK AND STATION, PETOSKEY, MICH.; postmark: BOYNE CITY, MICH., SEP15 / 7-PM / 1917

The postcard is addressed to "Miss Marcelline Hemingway / Barrows' House / Oberlin / Ohio." That fall she attended Oberlin Conservatory at Oberlin College, Clarence Hemingway's alma mater (Sanford, 154). On 17 September Grace wrote to EH that Marcelline had left for Oberlin that day (JFK).

1 On the front of the postcard, EH drew an "X" on the pictured bank of Bear River and penciled the note, "Cross shows my room." In her letter of 18 September 1917, Marcelline responded, "Your P.card created una riot with my room mate. She's from a 13000 acre ranch in Colo" (Sanford, 265–66).
2 EH signs the letter as "Aunt Grace," a reference to his paternal aunt, Grace Adelaide Hemingway.
3 EH's "signature" is a playful reference to one of his nicknames, "Stein," short for "Hemingstein." As Baker notes, this was EH's preferred nickname, one that he adopted in high school and kept all his life; it "originated before anti-Semitic jokes had become unfashionable and when, indeed, a few were even permitted in high-school publications" (Baker *Life*, 19).

To Clarence Hemingway, [16 September 1917]

Walloon Sun. Eve. 8 P.M.

Dear Dad—;

I am writing this from Ransoms where I just bought $24d worth of groceries. Tomorrow I start digging spuds on our place. Frost hasnt touched us but has cleared out Drayton and Ehrfoot.[1] Am Batching it at the farm.[2] Have paid for my groceries and two weeks board and am 5.75 ahead. Fish done it! Am feeling good and peppy now. Everything is great up here. Fine fall weather.

Love to all.

Ernie

IndU, A Postcard S; postmark: WALLOON LAKE, / MICH., SEP / 17 / 8 AM / 1917

1 The Hemingways bought supplies at Ransom's, a country store in Walloon Village at the south end of Walloon Lake (M. Miller, 21). Erfourth and Drayton were Horton Bay area

farmers. W. Erfourth was an early settler of the region, and children of both families attended the one-room Horton Bay School (Ohle, 7, 49; William H. Ohle, *100 Years in Horton Bay, Charlevoix County, Michigan* [Boyne City, Michigan: William H. Ohle, 1975], 33, 37).
2 I.e., living alone as a bachelor at Longfield.

To Anson Hemingway, 19 September 1917

Wed Morning

Sept 19 '17

Dear Grandpa—;

I certainly appreciate your sending me papers and magazines and your encouraging cards.[1]

Things are going very well up here. I am working on our farm now and cooking my own meals. The last two days I dug about 1/2 an acre of potatoes and there is about 3 days more work on them. All early potatoes are very poor in spots this year. The weather up here is glorious. Bright and clear sky but too warm for comfort while working. Thanks for the compliment about the fish and I only wish you could have some.[2] The week I was sick and couldnt work I kept my board paid up by going out a couple of times for fish for Dinners. Mrs. Dilworth gave me 18¢ a lb. dressed and I made over $5.00

We will get about 4 bbls. of apples off the farm. I have shipped one barrel already and some of them are for you

Probably I will see you in two or three weeks as I expect to get home in time for the Worlds Series.

Believe me I am always glad to hear from you and to get the papers. Give my love to grandmother and Aunt Grace.

Your Grandson

Ernest Hemingway

JFK, ALS

1 In surviving postcards to EH dated 4, 7, and 19 September (JFK), EH's grandfather sent good wishes, encouragement, and family news. In his 7 September letter he wrote that he was sending papers and "Leslie's" (*Leslie's Weekly*, an illustrated magazine published 1855–1922).
2 Anson Hemingway wrote EH on 4 September, "Your Big Fish story beats all" (JFK), probably in response to EH's letter of 6 August.

To Clarence Hemingway, [19 September 1917]

Wed Morning

Dear Dad—:

I came in here last night from Walloon to get the mail and some more cloths. There will be about 60 bushel of marketable potatoes the way it looks now. Those 60 bu however will be very good. You see there are strips of very good ones and then a lot of little nubbins.

I would advise shipping all the good ones home as Wesley is only paying 85¢ per bushel.

I am digging them all myself as Warren is all crippled up. In his joints.

I expect to finish them all and haul them over to the Bay by Sat night. It is very dry here just like powder and I am afraid our late beans will never get ripe. Our early ones are ready to pull now. Wesley advises shipping the spuds to O.P. I dig them then pick up the good ones and put them in crates and then sack them. Warren comes down for an hour or so in the evening and we put them on the stone boat[1] and haul them in the barn.

Today on the Missouri go down to you the barrel of apples I spoke about on the card. Also I thot you could use a sack of spuds. That sack shows the general run of the good ones.

Please write your instructions right away so if you want them shipped down I will send them next Wed. on the boat.

I am planning to leave some time during the first week of Oct.

I wanted to hire the polocks to pick up but they wanted 5¢ a bush so I told em nothing doing.

Yours

Ernie

P.S. Send me a Trib occassionally why not?

EMH

JFK, ALS; letterhead: Pinehurst Cottage / CHARLEVOIX COUNTY / HORTON BAY, MICH.; postmark: BOYNE CITY, MICH., SEP19 / 12-M / 1917

On envelope verso EH wrote, "Warren wants to hear from you. I won the prise I heard today." As EH wrote to his father on 11 September 1917, Bump and McCabe's hardware store offered the prize for the largest trout of the season.

1 A flat-bottomed sled used for transporting rocks.

To Clarence Hemingway, 24 September 1917

Mon. 8 A.M.

Sept 24 1917

Dear Dad—;

By tonight we will have all the spuds hauled over to the Bay and the early beans pulled. There will be about 60 bushel of good ones and they ought all to be shipped home as the market is only 70¢ now here. Will send down also 3 barrels of apples[.] This stuff leaves on the Missouri Wednesday night. Tomorrow I start digging for Wes. Weather is still great. Like a warm June Day at home but very cool nights. I am digging carefully and saving the small ones for seed. None of the potatoes are scabby and the 60 bushel are <u>very</u> good ones. Nice and big. The trouble is there are only 3 or 2 big ones in a hill where there ought to be about 10. Wesleys early ones are poor (<u>very</u>) and late ones are very bad on account of no rain for three weeks. They havn't grown since you left hardly any. Sat night Bill Smith and I caught 3 more rainbow. 4 lb. 3 and 2 1/2[.] Your little son caught three of them.

They will help kid along the board Bill. I am in great shape now and feeling lots of the old Jazz.

Al Walker went home two weeks ago and you might say it was a trifle lonesome on the Beloved Longfield. Gee this a great month up here.

Your letter and papers were much appreciated. Come again say we. Give mother my love and tell her I'll write her. The boy she speaks of is probably Bob Preble.[1]

Love—

Ernie

Thanks for stamps and my regards to the infants.

The late Beans are not coming out worth a chit. Fox's forty acres are N.G. and there will be acres and acres this year that will never be pulled.

Potatoes up here are very poor and low prices are caused by manipulation of Chicago market.

EH.

PSU, ALS; postmark: BOYNE CITY, MICH., SEP 24 / 1917

1 Oak Park acquaintance of EH and Marcelline (Sanford, 286, 304). In her letter of 17 September, Grace wrote, "Robt—can't remember his name, came to see you last week from Illinois." A "nice chap" in her words, he had done newspaper work and enlisted in the Aviation Corps (JFK).

To Clarence Hemingway, 25 September 1917

Charlevoix

Sept 25, [*191*]7[1]

Dear Dad—;

I just Brought 30 bags of Potatoes to here and 3 barrels of apples. I enclose bill of lading. Potatoes are marked at 62 bushel in Bill but there is nearer 90 bu. We save money on 62 bu tho.

Apples are crabs 1 barrel and winter apples 1 Barrel and fall apples 1 Barrel. Drayton took half of the hay (estimated). It appears to be lighter than we thot.

The Missouri gets in Saturday morning. leaves here Wed. night.

Potatoes are very good.

Love

Ernie.

IndU, ALS; letterhead: United States Post Office

1 "191" is preprinted on the stationery; EH wrote in the "7."

To Hemingway Family, 17 October [1917]

KC

Wed.

Dear Folks—.

I suppose you have got my first letter by now. I had a good trip and got in OK. Carl Edgar met me the first evening I was here and I sure am glad he is here.[1] He sends his love to all the kids. Aunt Arrabell wants me to stay here untill the end of the week.[2] Today I had 3 stories in the star. It seems like a pretty good paper. They have a very big plant.[3]

I start work at 8 AM and quit at 5 P.M. and have the Sabath off. So far I leave wit all I spent. Carl and I are going to try and get rooms together as we are both alone here.

All the relatives send you their kind regards.

With Love,

Ernie

My new address will be
3733 Warwick Boulevard
K.C.,
Mo.[4]

JFK, ALS; postmark: KANSAS CITY, MO., OCT 18 / 12 M / 1917

At the top of the first page of the letter, Clarence wrote, "Oct 17. 1917." and on the envelope, "1st letter From <u>K.C. Mo.</u> / Rec'd 2 pm Oct 19. 1917. / CEH." The envelope is pre-addressed to "C. E. Hemingway, M. D." at the family's Oak Park address.

1 EH traveled by train from Chicago to Kansas City, Missouri, on 15 October 1917 to begin work as a reporter at the *Kansas City Star*. He secured the job through his Uncle Tyler, an Oberlin College classmate of Henry J. Haskell, the paper's chief editorial writer. J. Charles "Carl" Edgar, whom EH nicknamed "Odgar," was a summer friend from Horton Bay. He worked at a fuel oil company in Kansas City and had encouraged EH's move, proposing that they share the apartment he rented there (Baker *Life*, 30–32, 570; Fenton, 28–29).

2 Upon his arrival in Kansas City, EH stayed for a few days at the home of his Uncle Tyler and Aunt Arabell Hemingway, at 3629 Warwick Boulevard.

3 Most of EH's writing for the *Star* consisted of short news stories generated by routine assignments given to cub reporters; none was credited in a byline (Bruccoli *Cub*, xii). The *Star* building at Eighteenth Street and Grand Avenue occupied most of a city block; the printing plant was in a lower level of the building.

4 Address of Gertrude Haynes's boarding house, a block from the home of EH's aunt and uncle.

To Clarence Hemingway, 25 October 1917

Oct 25th 1917

Dear Dad—;

I'm writing you this from No 4 Station.[1] I finished a week of work here yesterday. It is enjoyable. This morning Lord Northcliffe was in the office with his staff and Maj. General Leonard Wood too.[2] You ask about Carl Edgar. He is 28 and is running the California Oil Burner Co.[3] He is a peach of a fellow and is a good pal of Bill Smith's too. Everybody at the Star says that 35 a month for two meals and a bed is Robbry. At the end of the month I will change. I am sending you a Times for this morning with some of my stuff marked.[4] I have a desk and typewriter at the office. It is used at night by the Movie Editor. Everything we write is on the Typewriter. The star gets out a morning paper The Times 4 editions and the Evening Star in 5 editions also a weekly on Wednesday and a Sunday paper. It has a very large circulation and is pretty influential I guess.

Write me confidentially some time about Sue Kapps will you? I'm glad you have Bayley Savage as a patient but am sorry the Bayley is injured[.][5] tell him to write to me.

Much obliged for the Line O'Type they are always very welcome you bet. I got a scoop on the other papers yesterday about a troop train of soldiers to Fort Doniphan. I got thru the lines and talked with the Captain and got all the Dope. No body was supposed to see him and the troops couldnt leave the train. He told me that officially he couldnt say a thing. Then he went off aways with me and told me everything (Dont tell this around everywhere) where they were from where going, etc. Nobody else had it. I promised him I wouldnt publish it untill the train had gone so it was O.K.[6]

Much Love

Ernie

JFK, ALS; postmark: KANSAS CITY MO. / GATEWAY STA., OCT 26 / 10^{30} AM / 1917

EH wrote this letter on the back of the 24 October 1917 issue of the *Daily Bulletin*, subtitled "OFFICIAL PUBLICATION METROPOLITAN POLICE DEPT. / FOR THE INFORMATION OF COMMISSIONED EMPLOYEES ONLY."

1 EH's newspaper beat, which he later called the "short-stop run," included Police Station No. 4, Union Station, and the General Hospital (Fenton, 35). Although EH elsewhere referred to it as the Fifteenth Street Station, Police Station No. 4 had moved in July 1916 from 1430 Walnut Street to a building at Nineteenth and Baltimore (Steve Paul, "Annotation Added to Hemingway History," *Kansas City Star*, 4 July 1999).

2 Alfred Charles William Harmsworth, Viscount Northcliffe (1865–1922), popular British journalist and newspaper magnate, wielded strong political influence through his Amalgamated Press, which included the *London Evening News, Daily Mail, Daily Mirror,* and *Times.* In 1917 he traveled to the United States as head of the British War Mission, which placed propaganda items in American newspapers. Leonard Wood (1860–1927), U.S. Army officer and administrator, founding commander of Theodore Roosevelt's Rough Riders,

military governor of Cuba (1899–1902), and army chief of staff (1910–1914). After the outbreak of WWI in Europe in 1914, he led the movement for preparedness in the United States and advocated the creation of civilian training camps.

3 The company, at Thirty-first and Main streets, advertised its oil burners (manufactured locally since 1911) as a more efficient alternative to coal or gas heating.

4 EH enclosed clippings of short articles titled "Negro Methodists Meeting Here," "Little Help for Chief Vaughan," and "Glaring Lights May Return. "

5 Sue Kapps was a member of the OPRFHS class of 1916; her piece "How the Sphinx Lost Its Voice" appeared in the February 1916 issue of the *Tabula* literary magazine along with EH's story, "The Judgment of Manitou." On 12 October 1917, Marcelline had written to EH, "Tell the family to give S. Capps a wedding present for me" (Sanford, 268). Clarence Bayley Savage, Jr., known as "C. Bayley," was a member of the OPRFHS class of 1918 and captain of the football team during his senior year.

6 A piece in the 30 October *Star* "by a Staff Correspondent," datelined Camp Funston, Kansas, reported that the last quota of 6,000 drafted men would leave that day on "a special train" bound for Camp Kearney, California, as part of a troop transfer that already had sent 3,000 men to Camp Doniphan in Fort Sill, Oklahoma ("Finish Transfers This Week," 10).

To Marcelline Hemingway, [26 October 1917]

No.4 Police Station.

2.25 P.M.

Dear Old Ivory—;

And how is it at that most dear Oberlin huh? I also am working hard. Yesterday morning I had six yarns in the sheet and 1 on First page. A veritable reporter the old Brute. But nix on Fatimas for even they have went up to 18¢.[1] Carl Edgar and I jazz forth with Frequency. On Sunday last at St. Joe[2] we were and one Ada Lyon sent to you here love Also that Helen and this Auryllus. In truth it is the life at this place

All cops love me like a brotherhood. I am Editor of Public Mind like Vox of the Pop. but am now promoted and edit mind with less frequency.[3] This is copy paper. On it is written with a typewriter solely. Poor hand-writing has not handicapped me yet. At St. Josephine I was and have chance to work on St. Josephine Gazette.[4] But the Salary! Merci! It is nought. A mere pittance! Here I recieve 60 of them per month. A princely stipend.

and why is it I hear from you not? Loneliness consumes me theoretically; practically I am all business and have no time but at the office there is a frequency of the Tempus. Write me care the Star Ed department and you will be answered I swear it. Are there any he men with pants at that your school? Write me concerning them. I think not of Damsels but when the Spring cometh when no man can work, Ah then.[5] It is!

Yours,

The Brother

phJFK, ALS; postmark: KANSAS CITY MO., OCT 26 / 1917

1 A U.S. brand of Turkish tobacco cigarettes made by Liggett and Myers. Demand and prices for tobacco escalated during WWI, when it was distributed in daily rations to soldiers. EH is responding to Marcelline's complaint in her letter postmarked 12 October 1917 that most of the "callow youths" at Oberlin "have never seen a coffin nail except in picture books & their idea of heavenly bliss is a glass of milk and a doughnut on Sat. afternoon"; however, she confided, many of the girls "have other methods than looking at a mag's back cover in order to scent the sweet odor of Fatimas" (Sanford, 267–68).
2 St. Joseph, Missouri, about 55 miles north of Kansas City on the Mississippi River, famous as the eastern terminus of the Pony Express.
3 "The Public Mind" was the letters-to-the-editor section of the *Kansas City Star*. "Vox of the Pop," from *vox populi* or "voice of the people" (Latin), was the letters-to-the-editor section of the *Chicago Daily Tribune*.
4 *St. Joseph Gazette*, established in 1845, was one of the longest-running newspapers in the state.
5 Allusion to John 9:4: "I must work the works of him that sent me, while it is day: the night cometh, when no man can work."

To Madelaine, Ursula, Carol, and Leicester Hemingway, [5 November 1917]

Dear Kids:

Hy Nunbones, Howdy Urra, How are you Nubs, well how is the Bipehouse? Your large and Brutal brother is writing you this in the office where he labours. He is supposed to be laboring, is He? He is not. Enclosed are three transfers, which Ura will divide evenly among Carol and the Jazz. They are very special transfers being from St.Joe and K.C. and Nubs should take them to school to show the teacher that her burly brother paid his fare.[1] He is still living at Miss Haines but not for much longer. Also he is a beautiful soldier, and much to be admired.[2] This is how he will feel when all dolled up J-Z-Z-Z-Z-Z-Z-z-z-z-z-z-z-zy. Now Urra thinks this is very foolish but she is not wise like us is she Nunbones? She does not see the deep and hidden meening in all our remarks, does she Nubs? No she does not. Bipehouse, how would you like to shoot a great big dunga? Cracatua.

Mr. and Mrs. Edgar[3] sent you all their love but they did not know the Bipehouse or Nubs but they were sure they must be great being related to the great litterateur Stien and the Noted Ukalaliest Nunbones and the Noted smiler and latin shark, Ura. Now your stupendous and very magnisifant brother must go back to work, so called, and so he bids thee all farewell and hopes you will send him many Christmas, thanksgiving and any other presents that are fitting. So begin to save your money now my children for the Harvest is heavy and the Labourers few.[4]

Your Well known fraternal brother

Ernie.

JFK, TL with typewritten signature; postmark: KANSAS CITY, MO., NOV 5 / 1917

1 Among the Hemingway siblings' many nicknames were "Nunbones" for Madelaine (Sunny), "Urra" or "Ura" for Ursula, "Nubs" or "Nubbins" for Carol, and "Bipehouse" for Leicester. EH used "Jazz" as a nickname for multiple people, himself included; here, it is unclear to whom he is referring. Three train transfer coupons dated 4 November survive with the letter.
2 EH joined the Missouri Home Guard shortly after arriving in Kansas City and participated in practice drills and maneuvers over the next several months.
3 Carl Edgar's parents.
4 Luke 10:2: "Therefore said he unto them, The harvest truly is great, but the labourers are few: pray ye therefore the Lord of the harvest, that he would send forth labourers into his harvest."

To Marcelline Hemingway, [c. 30 October and 6 November 1917]

Written 1 Week Be Fore Being Mailed

Dear old Ivory:

Of course I wont say anything you old abysmalite. Sure I run the Public Mind, Honest to Godfrey. Glad you could have such a rzre time in Cleveland it must be quite a burgundy.[1] Tonight Carl and I go to Turn To the Right[2] What show did you see in Cleve? Does Red Milliken play on the O team? Today was pay day and I just dragged down $30 for the first two weeks work.

I got the negatives from G. AL walker today of those two pictures he took and am having a print made today. The Blight and Jock and the Mick have all written me this week.[3] Jock is at MIchigan and is having a rare time. Blight is still at Allentown, the Mick is working at Western Electric.

I am having a good time down here old kid and hope you get lots of joy out of the Alum Mattress.[4] But take it from tha Brother; be muchly careful and exercise discretion if not not absolute conformance to all rules and regulations. Carl is a good guy and not a suds downer,[5] he smokes the pills aw you are aware but he is 27 and I believe his life will not be ruinated thereby. Your kid brother leaves the fiery stuff alone and is about the only one down at the office that does not work with his face equipped with one of the filthy weeds. His vices are buying an occasional magazine and going to the debasing theayters ever and anon, also eating apples. I intend to enlist in the Canadian Army soon but may wait till spring brings back Blue days and Fair.[6] Honest kid I cant stay out much longer, the Canadian Mission Down here are good pals of mine and I intend to go in. Major Biggs And Lieut. Simmie are the officers in charge. If you enlist in the Canadian forces you are given as much time as you specify and then go to either Toronto or Halifax and the[n] to London and in three months you are in France. They are the greatest fighters in the world and our troops are not to be spoken of in the same breath. I may even wait untill the summer is over but believe me I will go not because of any love of gold braid glory etc. but because I couldnt face any body after the war and not have been in it.

You probably cant get me but cheer up because I am next to myself anyway. None of the above is for Family consumption, you know me Al.[7]

Your old Brute
Ernie.

A week later.

Hey old Brute. Glad Mother was there. Kiss all your room mates for the Stien. I joined the Mo. National Guard for State Service only.[8] Have a 40 buck uniform and 50 dollar overcoat. Some youth.

The Human Stien.

phJFK, ALS/TLS; postmark: [Kansas City, Missouri, 6 November 1917]

1 Burg, or town. Cleveland is about 35 miles northwest of Oberlin, Ohio, where Marcelline was attending Oberlin College.
2 The melodrama *Turn to the Right* (1916), by Winchell Smith (c. 1872–1933) and John E. Hazzard (1881–1935), was playing the week of 28 October at the Shubert Theatre in Kansas City, with the original Broadway cast. The Shubert, at West 10th Street and Baltimore Avenue, opened in 1906 and seated nearly 1,700.
3 EH refers to his friends George Alan Walker (Al), Fred "the Blight" Wilcoxen, and Jack "Jock" Pentecost. "The Mick" remains unidentified.
4 Alma mater.
5 Beer drinker.
6 Allusion to the lines, "I have a rendezvous with Death / When Spring brings back blue days and fair," from "I Have a Rendezvous with Death" by American poet Alan Seeger (1888–1916), published posthumously in 1917. Before the United States entered WWI, Seeger joined the French Foreign Legion and was killed in France.
7 Allusion to Ring Lardner's book, *You Know Me Al: A Busher's Letters* (New York: Doran, 1916). In stories for *The Trapeze*, EH often imitated the style of Lardner (1885–1933), American sports and short story writer who wrote a popular column for the *Chicago Daily Tribune*. EH also later imitated the busher's letters in *CIAO*, an irreverent broadside published sporadically by the American Red Cross (ARC) Ambulance Service Section 4 ("Al Receives Another Letter," *CIAO*, June 1918).
8 During WWI, National Guard units made up much of the American Expeditionary Forces, including 40 percent of the combat divisions in France.

To Clarence and Grace Hall Hemingway, 15 November [1917]

Nov. i5

Dear Dad and Mother:

I sure was glad to get your good epistles and the nifty cookies. Last night I had to stay late at the office to do a little work and they sure tasted good, Maw you are the rare cook, try me on some more stuff, let me get a sample of all your stupendous successes. If you want to why not send one of those war cakes?[1] I had to go out of the office while I was typing this letter hence the change.[2] All the Guard were ordered to report Tuesday and we had an all day maneuver and sham battle in the woods outside of town we marched and skirmished and had bayonet charges and sent out spies and all. Regular Army officers were the judges and it was very thrilling and instructive too. I will send you some of my stuff if I ever remember. I have had a couple of things that ran over Half a column. I saw the Trib about the High School Auto Smash.[3] Glad C Bailey was up Sunday. I heard from Cohan yesterday.[4]

We will get our winter uniforms soon and then I will get snapped and send to you. At Present I am using a borrowed khaki. Our new uniforms are olive drab wool and overcoats the same just like Regular Army and we wear regular army hat cords but have a MO. State shield on our hats. They should come soon. Can you send down my big shoes parcel post that are in my room? Send any packages and mail care the star as I dont know how long I will be at Miss Haynes.

It is fine that Bailey's team cupped the Champeenship.[5] I get better assignments all the time now and am going good. I will plan to work here until Spring and then get in one more good summer before Enlisting. I couldn't posibly stay out of it any longer than that under any circumstances. It will be hard enough to stay out till then. now be good and take care of your selves

much Love.

Ernie.

JFK, TL/ALS; letterhead: THE KANSAS CITY STAR.; postmark: KANSAS CITY MO., NOV 16 / 1917

1 In August 1917 President Woodrow Wilson created the U.S. Food Administration to assure the supply, distribution, and conservation of food during the war. Under the slogan "Food Will Win the War!" Chief Administrator Herbert Hoover launched a campaign of voluntary sacrifice, and Americans signed food-conservation pledges, adopted meatless Tuesdays, and devised "war" recipes without eggs, milk, and butter.

2 EH switched from typing to writing by hand after "stupendous successes."

3 The *Chicago Daily Tribune* ("Autos Driven by Girls Crash and Eight Are Hurt," 14 November 1917, 17) reported that eight students "were dangerously—one girl perhaps fatally—hurt" when the automobiles in which they were riding collided in front of OPRFHS. Several hundred pupils were thrown into a panic.

4 "Cohan" is probably EH's Oak Park classmate Ray Ohlsen. Ohlsen, Lloyd Golder (1899–1980), and EH had adjoining school lockers, on the doors of which EH drew circles in yellow chalk to represent a pawnshop, and the three boys dubbed themselves Cohen, Goldberg, and Hemingstein (Baker *Life*, 19; Sanford, 128).

5 On 10 November, led by team captain C. Bayley Savage, OPRFHS won the suburban heavyweight football title by beating Evanston High School 24–20 (George Schaffer, "Oak Park Takes Heavies Title in Prep League," *Chicago Daily Tribune*, 11 November 1917, A1).

To Hemingway Family, 19 November [1917]

November 19

Dear Folks:

This is about the third letter that I have started and had to stop all the others so am writing this right after work about 6:20 and so will try to finish.

The last two weeks have been awfully busy with me, doing something evry minute. Last Tuesday we all were called out and had drill and maneuvers allday. Yesterday I was up to Uncle Ty's for dinner, in the morning there was a big fire right next door to their new house, a large barn burned and I got there about the same time as the fire dept. and helped chop in the door and carried the hose up on the roof and had a good time generally. Probably I will stay at Miss Haines two weeks longer, I have been there a month today and by two weeks I will be able to get away all right. Glad the Bayley was up last Sunday, I had a good letter from him and from Al Walker, Al sent you all his love. He is at Olivet and they cant getany coal and unless some comes soon they are going to have to close the college.[1] There is no danger of the Star running out of coal. Much obliged for the stamps, they come in handy for mailing letters. This last week I have been handling a murder story, a lot of Police dope and the Y.W.C.A. fund stuff a couple of times so am mixint em up.[2] How is every thing going at home?

That sure was a bad accident but it was a good job to smash up the Atwood—Rogovsky auto bandits any way.[3] I have ridden in the Ambulance several times and as there is an epidemic of small pox here I think I will get vacinated again tomorrow. Aunt Arrabel is doing lots of Food conservation work and is quite high up in the Food ring. We have been having a swell lot of fun down here with a new fellow named Johnson who is about Baby Dales[4] speed and we have sure pulled some rare ones on him. There is a dandy bunch of fellows down here. I intend to go out to Camp Funston[5] soon and look up Pinckney. he is head of the motor truck unit there. Also I am going down to Oklahoma some time before I go home up North. Now if I am going [t]o get any supper I will have tosay good bye, The cookies were great try me again. Lots of Love

Ernie.

JFK, TL with typewritten signature; letterhead: THE KANSAS CITY STAR.; postmark: KANSAS CITY / MO., NOV 20 / 12 PM / 1917

On envelope verso EH wrote, "P.S. got your letter. Much obliged for package sent. It will arrive tomorrow probably. / EMH."

1 Olivet College, a liberal arts college in Olivet, Michigan, founded in 1844 by John J. Shipherd, a Presbyterian minister who had founded Oberlin College eleven years earlier. From the beginning both schools were open to men and women of all races.

2 The fatal shooting of a Kansas stockman, Claud C. Pack, was reported that week in the *Kansas City Star* ("Mystery in a Shooting," 15 November 1917, 1; "Mystery Shooting Was Fatal," 16 November 1917, 1). On the day EH wrote this letter (19 November), both the *Star* and the *Kansas City Times* (the *Star*'s morning edition) reported on the front page that police had killed two thieves and captured a third during a cigar-store robbery: "police dope" that later informed EH's vignette of cigar-store bandits (*iot*). Beginning on 11 November, the *Star* had featured a number of stories reporting the launch and progress of a week-long fund-raising campaign in Kansas City by the Young Men's Christian Association (YMCA) and Young Women's Christian Association (YWCA) to support the war effort. EH may have written or contributed to three stories in the 16 and 17 November *Star* that focused on the YWCA, which exceeded its goal of raising $50,000 for a Camp Recreation Fund (while the men's organization did not meet its $350,000 quota). The YMCA and YWCA were founded by evangelicals in mid-nineteenth-century London to counter negative social effects of the Industrial Revolution, and both organizations were established in the United States in the 1850s. During WWI they offered morale and welfare services to the troops.

3 Eleanor Atwood, a sophomore at OPRFHS, was driving one of the autos that collided in front of the school on 13 November; Florence Rogovski, a neighbor riding in the car, sustained a broken leg. According to the *Chicago Daily Tribune* (14 November 1917), Atwood was "mistress of four speedy cars, the largest of which she was driving to school." Her father was president of the J. C. Whitney Manufacturing Company, an auto parts company founded in Chicago in 1915.

4 EH's OPRFHS classmate Dale Bumstead, Jr.

5 Camp Funston, built during the summer of 1917 at Fort Riley, Kansas, was one of sixteen Divisional Cantonment Training Camps established in the United States. During WWI nearly 50,000 recruits were trained at the site, about 120 miles west of Kansas City.

To Grace Hall Hemingway, 21 [November 1917]

Wed 21 1:40 PM
Star Office

Dear Maw:

The great package and your fine letter came today. Im glad you see things the way I do and you are doing the real stuff for Fat. He has a good bass voice dont you think? I got vacinated yesterday at the General Hospital where I go nearly every day. They did a good job. Im writing this at noon but dont know when I can get it finished. You see we have no regular lunch time but just grab some grub whenever we can. The reason that I havnt written oftener is that every waking hour I am working and the days go before you realize. I have been so busy that this is the way it goes, get up at 7 breakfast at 720 and

have to be at the office downtown by 8 then get my assignments tha[t] keep
me moving until about 1pm then I have about 20 minutes for lunch and
then get my afternoon assignments that are supposed to be off at 5 p m but
usually I get after something and am on the go until 6 and supper is at 6:30
and right after supper I usually try and read a little and fall asleep and hit
the hay and that way the days just shoot by. I havnt seen a girl in Kansas City
yet and that is a hard predicament for a guy that has been in love with
someone ever since he can remember. On my way back from work I usually
stop off at Carl's office and see him for a few minutes. He is a peach mother
and you would sure like him. His mother is like Grandmother Hemingway.
I like Aunt Arrabel awfully well but Uncle Ty and his stupendous egoism
and ways etc. get my goat. However he would never suspect it as I am always
very courteous. There are a bunch of dandy fellows down here at the Star
and we have all kinds of fun in the office. There was a big Y.M.C.A campaign
here too.[1] I am sorry that the feeble one has went and that you are so
busy, but better to stoke on a liner than look at that face much, Gee it haunts
me yet.[2] Ura must be getting to be a regular roarer amongst the
Jaz-z-z-. It is 2 p.m. now and I will get sent out any minute now so will write
along so I can Quit any minute. Your cookies were fine, I gave a few to the
fellows that were in here at night [w]hen I opened the box they thot they
were great. Now I have to go now so Good Bye and Lots of Love to every
body and yourself in particular

Ernie

JFK, TLS

1 EH may be comparing the YMCA fund-raising campaign in Kansas City to one in Oak Park
(perhaps mentioned in his mother's letter, which remains unlocated). Or he may be clarify-
ing that the YMCA, as well as the YWCA, held a campaign in Kansas City (since he had
mentioned only the women's organization in his previous letter).
2 I.e., better to shovel coal on a ship than look at that face much. According to Griffin (45), the
departure of the "feeble one" refers to the death of Grace's Aunt Emma Hall. However, given
that Emma S. Hall (1844–1917), the widow of Grace's uncle Miller Hall (b. 1835), had died
nearly six months earlier (on 28 May), EH more likely is referring to the departure of one of
the family's servants.

To Hemingway Family, [24 November 1917]

saturday 6:30

Dear Folks: The cake that Mother sent was sure great, I gave some to Aunt
Arrabel and Uncle T. and the Kids and Carl and they all agreed that Mother
was Some cook. Thanks ever so much. Today was a Day. The big Army and
Navy Game was played here and there were about 5,000 soldiers intown.
General Wood and Governor Capper of Kansas were up at the office and
the Governor came over and introduced himself to me and two other
fellows that were here at the time. They were going to have a big pqrade and
had a reviewing stand built on the steps of the Star Building but there wasa
wreck and the troops couldnt get here in time for it.[1] But we have sure been
tearing around today. Yesterday I had 6 stories in the Main edition, two on
the front page, if I had postage I would send you one, Pay day is next Sat.
and then I will buy a lot of stamps and send you some papers. Got Uras
letter today and much obliged, will answeer it soon. Carl went down to
Columbia today to see Bill Smith and Kate and Mrs. Charles, he will stay
over Sunday there.[2] I go on duty again at 7:30 untill 12:30 getting out the
. sabath sheet. It snowed here today and a regular London Fog. (I had to
change Typewriters).

Now I had better knock off and go out and assimilate some fodder.

I have a good place to write letters down here when I am not at the[3]

At the Muelebach Hotel here which is as swell as the Blackstone, They
have a press room for all the newspaper men fitted upwith desks and a
typewriter and telephones and lots of paper and that is where the fellows
hang out. You feel like a million bucks to have a private room at the
Muelebach, there is also one at the Baltimore, which about corresponds to
the Auditorium.[4] If there is anything you want to know about this Burg, why
ask me. My vaccination itches right merrily and so I guess it is taking good.

Lots Of Love

Ernie.

JFK, TL with typewritten signature

1 An Army football team from Camp Funston played a Navy team from Great Lakes Naval
   Station before nearly eight thousand people in Kansas City on 24 November. A scheduled

parade was canceled when one of the army troop trains crashed and delayed the soldiers' arrival, as the *Star* reported on the front page that day. Major General Leonard Wood was the commander of Camp Funston; Arthur Capper (1865–1951) was governor of Kansas from 1914 to 1918 and U.S. senator from 1919 to 1949.

2 Bill and Kate Smith both studied at the University of Missouri in Columbia. Kate graduated in 1917 with an A.B. degree in English and journalism, and Bill graduated in 1918 with a B.S. degree in Agriculture. Mrs. Charles, their maternal aunt, had served as their guardian since their mother's death in 1899; she had married Joseph William Charles, a St. Louis physician, in 1902. The family spent summers at their renovated farmhouse in Horton Bay.

3 EH ran out of room at the bottom of the page, leaving the sentence incomplete.

4 The twelve-story Muehlebach, which opened in 1915 at Twelfth Street and Baltimore Avenue in downtown Kansas City, was one of the finest hotels in the Midwest. The Blackstone, a luxurious Chicago hotel on South Michigan Avenue, was built in 1910 by Timothy Blackstone, president of the Illinois Central Railroad. The Baltimore, a grand hotel completed in 1899, was at Eleventh Street and Baltimore Avenue in Kansas City. The Auditorium Building in Chicago, designed by Adler and Sullivan and completed in 1889, housed a hotel, offices, and a theater.

To Hemingway Family, [c. 28 November 1917]

Thursday. morning[1]

Dear Folks:

Mr. Duke Hill aws here yesterday and I spent about an hour with him at the union station.[2] I am sorry that we could not have gotten together sooner. He will tell you all about it, he took a star for that evening thqt had a couple of things of mine in it. This is going to be a short letter as I am trying to write it before I get my afternoon assignmwnt. Bill Smith is coming here a week from Friday, Kate has gone to Chicago to hunt a job so you will probably see her soon. We have had no really cold weather yet, tho there is a frost every night now.

These soldiers are for Nubs and the Bibe house, tell Nubs I got her letter and thing she is a wonderful letter writer, no kidding. I got Ura's too and will write her soon. I am so busy now that I have a hard time to write any body at all. Tomorrow is Thanksgiving, but wewill work the same as usual, also Christmas and New years. I enjoyed your letter Dad very much and the Pictures too, and have shown them to a lot of people. IT would be great if you could get me a pair of army shoes all right. I want to write to all of you sepapately but I am so blame busy that I never have any time any more.

Saturday is payday again and it will be quite welcome, extraceedingly welcome, very welcome as I am reduced in circumstances, quite reduced in circumstances. Therewerea big bunch of soldiers from fort Sheridan[3] got in here this A.M. a lot of K.C. men got commmisions. I got a couple of short items there this A.M. and they are the only things of mine in the First edition today, some days are better than others however. The guards get overcoats and wool uniforms soon this next week I guess. Now I have got to go out so

So Long Mucha Da Love

Ernie.

JFK, TL with typewritten signature

1 EH likely added this handwritten notation after typing the letter, in which he says, "Tomorrow is Thanksgiving." (In 1917 the holiday fell on Thursday, 29 November.) EH apparently mailed this in the same envelope as the following letter to his father, written 30 November.
2 Duke Hill, Sr. (c. 1873–1947), with his wife and five children, lived a few blocks from the Hemingways in Oak Park. A resident of Oak Park since 1895, he was employed by the Montgomery Ward Company. Union Station, built in 1914 at Pershing Road and Main Street, was the main railroad station in Kansas City and often part of EH's newspaper beat.
3 Army training and mobilization center established in 1887 on the shore of Lake Michigan north of Chicago, named for Philip Henry Sheridan (1831–1888), Civil War Union general and commander of the U.S. Army during the Indian Wars on the Great Plains.

To Clarence Hemingway, 30 November [1917]

Friday Nov. 30

Dear Dad—; Much obliged for the stamps and cards. Yesterday was Thanksgiving but I worked all day. We all went to Woolf's famous place where they served a 5¢ pig and turkey dinner at noon.[1] All the reporters went up. Then in the afternoon I was assigned to cover a big foot ball game but the game didnt come off; it was postponed. I had a good visit with Duke Hill and hope to see more of him the next time he is down here. Tomorrow is Saturday and Pay Day. I hope to move Monday as where I am it costs so much to live I havn't hardly enough left for necessities. Am going to get my winter wool. O.D.[2] uniform and overcoat tomorrow. They are the same as the regular Army except have Mo. State Shield on the collar instead of

U.S. Will try and send you a snap If I can get anybody to snap me. Have been awfully busy all week. At my room is a letter I wrote you a couple of days ago that I will mail tomorrow, as I have a stamp now. I will mail this now at the Union Station.

You can buy ~~rabbit~~ Peter Rabbit sandwiches here from the hot dog wagons, tell the Bipehouse I'll eat one for him. Congratulate Nun bones for me and tell her to go buy herself a birthday present and think of me.[3] Will send some stuff soon.

Yours,

Ernie

The book you send is very good. Thanks.

JFK, ALS; postmark: KANSAS CITY, MO., DEC 1 / 1917

This letter is written on the verso of blank report forms bearing the heading, "Metropolitan Police Department, Kansas City, Mo." On the back flap of the envelope, addressed to "Dr. C. E. Hemingway," EH wrote, "P.S. I mailed <u>Both</u> <u>Letters</u> <u>Together.</u> / Ernie." (apparently referring also to the previous "Dear Folks" letter).

1 The 1917 Kansas City telephone directory lists a Wolf's Famous Place at 117 West Ninth Street, and Wolf's Famous New Place at 1327 Grand Avenue. The narrator of EH's "God Rest You Merry, Gentlemen" (*WTN*) recalls walking to the hospital in Kansas City from "the Woolf Brothers' saloon where, on Christmas and Thanksgiving Day, a free turkey dinner was served."
2 Olive drab.
3 EH's sister Sunny had celebrated her thirteenth birthday on 28 November.

To Clarence and Grace Hall Hemingway, [6 December 1917]

Dear Dad and Mother:

I sure have enjoyed and appreciated both of your's letters and have been so busy before that I havnt had time to answer. The cake hasn't come yet but I know it will be great. I have moved and Carl and I have a nice big room with easy vhairs and a table and dreswer and a sleeping porch with two big double beds for $2.50 apiece per week and am boarding at restaurants.[1] It sure is an improvement and lets me give the necessessary time to my work, as I dont have to quit on a story to ride 5 miles to supper. We got our Woolen O.D. Winter Uniforms and overcoats, and they are the regular army stuff, we ahve the Black and Gold hat cord of Missouri state. (I had to go out there and am continuing now)

the Oak leaves that dad sent didnt come yet. It probably will tho, I have been handling some pretty good stories this week, and am sending you a couple of clippings. The suicide note was alot of fun, as I [got ?][2] to go and interview the girl in the case, and I had the regular police star thwat we keep here for emergencies, and so whe told me everything she, knew, thwn i got a story from the man Bowman, and had him give me samples of his hand-writing and, scared him pea green.[3] This afternoon the bosss, sent me out on my regular run and then told me to tear along as fast as possible, because he wanted me to get back inside, because he wanted to hold me in reserve. So I dont know what is going to come off. We drill tonight, and it is sure cold. About 15 above and a wild wind. The spelling in this is not to be watshed as I am pounding in s big hurry and not stopping to correct mistakes. Heard from the old Ivory and she must be getting to be some journalist herself.[4] She sure is stepping along. The clippings I am enclosing are all in the last few days except the coal story, which I wrote some time ago.[5] Our overcoats surely are good. Tehy are Regulation like the unilform and are warm as the dickens. If it ge[t]s much colder on the sleeping porch I am going to have to wear mine to bed. OH Gee I forgot something goood. My army shoes arrrived and I am wearing them Now so they will be good and comfortable for hiking. They are great and I am much ogligated to you for sehding them Dad. I got another Army thing the other day too that is great. An Army slip on sweater. Khaki Wool. Marge Bump knitted it for me, and it is a peach of a sweater. She and Pudge[6] are making one for Carl too. They adopted us to supply with knitted stuff and Carl doesn't get his until he is drafted, or enlists, but I got mine sooner because of the Guard.

> Now I have got to say So Long
> my love to every body
> Ernie.

IndU, TL with typewritten signature

1 EH and Carl Edgar had begun sharing an apartment at 3516 Agnes Avenue.
2 EH seems to have dropped a word as he typed to the bottom right edge of the first page, then changed the sheet of paper in the typewriter to begin the second page.

3 The 5 December 1917 *Kansas City Times* reported in a front-page story that an usher at
Union Station had found what appeared to be a suicide note from a spurned lover, requesting
that an Eva Frampton be notified of his death. Frampton had testified in an assault trial
against W. C. Bowman, whose conviction on the charge had just been overturned by the state
supreme court. Frampton believed that Bowman wrote the note. No suicide actually
occurred.

4 Marcelline recalled that she enjoyed a "brief experience writing for the college paper" at
Oberlin (Sanford, 154).

5 No clippings survive with this letter.

6 "Pudge," nickname for Georgianna Bump, Marjorie's younger sister.

To Clarence and Grace Hall Hemingway, [17 December 1917]

Dear Folks:

I am sorry that I didnt get a letter off oftener last week but I aws right up to
my neck in work and havn't had a single minute¾ It was sure cold downhere
too, for pretty near two weeks it was below zero all the time¾ Just think that
a week from tuesday is Christmas. I suppose that I will have towork all day
but probably not very hard as we will not put oit as maby editions. Last night
I saw the negros that were sentenced to life inprisomment being taken to
Fort Leavenworth¾ There weere three special cars of them and three guards
armed with rifles at each end of each car. They came into the Union Station
last night on there way up from Hpuston.[1] There has not been anything
s½pecial doing. just the regular line of stuff, but plenty of it. I am writing thid
from the press room of the Hotel Muehlebach Sunday Fternoon. It is a hOtel
about as good as the Blackstone and they have a room with bath and easy
chairs and Typewriter fixed up for the newspaper meb¾ I am glad the Ivory
will get home soon fpr Christmas. I would sure like to but there isnt any
chance. This typeing is a little woosy, but the light is bad and I am trying to
make speed. I owe a lot of peolpe letters as I have been so blame busy and this
aft J aj going to try and clear some of them up. It has been so cold here that
I have been wearing my Big red sweater under my Mackinaw and it wasnt a
bit too hot. I am hoping to get a raise soon as all the fellows say that there
ought to be one coming to me. I hopeso any way¾

Say expect my package of Christmas things to arrive about week late as
pay day is just one week after Christmaw. Last night I didnt get to bed until

two bwlls this morning and so I slept until about 10 30 and am beginning to get a little pep back now. Now I have got to stop but will write again right soon.

Lots of Love, Ernie.

JFK, TL with typewritten signature; postmark: KANSAS CITY, MO. / GATEWAY STA., DEC 17 / 5³⁰ PM / 1917

1 On 23 August 1917 a riot erupted in Houston, Texas, when members of the Twenty-fourth Infantry Division, Third Battalion (a U.S. Regular Army unit made up of African-American soldiers), stationed nearby, entered the city in protest against alleged maltreatment of black soldiers by local police. The incident, which resulted in the deaths of sixteen white civilians and policemen and four black soldiers, was declared a mutiny. In three court-martial hearings held between November 1917 and March 1918, 110 soldiers would be found guilty and nineteen hanged, the majority of the rest receiving life sentences in the federal penitentiary at Leavenworth, Kansas.

To Hemingway Family, 2 January 1918

January 2 1918.

Dear Folks— ;

Happy New Year! How is everything. I saw the old Aunt Grace yesterday and she told me all the latest dope[.] I had dinner at Uncle Ty's and was off yest aft. because I worked Christmas. I am glad the Bipehouse is better and the Ivory too. Everything here has been all swifty. Bill Smith was down Friday and went back Monday. I was glad to see the old dear again. He and Carl went up to St. Joe Sunday. We are all going up North together 1st of May and the three of us enlist together in the Marines in the fall unless I can get into aviation when I am 19 and get a commission. The W.K. Aunt is looking fine. A bunch of us saw the old year out and New vice versa in regular style. We had an rare time.

Tomorrow is drill night and we have to drill Sunday morning now too. Why doesn't Dad get a commission in the M.O.R.C?¹ He could get a captain's commission and that pays $2,700 a year. Nearly all the MD's down here have commissions. All you have to do is apply for one. Not go to any camp or anything. There are a bunch that are married and fat and a lot older than Pop too. I'm glad that Uncle Leicester has got his Second Lieut.[2] The reason Carl has not enlisted yet is because he was a Lieut. in Nat'l. Guard and then had tropical malaria and got a discharge and has tried to get in 2 officer's training camps but got thrown down of P. Exam.[3] He is all right now tho so he and Bill and I can get in. But we want one more summer first if possible.

It is warmer here now. Only 4 more months till the first of May. Yippi Yeah!

Give my love to everybody.

Ernie

P.S. I'm sending some stuff tomorrow—Xmas

E.M.H.

. P.S.S—Tell Ura to give my love to Ginny[4] and tell her I'll write her soon.

JFK, ALS; postmark: KANSAS CITY, MO. / JAN 2 / 1917[5]

1 Medical Officers Reserve Corps. While no evidence has been found to indicate whether Clarence Hemingway ever applied for or received such a commission, he did serve as a medical examiner for the local draft board in Oak Park (Sanford, 158).
2 Leicester Hall was a supply officer with the U.S. Army's 617th Aero Squadron (Grace Hemingway to EH, 20 May 1918 [JFK]).
3 Physical examination for induction into the service.
4 Probably cousin Virginia Hemingway (1903–1975), daughter of George R. and Anna Hemingway, who lived a few blocks away from EH's family in Oak Park.
5 The year on the postmark stamp had not yet been changed to 1918.

To Madelaine Hemingway, [c. January 1918]

Dear Kid Nun Bones:

Was the old brute glad to hear ffn you.? Hw was that. He was that. He surely was that. And give my love to the old Jiggs[1] and te/ll her that yust as soon as I can I will write her thst to fear not all is not lost. And when she sent me that candy I ate it and passed some of it to the best fellows here and told them it was from my best girl and they said, some damsel Steimway. Some Damsel. Show this to jigggs will you.&%$#"_(&) How goes all with you. Are you love smit by some youth yet? If not why not? So you would yearn to see the stein in a snappy uniform? Weell so does the greatest of the Hemingsteins. It may be the Navy blue, or the olive green of the Matrine Corps, or the Khaki of the Army or the snappy O.D. and officers belt of an american ambulance man in the Italian service which it may.[2] Nun bones there is a good chance of the antiquw brutality making that service. Ted Brumback who drove on the 'erdun front[3] and is now working here on the Star and the Steinway are planning to pull off something of the sort in the nest five or six months. You will probably glimpse this scion of the Hemstich family about the foist of May as he tarries a couple of days in Oakus Parkus on his way to the land of the rainbow trouts. Oh nunbones such fish as will be drug firth in this maybe the last fishing trip. Aint It.

Well muy Love Faret thee well old Minga And Cavironi till the Chingi's come home and tont forget to breath a Cracatua now and then as you keep the pour L'Diablo's burning.

> YouR WEll Known and Justly famous lovink Brother?
> ERNIe.

PSU, TL with typewritten signature

1 Probably their sister Ursula, who as a young child had been called "Mrs. Giggs" or "Giggs" (Sanford, 127).
2 "O.D.," olive drab; officers wore a "Sam Browne" belt, supported by a strap going diagonally over the right shoulder.
3 A fellow reporter at the *Star*, Theodore Brumback had served July–November 1917 as an ambulance driver with the American Field Service in France. The Verdun front in the northeast was the scene of some of the worst fighting in WWI in 1916. For details of Brumback's WWI service and his association with EH on the newspaper, see his piece, "With Hemingway Before *A Farewell to Arms*" (Bruccoli *Cub*, 3–11) and Steve Paul's "'Drive,' He Said: How Ted Brumback Helped Steer Ernest Hemingway into War and Writing" (*Hemingway Review* 27, no. 1 [Fall 2007]: 21–38).

To Marcelline Hemingway, 8 January [1918]

Tuesday Jan. 8

Dear Kid Ivory:

Gee kid I'm sorry to hear you had the pendacidis and were maybe going to have to stay out of school for a while.[1] I sent you a christmas, new years and birthday present to Barrows house, thinking you would be there by the time it got there.[2] You maybe better write to there and have them forward it. It is that New Book by Jeffrey Farnol, I hope you havn't read it.[3] How is evrything. mit the old dear? Don't think because you never hear from the Stien that he doesn't love you because he does, better than eny other dame in the woild, so far any way. And it looks as tho it would be for quite a while.

You know the only dames I ever really gave a dam about never gave two whoops in the old moratorium for the Stien. Doubtless you know to who I am referring Aknt it? Well kid you dont want to join thw crowd. Does yer? Naw yer doesn't. Hello no. All is well with the old Jazzz here[.] I scooped the world on a big, roarer of a story and nearly got bumped off doing it. It ran only a little more than a colyum on the Front page of the Sunaday Star and they wired it to the Associated Press and the ST.Lois papers as fast a[s] I wrote it. I am enclosing an clipping.[4] Understand this is a private letter and do not read the same aloud to the family, you can show them the clipping andgive them all my love.

Now Kid I want to have you writ me ane tell me all about the party you had at tye hovel and who was there a[n]d what did they do and did they ask for me and what did they say and have you seen Annette[5] and any body else and go into details. And do it soon and at lenghth.

The old Carl and I are living in our dump and having the jazzy time. I may be leading an speedy existence but watch my step and take care of meself. Pop writes that he may not run old farm next summer and so that I should not plan to beat it North the 1st of May. But kid one William Smith desires my presence on his farm and I am enlisting in the most dangerous branch of the service in the fall and may have only one more summer I yearn for a regular one and hope to garner several more of the finny monsters before being garnered by the huns. I dont object to vroaking if I can get one more good summer first and Cark and Bill feel the same exactly and so we are going to have thet little summer of the old Government will allow.

What think you woman. The Well known aunt Grass[6] was here a[n]d I seen her 2s t[.] The first time was on new years day and as I had been up till 5 am New years morning I may not have made much impression. However I am not worrying and if she tells any wild tales discount em. discount em.

The old Carl is an Whizz and a rare good pal and a heller and a peach and anuthing else you want to designate him as. Him and me are Pals. Now write me soon and at lenghth and include a,ll the dames and just what they say about the old bird. Where dod you get that stuff that L.A.Dick was keen about me.[7] She doesn't give an Tinkers ptofanity is my own personal opinion, but dont let that slip. GEt me. Write details.

James Sanford, TLS; letterhead: THE KANSAS CITY STAR.; postmark: KANSAS CITY, MO. / GATEWAY STA., JAN 9 / 12^{30} PM / 1918

On the envelope, addressed to "Miss Marcelline Hemingway / 600 North Kenilworth / Oak Park / Illinois," EH wrote, "Private. Personal."

1 Marcelline recalled that after she returned to Oak Park at Christmas time following an attack of appendicitis, Clarence and Grace announced that she was not going back to Oberlin because her semester there had cost more than they had expected (Sanford, 159–60).

2 Marcelline's birthday was 15 January. At Oberlin she had lived at Barrows House, former home of President John Henry Barrows, which the college purchased in 1916 and remodeled to serve as a women's residence for Conservatory students.

3 Jeffery Farnol (1878–1952), English author of best-selling romance and adventure novels. The book was probably *The Definite Object: A Romance of New York* (Boston: Little, Brown, 1917).

4 The unsigned article, "Battle of Raid Squads," appeared on the front page of the *Kansas City Star*, Sunday, 6 January 1918. A facsimile of a clipping bearing Clarence Hemingway's handwritten note, "Ernest's work entire column," along with the full text of the article, is included in Bruccoli *Cub* (20–26).

5 Probably EH and Marcelline's high school friend Annette DeVoe.

6 Aunt Grace (Grace Adelaide Hemingway).

7 Lucille Dick, a close friend of Marcelline.

To Grace Hall Hemingway, 16 January 1918

Jan 16 1918.

Dear Mother—;

I just got your letter today.[1] I was beginning to wonder why I didnt hear from the folks but the trains have all been tied up in bad shape. It was 20° below here too tho not so much snow. In Kansas they had two and three feet in most all the country. No trains got thru at all from the West or East. We were sure cut off for a while. The coal shortage is still pretty bad here. However we should cogitate for it will soon be spring. Now dry those tears Mother and cheer up! You will have to find something better than that to worry about.

Dont worry or cry or fret about my not being a good Christian. I am just as much as ever and pray every night and believe just as hard so cheer up! Just because I'm a cheerful Christian ought not to bother you.

The reason I dont go to church on Sunday is because lots of time always I have to work till 1 a.m. getting out the Sunday Star and Every once in a while till 3 and 4 A.M. And I never open my eyes Sunday morning until 12.30 noon anyway. So you see it isnt because I don't want to. You know I don't rave about religion but am as sincere a Christian as I can be.

Sunday is the one day in the week that I can get my sleep out. Also Aunt Arabells church is a very well dressed stylish one with a not to be loved preacher and I feel out of place.

Now Mother I got awfully angry when I read what you wrote about Carl and Bill. I wanted to write immediately and say every thing I thot. But I waited until I got all cooled off.

But never having met Carl and knowing Bill only superficially you were mighty unjust.

Carl is a Prince and about the most sincere and real christian I have ever known and he has had a better influence on me than any one I have ever known. He doesn't drool at the mouth like a Peaslee with religion but is a deep sincere Christian and a gentleman.[2]

I have never asked Bill what Church he goes to because that doesn't matter. We both believe in God and Jesus Christ and have hopes for a hereafter and Creeds dont matter.

Please don't unjustly critisize my best friends again. Now cheer up because you see I am not drifting like you thought.

with Love

Ernie.

Dont read this to any one and please get back to a cheerful frame of mind!

JFK, ALS

1 Grace's letter remains unlocated.
2 The Herbert C. Peaslee family, which included five children, were members of the Hemingways' church in Oak Park (Madelaine Hemingway scrapbook, PSU). Walter Peaslee was in EH's graduating class, and in EH's humorous "Class Prophecy" in the 1917 *Senior Tabula*, he figures as a disciple of a "new religion called Jazzism" (Bruccoli *Apprenticeship*, 111).

To Hemingway Family, [c. 30 January 1918]

Hem_ _ _ _ _ _ y.

ver.

Welll Known and Dear Family:

Much obliged for all the foodstuffs mother! They were awfully good and Carl and I hada feast last night. I didnt think at first that the buns would have kept so long but they were great. I opened the package at the office last night and padded the cookies around to some of the fellows and they Said ["]thet Ma Hemingstein must be some Cook" and to give her their regards. Which are hereby given. There is not much doing here now except qork which is busy as the deuce now. They are short on men and we tha[t] are here are having to work hard and ofteh. I am glad the appendix of the old ivory is good again[1] and that the Bipe House no longer suffers the qualms of whatever ailed him. Also that you all have plenty of coal. It sure is a scarce article here. And they cant get any of their famous natural Gas because it is so cold and all there is is the Fuel Oil that Carl sells.

There isn't any thing to tell you as all is peace able. There is going to be lots doing soon when the spring campaign for the city elections starts. This is as dirty a political town as the old smoke ville on the lake Mich. And they have just as jazzy fights as the one the Trib conducted on Big Bill Thompson.[2]

Right now there is a big Hospital and Health Board fight which I am in the middle of[3]

this town when I came down I thot was some what to th[e] South but for one whole ten days it never got above zero. And the old icy winds blow straight down from Athabasca[4] down the Mo. River valley and penetrate to the bones of the frigid Stein way. In other words she are cold. Tis two more days until the Ghost walks, i.e. pay day. Your box came in the nick of time. Those sox that Grandmother sent me were great. I will write her right away and thank her for them. I woke up to hear the telephone ring and it was the boss telling me that their was a big fire at 18th and Holmes street and that on my way down to the office to go over there and get a story on it.[5] Well I went and got tge yarn and telephoned for a photographer and got soaked all through my shoes in the icy water and then came into the office and there were my warm wool sox that I had put in my locker the night before. Well I beat it into the room where such things are done and changed my soaked, froze cotton ones into the warm wool jazzy ones and was ready to step forth among them.

Love

Ernie.

IndU, TLS

Written in Clarence's hand at the top of the letter is "K.C. Mo. 1/30/918."

1 Marcelline would have an appendectomy in 1920.
2 "Old smoke ville," Chicago. William Hale "Big Bill" Thompson (c. 1869–1944) was mayor of Chicago 1915–1923 and 1927–1931. After the United States entered WWI, his outspoken opposition to sending American troops to fight in Europe generated accusations of disloyalty and of pro-German activities; the *Chicago Daily Tribune* frequently ran articles critical of his administration.
3 Twenty-nine unattributed stories about the hospital fight and corrupt politics appeared in the *Star* between 2 January and 4 February 1918, some of them probably EH's work (Bruccoli *Cub*, 65–66).
4 Lake Athabasca, the fourth largest lake in Canada, is fed by the Athabasca River and spans the far northern border between Alberta and Saskatchewan.
5 EH's account, "Fire Destroys Three Firms," appeared in the *Star* on 26 January 1918 and included a three-level headline and three-column photograph.

To Marcelline Hemingway, [c. 30 January 1918]

Two Days before
Pay Day—

Dearest of Ivories—;

Tickles and pleasings enveloped me to get your sun dried and windblown epistles. Gosh I am glad to know the old Al is coming down.[1] I love him like a brother! Tell him to write me tho will you! How long is the dear lad going to step around that dear dump.

If the parents get rough explain to the old Al and he is a peach and will understand. Give him my love.

Say kid this newspaper business is the life. Since being here I have met and talked with Gen. Wood, Lord Northcliffe, Jess Willard, V. Pres. Fairbanks, Capt B. Baumber British Army, Gov. Capper of Kas. and any amount of others.[2] Tis the life. Also I can distinguish chianti, catawba, malvasia, Dago Red, claret and several others sans the use of the eyes.[3] Some days when I review shows I see three shows in a single day, all Theaters very class. Show of Wonders, Orpheum Circuit Vaudeville and Gayety Theater.[4] I can tell Mayors to go to Hell and slap Police commissioners on the Back! Yeah tis indeed the existence. Today got a letter from old Bill Smith. He speaks muchly concerning that joyous day the first of May on which we flea unto a far country.

I havnt written a soul except one slight epistle to the Fambly for a week. There is a devil of a big political fight going on and I havn't had a minute even to think. Lucile and K will be mad as the stuff they make the malt from.[5] If you see any of them tell them the Darn stien has been so busy that he hasnt even writ his family! Will you? Tell them that is the straight stuff. Damme Kid did you know they call me Hemingstien down here too? Even the Boss! Also Stienway and Hemstich. Also Hopkins the city Ed of the Times[6] addresses me as Mr. Goldfish! Reason unknown. Most of them call me The Great Hemingstien of Hospital Hill. That being one of my hang outs. There are a swell bunch of buds here ivory. Almost as good as the old gang. They are all abit to the wild but a peach of a gang. That Mrs. Hunter stuff seems all to the Rosy.[7] Do what ever you think best my dear!

Do you know I have to Pack a Colt gat? Dont spill it to the folks they might worry. Wm S. Smart or Bug Faced Bareshanks have nought on me.[8]

Fare well.

Your true love

The Old Brute.

phJFK, ALS; letterhead: UNION STATION HEADQUARTERS / SOLDIERS AND SAILORS / KANSAS CITY, MO.; postmark: KANSAS CITY / MO., JAN 31 / 12 PM / 1918

1 Probably Al Walker.
2 Willard, the "Kansas Giant" (1881–1968), became World Heavyweight Boxing Champion after defeating Jack Johnson in 1915; he would remain champion until his title bout with Jack Dempsey in 1919. Charles W. Fairbanks (1852–1918), senator from Indiana (1896–1905) and U.S. vice president under Theodore Roosevelt (1905–1909), ran unsuccessfully for vice president on the Republican ticket with Charles Evans Hughes in the 1916 presidential election.
3 Varieties of wine. This is not information EH would have shared with his parents.
4 *The Show of Wonders* (1916), a musical revue (book and lyrics by Harold Atteridge; music by Sigmund Romberg, Otto Motzan, and Herman Timberg), was playing the week of 27 January at the Shubert Theatre in Kansas City. The Orpheum Circuit, founded and headed by Martin Beck (1869–1940), included more than sixty theaters and dominated the vaudeville scene west of Chicago; Kansas City's Orpheum Theater, at Twelfth and Baltimore Avenue adjacent to the Muehlebach Hotel, was built in 1914 to resemble the Paris Opera house. The Gayety Theatre, also adjacent to the Muehlebach, was built in 1909 at the corner of Twelfth and Wyandotte; in addition to running vaudeville acts, it was a burlesque house.
5 Lucille Dick and Kay Bagley, close friends of Marcelline. An ingredient of beer (or "malt") is hops; EH means that the girls will be "hopping mad."
6 Charles Hopkins (d. 1956) joined the staff of the *Kansas City Star* in 1915, left to join the Navy in 1918, and returned to the newspaper after the war. He was assignment editor for the *Star*'s morning edition, the *Kansas City Times*.
7 While the "stuff" to which EH refers is unclear, Maria Cole Hunter was director of young people's work at the First Congregational Church in Oak Park and was popular among the youth for her warm manner and encouragement of social activities (Sanford, 148).
8 "Gat," American slang for a handgun, in this case probably a .45-caliber Colt automatic pistol, the standard-issue sidearm of the U.S. Army during WWI. "Wm. S. Smart" may be a reference to one of the first great stars of silent films about cowboys, William S. Hart (1864–1946), said to have owned one of Billy the Kid's six-shooters.

To Marcelline Hemingway, [12 February 1918]

Dear Ivory:

Well kid how goes it all with thee? And did that great Al of qhom I entertain the fondest thoughts appear as per scahedule? Let us hpoe. What I am writing to you for kid is to tell you that one of my best pals here

D. Wilson is soon coming up to the Great Lakes as a Radio Operator and as soon as he is out of detention camp he is goin to come out to the house and you are going to show him a good time.[1] Do you hear me child? As soon as you meet him you will like him as he is a heller of a good feller and will tell you all about the greatest of the Hemingsteins. You and Kay[2] should get together on Woodrow and paint the town red with him. He issuch another one as you cannot begin to appreciate he is such a peach. And the only draw back is that his foist name is, prepare to faint, Dale. But he is a living wxample that a regular he guy and a good guy and a swell guy can have such a monicker. I will give him an letter of introdiction to you and Also another good star guy Harold Hutchison[3] who is there now and you will slay the fatted goat. Wilt not sister of my bosom? Aint it? Sure Kiss me kid, I'm offn the old Garlic and know onions only by hear say. Look forward with the customary eagerness for Woodrows advent.

Thine ownest Own.

Stein the antique Brute.

P.S. I have got a bad case on Mae Marsh.[4] I have met the fair one and have fell hard. Ivory if you hear of me plunging off into Matrimony be not surprised. And Ivory if you would see the future Mrs. Hemingstein go to any movie that she is in and you will agree with me. And she is not half as good in the movies as in real life. Wilson Hicks the Movie Ed has fallen with a resoinding splash too.[5] But she loves me a whole lot better or else she is a darn liar. Gee Ivory I am comfortable now that I am in love again. It is the only state, next to _ _ _ _ _ _ _ _ication. Oh Ivory but I have got it bad. Miss Marsh's real name is Mary and she is twenty years old and very much unmarried tho not likely to remain so. I met her at the Muehlebach hotel. And Ivory such an Jane. Frances Coates? Annette DeVoe etc. will please march to the rear. She is as nice as Frances C. and far more charming than Annette and as for looks and good breeding etc. But tell not the Family. My only hope to remain single is to get in old War. That is probably the best thing to do but Miss. M.M. says that she will wait for me. And who says ought against the life of a newspaper man? Who indeed. When such opprtunities are brung forth.

Oh Boy. Oh Man. Oh Hemingstein.

I could rave on for hours. But Ivory go to see her in anything and then think of the Hemingstein that gets a letter at least twice a week from M.M. Oh Ivory. If you could see the picture that she sent me. Straus Peyton.[6] $75 per dozen and what is written on it! Understand Ivory she is not the rough stuff kind at all but is a peach. She is down on the coast near Woods Hole now making a picture but will be through here on the way back to the Coast agoin and then Ivory? I dont see what anybody can see in the brutal Steinway but I hope she keeps on seeing it.

Love From
Ernie.

Pull for me Ivory!

PSU, TLS with autograph postscript; letterhead: THE KANSAS CITY STAR.; postmark: KANSAS CITY / MO., FEB 12 / 12 PM / 1918

1 Dale Wilson, a twenty-three-year-old Missourian who worked as a copy reader at the *Star*, had been drafted into the Navy. EH dubbed him "Woodrow," after U.S. President Woodrow Wilson.
2 Kay Bagley.
3 Harold Hutchinson. At the *Star*'s Kansas City office, his name appears with EH's on a bronze plaque marking the roster of editorial staffers who served in WWI.
4 Silent-film actress Mae Marsh (née Mary Wayne Marsh, 1895–1968), best known for her appearances in *The Birth of a Nation* (1915) and *Intolerance* (1916). EH may have seen her during a vaudeville show in Kansas City. When asked years later if she ever met Hemingway, she replied, "No, but I would have liked to" (Dale Wilson, "Hemingway in Kansas City," *Fitzgerald/Hemingway Annual 1976*: 216).
5 A *Star* staffer and the movie editor; he later became executive editor of *Life* magazine and in 1952 would acquire the magazine rights of *OMS* (Wilson, "Kansas City," 213).
6 Photographers Benjamin Strauss (1871–1952) and Homer Peyton (d. circa 1930) became business partners and established a portrait studio in Kansas City in 1908, opening a second studio in 1915 in the luxurious new Muehlebach Hotel downtown. They were renowned for their artful portraits of theater celebrities, including the many performers who passed through Kansas City on regional and national tours.

To Adelaide Hemingway, [12 February 1918]

Lincoln's Birthday.

DEarest Grandmother:

This is a long long time to wait before writing to you to thank you for those great sox but here are the thanks. All that the paper will hold. They are wonderful and sure seved my life in the 20 below weather that we had for a long time down here. How is everything in Oak Park? I gope you are all well and know you are all happy. Give My love to Grndafather and Aunt Grace.

I am working hard now and having a fine time at the same time. It is like Spring here now and the nights are warm and balmy. The days are like May in Oak Park. This typewriter is easier to read than Uncle Bills[1] even if it doesn't write as good stuff. I suppose you are all busy on the Red Cross work and the Borrowed Time Club you work harder on those things than I do down here.[2] They are having a big Auto and Tractor show here now. The TRactor show is the funniest thing you ever saw. I thought I was having a night mare. There are such wierd looking machines. Some regular Tanks. They pull twenty plows at a time. There are about 150 different kinds of them at the show and a lot of them look unreal, like great big autos with wheels 15 feet high. They sure are funny. I would like to send one to Lester for a play thing. Well I have to catch a car out home and so will wrote you again. Thanks ever so much for the sox.

with Love.

Ernie.

IndU, TLS; letterhead: THE KANSAS CITY STAR.

"1918." is written in another hand below the letterhead.

1 EH's paternal uncle, Willoughby Hemingway (1874–1932), a physician and missionary who settled in China in 1904 with his wife, Mary Eliza Williams (1875–1974), and founded a hospital and school of nursing in Taiku, Shansi province (P. Hemingway, 294).
2 Work in these organizations included making bandages and raising funds for the war effort. The Borrowed Time Club of Oak Park, founded in 1902, initially was open only to men over the age of seventy. Anson T. Hemingway served as "Honorary President."

To Grace Hall Hemingway, [23 February 1918]

Daer Mother:

Dinna Wurra Mither abooot me not kennin the worth of your cookin. Twas Grand and the cookies and the tea cake and the pea nuts all were great and please do not make any resolve notto send me any more because I and Carl both are over jouyed when a box comes in. So you know me al. I am

glad the dee fish[1] is better and on the way to rosy cheeks and rough stuff
again. It was quite cold here for a time lately but is warm and nice agin.
Today The 2nd Mo. were reviewed by GoV. Gardner[2] and we had a big
review and parade and so I did not work in the A.M. I have just come dowm
to thw office now and will not have to go out this afternoon I believe as I feel
kind of bushed. I'm glad 6yat Old Al Walker and his pal could be down for a
couple of days and come out and see you folks. AL sure is a great pal of mine.
We had great fun together last fall when I was up there alone and when I was
pretty blame sick he sure took care of me. There isnt much to erite about
here. We are making a big fight on the Hospital and Health board. I am
writing the stuff for it and making the investigations. things are unbelievably
rotten. A small pox epidemic of 2,000 cases. A meningiti[s] epidemic, no
antiseptics at the hopital. No chemicals to develop X.ray plates. Fractures
andbullet wounds being treated without the use of the X.Ray for the last four
weeks. NO alchohol since Jan. 18th. And the politicians in the Board have
grafted $27,000 since the first of the year. I had a conference with
Mr. Latchaw the managing ed of the Times, the morning star, night before
last and he decided to fight them for fair and Albert King, Smith the Beamer,
and I have been put on it.[3] I cover all the Hospital and investigation end
of the hospital graft end. King the City Hall end in the P.M. and Smith, t/b/,
the health board office. I have had At least 1/2 column every day for the last
week in my end. We have got them on the run I think.

That is what I have been so busy on. As it takes lots of hard work to get and
verify dangerous facts and prove them beyond the shadow of a libel suit. It
does for fair.

Now I have to say good bye and give my love to dad and all the kids and
Nubs especially and don't cheat yoyrself when you are apportioning it.

:LOVE

Ernie.

JFK, TLS; postmark: KANSAS CITY MO., FEB23 / 1918

1 A nickname for EH's sister Carol; as his sister Sunny recalled, "Carol called herself Dee,
  then it got to be Deefish, then Beefish, until finally Beefy seemed like her real name"
  (M. Miller, 57).
2 Frederick D. Gardner (1869–1933), governor of Missouri, 1917–1921.

3 D. Austin Latchaw (d. 1948) became drama and music editor of the *Kansas City Star* in 1902 and also served as managing editor of the *Kansas City Times*, the *Star*'s morning edition, 1911–1922. He would go on to serve as editorial writer (1922–1928) and as associate editor of the *Star* from 1928 until his death (Felicia Hardison Londré and David Austin Latchaw, *The Enchanted Years of the Stage: Kansas City at the Crossroads of American Theater, 1870–1930*, Columbia: University of Missouri Press, 2007, ix). Albert King and H. Merle "the Beamer" Smith, fellow *Star* reporters.

To Grace Hall Hemingway, [2 March 1918]

Dear Mither:

The box came tonight and we just opened it atthe Press room the cake sure was great. Therewere about four of the fellows here and we opened the box and ate the cake. It was a peach. I am going to take the rest of the grub home and Carl and I will finish it up. The fellows all agreed that Mother Hemingstein must be some cook. your praises weere sung in loud and stentorian tones. The cake sure fed a multitude of starving and broke newspaper men tonight. There is not much doing here now except my hospital fight. Things are going great in that. I was officially barred from Entering the institution by the Manager yesterday and the Boss and the big political men are sure raising the mrrry deuce. We are panning the hide offn them for fair. But the boss said to disregard that fact that I am barred and sent meout there any way to get the dope on them. And so we are havin all soorts of rows. I have about five conferences withthe managing Ed per day and am getting along swell. We sure are making them hunt cover. The reason the[y] are trying to keep me out of the joint is because I have enough on them to send them all to the pen pretty near. Any way they sure hate the great Hemingstein ajd will do [a]ny thing they can to frame on him.

But we fight them High wide and handsome.[1]

I'm gkad the kids are all better. My love to Dad and I will write him next. Glad the old Ivory is having such an good time.

Good Luck

Ernie.[2]

Ernie

Love to Everyone.

Ernie

JFK, TLS; postmark: KANSAS CITY, MO., MAR 2 / 1918

The letter is written on the verso of stationery bearing the heading "Hotel Muehlebach / Baltimore Avenue and Twelfth Street / Kansas City, Mo."

1 In a carefree, stylish manner (U.S. idiom).
2 The rest of the valediction is handwritten.

To Marcelline Hemingway, [2 March 1918]

Daer Kid Swester.[1]

Love from the great Hemingstein to you all. And how is all with you? and that Sam how is he.?[2] Fall not for any such as Sam Ivory beacuse there are far better fish in the world than yon sucker, any way, think of the great Hem_ _ _ _ _ _y acting ad brother in law to such. Far better aL or some one or the real jazz. I can hear you rave, but the Kid brother, while a mere infant has been out in this old sphere considerable lately. And has seen many [a]nd various types. Also he has had many and varied experiences, it is the truth for a fact. No kidding, kid. Think twicw about Sam. I hae seen his breed before. Of course if he likes and loves you, theremust be some great good in him, that stands to reason. Aint it. Sure, but there are so many that are such a Damn sight Better Kid. Take it frpm the Great HemO_ _ _ _ _y. That is the way all my copy is signed. It takes too darn lomg to write out Heminbway. Any way Kid that was no idle Jest about the Great Hem_ _ _ _ _ _ _ _ _ _y being in love. And the one thqt he is in love with is none other than that Mae Marsh, ehom you and Sam glimpsed. If she would ever become Mrs. HemOOOOOOOO_ _ _ _y joy would reign supreme. Such is the state of affairs. Maybe she will love me enough some day. What id you and the Sam think of the Beloved Traitor?[3] I havn8t seen it yet and so cant tel.if it is up to her former standard. But I dont careif it is poor because that [m]akes no difference by me. Did you tel Sam that I was in love with she who you were glimpsing? And what did he say? Have you slippedany pne else the glad news? IF so, ley me know the results. I am glad that L. Dick is bats obout the Grimes if that is what you intended to infer.[4] Adhes to ashes and dust to dust is the Whiskey dont get you the cocaine, must. etc.[5] That meabs nothing to you anint it. Any way did I tell you that I was enlisted as an Ambulance driver for the American Ambulance service in Italy? Yes it is an fact. Mit me

my love but say nought ot the fambly. They might worry and I probably
wont br called for some time. Any way it is a big relief to be enlisted in
sometging. I enlisted for immediate service but got gypped on the immediate
end of it. You see it is like this there are only five jobs for immediate service
and my telegram got in sixth so I and the great Ted Brumbcak, who drove on
the Aisne for Six months will he next in line.[6] The St. Louis Headquarters
said that our enlistments were received, in response to our wire they sent
blanks, andthat they would let us know when they should avail them selves
of our services. The rank of a first Lieut. expense paid, an officers Italian
uniform, and a [p]robable Fifty amnonth for spending money. Aint it the
lofe. Any way promise on your word of honor not to say ought to any one asI
want not to be gyppeed. I now study French and Italian and have learned to
drive an ambulance. right jazzzy. Pull for the old bird. Isn't Mary M. a
wonder? HuH? HUH?HUH?HU?HUHU? Oh Boy. Brumstein andthe Great
Tubby[7] and the stupendous Hix all envy the gt. Hem_ _y. Is it not an just
cause? Oh man. Dale Wilson, has not yet left for Gt. Lakes and he is the bird
that I yearn to hace you have out? He is? But they are filled up there now and
so he is delayed leavibg. I yet hope to have a part of next summer up North.
Maybe, Maybe Not.

So write me right away and Good Luck with your A"mours

Old Kid it is none other than the great Hemingstein what signs this.

The Antique Brut.

James Sanford, TLS; postmark: KANSAS CITY, MO., MAR 2 1918

The letter is written on the verso of stationery bearing the heading "Hotel Muehlebach /
Baltimore Avenue and Twelfth Street / Kansas City, Mo." The envelope is addressed to "Miss
Marcelline Hemingway / 315 S. Ashland Boulevard / Chicago / Illinois," the address of the
Congregational Training School, where she was enrolled.

1 Probably a play on *Schwester*: sister (German).
2 Sam Anderson, a friend of Marcelline's whose attentions she mentions a number of times in
   1918 letters to EH (Sanford).
3 Silent film (1918) starring Mae Marsh and E. K. Lincoln (1884–1958). Later in this letter EH
   refers to Marsh (née Mary Wayne Marsh) as "Mary M."
4 George Grimm, a classmate who was close to Marcelline's friend Lucille Dick. Marcelline
   reported to EH on 11 May 1918 that Lucille and "George G. are still thick as butter" but by
   25 August, Grimm had been "canned from the Dick residence" (Sanford, 279, 284).
5 Lyrical phraseology common to many blues songs, notably W. C. Handy's "St. Louis Blues"
   (1916): "I said ashes to ashes, and dust to dust. / If my blues don't get you, my jazzing must."

6 EH was ineligible for service in the U.S. military because of his poor eyesight. The American
   Red Cross, however, accepted both EH and Brumback, who had lost an eye in a golfing
   accident. The Aisne River in northeastern France was the site of the Second Battle of
   the Aisne (16 April–9 May 1917), a failed French offensive. Brumback had served
   July–November 1917 as an American Field Service ambulance driver in France.
7 Nickname for T. Norman Williams, *Star* staffer and friend of EH.

To Marcelline Hemingway, [8 March 1918]

Daer Kid Sister:

Well Kid let me slip you an ear full. First I have not to my knowledge got
the Big Head? I was just trying to let you know how I was getting along.
Every time Hicks and Wilson and I get our pay checks it effectually fore stalls
any tendency toward the big head. Secondly old Sweetheart, incline and ear.
I dont want you to tell the family because I may yet get gypped on the
Ambulance Service as it may be taken over by the U.S. Govt. tho not
probably, and this is the point, YOu dont get any service flag[1] until it is for
sure, and I am not going to have any tears shed or letters written and then be
gypped. Do you get me? HUH? And Iwill let the folks know as soon as I a[m]
certain, if you think I am jesting or as it were kidding with you, why I will
enclose my correspaondence with the St. Louis and Washington depots.[2]
I did think kid that you had a little more faith in me than that. Uncle Tyler is
out of the City but I told Aunt Arrable and got a letter of recommendation
from Capta. J. B. White, the noted lumber hound and relative. Also from
Boss R. E. Stout, and Boss C. G.Wellington.[3] would I idly jest with the Boss
Stout one of the greatest newspaer men in the world ortrifle with my boss to
send letters? Also the W. K. J. B. White. However I[f] you think that I am
kidding and it makes you any more happy why go ahead. Also if you dont
like Mae Marsh, why go plumb to and take a long leap and see if it affects me
in the least. I am in love with her and while as I usually do I may get over it
yet she right now is the most wonderful in the world. Also in the Beloved T.
she was if you remember playing a character part and in real life, there is a
just a bare possibility that a wonderful character actress looks a trifle
different from playing the part she played in the Beloved Traitor.[4] I only
have pulled one boner in picking them and that was the late lamented D

Davies.[5] In other respects, fer exam[p]le, Annette DeVoe, Frances Coates, my judgment has been fairly sound. Ajd Mary Marsh, is far from an error in judgement. Also What did you tell me that Frances Coates wanted to hear from me for? I had no intention of writing her beyond the i[m]pression that you gave me. But going under that assumption I did write her about two weeks ago, which was a darn poor thing to do if she didnt want to hear from me and also you might say atrif[l]e humiliating, under circumstamces, about which you know nothing, not being home while I was. And she has not replied to the letter. I[t] makes no difference to me except maybe a matter of pride. And so dear old kid in your sheerful manner you have caused the beans to roll dorth frae the pot.

This is indeed a cheerful epistle. Any way I yearned to tell you about aby amount of things here but fear to because of a fear that you wil think that I have the Big Head or that I am kidding you. And so dear old thing write me and epistle and see if you can ease my mind, and dont kid me sweetest.

Thanks for asking HUtch out to the house wilson is still down here. also dont get the BIg head

phJFK, TL; postmark: KANSAS CITY / MO., MAR 8 / 12 PM / 1918

1 Beginning during WWI, families would display in their windows a flag with a blue star for each family member in active military service; a gold star symbolized a family member who had died in service.
2 Enlistment centers for the American Red Cross.
3 Arabell Hemingway's father, John Barber White (1847–1923), was in the lumber business. Ralph E. Stout was editor of the *Star*. C. G. "Pete" Wellington, assistant city editor and "keeper of the *Star* style sheet," was the editor most in daily contact with EH, who later expressed his gratitude for what he had learned working for him (Fenton, 31–34).
4 In *Beloved Traitor*, Marsh played Mary Garland, the heroine of the story.
5 According to Grace Hemingway, Dorothy Davies of Oak Park was the first girl in whom EH took a romantic interest, when he was fifteen years old (Baker *Life*, 19).

To Clarence Hemingway, 14 March 1918

March 14.

Dear Dad—;

The Oak Leaves and Trapezes arrived O.K. much obliged[.] I enjoyed them greatly. For the last three of four days it has been hot here. 85° in the shade official. Yesterday I was sent down to meet the Chicago Cubs coming thru to Caifornia and had a long talk with Manager Mitchel and a number of the players. I was sent down to see Grover Cleveland Alexander the worlds greatest pitcher who was sold to the Cubs for $75,000 from Philedelphia. He is holding out for a $10,000 bonus.[1] We met and talked for a half hour before the special train came in that he was to get on. While the train was stopped I met a number of the Chicago Base ball writers on the Trib, News[,] Examiner, Post, and Herald and they gave me a royal welcome.[2] I met all the players and had a fine time and wrote my story for the Associated and United Press so you ~~probably~~ could read it in Chicago if you wanted to or any where in the world. I bought Alex and Pete Kilduff and Claude Hendrix coca colas and they purchased me a lemon phosphate all of which goes on the expense account. Drinks purchased to get a story are by order of the boss called car fare.[3]

We are having a Laundry Strike here and I am handling the police end.[4] The violence stories. Wrecking trucks, running them over cliffs and yesterday they murdered a non Union guard. For over a month I have averaged over a column a day.

This warm weather is great! Just like summer. How is it with you? It is very busy now but I will write as often as I can.

Love to all
Ernie

any more Traps or Oak Leaves much appreciated.

JFK, ALS; letterhead: THE KANSAS CITY STAR.; postmark: KANSAS CITY, MO., MAR 14 / 1918

EH enclosed with this letter clippings of *Kansas City Star* stories: "'Alec' Left with the Cubs," "Hospital Clerk Let Out," and "Slay a Laundry Guard."

1 The Cubs were en route to spring training in Pasadena, California, and Fred Mitchell (né Frederick Francis Yapp, 1878–1970) was in his second year as team manager. The team finished first in the National League but lost to the White Sox in the World Series. In December 1917 the Philadelphia Phillies sold the Cubs the contract of pitcher Grover Cleveland "Pete" Alexander (1887–1950), later inducted into the Baseball Hall of Fame. He was drafted into military service in April 1918, after starting for the Cubs in only three games that season.

2 The *Chicago Daily Tribune, Daily News, Examiner, Evening Post,* and *Herald.*

3 Cubs infielder Kilduff (1893–1930) and pitcher Hendrix (1889–1944). Phosphates were
soda-fountain drinks made by mixing carbonated water with flavored syrups and a small
amount of phosphoric acid.

4 EH's "Laundry Car Over Cliff" appeared in the *Star* on 6 March 1918. An older reporter sent
with him to cover the laundry strike recalled that EH antagonized a mob of strikers by
identifying a rock thrower to the police (Bruccoli *Cub*, 37).

To Hemingway Family, 23 March [1918]

Sat March 23

aft

Dear Folks—;

I've just time to scribble a little to you. We are awfully busy. All the stuff
about the big German drive is coming in and we are short of men. Only have
12 men for the entire city.[1] The big Heney Packer inquiry is on, and the city
campaign and Henry Lauder here.[2] I am working like the deuce. The
German push looks awful. As I write we just got a bulletin that they were
shelling Paris.[3] I'd give details but you get it before you get this letter. The
Star office is some busy place, we are all pounding on the typewriter, and the
phones ringing, and the copy boys running and whenever we are free we go
over to the telegraph desk where the bulletins come in.

There's a General Strike of all Union labor in the city called for Monday.[4]
Then there will be more ____. The home guard has been formally taken into
the National Guard and take the Federal Oath Monday.[5]

Love to All.

Ernie.

Ill write as soon as I get time. Let me hear from all of you.

JFK, ALS; postmark: KANSAS CITY MO., MAR 23 / 1918

1 Hoping to defeat the British and French before the American Expeditionary Forces were
ready to fight, the Germans launched their last major offensive of the war on 21 March. They
initially gained considerable ground and captured many prisoners, but the Allies held with
the assistance of American forces. The *Star* was short of reporters because of increasing
enlistments and the draft.

2 Francis J. Heney was appointed in 1918 as special counsel for the Federal Trade Commission,
then investigating charges of price fixing and market manipulation by the meat-packing
industry. Hearings in Kansas City began on 21 March ("Ready in Packer Probe," *Kansas City
Star*, 21 March 1918, 2). Sir Henry (Harry) MacLennan Lauder (1870–1950), popular

Scottish comedian and vaudeville entertainer, performed at the Garden Theater in Kansas City, 21–23 March, as part of his "farewell America tour" (*Kansas City Star*, 16 March 1918, 3).
3 The Germans were using a 210-mm "Paris Gun," a 256-ton Krupp howitzer that could send a shell of more than 200 pounds over a distance of 75 miles.
4 The general strike was called in sympathy for the laundry workers' strike and lasted a week after laundry owners agreed to raise the workers' wages but refused to recognize their union.
5 The National Defense Act of 1916 required members of the National Guard to take a dual oath—to their state and to the nation. The federal oath required the Guard member to serve as directed by the president of the United States, including serving overseas.

To Clarence Hemingway, 16 April 1918

April 16 1918

Dear Old Pop:

How are you? Much obliged for the Oak Leaves[,] trap, and Tabula, but what was the idea of that camouflage about while only 18 he is etc. That made me pretty sore and I eish you hadnt done it.[1] This is the way things are lined up at present. I have been down here about seven months, granted. Until lately I have neen making not enough to live on. See High Cost of Living figures. I am only a kid of nearly 19 granted, and have been hitting the pace pretty blame hard. Working in competetion with men with threee to ten years more experience than I have. I have had to work like sin and have concentrated about three years work into one. Through good luck and some natural ability I have been able to get onto the game pretty well. In fact I have been having better assignments than a number of men from three to 8 years older than I am. and according to the way they are letting my stuff get by I am making good. I am now drawing $75 per month, the Star by a rule layed down by Col. Nelson, only gives one raise a year.[2] If I stayed intil mext April 1st I would get another raise of 15 or 20 beans. Making at the most $100 per month. Well I have an opportunity to go to Dallas at $30 a week, to Topeka at $30 a week and to St. Louis at $30 a week or to start as an out side man for the United Press at $25 a week. And every fellow on the staff tells me that I am a fool to stay here. I have had a lot of valuable experience and have done some good work and have hit it pretty blame hard. And now Pop I am bushed! So bushed that I cant sleep nights, that my eyes get woozy, and that

I am loosing weight and am tired all the time. I'm mentally and physically all in, Pop, and there isn't any body Knows it better than myself. Look at it this way. It is as though I had gone to college and been under the strain of cramming for an examination for seven months straight. For that is the way it is. Responsibility, absolute accuracy, thousands of dollars hinge on your statements, absolute truth and accuracy. A middle initial wrong may mean a libel suit. And allways working under a strain.[3]

This is what makes you mentally fagged. Having to write a half column story with every name, address and initial verified and remembering to use good style, perfect style in fact, an get all the facts and in the correct order, make it have snap and wallop and write it in fifteen minutes, five sentences at a time to catch an edition as it goes to press. To take a story over the phone and get evrything exact see it all in your minds eye, rush over to a typewriter and write it a page at a time while ten other typewriters are going and the boss is hollering at some one and a boy snatches the pages from your machine as fast as you write them. How long would a lot of people I know last at that before going wild. Or work from 8 am sat staright through to 1 sunday morning and then be so bushed you cant sleep. And remember Pop Ive been down here seven months and hadnt ever done anything more strenuous before in the line than have five or ten hours to ge[t] up a trapeze story.

I've got to have a vacation or bust and so on the first of May I am leaving on the Santa Fe for Chicago.[4] If you folks want me to I will be glad to spend a couple of days in O.P. And see youall again and all my old pals. But I cant stay more than a couple of days in Oak Park for I'm going way up North and work with my hands and rest and go fishing and give my buszing, cracking, bushed high tension, twin six brain a rest.[5] When I get rested and all back I'm coming back. I can always come back to the Star and may get more money. They may not pay more because of their hide bound old policy but there are other papers in the country that will pay me what I am capable of earning. There is the greatest dearth of newspaper men now such as there never was in the world. A man with any experience can go into any paper in the country and go right to work. After the next draft there is going to be a still worse lack of men. I am not telling you just my own opinion but the facts from dozens of men. And when I am telling you about my ability to work on other papers I am quoting the men in the office, the city editor of the Times, Hopkins, Meyer of the Globe Dmocrat St. Louis said I could have a job down there whenever I wanted it.[6] It seems blame funny that I that was writing for the Trapeze, bunk and bull should be doing some of the things I am now at my age. But it is so, and I am not telling you this because I think that I am any star or anything of the kind but just so you see the situation.

So Dad I hope to see you the second of May. Good luck and much obliged for the papers. Let me have a letter.

Ernie.
I'll write Mother soon.
Ernie.

Zieman, TLS with autograph postscript; letterhead: Hotel Muehlebach / BALTIMORE AVENUE / AND TWELFTH STREET / Kansas City, Mo.

1 The 6 April 1918 *Oak Leaves* reported that EH had been called out to serve with the Seventh Infantry, Missouri National Guard, during the "big strike" there the previous week. He apparently assumed his father was the source for this statement, which he found objectionable: "Altho but eighteen years of age, he is one of the star reporters on the Kansas City Star, which is considered by newspaper men everywhere to be one of America's greatest and most valuable news journals" ("Hemingway in Kansas City," 37). By "trap" EH means the *Trapeze*, the OPRFHS newspaper.
2 William Rockhill Nelson (1841–1915) founded the *Star* in 1880 and served as its publisher and editor until his death.
3 At the end of this sentence, EH drew a line and wrote "Insert" in the right margin of the page. The following paragraph was typewritten by him on a separate page and titled "Insert." It appears here in the sequence that EH indicated.
4 The Atchison, Topeka, and Santa Fe Railway connected Kansas City and Chicago.
5 EH is comparing his brain to a Packard Twin Six automobile, introduced in 1915 and named for its revolutionary high-powered 12-cylinder engine.
6 EH's colleague T. Norman "Tubby" Williams recently had gone to the *St. Louis Globe-Democrat* and might have had a contact or knowledge of job offers there.

To Clarence and Grace Hall Hemingway, 19 April [1918]

April. 19.

Dear Folks:

I sure was glad to hear from you both Dad and Mother.[1] Everything is going fine down here. It is raining hard now and has been all day. I put my old mackinaw on and turn the collar up and let it rain. All this week I have been handling recruiting. Writing the stories about the Army, Navy, Marines, British-Canadian and lately the new Tank Service. I'm enclosing a couple of the Tank Stories.[2] Some of them go pretty good. I'll hope to see you about the 2nd. I'll let you know when as soon as I find out. How is everything now?

Good night
Ernie

UMD, TL/ALS; letterhead: Hotel Muehlebach / BALTIMORE AVENUE / AND TWELFTH STREET / Kansas City, Mo.

1 Clarence and Grace each wrote to EH on 17 April in response to his letter of 16 April, expressing their pride in him and his accomplishments, their confidence in his good judgment, their understanding of his need for a rest in Michigan, and their eagerness to see him on 2 May (JFK).

2 EH enclosed clippings of five of these stories, published in the *Kansas City Star* on 17 and 18 April 1918 (Bruccoli *Cub*, 40–55). EH would draw his last pay from the Star on 30 April and then travel to Oak Park for an overnight visit with his family before he and Ted Brumback left on a fishing trip to northern Michigan with Charles Hopkins and Carl Edgar (themselves waiting to be called up by the Army and the Navy) (Baker *Life*, 38).

To Anson and Adelaide Hemingway, [12 May 1918]

Dear Grandfather and Grandmother—;
We are at Cleveland and having a great trip.[1] It is a fine bunch of fellows. My love to all.

Ernie

JFK, A Postcard S; postmark: N.Y. & CHI. R.P.O. / M.D., TR4 / MAY / 12 / 1918

Preserved in EH's grandparents' scrapbook, the postcard is dated "May 12 1918" in another hand. It is rubber-stamped on the verso with this address: "THE BORROWED TIME CLUB / A. T. HEMINGWAY, HONORARY PRESIDENT / 400 NORTH OAK PARK AVE. OAK PARK, ILL."

1 EH was en route by train to New York City to report for duty with the Red Cross. His Michigan fishing trip was cut short when he received a letter from his father, dated 8 May and sent to him in Horton Bay in care of James Dilworth (JFK), saying that a telegram had arrived that day from Red Cross Headquarters in St. Louis with orders that EH should start for New York. EH returned briefly to Oak Park to get his things before heading east.

To Hemingway Family, [12 May 1918]

Approaching Buffalo

Dear Folks—;

We are having a great trip and the bunch is very good. There are 15 fellows from mostly New Trier and Evanston and they are a dandy bunch.[1] I hope you saw Ted and had Hop out to dinner all O.K.[2] The road bed sure is rocky and we are going fast coming into Buffalo so the writing is a little more rotten than usual. We left Toledo after Breakfast and have been running along Lake Erie all day. We hit Buffalo at about 4 oclock and will be well into New York.

At New York I am going to get a canvass water proof Duffel bag with a chain and lock to keep all my stuff in. The meals have been very good so far. Well good bye and love to all.

Ernie.

JFK, ALS; postmark: BUFFALO / N.Y., MAY 12 / 12 PM / 1918

1 New Trier Township and Evanston Township High Schools (located, respectively, in Winnetka and Evanston, Illinois, immediately north of Chicago) were athletic rivals of OPRFHS in the Suburban League.
2 Ted Brumback and Charles Hopkins. In a letter to EH also written on 12 May, Clarence reported that he had spent an hour with Brumback, who was en route to join EH, and that "Hop made a grand visit at 600 [Kenilworth Avenue] with us today" (JFK).

To Anson, Adelaide, and Grace Adelaide Hemingway, [13 May 1918]

Dear Grandfather, Grandmother, and Aunt Grace—;
    We are stopping at a hotel in Washington Square and are being completely equipped and uniformed.[1] New York is a beautiful ____ etc. Everything is lovely. I don't know my overseas address yet.

Ernest.

JFK, A Postcard S; postmark: NEW YORK, N. Y. / STA. D, MAY 13 / 12 PM / 1918

Preserved in EH's grandparents' scrapbook, the postcard bears the notation in another hand, "New York May 13–1918." It is rubber-stamped on the verso with this address: "THE BORROWED TIME CLUB / A. T. HEMINGWAY, HONORARY PRESIDENT / 400 NORTH OAK PARK AVE. OAK PARK, ILL."

1 The Hotel Earle, 103–105 Waverly Place, New York, New York, opened in 1902 and was named for owner Earle L'Amoureaux; it was renamed the Washington Square Hotel in 1986.

To Hemingway Family, [14 May 1918]

Tuesday night

Dear Folks—:
    We are quartered here at a very nice Hotel in Washington Square. The heart of Greenwich Village. It is just a half block from 5th Ave and the arch and right on the square.[1] The Harvard Bunch left this morning[2] and we leave next Tuesday according to the latest dope. In the mea[n]time we are in New York with all our Hotel bills, meals paid for. We have been given each an officers trunk, 1 regular U.S. officers uniform with full U.S. officers' insignia, my name and unit stencilled on the trunk, 1 officers overcoat $60 value, 1 rain coat, 1 cocky field service cap, 1 Dress cap, 4 suits heavy underwear, soft buckskin driving gloves, 1 pair Cordova leather aviators puttees, 2 pair officers shoes, 1 knitted sweater, 6 pair heavy woolen socks, 2 khaki shirts, 1 woolen shirt and a lot of other stuff I cant remember. Well over $200 worth of equipment issued to each man. Our uniforms are regular United States Army officers' and look like a million dollars. Privates and non coms must salute us smartly

We may wear our uniforms as soon as our pass ports arrive and we get them vized. None of the Chicago passports have come yet. I will get my picture taken as soon as I wear my uniform. Everything is packed in my officers trunk now.

I met Ted all right yesterday and we are rooming together here. We have a bunch of dandy fellows in our unit and are going to have a wonderful time. Ted was very glad that Dad met him and was very sorry he couldn't see you folks.

We have all our time to ourselves and have to report to no one. This morning I had my uniform fitted and then in the aft Ted and How Jenkins, Harve Osterholm[,] Jerry Flaherty and I rode down to the Battery and went thru the aquarium. We bummed around and went up in the top of the Woolworth Tower 796 feet—62 stories high. We could see the camouflajed boats going in and out of the harbor and see way up the East river to Hell's Gate.[3]

And over at Hoboken the "Vaterland" now being used as a transport is docked. She made her last round trip to France in 14 days.[4] I have been all up and down Riverside Drive and seen N.Y. from the Harlem River on North and Grant's Tomb on West to the Libber of Goddesty in the South.[5] It is a wonderful sight from the Woolworth Tower. As soon as I don my officers' uniform I have an engagement with the Mrs. and have already investigated the possibility of the Little Church around the Corner.[6] I've always planned to get married if I could ever get to be an officer you know. It is a new ruling that makes us officers. We are kind of camouflajed 1st Lieuts.[7] We are like aviators in that we have no commands. The war department ruled for the wearing of the uniform in foreign service and just before we sail. 3 or 4 days. Hence the wait for pass port vises. Write me here at the Hotel.

Much love
Ernie

JFK, ALS; letterhead: Hotel Earle, 272 Washington Square North / NEW YORK; postmark: NEW YORK, N.Y. / STA. D, MAY 14 / 12 PM / 1918

Above "Tuesday night," Clarence wrote, "May 14, 1918." Printed on the envelope verso is the slogan, "The Washington Square Park Hotels, Under One Management / Hotel Judson The

Holley Hotel Earle" and an image of the park and surrounding buildings. EH wrote an "X" on the image to mark the Earle.

1 The marble arch in Washington Square Park, at the foot of Fifth Avenue, was modeled after the Arc de Triomphe in Paris and was completed in 1892, replacing a wooden arch erected in 1889 to commemorate the centennial of George Washington's inauguration as first U.S. president.

2 In the spring of 1918, a group of volunteers from Harvard University, mostly members of the class of 1921 and under-age for military service, enlisted in the ARC Ambulance Service. They enlisted for a three-month period over the summer (instead of the usual six months) with the intention of returning in time for fall semester classes. Among the Harvard group that left New York on 14 May was Henry S. Villard, who would meet EH in the hospital in Milan in August 1918 and decades later would write of the experience (Villard and Nagel, 206–9).

3 Howell Jenkins and Jerome Flaherty were fellow members of the ARC Ambulance Service Section 4, and Harvey G. Osterholm was in Section 1. Battery Park, at the southern tip of Manhattan, was the site of the New York City Aquarium, 1896–1941. The Woolworth Building, at 233 Broadway, was the world's tallest building from the time of its construction in 1913 until 1930. The Hell Gate Bridge, spanning the northern portion of the East River, opened in 1917 to provide the first uninterrupted rail service between Washington, D.C., and Boston; until 1931, it was the longest steel arch bridge in the world.

4 The German passenger ship *Vaterland* arrived in New York on 29 July 1914, just days before WWI broke out in Europe, and was laid up in Hoboken, New Jersey, for almost three years. When the United States declared war on Germany in April 1917, the ship was seized and turned over to the U.S. Navy, renamed *USS Leviathan*, and used as a transport ship during the war.

5 Burial place of U.S. President Ulysses S. Grant (1822–1885), in Riverside Park on the Upper West Side of Manhattan. "Libber of Goddesty," a play on "Goddess of Liberty," another name for the Statue of Liberty in New York Harbor.

6 The Church of the Transfiguration, built in 1849 at One East Twenty-ninth Street and known as "The Little Church Around the Corner," counted many theater people among its parishioners and was a popular site for weddings. It was the subject of the 1871 song "The Little Church Around the Corner" (music by George S. Dwyer; lyrics by Arthur Matthison). EH's claim to be engaged distressed his parents, who immediately sent letters and telegrams expressing concern and urging him, as Grace wrote on 16 May, to "think hard before making such a mistake as to marry at 18" (JFK; for details of the correspondence see Griffin, 57–60).

7 Members of the ARC Ambulance Service held the rank of honorary second lieutenant.

To Hemingway Family, [17–18 May 1918]

Dear Folks—;

I received your telegram and it was merry good.[1] We have all our equipment issued now and are wearing our officers uniforms. Yesterday afternoon we were told our sailing date and given a permit to wear our uniform. Our sailing date cannot be given out but we will not leave before Wednesday.

It was funny yesterday when we donned our uniforms. We put them on yest aft and went to supper and then in the evening walked up 5th Avenue to Broadway and then over. We thought at first it would be fun because all privates and non commissioned officers have to salute us. But by the time we had returned about 200 salutes it had lost all its fun. But it was fun to have the men snap up to salute. Ted and I had a couple of pictures snapped in a cheap joint and I'm sending it on. Ted is wearing his old American Field Service uniform that he wore with the French Army. Tonight I am invited out to Ellis Island to a dance and Dinner by the sailors there.[2] Also the Championship boxing bouts. Tomorrow we have to march in a parade for the big Red X drive. 5 miles down 5th Avenue from 85th Street to the Battery.

A lot of the men have not had any military training and so we have been drilling on the Roof of a big 4th Ave building.

We report at 9 AM and drill an hour and again at 4 PM. We are treated the same as aviators and while all honorary officers we have non coms in our co. to drill the men. I am corporal of the 1st Squad and will be at the head of the parade. They have a big reviewing stand at Union Square. I am invited to Trumbull White's for supper Sunday.[3] Ted and I are still rooming together. I will appreciate it Dad if you will send that check to Carl. He is J. C. Edgar, Care W. B. Smith Jr.

RFD. No2 Boyne City Mich.

Best Love,
Ernie

I am sending the pictures tomorrow under separate cover.

Ernie

Give my love to all the goils because I am too busy to write. Lots of time on board ship.

Much love
Ernie.

Saturday eve—

Dear Dad, Mother and Les Infants—;

I forgot to mail ye other epistle so this is an add. I got your telegram and you may think of me on the briny =(sea) on Thursday.[4] That is all I can tell. We paraded 85 blocks down 5th ave today and were reviewed by President Wilson. About #75,000 were in line and we were ye star attraction. I was made a sergeant in ye squadron and led the 2nd Platoon out In the middle of the avenue all by myself and saluted Ye Great Woodrow.[5] I felt lonesome.

I go to Trumbull White's tomorrow for supper. Have decided against ye little choich around the corner temporarily. Much nicer to be engaged. Have a $1,000 insurance policy—life—also a $20 a week decedent policy. Ye noted

Scion,

Hemingstein

JFK, ALS; letterhead: Hotel Earle / 103–105 WAVERLY PLACE / NEW YORK; postmark: NEW YORK, N.Y. / STA. D, MAY 18 / 9 PM / 1918

Clarence Hemingway dated both sections of the letter: "Friday May 17. 1918." and "May 18. 1918." EH wrote on the back of the envelope, "Ernest M. Hemingway / Care Italian Ambulance Service," and provided two return addresses: "222 4th / Avenue / New York City" and "American Red Cross / Milano / Italy."

1 On 16 May Clarence wired EH: "YOUR NEWYORK LETTER RECEIVED HAPPY SUCH EXCELLENT EQUIPMENT MAY GREAT SUCCESS FOLLOW PLEASE CONSIDER MOST SERIOUSLY ANY ADVENTURE THAT MIGHT TEMPT YOU MUCH LOVE DR C E HEMINGWAY" (JFK).

2 When the United States entered WWI, the U.S. Navy and Army Medical Department took over the complex of the Ellis Island Immigration Station in New York Harbor, in operation since 1892.

3 White was among several family acquaintances whom Clarence urged EH to see while he was in New York (letter to EH, 15 May 1918, JFK).

4 In a telegram of 18 May, Clarence asked his son to "Please write and wire before sailing giving your Exact status" (JFK).

5 On 18 May, President Wilson unexpectedly led the parade on foot for nearly 2 miles before assuming his place in the reviewing stand at Twenty-third Street; more than 70,000 participated in the parade, which lasted nearly six hours (*New York Times*, "Red Cross to March by President Today," 18 May 1918, 11; "President Leads Red Cross Parade," 19 May 1918, 8).

To Clarence Hemingway, 19 May [1918]

DR HEMINGWAY
600 N KENILWORTH AVE
CHEER UP AM NOT ENGAGED MARRIED OR DIVORCED THIS IS
AUTHENTIC JUST JOKING HERE TILL WEDNESDAY[1]

ERNIE
345P

JFK, Cable; Western Union destination receipt stamp: OAK PARK, ILL.; NEW
YORK / 124P MAY 19

1 Clarence responded in a letter of 19 May, "Your wire explaining the 'joke' which has taken
five nights sleep from your mother and father received about half hour ago. —So glad to
receive it, hope you have written your dear mother, who was broken hearted" (JFK).

To Clarence Hemingway, [19 May 1918]

Sunday

Dear Dad—;

I got your good letters and telegrams o.k. Cheer up Ye Old Pop for nobody
gets my insurance save yourself.[1] Also me matrimonial status is negative and
will be for some years. Sound ye loud timbrels. Everybody knows it so I guess
it wont hurt you if you dont tell any one that I told you so we sail Wednesday
via France. Landing at Bordeaux. Go to Paris, and then to Milan. Were going
on a rotten old tub on the French line.[2] It takes ten days but we travel 1st
class. I am going to Trumbull White's tonight. Try and see Bruce Barton
tomorrow.[3] Will send home what I dont need. We are having a great time.

Dont worry about me whatever you do and trust my good judgement. I'll
write before I go. Arthur Newburn is a nice enough fellow but not in our
bunch.[4] We have a great bunch of rare birds. Thanks for sending the Ten to
care very much. I may have you send the proceeds of my Lib Bond to me in
Milan.[5]

Much Love.

Ernie

P.S. I dont know my over seas adress yet
Pass port came yesterday

JFK, ALS; letterhead: 27 2 Washington Square North / NEW YORK; postmark: NEW
YORK, N.Y. / STA. D, MAY 19 / 4 PM / 1918

Clarence Hemingway dated the letter, "May 19.—1918."

1 In 1914, to provide insurance coverage for cargo ships and crews supplying materials to the
Allied forces, Congress passed the War Risk Insurance Act. When the United States entered
the war in 1917, the act was amended to include a voluntary life insurance program for
service members.
2 EH shipped to France on the *Chicago*, a French Line steamship launched in 1908, "one of the
many smoky, ungainly, unglamourous war workships of France's Atlantic fleet of converted
passenger liners" (C. E. Frazer Clark, Jr., introductory note to Col. C. E. Frazer Clark, Ret.,
"This Is the Way It Was on the *Chicago* and at the Front: 1917 War Letters," in Matthew
J. Bruccoli, ed., *Fitzgerald/Hemingway Annual* 1970 [Washington, DC: Microcard Editions,
1970], 153). Sources vary as to the actual date the *Chicago* sailed for Bordeaux. While EH says
here that the date was set for Wednesday (22 May), in his next letter home, posted on
20 May, he would report that the departure had been postponed a day (presumably to
Thursday, 23 May). Baker dates the departure as 21 May (*SL*, 10) or 22 May (*Life*, 39);
Sanford as 28 May (150); and Villard and Nagel as 24 May, citing the recollection of
Frederick Spiegel, EH's roommate on the ship, but also noting the discrepancies in various
accounts (204, 284n).
3 Barton (1886–1967) was the son of William E. Barton, pastor of Oak Park's First
Congregational Church. A journalist, religious writer, and magazine editor, he became
publicity director for the United War Work Agencies in 1918. Later the author of the
best-seller *The Man Nobody Knows* (1925), he would go on to become an advertising
executive and a U.S. congressman. On 13 May, Grace wrote to EH that she had received a
nice letter from Barton and suggested that EH visit him in New York to "let him know you're
writing . . . It may mean a great opening for you in magazine work" (JFK).
4 Arthur C. Newburn, a fellow Oak Parker, was a member of ARC Ambulance Section 2 in
Italy (Bakewell, 222).
5 Liberty Bonds were issued by the U.S. Treasury during WWI to help fund the Allied war
effort; citizens were encouraged to buy bonds as their patriotic duty. In April 1918, the Third
Liberty Loan offered $3 billion in bonds at 4.5% interest, and at least half of all American
households subscribed.

To Dale Wilson, 19 May [1918]

Dear Wilse—;

Ha Ha! Ha! Ha! Ha! Ha! Tis none other than the greatest of the
Hemingsteins that indicts this epistle. Woodrow me lad, comma how are
you. Much obliged for your sending ye old Liberty Bond. In the words of

Smith ye beamer it was most good of you. And the great Hicks. He of the tortoise shelled disposition and the sad lack of anal covering. What of him? Does he still classify the great Chicagoan Noblest Scion of the windy city as a—well meaning fellow—quotes— Tell him I bury the Hatchet. But also Do me this favour. When the story of Brumstein's and my sad end comes in let not he that is known as Lackpantz read copy on it. For it is feared by me that he would cut even the names of ye deceased.[1] Not diseased tho sad luck would lead one of gum gashing proclivities to infer that.

But to get down to the bare, naked, unclothed facts does Tod N. Ormiston, the journalistic white Slaver still take the bi menstrual stipend from William Moorehead. He that is yclept Broken Bill? And does Smith the Beamer slip the great Gus the warm palm and tell him Gus, how he Smith, likes to work for the paper he Gus manages?[2]

And does Peg Vaughn still fare forth in search of booty and Leo Lovely still be haunted by booty searching for him? And does the G't Fleisler still dog the shadow of the wily Godfrey searching for the pearls of journalistic wisdom which might be cast before the porcine Hebrew? And what does Tannenbaumb without the Tasmanian Snobelater woodsman and Boomerang thrower?[3] Huh? I ask you?

Well they have slipped us our uniforms and we are now Honorary 1st Lieuts. Ye G't Hem's'n stalked down Broadway and returned 367 salutes night before last. Since then he rides on a bus. It's easier on the right arm. Today we paraded down 5th avenue, from 82nd Street to 8th Street and were reviewed by Woodrow Senior and the Mrs. Also a bunch of large insects. Slang for Big Bugs. Woodrow resembles nothing so much as his pictures. While we all are commissioned yofficers yet we are in an squadron and have non coms. By virtue of his manly ~~bull shit~~ form and perfect complexion the one and only Hemsticth has been made Ye Top Cutter and you all should hear his rasping voice. Me duties consist largely of being ye right guide of ye 1st or initial platoon. Today as ye right guide I stalked all alone down the old avenue and felt lonesome as hell. But at eyes right I had a fine look at Woodrow.

This is not for publication kid but we are plowing the briny Wednesday. My passport arrived today and I get the French and Italian vises Monday.

This also is not for publication but I have been out to see Mae several times and am out there for dinner tomorrow evening. I have spent every damn cent I have too. Miss Marsh no kidding says she loves me. I suggested the little church around the corner but she opined as how ye war widow appealed not to her. So I sunk the 150 plunks Pop gave me in a ring so I am engaged anyway. Also broke. Dead. I did have about another 100 but I bought a pair of 30 buck cordovan leather boots a few sundries and a coupla drinks and now all is gone. Any way my girl loves me and says she believes I am going to be a great newspaper man and says she will wait for me, so What the Hell Bill. And maybe I can win an honest to God commission. Gee she is a wonderful girl, Wilse! Too damn good for me. You can tell Punk Wallace about my being engaged if you want to.[4] But for God's sake dont let it get out amongst the gang and in the sheet.

Well so long old Kid and my love to Hop and remember me to Pete and the Boss and Harry Kohr and John Collins and Punk, and Bill and Harry G. and Swensen and Smith.[5]

Good Luck

Hemingstein

Address care
Italian Ambulance Service, American Red Cross.
Milan Italy.

PUL, ALS; letterhead: Hotel Earle / 103–105 WAVERLY PLACE, NEW YORK; postmark: NEW YORK, [N.Y.] / STA. [D], MAY 19 / 4 PM / [1918]

On the front of the envelope, addressed to Wilson at the *Kansas City Star* office, EH wrote, "If he Be in Service To Be opened By H. Merle Smith. (The Beamer)." Smith was known as a "grinning backslapper" (Baker *Life*, 35). EH's inventive nicknames for his associates at the newspaper run throughout the letter.

1 Copyeditor Wilson Hicks earned EH's ire for editing out parts of his news stories; EH dubbed him "Lackpants" because his only pair of trousers was wearing thin (Wilson, "Kansas City," 213). "Brumstein" is Ted Brumback.
2 Todd N. Ormiston (1890-1969), *Star* reporter until 1920, when he joined the staff of the governor of Missouri; he was called the "White Slaver" for his "adroitness with girls the talk of the office" (Wilson, "Kansas City," 213). William "Broken Bill" Moorehead, an unlucky poker player, was the police-court reporter. August (Gus) Seested was the *Star*'s business manager, a position he would hold for four decades.
3 Miles W. "Peg" Vaughn, a former *Star* reporter, was United Press bureau chief in Kansas City during Hemingway's apprenticeship and later a foreign correspondent. Leo Fitzpatrick,

a smartly dressed Irishman, "was something of a dude and a girl charmer" (Baker *Life*, 36). The "G't [Great]" Fleisler was known as "the pensive Hebrew" (Wilson, "Kansas City," 213), while Harry Godfrey was a bespectacled copyreader who liked to give advice. The "Tasmanian" was a young Australian reporter (Baker *Life*, 36).

4 George "Punk" Wallace was another staffer at the *Star*. Mae Marsh, who would later say that she regretted never meeting EH, married Lee Armes in New York in September 1918.

5 In addition to the aforementioned associates at the *Star*, EH refers to afternoon assignment editor Charles Hopkins, assistant city editor C. G. "Pete" Wellington, and telegraph editor Harry Kohr. "The Boss" could be the city editor George Longan, who hired EH, or R. E. Stout, the managing editor.

To Hemingway Family, [20 May 1918]

Monday aft night

Dear Folks—;

All day today we have been out getting our pass ports vised and war zone passes and so forth. A big lot of the fellow's passports have not come and so they have to go on the next boat.

Our sailing has been delayed one day so that gives us a little more time. There are a few awful mutts in the unit but the majority are a swell bunch and we are having le grand time. Anything you want to know about N'Yawk ask me. I may take everything with me as I havnt any extra clothes to send really and I may need that old Brown suit back of the lines. I don't know yet I may send it along. We are certainly well outfitted all right. The biggest bore is the constant returning salutes. If you go up town at night it is awful because there are thousands of soldiers in town. Capt. Utassi[1] went over with the Harvard Bunch that left last week.

We are under a bird named Morrison. Ted and I will be together and will be driving partners. Latest dope is that we drive from Paris to Milan. Maybe we do I'm sure I dont know. Nor does any one else.

I was up along Riverside Drive this afternoon and saw the big French war ships in the Hudson River. There are 3 French Cruisers and a US. Dreadnought.[2] The transports are going in and and out all the time. The society girls are very nice to the officers here. One took 3 of us in her big car for a long drive this aft. They make us have as much fun as possible. It may be cheering news to you that the U. Boats have not sunk a ship between the US. and France since the Last of March.[3] They are pretty jolly well bottled up.

Much Love

Ernie

JFK, ALS; letterhead: Hotel Earle / 27[2] Washington Square North / NEW YORK; postmark: NEW YORK, N.Y. STA. D, MAY 20 / 630 PM / 1918

At the top of the first page, Clarence wrote "May 20. 1918" and noted, "Last Rec'd before he sailed."

1 Captain George Utassy, quartermaster general of Ambulance and Rolling Canteen Services in Italy, had been sent to New York City to recruit 100 ambulance drivers before the end of April (Bakewell, 221; *New York Times*, 14 April 1918, E3).

2 After the 1906 launch of the British warship *Dreadnought*, the term came to apply generally to battleships of that new design, built for high-speed operation and armed entirely with big guns of the same caliber. In August 1916, the U.S. Congress authorized a naval construction program that included ten Dreadnoughts.

3 German military submarines, or U-boats (the term short for *Unterseeboot*, "undersea boat"), posed a grave risk to Allied troop transport ships crossing the Atlantic. More than 200 U.S. servicemen died in the sinking of the *Antilles* in October 1917 and the *Tuscania* on 5 February 1918, and three more U.S. troop transports would be sunk between 25 May and 2 July 1918. EH's optimism may reflect his reading of a front-page story in the 15 May 1918 *New York Times*, reporting that convoy tactics and technology had made the passage safer and that twelve German submarines had been sunk or captured during the month of April ("U-Boats on Defensive / Dozen Sinkings in a Month Officially Reported, Two Others Known," 1).

To Hemingway Family, [c. 31 May] and 2 June [1918]

So[mew]here on les briny.

Dear Folks

Well we wre approcahing our port of deebarkation and are entering the widely known submarine zone[1] so I will get this epistle off so you will besure and get one any way. Very cheerful thought what aint it? This is the rottenst tubin the world and so it may be revealing a military secret to tell you. But it is absolutely. Now think what the rottenest ship in the world is and you know what I am on. Wehad two days of glorious weather ! warm and calm, just a pleasant breeze ! regular waloon lake days. 5hen we ran into a storm that cleared the dining rooms with grea regularity. I would report for a meal and be alright until I would se my next door neighbor clap his hand to his mouth and make a sudden break for the door and then the power of suggeston would be too much and I would break for the rail. Ho[w]ever we had two days of regular storm when she pitched, rolled ! stood on her ear and swung in wide legubrious circles and I heaved but four times. An record what? Howa are you all including the massive Ivory and the widely known Dessie.[2] Ted and I and Howell Jenkins are paling together and having thegrand time. The storm is over now ans for the last two days it has been very pleasant weather.

WE are also paling with two polish Lieutenants. Count Galinski and Count Horcinanowitz altho [i]t is not spelled that way.[3] And they are dandy fellows. and being with them has tought us that there is a big difference between poacks and Poles. THey have invited us to visit them in Paris and we il put on ze grand party. We are expected to land over seas about four days from now. I will mail this at our port and it will be the only letter that I will send from there so worry not. We had the grea time in little old Gotham[4] and are confirmed broadwayites. The Croix Rouge[5] took very good careof us while we were there and we lacked for nothing. The Y.M.C.A, who are just the same here as they are at home and you know what that means are ever present aboard the ship. also several nigger Y.M.C.Aers.[6] The Kinights of Columbus[7] have several representaives aboard and they seem a whole lot more human. 5ed and Jenks[8] and I had our second inoculations day before yesterday nd my arm is nearl[y] over the strain by now. We have only one more to tak[e] now. And wi[l]l get that in either FRance or Italy. Each one has made me sick as a dog. THey are triple typhoid and a lot stiffer than those I had while in school. A little while ago a big american cruiser came into sight headed toward home andwe heliograph to her and broke out a number of signal flags. She is the first boat we have passed since coming out in the atlant. It is very good to look upon at night when the phosphorescent waves break out from the bow. The wake [i]s also a welter of phosphorous and when it is rough the crests of the waves will blow away lookinh like brands from a camp fire. WE have s[e]en several popoises and a number of flying fish. one bunch that got up very e[a]r,y in the morni[n]g claim to have glipmsed a whale, but we look upon hthme with suspicion.

THe food aboard is very good but we get only two meals a day. At ten o'clock and at five. You can get coffee and hard bread for breakfast if you want it but it isnt worth getting up for. According to the latest dope we [a]re going right down to our he[a]dquarters after we leave Paris andthen go right out to the lines. To take the placeof the gang whose time is up. Our six months start from the day we start driving so it will probably carry us pretty well into the winter. Address me care the American Consul Milano Italy, Italian Ambulance Service American R[ed] Cross.

MUCH LOve Ernie.

P.S. June 2.

We are getting into Port tomorrow. Nothing new on the trip. Ill write from Paris. Write me at Milan address.

Love to you all.

Ernie.

IndU, TLS with autograph postscript

1 The *Chicago* was bound for Bordeaux. The danger of attack from U-boats increased as transports approached Europe.
2 Nickname for EH's brother, Leicester Hemingway.
3 Two Polish officers, Anton Galinski and Leon Chocianowicz, are characters in the opening of EH's abandoned WWI novel "Along with Youth," the pencil manuscript dated 15 June 1925 (Philip Young and Charles W. Mann, *The Hemingway Manuscripts: An Inventory* [University Park: The Pennsylvania State University, 1969], 11). The piece was published for the first time in 1972 as "Night Before Landing" (*NAS*).
4 New York City.
5 Red Cross (French).
6 During WWI the YMCA hired more than 25,000 workers to provide morale and welfare services to the American forces in Europe. Services included operating centers for recreation and religious services, sponsoring entertainment for the troops, setting up canteens immediately behind the front line, and offering relief to prisoners of war and refugees. The YMCA had a reputation at the time for being overly moralistic, and EH would come to regard the organization as synonymous with mismanaged efforts (Reynolds *YH*, 22–23; *GHOA*, 191). Like many organizations at the time (including the U.S. armed forces), YMCA units generally were segregated by race.
7 Alongside the Red Cross and YMCA, the Knights of Columbus, a Roman Catholic fraternal organization established in 1882, also provided social and spiritual services to soldiers during WWI.
8 Ted Brumback and Howell Jenkins.

To Hemingway Family, [c. 3 June 1918]

[*Letter begins here:*] effect on the French by the Hun long range artillery: The people accept the shells as a matter of course and hardly show any interest in their arrival. We heard our first shell arrive soon after Breakfast. Nothing but a dull boom (like blasting at Summitt[)]. We had no means of knowing where it hit but it was a long way away.

There were several more during the day but no one evinced any alarm or even interest. However about 4 oclock Booom came one that seemed about 100 yards away. We looked to see where it had fallen but an English artillery officer told us it alighted at least a mile away.

This afternoon Ted and Jenks (who you met at the train Dad) went all through The Hotel Des Invalides. Napoleons Tomb. They have a wonderful exhibit of captured enemy artillery and air planes there. It covers several acres.[1] We have been all over the city in the ancient two cylinder busses that pass for taxis. You can ride for an hour for about 1 Franc. Have seen all the sights. The Champs Elysee. Tuilleries, Louve Invalides Arc D'Triomphe etc.[2] Our Hotel is right on the Place D'La Concorde where the[y] guillotined Marie Antoinette and Sidney Carton.[3] Paris is a great city but is not as quaint and interesting as Bordeaux.[4] If the war ever ends I intend to bum all through this country. I have picked up a lot of French and can sling it pretty fast. I dont know what it looks like and cant write it but can speak fairly well and read easily. On the boat all the Garcons and Femmes De Chambes[5] and every one spoke nothing but French and it was a case of learn or starve. Ted and Jenks and I are having Le Grande Time. Tonight we went to the Follies Bergert.[6] Hot puppums. But ye Straight and narrow for me. I got my cocky cap and Sam Browne Belt today and now look Like the proverbial million dollars. We leave for Milan tomorrow—Tuesday—night. Travel first class all way. Tis Ye gay life.

Write me at Milan.

Much Love to All and Every One.

Your Old Kid

Ernie.

"Thank God He Writes From The Y.M.C.A!"[7]

IndU, AlSFrag; letterhead: Y.M.C.A. / HOTEL FLORIDA, / 12, BOULEVARD MALESHERBES, / PARIS

The conjectured letter date is based on EH's statement that they would leave for Milan the next night, a Tuesday (4 June). The first page of this letter is missing. It begins on the numbered page "II."

1 Established in 1670 by Louis XIV to house wounded, aged, or infirm military veterans and covering more than 30 acres, the Hôtel des Invalides is also the site of a military museum and the tomb of Emperor Napoleon I (Napoleon Bonaparte, 1769–1821) and other national heroes.

2 On the Right Bank of Paris, the Avenue des Champs-Élysées extends more than a mile between the Place de la Concorde and the Arc de Triomphe, the grand monument commissioned in 1806 by Napoleon I to honor those who fought for France. The gardens of the Tuileries extend from the Place de la Concorde to the Musée du Louvre, a former royal palace and the national museum and art gallery of France.

3 The Place de la Concorde, then called the "Place de la Révolution," was the site of thousands of executions carried out in the Reign of Terror (1793–1794). Queen Marie Antoinette (1755–1793) was guillotined there, as was her husband, King Louis XVI (1754–1793). Sidney Carton is the hero of *A Tale of Two Cities*, the 1859 novel by Charles Dickens (1812–1870).

4 An active port city on the Garonne River in southwest France, Bordeaux is distinguished by its well-preserved eighteenth-century historic center (in 2007 designated a World Heritage site by UNESCO, the United Nations Educational, Scientific and Cultural Organization).

5 *Garçon*: boy (French); a term often applied to a waiter. *Femmes de chambre*: chambermaids (French).

6 The Folies Bergère, Paris music hall renowned for its risqué performances.

7 EH's handwritten postscript, on the verso of the last page of the letter, is a joking reference to the YMCA stationery he is using. In letters to EH of 18 and 19 May, Clarence had praised the war work of the YMCA, as well as the Red Cross, and urged his son to be "active and helpfull in Both" (JFK).

To Clarence Hemingway, [9 June 1918]

DeAr DAD:

Everything Lovely. We go to the Front tomorrow.

I'm in the mountains[.] Ted and I were split up[.] Everything quiet now they say. We've been treated like Kings. Been two days here. Wonderful in Alps.[1] My love to all.

Ernie

Ernest M. Hemingway
Section 4. Italian ambulance
Croce Rosa Americana. Milano. Italy.

PSU, A Postcard S; verso: MILANO—Duomo e Torre S. Gottardo [Milan—Cathedral and Tower of San Gottardo]; postmark: MILANO / PARTENZA, 11–12 / 9·VI / 1918

After arriving in Milan, EH was assigned to the Red Cross post in Schio, a town northeast of Milan and about 10 miles from the front line at the time. The front ran from the mouth of the Piave River on the Adriatic Sea to the town of Triano on the Swiss border.

1 Schio is at the edge of the Italian Prealps, or "Little Dolomites."

To a friend at the *Kansas City Star*, [c. 9 June 1918]

Having a wonderful time!!! Had my baptism of fire my first day here, when an entire munition plant exploded.[1] We carried them in like at the General Hospital, Kansas City. I go to the front tomorrow. Oh, Boy!!! I'm glad I'm in it. They love us down here in the mountains.

Postcard excerpt as published in *Kansas City Star*, 14 July 1918

Appearing in an article headlined, "WOUNDED ON ITALY FRONT: Ernest M. Hemingway Formerly Was Reporter for the Star," the excerpt is preceded by this explanation: "Friends at The Star received a half dozen postal cards from Hemingway yesterday, the same day the message arrived telling of wounds. An extract from the cards, dated Milano, Italy, less than a month ago." The conjectured date of this postcard and the next (excerpted in the same article) is based on EH's mention of going to the front the next day, as he also noted on the card he sent to his father from Milan, postmarked 9 June 1918 (PSU).

1 On 7 June 1918, thirty-five people were killed in an explosion at the munitions factory of the Swiss firm Sutter and Thevenot, at Bollate, a small town about 12 miles from Milan (James R. Mellow, *Hemingway: A Life Without Consequences* [Boston: Houghton Mifflin, 1992], 57; Miriam B. Mandel, *Hemingway's "Death in the Afternoon": The Complete Annotations* [Lanham, Maryland: Scarecrow Press, 2002], 297; Luca Gandolfi, "The Outskirts of Literature: Uncovering the Munitions Factory in 'A Natural History of the Dead,'" *Hemingway Review* 19 [Spring 2000]: 105–7). EH would later describe this incident in "A Natural History of the Dead" (*DIA*).

To a friend at the *Kansas City Star*, [c. 9 June 1918]

I'm in the Alps riding in a Fiat; Ted is on the plains in a Ford.

Postcard excerpt as published in *Kansas City Star*, 14 July 1918

Appearing in an article headlined, "WOUNDED ON ITALY FRONT: Ernest M. Hemingway Formerly Was Reporter for the Star," the excerpt is preceded by this explanation: "Another card from Hemingway today read . . . ."

To Ruth [Morrison ?],[1] [c. late June–early July 1918]

On The Piave.[2]

Dear Ruth—;

How is everything in Ye olde village? It all seems about a million miles away and to think that this time last year we had just finished graduating. If anybody had told me when I was reading that damn fool prophecy last year that a year from date I would be sitting out in front of a dug out in a nice trench 20 yards from the Piave River and 40 yards from the Austrian lines listening to the little ones whimper way up in the air and the big ones go scheeeeeeeeek Boom and every once in a while a machine gun go tick a tack a tock I would have said, "Take another sip." That is some complicated sentence but it all goes to show what a bum prophet I was.

You see I'm ranked a soto Tenente or Second Lieut. in the Italian Army and I left the Croce Rosa Americana Ambulance service a while back, temporarily, to get a little action down here.[3] Don't publish this to the family who fondly picture me chaufing a Ford through Sylvan glens.

I'm quartered at a nice house about 1 1/2 miles from the Austrian lines. The n.h. had 4 rooms; 2 down stairs and two up. The other day a shell came through the roof. Now there are three rooms. Two down stairs and 1 up. I was in the other one. The moral is: sleep up stairs. The big Italian guns are all back of us and the[y] roar all night. What I am supposed to be doing is running a posto Di ricovero. That is I dispense chocolate and cigarettes to the wounded and the soldiers in the front line. Each aft and morning I load up a haversack and take my tin lid[4] and gas mask and beat it up to the trenches. I sure have a good time but miss their being no Americans. Gee I have darn near forgot the English language. If Cannon or old Loftberg[5] could hear me speak Italian all day long they would roll over in their graves. Gee but I do get lonesome for the sight of a real Honest to Gawd American girl though. I would give my captured Austrian officers automatic pistol, my German helmets, all my junk I've captured and my chances for the war cross for just one dance.

Believe the writer if you want to do some kind deed write me at the address on the envelope and it will be forwarded to me. And Ruth if you know of any body that I know in Oak Park that by any stretch could be induced to write me brow beat them into it and promise them from me that I will be a prompt answerer. I havn't had a letter from the States yet and have been here since the 4th of June.

I crawled out over the top this afternoon and took some darby[6] pictures of the Piave and the Austrian trenches. If they're any good I'll send you some. The hour of food draws nigh and I am of a great hunger.

So,

(you know I always used to get fussed when I'd say good bye so I'll sneak out quick, and leave you alone with the letter

Ernie.

UMD, ALS

The internal evidence for dating the letter is somewhat contradictory. EH suggests that he is writing this letter a year to the day after delivering his "Class Prophecy," which can be dated 13 June 1917 from the printed "Class Day" program preserved in his grandparents' scrapbook (JFK). His WWI service record states (on a form he completed himself) that he "participated in Piave Major Defensive June 15–July 8, 1918" (JFK; *SL*, 11).

1 Of the four girls named Ruth in EH's high school class, the likeliest recipient appears to have been Ruth Morrison (*SL*, 11), a member of the Girls' Rifle Club and one of two Ruths EH mentioned in his "Class Prophecy" (published in the June 1917 *Senior Tabula* and reprinted in Bruccoli *Apprenticeship*, 110–17).
2 River northeast of Venice, site of the Battle of the Piave, the last major Austro-Hungarian offensive on the Italian front (launched 15 June 1918), which the Italians successfully resisted. Within a week, the Austro-Hungarian forces had withdrawn to the east side of the river.
3 With little fighting in the mountains, EH and other ambulance drivers stationed in Schio volunteered to operate canteens near the line of the Piave.
4 Metal helmet.
5 Lucelle Cannon, EH's high school Latin teacher; J. O. Lofberg taught Latin at OPRFHS from 1914 to 1917.
6 1920s U.S. slang for "excellent" or "terrific."

To Clarence and Grace Hall Hemingway, 14 July 1918

[*Brumback writes:*]

Milan, Italy
July 14th 1918

Dear Dr. Hemingway,

I have just come from seeing Ernest at the American Red Cross hospital here. He is fast on the road to recovery and will be out a whole man once again, so the doctor says, in a couple of weeks. Although some two hundred pieces of shell were lodged in him none of them are above the hip joint. Only a few of these pieces was large enough to cut deep; the most serious of these being two in the knee and two in the right foot. The doctor says there will be no trouble about these wounds healing and that Ernest will regain entire use of both legs.

Now that I have told you about his condition I suppose you would like to know all the circumstances of the case. Let me say right here that you can be very proud of your son's actions. He is going to receive a silver medal of valor which is a very high medal indeed and corresponds to the Medaille Militaire or Legion of Honor of France.

At the time he was wounded Ernest was not in the regular ambulance service but in charge of a Red Cross canteen at the front. Ernest, among several others in our section which was in the mountains where there was not very much action, volunteered to go down on the Piave and help out with the canteen work. This was at the time when the Italians were engaged in pushing the Austrians back over the river so he got to see all the action he wanted.

Ernest was not satisfied with the regular canteen service behind the lines. He thought he could do more good and be of more service by going straight up to the trenches. He told the Italian command about his desire. A bicycle was given him which he used to ride to the trenches every day laden down with chocolate, cigars, cigarettes and Postcards. The Italians in the trenches got to know his smiling face and were always asking for their "giovane Americano".

Well, things went along fine for six days. But about midnight on the seventh day an enormous trench mortar hit within a few feet of Ernest while he was giving out chocolate. The concussion of the explosion knocked him unconscious and buried him with earth. There was an Italian between Ernest and the shell. He was instantly killed while another, standing a few feet away, had both his legs blown off. A third Italian was badly wounded and this one Ernest, after he had regained consciousness, picked up on his back and carried to the first aid dug-out. He says he does not remember how he got there nor that he had carried a man until the next day when an Italian officer told him all about it and said that it had been voted upon to give him a valor medal for the act.

Naturally, being an American, Ernest received the best of medical attention. He had only to remain a day or so at a hospital at the front when he was sent to Milan to the Red Cross hospital. Here he is being showered with attention by American nurses as he is one of the first patients in the hospital. I have never seen a cleaner, neater, and prettier place than that hospital. You can rest easy in your mind that he is receiving the best care in Europe. And you need have no fear for the future for Ernest tells me that he intends now to stick to regular ambulance which, to use his own words, "is almost as safe as being at home".

Since writing the last lines I have seen Ernest again. He told me the doctor had just seen him and made another careful examination. The result showed that no bones were broken and the joints were unharmed, all the splinters making merely flesh wounds.

By the time this letter will reach you he will be back in the section. He has not written himself because one or two of the splinters lodged in his fingers. We have made a collection of shell fragments and bullets that were taken out of Ernie's leg which will be made up into rings[.]

Ernie says he'll write very soon. He dictates love to "Ye old Ivory", Ura, "Nun-bones", "Nubbins", "Ye Young Brute[.]"

Please include my love also although I hav'nt had the pleasure of meeting the foregoing. Tell Mrs. Hemingway how sorry I was that I didn't get to see her while in Chicago.

Sincerely,
Theodore B. Brumback

[*EH writes:*]

P.S.

Dear Folks—

I am all O.K. and include much love to ye parents. I'm not near so much of a hell roarer as Brummy makes me out.

Lots of Love.
Ernie.

Sh _____ Dont worry Pop.

PSU, ANS (EH's postscript to ALS from Theodore Brumback to Clarence Hemingway)

EH was wounded on 8 July 1918. This letter would be published in EH's hometown newspaper, *Oak Leaves* (10 August 1918) and reprinted in the *Kansas City Star* (11 August 1918).

To Hemingway Family, [16 July 1918]

Wounded in legs by trench mortar; not serious; will receive valor medal; will walk in about ten days.

JFK, Cable as published in *Oak Leaves*, 20 July 1918

In a front-page article headlined, "THREE ARE WOUNDED / Ernest Hemingway First on Italian Front: Harold Beye and Arthur Giles Hit in Marne Battles," accompanied by photographs of the three men, the cable text is preceded by this explanation:

> Ernest Hemingway, son of Dr. and Mrs. C. E. Hemingway of 600 North Kenilworth and a member of the Red Cross Ambulance Corps in Italy, received his baptism of fire just five weeks after his arrival overseas and, moreover, has won a citation for bravery.
> Last Saturday evening Dr. Hemingway received an official telegram from Washington stating that the young Oak Park man had been wounded while doing rolling canteen work in Italy. On Tuesday the family was reassured by a cable from Ernest himself, which ran: . . .

Among the newspaper clippings in EH's grandparents' scrapbook concerning his WWI service is another article, also dated 20 July 1918 and presumably from a different local paper, headlined "HEMINGWAY, WOUNDED, TO BE REWARDED FOR VALOR." That article also quotes EH's cable, with slightly different wording and punctuation. Two other clippings dated 16 July 1918, one of them from the Chicago *Evening Post*, report the family's receipt of the cable that morning (JFK).

To Hemingway Family, 21 July [1918]

July 21.

Dear Folks—:

I suppose Brummy has written you all about my getting bunged up. So there isnt anything for me to say. I hope that the cable didnt worry you very much but Capt. Bates thought it was best that you hear from me first rather than the newspapers. You see I'm the first American wounded in Italy and I suppose the papers say something about it.[1]

This is a peach of a hospital here and there are about 18 American nurses to take care of 4 patients.[2] Everything is fine and I'm very comfortable and one of the best surgeons in Milan is looking after my wounds. There are a couple of pieces still in. One bullet in my knee that the X Ray showed. The surgeon, very wisely, after consultation, is going to wait for the wound in my right knee to become healed cleanly before operating. The bullet will then be rather encysted and he will make a clean cut and go in under the side of the knee cap. By allowing it to be completly healed first he thus avoids any danger of infection and stiff knee. That is wise dont you think Dad? He will also remove a bullet from my right foot at the same time. He will probably operate in about a week as the wound is healing cleanly and there is no infection. I had two shots of anti tetanus immediatley at the dressing station. All the other bullets and pieces of shell have been removed and all the wounds on my left leg are healing finely. My fingers are all cleared up and have the bandages off. There will be no permanent effects from any of the wounds as there are no bones shattered. Even in my knees. In both the left and right the bullets did not fracture the patella. One piece of shell about the size of a Timken roller bearing[3] was in my left knee but it has been removed and the knee now moves perfectly and the wound is nearly healed. In the right knee the bullet went under the knee cap from the left side and didnt smash it a bit. By the time you get this letter the surgeon will have operated and It will be all healed. And I hope to be back driving in the mountains by the latter part of August. I have some fine photographs of the Piave and many other interesting pictures. Also a wonderful lot of souvenirs. I was all through the big battle and have Austrian carbines and ammunition, German and Austrian medals, officers automatic pistols, Boche[4] helmets[,] about a dozen Bayonets, star shell pistols and knives and almost everything you can think of. The only limit to the amount of souvenirs I could have is what I could carry for there were so many dead Austrians and prisoners the ground was almost black with them. It was a great victory and showed the world what wonderful fighters the Italians.

I'll tell you all about everything when I get home for Christmas. It is awfully hot here now. I receive your letters regularly. Give my love to everybody and lots to all of you.

Ernie

Write to the Same address.

The medal that I have been recommended for and favourably voted on is a great honor of Italy and I am very proud to have been recommended for it. They were to present it to me at the other hospital in the field but I got away a day ahead of the time set for the presentation. Now they say it will occur in Milan. ~~Things like that take time and red tape.~~

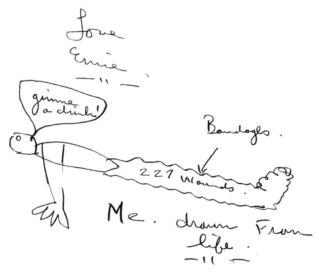

IndU, ALS; letterhead: AMERICAN RED CROSS / LA CROCE ROSSA AMERICANA / VIA MANZONI, 10 / MILANO

"1918." is written in as part of the date, in another hand. This letter was written on EH's nineteenth birthday.

1 Robert W. Bates, director of the ARC Ambulance Service in Italy (Bakewell, 216, 221). EH was not, in fact, the first American casualty in Italy, but was the first to survive his wounding; on 16 June 1918, Edward Michael McKey of the ARC Rolling Canteen Service was killed by an Austrian shell while on duty near Fossalta, the site of EH's wounding (Villard and Nagel, 22–23; Bakewell, 225).

2 EH had been transferred from a field hospital at the front to the Ospedale Croce Rossa Americana (American Red Cross Hospital) in Milan.

3 In 1899, carriage maker Henry Timken patented a tapered roller bearing design, originally applied to mule-drawn wagons, and founded the Timken Roller Bearing Company in Canton, Ohio.

4 Derived from a French slang word for "rascal," this term came into wide use during WWI to mean "German."

To Grace Hall Hemingway, 29 July [1918]

A.R.C.
Hospital
Milano
July 29

Dear Mom—;

I just got your letters of July 2 and June 22. Hurray for Nun bones and three rousing ones for Ura and Uncle Geo[r]ges.[1] Tell the Ivory for me to regard Sam in the cold light of reason and not to get too enthusiastic and also to remember ye old proverb about the great magnitude of the unhooked inhabitants of the ocean.[2] Also what was the Pater doing enroute to Georgia? I got his cable of congratulation yesterday.[3] There is nothing new to report on the Hemingstein Front. The latest dope is that I will step forth from the Hospital on or about the 1st of September. The wounds are coming on in rare shape. However from present indications I will never look well in kilts as the old limbs present a somewhat cut up appearance. They look a bit disgruntled. For a time Maw I resembled a walking blacksmith shop. Nearly everyone in Northern Italy has some souvenir from the Wounded Stein. Never mind Maw while the master woodsman was putting in his week in the trenches he managed to strike several slight blows towards discouraging the Austrians. Also I have glimpsed the making of large gobs of history during the Great Battle of the Piave and have been all along the Front From the mountains to the Sea.

Oh yes I've had to speak Italian ever since I've been over here and so I just naturally learned it. I can now carry on a conversation for just as long as the other fellow wants to talk. I've also got a pretty good working knowledge of French. It may seem funny after my showing in Latin but languages have been a cinch for me. And I can get by as an interpreter in Italian now. The trouble is I have it all by ear and cant write it a bit. But I can read the Italian papers easily.

Milan is a peach of a town. It's about the most modern and lively city in Europe. It sure does get hot though. We have lots of cool drinks though and they pull my bed out on the veranda under the awning. From our porch here we can see the dome of the cathedral. It is very beautiful. Like a great forest inside. The columns seem to go way up into the sky like the "Murmuring Pines and the Hemlocks." However I prefer Notre Dame.[4] They are going to send me down to the Riviera to convalesce after I get so I can walk so I'll get some sea fishing and boating and swimming in September. All the advantages of Foreign travel. Eh? A lot better than waiting to be drafted Eh what?

If you can mother we would appreciate it if you could send us some magazines. There isnt any U.S. Reading matter. Also ask about three of my kid sisters why they dont write to me?

Well good night old dear and God Bless you. I'm a good boy.

Much Love.

Ernie.

IndU, ALS

The year is written in another hand below "July 29."

1 In letters to EH of 11 June, 23 June, and 2 July (JFK), Grace reported that Sunny was graduating (presumably from the eighth grade) and that Uncle George, who was home for two days from Pine Lake, took Ursula back with him for a two-week visit at his family's summer home "up North."

2 In his letter to EH of 16 June, Clarence noted the attentions that Marcelline was receiving from her friend Sam Anderson, who was in Oak Park on his way home from Williams College and trying to join the Navy (JFK).

3 In late June, Clarence traveled on a troop train to Camp Wheeler, near Macon, Georgia, accompanying 700 young men from Illinois who had been drafted into military service. As a doctor and "Y.M.C.A. man," he provided moral support and medical care (Grace to EH,

2 July 1918, and Clarence to EH, 5 and 9 July 1918; JFK). In a cable forwarded to EH by the American Red Cross (26 July 1918), Clarence sent "LOVING SYMPATHY BIRTHDAY CONGRATULATIONS" (JFK).
4 In describing the Duomo di Milano, the world's second largest cathedral, EH is quoting from the opening line of Longfellow's "Evangeline: A Tale of Acadie." Notre-Dame de Paris is another soaring Gothic cathedral.

To James Gamble, 31 July [1918]

A.R.C.Hospital.
Somewhere in Milano
July 31

Dear Capitano;

Salute! On our front there is nothing to report. On our rear however all is healed and the bandages have been removed. We are also permitted to announce strong improvement on our right and left wings. Dr. Castiloni, spelling not verified, the surgeon from the Hospital Maggiore, came in today. According to him, or he, I will have to wait another two weeks before he, or him, will operate on the right knee and foot. That is a bit discouraging because it means a month and a half more prone. Doc C_ _ _ _ _ _ _ _ _i spoke learnedly and at length in Italian on the great pericolosa[1] attending the opening of the knee joint when there is any infection present. So it is probably for the best that I wait the two weeks.

If you look up at the left hand margin of this typewriting it looks quite a bit like Verse Libre? Come?[2]

By the clipping enclosed from the N.Y.Times of the 9th it is apparent that the Camouflage Captain is bursting into print in the metropolis.[3] Klaw and Erlanger please Copy.[4] By the way, does he still sport his three stripes? Milan is about as quiet now as the Sabath in your native town. Seeley and I have been earnestly reading the Delineator of 1916 and 17 and our meals are enlivened by viscious discussions of gussets and cutting on the bias. I have become the recognized authority on Crepe de chine in Northern Italy.[5] Seeley is soon to issue a monograph on Lingerie as She Is. "Lingeries I have met" would be better. Seriously, Capitano, I want to tell you how much I appreciate the things you did for me and the way you looked after me when I was hurt. I appreciate it much more than I can tell you so I wont try.

Give my love to Van Der Veer and the Vincenza bunch.[6]

Yours very torridly

Ernest M. Hemingway.

phJFK, TLS

1 *Pericolosa*: Dangerous (Italian); the word for "danger" is *pericolo*.
2 *Verse libre*: free verse (French), poetry with no fixed metrical pattern. *Come?*: What? (Italian).
3 Although the enclosure is no longer with the letter, EH apparently refers to "Our Aviators Tireless in Italian Fighting" (*New York Times*, 9 July 1918, 3), which reports the heroism of two American airmen selected for recognition by Captain Fiorello LaGuardia (1882–1947), who had left the U.S. House of Representatives to serve with the U.S. Aviation Corps as a bomber-pilot in Italy. LaGuardia was charged by President Wilson with delivering a series of rousing speeches to assure the Italian public of U.S. support in the war effort, and he received publicity and praise as an "orator and patriot" ("La Guardia, America's Congressman-Aviator," *New York Times*, 30 June 1918, 58).
4 Theatrical entrepreneurs and producers Marc Alonzo Klaw (1858–1936) and Abraham Lincoln Erlanger (1860–1930) established a partnership in the late 1880s and controlled most of the bookings in the United States into the early 1910s.
5 Coles van Brunt Seeley, member of ARC Ambulance Service Section 1, had served under Gamble in the Rolling Kitchen Service (Bakewell, 222, 225). He was in the hospital with EH after being injured by a live shell while collecting battlefield souvenirs (Villard and Nagel, 13–14). The *Delineator* (subtitled *A Journal of Fashion, Culture, and Fine Arts*) was a leading American magazine for women, published monthly from 1873 to 1937 by Butterick Publishing (originator and manufacturer of sewing patterns for home use) and featuring color illustrations of women modeling the latest styles. Crêpe de chine is a fine silk dress fabric.
6 John S. Vanderveer served in the ARC Ambulance Service Section 5 (Bakewell, 224). Vicenza lies about 15 miles southeast of Schio.

To Hemingway Family, 4 August [1918]

ARC. Hospital

Milano

August 4th

Dear Folks—;

Mothers letter of July 8th, the day I was wounded, came day before yesterday. There isn't a blame thing to write about because I'm still in bed and will be for a month or so.

The surgeon says that my leg is coming on very good and he plans now to operate on the knee and right foot on August 15th. I sure wish he would hurry up because it is very tiresome waiting in bed with the legs in splints. There was a big parade last Sunday and they took me out with my legs strapped to a board.

With a body guard of about six Italian officers I sat on the plaza and reviewed the troops. The crowd cheered me for about ten solid minutes and I had to take off my cap and bow about 50 times. They threw flowers all over me and every body wanted to shake my hand and the girls all wanted my name so they could write to me. The master journalist was known to the crowd as the American Hero of the Piave. I'm nothing but a second Lieut. or Soto Tenente but all the Captains saluted me first. Oh it was very thrilling. I tried to act very dignified but felt very embarrased.

I heard today that I had been recommended for the valour medal of the Duke of Aosta who is the brother of the King.[1] That is the in addition to the silver medal which I have also been recommended for. The silver medal is next to the highest Decoration that any man can receive. I think it carries a pension with it but I'm not sure. Only 9 men have the highest decoration. The silver valour medal is corresponding to the Victoria Cross. It is higher than the French Croix D'Guerre and Medaille Militaire and ranks with the Legion of Honor they say.[2]

I hope I am up and out soon so I may receive the one I have been recommended for. Usually they are presented by the King.

The rainbow trout up in Hortons Bay can thank the Lord there is a war on. But they will be all the bigger next summer. Gee I wish I was up there fishing off the old dock.

Maw, you seemed very enthusiastic over that last Jacky! The one with the tenor voice. Beware of tenors![3]

Say if it were not too difficult, send the Oak Leaves every week, will you? Also the Tribune occassionally. Newspapers and magazines are the only things you can send over here. Also ask why my four beautiful sisters dont write once in a while.

Here's looking at you all,

Lots of love to all and kiss Dessie for me.

Ernie.

PSU, ALS; letterhead: CAMPO AVIAZIONE-CASCINA MALPENSA; postmark:
MILANO CENTRO / PARTENZA, 88 18. 18

1 Prince Emanuele Filiberto (1869–1931), the second Duke of Aosta, commanded the Italian
   Third Army during WWI. He was a first cousin of Victor Emmanuel III (1869–1947), the
   king of Italy, who reigned from 1900 to 1946.
2 Italy's *Medaglia d'Argento al Valore Militare* (Silver Medal of Military Valor), established in
   1833 and awarded for exceptional bravery in combat. Victoria Cross, the United Kingdom's
   highest award for gallantry, established in 1856 by Queen Victoria. *Croix de Guerre* (Cross of
   War), established in 1915 for heroism in the face of the enemy and commonly given to
   foreign soldiers and units allied with the French. *Médaille Militaire* (Military Medal), French
   award instituted in 1852 and issued only to noncommissioned officers and enlisted personnel. *Légion d'Honneur* (Legion of Honor), the highest order of France and the first modern
   order of merit, established in 1802 by Napoleon I and awarded for distinguished civilian or
   military service. EH actually received two Italian decorations: the Silver Medal and the *Croce
   al Merito di Guerra* (War Cross of Merit). Reportedly the silver medal was awarded to all
   soldiers who were wounded, and the war cross, like U.S. Army campaign ribbons, to all who
   were engaged in action (Robert W. Lewis, "Hemingway in Italy: Making It Up," *Journal of
   Modern Literature* 9, no. 2 [May 1982]: 223–24; Villard and Nagel, 256–57).
3 In her letter to EH of 7–8 July, Grace spoke of the various "Jackies" recently visiting
   Marcelline. Of Sam Anderson (who "is quite taken with Marce"), she wrote, "He is a big
   athletic blonde, finished 2 yrs college, plays some & sings tenor & is an all round peach"
   (JFK).

To Clarence, Grace Hall, and Marcelline Hemingway, 7 August [1918]

August 7.

Dear Folks and Ivory—;

Your Epistles of July 9th and 13th received today. I greet you. The July
13th letter from Dad beat the July 5th from Ivory.[1] Such are the wonders of
the Postal System.

Gunnar Dahl was one of my best friends and played Tackle next to me on
the old Light weight team. He was a peach of a jolly good scout. I hope
God will give me a chance at some of the German Swine that killed him.[2] I'm
glad Pop had such a good time with the drafted men. If they're anything
like most of the contingents I've seen off he must of had a busy time.[3]

Ed Welch who was Sou chef, a in Englesi, Second Lieut, a second in
command of our section is leaving for home next week. He lives in Roge[r]s
Park and will come out to see you folks as soon as he gets home.[4] He is a

peach of a fellow and will tell you all about me and our bunch. He is a Catholic so dont pull any boners.

Charles Griffin a chef, or head of the section, is also going back to the States.[5] He lives in N.J. but may come to Chicago to see you folks. He and Eddie are both fine fellows.

Day after tomorrow I am to be operated on for my right knee joint and right foot. I'll tell you all about it afterwards. I've been in bed a month tomorrow and it is getting pretty darn tiresome. However I ought to get out in a month now so as to be on crutches. I'll convalesce at Riviera where I can get some good swimming and fishing.

Then in the Last of September I get a two weeks "permission" or leave with all railway travel free. So Brummy and Jenks and I will probably go down to Naples and Rome and cover Southern Italy. I've seen all of Northern Italy and Southern Italy will have to show some pep to come up to the North.

You would be surprised all right family to hear me talk Italian. I really can by the hour. I'll show you when I get home down at the fruit Stands. I also have my French down pretty well. I write a letter or so in Italian every day.

I think I'll stay down here this winter. Maybe I'll go to Mesopotamia. It all depends on how strong I feel. Mesopotamias nice in the winter. But reputed to be hell in the summer. It would be fine to take in Bagdad and Jerusalem etc. during the winter though. If I can enlist for Six Months I'll go down. But not for a year. Some of us may go down into Serbia too.[6] I'd like to get a Serbian medal.

Well have a good time while Papa is away children,

Much love.
Ernie.

P.S. You see were in the Italian not the American Army. Dont address my mail Lieut. That confuses it with the American Army Ambulance.[7] What our rank is is Soto Tenente. Abbreviated S. Ten. or Soto Ten. That is the Italian for 2nd Lieut. Our mail is separate from the U.S Army as S. Ten. Ernest M. Hemingway. Use my new Italian address too.

IndU, ALS; letterhead: AMERICAN RED CROSS / LA CROCE ROSSA AMERICANA / VIA MANZONI, 10 / MILANO

1 These incoming letters survive in the Hemingway Collection at JFK; Marcelline's is included in the 1999 edition of her memoirs (Sanford, 279–80).

2 Clarence wrote on 13 July that David Thor and Gunnar Dahl of Oak Park had been killed in France. He likely got the news from the front-page story of that day's *Oak Leaves*, which reported that the men, "comrades since marble days," had enlisted together in the U.S. Marines in April 1917 and were manning the same machine gun when they died. Dahl graduated from OPRFHS in 1916; Thor did not complete high school, but his younger brother Joseph was in EH's class of 1917.

3 In his 9 July letter, Clarence wrote of his "great trip" accompanying the Illinois draftees on the troop train to Camp Wheeler, Georgia, and enclosed a typewritten copy of his 1 July letter to a YMCA officer describing the experience in detail.

4 Edward J. Welch, Jr.; Rogers Park, far northeastern neighborhood of Chicago, on the shore of Lake Michigan and bordering Evanston, Illinois, just to the north of the city line.

5 Lieutenant Charles B. Griffin (Baker *Life*, 42).

6 The war in Mesopotamia and Palestine was primarily between forces of the United Kingdom and the Ottoman Empire. By this point in the war, the Allies were routing forces of the Central Powers throughout the Middle East. Austria-Hungary's declaration of war against Serbia on 28 July 1914 had precipitated WWI.

7 The envelope of Grace's 23 June letter, addressed to "Lieut. Ernest Miller Hemingway / Italian Ambulance Service / American Red Cross / Milano / Italy / c/o American Consul," had been been rubber-stamped, "NOT U.S. ARMY AMBULANCE SERVICE / ITALY" (JFK).

To Marcelline Hemingway, [8 August 1918]

Ospedale Americana

Cara Mio—;

Perche non scrivere a eo? Multo giorno niente Epistola! An altro tenente amata. Come? Dearest Ivory the foregoing is but to illustrate a sample of the letters I am compelled to write daily. Translated it means my dearest—; why my love have you not written. Many days I wait and nothing of letters. Is it that you love another Lieutenant?[1] Tis thus that the Old Master learns the Italian language. He can speak it with great fluency and on my return we shall journey to Italian restaurants down town where I will demonstrate. When I tell of the many Austrians that have fallen at my hammy feet they will feed us free. Scorning any emolument.

Why oh bright beam of an August moon have you not written me? Is it that you love me not? Or is it but neglect? If but the girls of our village could see me in my dress uniform, I am of a great fear that the men would be wifeless. However for them to appreciate my scars it would be necessary for me to wear no pants (i.e. trousers); or else to have flaps sown the length of the knees that they might be unbuttoned at will to show the marks of valour which be many and various. Ah Hah! I will wear nothing but my tank suit! Then will all be revealed. N'Espa?[2]

Dear Ivory call up on the telephone all my former sweet hearts! Tell them that the master woodsman, now known as The Heero of the Peehave, loves them with an undying love. Convey to them my undying fealty and fillial devotion.

Tell them that I will return, God willing and woo and perhaps wed them all. Inform them that it is only lack of interest that keeps me from writing them. Write me their replies.

Also call up Frances Coates and tell her that your brother is at Deaths door and that she will please, no excuses, write to him. Make her repeat the address after you so that she will have no alibi! Tell I love her or any damn thing! You know me Ivory.

Sweet sister, why not do you not dip the quill and sling me a screed yourself? Merely because I am a great man do not stand in awe of me! I am democratic or nothing. Si! Mostly nothing.

Here are my kisses,

Arevedechi, Bon Giorno![3]

I kiss again—

The Old Brute.

phJFK, ALS; letterhead: AMERICAN RED CROSS / LA CROCE ROSSA AMERICANA / VIA MANZONI, 10 / MILANO; postmark: MILANO / PARTENZA, 8.8.18

Letter is dated "Aug. 8, 1918" in another hand.

1 EH's Italian is riddled with errors.
2 *N'est-ce pas*?: Is it not? (French).
3 *Arrivederci, buon giorno*!: Goodbye, good day! (Italian).

To Clarence Hemingway, [c. 14 August 1918]

Washington. D.C

Aug 14 /918

Dr. C. E. Hemingway

Cable from Italy for you says Operation on legs completely successfull. progressing faster/.— Cable singed Ernest Hemingway.

W. R. Castle jr[1]

Red Cross

JFK, Handwritten transcription of EH Cable

This transcription is preserved in EH's grandparents' scrapbook, along with a number of newspaper clippings about his wounding and hospitalization in Italy. EH underwent surgery on 10 August, as noted that day in the diary of Henry S. Villard, a fellow patient at the hospital (JFK; Villard and Nagel, 31).

1 Formerly assistant dean of Harvard College, William R. Castle, Jr. (1879–1963), became director of the Bureau of Communications of the American Red Cross when the United States entered WWI.

To Elizabeth Dilworth, 14 August [1918]

Aug 14.

Dear Aunty Beth—

Save a place at the table for me because I'm coming up in time for next Springs fishing. I've had a great time here and hope to get out of the hospital and back to the Front again in a couple of months. I hope you have a good summer. Lots of love.

Ernest.

S. Ten. Ernesto M. Hemingway.

Croce Rosa Americana Ospedale.

Milano, Italia

Robert and Susan Metzger Collection, A Postcard S; verso: Milano—Galleria Vittorio Emanuele II.; postmark: MILANO / CENTRO, 19–20 / 15·VIII / 1918

The postcard is addressed to "Mrs. James Dilworth / RFD No. 2 / Boyne City / Michigan / U.S.A." It was found in 1995 in the attic of the detached "summer kitchen" of the Dilworths' home in Horton Bay.

To Hemingway Family, 18 August [1918]

American Red X
Hospital,
Milano
Aug 18

Dear Folks—;

That includes Grandma and Grandpa and Aunt Grace. Thanks very much for the 40 lire! It was appreciated very much. Gee Family but there certainly has been a lot of burble about my getting shot up! The Oak Leaves and the opposition came today and I have begun to think, family, that maybe you didn't appreciate me when I used to reside in the bosom. It's the next best thing to getting killed and reading your own obituary.[1]

You know they say there isn't anything funny about this war. And there isn't. I wouldn't say it was hell, because that's been a bit overworked since Gen. Sherman's time, but there have been about 8 times when I would have welcomed Hell.[2] Just on a chance that it couldn't come up to the phase of war I was experiencing. F'rexample. In the trenches during an attack when a shell makes a direct hit in a group where you're standing. Shells aren't bad except direct hits. You just take chances on the fragments of the bursts. But when there is a direct hit your pals get spattered all over you. Spattered is literal.

During the six days I was up in the Front line trenches, only 50 yds from the Austrians I got the rep of having a charmed life. The rep of having one doesn't mean much but having one does! I hope I have one. That knocking sound is my knuckles striking the wooden bed tray.

It's too hard to write on two sides of the paper so Ill skip—[3]

Well I can now hold up my hand and say I've been shelled by high explosive, shrapnel and gas. Shot at by trench mortars, snipers and machine guns. And as an added attraction an aeroplane machine gunning the lines. I've never had a hand grenade thrown at me, but a rifle grenade struck rather close. Maybe I'll get a hand grenade later. Now out of all that mess to only be struck by a trench mortar and a machine gun bullet while advancing toward the rear, as the Irish say, was fairly lucky. What Family?

The 227 wounds I got from the trench mortar didnt hurt a bit at the time, only my feet felt like I had rubber boots full of water on. Hot water. And my knee cap was acting queer. The machine gun bullet just felt like a sharp smack on my leg with an icy snow ball. However it spilled me. But I got up again and got my wounded into the dug out. I kind of collapsed at the dug out. The Italian I had with me had bled all over my coat and my pants looked like somebody had made current jelly in them and then punched holes to let the pulp out. Well the Captain who was a great pal of mine, it was his dug out, said "Poor Hem he'll be R.I.P. soon." Rest In Peace, that is. You see they thought I was shot through the chest on account of my bloody coat. But I made them take my coat and shirt off. I wasn't wearing any under shirt, and the old torso was intact. Then they said I'd probably live. That cheered me up any amount. I told him in Italian that I wanted to see my legs, though I was afraid to look at them. So we took off my trousers and the old limbs were still there but gee they were a mess. They couldn't figure out how I had walked 150 yards with a load with both knees shot through and my right shoe punctured two big places. Also over 200 flesh wounds. "Oh," says I in Italian, "My Captain. It is of nothing. In America they all do it! It is thought well not to allow the enemy to percieve that they have captured our goats!"

The goat speech required some masterful lingual ability but I got it across and then went to sleep for a couple of minutes.

After I came to they carried me on a stretcher three kilometers back to a dressing station. The stretcher bearers had to go over lots because the road was having the "entrails" shelled out of it. Whenever a big one would come, wheeeee whoosh—Boom—they'd lay me down and get flat. My wounds were now hurting like 227 little devils were driving nails into the raw. The dressing station had been evacuated during the attack so I lay for two hours in a stable, with the roof shot off, waiting for an ambulance. When it came I ordered it down the road to get the soldiers that had been wounded first.[4] It came back with a load and then they lifted me in. The shelling was still pretty thick and our batteries were going off all the time way back of us and the big 250s and 350's going over head for Austria with a noise like a railway train. Then we'd hear the bursts back of the lines. Then shreek would come a big Austrian shell and then the crash of the burst. But we were giving them more and bigger stuff than they sent. Then a battery of field guns would go off just back of the shed boom, boom, boom, boom. And the

Seventy Fives or 149s would go whimpering over to the Austrian lines and the Star shells going up all the time and the machine going like rivetters.[5] Tat a tat, tat a tat.

After a ride of a couple of Kilomets in an Italian ambulance, they unloaded me at the dressing station where I had a lot of pals among the medical officers. They gave me a shot of morphine and an anti tetanus injection and shaved my legs and took out about twenty 8 shell fragments varying from to about in size out of my legs. Then they did a fine job of bandaging and all shook hands with me and would have kissed me but I kidded them along. Then I stayed 5 days in a field hospital and was then evacuated to the Base Hospital here.

I sent you that cable so you wouldn't worry. I've been in the Hospital a month and 12 days and hope to be out in another month.[6] The Italian Surgeon did a peach of a job on my right knee joint and right foot. Took 28 stitches and assures me that I will be able to walk as well as ever. The wounds all healed up clean and there was no infection. He has my right leg in a plaster splint now so that the joint will be all right. I have some snappy souvenirs that he took out at the last operation.

I wouldn't really be comfortable now unless I had some pain. The Surgeon is going to take the plaster off in a week now and will allow me on crutches in 10 days.

I'll have to learn to walk again.

You ask about Art Newburn. He was in our section but has been transferred to II. Brummy is in our section now. Dont weep if I tell you that back in my youth I learned to play poker. Art Newburn held some delusions that he was a poker player. I won't go into the sad details but I convinced him otherwise. Without holding anything I stood pat. Doubled his [word ?] sweetened openers and bluffed him out of a 50 lire pot. He held three aces and was afraid to call. Tell that to somebody that knows the game Pop. I think Art said in a letter home to the Oak Parker that he was going to take care of me.[7] Now Pop as man to man was that taking care of me? Nay not so. So you see that while war isn't funny a lot of funny things happen in war. But Art won the championship of Italy pitching horse shoes.

This is the longest letter I've ever written to anybody and it says the least. Give my love to everybody that asked about me and as Ma Pettengill says, "Leave us keep the home fires burning!"[8]

Good night and love to all.

Ernie

I got a letter today from the Helmles[9] addressed Private Ernest H— what I am is S. Ten. or Soto Tenenente Ernest Hemingway.

That is my rank in the Italian Army and it means 2nd Lieut. I hope to be a Tenente or 1st Lieut. soon.

Dear Pop—; Yours of July 23rd Rece'd[.] Thanks very much. But you need the Kale[10] worse than I do. If I ever get really broke I'll cable. Send any money that others send me Pop, but dont you give me any unless I cable for it. I'll cable if I need it.

Love

Ernie.

IndU, ALS

1 *Oak Leaves* had reported EH's wounding in "Three Are Wounded" (20 July 1918), a front-page story featuring EH's high school yearbook photo, and "Wins Italian Medal / Ernest Hemingway to Receive Valor Badge for Exploit at Piave River: Recovering in Milan" (10 August 1918), which contained Brumback's 14 July letter to the Hemingways, with EH's postscript. In the coming weeks, *Oak Leaves* would publish more stories about EH: "With Our Wounded / Hemingway Is Italian Hero" (7 September 1918) and "Wounded 277 Times" (5 October 1918), which included the present letter and a photograph of EH in his Milan hospital bed. "The opposition" likely refers to the *Oak Parker*, a competing local newspaper, founded in 1884.
2 The statement "War is hell" is attributed to William Tecumseh Sherman (1820–1891), U.S. Civil War Union general most famous for his 1864 "March to the Sea" from Atlanta to Savannah, Georgia, in which his men destroyed anything of possible value to the Confederate war effort.
3 EH wrote on only one side of the paper for the rest of the letter (with the exception of a postscript, written on the back of the last page).
4 Hemingway "rendered generous assistance to the Italian soldiers more seriously wounded by the same explosion and did not allow himself to be carried elsewhere until they had been

evacuated," as described by the U.S. official history and quoted in Martin Gilbert's *The First World War: A Complete History* (New York: Henry Holt, 1994), 438.

5 The seventy-fives were the most widely used French field guns because of their rapid-firing capabilities and maneuverability; "149's," the 149-mm Italian Obice 149. Star shells, or flares, were used for signaling and illumination.

6 Assuming EH dated this letter accurately, he apparently misstates the length of his hospitalization, as he was wounded on 8 July, a month and ten days earlier.

7 In his letter to EH of 23 July, Clarence had asked, "Was Newburn near you? Where is Ted Brumback?" A letter from Newburn to his mother, dated 9 June 1918, was published in a newspaper article (presumably from the *Oak Parker*) and later preserved along with other clippings about EH's WWI service in EH's grandparents' scrapbook. Newburn had told his mother, "Hemingway will be in the same section with me, so you can tell his father that I will be able to look after him" (JFK).

8 Ma Pettengill is one of the colorful characters created by popular American humorist Harry Leon Wilson (1867–1939), whose work appeared regularly in the *Saturday Evening Post*. She speaks this line in "Red Gap and the Big-League Stuff," a story that appeared in the 15 June 1918 issue of the magazine and would be included in Wilson's 1919 collection, *Ma Pettengill*. The line alludes to the popular WWI song, "Keep the Home-Fires Burning ('Till the Boys Come Home)" (1914), music by Ivor Novello (né David Davies, 1893–1951) and lyrics by Lena Ford (c. 1866–1918).

9 Robert K. Helmle was a member of the OPRFHS class of 1915 and editor of the *Trapeze* in 1914–1915 (Buske, *Hemingway's Education*, 77); his "Boyhood Recollections of Ernest Hemingway and His Father" appears in *The Toe River Anthology* (Robert K. Helmle and Francis Pledger Hulme, eds. [Burnsville, North Carolina: Toe River Arts Council, 1979], 83–94).

10 Kale, North American slang for money. In his letter of 23 July, Clarence wrote that Uncle Tyler and "Grand Pa" each had given EH ten dollars for his birthday; Clarence said he would forward the money to EH via American Express, along with his own monetary gift (JFK).

To Grace Hall Hemingway, 29 August [1918]

Agosto 29

A.R.C. Hospital

Dear Mom—;

I havn't written before for quite a while because I aint got no pep. The old limbs are coming along fine. My left leg is all healed up and I can bend it finely and I now get around my room and this floor of the hospital on crutches. But I can only go a little bit at a time because I'm awfully weak yet. My right leg was taken out of the cast a couple of days ago and it's still as stiff as a board and awfully sore from so much carving around the knee joint and foot. But the surgeon, whose name is Sammarelli, hes the best in Milan and knows Beck of New York, now Dead, and one of the Mayo's.[1] Says that eventually it will be all right. The joint gets better every day and I'll be moving it soon.

I'm enclosing a picture of me in bed. It looks like my left leg was a stump but it really isnt just bent so it looks that way.[2]

They have been wonderful to me here. All the Americans have made an awful fuss over me. A Mrs. Stucke who has lived here some years has been particularly indescribably nice. Brought me books, and cakes and candy and with her daughter visits me about 3 times a week. She is a peach and is writing to you about me. Then there is a Mrs. Siegel, a nice dear old jewess who has been up to see me a lot. And a Mr. Englefield, a brother to one of the Lords of the Admiralty, who is about 52. He has been younger sonning it in Italy for about 20 years and has adopted me. He is very interesting and seems to have taken a great fancy to me. He brings me everything, from Eau de Cologne to the London Papers. And a peach of a Catholic missionary Priest from India, a regular good old scout like Mark Williams, comes in to see me very often and we have great old gab fests. And there are a number of jolly good Italian officer pals of mine that blow in all the time. One of them a Tenente Brundi is a famous artist and wants to paint a portrait of me. It will be a darn nice souvenir.

Now Mom you may not believe it but I can speak Italian like a born Milanese. You see up at the trenches I had to talk it, there being nothing else spoken. So I've learned an awful lot and talk with the officers by the hour in Italian. I suppose I'm shy on grammar but I'm long on vocabulary.

Lots of times I've acted as interpreter for the hospital. Some body comes in and they cant understand what they want and the nurse brings 'em over to my bed and I straighten it all out. All the nurses are American.[3] This war makes us a lot less fools than we were. For instance Poles and Italians. I think the officers of these two nations are the finest men I've ever known. There isn't going to be any such thing as "foreigners" for me after the war now. Just because your pals speak another language shouldn't make any difference.

The thing to do is learn that language! I've gotten Italian pretty well. I've picked up quite a lot of Polish and my French is improving a lot. It's better than 10 years of college. I know more French and Italian now than if I'd studied 8 years in college. And you want to be prepared for a lot of visitors after the war now because I've got a lot of pals coming to see me in Chicago. That's the best thing about this [old mess ?], the friends that it makes. And when you are looking at death all the time you get to know your friends too.

I don't know when I'll be back. Maybe for Christmas, probably not. I cant get in the Army or Navy and they wouldn't take me in the draft if I'd go home. One bum lamp and two shady legs, so I might as well stay over here and play around the old conflict for a while.

Also Mom I'm in love again.[4] Now don't get the wind up and start worrying about me getting married. For I'm not; as I told you once before. Raise my right hand and promise! So dont get up in the air and cable and write me. I'm not even going to get engaged! Loud cheers. So don't write any "God bless you my children" not for about ten years.

Your a dear old kid and your still my best girl! Kiss me. Very good, now good bye and God Bless you and write me often. I heard from you, last letter of July 21 about a week ago. Send B.L.T. often.[5] The papers Pop sent came. 2 packages. Much obliged to him. Also the two money orders from Gramp and Uncle Ty. I'm going to buy diamond studded radium dumb bells with the Kale.

So Long old dear.

I love you

Ernie.

IndU, ALS; postmark: 3 MILANO 3 PARTENZA, 21–22 / 28.VIII / 1918

Clarence wrote in "1918." as part of the date and added "Milan, Italy" below "A.R.C. Hospital."

1 Carl Beck (1856–1911), well-known German-born New York surgeon and a pioneer in medical applications of x-ray technology. William J. (1861–1939) and Charles H. Mayo (1865–1939), along with their father, William Worrall Mayo (1819–1911), had founded the renowned Mayo Clinic in Rochester, Minnesota. During WWI the brothers served in the U.S. Army medical corps, alternately serving as chief consultant to the Army's surgical services and dividing their time between Washington, D.C., and Rochester.

2 The photograph survives with the letter.

3 Although several of the nurses were from the United States (including Ruth Brooks, Loretta Cavanaugh, Charlotte M. Heilman, and Agnes von Kurowsky), Elsie MacDonald was from Scotland, and Katherine C. DeLong, the nurse in charge, was Canadian (Bakewell, 228–45; Baker *Life*, 46–47; Villard and Nagel, 29).

4 EH is speaking of Agnes von Kurowsky (1892–1984), the Red Cross nurse who would serve as a model for Luz in "A Very Short Story" (*IOT*) and for Catherine Barkley in *FTA*. EH's hospital mate Henry Villard, a member of ARC Ambulance Service Section 1, later described Agnes as "cheerful, quick, sympathetic, with an almost mischievous sense of humor—an ideal personality for a nurse" (Baker *Life*, 47).

5 Each of his parents wrote a letter to EH on 21 July, his nineteenth birthday. Bert Leston Taylor used his initials to sign his popular *Chicago Daily Tribune* column, "A Line o' Type or Two."

To Henry [S. Villard],[1] [c. August 1918]

A M E R I C A N   R E D   C R O S S
LA CROCE ROSSA AMERICANA
TELEFONO 49-64

Croce HL Tevito Dr Ospedale, VIA MANZONI, 10

M I L A N O

Dear Henry—;

I just started for your room and was grabbed by at least six nurses who informed me that I am isolated and can't leave the room. But Henry, why this influx of Kale? And how are you feeling? Also what news of Bake and my baggage? I gave BAKe an hundred lire to settle with Pop and Knapp.[2] That is why the money mystifies me. The Croce is a thing not of beauty, but a joy forever.[3] Gee I'm glad all the fellows pulled 'em. Consider yourself kissed on either cheek. The Doc after a lengthy commune with nature and the late medical bulletins decided yesterday that I have Vincent's Angina.[4] Though who Vincent is or what I am supposed to have done to his Angina are still shrouded in darkness. Now if it was Rabbits Blondy it would be easily diagnosable. Also did the medaglia D'Argento fall through or what?

Give me a general line on the Situation Henry when you get the Pep.

Hope you'r feeling better.

Hem

JFK, ALS; letterhead: AMERICAN RED CROSS / LA CROCE ROSSA AMERICANA / VIA MANZONI, 10 / MILANO

EH's sketch of a ribbon above the Red Cross emblem on the letterhead makes the cross resemble a military medal. His caption, "Croce Al Merito Di Ospedale" (Hospital Cross of Merit), is a play on "Croce al Merito di Guerra," the Italian War Cross decoration that he received.

1 The recipient of this letter was likely Henry S. Villard (1900–1996) of Ambulance Service Section 1, who was admitted to the Red Cross Hospital with jaundice and malaria on 1 August 1918 and occupied a room adjoining EH's. A handwritten response signed "Henry" at the end of this letter refers to their mutual ARC friends Brumback and Gamble, noting, "Gamble says he is on track of the Silver Bene, and it will come shortly." Villard returned to duty at the front on 23 August and would not see EH again (Villard and Nagel, 34–36, 232).
2 "Bake," probably either James H. Baker, who served in Sections 1 and 4, or Edwin H. Baker, Jr., of Section 4. "Pop" may be G. W. Harris of Section 4, an older volunteer whom the men dubbed "Dad Harris" (Brumback to EH, 1 September 1918, JFK). Harry K. Knapp, Jr., served in Section 1.
3 Allusion to a line in "Ode on a Grecian Urn" (1820) by John Keats (1795–1821): "A thing of beauty is a joy forever."
4 Also known as "trench mouth," a painful inflammation of the gums and throat caused by bacterial infection and common among WWI soldiers. It is named after French physician Jean Hyacinthe Vincent (1862–1950).

To Clarence Hemingway, 11 September 1918

Sept. 11 1918
A.R.C. Hospital
Milano

Dear Dad—;

Your letters of Aug 6th and 11th came today. I'm glad you got that one from Ted and know he will be glad to hear from you. He came in from the front as soon as he knew I was wounded and at the Base here and wrote that letter to you in Milan.[1] It was before my leg had been X Rayed or operated on and so I dont know just what he told you about it all because I was too sick to give a darn.

But I hope it was all right. I had a letter from him from the front a couple of days ago and they are having a good time. Mother wrote me that you and

she were going up North and I know you had a good vacation. Write me
all about it if you did any fishing. That is what makes me hate this war.
Last year this time I was making those wonderful catches of Rainbow at
the Bay

I'm in bed today and probably wont leave the hospital for about three
weeks more. My legs are coming on wonderfully and will both eventually be
O.K. absolutely. The left one is all right now. The right is still stiff but
massage and sun cure and passive movements are loosening up the knee. My
surgeon Captain Sammarelli, one of the best surgeons in Italy, is always
asking me whether I think that you will be entirely satisfied with the
operations. He says that his work must be inspected by the great Surgeon
Hemingway of Chicago and he wants it to be perfect. And it is too. There is a
scar about 8 inches long in the bottom of my foot and a neat little
puncture on top. Thats what copper jacketted bullets do when they "key
hole" in you. My knee is a beauty also. I'll never be able to wear kilts Pop.
My left leg thigh and side look like some old horse that has been branded and
rebranded by about 50 owners. They will all make good identification marks.

I can get around now on the streets for a little while each day with a cane
or crutch but cant put a shoe on my right foot yet. Oh yes! I have been
commissioned a 1st Lieutenant and now wear the two gold stripes on each of
my sleeves. It was a surprise to me as I hadn't expected anything of the sort.
So now you can address my mail either 1st Lieut. or Tenente as I hold the
rank in both the A.R.C. and Italian army. I guess I'm the youngest 1st Lieut.
in the Army. Anyway I feel all dolled up with my insignia and a shoulder
strap on my Sam Browne Belt. I also heard that my silver medaglia valore is
on the way and I will probably get i[t] as soon as I'm out of the Hospital. Also
the[y] brought back word from the Front that I was proposed for the war
cross before I was wounded because of general foolish conduct in the
trenches I guess. So maybe I'll be decorated with both medals at once. That
would not be bad.

I'm awfully glad that Hop and Bill Smith are going to be near where you
can be nice to both of them. They are the two best Pals I have about and
especially Bill. So have him out often because I know you will like him and he
has done so much for me. I will probably go back to the ambulance for a

while when I get out because the gang want me to visit them and they want to put on a big party.

I got a long letter the other day from every fellow in the section. I would like to go back to the ambulance but I wont be much use driving for about Six months. I will probably take command of some 1st line post up in the mountains. Anyway dont worry about me because It has been conclusively proved that I cant be killed. And I will always go where I can do the most good you know. And thats' what we're here for.

Well, So Long Old Scout,

Your loving Son
Ernie.

P.S.

If it isnt too much I wish you'd subscribe to the Sat. Eve Post for me and have it sent to my address here. They will forward it to me wherever I am. You need American reading an awful lot when your at the front.

Thanks,
Ernie

IndU, ALS

1 In his letters to EH of 6 and 11 August, Clarence wrote how pleased and relieved the family was to receive Brumback's detailed letter of 14 July with EH's postscript; Clarence reported that the letter had been published in both *Oak Leaves* and the *Oak Parker* and that he was sending copies of the articles to EH's out-of-town friends. On 11 August he wrote that he had received a letter from Hopkins, who had joined the Navy and would be passing through Chicago soon; Clarence had invited him to visit the family at Oak Park "early and often" (JFK).

To Ursula Hemingway, 16 September [1918]

Sept.16.

Dear Ura—;

You'r probably just going to school now huh? So'm I, in bed. Probably I'll get out of the hospital in about 20 days [*MS torn*: now ?]. I sure was glad to hear from you kid. Only they dont use bugs in Botany! You mean Zoology.

Are you breaking all the sophomores hearts now? Give my love to Ginny and Margaret[1] and tell 'em I'll write 'em soon. They both wrote me fine letters for the train. Remember me to Simmie[2] and Kewpie.

Also you might kiss Mac[3] for me.

Your brother is now a full fleged 1st Lieut. and all the 2nd Lieuts. salute him. So when you write to the Old Brute address him as Lieut. Not so bad Eh?

He wears two gold Bars on his sleeve and a Sam Browne Belt and is going to have command of a post of his own.

So now will you be good[.] Write me soon and long.

Love to you and Nunbones and Nubs and Dessie

Ernie

Exploding shrapnel

Schnack, ALS; postmark: MILANO / CENTRO / 21–22 / 16 IX / 1918

1 Cousins Virginia and Margaret Adelaide Hemingway (1901–1980), daughters of EH's Uncle George and Aunt Anna Hemingway.
2 Possibly Isabelle Simmons, then a junior at OPRFHS and the Hemingways' next-door neighbor in Oak Park.
3 OPRFHS principal Marion Ross McDaniel, whom EH disliked.

To Marcelline and Madelaine Hemingway,
21 September 1918

Hospital
Sept 21 1918.

Dear Ivory and Nun Bones—;

Your epistles of Aug 25th just arrived and oh women I was glad to hear from you! I'm still in the hospital and probably will linger for about 3 weeks more. Believe me kids, the Old Master is an authority on hospitals. Darn near three months already. It's funny that I've only had two letters offn. you since the war started, Aug 19 and 25.

There isn't a thing to relate. I know where your friend Bill Hutchins is and will try and look him up.[1] The Captain in charge has invited me to come and visit him so I'll strive to lamp Bill.

You know Milano is some town. About 690,000. Good opera and everything. I go out and walk around town almost every aft and sure know the old burg. After the war I'll be qualified to run a rubber kneck wagon through Itakly. When I walk it looks like I had a locomotor ataxia[2] but that will all clear up. My right knee bends a little now. Gee but I get anxious to get back to the front. I dont know exactly what I will do now that I have been commissioned at 1st Lieut. but know I will have charge of a front line post some where. Arn't things going great in France?[3] Next fall will see the Germans smashed completely. And the Italians will anihilate the Austriens. Now Ivory I will give you a full list of the old master's titles and other stuff. Tenente Ernesto Hemingway: Proposto Al Medaglia D'Argento, (valore) proposto per Croce D'Guerra Ferito Da Prima linae D'Guerra. Promotzione for Merito D'Guerra. Translated that means that the old Jazz hound is a First Lieut, cited for the Silver valour medal, cited for the war cross, wounded in the first lines and promoted for merit.

Now aint he stuck up? He aint though, I hope. I've only got one ambition though, but then I better not tell it. Huh?

Thank everybody that asked about me and give 'em all my love. I know a wonderful american girl over here so I'm not a bit lonesome for any of the X ones. None of them have a prayer. Which reminds me of a good yarn.

A nigger recruit was talking to a nigger veteran. "Say, what does this going "over the top" mean Boss?"[4]

"It means just this nigger, just this, good mownin' Gawd!"

Not Bad eh? I'll bet you kids had a rare time while the parents were away, what?

Well be good and write me soon and don't break too many Jackies hearts! What do they do anyway besides go to dances?

So Long Kids,
Ernie.

Cohen, ALS; letterhead: AMERICAN RED CROSS / LA CROCE ROSSA AMERICANA / VIA MANZONI, 10 / MILANO; postmark: MILANO / CENTRO, 17–18 / 23·IX / 1918

On envelope verso EH wrote, "DA Tenente Ernest Hemingway / Croce Rossa Americana / Osepdale Milano / Italia 1."

1 One of Marcelline's suitors and a Yale undergraduate. She reported in her letter of 25 August 1918 that he was in Section 587 of the U.S. Army Ambulance Service (Sanford, 285). EH would meet Hutchins in Italy and report his impressions in a 23 November letter to Marcelline.

2 Degenerative disorder of the nervous system (also called *tabes dorsalis*), marked by an unsteady gait and commonly resulting from untreated syphilis infection.

3 Beginning in August, a series of Allied offensives along the Western Front in France had steadily driven back the German forces.

4 To "go over the top" was to leave the front-line trenches to attack the enemy. Casualties from this type of attack were high.

To Marcelline Hemingway, [26 September 1918]

Dear Ivory—;

We are here for the Day. It is of a Great Beauty. Above the clouds in sight of Switzerland—right next door. I am here on a permission at the Lakes. Fishing Bathing. I love you Kid.

Ernie.

JFK, A Postcard S; verso: Grand Hôtel Mottarone. Kulm (m. 1500); postmark: MOTTAR[ONE], [*date illegible*]

The conjectured postcard date is based on the close resemblance between this and the following postcard to his parents (clearly dated in EH's hand and legibly postmarked 26 September 1918). They are similar in content and written on identical picture postcards, bearing a color image of the Grand Hôtel at the summit of Mount Mottarone.

EH was on convalescent leave in the resort town of Stresa, northwest of Milan on Lago Maggiore—a setting that would play a significant role in Book 4 of *FTA* From the nearly 5,000-foot summit of Mount Mottarone, a day trip from Stresa by cog railway, EH would have had a panoramic view of the Swiss frontier to the north and west.

To Clarence Hemingway, 26 September [1918]

Sept. 26.

My Dear Pop.

We can see Switzerland from here. Convalescing with some awfully nice Italian People. Back to the front in about a month. Electrical treatments.[1]

Good Luck.

Tenente Ernesto Hemingway.

Croce Rossa Americana

IndU, A Postcard S; verso: Grand Hôtel Mottarone. Kulm (m. 1500); postmark: MOTTARONE, 26.9.[18]

"1918" is added in Clarence's hand following EH's date.

1 EH was receiving electrical treatments on his leg as part of his rehabilitation therapy in Milan. He would draw upon the experience in his 1927 story "In Another Country" (MWW).

To Hemingway Family, 29 September 1918

Sept 29 1918.

Dear Folks—;

I'm up here at Stresa a little resort on Lake Maggiore one of the most beautiful of the Italian Lakes. I have ten days leave from the hospital and am resting up here. After 4 more days here I must return to the Milan hospital for more electrical treatments for my leg.

This is a wonderful place. The hotel is about as big as the Chicago Beach on the South Side.[1]

In spite of the war it is very well filled with an awfully good bunch. There are several contessas or countesses and one the Contessa Grecca has taken a great fancy to the old master and calls me "dear boy" etc.

Also a Signor Bellia, of Torino one of the richest men in Italy is here with three beautiful daughters. He and mother Bellia have adopted me and call themselves my Italian mother and father. He is a very jolly old scout and looks kind of like Grandpa Bacon.[2] They and the daughters take me everywhere and don't allow me to spend a cent. They have invited me to spend

Christmas and my two weeks leave with them at Torino and I think I shall probably go. The girls are named Ceda, Deonisia and Bianca and want to be remembered to my sorelli Marcelline Ursula Sunny and Carol. They all ask questions about my sisters and my "piciolo frattellino" Leicester.[3]

The second night I was here the Old Count Grecco who will be 100 years old in March took charge of me and introduced me to about 150 people.[4] He is perfectly preserved, has never married, goes to bed at midnight and smokes and drinks champagne. He told me all about his dining with Maria Theresa the wife of Napoleon the 1st.[5] He has had love affairs with all the historical women of the last century it seems and yarned at length about all of them.

He took me under his wing and gave me a great send off.

I limp pretty badly but can row on the lake and sit around under the trees and listen to the music and go on trips up the mountain in the cog railway. We went up the Mottarone and saw Monte Rosa.[6] From the front garden of the hotel you can see Switzerland the mountains just a few Kilomets away.

Gee I'm afraid I wont be good for anything after this war! All I know now is war! Everything else seems like a dream. I speak Italian all Day long and write two or three letters a day in it. It really is awfully easy for me now just like English.

You see at first I only knew the Italian of the front—all the language of the trenches and camp. But being with a crowd like this and being three months in Milan with Italian officers I have learned "polite sassiety" Italian now. And can flirt and fish in Italian with great ease.

I know you all had a good time up north and I hope next September that I will be at home and we'll all be up north. Probably not though. But by next Christmas it will be all over and there wont be enough Germans left to wind the watch on the Rhine [7]

Love to you all and to Grandma and Grandpa and Aunt Grace and P.L. Storm & Family.[8]

Love.

Ernie.

IndU, ALS; letterhead: GRAND HOTEL ET DES / ILES BORROMÉES / LIGNE DU SIMPLON / STRESA / (Lac Majeur); postmark: STRESA / NOVARA, 29[·]9·18

1 On the shore of Lago Maggiore, the large and opulent Grand Hôtel et Des Iles Borromées dates from 1861. EH would use it as the scene of several chapters in Book 4 of *FTA*. The exclusive Chicago Beach Hotel, on the shore of Lake Michigan at East Hyde Park Boulevard (Fifty-first Street), opened in 1893 near the site of that year's Chicago World's Fair.

2 EH was befriended by Pier Vincenzo Bellia and his family, and they would remain in touch throughout EH's stay in Italy (Villard and Nagel, 249–50). In 1898, Clarence and Grace had purchased their shoreline property at Walloon Lake from Henry Bacon. The Bacon family farm was up the hill immediately behind Windemere. EH's sister Sunny later recalled that their parents encouraged them to call older family friends "Aunt" or "Uncle" and "Grandma" or "Grandpa," and "our farmer neighbor was Grandpa Bacon from the beginning" (M. Miller, 46).

3 *Sorelle*: sisters; *piccolo fratellino*: small younger brother (Italian).

4 Count Giuseppe Greppi (1819–1921), a prominent Italian diplomat and social figure, would be the model for the sage old Count Greffi in *FTA*. Michael Reynolds notes that although Carlos Baker misidentified the real-life count in *Life* (572–73) as Emanuele Greppi (1853–1931), he discovered his mistake and pointed this out to Reynolds (Michael S. Reynolds, *Hemingway's First War* [Princeton, New Jersey: Princeton University Press, 1976], 166–69). EH would later claim that he was "brought up politically by old Count Greppi" (31 July 1950 letter to Charles Scribner, PUL).

5 Marie Louise (1791–1847), daughter of Francis I of Austria and Maria Theresa of Naples– Sicily, became Empress of France with her marriage in 1810 to Napoleon I (after his divorce from Joséphine). She bore a son, the future Napoleon II, and later became Duchess of Parma. Greppi was appointed her diplomatic advisor in 1840, as noted in his obituary (*New York Times*, 10 May 1921).

6 At more than 15,000 feet, Monte Rosa, part of the Monte Rosa massif on the border between Italy and Switzerland, is the second highest mountain in the Alps.

7 "When We Wind Up the Watch on the Rhine" (1917) was among the patriotic WWI songs written by Canadian music publisher Gordon V. Thompson (1888–1965).

8 Pierre L. Storm and his family were fellow members of the Third Congregational Church in Oak Park.

To Hemingway Family, 18 October [1918]

October 18

Dear Folks,

Your letter of September 24 with the pictures came today and family I did admire to hear from you. And the pictures were awfully good, I guess everybody in Italy knows that I have a kid brother.[1] If you only realized how much we appreciate pictures, Pop you would send em often. Of yourselves and the kids and the place and the Bay. they are the greatest cheer producers of all, and everybody likes to see everybody elses pictures.

You Dad spoke about coming home.[2] I wouldnt come home till the war was ended if I could make fifteen thousand a year in the states[.] Nix, here is the place. All of usRed X men here were ordered not to register. It would be foolish for us to come home because the Red X is a necessary organization and they would just have to get more men from the states to keep it going. Besides we never came over here until we were all disqualified for military service you know. It would be criminal for me to come back to the states now. I was disqualified before I left the states because of my eye. I now have a bum leg and foot and there isnt an army in the world that would take me. But I can be of service over here [a]nd I will stay here just as long as I can hobble and there is a war to hobble to. And the ambulance is no slackers job. we lost one man killed and one wounded in the last two weeks.[3] And when you are holding down a front line canteen job, you know you have just the same chances as the other men in the trenches and so my conscience doesnt bother me about staying.

I would like to come home and see you all of course. But I cant until after the war is finished. And that isnt going to be such an awful length of time. There is nothing for you to worry about, because it has been fairly conclusively proved that I cant be bumped off. And wounds dont matter. I wouldnt mind being wounded again so much because I know just what it is like. And you can only suffer so much you know. And it does give you an awfully satisfactory feeling to be wounded, its getting beaten up in a good cause. there are no heroes in this war. We all offer our bodies and only a few are chosen, but it shouldnt reflect any special credit on those that are chosen. They are just the lucky ones. I am very proud and happy that mine was chosen, but it shouldnt give me any extra credit. Think of the thousands of other boys that offered. All the heroes are dead. And the real heroes are the parents. Dying is a very simple thing. I've looked at death, and really I know. If I should have died it would hve been very easy for me. Quite the easiest thing I ever did. But the people at home do not realize that. They suffer a thousand times more. When a mother brings a son into the world she must know that some day the son will die. And the mother of a son that has died for his country should be theproude[s]t womanin the world, and the happiest. And how much better to die in all the happy period of undisillusioned youth, to go out in a blaze of light, than to have your body worn out and old and illusions shattered.

So dear old family dont ever worry about me! It isnt bad to be wounded, I know because I've experienced it. And if I die, I'm lucky.

Does all that sound like the crazy wild kid you sent out to learn about the world a year ago? It is a great old world though and Ive always had a good time and the odds are all in favour of coming back to the old place. But I thought I'd tell you how I felt about it. Now I'll write you a nice cheerful bunky letter in about a week so dont get low over this one.

I love you all,

Ernie.

IndU, TLS; letterhead: AMERICAN RED CROSS / LA CROCE ROSSA AMERICANA / VIA MANZONI, 10 / MILANO

This letter was published in the *Oak Parker*, 16 November 1918, along with a photograph of EH in uniform riding in a motorcycle sidecar in front of Milan's Arco della Pace; clippings of both are preserved in his grandparents' scrapbook (JFK). In his letter to EH of 13 November, Clarence would write that he was delighted by EH's "wonderful letter of Oct. 18th" in which he expressed his "real thoughts and ideals." He added, "the foto of you in the side-car was superb," but wished EH had written more details, including who his "Pal" on the motorcycle might be (JFK).

1 In a letter to EH of 24 September, Clarence had enclosed a photo of Carol and Leicester in the field at Longfield Farm and one of Leicester on Wesley Dilworth's thrashing engine (JFK).
2 In a letter to EH of 22 September, Clarence wrote, "Don't hurry about getting around. It takes a long time to get yourself after being seriously wounded" (JFK).
3 Joseph M. King of ARC Ambulance Service Sections 1 and 5 was killed by an Austrian shell at Bassano on 29 September 1918 (Bakewell, 222).

To Hemingway Family, 1 November [1918]

Nov 1.

Dear Fambly—;

Back to bed again for a little while. Dads and Mothers letter of Oct 12 came today. Also ones from Bill Smith and Frances Coates. Frances doesn't mention being engaged and so I guess she thinks I dont know it.[1] Well I might as well tell you why I'm in bed again. Nothing bad. You see I got a leave of absense from the Hospital the day the offensive started and blew for the front.[2] Worked hard day and night where the worst mountain fighting was and then came down with jaundice. It makes you feel rotten and look

like an inhabitant of the flowery kingdom but is nothing to worry about.[3] I
had the satisfaction of being in the offensive any way and now I can rest up in
the hospital and get cured and finish the treatments on my leg. Then I'm
going to take my two weeks leave down "licenzia," in Italian, "permission" in
French down in the South of Italy Somewheres.[4] Give Rome and Naples
and Sicily and Florence the once over and get lots of pep for the next crack at
the front. Brummy and I were working together during this last offensive.
And the Italians have shown the world what they could do. They are the
bravest troops in the Allied Armies! The mountain country is almost
impassible to skilled Alpine climbers and yet they fight and conquer in [it]
and by the time you get this they'll have the Austrains all the way out of Italy.
Italy has been fighting her own war all along and deserves all the credit in the
world!

It is getting p[r]etty chilly here now and quite rainy. But I have my old
mackinaw and am going to get it fixed up with some very jazzy buttons. At
the front they had never seen a mackinaw before and I wore it all the time.
They figured it was some kind of a camouflage coat for sniping.

Well Lots of love to All,

Ernie.

IndU, ALS; letterhead: AMERICAN RED CROSS / LA CROCE ROSSA
AMERICANA / VIA MANZONI, 10 / MILANO

1 On 5 July, Marcelline had written to EH that his high school friend Frances Coates was
  engaged to Jack Grace, and on 25 August she reported that she had urged Frances to write to
  EH (Sanford, 279, 285).
2 On 24 October 1918, the Italian Army launched what would be its final offensive, to be
  known as the Battle of Vittorio Veneto. In a letter to EH of 26 October, Agnes wrote, "I got
  your letter of the 24th & I know now for sure that you have gone back to be in the thick of the
  action" (Villard and Nagel, 113). Austria-Hungary would initiate armistice negotiations on 1
  November, and hostilities on the Italian front would officially cease on 4 November, by
  which time 300,000 Austro-Hungarian troops had been taken prisoner.
3 Jaundice, a medical condition associated with liver impairment and caused by an excess of
  the pigment bilirubin in the blood, is marked by yellowing of the skin and the whites of the
  eyes. "Flowery kingdom," a term for China. The character Frederic Henry develops jaundice
  in *FTA* and likens it to being kicked in the scrotum.
4 The Italian word for "military leave" is *licenza*; EH's French is correct.

To Hemingway Family, 11 November [1918]

Hospital
Nov 11. 9 P.M.

Dearest Family—;

Well it's all over! And I guess everybody is plenty joyous. I would have liked to see the celebration in the States but the Italian Army showed the wonderful stuff it is made of in that last offensive.[1] They are great troops and I love them!

I have about a month and a half more mechanical treatments on my leg. The machines are especially designed for the remaking of us mutilatis and they do wonders. Nothing like it in the States. So I will finish my treatments and by their conclusion the surgeon informs me, my leg will be practically as good as ever. Of course I will never be able to run races or anything but it's a fine workmanlike leg. After my treatments are finished I've been invited by an Italian officer to take two weeks shooting and trout fishing in the province of Abruzzi. He wants me to spend Christmas and New Years at his country home and guarantees fine quail, pheasant and rabbit shooting. Abruzzi is very mountainous and is in the south of Italy and will be beautiful in December. There are also several good trout rivers and Nick claims the fishing is good. So I'll take my permission there.[2] After that I'll come back to Milan and out to the X front and when I'm not needed I'll come home. Maybe in February or March, but probably not until May.

I dont like the Atlantic in the Winter! Now I'm wearing the ribbons of two medals and my chief was in from the front today and congratulated me and said that my Silver Medal had all gone through and would arrive in about three days. He brought a telegram telling of my war cross or Croix D'Guerre or Croce D'Guerra which I picked up this final offensive. The cross and citation are out at the section now and I'll have 'em in a couple of days. He brought the ribbon which is blue and white.

The Distinctive Service Medal Ribbon is green white and Red and is pretty good looking. The Silver ribbon is

Blue with a Silver Star.

You wear the ribbons of the medals in a row above your left breast pocket and I'm getting quite a railway track. But it is kind of embarrasing because I have more than a lot of officers that have been in three and four years. But then "for what we are about to receive may the Lord make us truly thankful" as we used to hustle through before flying at the pan cakes. But seriously I did come very close to the big adventure in this last offensive and personally I feel like every body else about the end of the war. Gee but it was great though to end it with such a victory! And by Gosh I'm going fishing all next Summer and then make the fur fly in the fall. The living allowance for a 1st Lieut is 800 Lire a month or about $160. I don't receive that while in the hospital but $20 a week insurance after 1st four weeks. This has been held up and delayed and I havn't had a Chit for four months [*EH insertion:* Dead broke.] but the first payment of 500 lire was transferred through today. There is about 1500 more coming. So when it all comes through I will have the world by the tail with a down hill pull.

This payment I recieved today helped me pay off my debts and left a small surplus which will last until it all comes through. I don't believe that you can get any Christmas presents through to me. So if anything is coming from any of the out side family or anybody have them buy me Am. Ex. Money orders as presents. Then I can get the presents over here. It is useless to try and send a Xmas box the way things are going now and besides it is prohibited unless you have a ticket sent from me. And we being with the Italian army dont have the tickets. I'm enclosing some pictures taken while on my convalescence. I've been hearing from you folks pretty regularly and I'll try and get you a letter oftener. The jaundice is all cleared up and I'm pulling through my annual tonsilitis now so feel bokoo[3] rotten.

Pop can experiment on my one tonsil after I get home if he wants to. I'll save it for him. The other night feeling around in my leg I located a bullet but it is in a comfortable place and quite unobjectionable. To be exact, the back of my lap. So I'll save it so Pop can take one out. Keep on writing me at the same address and be very good all of you and eat lots on Thanksgiving for me and it is a 100 to 1 shot I'll see you this Spring. I want to see some of Italy and Austria now as I'll not be back for several years. Because about next fall I am going to commence the real war again. The war to make the world Safe for Ernie Hemingway and I plan to knock 'em for a loop and will be a busy man for several years. By that time my pension will have accumulated a couple of thousand lire and I'll bring my children over to view the battle fields.

> Well toodle-oo family,
> Lots of Love.
> Ernie.

IndU, ALS; letterhead: AMERICAN RED CROSS / LA CROCE ROSSA AMERICANA / VIA MANZONI, 10 / MILANO

1 WWI ended that morning with the signing near Compiègne, France, of an armistice between Germany and the Allies, to go into effect at the eleventh hour of the eleventh day of the eleventh month. Austria-Hungary and the Ottoman Empire had ceased fighting earlier. On 7 November the United Press Association had falsely reported the end of the war, touching off premature celebrations across the United States ("City Goes Wild with Joy / Supposed Armistice Deliriously Celebrated Here and in Other Cities," *New York Times*, 8 November 1918, 1).
2 Nick, probably Nick Neroni (or Nerone; sources vary), an Italian captain and decorated war hero who later would work at the Italian consulate in Chicago and become one of EH's companions there in 1920–1921 (Baker *Life*, 60, 77; Sanford, 185, 211; Villard and Nagel, 282). EH later would use Neroni's name and his experiences in some of his postwar fiction, including "The Woppian Way." In *FTA* the priest comes from the Abruzzi, the mountainous

region east of Rome, and Frederic Henry regrets not having spent his leave there, as the priest had invited him to do.
3 A play on *beaucoup*: much; plenty (French).

To Marcelline Hemingway, 11 November [1918]

Nov. 11.

Dear Ivory—;

Noted sister it is with a feeling of deep humiliation and esteam that I endite these few words to your sympathetic if not over ample ears. Your effulgence in Italian greeted me with all the joy of a man drowning in a sea of Schlitz (t.b.t.M.M.F.) on having a bottle of beer flung to him.[1] Oh why, beautiful and handsome creature, must you write me in Italian when sempre giorni[2] I eat, drink, sleep, drink some more and have my being in it? Also you are learning the lofty brow type of Italian while I speak the common or garden variety. However on my return, which may be expected within 3 or 4 or 5 or Six months, we will hie us to a spaghettery and try our respective linguistic abilities upon the chianti vender. Capito? Tesora mea lo piace le tanta! Il scuolo sta melia?[3]

In regard to the question you asked I will reply. Yes. She is a Cross Red Nurse. Further more I cannot state I am of a dumbness.[4] However, Frances Coates, A. DeV. and all others can take a back seat.

However from long experience with families etc., I don't talk about things anymore. So guess anything you want to. But I don't wear my heart on my

sleeve anymore. But all Oak Park damsels are going to have to show something. I'm off of them the whole bunch. I'm afraid to come home and
have 'em pulling this blooming 'live stuff. All the fair maidens that wouldn't
give a damn about me before you write what drag I have. Child, I'm going to
stay over here until my girl goes home and then I'll go up North and get
rested before I have to go to work in the fall. The Doc says that I'm all shot to
pieces, figuratively as well as literally. You see my internal arrangements
were all battered up and he says I wont be any good for a year. So I want to
Kill as much time as I can over here. If I was at home I'd either have to work
or live on the folks. And I cant work. I'm too shot up and my nerves are all
jagged.[5] So I'll stay over and then can rest up all summer and be fit for fall.
Cause I'm going to work like a dog for I want to make good. Got a lot of
reasons to. All kinds of secrets. Nothing to revere though. Nothing definite.
But I want to knock them for a loop anyway.

Well Kid, have a good time and take care of yourself and steer clear of the
Flu and I love you a lot Kid.[6] Also you wont know me. I'm about an 100 years
older and I'm not bashful and I'm all medalled up and shot up.

So So Long Ivory Old Kid,

Yours (partially) ever.

Ernie.

James Sanford, ALS; letterhead: AMERICAN RED CROSS / LA CROCE ROSSA
AMERICANA / VIA MANZONI, 10 / MILANO; postmark: U.S. ARMY M.P. / 702,
1918 / NOV 18 / 5 PM

The front of the envelope bears the inked stamp "PASSED BY BASE CENSOR." On the verso
EH wrote, "Ten Ernesto M. Hemingway / Croce Rossa Americana Ospedale / No. 40 Via
Cesare Cantu / Milano—Italia."

1 In her letter to EH of 2 October 1918, Marcelline wrote several sentences in Italian, which she
   was studying at the time (Sanford, 290–92). The slogan of the Joseph Schlitz Brewing
   Company, established in the late 1850s in Milwaukee, Wisconsin, was "The Beer That
   Made Milwaukee Famous."
2 EH likely intends "every day"; *sempre giorni* would translate literally as "always days."
3 EH's imperfect Italian translates roughly as "You understand? My dear, I like you so much! Is
   school going better?"
4 In her letter of 2 October, Marcelline sent her devotion to EH's "newest love" and said he had
   a talent for "picking winners." In a postscript she added, "Is it a Red † nurse? I won't tell!!"
   (Sanford, 292).

5 EH's handwriting is ambiguous; it is unclear whether he intended to write "jagged" or "jazzed."
6 Marcelline reported in her 2 October letter that a mutual acquaintance had died from the "spanish flue" and that "mobs of people have it in Oak Park" (Sanford, 292). The 1918 influenza pandemic, the worst in recorded history, caused an estimated 50 million deaths worldwide.

To Clarence Hemingway, 14 November [1918]

Nov. 14.

Dear Pop—;

Yours of October 21 and the check for 40 L. came through today. Thanks very much and it came in very handy. One months insurance of 509 Lire has come through.[1] But I used it nearly all paying off my debts. There are two more payments to come and may be a third it has to go from Rome to Paris and then Back to Rome and then to me and they are slower than Dinky Dyle. First payment only 3 months late. It will take about one more payment to put me entirely clear. Then the third will have me sitting pretty. The tonsolitis is still pretty bad but I'm over the jaundice and 3 or four more days and my throat will be all cleared up. Then I'll start on my treatments again at the big Italian hospital.[2] I walk over about a half mile every afternoon and the treatments take about an hour and a half and then I have a good massage. Grandma's big Illustrated Thanksgiving letter came today too. Give her and Grandpa my dear love and thank her very much. When my Doctor heard about my latest medal, the Croix D'Guerre, he kissed me tonsolitis and all. My "Italian Father", Papa Count Bellia, sent me a wonderful big box of choclate. I havn't been able to eat it but the nurses like it very much. About a ten lb. box must of cost 150 lire. He and the family are very good to me.

You see I didn't get any living allowance all during my time in hospital and all my convalescence because I was supposed to be getting insurance. But the insurance was so blasted slow that I had to borrow quite a little to live on.

But now that the first payment has come it will all be through soon and everything will be all O.K. You see I figure it this way Pop. I will have to work so hard when I start in for the next few years that it may be quite a time before I see Europe again. So now while I am here with the privilege of free railway travel, we can have an order of movement written to any place or places in Italy, and all the privileges accorded an officer and honored by the Italian gov't and people I ought to see as much of Italy as possible. Rome and Naples and Sicily etc. It wouldn't be fair if I didnt. And you'll be just as glad to see me in May or June as you would be in February.

So after I've finished the cure for my leg in a couple of months. And the Doc said today he was going to take my tonsils out after a while, why I'll have a look around Italy. Also that will be a nice trip to Abruzzi for Christmas and the Count Bellia wants me to spend a couple of weeks with them at Turino. He has an awful lot of dough and is a peach of an old scout. The whole family are great and they treat me just like a son or like a prodigal son!

I got the Oak Leaves of Aug 31st and Forest & Stream today.[3] Thanks. The Oak Leaves with my letter hasn't come through yet.[4]

Good luck Pop and I'm glad your doing so well,

> Much love.
>
> Ernie.

IndU, ALS; letterhead: AMERICAN RED CROSS / LA CROCE ROSSA AMERICANA / VIA MANZONI, 10 / MILANO

1 In his letter to EH of 21 October, Clarence said he would be sending an American Express money order for 40 lire and asked about EH's accident insurance (JFK).
2 EH received physical therapy at Milan's Ospedale Maggiore (Villard and Nagel, 219, 223).
3 *Forest and Stream* was published in New York 1873–1930, then purchased and absorbed by its competitor, *Field and Stream* (1896–).
5 EH's letter to his family of 18 August was published in the 5 October 1918 issue of *Oak Leaves*; he may have learned of the publication in an incoming letter that remains unlocated.

To Marcelline Hemingway, 23 November [1918]

> Nov. 23.

Dear Old Sister—;

Well Kid yesterday I got your letter and today I met your friend Bill Hutchins.[1] Bill is quite an estimable youth although slightly fussed at meeting the Old Master. We found him quite cold and chisly and took him up to the ho[s]pital and gave him one of our knitted sweaters and a pair of heavy sox. He is a very nice kid and has had hard luck and a bunch of mean jobs. He thinks a lot of you and especially as a correspondent. Don't marry him but be very nice to him because he likes you a lot. Maybe he loves you, I didn't ask him. He has a mustache that looks kind of discouraged. I approve of him. He will probably write you about me so you can see myself as ithers see me.

From your letter Kid you surely must be working. I never thought you were pulling the butterfly stuff— Don't worry. I only wish you could.[2]

Salute your Italian teacher for me.[3] Tell him your kid brother is tre volte ferite, decoratio due volte per valore ance promosso Tenente per merito di guerra and see what he says.[4] Tell him Ciaou for me. Pronounced <u>Chow</u>.

I'm sorry you are so strong for Sam Anderson. He seems an awful simp to my humble view. But Al Walker is a peach and you have lots of time.[5] You aren't more than 21 yet are you? I don't know what I've written you about my girl but really, Kid Ivory I love her very much. Also she loves me. In fact I love her more than anything or anybody in the world or the world its-self. And Kid I've got a lot clearer look a[t] the world and things than when I was at home. Really Ivory you wouldn't know me. I mean to look at or to talk to. You know those pictures we took at home before I left? Well showing them to Ag the other day she didn't recognize me in them. So that shows I've changed some.

Really Kid I'm immensely older. So when I say that I'm in love with Ag it doesn't mean that I have a case on her. It means that I love her. So believe me or not as you wish. Always I've wondered what it would be like to really meet the girl you will really love always and now I know. Furthermore she loves me—which is quite a miracle in it's self. So don't say anything to the folks because I'm confiding in you. ~~But~~ I'm not foolish and think I can get married now but when I do marry I know who I'm going to marry and if the family don't like it they can lump it and I never will come home. But don't say anything for I'm not going to get married for two years.

Oh Ivory but I love that girl. Now don't ever say I'm not confidential—for I've written you what I wouldn't write anybody.

Now Kid who in hell is giving all my letters out for publication? When I write home to the family I don't write to the Chicago Herald Examiner or anybody else—but to the family. Somebody has a lot of gall publishing them and it will look like I'm trying to pull hero stuff. Gee I was sore when I heard they were using my stuff in Oak Leaves.[6] Pop must have Mal di Testa.[7]

The wife is up at the front in the invaded district dispensing medication from an ambulance and is awfully lonesome. They are going to shut up the American Hospital here shortly and then I'll probably live at a hotel.[8] I have to continue with the mechanical treatments on my leg if it is ever to be any good. Two months more of that. Then In a couple of weeks I'll be blowing back to the States. Probably get in some time in February–March maybe sooner. Frances Bumstead wrote me a letter also Alfred Dick and Aunt Grace.[9] All were full of bull. Give my love to the family and anybody else I ought to.

And I still love you Ivory Old Jazz.

The W.K. Brother.

Antique Brutality.

Da Ten. means <u>from</u> Ten.

James Sanford, ALS; postmark: MILANO / CENTRO, 13–14 / 25 · XI / 1918

1 In her letter to EH of 24 October 1918, Marcelline wrote that she hoped he would see her friend Bill Hutchins and urged EH to confide in her about his "new girl" (Sanford, 293–96).

2 EH means "social butterfly"; in her 24 October letter, Marcelline had described her busy schedule of work, church, and school activities, which left little time for going to dances with "fascinating sailor boys" (Sanford, 294–95).

3 Marcelline had remarked in her letter, "My Italian professor Senore De Luca is a perfect dear" (Sanford, 294).

4 Three times wounded, decorated twice for valor, promoted Lieutenant for merit of war (in EH's inexact Italian).

5 Marcelline had written that "Sam" would soon be graduating from the Naval Aviation Officers School and that she hoped he would visit her en route to his assignment in Florida. She also reported that Al Walker was in France and eager to hear from EH (Sanford, 294–95).

6 In her 24 October letter, Marcelline reported, "Your letter telling about your wounding in detail, ending with 'Leave us keep the house fires burning' was printed in last night's Chicago 'Herald.'" The faculty at her school had pinned it to the bulletin board, and she was "the object of many congratulations" (Sanford, 293). The *Chicago Herald and Examiner* began publication in May 1918 with the merger of the *Chicago Herald* and the *Chicago Examiner*. EH's 18 August letter to the family was also published in *Oak Leaves* (5 October 1918).

7 Headache (Italian).

8 On 21 November, Agnes von Kurowsky had traveled to take up a new assignment in a field hospital at Treviso, near Padua. The American Red Cross Hospital in Milan was soon to

close. Bakewell reports, "after the armistice, all delegates were instructed to begin at once to make arrangements for bringing the work in their districts to a close. By the first of March 1919, the Red Cross had withdrawn from all its war-time activities" (203).

9 Frances Bumstead, a classmate of EH at OPRFHS; Alfred Dick, younger brother (then about twelve years old) of Marcelline's close friend Lucille Dick.

To Hemingway Family, [28 November 1918]

Thanksgiving night 10.30

Dear Folks—;

There was a very good dinner and we all ate turkey, pumpkin pie and [fruital ?] and trimmings downstairs tonight. I imagined the dinner you were having with all the folks at dinner and I sure would like to have been there. There certainly is good cause for Thanksgiving this year. Probably you are all wondering when I will get home and really I don't know. About 7 weeks more treatments are necessary if I'm to have a fairly good leg.

Then I have so many invitations to various parts of Italy that I'll maybe take a month to fill them and to see the country. The Bellias want me to stay a couple of weeks at Turino. And I've promised Nick to go shooting with him in Abruzzi and there is a chance to go pig sticking in Sardinia.

They have wild boars there and you ride them down with a spear on horse back. It is regarded as quelque[1] sport. Captain Gamble wants me to go to Madiera with him for two months.[2] It is tropical there and very cheap living and a wonderful place. He paints and thinks we could dodge the rotten weather there. The weather is foul here. Fog today worse than London and snow day before yesterday. In the south of Italy the weather is great though they say. My blame leg is worse than a barometer, it aches with every change in temperature and I can feel snow two days in advance. That's why I hate to think of a Chicago winter. By the last of Jan. I ought to have about 1200 or 1500 lire and can take a good trip on that. It's impossible to obtain sailings now for the States. Everybody held up.

A lot of Chicago fellows from my old section have left for home and they have all promised to come out and see you. Also Brummy will be going through town. So probably by the time you get this letter you will see some of them. They are Howell Jenkins, Fritz Spiegel, Jerry Flaherty and Lawry Barnett and they'll all be out to see you.[3] They're all good pals of mine and Jenks especially. They'll give you all the dope about me.

If I get a chance I'll go up into Trieste and Trento and I may be able to.[4] Most of my souvenirs were stolen but I still have some good ones. I'm sure to be in Milan for Christmas and would like to send you all Christmas presents but with the present state of the mails you'd be sure never to get them so I'll just try and bring somethings when I come.

How is everybody? I hear from you about every week or so and Oak Leaves come through every once in a while. The flu epidemic is finished here. Thousands died—but I didn't have it. All I've had is Jaundice, Tonsilitis and Vincents Angina.

My girl is up at the front now and so I'm very lonely here—only about 3 other human Americans in town and nothing to do. I go to the opera though at the Scala. Have seen Aida, Ghismonda, Mose, Barbiere Di Seville and Mephistophele with Toscanini conducting. Going to see D'Annunzio's La Nave soon. Wish they'd give Carmen and La Boheme or something interesting.[5] I know lots of the singers who hang around the American Bar. Real chocolat Frappes there.

I'm feeling fine now and my knee is a lot better—I can bend it quite a bit— The machines are very good.

Well Cheerio and I'll write next Thanksgiving,

So Long.
Ernie.

Uncle Ty writes and asks me to write a "nice original letter," to him. Wonder who the devil he thinks I crib my stuff from.[6]

IndU, ALS

At the top of the first page Clarence wrote, "November 28, 1918." The envelope is missing a postage stamp but bears two rubber stampings: one reads, "Capt. R. H. Post. / Am. Red. Cross.," and another indicates that the letter had been "PASSED BY / BASE CEN[SOR]."

1 Some (French).
2 Madeira is the largest of the Madeira Islands, a Portuguese archipelago in the Atlantic Ocean about 350 miles off the northwest coast of Africa. Between Christmas and New Year's, EH would visit Gamble in Taormina, Sicily, where Gamble had rented a house (Baker *Life*, 55–56).

3 Frederick Spiegel and Lawrence Barnett had been classmates at New Trier High School in Winnetka, Illinois, a northern suburb of Chicago. Along with Jenkins and Jerome Flaherty, they were fellow members of ARC Ambulance Service Section 4 in Italy (Baker *Life*, 38, 41).

4 Both the Adriatic seaport of Trieste and Trento, a city in the Adige River valley just south of the Dolomites, were part of the Austro-Hungarian Empire until they were ceded to Italy after the war.

5 Milan's La Scala (Teatro alla Scala), one of the world's premier opera houses, opened in 1778. EH refers to the operas *Aida*, by Giuseppe Verdi (1813–1901); *Ghismonda*, by Eugen d'Albert (1864–1932); *Mosè in Egitto* (*Moses in Egypt*) and *Il Barbiere di Siviglia* (*The Barber of Seville*), by Gioachino Rossini (1792–1868); *Mefistofele* (*Mephistopheles*), by Arrigo Boito (1842–1918); *Carmen*, by Georges Bizet (1838–1875); and *La Bohème*, by Giacomo Puccini (1858–1924). Arturo Toscanini (1867–1957), renowned Italian conductor. *La Nave* (*The Ship*), a tragic drama by Gabriele D'Annunzio (1863–1938).

6 In his letter of 18 September 1918, EH's uncle Alfred Tyler Hemingway wrote to EH that his letters had been "most interesting" and asked him to "please write us one of your best and most original letters as we should be happy to learn all about what you are going through and how you are coming along" (JFK).

To Hemingway Family, 11 December [1918]

December 11

Dear Folks—;

I've booked passage for January 4th via Genoa, Naples and out through Gibraltar. So maybe I'll see you before you get this letter. Don't know how long the boat takes but ought to be home by the middle or last of January.

Your last letters were those of November 12. I've just returned from a peach of a trip. Today is Wed. Saturday morning I left Milan and rode in motor trucks and Staff Cars up to Padua. Stopping over night at Verona. Its a 12 hour run on the train and I reached Padua Sunday aft. Then I blew out to Torreglio to visit some British officers at the artillery camp there. They gave me a wonderful time and I rode the Colonel's hunter Monday morning. I ride pretty well now and got along great. We took fences and ditches and everything. Then in the afternoon we took the Staff car a "Vauxhall" and Lieut. Hey and I went up to Treviso about 50 miles to see the girl.[1] She is in a field Hospital there. We picked up her and a Miss Smith a friend of Hey's and went all up over the old battle field. And walked across the suspension bridge and saw the old Austrian front line trenches and the mined houses of Nervessa by moonlight and searchlight.[2] It was a great trip. After we came back the four of us got a big midnight supper cooked ourselves at the hospital and then about 1 oclock Hey and I started back to Torreglio. I had a great time while I was staying with the British and they treated me royally. We had horses and I inspected the guns and had a good servant to do me. With the car we went all over the country. It's the 105th Siege Battery. Capt. Shepard who invited me up is a famous artist for Punch, you may have seen some of his stuff.[3] Hey is a Canadian and a quite famous engineer.

I'd like to stay over here and bum a while as I may not get another chance for a long while. But I really feel as though I ought to get back and see you all a spell and then get to work.

For a while I was going to go down to Madiera and the Canaries with Capt. Gamble but I realize that If I blow down there and bum I never will get home. This climate and this country get you and the Lord ordained differently for me and I was made to be one of those beastly writing chaps y'Know. You know I was born to enjoy life but the Lord neglected to have me born with money—so I've got to make it and the sooner the better.[4]

So So Long and Good Luck.

Ernie.

IndU, ALS

1 Torreglia, a town about 10 miles southwest of Padua. At the Anglo-American club in Milan in early November, EH had met Eric Edward "Chink" Dorman-Smith (1895–1969), an Irish officer in the British Army then in charge of British troops in Milan. According to his biographer, in December Dorman-Smith "took some overdue leave to accompany Hemingway on a 200-mile journey east to visit [Agnes von Kurowsky], and organised a visit on the way to a unit of the Royal Garrison Artillery, some of whose officers he had looked after in Milan. Here they were put up on a couple of army horses for a day out with the local Montello Hunt." Dorman-Smith chose not to continue on to Treviso with EH (Lavinia Greacen, *Chink: A Biography*, London: Macmillan, 1989, 53–59). During WWI the British company Vauxhall Motors supplied the British Army with its 25-horsepower D-type model for use as staff cars.

2 Nurse Gertrude Smith recently had been transferred to Treviso from a hospital for refugees in Rimini (Villard and Nagel, 280). The town of Nervesa della Battaglia, on the Piave River about 10 miles north of Treviso, was the scene of heavy fighting and much destruction during the Battle of the Piave in June 1918.

3 The 105th Siege Battery, part of the British Royal Garrison Artillery, served in France since May 1916 before being sent to Italy. Ernest Howard (Kipper) Shepard (1879–1976), English illustrator who while serving in WWI sent drawings to *Punch*, the satirical weekly founded in London in 1841. After the war he would join the magazine's regular staff and later earn fame for his illustrations of A. A. Milne's *Winnie the Pooh* (1926) and the 1931 edition of Kenneth Grahame's *The Wind in the Willows*.

4 EH was planning to return home so that he could start saving money for his marriage to Agnes. This situation is replicated in "A Very Short Story" (*IOT*).

To William B. Smith, Jr., [13 December 1918]

Dear Jazzer—;

You do what a man of your bowells would in keeping on with the old air work. And you have my mitt on it Avis. But don't do anything damn foolish! And really bird you can be careful.[1] So be it.

The woodsman sails for the States on the good ship Giussipe Verdi on January the 4th. And probably will grace Mr. Chicago's city the later part of next month. Where will you be then? Oh plane punisher Oh potential destroyer of Boche whereinell will you be then? And the officer and the nee Gob? An reunion must be staged.

But Hark ye. I cannot stall until summer and must resume the battle for buns shortly. The tussle for tarts or the melee for meringue. One might even say the combat for cakes. And have no 210 a month. Nothing but an honorable discharge and 250 lire a year for life from the King. And 250 lire optimistically translated is $50.[2]

And 50 ferrous homo's[3] are not much to live on.

But listen what kind of a girl I have: Lately I've been hitting it up—about 18 martinis a day. And 4 days ago I left the hospital and hopped camions 200 miles up to the Front A.W.O.L. to visit some pals. Ossifers in the R.G.A. British outside of Padova.[4] Their batteries are en repose. They gave me a wonderful time and we used the staff car and I rode to hounds on the Colonels charger. Leg and all.

But Bill to continue. We went in the Staff Car up to Treviso where the Missus is in a Field Hospital. She had heard about my hitting the alcohol and did she lecture me? She did not.

She said, "Kid we're going to be partners. So if you are going to drink I am too. Just the same amount." And she'd gotten some damn whiskey and poured some of the raw stuff out and she'd never had a drink of anything before except wine and I know what she thinks of booze. And William that brought me up shortly. Bill this is some girl and I thank God I got crucked so I met her. Damn it I really honestly can't see what the devil she can see in the brutal Stein but by some very lucky astigmatism she loves me Bill. So I'm going to hit the States and Start working for the Firm. Ag says we can have a wonderful time being poor together and having been poor alone for some years and always more or less happy I think it can be managed.

So now all I have to do is hit the minimum living wage for two and lay up enough for six weeks or so up North and call on you for service as a best man. Why man I've only got about 50 more years to live and I don't want to waste any of them and every minute that I'm away from that Kid is wasted.

Now try and keep your finger off the trigger cause you may be in the same fix yourself sometime.

PUL, ALS; letterhead: BRITISH-AMERICAN CLUB, / 3 VIA MORONE, / MILAN; postmark: MILANO / PARTENZA, 21–22 / 13·X11 / 1918

1 After graduating from the University of Missouri in June 1918, Smith enlisted in the Marine Aviation Detachment for ground training at the Massachusetts Institute of Technology; he was discharged in November after the Armistice (*SL*, 20). EH is responding to Smith's letter from Boston of 27 October in which Smith laments that it would be six more weeks "until I take to the air" and adds, "probably the war'll end before I see service" (JFK). Avis is Latin for "bird," one of EH and Bill Smith's mutual nicknames.
2 It is unclear whether EH actually received a monetary award for his war service in Italy, and it would be some time before his silver medal was officially awarded. It was issued by the King of Italy in a decree dated 4 January 1920, but not formally presented to him until November 1921, when General Armando Vittorio Diaz visited Chicago. Marcelline recalled, "Ernie's medal carried with it a pension of fifty lira a year for life. It also made him, the General said, 'an honorary cousin of the King'" (Sanford, 211). Although the *Chicago Daily Tribune* of 20 November 1921 reported that Diaz would decorate EH at a banquet that evening ("Chicago Greets Italy's Hero as Her Own Today"), a small article in the 26 November *Oak Leaves* noted that the ceremony for decorating EH had been omitted because the general's program was so crowded (Reynolds *YH*, 257).
3 EH's Latin rendition of "iron men," U.S. slang for dollars.
4 "A.W.O.L.," absent without leave. "R.G.A.," Royal Garrison Artillery.

To William D. Horne, Jr., 13 December [1918]

December 13.

Caro Guililmus[1]—;

Your screed emitted before leaving for the briny was gratefully received.[2] Deeply did I sorrow [at] missing you but twas for [*hole in MS*] as that last night had battled with the Demon after a six weeks lay off and a liver weakened by jaundice and was overthrown. We offer no alibi's.

The Geusippy Verdy sailing for the alleged United States will carry what remains of the shattered frame of the old master toward his native heath. Exodus to take place January 6 from Naples.[3] How is all in them States William. [*hole in MS*] What of [*illegible*] what means [*hole in MS*]? Did the returning hero laden [*hole in MS*] Boche rifles and encumbered by Croces Di Guarixes have the proper effect? I hope for the non plush ultra.[4]

Last Saturday I scribbled a note to the Miss G.S. De Long[5] that I was leaving for a few days and pulled out of Milan.

Camions were hopped as far as Verona where a wop staff car was commandeered and the Old Master entered Padua triumphantly. Repairing to Terreglio about 30 kilos [*illegible*] we stopped with a British gunnery mess. The late John Walker[6] [*hole in MS*] non refillable was present [*hole in MS*] on the following morning I rode the colonel's hunter quite successfully in spite of a hangover and was well up during the run. In fact my nag cast mud quite effectively on 2 majors and any amount of Subs.

But Gawd was I stiff the next day! However Lieut Hey and I retained a staff car and pilgrimaged to the Hospital outside of Treviso where Ag is. A moonlight tour of the old Battlefield was staged. [*illegible*] feed afterwards. [*illegible*] Treviglio before Breakfast.

Ag was a trifle surprised to see me but bore it well. Hey is enamored of a Miss Smith she was present. We crossed the river on the pontoon bridge at Nervesa. Very effective.

I have conveyed your sentiments to the Missus.[7] She says that she will admire to have the W. K. Horne [grace the] Sunday supper table whenever [*illegible*] we will [*illegible*] for sure we [*illegible*] Ag in the course of [*illegible*] she would be [*illegible*] to marry me on $20 a [*illegible*] So startling events may come to [*illegible*].

Bill I have ever poured out to you—kidding to the side, I mean you know me pretty well. So pass judgement on this. Oh Hell no.

I'll tell you some other time. I was going on to give some instances of my Tedesci named wifes[8] [*illegible*]. But you know her—so why bother? [*illegible*] my short life I've [*illegible*] with some girl [*illegible*]. But never [*illegible*] [would] even think of [*illegible*] you to think that [*illegible*] any such thing and that [*illegible*] when my brow extended to the back of my neck I'd settle down with someone employed by Mr. Ziegfeld.[9]

Then thank God I got shot and you know the rest. That is you don't know the rest and never will but you know the result. [*illegible*] hadnt [*illegible*] bird that [built] that [*illegible*] over across the Piave. For [*illegible*] I give him the [yews ?] now with big leaves on the [side ?] of the sulphur bath.

And so I'm coming home and start the battle for buns or the skirmish for stew or the or the tussle for turnovers as soon as I can. Have to ring the family first. They love me dearly now I've been crocked and, reflects much credit [*illegible*] you know. But I'll not tarry long but hasten to send news [*illegible*] pound a vicious typewriter [*illegible*] the [*illegible*] which in spite of loves [young ?] [*illegible*] just twice that of one. And [*illegible*] 3,000 percent.

But Ag says we can have a wonderful time being poor together and we may have about 60 years at the most so want to start in as soon as possible. I'd be poor if I had 1,000,000 a year. Poverty's only comparative anyway.

Bill I am undoubtedly the most lucky bum in the world. The temptation comes to rave—but I wont.

If you know when the G. Verdi comes in sailing from here the 6th I may see you. I would admire to do so. If it can't be arranged why write me at

600 N. Kenilworth Avenue.

OAK PARK.

Illinois

All the damn luck in the world,

Hemingstein

Newberry, ALS; letterhead: BRITISH-AMERICAN CLUB, 3 VIA MORONE, MILAN.; postmark: 3 MILANO / PARTENZA, 21–22 / 15.XII / 1918

Letter has extensive water and mold damage and a large hole in the center of the main fold.

1 Dear William (Latin).

2 Horne had written to EH from Paris on 26 November 1918, lamenting that he had had to leave Milan on short notice before seeing EH again and reporting that he would sail for the United States on *La Lorraine* on 2 December (JFK).

3 EH would depart from Europe on the *Giuseppe Verdi* on 4 January.

4 *Non plus ultra*: perfection, the highest point or culmination (Latin).

5 Katherine C. DeLong, former Superintendent at the Bellevue Hospital School of Nursing in New York, was in charge of the American Red Cross Hospital in Milan. She was known among the patients as "Gumshoe Casey"; G. S. may be EH's abbreviation for "Gum Shoe." She would serve as a prototype for the authoritarian Miss Van Campen in *FTA*.

6 Johnny Walker, a popular brand of Scotch whisky marketed internationally since the 1860s.

7 In his 26 November letter, Horne asked EH to congratulate Ag for him "when it is safe to do so," and added, "You lucky stiff!"

8 *Tedeschi*: German (Italian), a reference to Agnes's family name. Her father, Paul Moritz Julius von Kurowsky, was a naturalized U.S. citizen of Polish, Russian, and German ancestry (Baker *Life*, 572).

9 Chicago-born theatrical producer Florenz Ziegfeld (1867–1932), whose spectacular stage shows, the *Ziegfeld Follies*, featured scantily clad women in musical and dance numbers.

To William D. Horne, Jr., [3 February 1919]

Dear Bill—;

It's hell—Oh gosh but it's hell. For gosh sake at once give me Jenk's address so I can relieve it. Barney is at Wisconsin U. Jerry can't be located. Spiegel is working and I cant find Jenks.[1] Jenks can save me—perhaps. Or how about yourself? Any chance of you coming out? Try and convalesce with 60,000,000,000 females mostly single and elderly and 80,000,000,000,000 males—mostly fat and exempt crying out for second hand thrills to be got from the front. These people that want to be vicariously horrified have captured the sheep of the EX Mountaineer. God but I'm sick of this country.

Ag writes from Toro Di Mosta beyond San Dona-Piave that she and Cavie are going to be there all winter.[2] I gave her your love. Bill I'm so darn lonesome for her I dont know what to do. All Chicago femmes look like a shot of Karo Corn Syrup compared to '83 Burgundy.[3]

I'll send you that picture as soon as I get stamps. The family raised much sentimental hell over my advent. In the 2 1/2 years since I'd lamped them much has changed. Dad now chuckles at my tales of Cognac and Asti. Indeed much has changed. I miss the old battles. Father has lost his fighting face. What hath Mars wrought?[4] Edgar Rice Burroughs who purpetrated

Tarzan + the Apes is trying to induce me to write a book.[5] If I do I'll not send you one—you'll have to buy it—cause the sales will need it.

I'll write more shortly and Bill I want to thank you for everything you done for me—

Newberry, ALS; letterhead: CLARENCE E. HEMINGWAY, M.D. / 600 KENILWORTH AVENUE. / CORNER IOWA STREET / OAK PARK, ILL.; postmark: OAK PARK / ILL., FEB 3 / 10PM / 1919

1 Howell Jenkins, Lawrence Barnett, Jerome Flaherty, and Frederick Spiegel.
2 ARC nurse Loretta Cavanaugh was nicknamed "Sis Cavie." In a letter of 21 December 1918, Agnes told EH that Cavie wanted her to go to "some forlorn little ruined place where she is setting up a little Hosp. & dispensary." Agnes joined her at the hospital in Torre di Mosto on 10 January; by 1 March she would be left in charge when Cavie moved on to Rome (Villard and Nagel, 146, 162, 281).
3 EH likens Chicago women to a common commercial sweetener (introduced in 1902 and heavily advertised to U.S. homemakers), as compared with Agnes, who is like a rare and costly vintage French wine.
4 Cognac, a fine brandy named for its town of origin in western France; Asti Spumante, an Italian sparkling wine. Mars, the Roman god of war.
5 Burroughs, American science-fiction and adventure writer (1875–1950), lived in Oak Park from May 1914 through January 1919, when the family moved to Los Angeles to be near the center of the motion picture industry. His book *Tarzan of the Apes* was published in 1914 (Chicago: A. C. McClurg); the silent film version premiered in New York in 1918 amid much fanfare and quickly became one of the first films ever to gross more than a million dollars.

To James Gamble, 3 March [1919]

March 3rd

Dear Old Chieftain,[1]

Gee you know I'd have written you before. In my day book for over a month you could open it up and find "Write Jim Gamble", scribbled[.] Every minute of every day I kick myself for not being at Taormina with you. It makes me so damned homesick for Italy and whenever I think that I might be there and with you. Chief, honest I can't write about it. When I think of old Taormina by moonlight and you and me, a little illuminated some times, but always just pleasantly so, strolling through that great old place and the moon path on the sea and Aetna fuming away and the black shadows and the moonlight cutting down the stairway back of the villa. Oh Jim it makes me so damn sick to be there, I go over to the camouflaged book case in my room and pour out a very stiff tall one and add the conventional amount of aqua and set it by my typewriter, slang for mill, battered key board etc., and then I look at it a while and think of us sitting in front of the fire after one of munge uova's dinners and I drink to you Chief.[2] I drink to you.

Don't for the Lord's sake come to this country as long as you can help it. That is from one who knoweth. I'm patriotic and willing to die for this great and glorious nation. But I hate like the deuce to live in it.

The leg is pretty bum, the family are fine, and it was great to see them again. They didn't recognize me by the way when I piled off the train. Had a stormy but pleasant trip home. Three great days at Gib. I borrowed some mufti from a British Officer and went over into Spain.[3] The usual hectic time in New York for a few days. Saw Bill Horne, who thinks a lot of you. They've tried to make a hero out of me here. But you know and I know that all the real heroes are dead. If I had been a really game guy I would have gotten myself killed off. And I know it, so it doesn't affect the size of the cranium I hope.[4] But the male youth of this village have either been in the Naval Reserve Force, the Student Army Training Corps or the Q.M.C.[5] All except AL Winslow and myself and a few birds of our old gang who got themselves killed with the Marines.

I've been doing the honors, but Al gets home next week and he brought down several boche and left an arm in a German Field Dressing station so I have announced my retirement from the public eye on his arrival.[6]

I've written some darn good things Jim. That is good for me. And am starting a campaign against your Philedelphia Journal the Sat. Eve. Post. I sent them the first story Monday last. Havn't written the wistaria yarn yet. And havent heard any thing yet of course. Tomorrow another one starts toward them. I'm going to send 'em so many and such good ones, no I havn't really got the big head, that they're going to have to buy them in self defence. Rea[l]ly Chief, I'm so homesick for Italy that when I write about it, it has that something that you only get in a love letter. A love letter, not a mash note.

One of the Kid sisters just brought up a plate of lobster salad sandwiches, the inference being that fish is brain food I guess. But they need Beer. Did you ever taste the beer at that little Birraria down near the rail way station at Schio? And we might be in Madiera now. Oh Damn it.[7]

Jenks is in town and we foregather pretty often. He sends you his regards as does Art Newburn. The Girl is still up at a God forsaken joint called Torre Di Mosta beyond the Piave. Straight up twenty kilomets from San Dona[.] She is running a visiting nurse field hospital, and kindergarten and between times acting as mayor of the town. She sent you the colours I guess tho she didn't mention it. Did you get them and the changed American Money? I felt bad about not attending to that [m]yself but I was tearing around so when they shifted the sailing of the Verdi that I had to turn it over to her. Did everything come through all right. If you ever get up in the Venezia I'd like to have you look her up. Agnes von Kurowsky, and the pass word is Hemingstein. Had a note from Harry Knapp the other day. He is looking around for something to do. Says Business is very unsettled. His arm is O.K. The cold weather plays hell with my leg and there has been some inflamation of the joint. All clear now though but Dad says to lay off of active work until the middle of the summer anyway.

Coming home with high resolves to start in at once on the battle for buns and expecting to find all finances very low I'm greeted with this from the Dad, "Never better. Everything going great. Why didn't you ask me for some kale and stay over if you wanted to!" That was the last straw. I had everything sized up wrong. And the Dear Uncle, missing believed killed, turns up alive and well in England and beats me home by a week. Damn him[8]

Dad was talking today about sending me down to the gulf for a while, the race meet closes tomorrow at New Orleans though and I'm working pretty hard with the typewriter so I think I'll stall here for a while. Maybe I'll go down the middle or last of March.

The Girl doesn't know when she will be coming home. I8m saving money. If you can imagine it. I can't. $172 and a fifty buck Liberty Bond in the Bank already. That's what comes from staying away from the ponies and having ones friends over seas.[9] Maybe she won't like me now I've reformed, but then I'm not very seriously reformed.

If you'r still at Taormina, give my regards to Madame Bartlett and the Maggiore and my salutions to the Duke of Bronte. Who, with the exception of your self is the only real guy in Sicily. Woods and Kitsen are perhaps good workmen but I should judge very fatiguing to Pal around with?[10] Is there anything over here I can send to you? Have you Tobacco? Sure you have Macedonias.[11] Wish I had. Bring some home with you! No, Do you need anything Jim? Really?

You Know I wish I were with you,

Knox, TLS with autograph postscript; postmark: OAK PARK / ILL., MAR 4 / 3:30PM / 1919

EH addressed the envelope to "CAPT. JAMES GAMBLE / CROCE ROSSA AMERICANA / TAORMINA / SICILIA" with the note, "PLEASE FORWARD." It was forwarded from Taormina to Gamble c/o H. C. Voorhes, Wellington Hotel, Elkins Park, Pa. U.S.A. On envelope verso a note in Italian (not in EH's hand and presumably intended for Gamble) translates as, "I send you warm greetings from all your friends in Taormina and a hug from your friend Giuseppe Cicala at the Post Office." The "4th estate," mentioned in EH's handwritten post-script, refers to the press.

1 Gamble was chief of the ARC Rolling Canteen Service when EH volunteered for emergency canteen service on the Piave River front in June 1918.

2 *Munge uova* is apparently an in-joke allusion to Gamble's cook, but the Italian is nonsensical. *Munge* is a form of the verb "to milk," and *uova* means "eggs."

3 Gibraltar, British dependency on the southern tip of the Iberian peninsula near the Spanish port city of Algeciras; strategically located at the entrance to the Mediterranean, Gibraltar was ceded by Spain to Great Britain in the 1713 Treaty of Utrecht.

4 The 1 February 1919 *Oak Parker* featured a story about EH's return from Italy, along with a photograph of him in uniform (clipping at PSU; Roselle Dean, "First Lieutenant Hemingway Comes Back Riddled with Bullets and Decorated with Two Medals," 12). On 24 February, EH, along with a French and an Italian officer, received a standing ovation after speaking to Oak Park's Nineteenth Century Club, as reported in both local newspapers; clippings of the articles are preserved in EH's grandparents' scrapbook at JFK ("Beware Propaganda: Three Lieutenants at Nineteenth Century Club Warn as to German Whispers—Friends of America," *Oak Leaves*, 1 March 1919; Roselle Dean, "France, Italy and America Well Represented at Nineteenth Century Club Monday," *Oak Parker*, undated clipping).

5 The Naval Reserve Force was created by Congress in 1915 so that the national government could call up reserve personnel to support the U.S. Navy's active-duty forces in case of war. The Student Army Training Corps program was enacted by the U.S. War Department in April 1918 to provide men with military training in addition to regular academic work at colleges and universities nationwide; it was demobilized when the war ended. During WWI, the U.S. Army's Quartermaster Corps provided battlefield support services and supplies.

6 Lieutenant Alan F. Winslow (1896–1933) of River Forest, Illinois, was decorated in April 1918 as the first American aviator to bring down a German plane in WWI. That summer he lost an arm when his airplane was shot down behind enemy lines, and he was taken prisoner by the Germans; for a time he was reported missing and presumed dead. The *Chicago Daily Tribune* closely covered the war hero's return ("Alan Winslow Back in the U.S. Wearing Honors / Chicago Flyer Returns After Period in Enemy Prison Camp," 1 March 1919, 7), and Winslow's portrait in uniform would fill the front page of *Oak Leaves* on 8 March 1919. By mid-March, both Winslow and EH would speak about their war experiences to an assembly of students at OPRFHS; the *Oak Parker* account notes that the audiences for "both warriors ... made the four walls echo with their cheers" ("From Italian Front, High School Student Body Hears Story of the Ardenti and of Fighting on the Piave," 22 March 1919, 54; PSU).

7 The stories EH mentions submitting remain unidentified; nothing he wrote would ever appear in the *Saturday Evening Post*. Published in Gamble's native Philadelphia, the magazine originated as Benjamin Franklin's *Pennsylvania Gazette* in 1728 and became known as the *Saturday Evening Post* in 1821. The "wistaria yarn" likely found its way into the story EH would call "The Woppian Way," in which the protagonist, Nick Neroni, recalls his wartime experiences, including drinking beer in a garden-like trattoria and smelling "those big purple flowers that mat over the white walls and just ooze perfume into the night" (Item 843, JFK; quoted in Zvonimir Radeljković, "Initial Europe: 1918 as a Shaping Element in Hemingway's Weltanschauung," *College Literature* 7, no. 3 [Fall 1980]: 306). Baker reports that during their first weeks in Italy, EH and fellow ambulance drivers had enjoyed "occasional evenings of beer drinking ... under a spreading wistaria bush in one of the back streets of Schio" (*Life*, 42). *Birreria*: beer-house (Italian).

8 The bulletin of Oak Park's First Congregational Church had reported that Grace's brother, Leicester Hall, was missing since 15 September (PSU; n.d.), and in a letter of 13 November 1918, Clarence told EH that his uncle might have been taken prisoner by the Germans (JFK). Just a few weeks later, Clarence was able to report not only that Uncle Leicester was "alive and well," but also that he had arrived in New York on the *S.S. Lapland* (letters to EH, 4 and 25 December 1918; JFK).

9 Once he had sufficiently recuperated, EH and Agnes, in the company of friends, enjoyed attending the horse races at the San Siro track near Milan, as she recorded in her diary (Villard and Nagel, 78–87). EH later would draw from these experiences in *FTA*.

10 According to Griffin, during EH's visit with Gamble in Taormina, they kept company with "Colonel Bartlett, a short, fat comrade with a walrus mustache Jim had known in Florence and who had also served on the Piave, 'Bartie's' pretty wife Louise, two English artists, Woods and Kisten, [and] a charming, generous aristocrat introduced as the 'Duke of Bronte'" (100). Among American Red Cross civil personnel in Italy, Bakewell lists Edward O. Bartlett, assistant to the director (and commissioner from 1 April 1919), and Mrs. Louise C. Bartlett, a social worker in Florence and Taormina, October 1918–March 1919 (227).

11 Macedonia cigarettes, made from Turkish tobacco, were among the brands distributed under Italy's state monopoly of tobacco sales.

To William D. Horne, Jr., [5 March 1919]

Egregrio Amicissimo,[1]

Par Baccho! Sporca Madonna![2] My heart within me leaps toward you to offer the congratulations. But why Oh, Carissimo, did you endite the great news in Wop? Being a little lit at the receipt of the fatal message I puzzled long. Your sentence structure, but then what is syntax to a man in your condition. But Bill I am Glad! Will you when it is safe offer my congratulations. And also Bill give me, in the lingua Anghilterrese, more details.[3] Are you rich? Or Happy?

I sure am glad though Bill. But then when guys knows guys like us guys do, why guys don't have to say much. Do they?

Now in regard to the cape. Ag's adress is Agnes von Kurowsky, Croce Rossa Americana, Padova, Italia—Please Forward. According to late advices from her, a certain small and too adipose Tenente of Artigleria is making an awful bid for her hand and fortune.[4] He is desperate. The securing of a cape through him should be facility its self. I would suggest your writing to her. I know that she will do it for you if she can.

Brother Jenks and I foregather constantly and are going under that good slogan "Bone Dry Forever—Drink Now For The Rest Of Your Life!" We are drinking.[5] Any former record that I might of enjoyed as an ultimate consumer have been supassed. The Chicago Wop Colony have given two great parties for us and from the last one I salvaged enough bottled goods to stock my camouflaged book case for years to come.[6]

(My) Ag does not know when she is coming home. She doesn't want to come home at all. I can't blame her cause I didn't either. But either one has to cross the ocean. I can't cross and have anything when I hit the other side. So I guess it will end i[n] the little C. around the C. You have first call as witness, best man, or whatever corresponds to best man at the Little Church. When I don't know. Eventually Why Not now doesn't apply. Bill I am writing. Honest to God writing. I wish you were here to give me your opinion on the stuff.

But one story made Brother Jenks cry, really, and he was cold sober. Maybe that was what was the matter. Really tho I'm writing stuff that I had no Idea I could write. I8m going to land in the Post. I'll bet you even money. That goes. Anything up to five bucks. Now when a hardened follower of the selling platers lays wagers upon himself, beware. The Stuff is Good. I almost wrote Goo. But it is. Good not Goo.

Saw Ed Dougherty and gave him your regards.[7] He retorted in kind. He was at the wop party and was quite stewed. Oh Bill it was quelque occasion. The old leg is giving me a lot of bother and hurts like hell in this weather. But I like it cause the pain reminds me of Ag.

So fair thou art—etc. [8] I'm still as much in love as ever Bill. Hope Ag stays that way. 'Cause if she shouldn't life wouldn't be worth living. Where are you going to live when you are married and more details on your Ag are eranestly desired by your humble and Ob't, etc.

Very have like the Buffalo once covered all Western Plains.

[*Typed on verso:*]
Any Chance of your getting out thus way?

Newberry, TLS with autograph postscript; postmark: OAK PARK / ILL., MAR 5 / 10 PM / 1919

1 Literally, "most esteemed friend" (a comical juxtaposition of formal and informal tones in Italian, comparable in English to "most esteemed pal").
2 *Per Bacco*: by Bacchus (Roman god of drink). *Sporca Madonna*, literally "dirty Madonna," indicates that EH had learned to curse fluently and idiomatically in Italian.
3 In his letter to EH of 23 February 1919, written entirely in Italian, Horne confided that he was in love. He wanted to give his girlfriend an Italian officer's cape and asked EH if Agnes might be able to buy one and bring it when she returned to the United States in the spring (JFK). *Carissimo*: dearest. *Lingua Anghilterrese*: in EH's inventive Italian, "English language" (correctly, it would be *lingua inglese*; *Inghilterra* means "England").
4 *Tenente di Artigleria*: Lieutenant of Artillery (Italian). In a letter to EH of 3 February 1919, Agnes had written, "The little tenente I spoke of before, is giving me a desperate rush—now don't get excited" (Villard and Nagel, 159). Likely he was Tenente Domenico Caracciolo (1891–1970), for whom Agnes would end her relationship with EH in March. In her letter of 21 January, she had reported having a "devoted admirer" named Domenico, but described him as "aged 14" (Villard and Nagel, 157).
5 On 16 January 1919 the U.S. Congress ratified the Eighteenth Amendment to the Constitution, prohibiting the "manufacture, sale, or transportation of intoxicating liquors,"

to go into effect a year from that date. In the meantime, under the War Prohibition Act passed by Congress on 21 November 1918, nationwide prohibition was mandated to take effect even earlier, on 1 July 1919. In the interval before either measure took effect, one of the largest liquor manufacturers in the United States coined the slogan, "Bone Dry Forever: Stock Up Now for the Rest of Your Life" (Ernest W. Young, *The Wilson Administration and the Great War* [Boston: R. G. Badger, 1922], 22). In October 1919, over President Wilson's veto, Congress would pass the Volstead Act to enact the amendment, and in December, the Supreme Court would uphold the constitutionality of the wartime law. Prohibition would be instituted in January 1920 and remain in effect until the amendment was repealed in 1933.

6 In EH's honor, a group of Italian-Americans from Chicago organized large, lively parties at the Hemingways' Oak Park home on two different Sundays, the first on 16 February 1919. After the second party lasted for more than twelve hours, Clarence, disapproving of the raucousness and free-flowing drink, insisted there be no more (Sanford, 185–87; Baker *Life*, 58).

7 Edward R. Dougherty served in ARC Ambulance Service Section 5 (Bakewell, 224).

8 Although the phrase appears in a number of literary works, EH most likely is alluding to the second stanza of "A Red, Red Rose" by Scottish poet Robert Burns (1759–1796): "So fair thou art, my bonie lass, / So deep in love am I: / And I will luve thee still, my dear, / Till a' the seas gang dry."

To William D. Horne, Jr., 30 March [1919]

Thirtieth of March

Caro Amico,[1]

It is kind of hard to write it Bill. Especially since I've just heard from you about how happy you are. So I'll put it off a bit. I can't write it honest to Gawd. It has hit me so sudden. So I'll tell you everything I know first.

Pease was in town.[2] Or maybe it should be Peas were in town. Jenks saw him. Spiegel is going strong. Jenks is still bartering securities. I'm—but I'll write it later. I havn't the guts to now.

Oh yes a letter came from Yak written from Fort Worth.[3] Think what the Bird is doing there? You couldn'T but after you think of Yak it becomes possible. He went to war at Fifty five or so. But that is nothing.

He is in Ft. Worth getting a divorce from Mrs. Yak! Can you feature it? He also bemoans the approaching aridity of the nation. He has been married twenty four years accordig to his own testimony. What can you make of that My Dear Watson if anything.[4]

Now having failed miserably at being facetious I'll tell you the sad truth which I have been suspecting for some time since I've been back and which culminated with a letter from Ag this morning.[5]

She doesn't love me Bill. She takes it all back. A "mistake" one of those little mistakes you know. Oh Bill I can't kid about it and I can't be bitter because I'm just smashed by it. And the devil of it is that it wouldn't have happened if I hadn't left Italy. For Christ's sake never leave your girl until you marry her. I know you cant "Learn about wimmen from me"[6] just as I can't learn from any one else. But you, meaning the world in general, teach a girl—no I wont put it that way, that is you make love to a girl and then you go away. She needs somebody to make love to her. If the right person turns up you're out of luck. That's the way it goes. You won't believe me just as I wouldn't.

But Bill I've loved Ag. She's been my ideal and Bill I forgot all about religion and everything else—because I had Ag to worship. Well the crash of smashing ideals was never merry music to any ones ears. But she doesn't love me now Bill and she is going to marry some one, name not given, whom she has met since. Marry him very soon and she hopes that after I have forgiven her I will start and have a wonderful career and everything.

But Bill I don't want a wonderful career and everything. That isn't really fair she didn't write "and everything"— All I wanted was Ag and happiness. And now the bottom has dropped out of the whole world and I'm writing this with a dry mouth and a lump in the old throat and Bill I wish you were here to talk to. The Dear Kid! I hope he's the best man in the world. Aw Bill I can't write about it. 'Cause I do love her so damned much.

And th[e] perfectest hell of it is that money, which was the only thing that kept us from being married in Italy is coming in at such an ungodly rate now.[7] If I work full time I can average around seventy a week and I'd already saved nearly three hundred. Come on out and we'll blow it in. I don't want the damned stuff now. I've got to stop before I begin feeling bitter because I'm not going to do that. I love Ag to much.

Write me Kid,
Ernie

Newberry, TLS; postmark: [OAK] PARK / [*date illegible*]; forwarding postmark: YONKERS / N.Y., APR 2 / 1130 PM / 1919

The envelope, addressed to "Mr. William Dodge Horne Jr. / 175 Park Avenue / Yonkers / New York," was forwarded to Horne at "University Club, / Bridgeport, Conn."

1 Dear Friend (Italian).
2 Warren H. Pease, a fellow member of ARC Ambulance Service Section 4; he would later achieve the rank of admiral in the U.S. Navy (Griffin, 73).
3 In subsequent letters to Jim Gamble (18 and 27 April 1919) and Lawrence Barnett (30 April 1919), EH would repeat this news about "Yak" Harris, most likely fellow section 4 veteran G. W. Harris of Yakima, Washington.
4 Reference to fictional sleuth Sherlock Holmes's mode of addressing his assistant, Dr. John H. Watson, in the detective stories by British author Sir Arthur Conan Doyle (1859-1930).
5 In her letter of 7 March 1919, Agnes told EH that her feelings for him were "more as a mother than as a sweetheart" and that she planned to marry someone else. "I can't get away from the fact that you're just a boy—a kid," she wrote (Villard and Nagel, 163-64). EH would fictionalize the situation in the piece published as Chapter 10 of *iot* and as "A Very Short Story" in *IOT*. In these early versions of 1924 and 1925, the nurse is named "Ag"; in the 1930 edition of *IOT*, EH changed her name to "Luz."
6 An allusion to Rudyard Kipling's poem "The Ladies," the third stanza of which reads: "I was a young un at 'Oogli, / Shy as a girl to begin; / Aggie de Castrer she made me, / An' Aggie was clever as sin; / Older than me, but my first un — / More like a mother she were — / Showed me the way to promotion an' pay, / An' I learned about women from 'er!"
7 After returning from Italy, EH had signed on with a Chicago agency that arranged speaking engagements; he earned five to fifteen dollars each for his "Reminiscences" about his war experiences (Griffin, 104; Sanford, 179).

To Howell G. Jenkins, 9 April [1919]

Big Nona, Of Aprile
A Five and Four. Another Gambler's Point.[1]
Professional Bondsman,[2]
The prospective ingress of the Barterer viewed from whatever angle fills the writer with a high joy beside which the joy of motherhood might be compared with the feelings of one receiving an advertizing postal in the mail. The above is a bit thick owing to the peerless inditer being without liquor for a period of two weekly periods. Merely an experiment. be not alarmed.

The Massif made out today an schedule of necessary tackle to be purchased. It includes a new steel Bristol Bait Rod, length ten feet, and a new Fly
rod, also bristol. A good camp ax, an Baldwin Camp Lamp. Which the writer
used very sucessfully on a canoe trip once. Heavy gut leaders. Sinkers. And
did I write of a Brook Hoop net?[3] It is indded an ideal mthod it would seem
to the enditer to take them from the places where they do not bite. Such as
below the cid[e]r mill.[4]

JFK, TL

1 *Nona*, ninth; *Aprile*, April (Italian). In the dice game of craps, an initial throw of 7 or 11 wins;
   a throw of 2, 3, or 12 loses; and a roll of any other number (including 9) establishes the
   "point." On subsequent rolls, a gambler must roll that point number before rolling a 7 in
   order to win. Jenkins earned the nickname "Fever" in "allusion to his fondness of crap
   games" (Baker *Life*, 40). "Fever Five" is a roll of five.
2 Reference to Jenkins's job; in a letter of 30 March 1918 to Bill Horne, EH had reported that
   Jenkins was "still bartering securities."
3 The Horton Manufacturing Company of Bristol, Connecticut, was known since the 1880s for
   its popular, high-quality steel "Bristol" fishing rods. The Baldwin Camp Lamp was a
   5-ounce acetylene lamp under 5 inches high that could be attached to a cap or belt, leaving
   the hands free; it was made by the John Simmons Company of New York and recommended
   by the Boy Scouts of America. A brook hoop net, used in small creeks or streams, consists of
   hoops of decreasing diameter held together by cotton netting; it is anchored underwater so
   that fish enter with the current through the large hoop but cannot pass through the other
   end.
4 Likely a reference to the mill on Horton Creek, built in 1910 by a founding resident of
   Horton Bay, Alonzo J. Stroud; for years the mill produced cider from apples grown in the
   area's many orchards (Ohle, 58–59). In *TAFL* and *UK*, EH would recall the cider mill and the
   pool below its dam, where he caught trout as a boy in Michigan.

To Kathryn Longwell, 22 April 1919

NOTHING is to be written on this side except
the date and signature of the sender. Sentences
not required may be erased. If anything else is
added the post card will be destroyed.

[handwritten: the Right Destroy it And See if I give a damn]

[Postage must be prepaid on any letter or post card
addressed to the sender of this card.]

I am quite well.

I have been admitted into hospital

{ *sick* } ~~and am going on well,~~ *[Bad]*
{ *wounded* } *and hope to be discharged soon.*
[OR will wreck the —— Hospital.]
~~*I am being sent down to the base.*~~

I have received your { *letter dated* __Christmas,__
{ *telegram ,,* __Easter__
{ *parcel ,,* __July 4th.__

Letter follows at first opportunity.

I have received no letter from you

{ *lately*
{ *or*
{ *for a long time.*

Signature } Leftenant E.M.Hemmingstoin .
only } 2nd Regiment Home Guards.
— ,, —

*Date*__ April 22 1919.__

Wt. W1566 R1619-18539 8000m. 6-17. C. & Co., Grange Mills, S.W

This Field Service postcard, of the type Frederic Henry mails to his family in *FTA*, presumably was a war souvenir that EH hand-delivered to a high school friend. The reverse side bears the printed heading "FIELD SERVICE/POST CARD" and these instructions: "The address only to be written on this side. If anything else is added the post card will be destroyed." In the address space provided, EH wrote, "Miss Kathryn Longwell." Baker reports that after Agnes broke off her relationship with EH, he "made a few dates with a pretty girl named Kathryn Longwell, resuming his prewar habit of canoeing on the Des Plaines River." Longwell later recalled that "we would come to my home and read stories he had written, while eating little Italian cakes he had brought from the city." He once presented her with his Italian officer's cloak, but his mother demanded its return (*Life*, 59).

To James Gamble, 18 and 27 April [1919]

April 18

Dear Jim,

Man it was good to hear from you! I'd been wanting to write you here in the states but couldn't figure but that you might be in Madiera. Why Chief I feel any amount more kindly toward this country now that you're in it. It isn't such a bad place now with the exception of the approaching aridity. But Taormina is not dry.[1]

I'm so darn glad to hear from you that I don't know what to write. The occasion is not one for writing but for grasping of the hand, greetings and perhaps the proposal of a toast. It is a time for the having of another. I'm writing this at my desk in my room. having hopped out of bed as soon as I'd read your letter a couple of times. On the left is a well filled book case containing Strega, Cinzano Vermouth, kummel, and martell cognac. All these were gotten after an exhaustive search of Chicago's resources. If it were not nine o'clock in the morning I would suggest the compounding of a Gamblers Delight. Cinquante—cinquante[2] martell and vermouth.

There is a good deal of news which should be retailed to you tho. First I am now a free man. All entangling alliances ceased about a month ago and I know now I am most damnably lucky —tho of course I couldn't see it at the time. Anyway everything is finished and the less said about it, as always with the unfair sex, the better. I did love the girl, though I know now that the paucity of Americans doubtless had a great deal to do with it. And now it's over I'm glad, but I'm not sorry it happened because, Jim, I figure it does you good to love anyone. Through good fortune I escaped matrimony so why should I grumble? Not being philosophical though, it was a devil of a jolt because I'd given up everything for her most especailly Taormina. And as soon as the Definite

Object was removed quelque kicks were implanted upon the w.k. ass for my ever leaving Italy. The first time you're jilted tho is supposed to be the hardest. At any rate I'm now free to do whatever I want. Go whereever I want and have all the time in the world to develop into some kind of a writer.

And I can fall in love with any one I wish which is a great and priceless privelege.

Here are a few bits of gossip of the old gang. Jenks is here in Chicago and we foregather every so often. Art Thomson[3] writes from Buffalo and is working at his old job. I stopped a couple of days with Bill Horne in Yonkers and he is engaged to some girl there. Bill alleges that she is the most wonderful etc. His remarks had a faintly familiar sound. Bill is a peach tho and an idealist which makes him too good for any woman to marry.

Idealists lead a rough life in this world Jim? But like hermit crabs they acquire shells that they cover their ideals with and that they can retreat into and protect the ideals with. But sometimes something comes along with a heavy enough tread to crush the shell and the ideals and all. Any way to return to the gang: I had a letter from Yak Harris and he is down in Ft. Worth Texas doing guess what? Getting a divorce from Mrs. Yak. There is a bit of real news. After twenty four years. Yak says, "I'm off all that stuff for life—At least I think I am." I think that "I think I am" is the best thing I ever heard. While separated from his family Yak may be addressed care Goldberg's Cigar Store, Yakima, Wash.

Corp Shaw[4] has been out at Coronado but is coming back for the fishing.

Sunday April 27th

Dear Jim,

Before I had a chance to finish this they took me off to the hospital and perpetrated another bit of carving. Throat this time.[5] Now I'm at home and darned sorry I didn't get this finished before I went to the hospital.

It was awfully good of you to ask me to Eagle Mere[6] and I know that we would have a great time, but this is the situation at present. A good pal, whom you'd like immensely. Good scout, wonderful sense of humor, and perfect pal is coming to town Wednesday next to stay for a week or so. Bill Smith. Then he is going up north where we go in the summer and open his place up.[7] I'm coming up about the middle of May and we've planned to bum and fish around together. I don't know just when my folks will be going up and we're not doing anything to the farm this summer, I think it is all rented out, there is nothing for me to do but go over and help them open up the shack on the other side of the lake. They wont be coming up until the latter part of June or first of July anyway and I doubt if I will stay with them.

But this is the idea. Bill has a farm which because he was in the service, Marine Flyer, he has rented out almost entirely. So that leaves him free for the summer. This is a priceless place Jim. Horton's Bay on Pine Lake[8] about twelve miles from Charlevoix. About three hundred miles north of here. It is great northern air. Absolutely the best trout fishing in the country. No exaggeration. Fine country. Good color, good northern atmosphere absolute freedom, no summer resort stuff and lots of paintable stuff. And if you want to do portraits. You shall do them. Bill has a Buick six that we can run into Charlevoix with when we long for the flesh pots. And it is equally good to run over to the Pine Barrens where it is absolutely wild and there are The Big and Little Sturgeon and the Minnehaha and Black Trout Rivers. It's a great place to laze around and swim and fish when you want to. And the best place in the world to do nothing. It is beautiful country Jim.

And let me tell you about the Rainbow fishing. I don't know whether you are a fisher man or not. But you might be a rank hater of the sport and you would like this kind of fishing.

Across the little Bay from where we would live is a point. And a little trout river comes into the Bay and makes a channel past this point. There is an old quay alongside and it is from there that we fish. And this is the manner of the fishing. We paddle over across the bay and stop at this old lumber dock. Just level with the water. And from the dock we run out about four or five lines into the channel. These are baited with a whole skinned perch which is dropped into the channel and sinks to the bottom. The lines are run out and then we put a weight on the butt of the rod they are run out from and set the click on the reel and wait. Do you get the scene. All the rods sticking out over the side, the clicks set, and the lines running way out into the channel. Then if it is night we have a camp fire on the point and sit around and yarn and smoke or if it is daytime we loaf around and read and await results.[9] And these are the results.

A reel goes screeee eeeech, the tip of the rod jerks under water, you run down and grab it up and thumb the reeel and then out in the lake a big rainbow shoots up into the air. And then the fight. And Jimthose trout can fight. And I've never taken one under three pounds out of the Bay and they run as high as fifteen. The biggest I ever took was nine and seven ounces. And you always get a strike. A nights fishing would average three of the big trout. Though I have taken as high as seven. It is the best rainbow trout fishing in America. Just this one bay and the only thing you can take them on is a skinned perch. And nobody knows it but us. People come down and troll all day for them from Charlevoix and never get a strike. While we will be taking them all day. And Indian taught it to me.

And they break water a dozen times and when you have one you have a regular fish. And it is the most comfortable kind of fishing I've ever found. When we feel like doing regular trout fishing we can fish any one of a half hundred good streams for brook trout.

But it's a great life up there just lazing around the old point and always having a line out or so for rainbow. There are trips in the car and runs around Little Traverse Bay to the old Indian missions and some beautiful trips. And Jimwe are going to have a wonderful gang up there. Bill who I told you of is a wonder. Then there is Carl Edgar, a Princeton man, of the same easy going humorous type as Bill Horne. Who reads fairy tales and swims and fishes when anyone else wants to. He's been an artillery officer during the late unpleasantness. Carl's coming up in July. Charles Hopkins a newspaper man and general good scout and mighty fisherman and loafer is coming up whenever I write him that everything is ready. Hop is the only one that takes his fishing seriously.

Bill and I have bummed together for years and the four of [us] got together on a trip last year before I went overseas. Bill is known as the Master Biologist, because some university dec[o]rated him with that degree, Carl as the Oil Maggot, because he owns some kind of oil business somewhere, Hop as the Wily Journalist, or the Bottle Imp and I as the Massive Woodsman. This title entitles me to cut wood and build fires while the Master Biologist and the Maggot lie on their backs and praise my skill.

It's a great gang Jim and I know you will like them. At Bill's place is his sister Kate, a rare good scout and good talker and game for any of the parties and Mrs. Charles, Bill's Aunt who is one of our own people.

Bill's place can't put us all up at once so when Hop comes up I'll move down to Dilworth's who have the leading house in the four house town of Horton's Bay and have plenty of beds, good rooms in a cottage and cooking that I've been wanting to get to ever since I came back from Italy. Very reasonable rates and the food and accomodations are splendid. We could have a great time Jim. Why can't you come up? We could work and we could have a wonderful time. I don't see why you can't. It is great up there all during June, July August and September. And I'll probably be up there all that time so I don't see any reason you can't come up and stay just as long as you can.

I'm all up in the air about what to do next fall. Wish a war would come along and solve my problems. Now that I don't have to go to work I can't decide what the devil to do. The family are trying to get me to go to college but I want to go back to Italy and I want to go to Japan and I want to live a year in Paris and I want to do so damned many things now that I don't know what the deuce I will do. Maybe we can go over and fight the Yugos.[10] It was very simple while the war was on. Then there was only one thing for a man to do.[11] Am having pretty good luck with my yarns. If you want I'll send you a couple.

I surely wish I were starting to meet you to go to Eagle Mere but I've promised Bill to go North now. If you don't withdraw the invitation I'd like awfully well to be there with you some time though. But why can't you come up North First? The good fishing and weather begins about the middle of June. I'll give you details about getting there later. Chicago is the only change you would have to make. I'd meet you at the station at the other end but when I think about that it makes me inarticulate and so I'd better quit.

Let me hear from you Chief,

As Ever,

Hemmy

Pardon the terrible typing will you Jim?

Corp Shaws fishing place isnt so very far from ours. He's over near the Barrens.

CMU, TLS with autograph postscript

1 EH is responding to Gamble's letter postmarked 16 April 1919 from Philadelphia, itself a response to EH's letter of 3 March. Gamble agreed with EH's negative assessment of life back in their "Glorious Country" and reminisced nostalgically about Taormina and the good time they had during EH's visit there. "Approaching aridity," a reference to the impending enforcement of nationwide Prohibition.

2 Fifty-fifty (French).

3 Probably Arthur E. Thomason, a fellow member of ARC Ambulance Service Section 4.

4 Carleton Shaw, a fellow member of ARC Ambulance Service Section 4 in Italy.

5 Clarence arranged for EH to have a tonsillectomy in hopes of curing his chronic sore throats. Nevertheless, in the decades after the surgery, EH continued to be "plagued with more sore throats than the average opera star," as his brother, Leicester Hemingway, put it (*My Brother, Ernest Hemingway* [Sarasota, Florida: Pineapple Press, 1996], 58–59).

6 In his 16 April letter, Gamble wrote that he hated city life and proposed that EH join him in May at Eagles Mere, a summer mountain and lake resort in northeastern Pennsylvania, where they could stay in one of his family's cottages. Jim's father, James M. Gamble, was one of the group that had purchased the lake and surrounding property in 1885 and founded the community (Joe Mosbrook, *Looking Back at Eagles Mere*, Eagles Mere, Pennsylvania: Eagles Mere Museum, 2008, 189).

7 Bill and Kate Smith's guardians, Dr. and Mrs. Charles, had bought and renovated a farmhouse near Horton Bay to "provide healthy summers" for their wards (Baker *Life*, 25); EH was a frequent visitor. The property, purchased in 1911, was across Horton Creek just to the northwest of the village (Ohle, 104).

8 In 1926 Pine Lake was renamed Lake Charlevoix after Pierre-François-Xavier de Charlevoix (1682–1761), a French Jesuit missionary and explorer.

9 EH's description matches the method and place of Nick and Marge's fishing in "The End of Something" (*IOT*).

10 The Kingdom of Serbs, Croats, and Slovenes was established in December 1918, incorporating lands of the former Austro-Hungarian Empire; it was commonly known as "Yugoslavia" before officially assuming that name in 1929. EH's sympathies would lie with Italy in its territorial disputes with the new country.

11 In "Soldier's Home" (*IOT*) Krebs recalls, "the times so long back when he had done the one thing, the only thing, for a man to do, easily and naturally."

To Lawrence T. Barnett, 30 April [1919]

600 N. Kenilworth Ave.

Oak Lark, Illinois.

April 30

Dear Lawrey,

Come Sta[1] Barney? How's everything? Everything is quiet in the village and there isn't much news of the gang. Bill Horne wrote me the other day from New Haven[2] and I see Jenks pretty often and Spiegel once in a while. Jock Miller, the great Scotch drunkard whom you may remember wrote from Minneapolis the other day. Pease was in town arrayed in purple and fine linen. Feder also blew in. Corp Shaw has been out at Coronado but should be back by now and we're going fishing together pretty soon. I called up your folks and Jerri's when I got home and they told me that you all were at school.[3] That gives me a bone to pick with you too. Do you recall giving K. Meyer, rather good looking and a pretty mean dancer but takes her self too damned seriously, a line of dope about the Great Hemingstein? Well anyway said Kate who lives directly across the street blew into the village of parked oaks and handed out quelque line in regard to me.[4] Had me practically married off and entangled with any amount of femmes. It created some sensation amongst all the nice Oak Park girls to whom I was swearing that I had always been true. You see I hand't been in Oak Park for over two years and they were ready to believe anything about me. So you owe me something for that and in return I am going to ask a favor. First let me tell you Barney that All bets with any of the women either wild or tame are off definitely. I am a free man! That includes them all up to and including Ag. My Gawd man you didn't think I was going to marry and settle down did you? Also just got out of the hospital here. Had another operation and everything is going great.[5] And I'm leaving for upper Michigan in about three weeks, or two weeks, to get in two or three months of fishing.

Now here is the dope. My Family, God bless them as always, are wolfing at me to go to college. They want me to settle down for a while and the place that they are pulling for very strongly is Wisconsin. I don't know anything about it except that there is nobody of the male sex from Oak Park that I recall that is worth a damn that goes there except Bob McMasters and perhaps Ruck Jones. And Bob Mac isn't there this year. However I know there are some very priceless femmes go there. And more will next year. So I wondered if you would write me all the dope on it. What kind of a gang there is and most anything you can think of about the place. Frankly I don't know where the hell to go. Wish I could go to Schio instaed of any of them. Anyhow write me Barney will you? I stopped with Bill Horne in N.Y. and he asked particularly to be remembered to you.

CIAOU KID
Stein

Pardon the bum typing and the pencil but I'm still laid up.

P.S. Yak Harris is in Ft. Worth Tex. getting a divorce from his wife he writes!!!

JFK, TLS with autograph postscript

1 How are you? (Italian).
2 A surviving letter from Horne to EH, dated 3 April 1919, is written on letterhead of the Locomobile Company of America, Bridgeport, Connecticut (JFK). Bridgeport is about 20 miles southwest of New Haven.
3 EH refers to John W. Miller, Jr., from Minnesota, an ambulance driver in ARC Ambulance Service Sections 2 and 3 whom he knew as a fellow patient in the Red Cross Hospital in Milan (Baker *Life*, 51), and Section 4 veterans Frederick Spiegel, Walter J. Feder, Warren Pease, Carleton Shaw, and Jerome Flaherty.
4 "Kate" is probably Catherine Meyer, whose family lived across the street from the Hemingways. Marcelline mentions "K. Meyer" in two of her letters to EH (postmarked 12 October 1917 and 25 August 1918), in the latter naming her among those in Oak Park who had been asking about him (Sanford, 268, 286).
5 EH's recent tonsillectomy.

To Clarence Hemingway, 24 [May 1919]

Ann Arbor 24th.

Dear Folks—,

Went down to Toledo yesterday and visited Carleton Shaw who was over in Italy with us. Leave for up North tomorrow be there when you get this card.

Have had a wonderful time here visiting with Jack. Michigan is a great school.[1] This aft I go to a base ball game. Michigan vs. Iowa.

Forward all my mail up North.

Love

Ernie.

IndU, A Postcard S; postmark: GRAND [RAPIDS & CHI] / [R. P. O.], MAY / 25 / 19[19]

Like a number of EH's communications home between May and September 1919, this is written on a prepaid two-cent postal card supplied by his father and rubber-stamped with the address, "C. E. Hemingway, M.D. / Kenilworth Ave. & Iowa St. / Oak Park, Illinois."

1 Jack Pentecost was studying at the University of Michigan in Ann Arbor.

To Clarence Hemingway, [25 May 1919]

Grand Rapids
Sunday 5 pm.

Dear Dad;

Got in here 7.15 this morning and Grand I. had just pulled out. No other train north until tomorrow morning. They [*EH insertion*: the MC.[1]] had promised to hold the train for us but the Pullman conductor was Drunk and forgot to wire ahead. This is the deadest town in the world bar none. Had a great time in Ann Arbor.

Ernie

PSU, A Postcard S; postmark: GRAND RAPIDS / MICH., MAY 25 / 10²⁰ PM / 1919

1 Michigan Central Railroad.

To Clarence Hemingway, 31 May [1919]

May 31

Dear Dad

[*Illegible, obscured by postal cancellation*] arrived yesterday. We are having [prettiest ?] weather 90° yesterday. A week's warm spell. Took some nice trout from the creek and yesterday afternoon a 4 lb. rainbow 28 inches long. Have him baked for dinner today. My leg feels OK except that I tire easily. Everything around the Farm is in shape. I'll take a look over Longfield soon and write you.

Dilworth's send their best. Bill and Mrs. Charles too.

Love
Ernie.

IndU, A Postcard S; postmark: BOYNE CITY, MICH., MAY 31 / 1130A

To Clarence Hemingway, 7 June [1919]

June 7. Saturday

Dear Dad,

Rain here today. First in two weeks. Tomorrow morning we'll go over to Longfield and I'll write you how it looks[.] Been too hot and bright for fishing. Have been doing a bit of gardening. Your letter came today.[1] When are you all thinking of coming up? I'm gaining weight and my leg is in pretty good shape. Dilworths send you their best regards. Congratulate Marce for me. Tell Ura I'll write her.[2]

Much Love

Ernie

P.S. Please give me Dr. Weber's Address in Kamerun![3]

PSU, A Postcard S; postmark: BOYNE CITY, MICH., JUN 9 / 8–30A

1 In his letter of 5 June 1919, Clarence asked EH to let him know "how things look on Longfield as to Hay and Fruit prospects" (JFK).
2 In her newsy letter to EH of 20 May, Ursula had mentioned that Marcelline would graduate that week from the Congregational Training School for Women, later incorporated into the Chicago Theological Seminary (JFK; also see Sanford, 193).
3 Kamerun was a German protectorate in West Africa from 1884 to 1916, when it was captured by British and French forces. In 1919 it was divided into British and French administrative zones, which in 1922 would become British Cameroons and French Cameroun under a mandate from the League of Nations. Dr. Weber may have been a missionary who spoke in Oak Park.

To Clarence Hemingway, [9 June 1919]

Monday

Dear Dad—

Went over to Longfield yesterday. Warren not there to speak to but talked to his wife. She said she had a letter from Mrs. Hemingway written Tuesday engaging Warren to Have the Lumber for the house she was going to build. She said Warren was hurrying through his week so as to be ready to do the hauling. Don't know whether you know about this or not. Is Mother going to do this selfish piece of damn foolishness? The Dilworths asked me about it when I first came up and I told them "No" knowing your ultimatum. They said they couldn't understand why she would wish to build there.[1]

The alfalfa on the field next to the Polaks looks very good and heavy— There will be quite a lot of hay. Orchard grass near the barn a good stand.

All the cherry trees are loaded. Should be 15 bushels or so at a guess. That is only a guess as I know nothing about cherries. But all the trees are loaded. Practically all of the trees in the old orchard will have fruit. All the northern spies. And the early harvest apples too. In the old clover field back of the old orchard there will be quite a few apples on the young trees.

The trees all look <u>good</u>. But need spraying if the fruit is to be salable. I asked Mrs. Sumner if Warren were going to spray them and she said she had heard nothing from you. So I told her to tell him to go ahead and spray. You ought to have a big fruit crop.

Bill and I have been spraying today and will tomorrow. It is a little cooler now and we had a rain yesterday. For ten days tho it hit 90° nearly every day. Have taken two big rainbows. Bill took one of them—17 inches long and a Sixteen inch Brook Trout. Lost a enormous one yesterday who ran out 75 yards of line and then came all the way in to the dock and then broke the leader.[2]

Give my love to Mother and tell her I'll write her

Love Ernie.

P.S. Don't forget Dr Weber's address and <u>Stand</u> <u>By</u> <u>Your</u> <u>Guns!</u>

CMU, ALS; postmark: BOYNE CITY, MICH., JUN10 / 3–30P

"June 9. 1919 / Horton's Bay, Mich." is written on the first page of the letter in Clarence's hand.

1 On 18 June 1919, despite her husband's objections, Grace began overseeing construction of a cottage on Longfield Farm that would serve as her retreat from the chores and family demands at Windemere; construction would be finished on 26 July (Grace Cottage guest book, Mainland). Although EH later would claim that the money for his missing college education went to the construction of the cottage, Reynolds notes that the money was there, but "four years in school did not fit with the self-image he was creating" (Baker *Life*, 78; Reynolds *YH*, 64, 69–70). Clarence stayed in Oak Park that summer, but when he came to Michigan in the fall, he graciously wrote in the cottage guest book, "A Beautiful View and Exquisite Cottage but the Family inside are best of all" (19 September 1919).

2 Clear filament that attaches the end of a fishing line to the fly or hook.

To Clarence Hemingway, [c. mid-June 1919]

[*Marcelline writes:*]

We are all going to land on Mother for lunch— I hope she won't care. We will bring out enough pink to make her cheerful. I'm going to try to call her up as soon as we get our shopping done—

Hop has been absolutely wonderful to us all, all thru the trip. He certainly is the perfect brother.[1]

—Urs wants to add a line now so adios— I'll send you expense acct. later—Very happily.

lovingly

Marc—

[*Ursula writes:*]

Dearest Dad;—

I havn't got time to write much but Marce has told you the news anyway I love you lots!!

Ura.

[*EH writes:*]

Dear Dad—

We've just met them and they look good.

Keep cheerful. We're taking them out to Windemere and then the Hop head over to the Bay. Good Luck.

Ernie

UT, ALS

"Summer—1918" is written at the top of the letter in what appears to be Marcelline's hand. This date is likely a later addition and apparently mistaken, as EH was in Italy in the summer of 1918. Other evidence places the letter in summer 1919: in her letter to EH postmarked 20 May 1919, Ursula wrote that after school was out on 11 June, she planned to get to Walloon Lake "mighty soon" (JFK). Clarence wrote to EH on 11 June that he had telegraphed Charles Hopkins, then at Fort Worth, Texas, to ask when he expected to come North (JFK), probably because they had planned for Hopkins to accompany the Hemingway sisters on the trip to Michigan.

1 Marcelline recalled that Hopkins became a family friend while he was training at the Great Lakes Naval Station, near Oak Park, during the time EH was in Italy (Sanford, 159).

To Howell G. Jenkins, 15 June [1919]

Sunday the 15th.

Dear Fever—:

Ciaou Kid.

I'm sorry I havn't written before but you know how it is. Anyway here's the dope. First I hope the malaria hasn't been bothering you.[1] Corp Shaw and I were on an enormous party at the Toledo Club. We both lay on the grass out side of the club for some time. Your old pal Hem established the club record. 15 martinies, 3 champagne Highballs and I don't know how much champagne Then I passed out.

It was a wonderful occassion. The night Toledo went dry.[2] Corp had a wire from Simmie[3] saying he and you were on a party. Wish I'd been along. Corp sends you his best and he'll probably be up here the latter part of July. You and he will get together up here.

We've had darby fishing. See the enclosure of Bill. The Buick is running well. Weve taken Six rainbow trout that would average about 3 lbs. The one in the picture is a four pounder.

And gosh Jenks but they can Fight. They are the Arditi[4] of the Lakes. It looks as tho we were going to get a respite from Prohibition. Dont you think? If not I'll send you down some kale to do a little laying in for me.[5]

Had a very sad letter from Ag from Rome yesterday. She has fallen out with her Major.[6] She is in a hell of a way mentally and says I should feel revenged for what she did to me. Poor damned kid I'm sorry as hell for her. But there's nothing I can do. I loved her once and then she gypped me. And I don't blame her. But I set out to cauterize out her memory and I burnt it out with a course of booze and other women and now it's gone.

She's all broken up and I wish there was something I could do for her tho. "But that's all shut behind me—Long ago and far away. And there aint no busses runnin' from the Bank to Mandalay."[7]

There is a russian cigarette shop on a cross street between Michigan and Wabash near Monroe. Where they sell Ivanoffs. There are some russian cigarettes there with a name I cant remember, 10 in a box and they are Brown paper, and a square box about the size of Pall Malls.[8] They are kind of shiny looking and the best weeds I've ever smoked. They cost 30¢ a box. I'm enclosing a buck and I wish youd mail me three boxes up here when you get time. If you don't know where the shop is ask some one. They have fruit and stuff in one window and Russian and Imported Cigarettes in the other. Perhaps it's Adams street. I can't remember. There's a shirt shop just beyond it toward Michigan Ave.

I sure would appreciate it if youd get 'em for me when you're over that way. They're the best pills of all.

Bill sends his best and says for you not to forget you're coming up here. We'll have a great old time! Kenley Smith's address is 800 Oak Park Avenue. North. 2 Blocks East and two blocks North of Our House. Their number is in the telephone directory under Oliver Marble Gale.[9] They want you to come out. I forgot to give Kenley your address!

Write me Kid.

Your old Pal.

Hemmy.

PUL, ALS; postmark: BOYNE CITY / [MICH.], JUN 16

1 In his letter to EH of 11 August 1918, Jenkins reported that he and Dick Baum had contracted malaria on the Piave (JFK).

2 As EH reported in his 24 May letter home, he had visited Shaw on 23 May in Toledo, Ohio, en route to Michigan. Under Ohio's prohibition law, the legal sale of liquor ended on Saturday, 24 May 1919. The private Toledo Club, established in 1889, is on Fourteenth Street downtown.

3 Probably Zalmon G. Simmons, who served with Jenkins, Shaw, and EH in ARC Ambulance Service Section 4 (Bakewell, 224).

4 Name for the elite special assault forces of the Italian Army during WWI. It is the plural form of the adjective *ardito*: bold, intrepid (Italian).

5 At the time, efforts to block enactment of the national War Prohibition Act, slated to take effect on 1 July 1919, were intense, as reported in the *Chicago Daily Tribune* the day of this letter ("Wets Mobilize at Capitol to Protest Dry Law: 10,000 Hear Gompers and Others Denounce Act as a Menace," 15 June 1919, 5). While it was still legal to buy alcoholic beverages in Illinois (Jenkins was living in Chicago), Michigan had gone "dry" in 1918.

6 Agnes von Kurowsky's letter does not appear to have survived. When Domenico Caracciolo took her to meet his aristocratic family in Naples, they forbade the marriage, supposing that she was "an American adventuress seeking the distinction of an Italian title" (Baker *Life*, 61).

7 EH is quoting from memory lines from Kipling's poem "Mandalay, " spoken by a British soldier in London who hears a "Burma girl" calling to him to return to Mandalay: "But that's all shove be'ind me—long ago an' fur away, / An' there ain't no 'busses runnin' from the Bank to Mandalay." The poem appeared in *Barrack-room Ballads and Other Verses* (1892).

8 Ivanoffs, a brand of cigarettes produced by the Rosedor Cigarette Company of Brooklyn, New York. Pall Malls were long cigarettes produced since 1907 by the American Tobacco

Company of Durham, North Carolina, after it acquired the premium brand from the British firm Butler and Butler.

9 Oak Park author (1877–1943) who wrote historical romances and edited *Americanism: Woodrow Wilson's Speeches on the War; Why He Made Them and What They Have Done* (Chicago: Baldwin Syndicate, 1918). The 1920 U.S. Census record of the Oliver M. Gale household in Oak Park includes not only Gale's wife and two sons, but also "Weyemga" K. Smith (probably "Yeremya" misspelled) as caretaker, along with Blanche E. Smith (caretaker's wife), Katherine F. Smith (sister), and Edith Foley (caretaker's friend).

To William D. Horne, Jr., 2 July 1919

Stone Crest Farm

July 2 1919

Dear Bill,

I should have written you a long time ago Bill. But some way I couldn't. Anyway now everything is all right. That is dependent on your conception of all right. After I wrote you last I went through a process of cauterization in which cognac and two or three girls I cared nothing about but violently rushed, took the place of the red hot iron. It wasn't a very devilish pleasant process but very thorough. Now for the last month and a half I've been up North here And "Ag" doesn't recall any image to my mind at all. It has just all been burnt out. So that is finito per sempre.[1]

How goes everything with you Amico? I went down to Toledo and with the Corp of Corps engaged in the last baccanallian rites of having a town go dry. It was an epic party. Jenks is coming up here to be wit us the first two weeks of August. Brummy according to late advices is running a grocery store in Kansas. It's a far cry from the Dolomites. Fratello[2] I get so damned lonesome for Italy that I don't know what to do/. How about you? Little Fever is even worse than I am. What Cheer from the rest of the gang.

Ieri mattina esta [n]otifica[z]ione ha arrivato da Commando Supremo con La Medaglia D'Argento proprio.[3]

Ernesto Miller Hemingway

Tenente Croce Rossa Americana

Ufficialle della Croce Rossa Americana, incarcicato di portare generi di conforte a truppe Italiane impegnate in combattimento, dava prova di corragio ed abnegazione.

Colpito gravemente da numerose scheggie di bombarda nemica, con mirabile spirito di fratellanza, prima di far si curare prestava generosa assistenza ai militari Italiani piu gravimente feriti dallo stesso scoppio e non si lasciavi transportare altrove se non dopo che questo erano stati sgombrati.

Fossalta (Piave) 8 Iulio 1918.

A Valore Militare.[4]

I get the gist of it but not the literal. We are catching some priceless fish up here and I wish you were around Bill. Is there any chance that you can makeit up here? Write me Kid,

Salute affetnosamente,[5] spelled wrong I guess,

Hemingstein

Newberry, TL with typewritten signature; postmark: BOYNE CITY, MICH, JUL 3 / 3–30 P

1 Finished forever (Italian).
2 Brother (Italian).
3 In his ungrammatical Italian EH probably means to say, "Yesterday morning this notification arrived from the Supreme Command with the actual Silver Medal."
4 EH apparently is copying verbatim from the letter he received with the medal; the Italian is correct, with a few misspellings that he likely introduced while transcribing. It can be translated as follows:

Ernest Miller Hemingway / Lieutenant in the American Red Cross / Officer of the American Red Cross, responsible for bringing various types of comfort to Italian troops engaged in battle, gave proof of courage and abnegation. / Gravely wounded by numerous pieces of shrapnel from enemy bombing, with an admirable spirit of fraternity, before seeking his own medical attention he lent generous assistance to the Italian soldiers more gravely wounded by the same explosion and did not allow himself to be transported elsewhere until these others had been moved away. / Fossalta (Piave) 8 July 1918 / For Military Valor.
5 *Saluti affettuosi*: affectionate greetings (Italian).

To Howell G. Jenkins, [15 July 1919]

Dear Jenks,

I'm darned sorry I haven't shot you a letter before but we have been tearing around so darn much and you know what a rotten correspondent I am. Bill and I were sure glad to know that you can come up in August. In regard to the boat way of coming the S.S. Manitou leaves from the municipal pier and comes direvt toCharlevoix where we will meet you. You can get the dope on the Manitou from the Northern Michigan Transportaion company agency at the Congress Hotel.[1] You get the dope and then write us when you will be here and we will be at the dock. How does it seem to have Chicago dry? It must be funny as hell—but then it will be wet again the first of October. Hope so anyway.[2]

We have just been on a peach of a fishing trip for about a week over on the Pine Barrens. Fishing the Black River and camping.[3] We went for five days without seeing a house or a clearing. Wild as the devil. Saw a bear on the Pidgeon River. That is where we want to go for a trip when you come up. We have all the fishing tackle so you don't need to bother about anything of that kind. We took all the trout we wanted to eat and then on the last day we were there we caught 64 to bring home[.] Some of them were hellers too. We sure will have a good time there as there are swell camping places along the river. The river is all clear—no brush and fast as the deuce good wading all the way. And I believe it is the best trout fishing in the states. We can guarantee you all you want to catch.

There are some deer and some [b]ear and if you want to bring up your Austrian Carbine with some shells it might be a good hunch. It would be a darn good thing to have around camp if we did pipe another bear. There are lots of partridges and I have my twenty guage shot gun and a twenty two rifle. Anche a 22 cal. Automatic pistol that is a whang.[4]

We can fish the rainbow around the bay here for a while and swim and have a good time and trk over to Walloon lake and see my folks and then we can put in a week on the barrens. I think we can guarantee you a pretty good time. The Corp[5] wants to come up and I think we can get him for the barrens trip. YOu and I and Bill and the Corp wouldn't make a bad gang?

If you can bring some grog up do it. Because I believe there is no danger. There is no search made aboard the boat and none at Charlevoix. Better bring up a couple of quarts.

We sure will be glad as hell to see you Jenks and Bill and I both and my family all send you their best.

Let me hear from you,
Hemmy

P.S. The papers and confirmation medal of my Medaglia D'Argento came through the other day. [*last sentence illegible*]⁶

phPUL, TLS; postmark: CHARLEVOIX / MICH., JULY 15 / 1919

1 The 274-foot-long steel passenger steamship *S.S. Manitou* was the premier vessel of the Northern Michigan Transportation Company. It made three round trips weekly between Chicago and Mackinac Island, Michigan, stopping at Charlevoix, Petoskey, and Harbor Springs. Congress Hotel, landmark Chicago hotel on the corner of Michigan Avenue and Congress Parkway; completed in 1893.
2 Anti-Prohibition forces had launched challenges in state courts and in the U.S. Congress in an effort to end enforcement of the national War Prohibition Act that went into effect on 1 July; these fierce battles between "wets" and "drys" were being closely covered in daily news reports. The U.S. Supreme Court, where some expected the final determination to be made, was then in recess and would not reconvene until October ("'Wets' to Rally and Give Justice a Taste of Beer: Will Stake Their All in Effort to Get Court Remedy," *Chicago Daily Tribune*, 6 July 1919, 8).
3 EH and Bill Smith drove to Vanderbilt, about 20 miles southeast of Horton Bay, and from there set out to fish and camp in the country to the east, traversed by the Black, Pigeon, and Sturgeon rivers. EH's fishing trips in the "Pine Barrens" and his expedition later that summer to the area around Seney in Michigan's Upper Peninsula would provide material for "Big Two-Hearted River" (*IOT*) (Baker *Life*, 61–63).
4 A 20-gauge shotgun is considered a medium-powered weapon, appropriate for hunting game birds. A .22-caliber gun would be used for small game like squirrels or rabbits. *Anche*: also (Italian).
5 Carleton Shaw.
6 On the verso of the first page of the source text, a photocopy of EH's letter in Carlos Baker's files at PUL, is the handwritten note, "The mill's not working." The note is likely Baker's transcription of the closing line, illegible on the photocopy. EH is probably commenting on the fact that the letter is rife with erratic spacing and other typographical errors.

To Howell G. Jenkins and Lawrence T. Barnett, 26 [July 1919]

Saturday the 26th.

Dear Jenks and Barney—;

Gee it's priceless that Barney can come up. Your letter just came and I showed it to Bill and we're going to send a wire this afternoon from Charlevoix. We'll have a priceless time.

Bill and I have a complete camping outfit for 4 men. Tents blankets cooking utensils, camp grate and so forth. Where we will go will be the Pine Barrens and camp on the Black River. It is wild as the devil and the most wonderful trout fishing you can imagine. All clear—no bush and the trout are in schools. The last time we were over Bill twice caught and landed two at once. Fishing a fly and a grasshopper and there are some hellers[1] too. We can fish all we want, and loaf around camp and maybe get a crack at a deer or a bear. Scared a bear out of our last camping place.

We have fishing outfits complete for 4 guys for lake fishing. But we have only 3 complete stream trout fishing outfits. We have 4 stream landing nets.

Barney should go to V.L and A's[2] and buy himself a 10 ft. fly rod. A fly reel and a fly line. That will be all he'll need.

I have a 22 cal. automatic pistol a 22 cal. rifle and my 32 automatic. Also a 20 guage shot gun. You birds better buy some 22 cal. cartridges.

These are the kind you want. 22 cal. "Lesmok" "Long Rifles". <u>Not</u> smokeless. Lesmok is <u>semi</u> smokeless.[3] Better get about 1,000 as they are cheap there and we will do a lot of shooting. Also get a box of 100 No 4 Carlisle spring steel hooks. That costs about 14¢ a hundred. Better get two boxes.

If you have some old Blankets or canvass bring them up. We have plenty but we can always use more. You want to bring all your old clothes too.

We are about 12 miles out of Charlevoix on Hortons Bay off Pine Lake. Mrs. Dilworth has a couple of cottages here and takes guests. You and I and Barney will put up there, Jenks. Bill's Farm is about a mile away. We will only be here two or three days to fish for Rainbow in the Bay and then avanti[4] over to the Barrens. It will not cost you anything Jenks as I have arranged for you to share my room. Barney can have a room next door. We'll have a crack at the Rainbow and you see from the Pictures what they are like.

You wont take any chances bringing the grog up as I don't believe that cars are searched at all. The best road to come up is the West Michigan Pike. It is pretty good. You can get the dope on it from any Blue Book.[5] It comes around through Michigan City and up the Shore through Muskegon, Ludington[,] Manistee[,] Traverse City and then on up to Charlevoix. You can drive it in less than three days. Probably in two days. All the roads up here are good. And on the Barrens they are fine. Because theyre not cut up by heavy traffic at all. You can nearly drive across the PineBarrens without any road just by compass. It is so free from underbrush.

Gee but we will have a good time. That Barrens' country is the greatest I've ever been in and you know that Bill and You and Barney and I will have some time. There are some great camping places on the Black. and we ought to get some Partridges. I can <u>guarantee</u> you and <u>Barney</u> both to catch all the trout you want. And Fever I can sure cook those trout. Bill will like Barney I know and I'll sure be glad to see him and you know what kind of a guy Bill is. Bring a camera and any junk you want to. We'll get some great action pictures.

Now tell Barney we want him and I'll guarantee that you and he both will have a good time. I'll write you again if I think of anything you need. Wire me when you leave. You can telephone me care Mrs. Jas. Dilworth, Hortons Bay when you get to Charlevoix and well come in and meet you. Or anyone in Charlevoix will tell you how to get to Hortons Bay. Its a straight road out and you can easily find it. Like a boulevard all the way.

Gosh Jenks it will be great to have you and Barney here.

Had a letter from the Corp yesterday and he has had to go to Rangeley Lake Maine because of his mothers health and he probably cant make it. He said to give his best to you.

Give my best to Barney and yourself and tear up here. We'll have everything ready for you. Shoot me a letter.

Hemmy.

P.S. Bill says to come up Multa Subito[6] and to bring heavy supplies of the grog. Picture us on the Barrens, beside the river with the camp fire and the tent. And the full moon and a good meal in our bellies smoking a pill and with a <u>good bottle</u> of Grog. There will be some good singing.

Hem.

I wont say anything to Spiegel.

phPUL, ALS

On envelope verso EH wrote, "P.S. Please hang onto the pictures." The pictures, presumably photographs, remain unlocated.

1 Grasshoppers are sometimes used as "flies" in fly-fishing. "Hellers" are the larvae of the hellgrammite fly, also used as bait.
2 Von Lengerke and Antoine, Chicago sporting goods firm established in 1891 by Oswald Von Lengerke (b. 1860) and Charles Antoine, with a store on South Wabash Avenue.
3 EH's rifle and pistol used "long rifle" cartridges, the largest size of .22-caliber ammunition. "Lesmok" was a type of gunpowder developed in 1911 by the E. I. du Pont Company of

Wilmington, Delaware, to produce "less smoke" than other powders used in .22-caliber cartridges; it was adopted by several ammunition manufacturers and was in use into the 1930s.

4 *Avanti*: forward, onward (Italian).

5 The West Michigan Pike ran along the shore of Lake Michigan from Chicago to Mackinaw City, Michigan. The *Official Automobile Blue Book: Standard Road Guide to America* (New York and Chicago: Automobile Blue Book Publishing Company), established in 1901, was billed as a "veritable motorist's encyclopedia." The annual regional volumes included maps of every motor road in the United States, along with information about state laws, local accommodations, and points of interest.

6 *Molto subito*: very quickly; right now (Italian).

To William D. Horne, Jr., 7 August 1919

August 7 <u>1919</u>

Dear old Bill—;

    I'm so damned sorry Bill. That doesn't do any good—but Bill I feel all broken about it. Why? Why? Why? Do such things happen.

    There's something wrong with us Bill—we're Idealists. And it makes us a deal of trouble and it hurts us. But we're that way and we can't help it. Mine were bent under the storm and some of them broken and it seemed a sorry mess. But out of the wreck I'm sticking to the same things.[1]

    Passing The Love of Women I cant be the same.[2] For me there are some things that when they are killed stay dead. Perhaps we can really fall in love with some other woman— But you know damned well we can't bring her the same things. Not when we think about it as we do.

    Bill if you want to keep the old ideals straight and cut loose from the damned dirty money grubbing for a year I'm your man. There is so much of this world we haven't seen and it is just a little while that we're here anyway.

    We are Simpatico Bill and we could go anywhere and have a good time. If you want to go out to Hawaii and the South Seas meet me in Chicago this fall. We'll bum—it may take us quite a while to get there. But you know we'll have a good time together. The more money we had to start with the better. But it isn't a necessity. We'll go through the South West to the coast and you can get to Hawaii for 45 dollars from the coast. And we'll discover every place we go. And we'll have thousands of adventures. And we'll work when we have to and we'll loaf. And we'll live Bill! We'll live! What doth it profit a man if he gains the whole world—and loses his soul?[3]

Bill I'll go anywhere with you this fall. Honest to Gawd I mean it. What do you say. We'll be gentlemen at large Bill.

Think it over and write me. I've bummed before and I know what its like. Come on Bill— Break away and we'll go and when we come back we'll write it. And it will be a classic.

Fever called up just now from Charlevoix. So we'll be starting soon. Wish to hell you were here. Is there any chance of your blowing up this summer? And come on this Fall Bill! Write me. And "Sempre Avanti!"[4]

Sua Amico[5]

Hemmy.

Newberry, ALS; postmark: BOYNE CITY, MICH., AUG 14 / 11 30A

1 Although no letter from Horne to EH has been located that would explain the situation, EH apparently is responding to news that Horne's romantic relationship had broken up. In his letter to EH of 23 February 1919 (JFK), Horne had written exuberantly of being in love with a woman from Wilmington, Delaware (see notes to EH's letter to Horne of [5 March 1919]). In the present letter, EH closely echoes the language and sentiments of Horne's consoling letter to him of 3 April [1919] (JFK), following EH's breakup with Agnes von Kurowsky.

2 2 Samuel 1:24, from David's lament on hearing of the death of Saul and Jonathan: "I am distressed for thee, my brother Jonathan: very pleasant hast thou been unto me: thy love to me was wonderful, passing the love of women."

3 From Mark 8:36: "For what shall it profit a man, if he shall gain the whole world, and lose his own soul?"

4 Ever onward (Italian). Horne used this same closing in his 3 April letter to EH.

5 *Suo Amico*: your friend (Italian).

To Clarence Hemingway, [16 August 1919]

Dear Dad;

Jock Pentecost, Jenks, Bill, Barney and I took 180 trout in 4 days on the Barrens. A dozen over 11 inches. Had a priceless trip. Jenks will call you up and tell you about it. Next week we're going up to the Upper Peninsula. How's everything? Sure wish you were along.

Ernie.

PSU, A Postcard S; postmark: CHARLEVOIX / MICH., AUG 16 / 7PM / 1919

To Clarence Hemingway, 27 August [1919]

Seney Aug 27

Dear Pop—

We caught some Brook trout $1\frac{3}{4}$ lbs. up here. 10 miles north in Schoolcraft Co. [1] Yesterday I caught 27 smallest nine inches. Lots of deer and game here. Going home to Horton's now. Jack Pentecost Al Walker and I. Hope to see you up this September. Have been out a week.

Ernie

CMU, A Postcard S; postmark: SENEY, / MICH., AUG27 / PM / 1919

1 County in Michigan's Upper Peninsula, organized in 1871 and named after Henry Rowe Schoolcraft (1793–1864), a prominent explorer of the region and early authority on its Native American tribes. He was married to an Ojibway and served as superintendent of Indian Affairs for Michigan 1836–1841.

To Howell G. Jenkins, [c. 31 August 1919]

Dear Shittle:

Jock and Al Walker and I just got back from Seney. The Fox is priceless. The big fox is about 4 or five times as large as the Black and has pools 40 feet across. The little Fox is about the size of the Black and lousy with them.[1] Jock caught one that weighed 2 lbs. 15 and a half of the inches. I got one 15 inches on the fly! Also one 14 inches. We caught about 200 and were gone a week. We were only 15 miles from the Pictured Rocks on Lake Superior.[2] God that is great country. I saw several deer and put three shots in one at about 40 yds. with the 22 machine gun. But didn't stop him.

Yesterday Bill and Kate and Jock and I and the Madam[3] went over to the Black and it rained like hell so we only got 23. Jock 8—I <u>nine</u> Bill 4—Kate 2. They weren't biting because of the rain. But we had some Darbs. 11-1/2 of the inches. We were over at the Black once before and rated 40. Bill had one that broke his leader on the stricture. Bill claims he was 3 or 4 of the pounds. A Hooper[4] is an easy article to lay hold of now that today is the last day of the season. The rainbow have come into the Bay and I expect some super whangleberries. You can see 'em jumping from Dilstein's[5] porch.

Joheesus an be Guy Mawd[6] Fever I lost one on the Little Fox below an old dam that was the biggest trout I've ever seen. I was up in some old timbers and it was a case of a horse out. I got about half of him out of wasser[7] and my hook broke at the shank! He struck on 4 hoopers. He was as big as any rainbow I've ever caught. I tried for him on 4 different days later but he only struck once and felt like a ton of the Bricks. There are no zanzaries up there and very few flack Blies.[8] Pock is going to get a Ford up next year and you'll be up there! We'll get the Corp and Bill Horne and Yak and the Bird and Jock and Marby and have a peach of a gang.[9] Take in both the Black and the Fox.

Say Shittle you and Marby owe 5 bones apiece on the grub. If you want to send it to me. I wouldn't mention it only I've only 5 to my name and dont see how I'm going to get out of the country.

These are damned good pictures e vero?[10]

Sua Amico

Hem. Hollow Bone Stein

Bill sends his best. Jock is home care J. L. Pentecost Jr. Elmhurst Ill. Call him up.

phPUL, ALS

The conjectured letter date is based on EH's references to fishing and on the dates of the 1919 fishing season in Michigan: the season for brook trout ended on 31 August, but for rainbow trout in Pine Lake it ended 15 September (*State of Michigan Game and Fish Laws*, 1919: 41, 126).

1 The Fox runs through Seney from the northwest to southeast; the "little Fox" is likely the east branch of the Fox River. This is the landscape of EH's "Big Two-Hearted River" (*IOT*), which takes its name from another river to the northeast of Seney.

2 Sandstone cliffs that are strikingly colored by mineral deposits and stretch for miles along the south shore of the lake.

3 Nickname for Bill and Kate Smith's aunt, Mrs. Charles.

4 Grasshopper, used for fishing bait.

5 EH's nickname for the Dilworths parallels the construction of his own nickname of Hemingstein.

6 A play on "Jesus" and "My Gawd."

7 Water (German).

8 *Zanzara*: mosquito (Italian); flack Blies, EH's play on "black flies."

9 The "gang" EH envisions would include old friends Jack Pentecost ("Pock" or "Jock") and Bill "the Bird" Smith, along with those he met in the war: "Corp" Shaw, Bill Horne, "Yak" Harris, and Larry Barnett ("Marby" or "Barney").

10 *È vero?*: Isn't it true? (Italian).

1 Grace Hall Hemingway with brother Leicester and father Ernest Hall, shortly before his death in 1905.

2 Anson and Arabell Hemingway and five of their six children: Antoinette (Nettie), Tyler, Clarence, George, and Grace (c. 1917). Willoughby lived in China as a missionary.

3 Clarence Hemingway with Marcelline and Ernest, six weeks old (11 September 1899).

4 Windemere Cottage on Walloon Lake, Michigan, where Ernest took his first steps on his first birthday and honeymooned with Hadley in 1921.

5 Ernest trout fishing at Horton Creek on his fifth birthday (1904).

6 Ernest, Ursula, Madelaine, and Marcelline on his sixth birthday.

7 The Hemingways' new house at 600 North Kenilworth Avenue, Oak Park, designed by Grace and built in 1906 with the inheritance from her father.

8 Family portrait taken "On the way home from Windemere," August 1909: Ernest, Ursula, Clarence, Madelaine, Grace, Marcelline.

9 Ernest writing on a camping trip in Michigan, summer 1916.

10 Grace and her six children at Windemere: Leicester, Carol, Madelaine, Ursula, Ernest and Marcelline, 1916.

11 "Portage at Riverside," Ernest on canoe trip to Starved Rock State Park, Illinois, April 1917.

ERNEST HEMINGWAY

Class Prophet; Orchestra (1) (2) (3); Trapeze Staff (3), Editor (4); Class Play; Burke Club (3) (4); Athletic Association (1) (2) (4); Boys' High School Club (3) (4); Hanna Club (1) (3) (4); Boys' Rifle Club (1) (2) (3); Major Football (4); Minor Football (2) (3); Track Manager (4); Swimming (4).

"None are to be found more clever than Ernie."

ILLINOIS

MARCELLINE HEMINGWAY

Commencement Speaker; Orchestra (1) (2) (3) (4); Glee Club (3) (4); Tabula Board (4); Trapeze Staff (3), Editor (4); Opera (1) (2) (3); Atalanta (1) (2) (3) (4); Girls' Rifle Club (2) (3) (4); Commercial Club (4); Drama Club (3) (4); Girls' Club (3), Council (4); Story Club (3).

"I'd give a dollar for one of your dimples, Marc."

OBERLIN

12 Ernest and Marcelline in 1917 *Senior Tabula,* the Oak Park and River Forest High School yearbook.

13 Warren Sumner and Ernest working at Longfield Farm, summer 1917.

14 Ernest (second from left) and fellow American Red Cross volunteers during a lifeboat drill on the *Chicago* en route to the war in Europe (May 1918). Ted Brumback recalled that the ship's French barman (far left) disdained the drills, but Ernest dragged him up on deck to be in the picture.

15 Ernest as an American Red Cross Ambulance Service driver, Italy, June 1918.

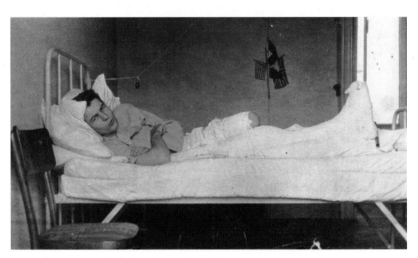

16 At the American Red Cross Hospital in Milan, summer 1918.

17 Agnes von Kurowsky, 1918.

LIEUT. E. M. HEMINGWAY
Taking an Airing in Milan, Italy

18 Photo enclosed in Ernest's letter home of 18 October 1918, both published in the *Oak Parker*, 16 November 1918.

19 Chink Dorman-Smith with his springer spaniel, George (c. 1919), in a photo he sent to Ernest.

20 Ernest's fishing gear, including the flour sack and the bottle hanging around his neck for grasshoppers, resembles that of Nick Adams in "Big Two-Hearted River," 1919.

21 Bill Smith and Ernest in downtown Petoskey, 1919.

22 Marjorie Bump, wearing Ernest's Italian beret, Petoskey, November or December 1919.

23 Grace Quinlan, one of the Petoskey high school girls in Ernest's social circle in the fall of 1919, whom he affectionately called "Sister Luke."

24 "Summer People": Carl Edgar, Kate Smith, Marcelline, Bill Horne, Ernest, and Bill Smith, 1920. Kate notices Ernest pointing his pistol at the camera.

25 Jack Pentecost, Howell Jenkins, (Arthur Meyer ?), Dutch Pailthorp, Ernest, Bill Smith,
Bill Horne, Carl Edgar, and Lumen Ramsdell on Ernest and Hadley's wedding day, 3
September 1921, Horton Bay.

26 Newlyweds Hadley and Ernest, 3 September 1921.

27 Hadley and Ernest at Chamby, Switzerland, 1922.

28 Sylvia Beach at her bookshop Shakespeare and Company on the rue Dupuytren, Paris. In July 1921 the shop moved to 12, rue de l'Odeon.

29 Ezra Pound at Shakespeare and Company, photographed by Sylvia Beach, c. 1922.

30 Alice B. Toklas and Gertrude Stein in their salon at 27, rue de Fleurus, photographed by Man Ray, 1922.

31 Ernest at Shakespeare and Company, photographed by Sylvia Beach (c. 1922).

To Clarence Hemingway, [3 September 1919]

Dear Dad

Hope you all had a good reunion. Chief Lore said he called you up. He is my pal on the motorcycle in the picture.[1] When you come up will you please bring my Medaglia D'Argento and the papers. I want to see it.

Saw Mother and the future brother in law Sunday.[2]

Love—

Ernie

PSU, T Postcard S; postmark: BOYNE CITY, MICH., SEP 3 / 3–30P / 1919

1 D. D. Lore, WWI acquaintance in the photograph that EH enclosed with his 18 October 1918 letter home (and published in the *Oak Parker*, 16 November 1918), showing EH riding in a motorcycle sidecar in Milan. The photograph appears in M. Miller (86).
2 Marcelline had become engaged that summer in Michigan to a man named Walter, who informed EH of that fact after Marcelline returned to Oak Park in late August. She wrote to EH that she should have told him herself earlier but feared that his reaction might "spoil our joy this summer" (Sanford, 306–7). According to Reynolds, EH told Grace that Walter was untrustworthy (*YH*, 77). The couple did not marry. A Walter Grover of Indianapolis frequently signed the Grace Cottage guest book during the summer of 1919, including on the page dated 31 August, suggesting that he is the "future brother-in-law" whom EH had met the previous Sunday (Mainland). Years later in a letter to his sister Ursula, EH named Walter Grover as "Marce's first love" (10 April [1933], Schnack).

To Ursula Hemingway, [c. 17 September 1919]

Dear Ura,

I meant to write you as soon as I got your "SO Long" note but you know the brother stein as a correspondent.

Anyway I'm writing you now. I spent over night with mother at the Frame and she told me about what a wild time you are having with the untameds at the old scolastic institution.[1] Keep it upwards. I havn't been doing anything much. The bird and I have fished a smidgeon or so and taken various and sun dried rainsteins.[2] One of the biggest weighed 7 of the pounds. I took Marge Bump fishing for Rainsteins and taught her how. Once when she and I were out we got one that weighed four and three of the quarters. Another time she went alone and used my rods and stuff and caught one that weighed five and a half of the pounds.

There is no one at the dilsteins now. Everybody gone but John K. Hollowbone. Which is my newest moniquer. It is quiet as hell, or rather as quiet as hell would be if we had some of the old time desk room teachers for devils. Marge went back Sunday to go to school. I miss her a lot as we were paling around together. She is a peach of a kid. Nespaw? Young Connie Curtis was out, I don't know whether you piped her this summer or not.[3] She tried to vamp the well known brother. Being the tender age of fourteen or fifteen the vampag[e] was not an unqualified success.

Since I started this I went into Peto with the Bird and the Madam and there piped Barge who informationed me that she had been screeded by you.[4] Why and wherefore cannot you screed me? Also shot a plover for the madam's breakfast. Probably I'll be alleying toward chicago somewhere around the first of Tocober. Will stop for a duet or trio of the diurnal periods and then allez[5] somewheres. I haven't any idea where. Perhaps Kansas City—perhaps Poland.

The writer just Broke.[6] Anyway Screed me and tell me all your troubles. 'Cause I love you.

Ernie — Black

My Love to Nunbones.

Ernest H. Mainland Collection at NCMC, TL/ALS

The letter is written on the verso of a bond dated 1 August 1918 for the Keo-England Drainage District No. 4, Lonoke County, Arkansas.

1 EH spent the night of 16 September 1919 at his mother's cottage at Longfield Farm; on 17 September she wrote in the Grace Cottage guest book, "Ernest left" (Mainland). Ursula was attending high school in Oak Park.

2 The bird, Bill Smith; rainsteins, rainbow trout.

3 Nespaw, playful spelling of *n'est-ce pas?*: Is it not? (French). Marjorie had returned to Petoskey, where she attended high school. During the summers, she and her sister,

Georgianna, stayed at the Horton Bay home of their aunt and uncle, the Ohles, who lived across the street from the Dilworths' Pinehurst resort. The girls and several of their friends from Petoskey, including Connie Curtis (1904–1973), worked in the dining room waiting on tables (Ohle, 104–5).

4 Peto, Petoskey. Barge, Marjorie Bump.

5 *Allez*, a form of the French verb *aller*, "to go."

6 EH's typewriter malfunctioned, and he switched to handwriting after the word "Kansas" in the previous sentence.

To Coles Van Brunt Seeley, Jr., [18 September 1919]

[Excerpt as published in Christie's catalog:]

". . . How's everything? By gosh I'd like to see you Capo. Didn't we have some damned good times . . . gosh I wish I were there now . . . After you left I went back out to the front, Mount Grappa,[1] and had a hell of a time. Then spent a couple of more months in the Ospedale Maggiore . . . Have cursed every day that I've been back in this god damned dry arid, friendless country! . . . Everything off betwixt Ag. and I. But it was a great life while it lasted . . ."

Christie's catalog, New York, 27 October 1995, Lot 74, published excerpt [ALS]; postmark: [Boyne City, Michigan, 18 September 1919]

According to the catalog description, the letter is signed "Hem" followed by the words "his mark" and a drawing of a stein of beer, and in the salutation EH addressed his friend (a fellow veteran of ARC Ambulance Service Section 4 and a hospital mate in Milan) as "Dear Capo." Henry Villard later explained that the "pronunciation of the name 'Seeley' identified its bearer with an area north of Venice known as Caposile, prominent in the war communiqués; the similarity between Seeley and the Italian *sile* led to the nickname 'Capo'" (Villard and Nagel, 275). The wordplay may go further: *capo* is also Italian for "leader" or "boss." The letter was returned to Hemingway because of a wrong address.

1 Monte Grappa, part of the Prealps in the Veneto region of Italy and strategically located near the Piave River, was the scene of some of the most fiercely contested battles on the Italian front in WWI.

To [Unknown], [c. late September 1919]

Still up North
or Perhaps
Silent up North.

At any rate Calamity has in the language of the Michigese Moss Back[1] "Laid hold of" the typer. It just let off a series of jarring whirrs like an annoyed rattler and quit frigidly. The main spring I imagine.

Fishing ended the fifteenth of this _ _ _ strual period.

However shooting has commenced. Nothing ever occurs, transpires, takes place, or happens up here. My pal and I have had a siezure of Poker. We've just terminated the 97th hour. The game played is Deuces wild and three jokers also untamed inserted in the Pack. A total of seven wild cards. It is a four bit, two shilling, limit.

Smith has paid me all he has with him and is under obligation for 220 dollars. This was incurred when he held four Aces against my five Queens.

In the Lingua Franca of the pastime he united a quartette of the deadly ones 'gainst a quinta of Vaginas.

In our 97 hours—some to recommend some rather good additions to the Lingua have transpired.

Two queens are monickered a "double duo of Breasts". A pair of Kings are yclept "A Brace of the Monarchs".

A full house is dubbed "an Asylum of Prostitution[.]" It is also known as a Jane Adams. A study of contemporary American Politics will reveal why.[2]

No one regrets the mortage of my mill more than myself—unless perhaps yourself. This will be a screed of the poorest type because

NYPL, AL

EH apparently is with Bill Smith and writing from Michigan to a mutual friend, likely one who spent time with them fishing and camping that summer: possibly Larry Barnett, Howell Jenkins, Jack Pentecost, or Al Walker. The conjectured letter date is based on the Michigan fish and game laws of 1919: fishing season ended on Pine Lake in Charlevoix County on 15 September; duck hunting season began the next day. The letter ends in midpage.

1 Mossback, U.S. slang for a rustic or provincial person (here, from Michigan).
2 Jane Addams (1860–1935), American social reformer best known as the founder of Hull House, a Chicago settlement house that provided assistance to women and children in a neighborhood of poor immigrants; in 1931 she became the first woman to receive the Nobel Peace Prize. Addams worked to remedy social and economic conditions that she believed drove women into prostitution, and she advocated women's suffrage—a matter then at the

forefront of "contemporary American Politics," as EH put it. In June 1919, Congress had passed the Nineteenth Amendment, giving women the right to vote; after ratification by the states, it would take effect in August 1920.

To Clarence Hemingway, 28 October [1919]

October 28th
Dilworths.

Dear Dad,

Had a very rough and stormy trip up on the Missouri. She got away about 4p/m/ and into Petoskey at midnight. Cold and stormy. I was not sick however.

Spent the night at the Cushman and went up and saw the Bumps in the morning and went to the Presbt. Church with old Mrs. Bump. Have a room located at 602 State Street where I wish you would forward my mail and anything else. It is small but heated and gives me a place to work. Monday I caught the train to Boyne Falls and thence to Boyne City and so via Wesley to here last night[.][1] Brought the typer from Charles's Shanty[2] and am departing with it and my other worldy goods to Petoskey on Thursday— Probably taking the same route I came out on. This afternoon I worked out the new front part of the "Woppian Way" that Balmer wanted me to do and will have it in shape to start on it's travells as soon as I am settled in Petoskey.[3] I typed off the new part this afternoon. It was snowing a little this evening and the only amusement offered is an Evangelical revival. There is some doubt as to whether I will attend.

Since leaving Oak Park I have read a volumne of stories by Guy de Maupassant one by Balzac, The Larger Testament of Francois Villon, Richard Yea and Nay by Maurice Hewlett and Little Novels of Italy also by Hewlett.[4] These are all things that are further along in college than Marcelline ever achieved so you see I have not been entirely idle.

Thank you very much for helping me so much and give my love to mother and the kids,

Lovingly
Ernie

If Manfredi calls tell him I was only home a day or so and called him several times.[5] I did but couldnt get him. Tell him I'll be down again and will write him.

Ernie

Phpsu, TLS with autograph postscript

At the end of the letter Clarence noted, "Rec'd 10/31/919 / Ans. 11/1/919."

1 Built in 1875 on Lake Street in downtown Petoskey, the Cushman House Hotel boasted a 250-foot-long veranda and its own orchestra; unlike most of the other first-class hotels in town, it was open year-round and served as a social center for townspeople (Michael R. Federspiel, *Picturing Hemingway's Michigan* [Detroit: Wayne State University Press, 2010], 33). During his two-month stay in Petoskey that fall, EH lodged in the two-story frame rooming house on State Street run by Eva D. Potter; the house is now on the National Register of Historic Places. The village of Boyne Falls, a stop on the main line of the Grand Rapids and Indiana Railroad, was connected by a local rail line to Boyne City, 5 miles to the northwest on Pine Lake. From there EH would have traveled 6 miles by road to Horton Bay.
2 The Horton Bay farmhouse owned by the Charleses, Bill and Kate Smith's aunt and uncle.
3 Also titled "The Passing of Pickles McCarty," the unpublished story is set in Italy during WWI; the hero of the piece gives up a promising career as a boxer to join an Arditi battalion (Reynolds *YH*, 58–59). Edwin Balmer (1883–1959)—novelist, later the editor of *Redbook* (1927–1949) and best known as the co-author of *When Worlds Collide* (1933)—had a summer place on Walloon Lake and had given EH the names of several magazine editors who might be interested in his work (Baker *Life*, 62, 574).
4 Guy de Maupassant (1850–1893), French novelist and short-story writer. Honoré de Balzac (1799–1850), French novelist best known for the series of more than ninety interconnected novels and stories that make up *La Comédie Humaine* (*The Human Comedy*). François Villon (1431–c. 1463), French poet and author of *Le Grand Testament* and *Le Petit Testament*. Maurice Henry Hewlett (1861–1923), English author of *The Life and Death of Richard Yea-and-Nay* (1900), an historical novel set in the time of Richard the Lion-Hearted, and *The Little Novels of Italy* (1899).
5 Pietro F. Manfredi, editor of *La Tribuna*, an Italian newspaper published in Chicago, was the organizer of the Italian festival held at the Hemingways' Oak Park home in February 1919 to honor EH's service in Italy (newspaper clipping in grandparents' scrapbook, JFK).

To Grace Hall Hemingway, 11 November [1919]

November 11th.

Dear Mother,

I was awfully glad to get your letter and am sorry that I have delayed answering it. For the last five days I've had what would have been tonsilitis if I had tonsils. Throat swollen so bad and so sore I couldn't swallow and white patches on both sides. I've gargled often and used the throat lozenges and tonight it feels a lot better. Today was armistice day and I prayed for all those that didm't live to see the armistice. It seemed as tho that were the proper thing to do. Poor old birds—I wonder what they think of us scrapping and haggling over the victory that they won. It must make them bitter to hear all the Congressmen talking about the "next war" when they thought they were dying to make an end to war. What do you think the 500,000 dear old wops that died think of Wilson robbing them of what they fought for?[1]

It has been a beautiful day, bright and clear. No snow yet. The weather up till today has been rainy and cold but today was a wonder.

I8ve written a lot and worked over my stuff quite a bit. Because of the linotyper's strike the eastern magazines aren't getting out at all and so it is useless to send anything to them.[2] So I'm getting stuff up for when the opening up again comes. The one yarn I sent to the Post I havn't heard from yet. Probably Lorimer won't take it but it is a really good yarn and I'm pretty sure some one will.[3] I havn't done anything the last couple of days—throat's been so bad. It does seem kind of rotten that the first magazine strike there ever has been should come off just when it should gyp me doesn't it? But then I8m working just as hard and getting in a lot of reading besides. Wish I were at Fiume tho.[4] Give my love to Ura, Nunny, Nubbins, the Jazz and Dad and tell Ura to write me. The Bumps have been awfully nice to me. Old Mrs. Bump is just like Grandmother Hemingway.

With Love,
Ernie.

Ernest H. Mainland Collection at NCMC, TLS; postmark: PETOSKEY / MICH., NOV12 / 1–30P / 1919

1 At the end of WWI, most of the Allies took a hard line against the defeated Central Powers, seeking heavy reparations and territorial concessions. Woodrow Wilson opposed these harsh terms, aiming to further a lasting peace. He lost most of his arguments for moderation both with the Allies and with the U.S. Congress, which refused to support U.S. membership in the League of Nations.
2 On 1 October, labor disputes involving New York City printers and other press workers, including a strike by linotype compositors, shut down publication of more than 200 nationally distributed magazines and trade papers ("Pressrooms Stop as Lockout Begins," *New York Times*, 2 October 1919, 3; "If You Fail to Get Magazines, Here's the Cause: 'Civil War' in Labor Ranks Closes Up All N.Y. Plants," *Chicago Daily Tribune*, 10 October 1919, 3).
3 George Horace Lorimer (1867–1937), editor of the *Saturday Evening Post*, 1899–1936.

4 At the end of WWI, Fiume, a major Adriatic seaport and industrial center formerly part of Austria-Hungary, was claimed both by Italy and by the newly created Kingdom of the Serbs, Croats, and Slovenes (Yugoslavia). It was given to Yugoslavia (with the strong support of Woodrow Wilson), outraging those who felt that Italy's sacrifices for the Allied cause had gone unrecognized. On 12 September 1919, Italian nationalists led by poet Gabriele D'Annunzio had seized Fiume, quickly establishing an independent city-state under authoritarian rule. The Treaty of Rome would cede Fiume to Italy in 1924. In EH's "The Woppian Way," protagonist Nick Neroni is bound for Fiume to fight for the Italian cause (Reynolds *YH*, 58–59).

To [Georgianna Bump], 23 November 1919

November 23 1919

Once upon a time I came to the front door and she was seated at the piano playing something very kind of well you know Dreamy like and when she heard my step on the front porch she started to play "Indian Blues,"[1] and that is not at all kind of well you know Dreamy like and I rang the bell. And she came to the door and smiled at me and—well IF you want to know the joke ask her— I'll never tell.

Ernest M. Hemingway.

Private Collection, Inscription

According to Marjorie Bump, EH wrote this inscription in her sister's autograph book (Georgianna Main, *Pip-Pip to Hemingway in Something from Marge* [Bloomington, Indiana: iUniverse, Inc., 2010], 21). Below the signature in another hand is the notation, "1230 N. State Street / Chicago / Ill." EH resided at that address from late October to late December 1920.

1 "Indian Blues," music by Edwin McHugh, lyrics by Carl Perillo (1919). Marjorie Bump speculated that the joke may have concerned the breakup of EH's romance with a Native American girl, Prudence Boulton, who "was rumored to be Ernest's first sexual partner" (Main, 21). Boulton is generally considered the inspiration for the character Prudence Mitchell, whose infidelity saddens the young Nick Adams in EH's "Ten Indians" (*MWW*), and for Trudy in "Fathers and Sons," who, an older Nick recalls, "did first what no one has ever done better" (*WTN*).

To Grace Hall Hemingway, 4 December [1919]

December Fourth

Dear Mother,

Thank you ever so much for the two boxes. They came all right, nothing smashed, and I appreciate them ever so much. I'll bet what made you think of sending them was hearing Tubby tell of the box of Cake we enjoyed at the Muelstein Press House? [1] Am I right? I'll bet I am. Don't you like Tubby? He is sure a good friend of mine and a whang of a newspaper man. I hope you will have him out at the house often. You can't get any one more amusing—and when Tubby tells you an incident it8s the truth—no matter how amusing. I was sure glad to hear that the old bird is in Chicago.

The weather here hasn't been bad at all. Also I'm aclimated now so that I don't notice the bad weather. But they are still running motor cars altho there is some snow. I've met a lot of nice people and have a pretty good time. Now that the magazines are resuming publication I should get rid of a yarn or so. I've written one that I'm tentatively calling "The Mercenaries" that is really good I think. I'm sending it out tomorrow. Even if I'm not making huge gobs of kale I'm serving a good apprentice ship. Have written an Anthology of the people out at the Bay that you might like. I'm going to send it out. [2] While the strike was on stuff accumulated and so I held mine up. Havn't been out to the Bay since I was laid up so havn't any dope on the people out there. Mrs. Joe Bacon is living here in Petoskey with Earl and the little girl going to school. That letter from the Star was sent out to Bacons on your old R.F.D. [3] schedule and stayed there a week and then Mrs. Joe Bacon brought it in here and sent it home. She had forgotten that I was here in Petoskey.

Thank you very much again for the presents and for writing me. My love to you and all the fambly. I'll write Dad next.

Lots of Love,
Ernie

My landlady here is awfully nice to me. Some nights when I come in early in the morning I find a lunch laid out on my table with a Thermos bottle full of hot cocoa. Cake and salad and cold meat. And she sends up pop corn to me. Hot and buttered. She treats me great. In return I try and do any things for her downtown and go around and pay her water, electric and telephone bills etc. She does any mending for me that I need too. She is a

Mrs. Potter and her husband is mort and she has a son with locomotor-ataxia—pretty far along with it poor devil. She surely is nice to me.

Ernie.

Ernest H. Mainland Collection at NCMC, TLS; postmark: PETOSKEY / MICH., DEC 5 / 8 AM / 1919

1 Comic reference to the press room at the Muehlebach Hotel, where EH and fellow staffers on the *Kansas City Star* once enjoyed a cake that Grace sent in one of several food parcels she mailed to EH in Kansas City (EH to Grace Hemingway, [2 March 1918]). One of EH's friends from the *Star*, "Tubby" Williams, recently had visited the Hemingways in Oak Park (Grace Hemingway to EH, 14 December [1919], JFK).
2 Neither "The Mercenaries" nor "Crossroads: An Anthology" would be published in EH's lifetime. They first appeared in print in Griffin (104–12; 124–27).
3 Rural Free Delivery, system established by the U.S. Post Office in 1896 to deliver mail directly to rural homes.

To William B. Smith, Jr., 4 December [1919]

December 4

Salesman Smith,

You are wrong I am not the prosecuting attorney.[1] But I may be deputy sherriff. I am doing to apply for the job. It only pays two of the neebs a day but you don't have to do anything. No word offn you eithet today nor testerday. Lorrie returned Wolevs and Doughnuts yesterday morning. I am getting it off to Adventure. Where it will be under the supervision of Arthur Sullivant Hoffman. No word from the Much Lauded Charles Agnew McLean anent the Woppian. Hope to God he may buy it.[2] Non hearage from him is a good sign at any rate. A better sign would be a large check. But what the hell Bill. Have been attending court here for the couple of days.

No new writeage has transpired. Largely because of lack of pep an[d] an inhibiyion gainst poundage. If sellage of anything should occur increased writeage would come like a shot. Did I tell yez of the devotee of the hand who has fallen for the writer? Tis a grewsome tail or tale rather. She is half injun and the other french and labors in the restaraw where I eat. Would you believe it? Grub is obtained at less than cost. A forty five cent meal is ofetn mangies for twenty five of the centimes. What would be your attitude? I am

certain the hand would stalk at my merest snuggestion. So far my attitude
has been that of a gentleman, but unless comeage through on my part takes
place how long will the present prices preveil? You should see the smiles
that are given the writer. The eagerness with which his every move is
anticipated. It is pitiful. She is about twenty of the years. Should the hand
stalk? She does an optic good. This is a good mill. I wish I could say as much
for ourn. But one should not examine a gift horse for hernia. Yesterday was
approximately Inju[n] summer. Guy Mawd avis the weather has realoy been
of the very penultimate quality. There could be no complaint. Cars are still
being run at all time all roads are passavle. Gee I tremble for the saftey of
your seeds next summer. I have practiced variations of the hand which will
insure your vanquishment if trickery is attempted. At straight play of course
I am your superior. You admit this of course? It would be useless for you
to attempt a denial. The big problem at present is the semi aboriginal hand.
Should the writer Don Jonah her?[3] A more or less poor rep is being obtained
by the writer among the locals due to association with known devotees of
the hand and widely known grog purveyors. To say that not three days has
ever passed without the vile stuff being pre[s]ent in some form or other
would be no exaggeration on the part of the [w]riter. Real groggage of the
Italian type has of course not been presnt but four or five drinks can be
obtained at almost any time. And as you know that is the real groggage. Have
you screeded the lever? Screed him. I have not and we do not want the
lever to think that we have neglected him. A little negelct on our part and
the immortal one might lapse into materimony. Do your best by the lever.
Tell me more of Odgars counsel. Also what is Stut[4] doing to obtain the
bread of life. Screed the enditer. Enlite to the Screeder.

WEMAGE.

Stanford, TLS; letterhead: OFFICE OF / PROSECUTING ATTORNEY / FOR
EMMET COUNTY / PETOSKEY, MICHIGAN

Under the letterhead, EH wrote "The Lever's address." "Lever" is a play on "Fever," i.e., Howell
Jenkins. On verso of the letter is a full-page handwritten reply from Smith that begins, "Wear
Demage: Take it not ill that I should use the reverse of your own screed for another."

1 Reference to the stationery on which EH wrote this letter.

2 "Wolves and Doughnuts" would be published for the first time in 1985 as "The Mercenaries" (in Griffin, 104–12). Lorrie, George Horace Lorimer, *Saturday Evening Post* editor. Hoffman (1876–1966), editor of *Adventure*, a popular pulp magazine established in 1910 by Trumbull White; Charles Agnew MacLean (1880–1928), Irish-American editor of *Popular Magazine* (1904–1931). "The Woppian Way" also would be turned down by magazine editors, and it remains unpublished.

3 Reference to Don Juan, legendary libertine and seducer of women. Responding on the verso of EH's letter, Smith advised, "Under no circumstances sacrifice your purity to a waitress' passion."

4 "Odgar," Carl Edgar. "Stut," Kate Smith (also known as "Butstein").

To Ursula Hemingway, [c. mid-December 1919]

Dear Ura,

You must be having a whangleberry of a time with that sledding, I8m glad you're such a good sport about getting hurt and I8M sure that the boys appreciate it too. I'm in very bad with all the old maid school tecahers here because a young teacher, aged twenty name Donley asked me to take her to the teachers party and ball and I went with her and she wanted to shock them because she is going away this week for good. So we shocked them all right, we didn't pull anything rough at all, but just danced cheek to cheek, you know etc. Not a thing that you couldn't get way with at home but all the old maidens who dance three feet away from each other and count, one, two, three, four, and then run eight, and one dances out to the side of the other! Well we gave them an eye full of the modern dences as they are stepped at the Friar's Inn and the Folies Bergere.[1] And they commented rather freely.

I'm enclosing $5.00 and I want you to go to Mrs. Snyder's on Mich. Boulevard, you know where it is, and get me two boxes of candy and parcel post them to me up here.[2] Get what ever kinds look the best to you. Those marshmallow nuts all over 'em things are good. A[ll] of her candy is good. Get the same amount of different kinds of candy for each box, I want them for Christmas for Marge ane Pudge. Do this right away will you please Ura? I'll do something for you sometime. Mrs. Snyder's candy runs around .90 a pound so you ought to be able to get at least two lbs and a half apiece. Have them wrap them each separately and thentogether. Then send them to me here. Will you do that right away? If there isn't enuf kale supply it and I will make it upwards to you. You see Pudge and Mrage have been awfully good to me here and I ought to give them something fairly decent.

I'm sending you Six rocks[3] to get something for each of the kids and dad and mother. It won't buy anything decent of course but I'm low on kale and get 'em each some kind of a trinket. Will you do this for me old thing. The reason I8m getting Marge and Pudge something that costs more than what I get for you all is just because I am under obligations to them and you know how it is. You know I love you anyway. And I'm one christmas ahead of the family anyway.

Tell the famile tht theycan't see this letter because it is about Christmas presents. I expect to be home for the fourth of January. Don't break your kneck! And have a good time, but you'll have that anyway won't you, kneck or no kneck. I'm going to Toronto, Can to be there the tenth of Jan. I have a good job and a chance to keep on with my writing.[4] I'll explain it in a letter to Dad. I'm going to write him tonight.[5] I hate to leave here as I've had a bludy good time and written some really priceless yarns. You know sometimes I really do think that I will be a heller of a good writer some day. Every once in a while I knock off a yarn that is so bludy good I can't figure how I ever wrote it. I'll bring the carbons down to show you all. Everything good takes time and it takes time to be a writer, but by Gad I'm going to be one some day. Well do this for me will you old Kid?

Shoot up the candy and screed the writer ir write the screedr

Lots of Love.

THE STEIN.

Ernest H. Mainland Collection at NCMC, TL with typewritten signature

The conjectured letter date is based on Ursula's letter to EH of 21 December 1919 (JFK), responding to this one.

1 Friar's Inn, a popular nightclub and jazz venue at Wabash and Van Buren in downtown Chicago; EH had seen a show at the Folies Bergères, legendary Paris music and dance hall, when he passed through the city en route to Italy in June 1918.
2 Ora H. Snyder owned a chain of candy stores in downtown Chicago.
3 Rocks, slang for dollars.
4 EH had received a job offer from Ralph and Harriet Gridley Connable of Toronto to serve as a companion to their disabled son, Ralph, Jr., while they spent a few months in Palm Beach, Florida. While visiting her mother in Petoskey, Harriet Connable heard EH speak about his war experiences at the December meeting of the local Ladies Aid Society (Ohle, 106); Ralph Connable was the head of the F. W. Woolworth chain of five-and-ten-cent stores in Canada (Baker *Life*, 67).
5 In her letter to EH of 21 December, Ursula replied, "What are you going to do in Toronto? We all want to know— You said you were going to write Daddy the nite of the day you wrote

me and you havn't yet!" However, a 22 December letter from Clarence to EH reveals that EH had, in fact, written to his father, who responded, "I was very pleased to hear from you this past week and to have your confidence that I have not disclosed to any one. No one knows I received the letter from you" (JFK). Clarence said he would leave it to EH to "give out what fact you choose" when he returned to Oak Park. EH's letter to his father remains unlocated, perhaps destroyed by Clarence to keep his son's confidence.

To Howell G. Jenkins, [20 December 1919]

Dear Fever,

I'll bet you've cursed the bird and me out for a couple of fine specimens when we havn't written. In every letter he's asked for your address and just the other day I remembered to give it to him. So I suppose by now you may of hward from him. Well how have they been rolling? I had a letter from Pock but he was raving about the Black and the little fox all the time and it was so full of such terms as Strictures, Whangleberries, Dehooperized, and Peeks, that I couldn't get much news out of it. To avoid my raving along on kindred topics I'd better get down to business. I'm getting home either the 2nd or 3rd of January and will be home for about five days. Then I'm going to Toronto. I'll explain all that when I come down. But the point is that I'll be in the city of sin, and sometimes gin, for about five days at any rate and we want to get together. We'll want to beve cognac at the Venice and take in a show. If you havn't made arrangements to go with anyone else I8d like to have us take in the follies together. What do you say. Why don't you get tickets now for some night between the 2nd and 8th and we'll take it in. First getting in the proper state of appreciation through the splitting of a flask of chianti at the Venice and imbibing a couple or three or four Cognaci. How about it? Get the tickets will you and then I'll settle with you when I come.[1] I'd send kale but I'm nearly flat but can tap the banco when I come home. This Toronto thing looks like the original Peruvian Doughnuts.[2] If you want to get in touch with Pock you can call him at John L. Pentecost, Elmhurst Ill. He's in the phone book or just ask central for long distance. Pock is John l/ Jr. Well I've got to ring off. See what you can do and Merry Christmas old cock.

Ciaou,

Stein

Stanford, TLS; postmark: PETOSKEY / MICH., DEC 20 / 1 – PM / 1919

On verso of the letter is the typescript first page of "WOLVES AND DOUGHNUTS: A Story," bearing EH's name, his 602 State Street address in Petoskey, and the notation "3400 words." The fragment appears in Baker *Life* (65–66).

1 According to Baker, the Venice Café at 520 South Wabash Avenue in Chicago, run by David Vigano, was a possible prototype for the Café Cambrinus, the setting of "Wolves and Doughnuts" (*Life*, 575). The *Ziegfeld Follies* annual revue was then playing at the Colonial Theatre in Chicago (Percy Hammond, "The Theaters," *Chicago Daily Tribune*, 14 December 1919, E1). EH and Jenkins would attend on 7 January (EH to Grace Quinlan, [1 January 1920]).

2 Harry Leon Wilson's story, "The Real Peruvian Doughnuts," appeared in the *Saturday Evening Post* (9 October 1915) and was included in his collection of Ma Pettengill stories, *Somewhere in Red Gap* (New York: Doubleday, 1916). EH uses the term in "Wolves and Doughnuts" (later titled and posthumously published as "The Mercenaries").

To Grace Quinlan, [c. 26 December 1919]

Dear G.E::—

According to Red's mother she Red not the Mother has to take a nap etc. to be in shape for tonight. The Judge is here with useless in spite of all our best efforts. You better rest up some too so as to be able to shake a very clever foot tonight with the smallest possible danger of going haywire. We're leaving and hope to be able to shake the Judge (Walter).[1]

Sorry you weren't here. Thanks for the note. The Book'll keep. We havn't started it yet. The Judge would ruin it anyway.

We'll see you tonight.

Pip Pip

Your Bro, Stein

Also Red

Useless

Yale, ALS; letterhead: American Central Insurance Company / IN SAINT LOUIS / THOS. QUINLAN & SONS CO., INC., / Petoskey, Mich.

On the envelope EH wrote, "Miss G. E. Quinlan. / Adressed" and, in the upper left corner, "After Five Days if not called for Take Down and Burn." EH apparently is responding to a note from Quinlan enclosed in an envelope addressed to "Pudge, Marge & Stein" below the notation, "STOP! / LOOK! / READ!" In her note, dated only "1:30 P.M," Quinlan wrote, "Just make yourselves comfortable until I get here and, Stein, please don't read them the story until I get home" (JFK). The conjectured letter date is based on a letter EH received from Evelyn Ramsdell (b. 1905), another of his teenaged friends in Petoskey, shortly after he left town. Her letter is in the form of a short play, "That Fatefull Day," set at the Quinlan house on 26 December 1919, 3:30 to 5:30 p.m., and with the following cast: EH as "Stine," Evelyn as "Eve," Grace Quinlan as "G. E.," Marjorie Bump as "Red," and Georgianna Bump as "Pudge" or "Useless" (JFK). The play features a gathering of friends bantering and dancing, presumably recalling the activities anticipated in EH's letter to Quinlan.

1 Possibly Walter Engle or Walter Gilbert, both classmates of Georgianna Bump.

To Grace Quinlan, [1 January 1920]

Thursday Evening

Dear Sister Luke[1]—

Been here since yesterday matin[2] and it seems like a million of the years. Gee up in your village a day went like a flash— here they're ages long. Gee Luke I do miss you a lot. I wonder if you're at the Elk's Dance tonight?[3] I've had a lot of fun already Luke but I do wish I hadn't left Teposkey.

A gang came down about an hour ago it's 10:30 or so now to get me to go to a dance at the Club but I begged off to write. My gambe[4] went hay wired in pretty hard shape after last nights hoof weilding. Had cramps in both calves of my legs nearly all night. Didn't turn in till after three. By George, Luke, Error didn't creep in. She galloped in.[5] So I'm off dancage for a day or so. The living grandfather, not the dead one, he's dead, toted me to luncheon with Harry Lauder yesterday.[6] 'Arry was in fine shape. He was very bitter about the non tryage of the Kaiser and demanded it in the name of Justice and all that sort of thing.[7]

Himmel but this is a pen of the very foulest. And the writer hates to write on this kind of paper too.[8]

The fudge was priceless, to properly use that much used word. But it wasn't a bit better than your letter which was a darb.

Gee I'm glad you're my Sister Luke.

I told all the family about what a peach you were and how you can ride and dance and swim and do everything just a whole lot better than anybody else and what a good scout you are and how good looking you are how much of the old think bean you have and oh everything. Then I raved about you when I took tea with Isabel Simmons this aft.[9] Everybody in the middle west will know that Stein Hemingway has a sister up North named Luke that is pretty darned nice.

Foregathered with Tubby Williams yesterday aft and he is the same old bird. Red Pentecost and the Fever called me up and were lunching Saturday at the Venice Cafe.

There's going to be an Arditi dinner of 15 of the old gang from all over the country at the North Side Saturday night. Jenks had arranged it and he was going to wire me today to come down. Called up to see when I'd be here. It'll be quelque occassion. A surmise that the hand of grog will stalk would not be far wrong. 15 of the old gang! Dad has 6 mallards that he's turned over to me to stage a game supper with Sunday night. And Monday I go to Pagliacci to hear Titto Ruffo and Tuesday have to step out Irene Goldsteen and Wed. the Follies with the Fever. So it doesn't look like there'll be much time spent studying the S.S. lessons.[10]

If this letter is too long Luke you can skip whatever you want to you know. But I miss you so I feel like talking to you so excuse all this ravege about what the screeder is doing etc. Wont it be great to get together again in the Spring? Havn't had any rows. But several girls got a bit miffed because I told 'em they couldn't dance as well as you all.

Maybe I'll not go to Toronto or K.C. either one. Kenley Smith was asked by the Firestone Tyre people to get 'em a publicity man to do some stuff on this "Ship by Truck" campaign and he asked me to do it. It may be too late as they asked 3–4 days ago. It pays $50 a week and expenses and involves goage to Cleveland, Toledo, Buffalo, Detroit etc. If it's still open I'll take it.[11]

Well I must shut offwards.

Good night Luke dear Sister

Love from your brother

Stein.[12]

Don't stall about writing. I'll take that trip for you.

(My best regards to your mother and father)

Yale, ALS; postmark: OAK PARK, ILL., JAN 2 / 3$\frac{30}{}$ PM / 1920

Quinlan wrote on the envelope, "My first letter from Stein."

1 EH is responding to an affectionate "train letter" from Quinlan, dated 27–29 December 1919, which she gave him to read during his journey from Petoskey back to Oak Park via the Grand Rapids and Indiana Railroad. In it she mentioned making fudge for him, asked him to remember that he was her "<u>very</u> only brother," and signed off, "Love, Your Sister Luke" (JFK).

2 Morning (French).

3 The Benevolent and Protective Order of the Elks, commonly known as the Elks Club, a charitable social organization founded in 1868 with local chapters across the United States.

4 Legs (Italian).

5 EH is echoing Quinlan's lament in her recent letter, "Error sure has crept in to my pen and mind."

6 Living grandfather, Anson Hemingway; EH's maternal grandfather, Ernest Hall, died in 1905. Scottish entertainer Harry Lauder was performing at the Studebaker Theatre in Chicago during the week of 29 December (Advertisement, *Chicago Daily Tribune*, 26 December 1919, 22; "Harry Lauder Here with a Title and a Brand New Joke," *Chicago Daily Tribune*, 30 December 1919, 15). EH's grandfather and Lauder may have known each other through YMCA connections. Anson Hemingway had served as General Secretary of the Chicago YMCA for ten years, and during WWI, Lauder often entertained the troops at military camps under the auspices of the YMCA.

7 German emperor Kaiser Wilhelm II (1859–1941) had abdicated on 9 November 1918 and fled to the Netherlands. Although the Treaty of Versailles provided for his prosecution, the Dutch government refused to extradite him for trial, and he would remain in exile for the rest of his life. Lauder, who had lost his only son in the war, was famous for his patriotic orations and anti-German sentiments as well as for his comedy.

8 *Himmel*: heaven (German). Ink smudges throughout the letter indicate that EH was having trouble with his pen. The letter is written on both sides of pinkish, cross-grained paper measuring about 5 by 6½ inches.

9 Isabelle Simmons's family lived next door to the Hemingways, at 612 North Kenilworth in Oak Park. She was then a senior in high school.

10 *Pagliacci* (*The Clowns*), Italian opera composed by Ruggiero Leoncavallo (1857–1919) and first performed in 1892; it played at the Auditorium Grand Opera in Chicago on 5 January 1920, with Italian baritone Titta Ruffo (né Titta Cafiero Ruffo, 1877–1953) in the role of Tonio ("The Opera: Concerts and Recitals," *Chicago Daily Tribune*, 4 January 1920, F4). Irene Goldstein, friend from Petoskey then attending Columbia College in Chicago. EH and Howell "Fever" Jenkins would have seen the *Ziegfeld Follies* at the Colonial Theatre (*Chicago Daily Tribune*, 7 January 1920, 13). "S.S.," EH's shorthand for Sunday School.

11 Advertising campaign created in 1918 by Firestone Tire and Rubber Co. founder Harvey S. Firestone (1868–1938) to encourage long-distance motor travel and support the creation of an interstate highway system. Eight brochures were published (December 1919–1921), but EH's work on these, if any, is undocumented. In a later letter to Quinlan (16 November–1 December [1920]), he would report having written some publicity for Firestone that year.

12 EH's following postscript ("Don't stall about writing. I'll take that swim for you") is in response to Quinlan's letter. She had written, "Don't forget that you were to take several swims for me and about five times as many dives."

To Edwin Pailthorp, [c. mid-January 1920]

Mr. Edwin Pailthorp
care Ralph Connable.
4 Queen Street West.
Toronto, Ontario.

Am throwing down forty a week and expenses to come to Toronto. Suggest you meet train with competent corps of alienists. Reserve room at best asylum. Reason has tottered.

Ernest M. Hemingway

UTulsa, TCD with typewritten signature

The conjectured letter date is based on a 12 January 1920 letter from Ralph Connable, Sr., to EH, offering him $50 per month in addition to expenses and assuring him that he could devote most of his time to his "literary pursuits" (JFK). Connable evidently was responding to a letter from EH that remains unlocated. Connable wrote: "Just received your letter and understand just how your father would feel when you have something definite in sight there and you know very little as to what your future would be in Canada." Pailthorp, one of EH's best friends in Petoskey, recently had moved to Toronto to work for Connable at the Woolworth Company (Baker *Life*, 65–66).

To Dorothy Connable, 16 February 1920

153 Lyndhurst,
February 16, 1920.

Dear Dorothy,

Ralph received a letter today from your mother portions of which he retailed to me. According to Ralph you visited the casino with five dollars and returned with seventeen and have taken a great interest in the game.[1]

So I'm stopping work on my magnum opus, "Night Life Of the European Capitols, Or The War As I Seen It" to place at your disposal the results of a mis-spent earlier boy hood.

Paragraph. Roulette is almost invariably honest. It doesn't need to be dishonest because they win anyway. The chances are 38 to 1 against your getting any single number that you select and it only pays 36 to 1 if you win.[2] So in the long run by the law of averages you will go broke.

Paragraph. There are many devices made for croupiers to brake or control a dishonest wheel. But the wheels at Palm Beach are straight so there's no use in going into them.

However there are one or two ways of playing roulette that give you a good chance of making money and you have the satisfaction of knowing that you are playing it well. Gee it makes me feel hungry just to talk about Roulette!

Hunches aren't any good. A hunch may be right once, but it's wrong a lot more times.

One good way to play scientifically is to watch how the wheel is running for a little while and what numbers are winning. The thing to do however is to watch what numbers aren't winning. Then take a number that hasn't been up for a long time, say 00 and put a chip on it, if you lose put on two chips, if you lose again four chips and so on until the number comes. You win at that if you stick—but it takes nerve. That's the way the real roulette player does when he is getting down low and want's to get capital to stage a comeback. You see it ought to come once in thirty eight spins and when the wheel has gone twenty or thirty times without a number showing it is a pretty good plan to begin to back it. There's nothing except the law of averages that evens everything up in the long run to prevent it going fifty more times without coming up, and sometimes it does, but the chances are that it won't.

That's a good way to play when the tables are crowded and you can't get in close and get a seat. When you can get a seat this is a pretty good way to do.

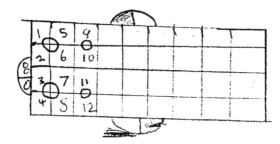

The wheel will probably be running, high, medium or low. That is the numbers will be running more often in one of the three thirds of the board. The first twelve, the second twelve or the third twelve. You want to pick which ever third they seem to be coming most often in and play as I have marked. In this way with four chips you are playing twelve numbers. The odds are roughly 1 in three that you will win, two to one against you, that is. But if you win on either of your chips that are covering four numbers it pays nine to one, and if you cash on either of your chips that are covering two numbers you are paid eighteen to one. So in the long run you win if you're lucky you are liable to make quite a lot of kale and at the worst you can play quite a long while at that system before you go broke.

Probably you already know all this and it's comparable to Edwin explaining that English on the right makes the ball go to the right etc.[3] But just on a chance that you didn't I whanged it out. It at least can claim the merit of not being theoretical but was worked out by bitter experience in the very best gambling hells in Yarrup.[4]

Goldwyn Gregory and La Belge were over last night and stayed till after eleven. We played billiards, played the organ yarned around and I committed ghetto french toward Yranne. Spelling very doubtful. Mrs. Dinnink, Dyssique or Derrick, whose name I'd love to spell if I could, called on the phone yesterday for your address. Mr. D_ _ _ _k, D_ _ _ _ _e or D_ _ _ _ _ _ _ck, her husband, has been quite ill. She and I are going to a musicale if there ever is one. She is going to write your mother.

£ are quoted @ three something or other. That remark is made through a desire to use the £ & @ which have never been used heretofore.

Will your mother keep up here bicycling when she returns to Toronto?

Let's see, you don't write letters do you? Neither do I. This is merely a treatise on the evils of gambling. Probably you aren't really interested in roulette any way. But it is the best game in the world, having the advantage over craps that in craps you are winning you friendVs money and consequently it is not so much fun. But in roulette you are bucking a wheel and there are no ethics against quitting when you are ahead. You can't do that in craps or poker. It is the loser who has to say when to quit. But in roulette when you get a decent way ahead—quit.

If you should play any along the line I've mentioned I'd like to know how you come out. Arte pour l'arte,[5] or however it is spelled, you know. Wire me collect or something.

My love to Mrs. Connable.

Hoping If luck is a raindrop you is the Mississippi,

Ernest Hemingway.

phPSU, TLS

1 Dorothy, sister of Ralph Connable, Jr., was vacationing with their parents in Palm Beach, Florida.
2 In the casino game of roulette, a croupier spins a wheel divided into thirty-eight numbered pockets (thirty-seven outside the United States), and players gamble on the number of the pocket in which a small ball will come to rest.
3 Edwin is "Dutch" Pailthorp. "English," a spin deliberately given to a ball along its vertical axis; in billiards, the player strikes the cue ball off-center to control its direction after it hits the object ball.
4 Playful spelling of "Europe."
5 *L'art pour l'art*: art for art's sake (French).

To William D. Horne, Jr., 25 March 1920

153 Lyndhurst Avenue.

Toronto Ontario.

March 25 1920

Dear Old Kid,

Why I wouldn't care what anatomical portion of the quadreped you alleged yourself to be so long as there isn't any good reason for your not writing me. The trouble is that when you lay offn me for six or seven months I know that there is noting wrong about you but begin to wonder where the hell I have fallen down.

How I would love to see you. You old low life why didn't you have the Fever wire me when you were in town? I'd have come down from the North like a shot. Anyway that's all right. Only the next time don't make your segregation from me so absolute.

Just at present I'm here in Toronto. The sheckels[1] are accumulating to a certain hardly perceptible degree. There will however be enough to take me North in the Spring.

That's all I'm living for. That's where you'd better come. We have the most wonderful trout fishing, swimming, hikes, loafing, any damn thing you wish including the best bunch of young Kids of the femme persuasion to pal aro[u]nd with when you're fed up with me.

Words can't describe the Fishing in the Black, Pidgeon and Big Sturgeon Rivers. Just take mine and Corp Shaw's word for it that the Black is the best trout stream in the States.

We camp at the Black way out on the barrens and you won't see a house or a soul. Nothing but the Pine Barrens with great wide sweep and ridges of pine trees rising up like islands. And the fishing is absolutely wonderful.

Come on up and stay for justas long as you can. If you decide to cut loose come on up and stay always and then go and bum with me in the fall. If you don't cut loose come on up when you get your vacation and you and I the Fever and the best bunch of guys you have ever known will have a trip that will eclipse even Schio in its Balmiest days.

I'll be here for a couple of months yet sweating to make the jack to buy freedom with this summer. You wouldn't like this town altho you might. But it is just like evry other damn city, a milling, stinking, sweating money grubbing place, and right now I'm one of the millingest, sweatingest, stinkingest, in spite of a morning tub, money brubbers of them all.

But two months from now I'm free Bill.

Come on Up for the love of the Lord. Or for anything else. We are located at Horton's Bay on Pine Lake Michigan. If you can't find that on the map look for—Boyne City and then work west along the Lake. The way you come is to take a train on the G.R. AND I. and Michigan Central to Boyne Falls. We tote you in from there. Or else come here and we'll go to Chicago together and see the Fever and absorb a few at the Venice and then go up together. Stopping in Chi long enough to give you a chance to observe the home life of the genus Hemingstein in their native habitat. And perhaps see a ball game or twa.

The Bay is the place for you Bill. Take it from the writer who should know.

It has the endorsement of such widely divergent boids as Barney, Jenks and myself. You'll just have to take our word for it.

Now write me and say that you are going to carry on for a brace[2] more of the months and then blow up North. Once our particular part of the North get's into you—life isn't a foul mess any more. I may be foul at the time but smash right through it thinking of the next summer's permissione.[3]

You'll just have to believe me—come on up—and then you'll be a new man from then on. I wouldn't give it up for all the wine, women and song in the world—and I was never opposed to any of the great trilogy. Although I was ever a poor singer.

Now write me subito[4] Bill at the Toronto Address.

Ciaou

Hemmy.

Newberry, TLS; envelope letterhead: RALPH CONNABLE / 4 QUEEN STREET WEST / TORONTO, ONT; postmark: TORONTO / ONT. / MAR 26 / 8 PM / 1920

EH enclosed three snapshots with these typewritten captions on versos: "One of Our Camps on the Barrens," "Jenks and Barney wit Trout," and "The Fever on the Black." On the envelope front EH crossed out the Connables' preprinted return address and wrote on the back flap: "Ernest M. Hemingway / 153 Lyndhurst Avenue / Toronto / Ontario."

1 Shekel: a coin based on a Hebrew unit of weight of the same name; used in the plural, slang for money or wealth.
2 Pair, a term usually applied to animals or birds killed in hunting.
3 EH apparently invented an Italian-sounding word to mean "leave of absence" (correctly, *permesso*).
4 Immediately (Italian).

To Grace Hall Hemingway, 6 April [1920]

Wednesday April 6.

Dear Mother,

Pardon this paper. It's all there is around just now. I'm glad you like the little lily. Thank you very much for the awfully nice letter you wrote.[1]

I've been laid up with a bad throat and working like the deuce at the same time so I havn't had much time for writing. My throat is still pretty bad and it knocks me out generally. A throat specialist has been working on it at four bucks a throw so I havn't been able to cache much of my earnings. It looked like the Vincent's Angina for a while and has been quite as sore as it ever was when I had tonsils. As soon as it gets decent weather again and I get in shape it will be all right

Sorry about the clippings. The next time I write I will send you some. It was the Sunday World I was writing for, not the Globe tell Dad. The Sunday Star is not called that but the Toronto Star Weekly.[2]

I've been doing some rather important political stuff for them lately. Will send you some. We're out to get the Mayor who is almost as much of an ass as Thompson and I've been riding him.[3]

Brummy may have called you up by now. He is in Chicago and is staying with Jenks until he gets located. I hope that you will be awfully nice to him and ask both he and Jenks out to the house. Brummy has been over in Paris and down in South America and in New Orleans since last spring. He worked his way all around and had a wonderful time. I am going to start out with him in the fall and have a look around. It will be good for me and almost a necessity for my writing. Absolutely invaluable.[4]

Brummy knows the ropes now. He never knows that I was at all peeved at him when he left Italy and it was a misunderstanding rather than anything else. He would have looked after my stuff but didn't understand exactly what I wanted. Brummy is a peach all right and I hope that you can have he and Tubby and Jenks out to dinner together.

Jenks adress is 6702 Newgard Avenue, Rogers Park and you will find his number in the phone book. Under Jenkins.[5]

For a while we had very nice weather here but now it has turned cold and snow again. Probably the same with you. While the good weather was on I played tennis and had a lot of fun. I'm not getting any kale from Mr. Connable now at my own request and am living off the money I get from the Star. My Doctor bill has pretty well gypped that and so I havn't any kale now or I would send Dad some tell him. I owe him about thirty some bucks. But please tell him that when I come north I will have plenty of kale and will pay him then. I have to spend about a buck a day on my lunch at noon and am always needing clothes and things so it keeps me pretty well down. The Doggone Star only pay once a month which is very inconvenient.

However on the first of may I'll be very Jake.[6] Will probably blow from here about the first of June or thereabouts and go North through Chicago. Meeting Bill there and driving up.

Lots of love to you and the Kids and Dad,

Ernie

PSU, TLS; postmark: TORONTO / ONT., APR 7 / 3[30] PM / 1920

1 The letter is on poor-quality paper, now yellowed, cut irregularly on one side. EH is responding to Grace's letter of 3 April 1920 thanking him for the beautiful Easter lily he had sent and asking him to send clippings of his newspaper work (JFK).
2 The *Sunday World* was the weekly feature magazine of the *Toronto World*, a daily newspaper that began in 1880 and would cease publication in April 1921. Any writing EH may have done for the *Sunday World* remains undocumented; none is identified in Hanneman's bibliography, and available microfilm copies of the *World* do not include Sunday editions. The *Toronto Globe* was founded in 1844 as a weekly newspaper and by 1853 was published daily; in 1936 it merged with another paper to become the *Globe and Mail*. The *Toronto Star* (founded in 1892) was then the city's largest newspaper and published the Sunday magazine *Star Weekly*. In all, 172 identifiable pieces by EH appeared in the *Star Weekly* from 14 February 1920 until 13 September 1924, and in the *Daily Star* from 4 February 1922 until 6 October 1923 (*DLT*, xxix).
3 Thomas Langton Church (1870–1950), mayor of Toronto from 1915 to 1921. EH lampooned him in "Sporting Mayor at Boxing Bouts" (*Star Weekly*, 13 March 1920; *DLT*, 8–9) and "Trading Celebrities" (*Star Weekly*, 19 February 1921; *DLT*, 67–69). William "Big Bill" Thompson (1869–1944) was mayor of Chicago 1915–1923 and 1927–1931.
4 EH would not make this trip.
5 On the envelope, probably in Clarence's hand, is this note: "Phoned 8[30] pm 4/14 1920 Roger's Park 3411." Rogers Park, a Chicago neighborhood.
6 Slang term for "excellent" or "fine."

To Clarence and Grace Hall Hemingway, 22 April 1920

April 22.

Dear Dad and Mother,

Both of your good letters came yesterday and I was very glad to learn that Brummy and Jenks had been out and had such a good time.[1]

I'm quite tired tonight and so I'm not going to attempy much of a letter—but just a line to let you know I'm well and everything is going well. A week ago Sunday I went over to Buffalo and saw Arthur Thomson one of the old Wop gang.[2] If I have anything any good in the weekly tomorrow I'll clip it out and stick it in this.

While the weather was good have been playing lots of tennis. My leg is in very decent shape altho it swells quite a bit after a hard day it doesn't bother me much. Friday I played seven sets and Saturday nine sets. Went to the Opera Saturday night, Cavaleria Rusticana and Pagliacci. De Frere, Du Franne, and a tenor named O'Sullivan who was a perfect whang. Anna Fitziu too.[3] None of the very high salaried stars, but very decent opera. O'Sullivan is a bear he sang Vesti la Guibba better than Enrico.[4]

Played bridge last night at Elsie Green's with her father and mother. Went on a picnic way into the country sunday aft with Bonnie Bonnelle.[5] Went to a dance with Doris Smith and to the Opera with Dorothy Connable. Ralph has had the mumps very badly. I didn't catch them thank the Lord. I've had about everything else.

Give my love to the kids and yourselves.

Your always loving son,

JFK, TLcc

1 In her letter to EH of Monday, 19 April 1920, Grace reported, "Yesterday we invited Jenks and Ted Brumback to dinner—they seemed to enjoy it very much, so much so, that they stayed 'til after supper" (JFK). EH also may be referring to a letter from his father that remains unlocated: a 13 April 1920 letter from Clarence to EH survives (JFK), but it seems unlikely that it would have arrived the same day as Grace's later letter.
2 Arthur E. Thomason, a fellow member of ARC Ambulance Service Section 4 who served with EH in Italy in WWI. Buffalo, New York, is about a 100-mile journey from Toronto.
3 *Cavalleria Rusticana* (*Rustic Chivalry*), a one-act opera by Italian composer Pietro Mascagni (1863–1945) that premiered in Rome in 1890 and is frequently performed along with Leoncavallo's *Pagliacci*. Désiré Defrère (1888–1964) and Hector Dufranne (1871–1951), tenors with the Chicago Opera; John O'Sullivan (1877–1955), an Irish tenor with the Paris Opera, was performing in North America in 1920. American soprano Anna Fitziu (1888–1967) made her debut with the Chicago Opera in 1917.
4 *Vesti la giubba* (*Put on the costume*), tenor aria sung at the end of Act I of *Pagliacci*. Italian tenor Enrico Caruso (1873–1921), affiliated with New York's Metropolitan Opera Company and a pioneering recording artist, was then the world's most popular and highest-paid singer. His 1904 recording of *Vesti la giubba* was the first phonograph record to sell more than a million copies.
5 Bonnie Bonnell was related to the wealthy Massey family, who had endowed Toronto's Massey Hall, a large venue for concerts, conventions, and sporting events that opened in 1894. She and EH rode horses through the western suburbs and called themselves the Bathurst Street Hunt Club (Baker *Life*, 69; William Burrill, *Hemingway: The Toronto Years* [Toronto: Doubleday Canada, 1994], 34–35).

To Clarence and Grace Hall Hemingway, 27 April [1920]

Star Office
April 27th.

Dear Dad and Mother:

I had written you several letters but neglected to mail them.[1] Going to try and get this one off. Glad Brummy and Jenks could be out Sunday.

Have been playing a lot of tennis here lately. Ralph has had mumps very badly—but I didn't catch them.

I made a trip to Buffalo a couple of weeks ago and saw Arthur E. Thomason who was with me in Italy.

Have been working hard on the Star lately and enclose a clipping or two. One I wrote yesterday was quoted almost entirely today by The Globe in an editorial. Mr. Atkinson who owns The Star complimented me on it.[2]

I plan to hit Chicago about the 17th or Eighteenth and leave the 20th or 21st of May for the North. Driving through with Bill. Am going to do some more out Door stories for the Star up North. I'm recognized as an authority on Trout Fishing and camping here. Have one every week like Larry St. John in the Trib.[3] I work Bill and Jacque Pentecost into the yarns and the Boss doesn't know who they are. I'm crazy to go fishing.

Whats all the dope? I've another letter written to you 3 or four days ago at home that I'll try and remember to Post.

Lots of Love
as ever
Ernie.

PSU, ALS

1 The unmailed letters may include the previous one, dated 22 April, as EH here repeats some of what he had written earlier.
2 No clippings survive with this letter. The 27 April 1920 *Toronto Globe* editorial, "A National Purchasing Board," advocated centralized government purchasing of supplies, as did EH in his unsigned article "Buying Commission Would Cut Out Waste," published the previous day (*Toronto Star Weekly*, 26 April 1920; *DLT*, 25–26). EH's claim that the *Globe* extensively quoted his article is not entirely accurate: rather, both pieces quote a published statement on the topic by Ralph Connable, Sr., who had been appointed by the Canadian War Purchasing Commission to investigate the question (the *Globe* quoting Connable directly and EH quoting him indirectly). Joseph E. Atkinson (1865–1948) became manager and editor of

the *Star* in 1899 and principal shareholder in 1913; his editorial policies reflected his belief that a newspaper should promote social and political reforms.

3 St. John, outdoor-life columnist for the *Chicago Daily Tribune* and author of *Practical Bait Casting* (New York: Macmillan, 1918). The *Star Weekly* had already published two outdoor pieces by EH: "Are You All Set for the Trout?" (unsigned, 10 April 1920; *DLT*, 14–16) and "Fishing for Trout in a Sporting Way" (24 April 1920; *DLT*, 22–24). Five more articles by EH on fishing and camping would appear in the *Star Weekly* from June through November 1920 (*DLT*).

To Harriet Gridley Connable, 1 June [1920]

600 Kenilworth
June 1st.

Dear Mrs. Connable,

I must apologise for not having written sooner to tell you how much I enjoyed and appreciated being in your home.

You were awfully good to me and I want you to know how much it meant to me to know you all in addition to the priceless time I had.

Bill Smith was delayed getting here—just blew in yesterday, and shot a main bearing in the car so it's in the garage for a couple of days. We expect to shove off Thursday.

Brummy has been out at the house constantly and we've had a good time. He is all set on going in the fall and wants to leave from San Francisco. He says that as ordinary seamen we will make 70 seeds a month and should hit Yokahama with quite a little money even if we leave San Francisco broke. I am going to try and sign on as a stoker as there is more money in it. He says I only need the fare to Frisco.

Brummy has his pass port and I'm getting mine for China, Japan and India.[1]

I stopped in Ann Arbor and saw Jacques Pentecost and he and Brummy are coming North together about the fifteenth or twentieth of June.

It has been great to get all the gang together again.

All the family are jake and are going North the Seventh of June. Marcelline, my older sister and I are the best of pals now so I've no one at all to row with.

I miss Toronto and you and Mr. Connable and Dorothy and Ralph a lot and think of you very often.

It will be very good to see you in Petoskey and I look forward to having you come out to Walloon.

I've told the family many times that you are the very nicest people I have ever known and I look forward to having them meet you so they will agree with me.

At present the house is pretty badly shot to pieces. Jenny—our last bet in the maid line, couldn't stand the strain and so there is no one.[2]

At Walloon tho it doesn't matter.

Hope you and Dorothy have a darby trip and give my best to Mr. Connable and Ralph.

This letter is too long I know.

Yours very sincerely,
Ernest Hemingway.

phPUL, ALS

1 In a letter to EH of 23 April 1920, Brumback reported that during his recent visit with the Hemingways in Oak Park, he had "talked eloquently about the inestimable opportunity such a trip would give you in the writing game," but while Grace agreed in principle, she wanted her son to go to college (JFK; Reynolds *YH*, 99). They would not make the trip.
2 The 1920 U.S. Census record (dated 10 January) lists Jennie Fizek, age eighteen and born in Prague, as a servant in the Hemingway household in Oak Park. Reynolds reports that in seventeen years, the Hemingways employed ten new maids, which some have seen as a sign that Grace was "impossible to work for." However, the family frequently hired a new maid when they returned from Michigan in the fall, "indicating their previous girl had not wanted to be unemployed for two months of the summer" (*YH*, 108).

To Grace Hall Hemingway, [24] June 1920

Thursday

Dear Mother—

Went to the Beach with Jock and then he went South and Bill arrived with Brummy and grub to stay a week. Home at the Bay next Tuesday June 29. Will try and get over right soon to help you with the Dock.[1]

Write me at R.F.D. No 2
Boyne City

Love to all
Ernie

Came in here Mon to see Dr. Bad throat.

JFK, A Postcard S; postmark: [VANDERBILT] / MICH, JUN / [2]4 / 7 PM / 1920

EH addressed the postcard to "Mrs. Dr. C. E. Hemingway / care Joe Bacon / RFD / Petoskey / Michigan."

1 Although EH frequently stayed at the Dilworths' place in Horton Bay, bunking in a shed attached to the rear of the kitchen (Ohle, 104), Grace expected his help with chores around Windemere, including putting out the boat dock at the beginning of the summer season.

To Grace Quinlan, 1 August [1920]

August 1st.

Dearest G:

Awfully sorry old dear that I haven't written before—but so much has happened.

And now while I'm trying to write there are 8 cursed clacking tongued boarders talking.

Hope you're having a swell time at Camp G. You cant be homesick with Pudge and Ev and all there.[1]

Which reminds me that I haven't any home now. Literally you know. Kicked out quite permanently.

And fired from home for no decent reason even.

I'd write you all about it but probably it would bore you. Brummy was thrown out at the same time!

Makes a guy feel kind of rotten to know that he hasn't any home even if he doesn't use it. So I'm a bit blue—and is bad to be accused unjustly too.[2]

Urse my sister was in visiting Red and told her all the straight dope about it so may be youve heard.

Jacque and the Fever and Dick Smale are up and the Odgar comes the 14th or so.[3]

Aw Luke I feel low tonight. Sam Nickey and I were fishing together last week. Stayed at the Club and had great fishing. I took the record brook trout for the Vanderbilt Club.[4] A little over two pounds.

Tomorrow morning we're going out on the Black and then in a couple of weeks to Seney.

If you write me a letter here I'll get it when Bill comes out to camp
Thursday with the mail.

I want to write you a long letter G and tell you all about every thing but I'm
so cursed tired and sleepy—up all last night fishing—and cant write worth a
hang. And also feel low and lonesome in spite of the men—

Better go on a way tho 'cause this is a gloomy good for nawthing letter.

Brummy and I beat Bill and Dr. Charles in tennis at the Voix.[5]

Boxed last week and stopped Bob Loomis (178 lbs.) in 4 rounds. Didn't
have a mark.

Gee cant seem to get any thing but the most tiresome common places
in this. And there are so many big and interesting things to tell you. But
the[y] wont write.

Never can tell whether you give a darn about me or not and I hate to bore
you with a lot of troubles and so on.

Give my love to Useless and I think she owes me a screed.

All my love Gee,

Immer[6]

Stein.

Yale, ALS; postmark: BOYNE CITY, MICH., AUG 2 / 3–30 P / 1920

1 Quinlan was attending Camp Arbutus, a summer camp for girls near Mayfield, Michigan,
about 70 miles southwest of Petoskey. EH refers in this letter to other teenaged Petoskey
friends Georgianna Bump ("Pudge" or "Useless"), Evelyn Ramsdell, and Marjorie Bump
("Red").

2 As EH would explain in more detail in his letter to Quinlan of 8 August, his mother had
banished him from Windemere after a confrontation with him over a surreptitious midnight
picnic on 27 July involving Brumback, Ursula, Sunny, and four younger friends. Grace held
EH responsible for the incident and later that day handed him a letter (dated three days
earlier, 24 July 1920) outlining her grievances over what she regarded as his disrespectful and
rebellious behavior that summer. EH moved to a boarding house in Boyne City (Reynolds
YH, 135–38; Baker *Life*, 71–73).

3 Jack Pentecost, Howell Jenkins, Dick Smale (whom EH would identify in his next letter as a
"new guy"), and Carl Edgar.

4 Sam Nickey was probably a member of the A. B. Nickey family mentioned in Marcelline's
memoirs (Sanford, 84). The Nickeys appear in several Hemingway family photographs taken
at Windemere (PSU, Madelaine Hemingway Miller scrapbooks). According to the Otsego
County Historical Society, the Vanderbilt Club, or Vanderbilt Sportsman Club, was a
hunting and fishing lodge on the Pigeon River, 8–10 miles east of the town of Vanderbilt,
Michigan.

5 EH played tennis in Charlevoix with Brumback, Bill Smith, and Bill's uncle, Joseph Charles.
6 Always (German).

To Grace Quinlan, 8 August 1920

Aug 8 1920

Dearest G:

Well we were out on the Black and yesterday got back to the Bay and your letter was waiting.[1] And I'd rather get a letter from you than anybody else and I sure like to get letters so—

Gosh G what a hiker you are. 11 and 15 of the miles! That's real honest to [God] hiking. You must be having a peerless time.

It must be that thee and me are the kind that dont get homesick. Haven't ever been and yours was so far away as not to count.

We had a marvelous time this trip. Brummy and Jacques and the Fever and a new guy named Dick Smale.

Brum can play the mandolin wonderfully and in the evening he would play after supper in the Dark outside the camp fire.

And before we went to sleep we'd all be curled up around the fire[.] Often a wonderful moon and the guy's would have me read Lord Dunsany's Wonder Tales out loud. He's great.[2]

And Bill and Dr. Charles and the Madame came out one day and we caught about 50 trout and got a wonderful mess for them to take home.

Brummy and Dick were wading down the stream and Brummy was tired and wet and about two miles below camp. Brum's beard was blond and curly and Dick sez, "Gosh Baugh you do look like Jesus Christ!"

"Well," the Baugh comes back at him, "If I was I wouldn't wade. I'd get right up on the water and walk back to camp!"

That wasn't such a bad one Nespah? We rented a car and a trailer for a week. Jock and I took some Darby fish.

Came home yesterday and all went in to the Voix and played Cook's. I had only Six seeds to my name and was thinking I'd have to write to the Bank at home for more or work in the cement plant and then I played roulette until 2 a.m. this morning and won 59.[3] Was going strong playing the rouge

and noir, the way I learned in Algeciras—but the men made me quit as
they wanted to go home.[4] Hemingstein luck.

59 of the seeds would be several days at the cement plant.

8 girls must be a lot in one tent G. We have plenty when we put two guys
in one. But then they make you be neat Eh?

Didnt we rate a great moon the first of last week? It was great in camp
lying all rolled up in the blankets after the fire had died down to coals and
and the men were asleep and looking at the moon and thinking long, long,
thoughts. In Sicily they say it makes you queer to sleep with the moon on
your face. Moon struck. Maybe that's what ails me.

About the kicking out business. Ursula and Sunny and young Loomis kid
and a girl visiting her got up a midnight supper. They dragged the Baugh,
(Brummy) and I along. We didnt even want to go on the bludy thing. Pretty
much of a bore. And we all went out at 12 bells and had a big feed up at
Ryan's Point and came in about 3 am.[5]

Urse and Sunny and Bob Loomis and his Sister and Jean Reynolds and a
boy visiting Bob and Brummy and I went along.[6]

Mrs. Loomis missed the kids and was frantic and went to our house and raised
hell and accused the Baugh and I of getting up the party for the Lord knows
what foul purpose! And we were dragged along and really acted as chaperones!

So the next morning Brummy and I were kicked out without being
allowed to even tell them anything about it!

Mother was glad of an excuse to oust me as she has more or less hated me
ever since I opposed her throwing two or three thousand seeds away to
build a new cottage for herself when the Jack should have sent the kids to
college. That's another story. Fambly stuff. All famblys have skeletons in
their closets. Maybe not the Quinlan's but the Steins have heaps. "Heeps"
Red used to spell it.

Grandfather gambled away a fortune, have a great uncle that is a remittance man and cant go back to England and is never unsoused long enough
to endorse the checks he gets. His valet has to do it for him.[7] Oh all kinds of
fine scandals that we kept from the neighbors. And this is another one.

But isnt that the most ridiculous thing to get kicked out for? Have three or
four letters from them that I haven't even opened so Dont know what the

late dope is.[8] Am so damned disgusted I dont care to have anything more to do with them for a year at least.

The Baugh is all for Wopland[9] and I'm all for workage this winter. Jacque's going to work this winter and we might buy a car in the Spring and then cover all the country next summer. I hate jazzing all over Europe when there is so much of my own country I haven't seen.

~~But~~ And the Wopland gets in the blood and kind of ruins you for anything else. And I'd rather go later. You see I get so darned much fun out of working on a paper and writing and I like this country.

But then—It's all in the lap of the God's. I'm for a job in New York next winter. But then I'm also for the open road and long sea swells, and an old tramp steamer hull down on the oily seas.

And waking up in the morning in strange ports. With new delightful smells and a tongue you dont understand. And the rattle of shifting cargo in the hold.

And tall glasses and siphons. And rare new stories and old pals in far places. And hot nights on Deck with only pyjamas on.

And cold nights when the wind roars out side and the waves smash against the thick glass of the port holes and you walk on Deck in the flying scuds and have to shout to make yourself heard.

And laying chin down on the grass on a cliff and looking out over the sea. And oh such a lot of things G.

Anyway I'll bet no one else writes you such damned fool letters as I do.

We're here for about 3 or 4 days of tennis at the Voix. Bill and the Doc— Brummy and I, Jack and the Fever. We get some rare doubles. Also took a 4 lb rainbow this morning.

You played any tennis at camp? Were swimming a lot lately.

Must shut this off G old dear. What do you think about things.

And please write. I owe everybody else I know a screed.

Love (all Ive got)
Stein.

My best to Useless and Evalina.
PS. A.T.L. for you from Brummy.[10]

Yale, ALS; postmark: BOYNE CITY, MICH., AUG 9 / 1130A / 1920

1 EH is responding to a letter from Quinlan of 4 August 1920 (JFK) describing her activities at summer camp.
2 Edward Plunkett, the eighteenth Baron Dunsany (1878–1957), Anglo-Irish writer of fantasy whose works include *The Book of Wonder: A Chronicle of Little Adventures at the End of the World* (London: William Heinemann, 1912; Boston: J. W. Luce and Company) and *Tales of Wonder* (London: Elkin Mathews, 1916), published in the United States as *The Last Book of Wonder* (Boston: J. W. Luce and Company, 1916).
3 Cook's, a gambling establishment in Charlevoix (Constance Cappel, *Hemingway in Michigan* [Petoskey, Michigan: Little Traverse Historical Society, 1999], 185). EH is referring to the Petoskey Portland Cement Company, which began production in 1921 at its new plant just west of Petoskey on the shore of Lake Michigan's Little Traverse Bay.
4 Red and black (French), colors of most of the pockets on a roulette wheel; EH had briefly visited the Spanish port of Algeciras on his way home from Italy in 1919.
5 The group picnicked on the sandy point forming the Narrows on the west arm of Walloon Lake, about a mile up the shore from Windemere cottage. For Sunny's account, see "A Midnight Picnic" (M. Miller, 67–68); she notes that the next summer she was sent away to a girls' camp in Minnesota.
6 Jean Reynolds was a thirteen-year-old guest of the Loomis family at their lake cottage near Windemere, who reportedly had been flirting with EH. She and young Elizabeth Loomis invited EH and Brumback on the picnic (Baker *Life*, 71; Reynolds *YH*, 135).
7 Grandfather Ernest Hall and his brother-in-law William Randall had established the successful firm of Randall, Hall and Company Wholesale Cutlery in 1862; Marcelline recalled Grace's telling the children that in his retirement, Grandfather Hall had a "corner on wheat" in the stock market for a few hours and was a potential millionaire, but "lost it all" and thereafter returned to more modest investments (Sanford, 5). A "remittance man" is one living abroad supported by payments from home; "unsoused," sober. EH apparently is embellishing the family history for effect: his sole living great uncle, Benjamin Tyler Hancock (1848–1933), was born in England just months before his family emigrated to the United States, and he later worked as a traveling salesman of brass bedsteads (P. Hemingway, 520, 527).
8 Any letters EH's parents may have written between the date of the incident at Windemere and the date of this letter remain unlocated.
9 EH's slang for "Italy."
10 Evalina is Evelyn Ramsdell. A.T.L., perhaps "all tender love."

To Howell G. Jenkins, [16 September 1920]

Dear Mr. LeFever—The Carper:

Sorry as hell old bean that I haven't written you before—but then the men gave you all the dope up till when they left.

Since they left we have caught a lot of Rainsteins. A couple or so pretty near every day we fished for them. Also we have laid a hold of a high grade sailing craft and have sailed the ass offn it every day. Yesterday Kate and Odgar and I were sailing to the Voix and altho under a double reef we had such a hell of a storm that we had to put in at Ironton. Rain lightning thunder Tidal waves, typhoons and Gawd knows what.

Duck season opens today and we hope for a pogrom of the feathered ones. I expect to stay here until about the middle of October and will then flash down in the car with the Madam and the Bird and Stut. Having been barred from my domicile I know not where I will linger in Chi. Probably ask Vigano to leave me use a couple of blankets in the Venice. Will be in Chicago a few days and then allez to either Toronto or K.C. Had a letter from K.C. asking me to name my figure! As I can lay hold of fifty of the seeds four times a month in Toronto I am going to mention those statistics to them. Something tells me that they will come through. In that event I'll have plenty of Jack next summer. They offered the Baugh $175 a month and they always paid me more than the Baugh. Hope I can get some good sized Jack down there because I can clean up a hundred or hundred and fifty a month on the side out of my special correspondence. That's why I think that K.C. is the place cause I'll get a good salary there and supplement it with pretty near as much on the side from Toronto.[1]

Whadda you think?

In regards to Jack and Carp, don't let your enthusiasm run away with you.[2]

Remember this. Miske was a set up. He had been sick and was through in the ring and this was really a benefit given for him by Dempsey. They are very good friends and so Jack said. You have to give Miske the first crack at the title. It was ridiculous of course to expect Miske to do anything against Jack.[3]

Now Jack is going up against another good old war horse who is absolutely through[,] Gunboat Smith.[4] The Gunner was a hell of a good rough fighter altho a damned wild swinger. But now he is absolutely through. Somebody, some second rater knocked him out in Gra[n]d Rapids the other night.

Jack will polish him off in short order and then will knock out Bill Brennan who is one of the poorest fighters of all time.[5]

But what you want to remember Fever is that Geo. could take these set ups just as easily.

Geo. Went twenty rounds against Joe Jeanette, he's fought Billy Papke and Frank Klaus, he's knocked out Wells twice and Beckett in quicker time than Dempsey ever handled any one. He is no bloomer and no morning glory and don't go to think just because Dempsey is koing all the tramps that he is going to make an ass out of Mr. Carp.[6]

If you can get any one to give ten to one or anyhting like that that Dempsey will put him away in short order I'd snap it up like a shot. Because as soon as they pipe Geo. agin Battling Levinsky the price will tumble right through itself.[7]

Dempsey, fever, has never had a real fight yet, Geo. has a pile of them under his belt. Dempsey may be just as good as they say he is—but he has never proved that he is anything but a lightning fast puncher who packs a hell of a wallop. What he will do agin a man that is as fast a puncher as he is and that can stay away from him and hand out stuff in return is yet to be seen.

Ponder these things. Dempsey may beat his can off. But on the other hand there is a gaoddam good chance that he won't. And this is the first fight that Jack has ever been in that the result hasn't been determined before they stepped into the ring.

I sure enjoyed seeing Chic Take Francis Ouimet. To hell wit the Harvard Hedgehogs.[8]

What are you doing now? What is Poack doing? Is he going back to school? Do you ever see Dick?

How about the liquor problem?

Screed me carper and tell me what you think about my dope on Dempsey-Carp.

We have picked a lot of apples lately and also cut and set up Nine acres of sweet clover for seed. Oh Yes. I tore my gut on a cleat on the boat and had internal hemorrhages and yesterday the Doc lanced the navel and took out a lot of puss. Feels better today. They thought I was haywired tho for a while though.

We laid hold of some gloves and did a little boxing the other day. I went four rounds wit Honest Will[9] without getting a wallop, no only three rounds, and managed to swell Will's face up in nice shape. Will is fast and a hard puncher but don't know enough about the game. He is game though because I rocked him wit right and left hooks to the head and he kept coming in. We played three sets of tennis the other day and Will made me look worse on the courts tyan I made him wit the gloves.

Well I'll try and catch the official with this.

Screed and my best to your folks and to Dick.

Immer/

Stein.

phPUL, TL with typewritten signature; postmark: BOYNE CITY, MICH., SEP 16 / 1130A / 1920

1 EH never returned to work for the *Kansas City Star*, but he would continue to freelance for the *Toronto Star*.

2 On 2 July 1921, in a fight heavily promoted as the "Battle of the Century," American Jack Dempsey (1895–1983), world heavyweight boxing champion since 1919, would defend his title against French boxer Georges Carpentier (1894–1975). Despite EH's prediction of a Carpentier victory here and in an article for the 30 October 1920 *Toronto Star Weekly* ("Carpentier vs. Dempsey," *DLT*, 55–57), Dempsey would win that fight in a knockout, retaining his title until 1926.

3 William Arthur (Billy) Miske (1894–1924), who suffered from Bright's disease, a kidney disorder, was knocked out by Dempsey in a world heavyweight title bout on 6 September 1920 in Benton Harbor, Michigan ("Dempsey Visits Miskey at Hotel, Best of Friends," *Chicago Daily Tribune*, 9 September 1920, 18).

4 Gunboat Smith (né Edward J. Smyth, 1887–1974) lost his world heavyweight boxing title to Carpentier in July 1914. Dempsey and Smith reportedly were planning to meet in a title match in Boston, but it did not take place ("Dempsey Expects to Meet Gunboat Smith This Month," *New York Times*, 7 September 1920, 25; *Chicago Daily Tribune*, 9 September 1920, 18).

5 Bill Brennan (né Wilhelm Schenck, 1893–1924). EH predicted correctly: on 14 December 1920 Dempsey would beat Brennan by a knockout for the world heavyweight title.

6 In 1914 American heavyweight Joe Jeanette (né Jeremiah Jennette, 1879–1958) went fifteen rounds with Georges Carpentier and won on points. William Herman (Billy) Papke, "The Illinois Thunderbolt" (1886–1936), and Frank Klaus (1887–1948) each defeated Carpentier in middleweight championship title fights in France in 1912. In 1913 Carpentier knocked out English heavyweight "Bombardier" Billy Wells (1889–1967) in each of two bouts for the European heavyweight title. In 1919 Carpentier knocked out English boxer Joe Beckett (1892–1965) after one round to win the European heavyweight championship again. "Koing," boxing term for "knocking out."

7 American boxer Battling Levinsky (né Barney Lebrowitz, 1891–1949), world light heavyweight champion since 1916, would lose by a knockout to Carpentier on 12 October 1920.

8 Charles "Chick" Evans, Jr. (1890–1979), a Chicagoan, defeated Francis Ouimet (1893–1967) of Boston in the 1920 U.S. Amateur Golf Championship on 11 September. EH's disparagement of "Harvard Hedgehogs" may be an expression of regional pride; the *Chicago Daily Tribune* cast the win by Evans as a show of "Middle West Strength" over the Eastern golf establishment (Joe Davis, "Beating Ouimet Evans' Sweetest Win of Career," 13 September 1920, 14).

9 Bill Smith.

To Grace Quinlan, 30 September [1920]

September 30

Dearest G:

Your mither told me this morning that it was your birthday and so I at
once tore down town to get you something fitting. But haveing only fifty nine
centimes in my pocket I was seriously handicapped.

The gift of fifty nine one cent stamps was considered—or a months
subscription to the Evening Snewse or a bargain in special cut rate sale of
rubbers at Reinhertzes[1] but all were rejected on the grounds that you can
borrow stamps, have the paper anyway and probably dont wear rubbers.

So Kate and I and the Doc went to Martin's[2] and each had an alleged drink
and I requested that they drink to a very estimable lady of my acquaintance
whose birthday it was. And we drank and Kate wanted to know how old that
lady was and I said that she was approaching Thirty—slowly but surely. And
so on the strength of that we drank again and then all the money for your
birthday was gone.

But next time old bean I'll try and not go broke until after you celebrate.

This morning in your kitchen we were talking and in came Deggie and
discussion occurred in the course of which I was informed by Deggie that it
served me right to lose when I bet on the Sox last fall. Thinking the series was
honest. And that he didn't blame the sox for selling it etc.[3] And becoming
somewhat wroth, but not showing it I hope, a great and overpowering desire
to spank him laid hold of me. But it was conquered because thought I, "Sooth
and what will become of the snall remnants of my old drag if commit
spankage on a dear friend?"

Then Kate and I went to the catholic church and burnt a candle and I
prayed for all the things I want and won't ever get and we came out in a very
fine mood and very shortly after to reward me the Lord sent me Adventure
with a touch or Romance.

It was a very small adventure but it was unexpected and for a moment
thrilling and I was glad that I had burned the candle. For the details you'll
have to see Liz.[4]

As we drove home in the rain I thought long long thoughts about how fine
it is to be Fifteen and You.[5] And it raining quite hard and Kate going to sleep

I made a poem about you being fifteen and then when I got home I remembered how much more sense you have than I have and the rain having stopped and Kate having wakened up I thought that you would think that a poem would be a very foolish thing. And so I didn't send it.

Gee I'm awfully darned sorry that I've been such poor company this summer and so grouchy and I'm darned sorry that you don't like me as well as you did. And because I did like you better than anybody else it hurt when I heard that you were saying things about me behind my back

But that's not this which is your birthday and I hope it was a darned good one and that maybe if you don't feel too darned old you'll write me a letter

Good night

Love, old dear,

Stein

P.S. Burned a candle for you. Wonder if you'll rate any results. Told 'em to give you whatever you want.

Yale, TLS; postmark: BOYNE CITY, MICH., OCT 1 / 1130A / 1920

1 I. Reinhertz and Son, dry goods store at 410 East Mitchell Street in Petoskey. EH is referring to rubber overshoes, or galoshes.
2 Kate Smith and her uncle, Dr. Joseph Charles; Martin's Candy Corner in Petoskey.
3 In a gambling scandal that marred the 1919 World Series, eight Chicago White Sox players were accused of throwing the series to the Cincinnati Reds. They were formally indicted on charges of conspiracy by a grand jury in Chicago on 28 September 1920.
4 Liz, their mutual friend Elizabeth Shoemaker, also from Petoskey, then a junior in high school. In a letter to EH of 25 October 1920 (JFK), Shoemaker declared, "I'm thru with Harold Lee Ruggles!" a Petoskey boy who, she reports, was furious upon learning that EH had kissed her—probably the "adventure" EH alludes to here.
5 EH is mistaken about Quinlan's age; born in 1906, she was then turning fourteen.

To Grace Hall Hemingway, 9 October [1920]

October 9

Dear Mother,

Your letter came yesterday. I was very sorry about not getting over to Longfield the day that you left.[1]

I was working up at Bill's and was knocking off at noon to come over to the Bay to go with Charley Friend when Mrs. Charles told me that their time was nearly half an hour slow. I ran all the way over to the bay but Charley Friend had just gone. I felt very badly about missing you.

Dad has been over here a couple of times and I've seen him once. Yesterday a letter came for him from you and he called up last night. He may be over today to get the letter and if not we'll forward it to him. He is going home Saturday on the Pennsylvania I believe.[2] It has been wonderful weather all the time he has been up.

We are planning to start down this Tuesday driving by way of Grand Rapids if the weather is still good. Just now I am very busy cleaning up on the apples and so on at Bills as he is still unable to walk.

When Dad called up last night he mentioned that he had found the Camp Cooking book at Windemere.[3] That accounts for all of them.

Awfully sorry that you had a bad night about my family spot. I didn't think of its worrying you that way or I wouldn't have described it. It's all right now and hasn't bothered me for some time.[4]

As for my plans. I had a letter from Bill Horne, Carl Edgar's class at Princeton and one of my best pals, saying that he was coming to Chicago this winter to live and suggesting that we get diggings together somewhere. If it pans out and I can get a good enough job we'll probably live together somewhere in town. If not I'll probably allez down to Kansas City as I had a letter from Carl yesterday urging me to come down and saying that if I would come to Kansas City he would come down from St. Joe[5] and get a job there so we could live together again. He hasn't decided what he is going to do this winter yet. Waiting to hear from me.

In any event I'll probably see you all Thursday or Friday of next week unless things fall through themselves.

Hope you are feeling well and love to yourself and all the kids,

As Ever,

Ernie

P.S. I met a Mrs. Bassett the other day who knew your father and his brother, Uncle Miller I presume when they stayed the winters in Los

Angeles.⁶ She spoke of them very kindly and of how they used to take long walks together. She met you one time a long while ago with the Geof Von Platens.⁷

PSU, TLS

1 Grace wrote in the Grace Cottage guest book that she left for Oak Park on 27 September (Mainland). In a letter of 4 October (JFK), she told EH she had a nice lunch prepared for him that day and expressed her disappointment that she had missed seeing him.
2 To return to Chicago, Clarence could have taken a southbound Grand Rapids and Indiana (GR&I) train, then transferred to the westbound Pennsylvania Railroad (PRR) in Fort Wayne, Indiana.
3 In her letter, Grace wrote that she returned the books EH had borrowed from the public library, but asked him to look on the Windemere book shelf for "Camp Cooking," which was missing. Probably *Camping and Camp Cooking*, by Frank Amasa Bates (Boston: Ball, 1909).
4 Grace wrote that she could not sleep for "sympathetic nervous pain" the night after EH told her of his internal injury, probably the injury he described in his 16 September letter to Jenkins.
5 St. Joseph, Missouri, where Carl Edgar lived.
6 Grace's father, Ernest Miller Hall (1840–1905) had a brother named Miller Hall (b. 1835). They were among the nine children born to Charles E. Hall (1800–1872) and Mary Dunhill Miller (1806–1897) (P. Hemingway, 505).
7 Probably Godfrey (Guff) Vonplaten, a successful timber operator from Boyne City (William H. Ohle, *100 Years in Horton Bay, Charlevoix County, Michigan* [Boyne City, Michigan: William H. Ohle, 1975], 12–13).

To William B. Smith, Jr., 25 [October 1920]

Twenty Ficth.

Honest Will of Ottawa.

It seems unbelieveble. What transpired in the automobile? How much do they charge to stay in a hotel at Ottawa? How many days did you linger there? How did you ever levve there? I am stunned by condidtions there.

It seems hard that youse should be compelled to purchase a a domicile. Can't ought be did?¹

Ferexample why not continue to stay on at Hash's. For a nominal sum I would guarantee that Hash would never return to the apartmong. We are within a block of the Lake here. Anything might transpire.² Could you hold the apartmong in the event of Hash's demise? What will you offer?

Has the zist shoved off and to where?³

I have not yet layed hold of a job .. have been standing by in hope of a vertizing sitshooation that Yen is developing. In the meantime I have wrote a story for the Toronto Papier every day.[4] Four in total. A thousand to twelve hundred apiece. More than I did all summer. Have four more to write and am going to start as soon as this is milled.

Bill Horne and I have layed hold of a cile at 1230 N. State Street. It is a block from Yen's new hovel and just down and across the street from Stut's.[5]

Lamped Deek last Friday night. He is but a wraith of his former self. With little trouble he could make weight for Honest Abe Attell.[6]

They have also measured him for an Alpaca coat. Had you heard of it?

If something doesn't show subito in the vertizing line I'm going down and confront the city eds. Yen says that it is a cinch that I can hook up wit some agency but that it will take a little temps. In the meantime I'm making more money agin Toronto than if I were reporting but can't lay hold of it for a month. At one yarn a day at ten to twenty a yarn you have no idea how short a temporal it takes to lay up jacksonian. But the need for the ready is going to drive me in to tainted brothel of journalism again.[7] I'm going to lamp the Ed's tomorrow. So far production has held to a yarn a day. It is hard to believe.

Bill Horne throwed a party the other nocturnal at which a group of young people numbering Stut Hash the writer and he were present. We had dinner at the Victor House, two rounds of Bronix's, the acids, and liquers were enjoyed. Then we went to the College Inn and danced.[8] We were all in the finest of shape. It was a jovial affair. A private room in the victor and heavy singage by all the members. Hash is a good scout of the einst wasser[9] and a splendid hand with the grog. She can also in the writers opinion spot Doodles a trio of pianos and still be fighting for her head in the stretch. It was the fisrt time I had seen stut up agin the acids in a decision affair. What would have made Theodore bring up the subject of the emasculation of dumb animals found her serene and jovial.

What would have caused J. C. Odgar to attempt self mortage and enabled him at the same time to be unable to locate the morter left the sister in the finest of shape.

The adress is 1230 N. State. Leave me hear from you. My love to the Madame. How long do you want Hash to stay here? She'll be here all this week at any rate.

Waddiox

Miller

PUL, TL with typewritten signature

1 In his letter to EH of 21 October 1920 (JFK), Bill Smith waxed enthusiastic about the women of Ottawa, Illinois, where he and his aunt had stopped on their drive home from Michigan to St. Louis. Smith wrote that he planned to buy a house there because "rents are insane."

2 EH and Elizabeth Hadley "Hash" Richardson first met in Chicago in October 1920 when both were staying at the apartment of Bill and Kate's brother and sister-in-law, Yeremya Kenley ("Y. K." or "Yen") and Genevieve "Doodles" Smith. Hadley and Kate had attended school together at the Mary Institute in St. Louis; after their mother's recent death, Hadley was visiting Chicago for a few weeks at Kate's invitation. EH, just back from Michigan, had accepted Y. K.'s offer of temporary lodging at his 100 East Chicago Avenue apartment until he could find a job. Back in St. Louis, while looking for a permanent residence, Bill Smith was staying in Hadley's quarters in the house at 5739 Cates Avenue, which she shared with her sister and her family.

3 In letters to EH of 21 October and 2 November 1920 (JFK), Smith refers to "the Zist," the nickname of a mutual acquaintance named Gudakunst who was a doctor. (In answer to EH's question, Smith would respond on 2 November that "the Zist has went away to Santa Fe New Mexico" [JFK]). In later letters, EH would adopt the word "zist" as a slang term for "doctor."

4 Six articles by EH appeared in the *Toronto Star Weekly* from October through December 1920 (*DLT*, 53–66); the newspaper had published five of his pieces from June through August.

5 Cile, EH's slang for "domicile." He and Horne would share the apartment in October and November 1920. Kate "Stut" Smith was living at 1259 North State Street (K. Smith to EH, 7 October 1920, JFK), and Y. K. had just leased a seven-room apartment nearby in the "Belleville" at 63 East Division Street.

6 Abraham Washington Attell (1884–1970), a featherweight boxer known as "The Little Hebrew." EH ironically dubs him "Honest Abe" (evoking the nickname of President Abraham Lincoln) because Attell allegedly ran communications between players and gamblers in the 1919 World Series fix.

7 "Jacksonian," money; possibly EH's embellishment of the slang term "jack," or a reference to U.S. President Andrew Jackson (1767–1845), whose portrait has appeared on paper currency of various denominations since 1869. "Ready," ready money.

8 The Victor House, at 9 East Grand, was one of the most popular of the many Italian restaurants on Chicago's Near North Side. "Bronix's," probably a Bronx cocktail, made of gin, vermouth, and orange juice. College Inn, restaurant in the Hotel Sherman at Clark and Randolph streets, renowned for its jazz orchestra.

9 In imperfect German (which translates literally as "once water"), EH likely means "first water," a term for the highest quality of diamonds or pearls.

To *Chicago Daily Tribune*, 29 November [1920]

November Twenty Ninth

C 122

Tribune:

No attempt will be made to write a trick letter in an effort to plunge you into such a paroxysm of laughter that you will weakly push over to me the position advertized in Sunday's Tribune.

You would probably rather have what facts there are and judge the quality of the writing from published signed articles that I can bring you.

I am twenty four years old,[1] have been a reporter on the Kansas City Star and a feature writer on the Toronto Star and the Toronto Sunday World.

Am chronicly unmarried.

War records are a drug on the market of course but to explain my lack of a job during 1918—served with the Italian Army[2] because of inability to pass the U.S. physical exams. Was wounded July 8 on the Piave River— decorated twice and commissioned. Not that it makes any difference.

At present I am doing feature stuff at a cent and a half a word and they want five columns a week. Sunday stuff mostly.

I am very anxious to get out of the newspaper business and into the copy writing end of advertizing. If you desire I can bring clippings of my work on the Toronto Star and Toronto Sunday World and you can judge the quality of the writing from them. I can also furnish whatver business and character references you wish.

Hoping that I have in a measure overcome your sales resistance—

very sincerely

1230 N. State Street

Chicago—Illinois.

UTulsa, TL

EH is responding to this advertisement in the "Wanted—Male Help" section of the 28 November 1920 *Chicago Daily Tribune* (H2): "ADVERTISING WRITER. EXPERIENCE NOT NECESSARY. Prominent Chicago advertising agency offers unusual opportunity to men capable of expressing themselves clearly and entertainingly in writing. A real opportunity to enter the advertising profession and be promoted as rapidly as ability warrants. State age, education, experience, if any, whether married or single, what you have been earning, and, in fact, anything or everything which will give us a correct line on you. All communications considered strictly confidential. Address C 122 Tribune." Whether EH received a response to his application letter remains unknown.

1 EH actually was twenty-one.
2 EH does not mention that he served in the war as an American Red Cross ambulance driver.

To Grace Quinlan, 16 November and 1 December [1920]

November 16

Dearest Old G,

No the letter didn't rate sneers or groans nor anything like that. I was just dawgone glad to hear from you. Sure you're forgiven . . . . . . It seemed darned good to hear from you again.[1]

Nothing to forgive anyway. I just felt bad beacuse I thought that you didn't like me anymore . . . but there wasn't any particular reason why you should like me . . and if you still do why what the hell? There's nothing to forgive.

Yes I've heard quite a bit of Liz's affaires du couer, mis-spelled of course, and as you know mixed in them to a certain extent. Out of a love for adventure and the possible chance of battleage. But while there was a small trifle of adventure or so the battleage never materialized. And then that dirty big slob of a coward Ruggles had beat up a little chap like Gale Wilson.[2]

At least that's the report I got. Wish sometime when you feel like it you'd give me the straight dope on the whole business. You know Gee m'dear I have more faith and confidence in your judgement and opinions than in most anybody else.

And about experience being the best teacher Gee. It's true as true all right. But his tuition rates are terribly high. I've gone along that way too all my life and when you learn things you learn'em. But . . . . by Gad you do pay for a lot of 'em.

Frinstance, purely hypothetical, if somebody says that boiling tar will burn you if you want to learn for good and all that boiling tar will burn you stick your finger in it. That's learning by experience. It sure teaches all right.

But after a while you get to judging people and knowing what people and what books to believe and what ones not to. Then you don't have to stick your fingers in the tar kettle so much.

Don't see any chance to go hunting this fall. At present I'm trying to cinch an advertizing job that will pay me some real Jacksonian. About twice as much as I've ever made before. It is sure to come through but it takes time. Kenley Smith wants me in Gregg and Ward but is trying to land me with Erwin-Wasey as they can pay me more.[3]

Meantime I'm grinding out stuff every day for the Star. Am colloborating on a comedy with Morris Musselman on a fifty fifty basis. He sold one play to this guy and is doing this on order. This morning a guy called me up and wanted me to write a boy's story in six installments for a boys and girls feature page that he has syndicated with over two hundred newspapers. The boid mentioned a very decent amount of seeds so I'm going to get it right out.[4]

Then I've been writing some publicity for Firestone for Tubby Williams of Critchfield and have also written some newspaper stories to be syndicated as part of a big advertizing campaign for Handsen Gloves.[5]

That covers the work just about .. but Gee Gee we've been having a good time! Hadley Richardson was here for three weeks and we tore around together and had a terrible good time. She's a peach and I've been leading a kinda quiet life since she's gone. Seen all the shows that are any good, Ethel Barrymore in DeClassee and Happy Go Lucky and the Scandals and a couple others.[6]

Bill Horne and I have a darned good place to live and I'm rating a terribly good drag with my family and we go out there on Sundays. The town is in no sense dry .. in fact it's a long ways wetter than this time last year.

Now there's a whole page filled up with nothing but what I'm doing and you'll think that the guy's a worse egotist than ever. But honest to gosh Gee I'm not. I just got started on what is going on here and raved on. Sorry you thought I was one .. but Lord knows I don't mean to be. I'll try and cut all the I's out from now on. Sez he making three I's in the sentence.

Anway Gee this is a terribly good town and instead of hating it the way I used to I'm getting terribly fond of it. However there isn't going to be any permanent settlege down in it . . . because there are so many more most excellent towns in different places that I'd like to be. It takes seeds tho. But they're what I'm cornering now.

What all are you doing now? Who are you going around with? Like 'em much. little or so so? Hope you're over Bob Mudgett.[7] He's a phase in every girls life I suppose. But Gee he is sure the most fundamentally worthless . . . .

Nope . . . it isn't worth while to knock anybody. Petoskey is funny tho. The girls are so darned nice and most of the fellows aren't worth a hoot. Maybe I'm slandering 'em tho.

I'm mixing them up and stepping with Kate Smith and Hadley, only she's allezed, and tonight with two girls of Jenk's. Not me with two girls but the great Little Fever being along.

Got to stop. Jenks just telephoned that he and Jacques were waiting downtown for me to come to lunch.

So long Gee, wish you were down here. There's any amount of jolly things to do. Been some great football games too.

Dearest G

December 1

Thought this had been mailed months ago Gee. Terrible sorry. What's all the dope? What are you doing, thinking, having done to you, having thought about you, saying, having said about you etc?

Didn't get to go hunting. Dad went last week. Down south—wanted me to go but I didn't think I ought to bust away. He shot a lot of quail and a wild cat and they got some coons too. Mother's allezed to California for the winter. Taken the kid bro.[8] Marce threw a dance on Thaksgiving, been playing golf, but it's snowing today so that's shot. If you see Luman Ramsdell will you tell him for me Gee that I'm going to write him and send the book Drowsy back?[9] Thanks.

Going to the Opera tomorrow night, Andrea Chenier, saw it last week too. It's a zinger with Ruffo, Raisa, Johnson, VanGordon, same plot kinda like Tale of Two Cities.[10] Also lamped the Scandals with Ann Pennington getting a bit heavy, Ethel Barrymore in Declasse, a marvelous thing, all Ethel, and Happy Go Lucky with O.P. Heggie and Belle Bennett, it is great, went feeling low and grouchy and by the end of the second act had to nearly be carried from the building in hysterics . . Gee I wish you could see it. Any chance of you and your Mother getting down here this winter? Give her my love will you?

Love ZEver,
Stein.

Let's hear from you!

Yale, TLS with autograph postscript; postmark: CHICAGO / ILL., DEC 4 / 130AM / 1920

1 In a letter to EH of 14 November 1920 (JFK), Quinlan apologized and asked his forgiveness for not having written since receiving his "dandy birthday letter" [30 September 1920].

2 *Affaires de coeur*: affairs of the heart (French). Liz Shoemaker (who in her 25 October letter reported Harold Ruggles's fury on learning that she and EH had kissed) wrote to EH on 11 November 1920 that "R—s" had disillusioned her about men. Ruggles was a basketball star at Petoskey High School, then in his junior year (1920 *Observer*, school yearbook). Gale D. Wilson is listed as a clerk in the 1919–1920 *Petoskey City Directory*.

3 Chicago advertising agencies. Y. K. Smith was employed by the Critchfield advertising company in Chicago.

4 Morris McNeil Musselman (1899–1952), a high school friend of EH who, under the pen name Morris McNeil, published *Ouija: A Farce Comedy in One Act* (Boston: W. H. Baker and Company, 1920). He would go on to write several books and become a successful Hollywood screenwriter. The comedy on which he and EH collaborated, *Hokum: A Play in Three Acts*, was copyrighted by Musselman on 4 June 1921 and published for the first time in 1978 in a limited edition, with an introduction by William Young (Wellesley Hills, Massachusetts: Sans Souci Press). Any "boy's story" that EH may have written for newspaper syndication remains unlocated.

5 EH means Hansen gloves, manufactured in Milwaukee, Wisconsin, since 1871. Any advertising work he may have done for Firestone or Hansen remains otherwise undocumented. Williams had landed a job at the Critchfield agency in early 1920 with the help of their mutual friend Y. K. Smith (Williams to EH, [26 February 1920], JFK).

6 Ethel Barrymore (née Ethel Mae Blythe, 1879–1959), renowned American stage and screen star of the famous Barrymore family of actors; she starred in *Declassée*, a drama by Zoë Akins (1886–1958) that opened in New York on 6 October 1919 and played at Powers' Theatre in Chicago, October through December 1920, closing on Christmas Day. *Happy-Go-Lucky*, a comedy by Ian Hay, opened in New York on 24 August 1920 and ran in Chicago at the Playhouse Theatre from 1 November 1920 through February 1921, starring Oliver Peters (O. P.) Heggie (1879–1936) and Belle Bennett (1891–1932). *Scandals*, an annual musical revue similar to the *Ziegfeld Follies* and featuring American popular music and fast-paced sketches, was produced 1919–1926 by George White (1890–1968). *George White's Scandals 1920*, starring Ann Pennington (1893–1971), ran from October through December 1920 at the Colonial Theatre in Chicago.

7 Robert "Skinner" Mudgett, a 1918 graduate of Petoskey High School, where he was basketball team captain during his senior year.

8 Grace Hemingway had taken her five-year-old son Leicester to visit her brother, Leicester Hall, who lived in the town of Bishop in east central California.

9 Ramsdell (1900–1928), one of EH's closest friends in Petoskey and brother of EH's younger admirer, Evelyn; their father was a local physician (Baker *Life*, 65–66). *Drowsy* (New York: Frederick A. Stokes, 1917), a novel by John Ames Mitchell (1845–1918), who founded the American humor magazine *Life* (1883–1936) and served as editor-in-chief until his death.

10 *Andrea Chénier* (1896), opera composed by Umberto Giordano (1867–1948) with libretto by Luigi Illica (1857–1919). It was performed by the Chicago Opera Company at the Auditorium on 24 November and 2 December 1920, starring Titta Ruffo; Rosa Raisa (1893–1963), Polish-born soprano; Edward Johnson (1878–1959), Canadian-born leading tenor of the Chicago Opera 1919–1922; and Cyrena Van Gordon (née Cyrene Sue Pocock, c. 1897–1964), American mezzo-soprano. The opera is loosely based on the life of poet

André-Marie Chénier (1762–1794), who died at the guillotine during the French Revolution; Charles Dickens's novel *A Tale of Two Cities* also is set during that period.

To *Chicago Daily Tribune*, [2 December 1920]

F.G. 391 Tribune:

Your advertisment in today's Tribune looks to be the oppotunity I have been seeking to leave the Newspaper business and enter the magazine field.

I have been a newspaper man since 1916[1]—working on the Kansas City Star and Times as a reporter and on the Toronto Star and Toronto Sunday World as a feature writer.

At present I have left Toronto and am doing by-line feature stuff for the Sunday edition of the Star. These stories cover everything american that can have a Canadian angle dragged in. It pays well—but constantly writing Canadian stuff for inmates of Canada without yourself being in Canada palls after a time.

UTulsa, TLcc

EH is responding to this advertisement in the "Wanted—Male Help" section of the *Tribune* of 2 December 1920 (26): "NEWSPAPER MAN—YOUNG ONE WHO has had experience on dailies as reporter and who has written editorials and feature stories; unusual opening for man on live magazine in Chicago reaching 200,000 readers monthly, and we want an unusual young man; write a letter stating education, experience, age, and salary willing to accept at start. Address F. G. 391, Tribune."

1 As he had in his 29 November response to another classified advertisement, EH somewhat misrepresents his experience; in 1916 he was still in high school, albeit writing for the *Trapeze.*

To Grace Hall Hemingway, [22 December 1920]

Dearest Mother,

I didn't realize how close it is to Christmas before it is actually upon us. We'll all miss not having you here. Bill Horne is gone East but Kenley and Doodles are coming out for dinner.

I'm working on this magazine called the Co-operative Commonwealth which is the organ, mouth organ, not pipe organ for the Co-operative movement.[1] If almost any part of what they say about this movement is true it is quelque movement. The mag has 65,000 circulation and this month eighty pages of reading matter and about twenty of ads. Most of the reading was written by myself. Also write editorials and most anything. Will write anything once.

It was nice to get a letter from you and I'm glad Uncle Leicester thinks he might like me. I'd try and do the same toward him. Hope you can go swimming in the boiling, bubbling baths[2]—they sound like when we used to swim at Nantucket and I'd go in with the kelp and the horseshoe crabs and you'd swim in the salt water baths.

Dad lets me read your letters when I'm out at the hoose Sundays and so I keep fairly well informed of your doages. Can't seem to recall any news that would be news to you. I took Sun to the foot ball dance and she danced wonderfully well and looked great. Ura was there with Johnny and an apricot and white evening gown slashed like a court jester. She looks terribly well in evening dress because of being a well turned article.

Doodles is going to New York to study with Lawrence the Monday after christmas. I'm going to live there then. 63 East Division Street. It's a very extra comfortable apartment, seven rooms, and the priceless Della to cook for us. There will be five of us there in batchellor quarters.

Am being frightfully good in pursuit of your instructions. At least you told me to be good didn't you? Being so anyway. Very busy, very good, and very tired. It's fun to be the first but the second and third have a decreasingly stronger appeal. Hash was up here from Saint Louis for a week end. Came one Saturday night and allezed Monday night. We had a most excellent time. She wants me very badly to come to a big New Years eve dinner and party at the University Club in Sin Louis—but I can't negotiate the grade.[3] Being about as well seeded as the navel orange.

I'm getting a very fair wage but am busily engaged in getting through chrstmas, paying off the odd debt and must purchase badly needed clothes, both under and over.

Am giving the kids paper seeds in small denominations for Christmas—haven't had a minute to shop. It would be hardly fitting to send one's wealthy mother luxuriating in California paper seeds—so I'm getting you and Lessie[4] something and will hold it here or forward it out if you decide to stay longer. Give the kid my best love and wish he and Uncle Leicester both Merry Christmas for me. I wish I could see Uncle Leicester.

Had a letter yesterday from the Zist, Doctor Gudakunst, that is, perhaps you recall the fact that he is a physician? He is at Santa Fe New Mex and has been made manager of a Health Resort Ranch at a very good seed basis. He wants to wire me a ticket to come down there claiming that there are horses to burn and a man never has to shave and many other attractions.[5] He is anxious for me to allez down—but I ought not to play the role of the rats deserting the stinking ship yet—the odor from the ship is just begining to be perceptible. When it becomes a full blown stench I may chase down there. 'Nother words I havena all the confidence in the world in the Movement.

Well Merry Christmas to you old dear—won't wish you Happy New Year because New Year is just one lurch nearer the grave and nothing to be happy over.

Hope you have a priceless time.

Love

Ernie

JFK, TLS; postmark: CHICAGO / ILL, DEC 22 / 830 PM

EH typed "Ernest Hemingway." above the pre-printed return address on the envelope: "THE CO-OPERATIVE COMMONWEATH / RICHARD H. LOPER, PUBLISHER / 1554 OGDEN AVENUE / CHICAGO, ILL." The envelope is addressed to "Mrs. Grace Hall Hemingway / care Leicester C. Hall / Bishop / Inyo County / California." On it she wrote, "Letters from Ernest Received at Bishop. Jan 1921."

1 The magazine of the Co-operative Society of America, incorporated in Chicago by Harrison M. Parker on 20 February 1919. The society aimed to allow people to "avail themselves of the advantages of co-operation as a welcome escape from the unconscionable profiteering of rapacious tradesmen" (Colston E. Warne, "The Co-operative Society of America: A Common Law Trust," *University Journal of Business*, 1 [August 1923], 373). EH worked as writer and editor from December 1920 to October 1921, when the magazine folded and the Society was adjudged bankrupt amid accusations of fraud leveled against Parker. (For an account of the scandal, see "Parker Gave Wife $1,000,000 in Bonds," *New York Times*, 11 October 1921, 7.)

2 Likely Keogh's Hot Springs, a popular health resort that opened in 1919 at the site of geothermal hot springs near Bishop, California.

3 Private club in St. Louis housed in the former Edward Walsh mansion on West Pine Street. The party was being hosted by Hadley's longtime friend Helen Pierce Breaker (b. circa 1891)

and her husband, George Breaker (b. 1891), a St. Louis attorney, and Hadley had urged EH to
come (Diliberto, 49). He did not attend.
4 EH's brother, Leicester.
5 The 18 December 1920 letter from Gudakunst, written from Clovis, New Mexico, survives at
JFK.

To Hadley Richardson, 23 December [1920]

[*Letter begins here:*] I'd be much happier too Hash Darling—but I can't
come— You see I hate and loathe and despise to talk about seeds but I
haven't been home since 1915 I think and so I more or less threw a fairly
decent Christmas for the kids and am consequently broke—[1] Embarrassing of
course. Could have much easier lied to you and mentioned acceptance of half
a dozen New Years dates—all of which I'd have thrown out in a minute for a
sight of you—but have always had this beautiful truth talking habit with you—
    You can make me jealous—and you can hurt most awfully—'cause my
loving you is a chink in the armour of telling the world to go to hell and you
can thrust a sword into it at any time—
    Hate to think of you going to the party with Dick[2] instead of me—but I'm
broke because of the Lord's birthday! S' Not a question of regard for seeds or
anything you know—but why go into it?
    Feel terribly bad—but I've shot my Toronto check—wont have another
till the 15th of January—am in the intervening ones with Six members of the
famille—
    At present there's someone or other snoring in the big bed—we threw quite
a party to speed Saltzenbeck south. Gin hacks—Don[3] corked his Christmas
Scotch and a bottle or so of port. I hate gin! Onct it done me wrong.
    Saw tragedy tonight. I was in a drug shop opposite the Marigold Gardens[4]
and a girl was telephoning in a booth. She was kidding some one over the
wire, lips smiling. And talking cheerily away and all the time dabbing her
eyes with a handkerchief— Poor kid it was terrible bad whatever it was.
    <u>Dear</u> Hash you can surely hurt me a lot when you want to. About the
platform and the train. Lord— I thot I was loving you— If I wasnt I never
could and never would love any one.[5] Guess I was thinking too much about

how I didn't want you to go— Don't you believe I love you? Dunno how I can make you believe.

I didn't want to kiss you goodbye—that was the trouble— I wanted to kiss you good night—and there's a lot of difference. ' couldn't bear the thought of you going away when you were so very dear and necessary and all pervading.

Suppose when you tell me how nice Dick is and so on I ought to counter with how enjoyable it is to dance with Maydlyn and how nice she looks top-side of a horse and so on—but when I think of anyone in comparison with you it's like—You are so much dearer and I love you so much— that what odds kidding along about them.

'Course I love you— I Love you all the time—when I wake up in the morning and have to climb out of bed and splash around and shave— I look at your picture and think about you—and that's a pretty deadly part of day as you know and a good test of loving any one.

And in the evening— It's too much to stand— Sure go on—go to the party with Dick but maybe once pretend I'm there—

Discovered Siegfried Sassoon this afternoon and so feel kind of bitter[6]— I'm sorry about Bill and Ruth—if she's your Bill She has a lot. Poor old Bill—what a shame the warrrrrrrrrrr was drug in. He's better on almost anything else.[7]

Sounds as tho there was someat quite unforgiveable twixt you and Leticia[8]— If you think I couldn't I'll not try and understand.

How many seeds would we need for the open fire? The sloop doesn't need many but there's beach combing at the end of the cruise unless I make a heavy drive first. That's what I'm a tryin' to do of.

'Night my dearest Hash— I'd like to hold you so and kiss you so that you wouldn't doubt whether I wanted to or not—

Love you—
Sera[9]
Ernesto

2a.
December 23

Very sporting of you to bundle 600 N. Kenilworth. Jim Gamble is great— and I love him a lot—but not like I love you—you dearest, Dearest, Dear.[10]

JFK, ALSFrag

The beginning of the letter is missing.

1 EH is responding to Hadley's letter of 20 December 1920 (JFK), in which she wrote, "if you really want to know what I think I think I would be lots happier if you came for New Year's." He had last spent Christmas in Oak Park in 1916.

2 After EH told her he could not afford to come to St. Louis, Hadley invited Dick Pierce, Helen Breaker's brother, to accompany her (Diliberto, 49).

3 Probably Don Wright, who also boarded at Y. K. Smith's.

4 Popular beer garden at Grace and Halstead streets in a predominantly German-American neighborhood on Chicago's North Side; established in 1895 as Bismarck Gardens, it was renamed Marigold Gardens in 1915 in response to anti-German sentiment during WWI.

5 When Hadley and EH parted at the train station in Chicago after her visit the first week of December, EH did not kiss her as she expected, and she went away with feelings hurt: "I tho't maybe you didn't really want to kiss me good-bye," she wrote. "I was shot to pieces myself— cause I certainly didn't want to leave" (Hadley to EH, 20 December 1920 [JFK]; quoted in Diliberto, 46).

6 Sassoon (1886–1967), English poet and memoirist best known for his WWI poems.

7 Bill Horne was then visiting St. Louis and, Hadley reported to EH in a letter of 16 December 1920 (JFK), he "ast right away after Ruth. Startling possibility!" Ruth Bradfield, a twenty-five-year-old advertising copywriter for a St. Louis department store, shared Hadley's upstairs apartment in the family home on Cates Street (Diliberto 36, 42). However, the meeting Hadley arranged had not gone well, as she wrote in her letter of 20 December: "I love Bill, as always. I'd like to know (angrily) what chance Ruth had to be alluring— I tell you it was all Warrr— I was pretty mad— . . . There honestly wasn't a chance for decent fun and conversation" (JFK).

8 Letitia Parker, a wealthy classmate of Hadley's from the Mary Institute, had offered to accompany her from St. Louis to Chicago in early December and pay for the trip, but she canceled at the last minute, leaving Hadley to travel alone at her own expense (Diliberto, 44).

9 Night (Italian).

10 In her 20 December letter, Hadley said that the next day she would be mailing a "bundle containing small cadeau with findings" to his Oak Park address. She also wrote, "Jim Gamble sounds great if you like him so."

To James Gamble, [c. 27 December 1920]

James Gamble
256 South 16th Street
Philedelphia Penn.

Rather go to Rome with you than heaven Stop. ~~Not married stop~~. But am broke stop ~~Sad stop~~ Too sad for words stop Writing and selling it stop ~~Unmarried~~ but don't get rich stop all authors poor first then rich stop. me no exception stop Wouldn't we have a great time stop Lord how I envy you

Hemmy.

63 East Division Street
Chicago Illinois.
care Y.K. Smith

JFK, TCD

EH wrote this cable draft in response to Gamble's cable and letter of 27 December 1920 (JFK) that urged EH to accompany him to Italy, departing 4 January 1921 on the *S.S. Rochambeau*. Gamble's plans were indefinite, he said, and "can be formed according to your wishes": "Just think of the land of Romance, spaget and fleas again. Can you resist it?" He also asked, "What have you been doing since I heard last? Married? Writing? Making money or what?" Gamble assured EH that the trip would be inexpensive, with the lira "only worth three cents."

To Hadley Richardson, [29 December 1920]

Hemingway.

Wednesday.

Dearest Mr. Hash—

Hope it's just the Christmas tie up of mail service that accounts for my not having heard from you since Christmas day.[1] Tisn't so much fun whatever t's.

Things are all up in the air. I'm liable to leave Tuesday for Rome, not Rome N.Y. the other one, on the biggest chance of my career. Career hell—I haven't had one—but I'm liable to with this Rome thing—

If I allez I'll go to N.Y via Washington to pick up passport and will leave from here to St. Louis and then to Washington.

Here's the chance—5 months of writing under Ideal conditions—a chance that Gawd knows when I'd get again to play fiction clear across the board—an arrangement with the Co-operative whereby they announce that I'm gone to Europe for them to study the Co-operative movement abroad—and contribute Editorials to 'em—at a figure that the exchange rate will make livable—30 lire to a dollar approximately. And Rome per se isn't so very bad in the winter time—climate about like our October—and a pretty decent town.

Then in June I'd be coming back with a better job and the advantage of 5 months with the best. I'll be able to argue with you intelligently about [Berenson ?][2] after 5 months with Jim in Rome—

I can make quite a bit of Jack from Toronto—but think the play is to lay off of Hacking and slay the big stuff—

The whole proposition ought to appeal to any one who has ever rolled dice.

Yen is crazy to have me go. Says I'm an utter damned fool if I don't. My Dad favors it—Whadda you think?[3]

JFK, AL

1 On 24 December 1920, Hadley had sent EH a letter by special delivery mail so that he would receive it on Christmas Day (JFK).
2 Although EH's handwriting is not entirely clear, probably Bernard Berenson (1865–1959), Lithuanian-born, Harvard-educated art historian, connoisseur, and critic, best known for his influential studies of Italian Renaissance painting, the bulk of them published 1894–1909. Later, EH and Berenson became correspondents, beginning in 1949.
3 In a special delivery letter to EH of 31 December 1920, Hadley wished him the "best of New Years," adding, "Should you be in Rome or Buenos Aires the wish would be the very same." She also wrote, "I hope you can tell me the reasons for and against Rome" (JFK). EH did not make the trip with Gamble.

To Miss Conger, [c. 1921]

MISS CONGER—

The attached proofs have been seen by Mr. Parker and Mr. Loper for policy and form and I have read them for typographical errors.[1]

Will you look after the make-up and the continuations of the various stories?

Ernest Hemingway.

I wrote, under Mr. Loper's direction the squib to fill the bank story, which must be killed.[2] Will you be sure and catch that center baby's name? The relative of MrUnthank I mean.

E.M.H.

JFK, TL with typewritten signature

1 Harrison Parker, founder of the Co-operative Society of America, and Richard Loper, publisher of the *Co-operative Commonwealth* magazine. The galley proofs that they reviewed do not survive with this letter.

2 Squib, a short piece used to fill out a page in newspaper or magazine layout. Because only the
1 October 1921 issue of the *Co-operative Commonwealth* is known to survive (JFK), EH's
piece cannot be identified, nor this letter dated definitively.

To Grace Hall Hemingway, [10 January 1921]

Dear Mother,

I've been very busy lately or I would have written you before. I've moved,
guess I told you that, or was going to.

Now at 63 East Division. Haven't been out to the house since New Years I
think—now it's the tenth of January so I'll have to allez out soon

Yeseterday I meant to but we had Isaac Don Levine, the Daily News
correspondent in Russia at dinner at noon at the apartment and then went to
hear Benno Moseiwitch play at orchestra hall in the afternoon. Moseiqitch is
the best pianist there is now I think.[1] He's infinitely superior to Levitski or
Jeosh Hoffman and I think he has in on Rachmaninoff or Gabrilowitch—
he's in the first four anyway.[2]

He played a much better program than he did the last time I heard him,
Chopin's B. Minor Concerto and the sunken cathedral Cathedral Engloutie
or something like that by DeBussy and then two of Lizst with the
Campanella, and some modern stuff that I forget the names of.[3] I'm quoting
from memrory or I'd be more accurate.

Then Levine took Kenley and I to see Lenore Ulric in her new play at Powers.
Remember us seeing her in Tiger Rose? This new thing is The Son-Daughter—
and it is just as good a melodrama as Tiger Rose—don't know whether it is as
well constructed or not—but Lenpre is quelque actorine and the thing is filled
with notable things like FenCha the illustrious gambler and The Sea Crab—the
sea crab is very scary article—I was scared—you might be scared.[4]

Have seen Willie Collier in the Hottentot and Happy Go Lucky and a few
other shows and the Ulric twice.[5]

Levine is an excellent fellow and gave us the cold dope on Rooshia. He's
just been back for four days and goes to NewYork tomorrow.

I'Ve been raised ten paper seeds more a week. Ten seeds are ten seeds.
That makes me get fifty of the papered seeds every Saturday. Of course that
isn't many paper seeds but still it is a few paper seeds.

Horney Bill is still in the near East, Yonkers to be exact. The kids are all in good shape I believe. They seem happy. They act well. They look healthy. I am in good shape. I eat well. I sleep well. I do everything but work well. Interviewed Mary Bartelme today and she is the genuwind old darticle. An excellent woman and I fell hard for her and wrote a wonderful story. Will send it to you when it comes out.[6]

Did I send you one of the lousy magazines?

How is the Kid Leicester?

Give my love to Uncle Leicester and the same love and any remaining, there is undoubtedly much remaining on account of not being able to love Uncle Leicester except as something ebstract like a charcter of fiction, to yourself.

Always glad to hear offn you.

I'd stay out there as long as you can—we've been having wonderful weather here—which means that we have hells own weather enroute. We always get it sooner or letter and it hasn't come yet.

Love to you, pardon the rotten typer—it's a new one and stiff as a frozen whisker,

Ernie

JFK, TLS

1 Levine (1892–1981), Russian-born journalist who came to the United States in 1911; he worked for the *Kansas City Star*, covered the 1917 Revolution for the *New York Herald Tribune*, and again returned to the Soviet Union to cover the civil war there as foreign correspondent for the *Chicago Daily News* (1919–1921). Moiseiwitsch (1890–1963), Russian-born pianist who made his debut in New York in 1919 and performed at Orchestra Hall in Chicago on 9 January 1921.

2 Mischa Levitzki (1898–1941), American pianist and composer; Josef Hofmann (1876–1957), Polish-born pianist; Sergei Rachmaninov (1873–1943), Russian-born composer, pianist, and conductor; Ossip Gabrilovich (1878–1936), Russian-born pianist who settled in the United States in 1914 and became conductor of the Detroit Symphony Orchestra in 1916.

3 Fryderyk (Frédéric) Chopin (1810–1849), Polish composer and pianist who settled in Paris in 1831; his two piano concertos are in E minor and F minor, but he did compose other works in B minor. *La Cathédrale Engloutie* (*The Submerged Cathedral*), a 1910 composition for piano by French composer Claude Debussy (1862–1918). Franz Liszt (1811–1886), Hungarian composer and piano virtuoso; *La Campanella* (*The Little Bell*) is his transcription for the piano of the 1826 Violin Concerto in B minor by Nicolò Paganini (1782–1840). Of Liszt's several treatments of this material, the first composed in 1833, the most popular was his 1851 version. EH likely had read Bert Leston Taylor's preview of the program in his "Line

O'Type or Two" column in the 6 January *Chicago Daily Tribune*: "Mr. Moiseiwitsch, who presented a très punque programme the last time he was here, offers next Sunday one that is as good as the other was bad: Handel-Brahms, Chopin, Ravel, Debussy, Palmgren, and Liszt at his most endurable" (6).

4 Lenore Ulric (née Leonora Ulrich, 1892–1970), stage and screen actress who starred in the David Belasco production of *The Son–Daughter: A Play of New China*, a three-act melodrama by George Scarborough and David Belasco. The play opened on Broadway in November 1919 and ran at Powers' Theatre in Chicago 27 December 1920–19 February 1921. Fen-sha, a wealthy merchant whose secret identity is the "Sea Crab," is a character in *Son–Daughter*. Ulric earlier starred in *Tiger Rose* (1917), a play by Willard Mack (né Charles Willard McLaughlin, 1878–1934). EH would mention Ulric in *TOS*, and she would play the role of Anita in the 1940 Broadway production of EH's *The Fifth Column*.

5 William Collier (1866–1944), American actor, writer, and director, starred in *Hottentot*, a three-act farce he wrote with Victor Mapes (1870–1943) that opened in New York on 1 March 1920 and at Cohan's Grand in Chicago on 5 December 1920. EH had mentioned seeing *Happy-Go-Lucky* in his letter to Grace Quinlan of 16 November and 1 December 1920.

6 Mary M. Bartelme, Chicago-born lawyer (1866–1954) who specialized in cases relating to children. In 1899 she helped establish the juvenile court in Chicago, in 1914 founded the first "Mary Club" for the supervision of girls before their placement in foster homes, and in 1923 would be elected Cook County Circuit Court judge, the first woman in Illinois to hold such a high judicial position. EH's story about her, presumably published in the *Co-operative Commonwealth*, is not known to have survived.

To William D. Horne, Jr., [before 26 January 1921]

Horney Horney Bill—

Me and this typewriter are both sick so this isn't going to be much of a screed.

Suppose you've seen Doodiles by this time and she has informed you pretty well of the various states, the last are always worse than the first, of the men.

There is little to relate. Mrs. Seymour craves your key. She's asked me if I've received it from you severel times. Always I haven't but am expecting it. Now I can continue to say so with a better conscience.

Send it to me and I'll take it to her.

Most of the stuff is here at the club and the residooee is at Seymourses where the trunks are still housed—[1] I keep them there under the plea that you will sooner or later advise me what you want done with them. Don't advise me—they are all right there.

An ulcerated throat has smote me for an acre of Abyssinian Bungwad.[2] So I8m at the club recuperating.

How's all wit you?

Wish't you were here[.] We have an excellent time. Carl Sandburg and Sherwood Anderson come over,[3] we have wine in abundance, good claret every night on the table wit dinner, You'd better come home. You know how Della cooks.

The advertizing agency business is shot to hell—laying off men—Don is just now out of a job. I'm lucky to have this Loper job I guess. Men are walking the streets. So are women.

My sisters ask about you. My mother asked about you, in a Letter.

There's lots to tell you—but I'm too feeling rotten to tell it all.

Will write youse right away soon.

I'm still in love with Hash—she still declares that if we met she would not seek to hit me over the head with a slice bar.

Thass about all I know—

No that's a damned lie— I know lot's more but too darned tired to screed—

This is justa note— I've wrote some pretty decent stuff and been given a rear by the magazine.

S'Long,

Immer,

Oin

Newberry, TLS

The conjectured letter date is based on Horne's notation on the letter, "Answered Jan. 26, 1921," and by his response, postmarked 27 January 1921 (JFK), making reference to details in EH's letter.

1 EH and Horne shared an apartment at 1230 North State Street owned by the Seymour family, until Horne's employer, the Eaton Axle Company, called him to the Cleveland home office in early November (Horne to EH, [10 November 1920], JFK). Just after Christmas, EH moved to Y. K. Smith's place at 63 East Division (known as the "club"), joining several other young men already living there and accepting Y. K.'s offer of a free room while his wife, Doodles, was studying music in New York City. Horne had told EH that while he was home in Yonkers, New York, for a Christmas vacation, he planned to be in touch with Doodles (Horne to EH, 18 December 1920, JFK).

2 In his 26 January reply, Horne reported that in sharing EH's letter with Doodles, he had "properly censored" such "effusions" of EH's as "Abasynian Bungwad" (apparently an off-color private joke; "bungwad" was 1920s U.S. slang for toilet paper).

3 Sandburg, American author and poet (1878–1967) best known for his biographies of Abraham Lincoln and his poems about Chicago. Anderson, his career soaring since the 1919 publication of *Winesburg, Ohio*, had an apartment nearby on East Division and knew Y. K. Smith through their mutual association with the Critchfield advertising firm (Reynolds *YH*, 181–82).

To William B. Smith, Jr., [c. January 1921]

Kellner—[1]

It has just come to me that a new meaning to that famous spirituelle poem The Lost Chord might be read into it by starting it Thusly—

"Seated one day on my organ—etc."[2]

The heart, so called, was gladdened to hear from you— The writer had about resolved that unless the Enditee screeded some he the enditee could eternally urinate up a hauser. The writer was sure that you had started upon a campaign of exorcision of your old aquantainces. The writer felt that he had gone by the squard as far as you were concerned. Bitterness was stalking into the enditers cardiac valve.

If you want to play the newspaper game I can lay hold of letters to whatever city or managing eds you wish—if you wish. What paper's do you want 'em to? The letters will be from one with an air tight drag with the city and managing eds referred to.

Violate your new custom and leave me know if you crave them or not.

The maggot is like sulphur—pleasant stuff until a match is applied to it— then it stinks and sputters and burns with a blue flame. Keep him from the flame and there is no better—apply the flame and there is no worse—

If the flame is kept long enough away we disbelieve it's effect. But apply the flame and he'll stink.

The Guy, Carper, and I ate at Dick Smale's the other Nacht.[3] Pleasant feed. Fine young men.

This town is filled with wine—

The writer will say no more about Hash—of course appearances are agin me—I explained that— Even in the face of past performances a horse sometimes wins in a good race—maybe he carried too much weight—maybe the Jock didn't give him a good ride—maybe they pulled him up in the stretch—who knows? Past performances don't amount to much until you get along in years— Anyway the horse knows he can win—sometimes.

JFK, AL

The conjectured letter date is based on the verso of the second page, a mimeographed memo dated 7 January 1921 regarding parking on Michigan Avenue. EH's reference to his friend's interest in finding employment with a newspaper suggests that he wrote this before receiving Smith's letter of 30 January 1921, in which Smith reported that he had accepted a job with the Ever-Tight Piston Ring Company in St. Louis (PUL). EH may have abandoned his own letter and put it away unsent.

1 Waiter (German), a mutual nickname of EH and Smith.
2 Bawdy play on "Seated one day at the organ," first line of the poem "The Lost Chord" by Adelaide A. Proctor (1825–1864). The poem was set to music in 1877 by Arthur Sullivan (1842–1900) of Gilbert and Sullivan, and the song remained popular in the early twentieth century.
3 "The Guy," a variant on "the Ghee," a nickname for Jack Pentecost. *Nacht*: night (German).

To William B. Smith, Jr., [15 February 1921]

Written Tuesday—

Mailed Friday—

Smith—

Keep a stiff upper jaw. Altho your position appears to be death in its worst form show the dogs that a Smith knows how to die.[1] Boid you must see the Tevern[2]— My God I never lamped such an exhibition in all my life. Yen plus I and the Carper, i.e. Mr. LaFever, viewed it at a Saturnsday Mat. and at one time I thought Mortage of Yen was about to occur due to laughage. Mr. La Fever was so moved that he arose and struck the man next to him a blow in the face out of nothing but camaraderie. It is bar none, the best show I've ever lamped. What is Ruth like?[3] Does she aid or mar an optic? Does she cause tumescence? Would she appeal more to a sadist or a masochist? Is she a femme withwhom a man would be safe in broaching the subject of the prevalence of intracrural coitus among the Papuans?[4] What sort of a femme is she?

The enditer has not been without adventure. Thursday the enditer plus Gayle Aiken plus Yen went to Ruth Bush Lobdell's.[5] A rare time was enjoyed one of the features of which was the alcohloization of Aiken caused by 5 star liqueur blend Haig and Haig—and the defeat of Mrs. Lobdell and

Aiken at Bridge by Yen and the enditer—alcoholization perhaps aided but I
had two high balls up on the Bock. And a passage of a certain amount words
phrases and the like between the enditer and Mrs. Lobdell—these words
phrases and the like being calculated to produce in the minds of both the fact
that neither was homosexual. The proper effect was produced becasue
Saturday night I was summoned to the Lobdell's to play Bridge. Arriving
there found four at Bridge and Mrs. sitting out. She is a knockout. Was Ruth
Bush in New Orleans and four times queen of the Mardi Gras ball. We
repaired to the dining room and scotched up—also drank several
Benedictines, an apricot brandy or so and what not. My Gawd what a cellar.[6]
The up shot of the affair was non returnage by the enditer to the domicle
until the third hour! It seems that Charles the husband is a fine but quiet
article who loves bed better than all else in the evening. Ruth likes to dance
and step out. A splendid situation. Yen knew Ruth in New Orleans. She can
still give them a canter for their kale.

The enditer has laid hold of a job for Yen with us men on the magazine—
he works half time, things are dull at G. and W.,[7] thank God you men didn't
buy an agency, and Yen is to look after the mechanical end of the make up.
He is emolumated at the rate of Fifty seeds each Saturday night. Not bad for
an obtained job? I press agented him like mad as the greatestmechanical
make uper of any or all temporals and said that it was impossible for me to
do the work—for which I would have received not a centime more—, thus
bringing 50 additional seeds out of the arms of industry.

SIn Louie as a boxing center seems to me a place where the top notchers
go to stall through an exhibition—they have to fight in New York becasue
the scribes would pan them to death—but after staging a brilliant battle there
they say— "Now we will go down to Sin Louis and step Six rounds and
nobody gets nocked out and it is all all very much on the up and up."[8] That's
the way it looks to me. I migmt ask Kid Howard and Charley Cutler and some
of the guys I know who have the frigid on the financial conditions of the fight
game.[9]

Learned the other day from FitzSimmons the promotor, had lunch with
him, that Dempsey is broke in spite of heavy earnage becasue it cost him
several hundred thousand to square himself on the slacker charge on the

coast. It seems that he has to fight Carp whether he wants to or not—because he is a non seeded article and getting outta debt.[10]

That puts a new angle onto things huh? It is also rumoured that the well knowed wages have him in their grip and that he's a shadow of his former self. Fitz wouldn't confirm the wages dope but hinted at it.[11] And Fitz knows. He is a great bird. No defecator and intersting as hell.

I think that Tom Gibbons could trim Jack with ease—and I8m afraid he could trim Carp.[12] Personally I have never lamped a better fighter, faster puncher, with a more perfect style and hitting system than this guy Gibbons. He's only 165—but God he is a sweet article. I am absolutely mad about the guy as a ringster—and you know that I am a man who does not rave over a box fighter for no good reason. He hasn't a weakness. I would give five seeds to have you lamp him.

Yen has been in bad shape lately—but has pulled out of it and is feeling very good today. He's taking it easy now—was a ten day headache—like he had once before. He's all jake now and nothing to worry about. I see that he caresses the Ayfee and he has been out only two nights since Doodles departure—no—only one night!

The enditer encloses ten of the paper ones to apply on my debt to the madame— I will write her.

The dope on Stut is not at hand. She and I went to another of those Goddam breakfast's the other day—last Sabath. Last wednesday she said she was going home before the first of March—but you know her. She has suggested leaving and they applealed to stay but she is leaving all right. She and Yen are again on the good terms.

The Carper and the Ghee I see quite often—the ghee spent the nacht here recently and we had asession of bridge.

I will enjoy lamping you even if it is in the throes of death—you cannot stand the strain of such labor as you describe. No man can.

Yen went to work today and saw Palmer— Yen had to only stay in the office an hour—his days wage is $8.33. He urned it today in an hour. Shades of forty cents an hour on the apples.

I could think of more if I could think at all. But cannot. I am writing this at the cile, taking my usual siesta and must return to the office by 4. I am supposed to do a great deal of thinking and planning of editorials at home. My hours are elastic. Usually arrive at 9 to nine thirty—stay out two or three hours at noon and shove off at four or four thirty. Not a bad job—, but when we do have to work at the last of the month we have to work like hell.[13]

The enditer purchased a suit from Brooks Brothers—they were here at the La Salle last week. It is to be delivered C.O.D. on the first or fourth of March —as soon thereafter as I have the seeds I will allez to Sin Louis.[14] I could not face any one in present raiment—all shot to hell— I get by in splendid shape at the Lobdell's on account of the lights being dim and rugs such also dim— my garb cannot be seen in detail and the cut of my old blue suit is jake. This new suit will place you in a state of coma. It is the genuwind English—

I know naught of Hourismans but would be inclined to place a seed on Hoppy.[15] How is Hash? My love to the Madame.

Immer screed to
Marvelous Miller. the Miller.

PUL, TL with typewritten signature; postmark: CHICAGO / ILL., FEB 19 / 1230AM / 1921

Although EH notes that he mailed the letter on Friday, it was not postmarked until after midnight on 19 February 1921, a Saturday. On the envelope he wrote, "Special Delivery."

1 In his letter to EH of 13 February 1921, Smith complained of the long hours and tedium of his new job (JFK).
2 *The Tavern*, a satiric adaptation by George M. Cohan (1878–1942) of *The Choice of the Superman* by Cora Dick Gantt (b. 1877). Gantt's play premiered in New York in September 1920; *The Tavern* ran in Chicago from 31 January 1921 to 1 May 1921 at Cohan's Grand Theatre.
3 In his letter, Smith reported having dinner the night before with Hadley and Ruth Bradfield at their apartment before he took Ruth "along of me to the copy screeding class."
4 EH's questions reflect his reading of *Erotic Symbolism; The Mechanism of Detumescence; The Psychic State in Pregnancy* (1906), volume 5 of *Studies in the Psychology of Sex* by English sexologist Havelock Ellis (1859–1939). EH bought the book in Toronto in early 1920 and sent his copy to Smith, who was unimpressed and returned it almost immediately (Reynolds *YH*, 120–21).
5 Charles W. and Ruth Bush Lobdell lived at 2650 Lake View Avenue; formerly of New Orleans, she had been queen of the Mardi Gras ball before their marriage. The society page of the 30 January 1920 *Chicago Daily Tribune* (F4) prominently featured a portrait of her in evening dress, along with news of an upcoming charity ball that she was helping to plan.
6 Haig and Haig, a brand of blended Scotch. Highball, a term coined in the United States in the 1890s for an iced drink of whiskey and soda or other mixer served in a tall glass. Bock, a dark

German beer; perhaps a nickname for one of EH's companions. Benedictine, herb-based liqueur originally made by Benedictine monks in Normandy; a local merchant modernized the recipe in the 1860s, and it has been commercially produced since 1876 by the company he established, Benedictine S.A.

7 Advertising firm Gregg and Ward.

8 In his 13 February letter, Smith complained about the "stalling" he had seen in recent boxing bouts in St. Louis.

9 Kid Howard (né Howard Carr) operated boxing gymnasiums in downtown Chicago for nearly three decades, the first (1910–1925) at 32 South Clark Street ("Howard Gym Closes," *Chicago Daily Tribune*, 23 November 1939, 38); EH visited his gym as a teenager (Baker *Life*, 22). Charles "Kid" Cutler (b. 1883), boxer and world heavyweight wrestling champion (1913–1915), opened a training gym in Chicago in 1913 and himself boxed into the 1920s ("Time Mellows Kid Cutler, Mat King in Golden Age," *Chicago Daily Tribune*, 1 February 1951, B1).

10 Floyd Fitzsimmons, Chicago boxing promoter who organized the 1920 Miske–Dempsey fight. In early 1920, Dempsey's draft board classification that exempted him from military service during WWI came under question, and he was formally charged with draft-dodging. On 15 June 1920 a San Francisco jury found him not guilty, but the charges that he was a "slacker" remained a stigma on his reputation. Dempsey and Carpentier, a French war hero, met in a highly publicized fight on 2 July 1921, the first million-dollar fight in boxing history.

11 Allusion to Romans 6:23: "For the wages of sin is death; but the gift of God is eternal life through Jesus Christ our Lord."

12 Tommy Gibbons (1891–1960), an American light heavyweight. In 1923 Dempsey failed to knock out Gibbons, winning the match only on points, and in 1924 Gibbons beat Carpentier.

13 This comment suggests that the magazine was published monthly; yet the sole surviving issue of 1 October 1921 (JFK) carries on its masthead the description "the weekly magazine of mutual help," as Reynolds also notes (*YH*, 279). The format of the magazine may have changed over the course of its publication.

14 Brooks Brothers, New York retailer of high-quality men's fashions founded in 1818. Apparently a sales representative for the firm was at the LaSalle Hotel, one of Chicago's finest, at LaSalle and Madison streets, taking orders for custom-made clothing. C.O.D., cash on delivery.

15 In his letter of 13 February, Smith reported, "St. Louie pool sharks are picking Houremans to smear the original Hoppe! The dope is that the Belgian has it over Wiiliam when it comes to masse shots. . . . Somehow I still give Hop an outside chance." In November 1920, Edouard Horemans of Belgium, the professional billiards champion of Europe, arrived in the United States to challenge William Frederick (Willie) Hoppe (1887–1959) for the world title, which Hoppe had held for fifteen years. When they finally met in the world championship tournament in Chicago in November 1921, Hoppe defeated Horemans but lost his title in December to another American, Jake Schaefer.

To Grace Quinlan, 25 February [1921]

February 25

Dearest G—

Scuse the use of your letter—but I'm in bed and have the typer with me—but no paper. What do you send a little piffling letter like this for anyway? Dawgone you.

Don Wright little while ago brought me a fine three or four page feeling letter from you and I open it thinking "Ha. Fine letter from G." Then find this.

Whatta ya want to send the old book back for anyway? I'm through with it.

And "Very sincerely yours." Since when were you very sincerely mine? You want to tell me about those things. They shock me. You used to say "Love" which meant that you liked me—don't you like me anymore?[1]

I've been laid by the heels in bed for a week or ten days—nope not with Hemorraghes or any of the things that Petoskey periodically brings me to the point of death with—just sick with Grippe and fever—and haven't been getting a doggone letter. Haven't had the drive to write to any of you all— and I guess I owe everybody there is a letter.

What's all the news? Wish you could come down here and see The Tavern. It's the funniest show I ever saw in my life. It's a Geo. M. Cohan buresque on Melodrama and it's so funny that a couple of times in it it gets so terrible funny that you know that if they say another thing you'll die.

Huh. Come to think of it I firmly believe that you owe me a letter. Yeah. Therefore this one just received takes on a tremendous significance. It may mean any number of things.

It may mean that you have discovered the secret of my dretful past.

It may mean that you are seriously in love with somebody. It sounds a little like that. People lose their sense of humor so very completely when that happens. Hate to think of you in love with somebody in Petoskey.

It may mean that Liz has told you any of the numerous diatribes I might have written agin you when I was in a very remote and unreal seeming period profoundly irritated by you.

It may mean that you have became a christian scientist. That also removes the sense of humor automatically.[2]

It may mean nothing at all.

Hope it's the last and that I get a good letter from you. Because in spite of all, as the best melodramas say, I love you still—also moving—and dancing—and swimming—you do swim very finely you know— And we used to be terrible fond of each other. I thought you were the best kid sister I had. And cause I thought you were my kid sister, you thought I wasn't very exciting. Yeah I know about that. But it was cause I was very fond of you and because you were 14, even though remarkably grown up you know, that I always treated you like a kid sister. And therefore lost drag as not being trilling like the love making village yokels.

Can make love you know—but always figured you as a sister and a pal— then never felt very admiratious of guys like Bob Mudgett that go around spreading their calf love over all the little girls in town like Karo corn syrup.

Paper running out.

Write me a good letter G—or if for some bad or bitter reason you are off of me till death doth come—why write me a fine dramatic, cold and haughty letter telling me all about why you never wish to write to me again. I like a fine dramatic situation like that. Theres something about it.

Well, 'bye.

Wish you were here to cheer me up this aft—feel kinda little bit blue— Have excellent new job—tremendous lot of seeds.

Love

Stein.

phPDL, TLS

1 EH typed this reply directly on Quinlan's letter to him of 23 February 1921, but did not mail it until enclosing it with his letter to her of 21 July 1921. She wrote that she was returning his copy of *This Side of Paradise*, F. Scott Fitzgerald's debut novel (Scribner's, 1920) and one of the year's best-sellers. In contrast to her earlier letters (JFK), with such closings as "Lots of Love," this one is brief and businesslike, signed "Very sincerely yours, / Grace Edith Quinlan."

2 The Church of Christ, Scientist, was founded in Boston in 1879 by Mary Baker Eddy (1821– 1910) "to reinstate primitive Christianity and its lost element of healing." Christian Scientists usually practice methods of spiritual healing in preference to medical treatment. In "The Doctor and the Doctor's Wife" (*IOT*), EH portrays the doctor's wife, ironically and unsympathetically, as a Christian Scientist.

To John Bone, 2 March 1921

Chicago
~~February~~
March
second
Nineteen Twenty One.

Mr. John R. Bone,
Managing Editor,
The Toronto Star.

Dear Mr Bone—

I was very glad to receive your letter in regard to the projected special ~~articles~~ policy. for the Daily Star. It was especially interesting as it coincided with certain ideas I had been mulling over for a long time in regard to the Daily.

~~Of~~ As you say feature stories for a daily differ from those for weekly publication. But that, as well as the ~~other, various~~ varied uses you could make of a special writer working under the Managing Editor, could be discussed later.

The position, as you have ~~outlined~~ sketched it appears to have splendid possibilities and appeals to me strongly.

At present, I am making $75.^{00} a week at agreeable, though rather dull work. I would be glad to come with you at $85 a week and could report April 1.

Yours Sincerely
Ernest M. Hemingway

JFK, ALDS

Bone's letter to which EH drafted this response remains unlocated, as does a letter from EH to his friend Greg Clark, features editor for the *Toronto Star Weekly*, asking his advice on how to respond to Bone's offer of a job writing features for the *Daily Star*. In a letter of 28 February 1921, Clark advised EH to tell Bone he was "now making $75 a week at agreeable and easy work," and to ask for a weekly salary between $70 and $100 (JFK). The letter that EH actually sent to Bone has not been located, nor has Bone's response. But in a later letter, dated 17 May, Bone wrote to thank EH for his letter of 12 May, adding that the article EH had enclosed would better suit the weekly than the daily edition of the *Star* (JFK). The *Star Weekly* published seven feature articles by EH in 1921; his first piece for the *Daily Star* did not appear until February 1922 (*DLT*, 67–87).

To William B. Smith, Jr., 4 March [1921]

March 4

Ye Ossif

Smith—:

Well Smith you dont write to your Friends any more do you?[1] That is no way for you to do. Do not be the rats that desert the stinking ship. Tho very shamed the writer be compared to the stinking ship. The writer does not stink. Even the feet of the writer are of pure and rose like odour. The writer bathes daily.

Some clippings—nay whole newspapers shall be dispatched to you. In these you will discern by blue a black pencil marks those stories writ by the writer. In some cases you will observe the writers name.

Observe the fine style, the compactness, the virility, the artistry of the articles. Note how those articles writ by the writer excell those writ by others.

The writer boosts himself. No one will boost the writer.

How about further sellage? I have figured out that you should sell one car a week for 10 weeks and have 2,000 nubolums. This will purchase at a conservative estimate 200,000 Yellow Sallys.[2]

JFK, AL

1 The surviving letter from Smith that most closely precedes this one is dated 30 January 1921; Smith's next surviving letter to EH was mailed from St. Louis on 7 March 1921 (PUL).
2 Type of dry stoneflies used in fly-fishing.

To Irene Goldstein, 16 March [1921]

March 16

Dear Yrene—

That's pretty darned nice 'bout you coming up here—it'll be down here though—for July. Pavley—Oukrainskey. You must be good. Why've I never seen you dance?[1]

Bet it's nice to have Mrs. Rosenthal visiting with you. That was funny bout the letter. Wrote it from the office and thought of course Grand Island would catch you—thought you'd be well nough known by now.[2] I was wondering what the hell. Didn't hear from you or anything. Will wait till I get home to get your letter to send this so it'll get to you.

Week ended in Saint Louis last week. Back yesterday.[3] Been having an excellent time. warm there—didn't need coat all the time. Canoed and fooled around the country club.

Kinda nice here now. When you coming through? We're having a regular orgy of bridge just now. I've been holding the most unbelieveable cards. Have offered to make the men a flat montly rate on bridge. Also town is still damp. Been working hard. Your job sounds hard to. Are you tired at night? Me also. Sleeping like a log. We have the apartment till May 1st. Then going to spend the summer at Mrs. Aldis's. Very nice joint. Has this one beat on size—but can't tie that Divan. Gaw what a divan that is too. 100 E. Chicago is the new adress. Tisn't so yet though. Have Aldis's till November—so we're set on a place to live in. Course getting food is still a problem. I thought I was going to Toronto for good about a week ago—had a peach of an offer from them—but if you're going to be here during July I'll stay around. Be fine to see you. Bobb Rouse still seems fond of you—you know I am—write me a letter—huh?[4]

Stein

Stanford, TLS

1 Goldstein wrote to EH on 9 March 1921 that she would be in Chicago for the month of July to study at the Pavley-Oukrainsky Ballet School (JFK). In 1916, Andreas Pavley (1892–1931) and Serge Oukrainsky (1886–1972), both veterans of the Russian Imperial Ballet and then leading dancers of the Chicago Grand Opera, established the school to train dancers for the opera ballet; beginning in 1919, they directed a summer dance camp in South Haven, Michigan.

2 Goldstein was then teaching physical education at a public school in Grand Island, Nebraska (Diliberto, 50). She had written that her aunt, "Mrs. Rosenthal from Petoskey," was visiting and that EH's previous letter had been delayed two weeks at the Grand Island post office.

3 EH had visited Hadley in St. Louis for the first time on the weekend of 11 March (Baker *Life*, 77; Diliberto, 57–58).

4 EH and Bill Horne would move with Y. K. Smith when he returned to his former apartment at 100 East Chicago, owned by Mrs. Dorothy Aldis, "a wealthy, local patroness of the arts" (Fenton, 99). Robert (Bobby) Rouse was one of the young bachelors who shared Smith's apartment at 63 East Division, where Goldstein had visited EH over the Christmas holidays. Years later she recalled that as she was leaving, EH had flung himself upon her as they were sitting on a bed where she had left her coat (Diliberto, 50)—perhaps explaining his reference to the divan.

To Marjorie Bump, [after 7 April 1921]

~~My Darling~~

The vituperative vein is not so adaptable to your own naive inflexibilty of diction.

For instance, to grow Phillipic and then commit the indiscretion of spelling "abominable" in the wholly charming and ingenuous way in which you spelled it is fatal to the grand Bernhardtric manner.[1]

The pencilled addition of your address to the back of the envelop means of course that you wish an answer.[2]

Dear Red—

I tried hard in the above to give you something comparable to the tone of your screed. But it was Too difficult— These kind of letters, you know, went out with books on Etiquette. Not throwing off on the Etiquicy book we studied together.

~~If it was my abominable conceit that finally wrenched that letter from you after two months, it is only reciprocal to say that it was the shape of your mouth that, to my mind, parted us forever.~~

~~You made only one reference to the conceit so I only refer to the mouth but once.~~

~~That was a splendid point about seeking to discuss for two months. The vituperative vein—indefencible alliteration—but my Stenographer has a good deal of work to do and you have banned favorite phrases—is not becoming to your naive style.~~[3]

Abominable is not spelled Abomnable.

That should show, without 2 month's consideration, how I've been good for you. Was joking about that you know Red.

Wonder what the grand outburst was about anyway. Suppose I'll never know. What's the stuff about conceit? Am I really so doggone conceited?

Was going to write you a sarcastic letter—but don't feel like it now. Got started remembering that summer of 1919— Best ~~I've ever had~~ summer there ever was I guess— Not going to spoil that summer or fall for anybody. It was idyllic—perfect as some days in Spring are and mountain valleys you pass on puffing trains—and other impermanent things.

Afterward you reverted to type and I acted like a cad—and it all came out right.

You'll marry a sublimated Don Marcle[4] or something of the sort and live happily for ever after—and if you marry a sufficiently cheerful sufficiently boneheaded cheerful bonehead you may both live happily ever after. Charles Graham is a good example of the type—[5] You'll have a wonderful honeymoon and two years later you may occasionally get him out of the house to go to the movies. Can't depend on that though. He may be very fond of the movies. There's no formula.

Probably as you say I wasn't good for you—advocated moonlight swims—and fishing for rainbow off the point and gang dances at the Bean house and working in the orchard with Kate and Bill—while any sensible person would know that the proper amusements were Koulis' Ice Cream parlor and Jew dances at the Cushman and Spoony kid parties at Helen Sly's.[6]

Yup I was bad for you—shouldn't have had you read Richard Yea and Nay —remember that the Petoskey librarian said Hewlett was not nice. We shouldn't have read the other stuff we did when you could have been reading The American Magazine and The Ladies Home Journal.[7]

Chin up Red— I wasn't so bad for you— Except as Bill always said— But I won't repeat that because I never agreed with him.

This is getting to be a long letter

JFK, ALD

Apparently an unsent draft responding to Marjorie Bump's letter of 7 April 1921 (JFK), in which she said that after giving two months' consideration to his remark that he was good for her, she concluded she would have been better off had she never known him, adding, "it was wrong to think highly of a person of such abomnable conceit." Reynolds surmises that this letter to EH was in response to a now-lost letter from EH in which he told Marjorie of his plans to marry Hadley (*YH*, 174). However, H. R. Stoneback finds it more likely that EH and Marjorie had met two months earlier, perhaps during her school term break, and that he had broken the news to her in person ("'Nothing Was Ever Lost': Another Look at 'That Marge Business,'" in *Hemingway: "Up in Michigan" Perspectives*, ed. Frederic J. Svoboda and Joseph J. Waldmeir [East Lansing: Michigan State University Press, 1995], 74).

1 Sarah Bernhardt (1844–1923), French stage actress renowned for her dramatic roles.
2 An envelope does not survive with Marjorie Bump's letter.
3 This sentence is typewritten on the verso of the first page and is scratched out in pencil. It likely represents EH's first attempt at beginning the letter.
4 Donald Markle, a student at Petoskey High School, then in his senior year.

5 Charles S. Graham was married to Marjorie's mother, Mate Cecilia Bump Graham (c. 1872–1935), widow of Sidney S. Bump. According to the 1919–1920 Petoskey City Directory, Graham was a traveling salesman, living at 414 Grove with "Mrs. Matie C. Graham," who worked at Bump and McCabe.

6 Koulis Kandy Kitchen, at 325 Mitchell Street in Petoskey, advertised "Home-Made Candies and Ice Cream." Sly, a classmate of Marjorie Bump who also graduated from Petoskey High School in 1920.

7 *The Life and Death of Richard Yea-and-Nay*, by Maurice Henry Hewlett. *The American Magazine* (1906–1956) and *Ladies' Home Journal* (1883–), popular monthly magazines with wide readerships.

To Clarence Hemingway, 15 April 1921

Spril 15 1921

Dear Dad

I was very glad to get your two postals—by now you should be having a wonderful time.[1] Things are moving fairly fast here. I'm working very hard at my jawb and have a chanct of promotion and I suppose more seeds—can't go into the details as there is always some one liable to come in and look over your shoulder to see what you're writing. We have a new office in the loop— address room 205 Wells Building—128 North Wells Street Chicago Illinois will get me.[2] Chance of me being made managing editor of the poiper. That's private and very sub rosa.

Meantime I'm still dickering with Toronto and liable to shove for there any time.[3] The Italian Lira that I've bought around 3.50 and so on have risen to 5.00— I could sell at a good profit—but am buying them becasue I want the Lira—not as a gamble. Want to go to Italy in November if I've enough Lira. Manfredi was up last night. he's looking well and sent his best to you.

I had Ursula out to dinner one night and am going out to the house soon. But have been working like a dog. Going up to Wisconsin on a story next Monday.

They hanged Cardinella and Cosmano and some other Wop killer today. Lopez, who was to hang was reprieved. Cardinella is a good man to swing I guess.[4] Passed the County Jail this morning and there was a big crowd standing outside waiting for the event.

Have you been doing any fishing yet?

Give my love to Grandmother and Grandfather and Aunt Grace and
Carol. Hope they are all feeling well.

Get a good rest and some good fishing and go swimming for me— I surely
wish I were with you—eat a lot of shrimps too—Wish I could rate a vacation
—seems as though you work like a dog all week and it's barely Sunday and
you get a little sleep and it's back at the treadmill again— I'm going to beat
the machine by going to Wopland for a while in the fall.

The sun hasn't shown here for about two weeks. I'm writing you a swell
gloomy letter so that you'll appreciate what a fine time you're having. I hate
these guys that write to some one that's away on a trip and try and make
them feel they would have more fun if they were at home. It's not a bit of fun
here—and nothing to look forward to.

With that cheerful prospect I close—

Your affct son
Ernie

JFK, TLS; postmark: CHICAGO / ILL., APR 15 / 6 PM / 1921

1 Clarence was visiting Sanibel Island, Florida, with his daughter Carol, his parents, and his sister, Grace Adelaide Hemingway. In the one postcard to EH that survives from that trip, Clarence reported they were "oh so happy" and that there were plenty of fish (9 April 1921, JFK).
2 The office of the *Co-operative Commonwealth* was in the city's historic downtown business district, popularly known as the Loop because of the pattern of elevated train tracks encircling the neighborhood.
3 EH had been offered a job at the *Toronto Star* by managing editor John Bone.
4 Salvatore "Sam" Cardinella ("Cardinelli" in court records; 1880–1921), a Chicago organized crime leader, was hanged that day for the 24 June 1919 murder of saloonkeeper Andrew Bowman. Joseph Costanzo (not "Cosmano"), Sam Ferrara, and Antonio "The Game Cock" Lopez had been sentenced to death for the 14 January 1921 murder of Antonio Varchetto, a Chicago baker. While Costanzo and Ferrara also were executed on 15 April, Lopez was granted a thirty-day reprieve upon discovery of potentially exculpatory evidence ("Three to Hang Today; Lopez Is Reprieved," *Chicago Daily Tribune*, 15 April 1921, 1; "Bandit Killed, Three Hanged, in Crime War," *Chicago Daily Tribune*, 16 April 1921, 1). Lopez was later executed, on 8 July 1921. EH wrote of the hanging of Cardinella in *iot*.

To William B. Smith, Jr., [28 April 1921]

Gaw Bird you sound in ghastly shape. Far be it from the enditer to
count letters on a run down article. You oughta be able to pick up some

pretty good jack with this Zelnicker stuff this summer as a side line. You can give the Nicker a good line on the Michigan situation anyway. Does Ben Brown stock our rings?[1]

The enditer is stunned by the shape you sound to be in—the screeds shall flow freely. I'd no idea that you were in such carpy condition—though you looked bad when I was in the village. Laid non hearage from you to some form of displeasure with the enditer and so after a time stopped screedage on the theory that if a man didn't want to have nathing to do with a man a man ought not to give an imitation of Odgar in epistolary pursuit of Butstein. However if you're under the squord, as you obviously sound, the out put will be unrestricted.

Us men are moving to 100 E. Chicago forninst Saturday. Doodiles is coming home on the 28th of May. Yen is in swell shape—172 of the pounds —keeps twixt there and 174. Dcelares that he has never felt better since first laid by the heels.

Fedith[2] is in town and living with her parents at the Virginia Hotel. Stut hasn't seen her, to my knowlege, for a week or ten days. Stut has been with Yen or I nearly every night last week—we staged a swell party She and Yen and the enditer and a fine guy named Krebs[3] last saturday nacht at a series of German family resorts that I have never seen rivalled. I doubt if their equal exists in Germany. Moselle wine at 40 centimes the large beaker, regular prewar beer at 40 cents the stein. Man can get a good dinner for 50 cents. Not a word of English spoken. We'll make them when you stop here. Sunday Stut and the men Yen, Horne and Rouse went out to Oak Park, the parentals all being in Michigan. Swell Geramn vaudveel at the places I mentioned, Wurtz n'sepp's,[4] Komicker seppels and two other splendid places.

Fedith being here, she and Stut living apart and not seeing each other would indicate bustage up would it not?

The enditer is not in anyway in the pink hisself. For last two weeks have rated splitting head aches that damn near mort a man. Yesterday at the office rated haywireage of my good optic and had to go home to the domocile. Had to lay off the gloves on account of the headaches—been working like hell at same time as doing regular stuff here for Loper. Written more stuff in past two weeks tha[n] in preceeding 18 months. Physical doesn't seem to be bucking the mental—feel right up forninst the verge of complete haywireage however. When a man can go swimming here it'll be better. At present come home from the office, feed, shoot a couple or three rubberoids of bridge with the men and then go to bed, sleep a little while and then wake up and can't sleep for nawthing, so start working and keep going till get sleepy in the morning. Pastimed the Veronal[5] but it don't seem to have the wallop. Wish to hell I was going Nort when you men do. Doubt if I get up this summer— Jo Eezus, sometimes get thinking about the Sturgeon and Black during the nocturnal and damn near go cuckoo— Haven't the Odgar attitude on that. May have to give it up for something I want more—but that doesn't keep me from loving it with everything I have. Dats de way tings are. Guy loves a couple or three streams all his life and loves 'em better than anything in the world—falls in love with a girl and the goddam streams can dry up for all he cares. Only the hell of it is that all that country has as bad a hold on me as ever—there's as much of a pull this spring as there ever was—and you know how it's always been—just don't think about it at all daytimes, but at night it comes and ruins me—and I can't go.

Remember that day last summer when we hit the big school at that bend down below Chandler's? That's one of the worst that hits a man. and the day I fished alone with Sam Nickey down on another part of the creek and took all those tremendous ones in that stretch where you and I first butchered them, the day that Hoopkins and Odgar got their big bunch up the stream. Remember me breaking my rod on that place where you caught your big one and the fight we had before we netted him? Joe Eesus I'll bet there are trout in there a man wouldn't believe. Now I've gotten started thinking about it— ruined for the day.

This is carpy screed— Carper's making good seeds now—on a basis of strictly commision—making lot more than he ever did before and keeps it right up. Says he's going to take a month up North. Dirty Dick in pretty good shape—had lunch with him this noon. Don't know the Ghee's plans yet. What is the dope on Teodore? Had a screed from Theodore—postal rather— didn't give anydope.[6]

Spose one of the principal cuases that's haywired you is being to[o] tired at night to take any kind of exercise. Think that's one of the big things that ruins a man. He doesn't realize it till he's a ruint article too. You sure appear to have an air tight drag with Zelnicker. Good thing for a man to have— Well Waddyoh—shoot you a better screed shortly—couple of screeds of this character would topple a man into the casket.

Immer,
Wemedge

PUL, TLS; postmark: CHICAGO / ILL., APR 28 / 11PM / 1921.

1 Smith was employed by the Walter A. Zelnicker Supply Company of St. Louis, manufacturer of the Ever-Tight Piston Ring. Brown operated a garage in Charlevoix, established in 1898 as a harness shop.
2 Edith Foley (b. 1894), freelance writer and friend of Kate Smith from girlhood summers in Michigan; they had roomed together at Y. K. Smith's Chicago apartment and were collaborating on magazine articles (Fenton, 99–100). Later, Smith married John Dos Passos in 1929, and Foley married writer Frank Shay (1888–1954) in 1930, and they lived near each other in Provincetown, Massachusetts. The women collaborated on two books, *Down the Cape: The Complete Guide to Cape Cod* (New York: Dodge Publishing Company, 1936) and *The Private Adventure of Captain Shaw* (Boston: Houghton Mifflin Company, 1945), an historical novel.
3 Krebs Friend (1896–1967) a *Co-operative Commonwealth* colleague and WWI veteran who had seen action on the Western front in 1918 and suffered severe shell shock. EH encountered him again in Paris in 1924, when, having married an heiress, Friend became the chief financial backer of the *Transatlantic Review* (Baker *Life*, 131; Smith, 70). EH drew on some of his friend's war experiences in "Soldier's Home" (*IOT*), naming the protagonist Harold Krebs.
4 Wurz 'n' Zepp's, renowned beer hall on North Avenue in Chicago (Baker *Life*, 79).
5 Brand name of a barbiturate drug with a sedative or hypnotic effect, introduced in 1903.
6 A postcard from Ted Brumback to EH, postmarked Kansas City, 8 April 1921, was forwarded to EH by Grace Hemingway in her letter of 14 April 1921 (JFK).

To Marcelline Hemingway, [20 May 1921]

Dearest Carved Ivory—

Hope the 'domen is feeling in good shape. Gee I was sorry when I heard that you were to go under the knife. There's nothing bothers me like having a dear old friend or relative go under the knife.

Conversation with the male parent however elliceted the information that you had come out from under the knife in nice shape.

The men are going to screed you and I will be out shortly to see in what shape you have come out from under the knife.

Tonight the Carper, i.e. Mr. La Fever the Carper, and Yenlaw Smith and the wrter are going to be seated at the ringside while Frankie Schaeffer—of the Stock Yards—and Gene Watson—the Pacific Coast demon—maul ten rounds at 130 lbs. ringside.[1] It should be a good brawl. I look forward to viewing it.

I think that Al[2] had a good time with me here. Hope so—I took your tip that he was without seeds and financed the entire enetertainment—food drink etc. It must have schocked Al to learn that you were going under the knife.

Does Douglas Wilde know that you have gone under the knife? He ought to come through with something pretty handsome. Think of what you might have rated from him if you had only permitted kissage[.] Your going under the knife would then have rent him in such bad shape that he would probably have smothered the hospital in onions like a steak is smothered in onions.

All the men were broken up to hear that you had gone under the knife.

Last night Issy Simons and I had a swell party. Went to four of the best places in the city and while I was saddened at the thought of you being under the knife I managed to assume a certain false Gayety. We had a peach of a time. Issy is a priceless kid. It was a glorious night. We'd come out of some place where we'd been waltzing and into the outer air and it would be warm and almost tropical with a big moon over the tops of the houses. Kind of a warm softness in the air, same way it used to be when we were kids and we'd roller skate or play run sheep run with the Luckocks and Charlotte Bruce.[3]

I'm, and Horney's, going down to St. Louis next Friday night and stay three days at Hash's domocile. Ought to have a swell time—

The new Domocile is a wonder—much larger than the old one—and with an elevator and a view from my front window looking down over the queer angled roofs of the old houses on Rush street down to the big mountain of the Wrigley building,[4] green of the new grass along the street and trees coming out—wonderful view. Bobby's going to New York for good pretty soon—did you know that? Horney's working hard.

We've a fine song—wrote by me about the men—
    Bobby strolls round on La Salle street
    Carper spends money on sin
    Horney'll write ads for a quarter
    My Gawd how the money rolls in! [5]

Gee I'm sorry that you had to go under the knife. But still if a person has to go under the knife they might just as well go right under the knife without struggling. Sleepy as the deuce this aft—hot you know—and I didn't get in till all hours this morning. Gee had a good time—more fun to go out with Is than any body I know in this town. Youghta a seen us in the Grottenkeller waltzing round and round and all germans around and a fine beery, smoky, cheerful pound on the table with a stein for more music, atmosphere.

Scuse the rotten typeage and the probably tousands of errati—that's on account of me typing by the touch system—just learned it recently and it's faster but more inacurrate.[6]

Kate sent you her love and said that you were the last person she would enjoy having go und[e]r the knife. Me too I hate to think of you going under the knife—did you have 'em take anything else [o]ut too? I8d have had everything out at onc't. Coming out Sunday I think and will cast an optic on you—

Best love to you, dear old swester—and hope you're comfortable—

ever,

Ernie

phJFK, TLS; postmark: CHICAGO / ILL., MAY 20 / 630 PM / 1921

EH addressed the envelope, "Special Delivery / Miss Marcelline Hemingway / care Oak Park Hospital / Oak Park / Illinois / (A Patient With The Appendix Out)."

1 Frankie Schaeffer, a native Chicagoan, would win a lightweight boxing bout with Gene Watson of Los Angeles in Aurora, Illinois, on 15 July, but no record of a fight in May has been located.

2 Probably Al Walker.

3 The George and Emma Luccock family lived at 523 North Kenilworth, near the Hemingways and the family of Isabelle Simmons; their daughters Georgia and Emory were about four years older than EH. Charlotte Bruce was a member of the OPRFHS class of 1915.

4 Construction of the Wrigley Building, completed in April 1921, inaugurated the development of Chicago's "Magnificent Mile" business district on Michigan Avenue north of the Chicago River.

5 EH parodies the bawdy song, "My God How the Money Rolls In" (sung to the tune of the Scottish folk song "My Bonnie Lies Over the Ocean"), one version of which begins, "My father makes illegal whiskey. / My mother makes illegal gin. / My sister sells sin in the corner. / My God how the money rolls in."

6 The "all-finger" touch system of typing, developed in 1876 by Frank Edgar McGurrin, relies on feel and memory rather than sight. After he won a highly publicized typing competition against a four-finger typist in 1888, touch typing gained widespread acceptance as the most efficient technique.

To Marcelline Hemingway, [25 May 1921]

Hemingway

Dear Ivory Tower—

Enclosed is a biological missive from Yenlaw written at the Crear Library—there is nothing to report.[1] The maternal parent came up last night and she and the enditer placed away a chow mein at the Royal Cafe—it isn't hot any more—but you probably know that. Yen cut the end off his thumb with a razor but the writer, asssuming for a moment the role of a physicist, fixed it back on again and it is growing in nice shape.

Horney and I are showving off to SinLouis on Friday nocturnal. As you surmise I will be glad to clap my deadlights onto Hash. There is nothing of any moent at the office of the enditer. I have been laboring hard and it has been terrible hot—but a cool breeze from the lake has swept the heat away like a bad dream.

You are pr[o]bably in pretty good shape by now. Is a present indicate[d] in the event of our attending the wedding of the Passionate Blight and Cousin Maggie?[2] In such an event I feel that my attendance may be difficult to obtain.

Gee I wish it was Friday night—two entire diurnals to get through somehow before the evening cometh. It'll only be worse when I'm back again tho—that's the hell of it—to coin a phrase.

How's the 'domen?

Pardon the brevity and also the assiniinity of this screed and believe me always your devoted brother and sincere admirer—

your good friend,
Ernest M. Hemingway

James Sanford, TLS; postmark: CHICAGO / ILL., MAY 25 / 6 PM / 1921

1 The John Crerar Library, a free public reference library of scientific, technical, and medical literature, established in 1897 and originally housed in the Marshall Field and Company Building in the Chicago Loop. In May 1921, it opened in a new permanent building at Michigan Boulevard and Randolph Street. Y. K. Smith's enclosed letter remains unlocated.
2 The 11 June 1921 *Oak Leaves* announced the wedding that day of EH's second cousin Margaret E. Hall (b. circa 1901) to his classmate Fred S. "The Blight" Wilcoxen, Jr. Margaret's father, Fred E. Hall (b. 1877) of Oak Park, was Grace Hall Hemingway's first cousin, son of Miller and Emma Hall.

To Hadley Richardson, [7 July 1921]

Miss E. Hadley Richardson

5739 Cates Avenue

St. Louis Missouri—

Nothing better than your coming. Stop. Cheer up. Stop. Bill heart broken over Georges Carpentier.[1] Stop. Not me—Stop. Please come. Stop. Stay here. Stop. All my Love.

E.M.H.

JFK, ACDS

EH wrote this on the verso of a 7 July 1921 telegram from Hadley that reads, "WANT SO MUCH TO SEE YOU BUT AFRAID OF MAKING THINGS HARDER COULD COME FRIDAY NIGHT SEEING YOU SATURDAY AND SUNDAY CAN EASILY GIVE IT UP JUST WANT TO SEE YOU VERY MUCH KNOW IT IS PROBABLY NOT PRACTICAL ON ACCOUNT OF THROAT AND WORK VERY DEAR LOVE / E.H.R."

1 On 2 July 1921, defending heavyweight boxing champion Jack Dempsey knocked out Georges Carpentier in the fourth round of the much anticipated world title bout, touted as "the Battle of the Century." More than 80,000 spectators packed a stadium constructed especially for the occasion in Jersey City, New Jersey.

To Grace Quinlan and Georgianna Bump, [c. 21 July 1921]

Dearest G and Dearest Pudge—

Haven't any idea where you men are now—maybe at various camps and so I'm sending this to G's address and Lord knows what delays before you get it.

Exhibit A. is letter just came to me today from My Dad at Walloon— he told me 1st part of July that he'd forwarded a letter to me enclosing one from Petoskey—and it never came— I wrote him twice and it's finally come back for a decent address and just arrived this morning.

I feel terribly to have not answered your congratulation screed—but it's just come this morning and I'm answering it as fast as I can—

Cause I never wrote either of you men a letter together I don' know how to do it—so here ends the double letter with love to both of you and here starts two single letters to each of you— Just a minute—

The enclosure is for both of yez to see and if you'll send 'em back to me I'll be much bliged on account of they being the only ones I have—they're further evidence in the case—

I'm not writing to Red 'cause she wrote me a letter saying she didn't never want to even clap a deadlight on me again on account of my been so conceited, so naturally I'd feel uncomfortable writing to her on account of thinking whatever I said, she'd be thinking—"Ah, that's his insane conceit." However I'm not sore at her nor nawthing—anyway she said my conceit was "abomnable" not insane—so that's all right—[1]

Love to both of yez—
Stein

Yale, TLS

The conjectured letter date is based on the date of the following letter of 21 July 1921 from EH to Quinlan, which he evidently enclosed with this "double letter" to Quinlan and Georgianna Bump. The other enclosures he mentions, including a "single letter" directed to Georgianna ("Pudge"), do not survive with this letter. His comments in the following letter suggest that he had sent society column clippings from St. Louis newspapers announcing his and Hadley's engagement.

1 Reference to Marjorie Bump's letter to EH of 7 March 1921 (JFK).

To Grace Quinlan, 21 July 1921

July 21 1921

Dear Old Gee—

You musta thought me all sorts of a dirty bum because of not answering your and Pudges' priceless note—but guess the letter to both of you explained that.[1] Woulda written you both together—but can't very well—always been separated in my mind and sides there are things to tell both of you.

Just becuase you said about my not writing you I'm enclosing letter I wrote you one day last February when I was feeling low—that's so you won't think I just dropped you out of my mind.[2]

Suppose you want to hear all about Hadley—well her nickname is Hash—she's a wonderful tennis player, best pianist I ever heard and a sort of terribly fine article. Spite of the clipping prophecying a big wedding in the fall in St. Louis, we're going to fool them and be married at the Bay in that small, trick churchthere.[3] Then going to kinda bum arouud for about three weeks and then go back to Chicago—apartment there with Kenley Smith's—stay there through November I guess and then allez to Italy for a year or maybe two years. I've been saving seeds and buying Wop money since came down from Petoskey and I recently had a grant from the King and so I'm setting pretty well thataway.[4] We're going to Naples and stay there till it gets warm in the spring. Living at Capri I guess, and then go up into Abruzzi. Capracotta probably—there's a fine trout stream there—the Sangro River—and tennis courts and it's 1200 meters above sea level—most wonderful place you ever heard of. I've gotten all the dope on prices and so on from my best pal, Nick Neroni who's just come to this country, we were together in the war, and he's been staying around with me and given me all the dope. He's going back in the fall and will arrange everything for us.

It sounds pretty good? The date hasn't been set for the wedding, but it'll be early in Sept—some time the first week—and you'll be there of course. I can't invite a big lot of people because we're having it up North to get away from all that sort of thing—but you'll come won't you? Invitations and all that sort of thing'll arrive in course of human events.

You don' wanta think, Gee, that I've thrown over all the people I'm fond of up North because I've not been writing this winter. IT's been a regular hell of a winter in some ways—been pretty badly sick couple of times—been holding down one jawb days and one nights to get more seeds—been writing stuff on the side all the time and been so busy and tired and done in that I haven't written a line except to Hash all winter.

Have what's really a pretty darned good job now—maybe making a mistake to throw it over to go to Italy—but will have enough seeds to last a couple of years there—and with that time to write in I've a chance to get somewhere—

Irene Goldstein was here and we had one good session of tennis and I was going to see her again and then got suddenly ordere[d] east to the fight and hadda leave in a hurry—packing on the run and didn't even have a chance to call her upwards.[5] Lost 700 and some seeds on the battle—and that didn't help peace of mind any— It was a good bet at 3–1 though— Carp showed that when he nearly got him in the 2nd round. We were out of luck—if he hadn't busted his hand with that first right he landed—but what's the use of Post mortems? I'd rather you didn't say anything bout the seeds loseage—you know —there are too many people like to have a crack at you if you give 'em any chancet—

Well dear old bean I'D better close—must write Useless— I'll be seeing you in September— Irene tells me you're getting beautiful—wouldn't be anything new—you have to be pretty good looking tho to have other girls say so—

Write me will you? And remember me to your Dad and Mother. I'm terribly fond of all of you—you know how fond I am of you—

Always,

Stein

P.S. Maybe your father and mother could bring you and Pudge and who else? Red and Liz? Over to this here wedding. I'm not asking Mrs. Graham[6]—you know why—cause I don't want her. But didn't want Pudge to see this.

Immer

Stein.

Give me all the dope on whats going on—Huh?

Yale, TLS

1 On the accompanying envelope, EH typed simply, "Miss G. E. Quinlan / addressed." This letter apparently was enclosed in the preceding undated letter to "Dearest G and Dearest Pudge." Both letters were written on the same typewriter on identical paper and signed with the same blue crayon-like pencil.
2 EH's letter to Quinlan of 25 February 1921, typewritten on her letter to him of 23 February 1921 (PDL).
3 A note in the "Social Items" column of the *St. Louis Post-Dispatch* of 15 June 1921 reported that the engagement of Miss Hadley Richardson and "Ernest Miller Hemmingway" was announced the previous day at a tea hosted by Mrs. George J. Breaker and that the wedding would probably take place in the fall. EH is apparently alluding to the "Society News" piece in the *St. Louis Globe-Democrat* (15 June 1921), which predicted that "The wedding will be one of the notable social events of the autumn." EH and Hadley would be married on 3 September. Although the wedding invitation sent by Hadley's sister named the First Presbyterian Church in Horton Bay as the site, the wedding actually took place at the

Methodist church that once stood next to the Horton Bay general store. Ohle notes that by 1921 the Methodist church was used for services only rarely, "when a 'circuit rider' minister happened along" (106–8; Baker *Life*, 576).

4 Marcelline recalled that EH, decorated with the Italian Croce di Guerra, received a lifetime pension of 50 lira per year (Sanford, 211).

5 Apart from EH's claim here and in the absence of surviving copies of the *Co-operative Commonwealth* (other than a sole issue, 1 October 1920, at JFK), no evidence has been located to confirm whether or not he traveled to New Jersey to attend the 2 July title bout between Dempsey and Carpentier.

6 According to Ohle, his cousin Marjorie Bump did not attend because her mother, Mate Bump Graham, Ohle's paternal aunt, was not invited (Ohle, 108). Georgianna Bump did attend.

To Grace Quinlan, [c. late July 1921]

Dearest Old G—

It's kinda so fine to have you back again that I feel almost too good to write—wish you were here and we could go out to Wurz nSepp's and have dinner and go some where and dance and talk and make up all the time we've missed mis-understanding each other—

Sure I know how you feel about my getting married— Course I'm too young by the calendar and would seem terribly funny to be married and horrible to be domesticated and settled into a dead rut of seed getting and maybe children having and all that. Chance though that it won't be thatway at all— Good chance that it'll be just two people that love each other being able to be together and understand each other and bum together and help each other in their work and take away from each other that sort of loneliness of that's with you even when you're in a crowd of people that are fond of you. Think marriage might be a terrible fine thing you know— Anyhow Hash and I are going to have a very fine try at it—

Gee I'M sorry about whatever bumness of me lead up to that Sincerely Yours screed. And if I'd only sent the answer to it, it might have all cleared up then—wish I had—have wanted you to tell all about all this as it went along— You know there are thousands of things about this here getting married I'd want to talk over with the very best sister I have—Huh—don' tell anybody else I said you were that—will you? Cause you always knew I loved you so much better than all the rest of the gang that it made them jealous and they'd try and gyp you with me—could make me sore at you by lying to me

—and me believing—but couldn't make me not love you. That's funny. I dunno— You're such a terribly fine sort of a person— Think you make the finest fight against Petoskey—it's really something to fight. It's awful the mothers cutting Liz isn't it? I haven't written her for ages—will—but Mrs. Graham, that awful Mrs. Graham not letting Pudge be with Liz is so bad that it's funny.

Be fine at camp won't it? Gosh I wish I were up North. Sleep on the roof here—our apartment has a big, flat roof and all sorts of shaped chimney pots and at nights sometimes lie there in the moonlight and see the Bay with the moon coming up over a hill and us guys lying out on the dock and a big rainbow trout making a swirl in the moonlight on the bay—or think of the sweep of black country from the hill where we camp above the Sturgeon—or the pool in front of the shack we have out on the Black River—feel as though I'd like to step off the roof—

JFK, TL

Apparently abandoned and unsent. The conjectured letter date is based on EH's reference to his letter to Quinlan of 25 February (answering her "Sincerely Yours screed" of 23 February), which he finally sent to her enclosed in his letter of 21 July. In addition, EH refers in future tense to Quinlan's attending camp; in her letter to EH of 10 August 1921 (JFK), she would report that she had been at camp for two weeks.

To William B. Smith, Jr., [c. 3–5 August 1921]

Boid—

Your screed is not to hand but let me say that appreciate the fact that you are doing the best you can to make this a real wedding from start to finish. That's the way I like to do things. The weddee is on tap here during this week with a consequent loss of my seeds. Having a weddee on tap is as hard on a seed as anything the enditer has yet encountered. You probably by now have viewed a peper telling of the Hose aquital. Cook County what crimes are committed in thy name. Where else could it have been done? New York probably. You recall the Abe Attell angle? Acquitted in the face of Burns and Maharg's testimony and their own confessions![1] My Gawd Justice has about as much of a petition here as the Madame would have being tried for the murder of Lyle Shanahan before a picked Venire of Local Boys.[2]

I work like hell. You aint got no idea how I work. It's good as hell for me as I'm learning a lot from this Stockbridge—[3] You are probably in receipt of info from the males. Their allezing date is set for next Montag. They made an effort to get stut to flash with them but met with small success.[4]

Downey wan the titular all right, but how he is to get it I don't know. The whole thing was too foul for words. I have seen Bryan and he is a pretty fair boy, but Jo Eezus the middles can hardly be said to be much. He socked Wilson, who was fat as a hawg and under the protection of his own official on the button, all right, but Wilson trained and in shape might butcher him. Unless Wilson has went entirely by the squard I would not be a man to bet money on Downey in a return match.[5] Boid this whole box-fight game is more crookedly and ludicrously refereed than some of the pastimes you have hurled at the Voix. I've seen things a man wouldn't believe. 7 second counts and 18 second counts. Gaw. There's a sbx named Phil Collins that referees brawls locally that the boys are afraid to take nine from on account of once on the canvas with Collins counting you're gone. No one can arise before he will count them out. This Gardner must have had the viscera at that. Not that I admire that type but think of what the ringside musta lo[o]ked like, Wilson out cold, down three times for 13 and 18 second counts and this Gardner has the nerve to disqualify Downey while Wilson is out as cold as fish for Fouling! My Gawd.[6]

Things are fouler than ever at the cile. I can't write about it. Would like to park the Fanny beside you on the Sturge[7] somewhere and do a Bert Collier into your Lily White Ear— Can't talk to anyone here on it— I don' know what shape Yen's in—any remarks by me that he seems to be losing weight and oughta ease up or anything of that character are hooted by Diles. Besser than ever is her verdict. She's took him like the Wooden Horse took the Trojans. I8d rather have the horse in a matrimonial venture.[8] Jo EEzus— how blind you musta considered me when I would rally to her defence in former times. I should not speak in this manner when occupying their bed and board, but may be allowed to speak a very little on account of rarely rating any board and having no bed. Horney and I share a small room—the two big rooms are occupied by them, I aint throwing off on that—just killing the bed and board myth. I sleep on the roof. Thass all right if I can get into the bath room in the morning to Bozo out the soot which pours down on a man from the adjacent chimneys. Doodles told Hash happily that no matter what the weather Ernest had never had to come down from the roof. The frigid on that is that he aint got no other place to go. A man handles rain by pulling the blankets over the head. Part of the stuff I wanta tell you but aint got the verve to write is that we aint occupewing the cile with them this coming fall.

Wright! Goddam I would mort Wright except that it wouldn't do me any good and if I'd strike him they'd say how much smaller etc. All of that will go b[y] the squard some day and I will drown Wright in a donicker.[9] The enditer would sooner take his promised bride to the back room of the second floor of a brothel in Seney Michigan than to a cile inhabited or even frequented by Donal McCloud Wright. The frigid on Wright anon. Wright has conducted an intensive campaign with Diles on the grounds that the enditer is "no gentleman" Wright's words, ever since last fall. During part of that time said Wright was yencing[10] his nymphomaniac paramour, Harvey in Dile's own cile! Since the enditer spoke honestly to Wright for a few brief phrases he has posed asa martyr in Diles eyes and will not come into the cile as long as I am here. That is his ultimato—he calls her up ma[n]y times a diurnal however and she always has to go outside the cile to meet him on account of him refusing to come inside. Yen's words to me are "You can never understand what Don means to Doodles." Yen is right. I can't. He, Yen, and I aint had no falling out, he was just explaining to me a bitter attack on me by Doodles because I didn't love Wright. Have you ever heard her in an attack? You oughta. You would then go to Baffin Bay and with a high powered rifle shoot all women down as fast as they appear. Jo Eezus. This wright rates the rope. Who the hell is this Wright anyway?

Hash is in swell shape and looks in excellent condition. We've been having a high grade time. Don't say you told me never to live with them. I know you did. I'm just commenting. When I went there, however, Diles was in N.Y. and we had a high grade time. Yen is like a broken old man at present. Not a laugh outa him. Of course he ain't got nawthing to laugh at, but he usta laugh anyway. Not any more. Diles has barred popular music and all his bar room songs from the home. She plays worse than ever. If any of the above appears incoherent lay it to rage. The enditer has took a lot. I never was cut out for a catcher.

No prior request has been made to you to appear in the role of Best Male at this wedding due to oversight and assumption that of course you would be the best male. Look up his duties. You may have to exceed them even, I am busy ascertaining the duties of a groom, perhaps I oughta be an under-groom first, perhaps you can get the frigid from some hostler. Am I expected to groom the bride? Isn't that taking a chance that she won't be well groomed? Who will groom the groom? Ashdown probably.

The Ghee is shooting par golf. I'd back him against that Jew swine after the Ghee has shot the course a couple of times. There's something about the way the Ghee performs when seeds are wageredcon him that has always appealed to the enditer. He picked up $7.50 Sunday morning under my observation against a trio of males that were all the superiors of Deak Foley.

Did I tell you that I8d been ruptured learning Horney Bill to box and had been wearing an elsatic bandage under the care of a zist and that it was now healed and no longer protuberant? A sad end for a man. I was teaching the little feller to body punch, was not wearing no G string and kept after him to rip them in lower. He caught me about a foot below the belt with a really good swing and it had the usual result. About a month and a quarter ago—it began to swell got a Zist onto it and he fixed it without an operation—have done n[a]wthing till plaid some tennis Sunday for quite a little while— I didn't know it amounted to anything at first—is all right now—but I can't take no chances with it. Fate is swinging a nasty knuckle on the enditer of late months. Stockbridge was going to send me to the International Co-operative Convention in Basle Switzerland the last of August to cover it for the new Commonwealth—off on account of the Nooptials.[11]

Gotta allez now to step Hash to a meal— Jo Eezus, if it were not for the presense of Hash a man would tumble by the squard. Well I usta be lucky you'll remember. I shudder to think what you'd do to my seeds now, a small wax match wouldn't be the slightest deterrent to you. Keep your optic open— in a year you'll probably be as lucky as I usta be—when it comes grab it.

Liquor is all that has carried the enditer through the last month. By Gawd Liquor is a fine thing. Let there never be any throwing off on it. By Liquor mean wine of course—guy in the 19th ward[12] gave me a lotta cognac recently—alleaing to the old country and don' wanta sell it—gone—but aided a man.

Am not really inas bad shape as this sounds, but you know how a man gets, havta carp along wit cheerful facial all diurnal and seek relief in a screed. Shoot me one.

Immer,
Miller

PUL, TLS

The conjectured letter date is based on EH's reference to "having a weddee on tap" that week; according to Diliberto, Hadley was visiting EH in Chicago 1–6 August 1921 (78–80). EH also alludes to the 2 August 1921 acquittal of eight Chicago White Sox ("pale hose") baseball players in connection with the World Series gambling scandal two years earlier.

1 The outcome of the White Sox trial became front-page news on 3 August. The scandal broke in September 1920 when Bill Maharg, a former boxer, told a Philadelphia newspaper that he and Bill Burns, a former major league baseball pitcher, had acted as go-betweens for the Chicago players and the gamblers who sought to fix the games, including former feather-weight boxing champion Abe Attell ("Jury Frees Baseball Men / All Black Sox Acquitted on Single Ballot," *Chicago Daily Tribune*, 3 August 1921, 1). Chicago is the county seat of Cook County, Illinois.

2 Lisle Shanahan (b. 1875), a Michigan native, was a prominent attorney and civic leader in Charlevoix; considered a "broad-minded citizen of sterling worth" who enjoyed a "legion of friends," he was particularly admired for having achieved success despite a physical handicap caused by childhood illness (Charles Moore, *History of Michigan*, volume 4, Chicago: Lewis Publishing Company, 1915, 2107–8). The Madame, Bill Smith's aunt, was a summer resident of the area.

3 Frank Parker Stockbridge (1870–1940), editor and publisher of the *Co-operative Commonwealth*.

4 *Montag*: Monday (German). Stut, Bill Smith's sister Kate.

5 In the 27 July 1921 world middleweight title fight, defending champion Johnny Wilson (né Giovanni Francisco Panica, 1893–1985) was knocked down three times in the seventh round by Bryan Downey (né William Bryan Downey, 1896–1970); nevertheless, referee Jimmy Gardner (b. 1885) declared Wilson the winner and disqualified Downey, claiming that he struck Wilson while he was down. Before the fight, Wilson had insisted that Gardner be the referee. The Cleveland and Ohio boxing commissions overruled the referee and declared Downey the winner by a knockout ("Wilson Scrap Ends in Riot; Title Dubious," *Chicago Daily Tribune*, 28 July 1921, 13). On 5 September the boxers would meet in a rematch that ended in a draw, with Downey recognized as the champion in Ohio and Wilson widely recognized elsewhere.

6 A referee should count to ten when one of the boxers in a match is knocked down before awarding his opponent a knockout. Philip J. "Little Phil" Collins (c. 1885–1963) later would

referee the 1926 world lightweight title bout in Chicago between Sammy Mandell and Rocky Kansas, the first legalized fight in Illinois since the state outlawed boxing in 1900.

7 Sturgeon River.

8 EH's concern about Y. K.'s weight is likely related to Y. K.'s having had tuberculosis. *Besser*: better (German). In epic tradition, the Greeks captured Troy by concealing soldiers inside a hollow wooden horse ostensibly left as a gift; a Trojan horse is therefore a means of attacking stealthily from within. EH was angry that Doodles was having an affair with one of Y. K.'s boarders, Don Wright. According to Diliberto, EH did not realize that Y. K. and Doodles had an "open marriage" and were free to take other lovers. They had met at a tuberculosis sanatorium in the Adirondacks, and "their union was based more on shared illness than on mutual love"; they never married legally (43).

9 Slang for toilet.

10 EH's slang for having sex he used various forms of the term in various grammatical constructions.

11 The International Co-operative League Congress, attended by delegates from twenty countries and representing 42,650 cooperative associations, was held in Basle, Switzerland, 22–26 August 1921. The main topic of discussion was the creation of an international wholesale purchase organization ("Open Big Congress of Co-operatives," *New York Times*, 23 August 1921, 3).

12 At the time, the Nineteenth Ward on Chicago's West Side was home to a large Italian immigrant population and a haven for organized-crime figures.

To Grace Quinlan, [7 August 1921]

Dearest G—

All sorts of things for not having screeded you before of course. But—oh a bas[1] the alibis.

Isnt this a lovely place? My boss sent me down East to drive his car through to Chicago and I'm on the last leg of the trip.[2] Get in tomorrow noon I hope to Gawd— Sh—— — not meant to be sacrilegious—Just prayerful. Gee G. I'll be glad to see you at this here wedding. Dearest old Kid. Bet you're having a smashing time at camp.

Know how you feel about my being too young to be married. Felt exactly the same way until Hash and I realized that life would be about as interesting as this splendid hotel [see picture at head of stationery][3] unless we could have each other to live with. So in circumstances like those you hafta make allowances.

I never wanted to be married before, in spite of having faced it on numerous occasions.

Is Pudge at camp? Whyn't she answer my letter?

I'm glad your the same very dear, very beautiful, very much older than your years, very unsatisfied (Thank Gawd) with Petoskey person that you are. Also you're the best of all sisters. Don't ever tell this, blood or otherwise; and I knew you wouldn't be a Scientist.[4]

I'm tired from driving all day, and error has krept into the more bum of my bum legs; so I oughta go and take a long soak in the tub and see if I cant drown error.

Wish you were here to talk to. I'm lonely as the deuce. If you really want it, you can have that snap I sent you with the 'nouncement and picture of Hash. Leave me know if you do. It's at home.

Enclosed is a picture of Hadley in her wedding dress. Very improper to circulate prior to wedding I blieve but your my sister—aren't you?

Good night old Dearest— I love you a very much.

Always yours Bro.

Stein

Yale, ALS; letterhead (with illustration of building): ALDERMAN HOTEL. GOSHEN, IND.; postmark: GOSHEN IND, AUG 7 / 1 PM / 1921

1 Down with (French).
2 Goshen, Indiana, is about 120 miles east of Chicago.
3 Square brackets are EH's.
4 "Scientist," Christian Scientist.

To Grace Hall Hemingway, [8 August 1921]

Dear Mother—

I've just written Dad and told him to tell you that I'd write you as soon as I had a minute—but I realized that I haven't an idea when I would one, so I'm writing you now in lunch time so it'll be done. You see I love people just as much whether I write them or not, but they don't all remember that.

Between now and when I go North in addition to the thousand personal details I must attend to I have to write 8 five thousand word articles for serialization that are later to be made up into a book on European Co-operation— 100,000 word book altogether.[1] Must do the others when I get back. Am working like a dawg.

Hadley was here for a week and is now North in Wisconsin.² Won't see her again till the first of September. Wedding's the 3rd. Are you really going to rent Longfield to Al Walker's sister? Cause if you are I don't know where you all will stay while waiting for the wedding as Dilworth's is full. Is there any chance on getting the piano at Windemere tuned. Hash'll wanta play and a sour piano's a pretty bad article. Of course you may have it tuned already.

The handkerchiefs were excellent. Thanks very much. Cept for them and Dad'd fine check I din't know I hadda boithday. Missed going fishing on it the most, I guess.

Stockbridge is making a fine magazine out of this. IT's a pleasure to work for him. I'm learning a lot, only I wish all this strain and all was over. I'm in rotten physical shape and been having to keep stimulated [*EH handwritten insertion*: That sounds bad. It only means Black coffee and an occasional drink.] to keep awake to work nights. It don't aid a man none.

Tell Ura that I love her just as much whether I write her or not. She's not sore at me for not writing I hope. 'sides she hasn't written me.

This lousy Pageant of Progress is on, it does provide good fire-works for our roof every night.³

Hash and I are not going to live at Kenley's this fall—they're having to give up the partment—so that gives me something new to work on. Looking around for some place to park ourselves for three months. Guess'll be able to find it all right, only it's just another thing to think about.

I have to get started on this here first article now—have to have it in type in three days—so I must shove off.

'bye—

Ernie

PSU, TLS; letterhead: The Co-operative Commonwealth / ROOM 205 / WELLS BUILDING / 128 N. WELLS STREET / CHICAGO; postmark: CHICAGO / ILL., AUG 8 / 3 PM / 1921

1 Whether EH wrote these articles is not known.
2 On 7 August Hadley arrived at the Charles A. Brent Camp near State Line, Wisconsin, for a month's vacation with Helen and George Breaker and their infant son (Diliberto, 80).
3 Set on Chicago's 3,000-foot Municipal Pier (renamed Navy Pier in 1927), the Pageant ran from 31 July to 14 August 1921, drawing an average of 55,000 people daily to view some 2,000 business and trade exhibits.

To Marcelline Hemingway, [11 August 1921]

Dear Diseased Ivory—

The maternal parent has informed me that you are Haywired in New Hampshire.[1] Gaw. The letter came today, revealing for the first time your address, and I hasten to croouch over this chattering Corona[2] and with terrific speed and thousands of errors advise you of my undying fire of love for you, which at the moment of writing, courses through my veins like nigger gin.[3]

So you're haywired Eh ¢. That is supposed to be a question mark, which I will now insert ? You see this is a Corona, the gift of she who, I keep telling her, in a temporary lapse of all good sense, is to assume the difficult role of Mrs. Hemingstein. The Corona, however, is as yet too small for my hands which daily caress the bigger mills of commerce. Therefore pardon the multitude of mistakes which mar its marvelous melody.

The enditer is to become man and wife on September the 3rd at Hortense Bay, Michigan, as yet I do not realize all the full horror of marriage, which was plainly visible on the Blights face, you recall his face?, and so if you wish to see me break down at the altar and perhaps have to be carried to the altar in a chair by the crying ushers, it were well that you made your plans to be on tap for that date. It is a Saturday.

Come Ivory, for Gawd's sake, come. Be there. A choice array of young males will be present. Horney, the Ghee, The Carper, Art Meyer, others, Hoopkins I hope, Odgar I crave, Come at once and by all means. Be there. Answer at once in the affirmative that you will be there. I can count on you can't I? I will do everything in my power to make it as pleasant a wedding for you as possible.

Really it ought to be a high grade affair. Hash is in excellent shape. She is training in Northern Wisconsin and press reports say that she has never been better. I am working out daily at the Ferretti Gymnasium with a capable corps of sparring partners and Nate Lewis declares that he'll put me in there in the best shape of my career.[4]

Naw Ivory, seriously you know, come to this wedding. Please, Please, Please! You gotta come. I may call it off if you don[']t.

September 3rd is the date at 4 o'clock in the afternoon.

My love to youse and get well. Tanks for the birthday wire. Dear love to you—and be on tap.

Immer,

Oin

JFK, TLS; postmark: CHICAGO / ILL., AUG 11 / 11 PM / 1921

1 On 7 August 1921, Grace wrote to EH that Marcelline had to quit her job as a camp counselor and go to the Concord, New Hampshire, home of her longtime friend Marion Vose, for bed rest: "Nerves all gone to smash" (JFK; Reynolds *YH*, 245–46). Although in her 16 August response to EH's letter, Marcelline expressed her eagerness to come to Michigan for his wedding (Sanford, 315–17), she was unable to attend.
2 The most popular portable typewriter of the time, manufactured by the Corona Typewriter Company.
3 Slang for poor quality bootleg liquor distilled during Prohibition in the United States.
4 Ferretti, a boxing gym in Chicago where professional fighters trained. Lewis, a welterweight who lost by decision to Peter Cholke in Detroit a month earlier.

To Grace Quinlan, [19 August 1921]

Dearest G—

Sorry camp is sort of tunking out on you. Maybe it's better now though. Usually things aren't so much fun the second time are they? We oughta do 'em once and then go on to something new—only guess the new things would probably wear all out on us.

Sure I know somebody named Shorney. Two boys Gordon and Herbert. Herbert's older than I am, but Gordon and I were class mates at school. He's a very fine article. I just know the sister to speak to—

No, really, did they have me married in France? Gaw. Tell me all about it. Did I desert her, or what? D'ya think I'll be a bigamist? Tell me all about it. I'm frightfully interested.[1]

Why I'm going to leave here the 27th of August and get up North the next morning and probably tear right out to the Sturgeon for the last three days of the fishing season. They close it up on a man the 1st of Sept. and I haven't had any for so long that I'm starved and crazy for it. Then I'll be back and standing by till the 3rd when heavy marriage occurs. Oughta be a fairly high grade occasion, be a pretty good gang there. Not many people, but a lot of people we like.[2] I'll be trying to get into Petorskey to see you before der Tag.

Am enclosing the picture.[3] Look civilizeder than you ever knew me,
Huh? Been terrifically civilized for about twelve months now, and it's darned
near ruined a man.

Have to go down to interview the president of the U.S. Grain Growers Inc.
in a little while, and I'm writing this during lunch hour.[4] Guy I usually
eat lunch with is sick. So talking to you instead. You don't mind particularly
do you? Hash is somewhere up on the Upper Peninsula having all the fun
that's being had in the familly. I won't see her again till we're at the Bay.
Sunny is in Minnesota, Marce in Maine, the Hemingstein's are at Walloon.
All the guys I know here are left town, not a soul here, lonely as Boyne Falls.
Have to stick out two more weeks of it only though. That's a good thing.

Had a terribly funny dream about you last night. Can't remember it at all
now, one of those kind that sort of slither away from you, but it was a
very good dream and I wish I could remember it. Foist time I've had you
bumming around in my head in a dream in months. Funny that it should
come last night and then a letter from you first thing this morning. Maybe
the hand of the Maker stalking into the room.

Oh Yes. How about ministers, preachers, priests or prelates.?? In
your wide and diverse acquaintance can you recommend a capable minister
to perform this ceremony? Hash says she doesn't care particulalry what
breed of priest it is, but prefers one that doesn't wear a celluloid collar[5] or
chaw tobacco. We thought we could lay hold of Bishop Tuttle from St. Louis
that summers at Harbor Point, but he may be gone by then.[6] Remember
when selecting this Priest that he's gotta be able to read and be dignified.
Dignity's what we're going to pay this here prelate for, we don't want no
evangelist that's liable to shout out, 'Praise be the Lord' and start rolling on
the floor during a critical part of the ceremony. Presbyterian preferred, or
else Episcopal, doesn't make the slightest difference to me. What's the local
prelate situation. Give me a brief resume. Huh? Pick me a prelate.

Well I gotta eat something and start after this Grain Grower. We go to
press in three days. I've been working like a dawg on account of having to
get stuff up for all the time I'M going to be gone.[7] Gradually getting ahead
of the line though. Sure am sick of it all though. I'm writing a 100,000 word
book for them, being published serially in 5,000 word chunks. Deadly stuff.

You won' know me, a wreck, I tell you, a wreck. Slap a lotta thought, or not a lot if it don't take much, don't slap no more thought than you have to, on this here Man of God.

Write me G— I'm lonely as the deuce—

Great amount of love—

Stein

Yale, TLS; letterhead: The Co-operative Commonwealth / ROOM 205 / Wells Building / 128 N. Wells Street / Chicago; postmark: CHICAGO / ILL., AUG 19 / 12 M / 1921

1 EH is responding to Quinlan's letter of 10 August, written from Camp Arbutus, in which she says that camp is not half as interesting as it was the year before, asks if he knows anyone by the name of Shorney, and tells him that some time ago he was rumored to have been married to a nurse he met in France in a "warlike romance" (JFK). Gordon Shorney was in EH's 1917 graduating class at OPRFHS; his brother Herbert was a member of the class of 1914, and their sister Marian was in the class of 1921.

2 Baker reports that at one point the wedding invitation list had reached 450 (*Life*, 80). According to Ohle, EH and Hadley chose Horton Bay as the site to avoid the pomp that would have surrounded a ceremony in either St. Louis or Oak Park. Although Grace Hemingway invited the local families to help fill up the church, most were "too shy to appear" and no more than thirty people attended the ceremony (Ohle, 106, 108).

3 The photograph does not survive with the letter.

4 U.S. Grain Growers was a farmer-owned, nonprofit association that handled and sold grain for its members; it was incorporated in Chicago on 16 April 1921. No copy of the interview has been located.

5 Mass-produced, detachable, hard plastic collars for men's shirts, popular in the late nineteenth and early twentieth centuries.

6 Daniel Sylvester Tuttle (1837–1923) was presiding bishop of the Episcopal Church for the state of Missouri from 1886 until his death. Harbor Point is on the north shore of Little Traverse Bay, opposite Petoskey.

7 EH was given three weeks off from the *Co-operative Commonwealth* to get married, two with pay (Reynolds *YH*, 251).

To William B. Smith, Jr., [c. mid–late August 1921]

Boid—

My paternal running true to form. The g.d. kkkkk---------- Jo Eezus what a paternal to have spring from the loins of. He could only handle himself and another male could he? I hope to hell his goddamned ford burned up. Hes the yellowest guy I know—[1]

No time for a screed except to slip you the frigid. Am due in O. P. in an hour to get my trunk.

I have worked on St[u]t constantly to get her to allez but she has been bucked at the bank, they didn't want to let her off and I couldn get the dope on her leaveage to shoot you. She now sweara that she is leaving on Friday night and letting you know to that effect.

Yen no longer speaks to the enditer! Denmark, at the time of Hamlets foulest prime, was a pure paradise alongside of that cile. The Wright stuff is terrible. Yen is completely emasculated, Wright and Diles wielding the scalpel.[2] His latest stunt was to work heavily on Stut to not go to the weddage at all. He is dominated by Wright in every way, I aint got no time to go into it all— Stut will give you some of the dope and I'll give you the rest. It's worsen the worst imagination could picture.

The enditer has a ticket and berth on the G.R. and I. leaving here Saturday nacht, the 27th, arriving at Boyne Falls Sunday morning at 5.50 I believe. Will you handle meetage of me? Dont feel obligated to flash or nawthing, just see that meetage of some sort occurs.

Invite Bob and Wedna[3] by all means and forward their proper names and addresses to Hash at this address

Hadley Richardson

Care C.A. Bent

Donaldson

Vilas County

Wisconsin

and she will send them the genuwind dodgers. If you know of anyone else I oughta ask, ask 'em for me in my name as Jesus would say.

There is a episcopal prelate in Petoskey that oughta be able to handle spliceage. What the hell is the ring service?[4] Don't attempt an answer, tell me when I come.

I've been working so damned hard getting stuff ahead for four weeks that I'm sory that I've tunked out on stuff like thinking about asking Morrow— ask he and Wedna by all means. The bank has really had Stut in a bad way, she's tossing them over now however,

The ile situation is horrible— Did I tell you that I had laid hold a swell cile for Hash and I, no lease required, at 1239 N.Dearborn, snappy location, furnished complete, four rooms, living room, sun room, bed room, kitchen, lotsa windows, old joint made into aprtment for 75 seeds a month? A man wouldn't believe it. I have paid the guy an deposit on it already. Four people have tried to get it offen the enditer all ready. Elmore Brown, a magazine illustrator I know[5] turned it over to me, get posession Oct. 6—they're going to clean and decorate for us, no obligation to stay more than a month ahead. It's a pretty high grade shop. Wop consul has inhabited the ist Apt. this is the third. That's the old fortuna coming back huh?

I have to get back to work the 26th— Hash can stay at Dilstein's till the 5th and then allez down and move right into this place— I'll put up with Krebs while I'm here. 'll be kinda a good thing anyway as I'll have Gawd's own quantity of work to do that week.

The enditer will wanta flash out onto the streams as soon as possible after arrival. I have a rod etc haven't I? If the men are on the Sturg we can make it via the R.R.'d as the Ghee and I did. With Stut there you'll be able to flash wit me won't you? Means a hell of a lot to a man. Sort of an ultimate of the old Golden Age.

I gotta letter from the Hoop head. Negation.

I'm terribly sorry the Madame has fell slightly through hereself. Will you tell her so for me. It's a shame.

Odgar has tunked on us. I keep telling Butstein she has lost him. She intimates that she's been trying to.[6]

I won't want heavy roomage accomodations till the initial of Sept due to a hope that the stream 'll be played till then. probably wes or Mrs. west can handle me if Stilldeins are full.[7]

Your feat of snaring the lost linear was collossal.[8] damned nice work. I'm so mad at my paternal for that two men stuff that I can hardly write.

Glad the Guy made the 75.[9] How'd you get him to holdthem?

The Whissle wing, I take it, is a better boat als the one we had last summer.

Gotta mail this to you now as I'm due at the vale of P.O.'s Tell Dillstein's to hold my mail.

Ipiscopal for the priest. They're nice clean workers and dress the part.

It all seems damned strange to me. Like when they hanged Sam Cardinella—
he didn't realize it till the last moment. Then they carried him to the gallows and
hanged him in a chair. Was an impressive sight.

If there's anything you want in tackle wire me. Wire in regard to anything
else—

Immer—

Wemedge—

I got some nice clean clothes—
Excuse cursage of the paternal!

Meeker, TLS with autograph postscript

1 EH is angry with his father because of an incident that Smith relayed in a recent letter: "Your
paternal was to call for the males today with Al Walker and go out [fishing on the Black
River]. He come but said his Fraud [Ford] could only handle himself and Al. This placed it
before the Ghee and Carp who lined the greasy pockets of Charlie Friend and are being
hauled out by him. I will fetch them back. You see they expected to ride along with the
paternal" (c. August 1921, JFK).

2 EH alludes to the line in Shakespeare's *Hamlet*, "Something is rotten in the state of
Denmark" (1.4.90), in reference to the affair between Doodles "Diles" Smith and Don
Wright, a fellow boarder at the "Domocile," as the Smiths' residence was known.

3 In his letter to EH, Smith wrote of gambling at Cooks with Bob and Wedna and then going to
Wedna's place for alcoholic drinks. Smith asked EH if they could be invited to the wedding.

4 Smith had asked in his letter what type of "gospel dispenser" EH wished to preside at the
wedding, adding that "a good dispenser who knows the ring ceremony is rare." Traditions
involving wedding jewelry, including the bride and groom's exchange of wedding bands,
were developed in the 1920s by a growing wedding industry.

5 OPRFHS classmate Elmor J. Brown (1899–1968) had illustrated EH's story, "A Matter of
Colour," in the April 1916 *Tabula*, and went on to become an illustrator for national
magazines, particularly *Collier's*, where his work would appear regularly from 1933 to 1949.

6 Kate Smith had long been the object of Carl Edgar's unrequited love (Baker *Life*, 30; *SL*, 4;
Reynolds *YH*, 75). They appear as "Odgar" and "Stut" in EH's "Summer People" (*NAS*), a
story unpublished until 1972.

7 Wes, Wesley Dilworth, then living in Boyne City with his wife, Katherine (née Kennedy, a
schoolteacher whom he had married in 1915) and their two small children. Mrs. West is
likely Anna West, a widow who lived on a farm on Horton Bay Road with her three
daughters, son-in-law, and granddaughter (1920 U.S. Federal Census). "Stilldeins" is another
play on "Dilstein's," itself a play on "Dilworth's" (referring to James and Elizabeth Dilworths'
Pinehurst guest house in Horton Bay).

8 Smith reported that when he was fishing with Jack Pentecost and Howell Jenkins, a fish
hooked an unattended line, pulling their best rod off the dock and "into the depths." Smith
managed to snare the line and retrieve the rod after dragging the bottom of the bay with
hooks and sinkers.

9 Smith reported that in their recent gambling, "the Ghee" (Pentecost) had cashed in his chips when he was ahead $75, down from a high of $80.

To Y. K. Smith, [1 October 1921]

The Office

Saturday noon.

Dear Y.K.—

I understand from Mother, over the phone, that she mailed you an invitation to a reception at Oak Park tonight.[1]

There is no chance, of course, that you and Doodles would go, but on the chance that you might mis-interpret the bid, I'm taking a couple of minutes to rescind it personally.

Not that I wouldn't be glad to see you, as Doodles says in her often-read-aloud masterpiece, you are "A good-looking young man" but I feel, to quote your wife's universally admired output that "So mote it be"

I'll be over to collect the residue of my clothes and my probably well-thumbed correspondence while you and the good wife are out at the triangular little home in Palos Park.[2]

So mote it be

So mote it be

Go hang yourself on a Christmas tree.

Always,

JFK, TL

1 On 1 October, Clarence and Grace held a reception to celebrate their twenty-fifth wedding anniversary.

2 Y. K. replied to EH shortly thereafter that he could collect his things from the Aldis store room, adding "You can readily understand that your having written me as you have makes your presence in my house quite impossible, at any time, under any circumstances" ([2 October 1921], JFK). With this exchange, EH's friendship with Y. K. was effectively terminated. His friendship with Bill Smith also suffered a severe setback for several years; the men would resume contact in 1924.

To John Bone, 29 October 1921

Chicago, Illinois
October 29 1921

Mr. John R. Bone
Managing Editor
The Toronto Star

Dear Mr. Bone:
    Greg Clark has written me that he spoke to you about my hope of returning to Toronto and

Dear Mr. Bone—
    Greg Clark has written me that he spoke to you about my being desirous of returning to Toronto and obtaining a staff position on the Star.
    You very kindly suggested such a position last February, but at that time I was getting some ~~very~~ valuable experience and a very satisfactory salary here and in answering your letter named a salary figure which was more, I believe, than you wished to pay.

JFK, TLD

EH began each draft on a new side of a single sheet of paper. He had quit the *Co-operative Commonwealth*, as its sponsoring organization was going into bankruptcy amid charges of fraud. While the letter Bone actually received remains unlocated, "that note or some other communication to Toronto struck fire. By the Monday after Thanksgiving it was arranged that Hemingway should go to Paris as a roving correspondent for both *Star* papers, to be paid at regular space rates and expenses on most stories but at $75 a week and expenses when covering specific assignments" (Scott Donaldson, "Hemingway of *The Star*," *College Literature* 7, no. 3 [Fall 1980], 264–65).

To Hemingway Family, [8 December 1921]

Dear Dad and Mother & children—:
    Were writing this from the Hotel just before we leave.[1] Everything is very lovely. Fine trip and enjoyed the dates and apples Mother's check and Nunbone's and Massweene's letters tremendously.
    Had dinner with Bobby Rouse and met several other friends here both mine and Hashe's and I've checked all our baggage and seen the boat.

Walter Johnson is going to see us off at the boat.[2] I'll mail this from the pilot—

Everything is very lovely and we're getting off in excellent style. Wish you all a Merry Christmas.

Keep away from the stockyards is my advice until the strike is settled.[3] Keep all the kids away too. They must find a new playground.

Robby Rouse sends you his love as do

Ernie

and

Hash

Very dear love to all of <u>yez</u>.

JFK, ALS

In the upper right corner of the first page is this notation in Clarence's hand: "New York N.Y. Dec 8, 1921."

1 After long dreaming of returning to Italy, EH was persuaded by Sherwood Anderson that Paris was the place for an aspiring young writer. The newlyweds set sail from New York on 8 December aboard the French Line's *S.S. Leopoldina*, arriving in Le Havre, France, on 22 December.

2 EH's cousin, Walter Edmonds Johnson, of Montclair, New Jersey (Sanford, 149).

3 A strike by meat packers was underway at the Chicago Stockyards, where some 2,000 police officers had been advised to shoot the strikers if necessary; one striker was shot dead and several others were wounded (Reynolds *YH*, 259).

To Hemingway Family, 20 December 1921

[*A Bord*] SS. Leopoldina

[*le*] 20 December [*192*]1

Dear Famille—

We've had a fine trip. Stopped at Vigo in Spain and went ashore in a motor launch.[1] Only very rough one day. Then a regular hurricane. Good weather balance of time.

It was so warm in Spain I was too hot with only one sweater on. In the harbor were great schools of tuna—some jumped 6 and 8 feet out of water chasing sardines.

Hash is very popular aboard the ship because of playage of the piano. We had a show one night— Took out three tables in the dining room and made a ring and I boxed 3 rounds with Henry Cuddy a middleweight from Salt Lake City who is going over to fight in Paris.[2] We trained together on board and in the 3rd round I had him on the verge of a knockout. Got the decision. Cuddy wants me to fight in Paris. Hash was in my corner and wiped me off with a towell between rounds.

Coming up the coast of Spain off Cape Finisterre we saw a whale. Vigo harbor is almost landlocked and was a great hiding place for German Submarines during the war. I talked my Lingua Franca— [International Mediterranean Language][3] in Vigo and interpreted for all the passengers. ~~Bones~~ Hash can talk French so we get along beautifully.

Thank you all for your letters. We were greatly appreciative of all of them and are using dad's rubber bands—

Hash is playing the piano now while I'm writing but her fingers are very cold from the English Channel wind. We've been sailing across the Bay of Biscay and up the coast of France all day. Passing many ships that rolled badly but this boat is as steady as a rock.

There are a funny lot of people aboard but ~~many~~ a few very nice ones.

We land in Havre tomorrow about noon and will be in Paris tomorrow night. Will mail this from Havre—

Hash and I both send love to everyone and all of Grandfather's family.

Love to you all—

Ernie and Hash—

Hash is talking French to 3 Argentinians that are in love with her. Also an old Frenchman————

JFK, ALS; letterhead: Cie Gle / TRANSATLANTIQUE; postmark: LE HAVRE / SEINE-INFRE, 21^{30} / 25 XII / 1921

On envelope verso Clarence wrote, "Read and Return Promptly to Daddy Enclosed."

1 EH and Hadley had four hours to explore the town before the ship continued on to Le Havre (Baker *Life*, 83).
2 There is an apparent conflict in EH's story: he may have been fabulating, or his shipboard opponent may have misrepresented himself. Featherweight boxer Henry "Kid" Cuddy fought in Salt Lake City, Utah, on 19 December 1921; his defeat by decision was reported in the *Salt Lake Telegram* on 20 December 1921, the day EH wrote this letter.
3 The square brackets are EH's.

To William B. Smith, Jr., [c. 20 December 1921]

Boid—

Vigo, Spain. That's the place for a male. A harbor almost landlocked about as big as little Traverse bay with big, brown, mountains. A male can buy a lateen sailed boat for 5 seeds. Costs a seed a day at the Grand Hotel and the bay swarms with Tuna

They behave exactly like lainsteins—sardines for shiners—chase them the same way and I saw 3 in the air at once—1 easily 8 feet. The biggest one they've taken this year weighed 850 lbs!

Vigo's about 4 times the size of the Voix and there are three or four little places around the bay to sail to. Gaw what a place.

We're going back there. Trout streams in the Mts. Tuna in the bay. Green water to swim in and sandy beaches. Vino is 2 pesetas[1] a qt. for the 3 year old which can be distinguished by a blue label. Cognac is 4 pesetas a litre.

C'est la vie—

Immer—

Wemedge—

[*On verso:*]

Why not screed care the American Express Paris—France?[2]

Hash wielded a towel in my corner for a 3 round session with Young Cuddy—Salt Lake City 158 lbser—just grown out of the welter ranks—a wop who's going to Paris to fight— Has 3 fights there and 1 in Milan—

We trained daily throught the voyage.

They took up 3 tables in the dining room and made a ring between the posts and we went the 3 stanzas for the benefit of a French woman in the steerage who has a baby and 10 Francs to till France with. A.E.F. husband deserted her.[3]

They passengers claimed it was a good thing to watch.

You'll have to get Hash to tell you about the bout. If I wrote it you'd think it was fiction.

Wemedge.

PUL, ALS; letterhead: Cie Gle / TRANSATLANTIQUE / A Bord; postmark: LE HAVRE / SEINE-INFRE, 21$\frac{30}{}$ / 25 XII / 1921

1 Peseta, the official Spanish currency; in 1921 one dollar was worth approximately 7.3 pesetas.
2 American Express, which began in New York in 1850 as a private express delivery company, introduced money orders and travelers cheques in the 1880s and 1890s, and in 1895 established a Paris office, its first in Europe. During WWI its European operations expanded to include banking, mail, and travel services.
3 American Expeditionary Forces, the combined U.S. military forces in Europe during WWI, commanded by General John J. Pershing (1860–1948).

To Sherwood and Tennessee Anderson, [c. 23 December 1921]

Dear Sherwood and Tennessee—

Well here we are. And we sit outside the Dome Cafe, oposite the Rotunde that's being redecorated, warmed up against one of those charcoal brazziers and it's so damned cold outside and the brazier makes it so warm and we drink rum punch, hot, and the rhum enters into us like the Holy Spirit.[1]

And when it's a cold night in the streets of Paris and we're walking home down the Rue Bonaparte we think of the way the wolves used to slink into the city and Francois Villon and the gallows at Montfaucon. What a town.[2]

Bones is out in it now and I've been earning our daily bread on this write machine.[3] In a couple of days we'll be settled and then I'll send out the letters of introduction like launching a flock of ships.[4] So far we haven't sent 'em out because we've been walking the streets, day and night, arm through arm, peering into courts and stopping in front of little shop windows. The pastry'll kill Bones eventually I'm afraid. She's a hound for it. Must have always been a suppressed desire with her I guess.

We had a note from Louis Galantiere this morning and will call on him tomorrow. Sherwood's note was here at Hotel when we got in.[5] It was awfully damned nice of you to send it. We were feeling a little low and it bucked us up terrifically.

The Jacob is clean and cheap. The Restaurant of the Pre aux Clercs at the corner of the Rue Bonaparte and the Rue Jacob is our regular eating place. Two can get a high grade dinner there, with wine, a la carte for 12 francs. We breakfast around. Usually average about 2.50 F. for breakfast. Think things are even cheaper than when you all were here.[6]

We came via Spain and missed all but a day of the big storm. You ought to
see the spanish coast. Big brown mountains looking like tired dinosaurs
slumped down into the sea. gulls following behind the ship holding against
the air so steadily they look like property birds raised and lowered by wires.
Light house looking like a little candle stuck up on the dinosaurs shoulder.
The coast of Spain is long and brown and looks very old.

Then coming up on the train through Normandy with villages with
smoking manure piles and long fields and woods with the leaves on the
ground and the trees trimmed bare of branches way up their trunks and a
roll of country and towers up over the edge. Dark stations and tunnels and
3rd class compartments full of boy soldiers and finally everyone asleep in
your own compartment leaning against each other and joggling with the
sway of the train. There's a deathly, tired silence you can't get anywhere else
except a railway compartment at the end of a long ride.

Anyway we're terrible glad we're here and we hope you have a good
Christmas and New Year and we wish we were all going out to dinner
tonight together.

[*Hadley begins:*]

Every word that he says is true, especially the wishes for the jolliest kind of
a Xmas season. It feels like anything but a strange place here at the Jacob,
what with your note of welcome and the feeling that you two have lived here
so lately. We like it very much and also we think this the best neighborhood
we've seen. We're going out now, across this river to purvey for each others
Xmas stockings. I will try to keep from buying pastries for Ern. Here we go
pausing for an affectionate moment in passing to sign ourselves

Ernest and Bones

Newberry, TL/ALS

In this joint letter from EH and Hadley, the beginning portion was typewritten by EH, and
Hadley continued in longhand. Each of them signed the letter at the end.

1 The Café du Dôme and Café de la Rotonde, on the Boulevard Montparnasse, attracted
expatriates, artists, and political activists in the 1920s; both cafés would figure by name in
SAR. In his piece for the *Toronto Star Weekly*, "American Bohemians in Paris a Weird Lot,"
EH would condemn the clientele of the Rotonde as pretentious loafers, "the scum of
Greenwich Village, New York" (25 March 1922; *DLT*, 114–16).

2 In Robert Louis Stevenson's short story, "A Lodging for the Night" (1877), the medieval French poet Villon muses that it was the kind of weather "when wolves might take it into their heads to enter Paris again," and he is haunted by the aspect of the gallows at Montfaucon, the "great grisly Paris gibbet."

3 "Bones," nickname for Hadley. Although EH was working for the *Toronto Star* as a freelancer and foreign correspondent, the couple was supported in large part by Hadley's trust fund, which provided nearly $3,000 a year, more than enough to live on comfortably in Paris (Reynolds *PY*, 5; Gerry Brenner, *A Comprehensive Companion to Hemingway's "A Moveable Feast": Annotation to Interpretation* [Lewiston, New York: Edwin Mellen Press, 2000], 40).

4 Sherwood Anderson had provided EH with letters of introduction to his friend Lewis Galantière and other literati whom he had met earlier that year on his first visit to Paris: Sylvia Beach, Ezra Pound, and Gertrude Stein. In his letter of 28 November 1921 to Galantière, then employed by the International Chamber of Commerce in Paris, Anderson described EH as "a young fellow of extraordinary talent" (Baker, 82–83; Fenton, 118; Howard Mumford Jones and Walter B. Rideout, eds., *Letters of Sherwood Anderson* [Boston: Little, Brown and Company, 1953], 82–83).

5 Galantière had booked the Hemingways at the Hôtel Jacob et d'Angleterre, 44 rue Jacob, on the Left Bank, near the Place St. Germain des Prés and a few blocks from the Seine.

6 EH would describe how well tourists and expatriates could live in Paris, given the favorable exchange rate, in his 4 February 1922 piece for the *Toronto Star Weekly*, "Living on $1,000 a Year in Paris"(*DLT*, 88–89).

To Howell G. Jenkins, 26 December [1921]

Screed care of

American Express Company

Paris, France.[1]

[*PARIS, LE*] 26 Dec.

Dear Carpative—

Merry Christmas and Mille Grazie[2] for the muffler. Bones and I are located in this hostilery on the left Bank of the river just back of the Beaux Arts[3] and are in good shape.

Our room likes like a fine Grog shop—Rhum, Asti Spumante and Cinzano Vermouth fill one shelf. I brew a rum punch that'd gaol you.

Living is very cheap. Hotel room is 12 francs and there are 12.61 to the paper one. A meal for two hits a male about 12–14 francs—about 50 cents apiece. Wine is 60 centimes. Good Pinard.[4] I get Rum for 14 francs a bottle. Vive La France.

There's nawthing much to write. Paris is cold and damp but crowded, jolly and beautiful. Charcoal braziers in front of all the cafés and everybody in good shape.

Bones and I are going to buy a motor cycle with side car and go all to hell and gone over Yarrup next summer.

Screed a male. My love to the Ghee and Dirty Dick—

Sempre[5]

Steen—

Stanford, ALS; letterhead: HOTEL JACOB & D'ANGLETERRE / 44, RUE JACOB—PARIS

1 EH wrote this return address above the hotel's address on the letterhead.
2 *Mille grazie*: a thousand thanks (Italian).
3 The Ecole des Beaux-Arts, the premier official school of fine arts in France, traces its origins to the founding in 1648 of the Royal Academy of Painting and Sculpture; since the early nineteenth century it has been housed in a complex of buildings on the rue Bonaparte, across the Seine from the Louvre and close to the Hemingways' hotel.
4 "Pinard," French slang for any red wine of poor quality, specifically of the kind issued to French soldiers during WWI.
5 Always (Italian).

To Howell G. Jenkins, 8 January [1922]

[*PARIS, LE*] 8 January.

Dear Carpative—

Hash and I are moving to an apartment at 74 Rue du Cardinal Lemoine.[1] So you can address us care of the Cardinal. Suppose you have my last screed by now. We've been having a priceless time and I've been working like hell. Written a chunk of my novel and several articles.

Went around to the Florida the other day and often eat [at] a place near the Madeleine. I showed Hash the head that was knocked off while we were there. They've left it off.[2]

I'm drinking Rum St. James[3] now with rare success. It is the genuwind 6 year old rum as smooth as a kittens chin.

This apt. is a high grade place and were moving in tomorrow—but not going to keep house till we get back from Chamby Sur Montreaux in

Switzerland where we're allezing for a brace of the weeks to shoot some winter sports. It's in the mountains above Geneva and is a place sort of like Dilstein's—but with a better clientele. It would be a paradise with the men along. Gaw— Can you see us all with unlimited good liquor and skiing, bob sledding and skating? I wish you and the Ghee and the Boid and Dirty were coming.[4]

Must close. Screed a man. The muffler rates daily wear. I laid hold of a suit—made to measure with slacks and knickers—Irish hand made homespun—for 700 francs. As I bought Francs at 14 to a paper one that isnt bad. Cook and Co. are a famous London house.[5] You know 'em of course. This was the best stuff they had in the Cile.

Well screed me Carpative. I miss you like hell and am lonely for the men. This side is the place for a man to live.

Love.

Steen.

Hash sends you hers also.

Screed to the 77 Rue du Cardinal Lemoine address.

It is just back of the Pantheon and the Ecole Polytechnique— In the best part of the Latin quarter.[6]

Greet Dick for me and tell him I'll write him. Regards to the office.

Stanford, ALS; letterhead: HOTEL JACOB & D'ANGLETERRE, 44, RUE JACOB -:- PARIS; postmark: PARIS 115 / R DES SAINTS-PERES, 13 15 / 9–1 / 22

1 Galantière helped the Hemingways find a fourth-floor walk-up apartment at 74, rue du Cardinal Lemoine, in a working-class neighborhood near the Place de la Contrescarpe in the fifth arrondissement.

2 En route to the war in Italy in June 1918, EH and his fellow American Red Cross volunteers were quartered at the Hotel Florida at 12, Boulevard Malesherbes, in the eighth arrondissement. The nearby Madeleine (L'église Sainte-Marie-Madeleine, or Church of St. Mary Magdalene), commissioned in 1806 by Napoleon I as a "Temple of Glory" to honor his armies, was built in the style of a Roman temple on the site of an eighteenth-century church; the structure was consecrated as a church in 1842. EH presumably is referring to a statue damaged when German artillery hit the façade of the Madeleine during the bombardment of Paris that he described in his letter home of [c. 3 June 1918] (see also Baker *Life*, 40, for Ted Brumback's account of the shelling).

3 A brand of rum produced since 1765 on the French Caribbean island of Martinique.

4 Jack Pentecost, Bill Smith, and Dick Smale ("Dirty Dick").

5 Probably Alfred H. Cooke, London tailor and outfitter. Among the Hemingway papers at the University of Tulsa's McFarlin Library is a receipt from the Cooke establishment in Gibraltar dated 8 January 1919 for puttees, shirts, and collars, apparently purchased by EH on his return from Italy after the war. According to the 1924 Baedeker guide to Paris, many London tailoring firms had branches in Paris (*Paris and Its Environs*, 19th edn. [Liepzig: Karl Baedeker, Publisher, 1924], 51).

6 EH mistakenly wrote the street number as "77." The Panthéon, originally a church dedicated to St. Geneviève, the patron saint of Paris, was converted in 1791 into a memorial temple for the burial of illustrious French citizens. It stands on the Montagne Sainte-Geneviève, the highest ground of the Left Bank and one of the three hills of Paris (along with Montmartre and Montparnasse) that would give American journalist and publisher William Bird (1888–1963) the name for his Three Mountains Press. The École Polytechnique, a college of engineering founded in 1794, was then on the rue Descartes.

To Hemingway Family, [c. late January 1922]

Dear Family—

Bones and I are living up here at about 3,000 feet above sea level and having the most gorgeous time. Paris got sort of damp and rotten weather so we came down here in the Alps to get rid of our colds and get healthy. It is Les Avants, above Montreaux on Lake Geneva and wonderful mountain sports. We get an all day ticket on the little railroad and then coast down the mountain on a bob and take the train back up. With an all day ticket you can take as many rides on the train as you want. The Bob is only big enough for two and has a steering wheel and brakes and goes all the way down the mountain through the wildest country you ever saw. Black forests of Pine trees and gorges and the big mountain Dent du Jaman.[1] Snow is forty inches deep but you are never cold. Wear only sweaters and the air is bracing. The bob gets a speed of sixty miles an hour on some of the streches and there isn't a single stop till you hit the railway s[t]ation at the bottom. You ought to see us come down with Hash steering. She thinks it is a sign of cowardice to ever put on the brake! I use it every once in a while on account of the fine way it makes the slivers of ice fly up. On the curves you have to lean straight out to keep from going over and you skirt sheer drop offs for miles. It is the greatest sport I've ever had

I'm doing a lot of work too an this morning wrote two articles for the Star[2] and sent them off while Hash was coasting with Dorothy Beck a nice

American girl that is down here. We are staying at a place that is about like Dilworth's prices and all and have enormous meals twice a day. Drink lots of milk all the time and both Hash and I are getting into splendid shape. You leave Paris at 9 o'clock at night and are at Montreaux at ten the next morning. Montreaux, you remember, is right near the Chateaux Chillon.[3] Both of you have probably been there Dad and Mother. All of you would be mad about the coasting. There is skiing too and mountain climbing and skating but the coasting is the most fun. We make a twelve mile run in about 14 minutes! Beck is the only American here—she came down with us—all the rest are English Lawds. Very nice and fun to hoot at as you race with the bobs.[4]

Hash just came in and read this over my shoulder an says to send lots of love to you and tell you about our apartment. It is at 74 Rue duCardinal Lemoine. And is the jolliest place you ever saw. We rented it furnished for 250 francs a month, about 18 dollars and have a femme du menage who cooks dinner for us every night.[5] I think I wrote you about it, so I won't go on, You can send mail there and it will reach us. It is the most comfortable and cheapest way to live and Bones has a piano and we have all our pictures up on the walls and an open fire place and a peach of a kitchen and a dining room and big bed room and dressing room and plenty of space. It is on top of a high hill in the very oldest part of Paris. The nicest part of the Latin quarter. Just back of the Pantheon and the Ecole Polytechique. It has a tennis court right across the street and a bus line ends in the square around the corner so that you can get anywhere in the city. We were having an awfully good time in Paris, [b]ut the weather was so rotten that we were glad to come down here. It;s only seven dollars away from Paris. We came down here two days after we got settled and everything unpacked in the apartment so that we could go back to a place with no packing and work. For this trip we only brought rucksacks and a big suit case. Had some knickers made for Bones at the best man's tailor in Paris and they fit her wonderfully. She has a big white sweater with a roll collar and a white tam with an orange stripe. I put all that in for the females in the family.

You would be amazed how warm you are when it is so cold. We haven't had coats on since we were here and none of the men, hardly, wear hats. It is the healthiest and the nicest place you ever clapped a dead light on.

Bones and I both send you our love and to Grandmother, Grandfather, Aunt Grace and all of Uncle George's family. Hope to get some letters from you soon.

Love,
Ernie and Hadley[6]

[*Hadley adds:*]

P.S. Dear Family:—

Here we are filling our lungs with the cold dry air of the Swiss Alps and hiking and bobbing all day long—at night we are so weary we tumble into our beds, pull up the immaculate white feather beds—and drop off into the deepest sleep that doesn't break till they come in to light the stove and lamp at 8 o'clock in the morning. Breakfast in bed! Then a little reading or talking then out on the roads again or shopping in Montreux. We are feeling fitter each day— Hope to hear a little gossip about the family doings soon.

Always devotedly
Hadley

IndU, TLS

The conjectured letter date is based on the stamp in EH's passport indicating his entry to Switzerland on 15 January 1922 (JFK); on verso of the second page, Clarence wrote, "Rec'd 2/2/ 922." In content and language, this letter is quite similar to the following two, in which EH wrote that he and Hadley had been in Switzerland for ten days. Hadley signed the letter and added her own postscript.

1 The Dent de Jaman, a peak to the northeast of Montreux in the Bernese Alps, rises to more than 6,100 feet.

2 Nineteen pieces by EH would appear in the *Toronto Daily Star* and *Star Weekly* in February and March 1922, four of them about tourism and winter sports in Switzerland (*DLT*, 87, 101–4, 110–11).

3 The Château de Chillon stands on a rocky islet on the edge of Lake Geneva near Montreux. Made famous by Byron's poem "The Prisoner of Chillon" (1816), the castle became a tourist attraction in the nineteenth century; among its well-known visitors were Charles Dickens, Hans Christian Andersen, and Mark Twain.

4 In "The Luge of Switzerland" (*Toronto Star Weekly*, 18 March 1922, *DLT*, 110–11), EH noted the popularity of lugeing among the British expatriates living in Bellaria, near Vevey, about 5 miles northwest of Montreux on Lake Geneva.

5 *Femme de ménage*: housekeeper (French). The Hemingways employed Marie Rohrbach (nicknamed "Marie-Cocotte"), "a sturdy peasant from Mur-de-Bretagne," who lived in Paris with her husband Henri ("Ton-Ton") at 10 bis, Avenue des Gobelins (Baker *Life*, 123). Hadley later recalled, "the great feature of this apartment was that with it went Marie-Cocotte, our cook, emptier of various articles, water hauler, marketer, explainer of French manners and customs, and in later years, nou-nou to Bumbie" (the Hemingways' son) (Hadley interview, 1962, JFK).
6 "Ernie and" is in EH's hand; the rest of the letter is in Hadley's hand.

To Marcelline Hemingway, [c. 25 January 1922]

Chamby sur Montreux
Les Avants
Sonloup
Chateau Chillon
MontreuxOberland Bernoise Rail
Railroad Switzerland.[1]

Dear Ivory—

I send you this on your birthday from Suisse where we are very happy and wishing for your good health and continued prosperity.[2] I broke my hand in a couple of places yesterday and it is swoll big as a pumpkin so there will be no highgrade, and perhaps not very much, typing.

Switzerland is a swell place. See my articles in the Toronto Star. Where we are it is lousy with English Lawds all of whom we go to tea with. Hash is getting to talk English to beat hell and will constantly say something like "Run me a tub Ahthuh, for the glass is falling and I'm off to the cinema." We have a bob sled with a steering wheel and two hand brakes and a foot brake and ride up the mountin in a fine little train like the Peto-Walloon dummy,[3] climbing, winding, climbing, winding, till we get way to hell and gone above everything where the train stops and you get into another one that runs on cog wheels to the top tip of the mt. Then we shove the bob into the road and go down a drop that makes you're heart hit the roof of your mouth for seven kilometers. All through thick pine forests on the most wonderful roads. We get up to fifty miles and hour and Hash, who is now called Binney, and I take turns steering. The one who doesn't steer breaks. The Mountain is called Sonloup and it is in sight of the Dent du Jaman, the Dent du Midi, The Wetterhorn, the Jung frau and lots of big snow covered ones.[4]

We eat nice and are both getting as healthy as mt.goats. Been here ten days and going to stay about ten more and then go back to our apartment in Paris. It is a fine place. My hand hurts too much to type or I'd write you about it. I'm doing a lot of work and writing some good stuff. Sherwood Anderson's introductions didn't harm us any. This is the best country I was ever in for simply living. You have so much fun, out-doors all day, that you don't think at all, nor worry, nor do nawthing but a days work about four mornings a week and eat up the air and the swoops on the bob.

Again wishing you renewed prosperity and a continuation of your remarkeable career,[5]

I am,

your affect. Bro;

Ernie

James Sanford, TLS; postmark: CH[AMBY] / SUR [MONTREUX] / [*date missing; postage stamp and most of postmark torn away*]

The conjectured letter date is based on EH's statement that they had been in Switzerland for ten days; the stamp on his passport indicates that he and Hadley entered the country on 15 January 1922 (JFK).

1 The Montreux-Oberland Bernois, one of Switzerland's oldest electric railway lines, opened between Montreux and Les Avants in 1901 and by 1912 extended to Lenk. The Swiss Federal Railways were created 1 January 1902, when the country's many private railroads were nationalized.

2 Assuming the Swiss entry stamp in his passport is accurate, EH either misremembered his sister's birthday of 15 January or he was writing on the occasion of her birthday, rather than on the actual date.

3 The Walloon Lake "dummy train," a spur line built by the Grand Rapids and Indiana Railroad and in operation from 1892 to 1928, connected Harbor Springs, Petoskey, and the village of Walloon Lake.

4 From Les Avants, about 2 miles from Chamby by road and 700 feet higher, EH could take a six-minute ride by cable railway to the Col du Sonloup (elevation about 3,800 feet), which commands panoramic views of Lake Geneva and Swiss Alpine peaks (Karl Baedeker, *Switzerland Together with Chamonix and the Italian Lakes*, 26th edn. [Leipzig: Karl Baedeker, 1922], 286–87). The Dents du Midi ("Teeth of the South"), a rugged range of seven peaks, each rising over 10,000 feet, lie south of Lake Geneva near the France–Switzerland border. Like the Dent de Jaman, the Wetterhorn (more than 12,100 feet) and the Jungfrau (more than 13,600 feet) lie to the northeast of Montreux in the Bernese Alps.

5 Marcelline was then attending classes at Northwestern University and working as supervisor of the Kenilworth Community Center (Sanford, 213).

To Katharine Foster Smith, [27 January 1922]

Dear Butstein—

Here are the bare facts. We have an apartment in Paris at 74 Rue du Cardinal Lemoine for which we pay 250 francs a month. It is on the top of a tall hill in the oldest part of Paris and directly above a fine place called the Bal au printemps which is a french Frau Kuntz's. The noise of the accordian they dance to you can hear if you listen for it, but it doesn't intrude. We have a Femme du Menage whom I call a feminine menagerie who comes in and gets breakfast and cleans and empties in the morning and then goes away and comes back and cooks and serves dinner at night. She can cook the best meals you ever put into your mouth and I make out the menus, me and Bones, from all the things we've ever heard of or eaten and she does them all wonderfully. We got her on the recommendation that her husband is a great gourmet and gourmond too I believe. The apartment is larger than ours was in Chicago and very comfortable with an open fire place, an enorm[o]us french bed, nice dining room, dressing room, and a kitchen with 3,000 shiny pots and pans on the walls. But we aren't there.

We're in Switzerland for the winter sports. Suisse is a wonderful country, see my articles in the Toronto Star, and we've been hawb-nawbing with English Lawds and rating the most wonderful bobsled running you ever thought of. The roads are like iron with two feet of packed snow and you shoot down with a shreik, can go down half the day, dummy train service hauls you and the bob back up again. We have a two man bob with a steering wheel and two brakes and when you put on the brakes and lean way out you go around the turns in a slither of ice dust. Gaw. The country is as wooded as the big ridges and sweeps out on the barrens and is all high mountains with great blotches of forest on their flanks.

Hash has become Binney, through Bones, and is become healthy and strong as a goat. The bob's name is Theodore and we take turns steering. We live at a chalet run by an english speaking Swiss named Gangwisch and have breakfast in bed and two enormous meals besides, Mrs. is a high grade cook and we rate meals like roast beef, creamed cauliflower, fried potatoes, soup before and blueberries with whipped cream after for two seeds a day.[1] It isn nawthing to make a man cry the army and navy forever three cheers for the red white and blue!²

I haven't heard from Bill allthough I have wrote him four letters altogether without answer. If he wants to make it permanent I wish he would let me know in some way so that I can start forgetting him. As it is he is my best male friend and there isn't any one to take his place.

We've been here ten days and are going back any time now. It's an all day ride to Paris and we're going to take it in day time so we can watch the country. I'm begginning to get a little lonesome for Paris and will be glad to get back. Have had a wonderful time here though, but this town of Paris bites into a man's blood. Don'yt get to thinking I can't spell, I can ' but this is an accursed French typer and the key board is rotten to work. You'd be nutty about this country, it seems the only place fit for a male to live in. Seems so funny, our wailing about the jews coming and ruining the bay and here is country that has the bay lashed to the mast. Enormous forests, good trout streams, wonderful roads, and thousands of places to go instead of Boyne and the Voix. If the men were here, any three of them, we could make this place absolutely epic.

Yesterday Binney and I took a hike way up the mountain through tall pine woods, like aisles in a cathedral, they were as big and as bare of underbrush as the woods used to be just after you crossed the Sturgeon on the way [t]o the Black. When we were way up the mountain side we rolled boulders down; they would start jumping down like rabbits and then take great bounding leaps and then smash against the railroad at the bottom. We hoped we'd busted the tracks. There are deer and wolves in the woods and all sorts of strange birds. All new birds to me except great big ravens that teeter on the top of the pines and watch everything you do. Funny little brown and grey birds too. All the swiss birds seem sort of mumpbacked.

Binnes and I refer to each other as the male and the female Binney. A favourite saying is that the female binney protects its young. You are known as the Little Binney's Aunt Katherine and Harrison Williams as the Little Binney's Uncle Harrison. We have a hell of a lot of fun together and you ought to see the female binney steer the bob down from the col du Sonloup. Gaw she is a swell steerer.

We go down to Montreux, the town where the Chateau Chillon is, to have big liquor tea and go to the movies and yesterday we went to a movie of skiiers and they were all silhouetted in black and th[e] female Binney says "I wish I could see their faces so I would know whether I am personally interested in them." and I says, "Can't you see their legs?" And the female says, "Yes but one nose can often spell two legs." Ijust stuck that in to sort of give you the atmospehere of our stuff.

Deare old Butstein, wish to hell you were here. You must have all this before you die. There's no living in the States. Poison the Unc and come over here, poison the Madame and come over with Smith.[3] Gaw I can just see the way he would be all the time. It would be wonderful. What's the use of trying to live in such a goddam place as America when there is Paris and Switzerland and Italy. My gawd the fun a man has. When people lie to you and say America is as beautiful or as much fun to live in give them the razz. It is so beautiful here that it hurts in a numb sort of way all the time, only when you're wit somebody you're lovers wit the beauty gets to be jost sort of a tremendous happiness. It's so damn beautiful, Butstein, and we have so damn much fun.

Write me. I aint heard from you. I'll send you some of my stuff if you want; if you'll write me, that is. Please write a man. Aint I your best friend? Or aint I? Who's fonder of you than I am anyway?

So Long,

Love as ever

Wemedge.

UVA, TLS; postmark: CHAMBY / SUR MONTREUX, 27.1.22

EH sent this letter to "Miss Katherine Foster Smith" at Bill Smith's St. Louis address with the notation, "Please Forward." The envelope bears the forwarding address, "Chicago Beach Hotel / Chicago / Ill.," and on the verso, the forwarding postmark, "ST. LOUIS, MO., FEB 16 / 6 PM. / 1922." Accompanying the letter on a separate page is a poem written in what appears to be Kate Smith's hand. The third stanza reads: "I am not of the eagle's role / But you have driven me up / Alone / I do not even know / If you are above me / Or below." Next to these lines EH penciled the notation, "Undertow."

1 The German-born couple Gustav and Marie-Therese Gangwisch (1874–1951; 1880–1973) operated the pension in Chamby at the chalet that they owned from 1904 to 1933 (Hans Schmid, "The Switzerland of Fitzgerald and Hemingway," *Fitzgerald/Hemingway Annual 1978*, 265–67). In Book 5 of *FTA*, Frederic Henry and Catherine Barkley stay in a chalet

above Montreux and enjoy the winter sports; the characters of Mr. and Mrs. Guttingen strongly resemble the Gangwisches.

2 "The Army and Navy forever, / Three cheers for the red, white and blue!" are lyrics from "Columbia, the Gem of the Ocean," song copyrighted in the United States in 1843 by David T. Shaw.

3 The "Unc" and the "Madame," Kate and Bill Smith's uncle and aunt, Dr. and Mrs. Joseph Charles.

To Lewis Galantière, 30 January [1922]

Jan 30.

Dear Louis—

Bones and I are hiking up the valley of the Rhone and are going to walk home to Paris.[1] Only taking the train when we feel like it. This is our first halt for post cards.

Immer

Ernest M. Hemingway

Columbia, A Postcard S; verso: Château de Chillon; postmark: VEYTAUX-CH[*ILLON*], 30. 1. 22 · 19

1 The Rhône River originates in the Swiss Alps and flows into the east end of Lake Geneva about 5 miles from Montreux; at the far southwestern end of the lake, it flows from the city of Geneva through France to the Mediterranean. EH presumably is joking about walking back to Paris.

To Clarence Hemingway, 3 February 1922

Paris

February 3 1922

Dear Dad—

Hash and I are back in Paris from Switzerland after a 3 weeks stay and are both very well and in excellent shape. Found your letter of Jan 19 waiting for us this morning. Glad you are all well and things going along.

It is difficult for me to tell you how to get my stuff as I mail it all and so do not know the exact dates it appears. But if you were to subscribe to the Toronto Star Weekly you would probably see a good deal of it. Write to the Business office of The Toronto Star Weekly—Toronto Ontario and subscribe to the Weekly for 3 months or so and watch for my stories is the best way I know. Many of them are printed in the Daily Star but the mailing makes them quite irregular. The office decides whether to use the stuff in Daily or Weekly, but many go in the Weekly I'm sure and it would be easier for you to watch.

I sent ten or twelve good stories from Switzerland and they ought to be printed in about 3 weeks from the time I sent them.

Afternoon—

We are very comfortable in our apartment in Paris and have some good friends here. It is showery wet weather today but the showers only last while you wait under an awning to go on. I never had a better time than we had in Switzerland. We climbed the Dent du Jaman—and took some long hikes. Our trip up the Rhone Valley was halted by a great snow storm that made the roads impassable. In the Spring we are going up that way again and walk over the St. Bernard Pass. It is very wild and beautiful.

The Toronto Star Weekly of Dec. 19 has an article of mine on wedding gifts—(humorous) and is illustrated with a cartoon.[1] It is the last paper I've seen.

Must shut off now and get cleaned up. I've been writing at this different times during the day and have just come from the customs' office. Hash is out at a tea. We're happy and having a good time.

Love to you and Mother and all the family.

Ernie—

PSU, ALS

1 "On Weddynge Gyftes," actually published 17 December 1921 (*DLT*, 84–86).

To Grace Hall Hemingway, 14 and 15 February 1922

February 14 1922

Paris—

Dear Mother—

Dads letter of Feb 2 came today—a very fast crossing. It must have made the Aquitania. What boat a letter comes on makes any amount of difference in the time we get it.[1] Hash had a lovely letter from you that she is going to answer soon. She's in a great spell of working on the piano now and isnt writing at all. She is very well and strong and healthy.

Lately I've had a rotten cold and have been feeling very foul but as soon as we get some spring here it will clear up. We know a good batch of people now in Paris and if we allowed it would have all our time taken up socially; but I am working very hard and we keep plenty of time to ourselves. It is fun living in this oldest quarter of Paris and we have a wonderful time.[2] Paris is so very beautiful that it satisfies something in you that is always hungry in America.

I have such a cold in my head that it is quite impossible to think or write consecutively. That stuffed out moist but stupid feeling you know.

Gertrude Stein who wrote Three Lives and a number of other good things was here to dinner last night and stayed till mid-night[.] She is about 55 I guess and very large and nice.[3] She is very keen about my poetry— My Corona typewriter is being repaired. The femme de menage knocked off my writing table while she was cleaning and I dont get it until tomorrow[4]

Next day—

Madame came in yesterday while I was writing to clean the room and so I had to stop. Got the typewriter today again. Lunched this noon at the weekly luncheon of the Anglo-American newspaper men's association.[5] Tomorrow I'm getting four stories off to the Star and will have to work hard all day. Hash, who is now called Binney, is going shopping for a spring hat and a fur piece for her neck to we[a]r in the spring eith a suit and dresses as soon as she leaves off her coat.

Tell Dessie and Nubbins that we are living just two blocks away from the Jardin des Plantes which has the largest zoological gardens in the world. There are hundreds of animals and birds Oinbones has never seen before. Mountain goats from the Atlas mountains with horns that are curl three feet long and funny whiskers on their front legs. All sorts of hawks and eagles from South America and Africa and all sorts of South African animals. There is a big cage too full of Condors that have awful naked heads and red eyes and black wings twelve feet wide. It is the most wonderful collection of birds and animals I have ever seen and all thr cages are outdoors. There is a snake house that is as big as the largest building in the Lincoln Park Zoo.[6]

Friday we are going to tea at Ezra Pounds. He has asked me to do an article on the present literary state of America for the Little Review.[7] Binney is reading Lytton Strachey's Queen Victoria while I am writing this. You will enjoy it if you have not read it all ready.[8]

I am sorry to write such dull letters, but I get such full expression in my articles and the other work I am doing that I am quite pumped out and exhausted from a writing stand point and so my letters are very commonplace. If I wrote nothing but letters all of that would go into them. You know what Flaubert said, "The artist must live like a bourgeois and think like a demi-god."[9]

I hope you are very well and haveing a good time. Give my love to Dad and all the kids and the family. I'm writing Dad shortly. The stamps on this are for Carol with my love.

Ever so much love,

Ernie

PSU, AL/TLS

1 A Cunard Line ship designed to be the world's largest ocean liner and launched in 1913, the *Aquitania* could travel at 23 knots. During the 1920s it operated on the Southampton–Cherbourg–New York route across the North Atlantic.

2 From his kitchen window, EH could look down the rue Rollin and see the Arènes de Lutèce, the old Roman amphitheater built in the first century A.D.

3 *Three Lives: Stories of the Good Anna, Melanctha, and The Gentle Lena* (New York: Grafton Press, 1909) was Stein's first published book. At the time of this letter, she had just turned forty-eight and had published three other volumes, including *Tender Buttons: Objects, Food, Rooms* (New York: Claire Marie, 1914). This letter, new to scholarship, places the meeting of EH and Stein earlier than March 1922, as previously believed (Baker *Life*, 86; Reynolds *PY*, 34–36).

4 The letter is handwritten to this point; the remainder is typewritten.

5 The Anglo-American Press Association of Paris was founded on 16 December 1907 by correspondents of the *London Chronicle* and *Chicago Daily News*, who shared offices. Weekly lunches were established in 1914 and featured speeches by public officials from around the world, often speaking to reporters off the record.

6 The Jardin des Plantes, created in 1626 as a medicinal herb garden for King Louis XIII, was the first garden in Paris to be opened to the public, as early as 1640. After the Revolution, it became part of a new national museum of natural history in 1793, and animals were brought from the royal menagerie at Versailles to create a zoo. The zoo at Chicago's Lincoln Park, on the shore of Lake Michigan about 3 miles north of the Loop, was established in 1868.

7 The *Little Review* (1914–1929) was founded in Chicago by Margaret Anderson (1886–1973), who edited it with Jane Heap (1883–1964). In 1918, the magazine began serializing *Ulysses* by James Joyce (1882–1941); the editors were convicted on obscenity charges in 1921. As foreign editor of the *Little Review*, 1917–1919, Pound had introduced Anderson and Heap to Joyce's novel, and he continued to scout for new talent and to influence the direction of the magazine over its lifetime. If EH ever wrote such a piece, it was not published in the magazine.

8 In 1921, Strachey (1880–1932) was awarded the James Tait Black Memorial Prize for Biography by the University of Edinburgh for *Queen Victoria* (London: Chatto and Windus, 1921; New York: Harcourt, Brace, 1922).

9 Gustave Flaubert (1821–1880), French realist writer best known for his novel *Madame Bovary* (first published in book form in 1857). EH is closely paraphrasing a line from Flaubert's letter of 21 August 1853 to his lover, Louise Colet, articulating his artistic principles. The English translation of this letter was included in John Charles Tarver's *Gustave Flaubert: As Seen in His Works and Correspondence* (Westminster: A. Constable and Company, 1895).

To Lewis Galantière, [27 February 1922]

Cher Galantiére—

Thanks for your note. We're both fairly well. Me and Ezra Pound are getting to be great pals. Will you drop us a note to say what night this week you can dine with us?

Were both ashamed of messing your nice party so. Binney sends you her love.

Immer—
Ernest Hemingway.

Columbia, A Postcard S; postmark: PARIS / MONGE, 1630 / 27–2 / 22

To Sherwood Anderson, 9 March [1922]

March 9, 74 Rue du Cardinal Lemoine

Dear Sherwood—

You sound like a man well beloved of Jesus. Lots of things happen here. Gertrude Stein and me are just like brothers and we see a lot of her. Read the preface you wrote for her new book and like it very much. It made a big hit with Gertrude.[1] Hash says to tell you, quotes, that things have come to a pretty pass between her and Lewy—close quotes.[2] My operatives keep a pretty close eye on the pair of them.

Joyce has a most god-damn wonderful book. It'll probably reach you in time. Meantime the report is that he and all his family are starving but you can find the whole celtic crew of them every night in Michaud's where Binney and I can only afford to go about once a week.[3]

Gertrude Stein says Joyce reminds her of an old woman out in San Francisco. The woman's son struck it rich as hell in the Klondyke and the old women went around wringing her hands and saying, "Oh my poor Joey! My poor Joey! He's got so much money!"[4] The damned Irish, they have to moan about something or other, but you never heard of an Irishman starving.

Pound took six of my poems and sent them wit a letter to Thayer, Scofield, that is, you've heard of him maybe. Pound thinks I'm a swell poet. He also took a story for the Little Review.[5]

I've been teaching Pound to box wit little success. He habitually leads wit his chin and has the general grace of the crayfish or crawfish. He's willing but short winded. Going over there this afternoon for another session but there aint much joy in it as I have to shadow box between rounds to get up a sweat. Pound sweats well, though, I'll say that for him. Besides it's pretty sporting of him to risk his dignity and his critical reputation at something that he don't know nothing about. He's really a good guy, Pound, wit a fine bitter tongue onto him. He's written a good review of Ulysses for April Dial.[6]

I don't know whether he has much drag with Thayer so I don't know whether Thayer will take the poems or not—but I wish to hell he would.[7]

Bones is called Binney now. We both call each other Binney. I'm the male Binney and she is the female Binney. We have a saying—The Male Binney protects the Female—but the Female bears the young.

We've met and liked Le Verrier—he's done a review of the Egg for a french magazine here.[8] I'll get it and send it to you if he ha[s]n't done so already.

Your book sounds swell. Paid you to go to New Orleans—huh?[9] I wish I could work like that. This goddam newspaper stuff is gradually ruining me— but I'm going to cut it all loose pretty soon and work for about three months.

When you've seen Benny Leonard you've seen them all. Hope he was having a good night when you viewed him. I've seen this Pete Herman. He's blind in one eye you know and sometimes blood or sweat gets into the other and they cuff him all over the place—but he must have been seeing well the night you lamped him. He's a fine little wop and can hit to beat hell.[10]

Well this is getting too damned voluminous. Write us again will you? It puts a big kick into the day we get your letter.

Oh Yes. Griffin Barry is still in Vienna and living, they say, with Edna St. Vincent etc. The Rotonde is cluttered with the various young things, female, she's led astray.[11] Like Lady Lil, she piles her victims up in heaps.[12]

Well, bye-bye and any amount of love to Tennessee and yourself from us—

Ernest

I wrote some pretty good poems lately in Rhyme.
We love Gertrude Stein.

Newberry, TLS with autograph postscript

1 In his preface to Stein's *Geography and Plays* (Boston: Four Seas, 1922), Anderson wrote that hers was "the most important pioneer work done in the field of letters in my time" and that she had managed to "recreate life in words."

2 Probably Lewis Galantière.

3 The first two copies of *Ulysses* were hand-delivered to Sylvia Beach in Paris on 2 February 1922, Joyce's fortieth birthday. Michaud's, Joyce's favorite restaurant, was at the corner of rue Jacob and rue des Saints-Pères.

4 The discovery of gold on the Klondike River in Canada's Yukon Territory prompted a rush of prospective miners to Alaska and the Yukon beginning in 1897.

5 Pound was the paid European talent scout for the *Dial*. Scofield Thayer (1889–1982) purchased the magazine in 1919 (with James Sibley Watson, Jr.) and served as editor from the publication of their first issue in January 1920 until June 1925. Anderson certainly had heard of Thayer, as EH well knew: Anderson was the recipient of the Dial Award for 1921, the first of the annual $2,000 awards given to "acknowledge the service to letters" of a contributor to the magazine. Hadley wrote to Grace Hemingway on 20 February, "Ezra Pound has sent a number of Ernest's poems to Thayer of the 'Dial' and taken a little prose thing of his for the *Little Review* also asked him to write a series of articles for the 'Dial' on American magazines" (JFK, quoted in Reynolds *PY*, 26). Whatever the "little prose thing" might have been, EH's first contribution to the *Little Review* would not appear until the Spring 1923 issue: "In Our Time" (six vignettes that would be published with minor revisions as Chapters 1–6 of *iot*) and a poem, "They All Made Peace: What Is Peace?"

6 Pound's review, titled "Paris Letter" and dated "May, 1922," actually would appear in the June 1922 issue of the *Dial* (623–29).

7 Thayer rejected the poems (later published as "Wanderings" in the January 1923 issue of *Poetry: A Magazine of Verse*), and EH bore a long-lived grudge against the *Dial* and its editors. Thayer appears by name in *TOS* and *MF*.

8 Anderson's *The Triumph of the Egg: A Book of Impressions from American Life in Tales and Poems* (New York: Huebsch, 1921), republished as *The Triumph of the Egg, and Other Stories* (London: Cape, 1922). The book was reviewed in the 30 March 1922 edition of *Revue Hebdomadaire* by French critic Charles Le Verrier, who wrote that Anderson's work was sounding a wake-up call against the conformity and pragmatism that had stifled American letters (MarySue Schriber, "Sherwood Anderson in France: 1919–1939," *Twentieth-Century Literature* 23, no. 1 [February 1977]: 141).

9 Buoyed by the financial success of *The Egg*, Anderson was then in New Orleans working on *Many Marriages* (New York: Heubsch, 1923). That novel was serialized in the *Dial* before being published in book form the following February.

10 Leonard (né Benjamin Leiner, 1896–1947), a lightweight boxer from New York, and Peter "Kid Herman" Gulotta (1896–1973), a bantamweight boxer from New Orleans, both had won recent bouts in New Orleans (on 25 February and on 20 February, respectively). Evidently Anderson attended the fights and described them in a letter to EH that remains unlocated.

11 Griffin Barry (1884–1957), American journalist. Edna St. Vincent Millay (1892–1950), American poet and dramatist who in 1923 became the first woman to receive the Pulitzer Prize for Poetry. She toured Europe January 1921–January 1923. Barry and Millay had been lovers and were living together in Vienna in early 1922, but she was unhappy in the relationship and returned to Paris and "the Rotonde crowd" in late March (Nancy Milford, *Savage Beauty: The Life of Edna St. Vincent Millay* [New York: Random House 2001], 225, 229).

12 Lady Lil, an American folk poem character, competes in a "fornicating contest" with a man named Pisspot Pete. In several variants, it is said that "When [she] fucked she fucked for keeps / And left her victims all piled in heaps." A product of oral tradition, the poem first appeared in print in 1927 in *Immortalia*, a privately and anonymously published anthology of bawdy verse, where it was attributed to American journalist Eugene Field (1850–1895).

To Howell G. Jenkins, 20 March 1922

74 Rue du Cardinal Lemoine

March 20 1922

Cherished Carpative—

Your screed has dragged me to the mill from a bed of pain and I mill like a wild thing. Jo Eesus but I have been a sick male the last brace of diurnals, the same old throat trouble to the last yencing degree. You give a male a pile of news and it was fine as hell to hear from you Carper.

Lemme see, I don't know what the dope was. Oh yes, I was sitting on the Boulevard Madeliene morting an absinthe, they call it by another name, but it is the Genuwind, when I saw Feder going by.[1] I nailed the Duke with a few short ugly words and he and his jewine bride, picture the Duke honeymooning with that mouthful of false fangs, came up to our cile for dinner that night. They were Honeymooning all over Italy and Austria etc. etc and sailed for the states the day after we saw them. Hash and I took them to a couple of dives after we'd chowed and we morted a brace of champagne bottles and a few other things, Feder wouldn't get tight on account of his new respectability, but I, having been married a long time, acted as usual.

Hash sends her love to you and we both send you the picture. Ogilvey can't cut 'em like that suit carpative.[2] It is so homespun that you smell the genuwind peat smoke in the wool.

This damned typer ribbon is about worn out. I've worked like hell. The Star have offered me 75 seeds a week whenever I come home from here— would like to copy the letter, but it is too goddam long, but I hit that and over on space[3] so why the bloody hell ever go back until a male's spring-offs are ready to go to cawlegge, except to see youse men, and then why don't youse men come over here? A six pound trout was taken in a stream near Pau day before yesterday, and the guys who fish a wet fly are making some nice catches all along now. Season opens here the first of March.

The enclosed letter came from Smith after I'd written him about five in the old vein, this is the first answer I've had. You send it back to me when you're through with it, I want to file it. The temptation of course is to tell him to take his whole damned family and jam them as far as they will go up some elephant's fanny—but I'm still fond of him, so I'm making no answer. Isn't that a goddam hell of a letter from a guy whose been like Smith and I have been? Of course the Madam, damn her soul, has been poisoning him agin me for a couple of years now, but I din't know he would swallow propaganda like that! Christ! Do you think I am so goddam changed for the worse and all that? Didn't we have about the best time bumming around, You and Rouse and I that we ever had? Was I such a leper? Aw hell— It's hell when a male knifes you—especially when you still love him. Show the Ghee the screed. To Hell wit him if he's that way. I'd written him five letters, the regular old kind you know— I thought he was just too busy to answer.[4]

I'd like to have seen the Ketchell pics—he was a swell battler, but too small for that damned smoke.[5] I haven't seen a fight since I was here on acct no one to go with—but they have very good bouts all the time. I'm going to lay hold of some fight fan and get a season ticket or something.

By the way— Do you ever see Butstein? I haven't heard from her since we shived—she wasn't off of me then—and I left about eight hundred dollars worth of wop drafts with her to forward to me as soon as we had an address. She was to keep them in her saving's dep. vault and send them as soon as we wrote. Have written five times and no answer and need the money bad. Perhaps she never got the letters. Meantime the drafts are liable to be outlawed —some of them getting to be over a year old. It's a hell of a mess, also I need the money to go to the Genoa conference.[6] Have to pay my expenses and then they pay me. Will you look her up, either at the Chicago Beach Hotel or at the Co-op 128 N. Wells, and see if she got my screeds, and ask her to please send me the drafts. I'm worried as hell about them. Have them sent registered and insured. To 74 Rue duCardinal Lemoine or to the American Express Company, 11 Rue Scribe. By the time this screed gets to you the drafts may have come, but as I've heard nothing yet and been writing for two months now, you'd better have a look anyway. Will you please? Thanks ever so much Carp. You can show her Bill's letter if you want. I'm afraid to write her again for fear that she may be sore at me— I wrote Bill five letters and I'm fonder of Stut than of Bill, but a man gets a little bit bucked about pushing his mush in the dust after a certain length of time. Krebs may know where to lay hold of Kate—he does, I'm pretty sure. Tell her I still feel the same as ever.

We have a hell of a good time. I'm boxing regular with Ezra Pound, and he has developed a terrific wallop, I can usually cross myself though before he lands them and when he gets too tough I dump him on the floor. He is a good game guy and has come along to beat hell wit the gloves—some day I will get careless and he will knock me for a row of latrines. He weighs 180.

My stuff is coming along— I'll look out for a jawb for you over here. Do you speak frawg? Give the Baw my best— I'm going to screed him. I don't screed as much as I ought on account of writing s[u]ch a gawd awful lot on the mill every day. Day before I got sick four of us went out on a picnic way out on the Marne to Mildred Aldrich's—she wrote A Hilltop on the Marne—you know—a fine old femme.[7] We saw the woods where the Uhlans were in 1914 and bridges the English blew up and the whole thing.[8] It's a beautiful valley and the trees are all getting into blossom. Aldrich was there during the battle and she told us all about it. Wish you'd been there. I mor[te]d a fiasco of wine at lunch on the way out, we had a Ford, and we all were pleasantly lit and I drank a cup full of 3 Star Hennesey to see me homeward on the drive back to Paris. It was near Meaux we wnt. A lovely place.[9]

Well I goot go back to bed—this bitch of a throat is good for about three days more—two big pus sacs and white patches—

So long old Carpier and screed a male—

My regards to John and Dirty Dick—tell him to screed me and I'lll screed him, maybe I'll do it before then. Steer clear of women and bad liquor. Hash sends her love to Dick.

Sempre,

Steen

UT, TLS

1 Morting, EH's slang for finishing, or "killing," a drink. The drink of choice among Parisian café patrons and the artistic avant-garde since the 1890s, absinthe came to be seen as a dangerous drug and social problem and was outlawed in France in 1915. In "The Great 'Apéritif' Scandal," published in the *Toronto Star Weekly* (12 August 1922; *DLT*, 182–84), EH explained that despite the ban, absinthe was being sold in great quantities as a pale yellow syrup under the name of Anis Delloso. Walter J. Feder was a fellow veteran of the ARC Ambulance Service Section 4.

2 Probably Ogilvie and Heneage or Ogilvie and Jacobs, both listed in the 1923 Chicago city directory as purveyors of men's clothing with addresses on Jackson Boulevard in the Chicago Loop.

3 EH means that, paid by the column inch, he is making $75 per week already.

4 After EH sent Bill Smith an insulting letter about Y. K. Smith, Bill sided with his brother on the grounds that blood is thicker than water. In a letter to EH of 22 February 1922, Bill wrote that their friendship had undergone "profound and very unwelcome changes" and that he did not care for the "1922 edition of E.M.H.," which was as different from what he had been as vinegar was from champagne (phPUL; quoted in *SL*, 66, and Baker *Life*, 88). EH and Bill Smith did not reconcile until the fall of 1924.

5 Stanley Ketchel (né Stanislaus Kiecal, 1886–1910), American middleweight boxing champion from 1908 to 1910, nicknamed "the Michigan Assassin" and known for taking on larger opponents. As "the White Hope," Ketchel fought African-American heavyweight champion Jack Johnson on 16 October 1909, knocking him down with a surprise punch in the twelfth round; Johnson (whom EH derogatorily calls "that damned smoke") responded by knocking out Ketchel with a single punch. The next year, while in training and trying to arrange a rematch, Ketchel was murdered, allegedly by a woman's jealous boyfriend. EH wrote about the legendary fight in "The Light of the World" (*WTN*).

6 The Conferenza Internazionale Economica convened in Genoa, Italy, 10 April–19 May 1922. Delegates from more than thirty European countries met to discuss the postwar economic rebuilding of Europe and improvement of relations between Western Europe and the Soviet Union.

7 The Baw, Ted Brumback. EH and Hadley went with Stein and Alice B. Toklas to visit Stein's
   close friend Mildred Aldrich (1853–1928), American author whose books included *A Hilltop
   on the Marne, Being Letters Written June 8–September 8, 1914* (1915). Because the French
   government believed that her work was instrumental in persuading the United States to
   enter the war, Aldrich was awarded the *Légion d'Honneur* (Legion of Honor) in 1922.
8 Uhlans, German cavalry soldiers. The bridges were blown to stall the German army's
   advance on Paris.
9 Hennessy, cognac made in Cognac, France, since 1765, when the brand was established by
   Irish aristocrat Richard Hennessy (1724–1800). Meaux, a town about 25 miles northeast of
   Paris in the department of Seine-et-Marne.

To Howell G. Jenkins, 20 April 1922

Dear Carpative—

The flags of all nations out for the Conference.

Have been here two weeks working like hell.

sempre

Steen.

April 20 1922

phPUL, A Postcard S; postmark: PARIS / R. MONGE, 16 30 / [2]-5 / [22]

EH wrote this postcard and the next three in Genoa and mailed them after he returned to Paris
(as he explains to his mother in his letter of 2 May 1922); all are postmarked from the rue
Monge post office in Paris, 2 May 1922.

To Marcelline Hemingway, [c. late April 1922]

Dear Ivory: Leave here tomorrow for the old home town; worked hard as
compatable with temperament and will be glad to see Hash again.

This isn't a bad town if you don' hafta live in it and travel to it and from it
on the trains.

Ernie

James Sanford, T Postcard with typewritten signature; verso: Genova—Via G. D'Albertis;
postmark: PARIS / R. MONGE, 16 30 / 2–5 / 22

To Clarence Hemingway, [c. late April 1922]

Dear Dad:

If you've read the Daily Star you know all about this town.[1] I4m glad to get away from it altho the weather has been warm and fine. This is the old fort on top of the hilloverlooking the town.

Love,

Ernie

JFK, T Postcard with typewritten signature; verso: GENOVA—Righi—Castellacio; postmark: PARIS / R. MONGE, 16 30 / 2–5 / 22

1 Between 10 April and 13 May 1922, the *Toronto Daily Star* published twenty-two articles by EH on the Genoa Conference, seven of them unsigned (*DLT*, 127–35, 138–68).

To Madelaine Hemingway, [c. late April 1922]

Dear Nunbones:

Am glad to leave this burg where the old brother has been working like a horse.

Still, if you didn't have to work here; you'd go cuckooed.

Give my love to the relatives and believe me always your brother

Sincerely as always

PSU, T Postcard with typewritten signature; verso: Genova—Panorama; postmark: PARIS / R. MONGE, 16 30 / 2–5 / 22

To Grace Hall Hemingway, 2 May 1922

Paris May 2 1922

Dear Mother—

Thank you so much for the very lovely photograph. Hadley and I both enjoyed it tremendously and appreciate so much your sending it to us. It is very beautiful.

Enclosed are a bunch of postals I wrote to you all at Genoa and carried in my pocket, too busy to mail.[1] Got back here last week after skimming the cream from Genoa.

I was worn out and in fairly rotten shape from over-work and we went on a fine hike out through the country to Chantilly and through the forest to Senlis. Slept in the hotel in Senlis where Von Kluck stopped in 1914. Because he was there they didn't burn it when they set fire to the town. It is a lovely old to[w]n though with a beautiful cathedral and abbey and old chateau. Then we hiked through the woods and forested hills to Pont St. Maxense on the Oise river and went from there to Compiegne.[2] We were going on to Soissons and then down to Rheims[3] but it got rainy and I got sick so we came back to Paris and I've been in bed f[o]r three days with me throat. It was a fine long hike though and the woods are beautiful this time of year. It is great hunting country around Senlis, wild boar and stag.

We'll go out again soon as my throat is mended. Krebs[4] and Willard Kitchell are over here for six weeks and have gone hunting down in the South. Everybody shoots wild boars in this country.

I had a good time in Genoa and wrote and cabled some very good stuff. I suppose you see some of it in the Star. My first articles on Genoa (cabled dispatches) opened April 10. The mail articles started to run about April 22 or 23

I may be going to Russia for the Star in the very near future, am awaiting orders from them now.[5]

I'm sorry we've been so sloppy about writing youall lately. I thought that Binney was writing and she thought I was and as we were several hundred miles apart we didn't get together on it.

Hope everybody is in good shape and that Dad gets some good trout fishing in May. He's probably up there now. Seems funny Marce having such a gay time when she went down to be with Aunt Arrabel just after Uncle Tyler's death.[6] How did they manage to make a coming out party out of that?

We saw Mrs. Dr. Lewis thr other day.[7] Went and called at her hotel. She has had a wonderful trip and is fairly well.

Give my love to Dad and all the kids. IVm writing Dad shortly.

Love, as ever,

Ernie

PSU, TLS; postmark: PARIS / R. MONGE, 16 30 / 2–5 / 22

This letter is written on the verso of Co-operative Commonwealth stationery.

1 Evidently EH decided to mail the Genoa postcards separately rather than as enclosures; the postcards bear French postage stamps, and their postmarks show that they were mailed at the same time from the same Paris postal station as this and the following letter home.
2 General Alexander von Kluck (1846–1934) commanded the German First Army during the August 1914 invasion of Belgium and France, his forces coming within 15 miles of Paris before being halted in the First Battle of the Marne in September 1914. From the town of Chantilly, about 30 miles northeast of Paris, EH and Hadley hiked some 40 miles to Compiègne, passing through the towns of Senlis and Pont-Sainte-Maxence. Senlis is famed for its twelfth-century Gothic Cathedral de Notre-Dame, a château dating to the eleventh century, and the remains of Gallo-Roman walls. The armistice between the Allies and Germany ending WWI was signed in a railroad car in the forest near Compiègne.
3 Soissons (25 miles east of Compiègne) was the site of a fierce battle between U.S. and German troops in July 1918. The city of Reims (about 36 miles east of Soissons and 90 miles northeast of Paris) is noted for its thirteenth-century Gothic cathedral, where French kings tradition- ally were crowned; the city and cathedral were heavily damaged by German shelling in WWI.
4 Krebs Friend.
5 The trip to Russia never materialized.
6 EH's paternal uncle Alfred Tyler Hemingway died of pneumonia on 24 February in Kansas City.
7 Gertrude Lewis (b. circa 1863), widow of Oak Park physician William R. Lewis (b. circa 1849) and a member of the Nineteenth Century Club; Grace Hall Hemingway was also a member.

To Clarence Hemingway, 2 May 1922

May 2, 1922.

Dear Dad—

I was very glad to get your last good letter saying that you were going North in may to get some fishing. Hope you are up there now.

Spring has come quite definitely here although it took plenty of time about it. It was a great change getting back here from the warmness of Genoa where I didn't need to wear a coat at all.

Have been laid up in bed for four days with my same old bad throat and it has about run its course and I expect to go out tomorrow. May day was quiet here although the Comrades shot a couple of policemen.[1] I worked very hard at Genoa and wrote some very good stuff. Met L. George, Chicherin, Litvinoff and many others.[2] Star pays me 75 a week and expenses. Expect to go into Russia for them very soon. Waiting to hear now. I'll let you know as soon as I have details.

It's a rainy rotten day. The country outside of Paris and up into Picardy is beautiful.[3] Fields full of big black and white magpies that walkalong the plow furrows like crow[s] do. Lots of larks too. There are lots of common birds I don't know, but I go down to the Zoological gardens that's right near our house and identify them. Saw a crossbill the other day.

The forests are very wild and free of underbrush and cover all the hills and ridges. Hash and I took a forty mile hike through forest nearly all the way. Forests of Chantilly, Chatallate[4] and Compiegne. They have deer and wild boar and foxes and rabbits. I've eaten wild boar twice and it is very good. They cook it up into a pasty with carrots and onions and mushrooms and a fine borwn crust. There are lots of pheasants and partridges too. I expect to get some good shooting in the fall.

Krebs is down in the south of France wild boar hunting now. They certainly can move fast and look very mean when the dogs are after them.

On Hash's and my hike we went up the Oise river and through the forests and over the hills to where the Aisne comes in. They are working hard rebuilding the towns and are making many of them so ugly with the new, ugly French architecture.[5]

As I'm writing on my Corona in bed I have to stop because it gets so uncomfortable. Mrs. Lewis sent her love to you and spoke very highly of you. We have also seen your old patients the Winslows. Hash has been out with Marjorie Winslow and was at there house to tea while I was in Genoa. Alan has a new diplomatic post in Brazil.[6]

Much love Dad and I hope you have a good trip. I had the two World's Illusion volumnes mailed to Mrs. Dilworth before I left Chicago and will trace them up. If she does not, ot has not, received them I will send to Kroch's five dollars to send her two new ones, but I am sure she mutst have gotten them.[7] I left them with Krebs with Postage and Dilworth[']s address.

Excuse the bum spelling and typographicals.

Ernie

JFK, TLS; postmark: PARIS / R. MONGE, 16 30 / 2–5 / 22

Like EH's letter to his mother of the same date, this is written on Co-operative Commonwealth stationery. EH mailed the letters to his parents in separate envelopes to 600 North Kenilworth in Oak Park.

1 May Day, the first of May, was designated as International Workers' Day by the International Socialist Congress in Paris in 1889; since 1890 it has been observed as a day of activism and commemoration by various socialist, communist, and labor groups. In 1922 two policemen were shot while attempting to control the crowd during a "preliminary May Day demonstration" in Paris ("Two Policemen Shot at End of Reds' Meeting / Single Bullet Wounds Both: Expect Them to Die," Paris edn., *Chicago Daily Tribune*, 1 May 1922, 1.) In his unpublished "Paris 1922" EH wrote, "I have watched the police charge the crowd with swords as they milled back into Paris through the Porte Maillot on the first of May and seen the frightened proud look on the white beaten-up face of the sixteen year old kid who looked like a prep school quarter back and had just shot two policemen" (JFK; Baker *Life*, 91).

2 Prominent delegates to the Genoa economic conference included British Prime Minister David Lloyd George (1863–1945), Soviet Commissar of Foreign Affairs Georgi Chicherin (1872–1936), and Soviet Deputy Commissar of Foreign Affairs Maxim Litvinov (1876–1951).

3 Region north of Paris traversed by the Somme, Oise, and Aisne rivers.

4 Probably the Forêt d'Halatte, north of Senlis, between the Chantilly and Compiègne forests.

5 The valley of the Aisne River was the scene of three major battles during WWI.

6 The Winslows, William H. and Edith H. Winslow of River Forest and Chicago, Illinois. Their daughter Marjorie was then about fifteen years old. Their son Alan F. Winslow, the celebrated WWI aviator, was attached to the Department of State after the war and would spend several years in the U.S. diplomatic service ("Alan Winslow, 37, War Ace, Is Dead," *New York Times*, 16 August 1933, 17).

7 *The World's Illusion* (New York: Harcourt, Brace and Howe, 1920) is the English translation by Ludwig Lewisohn of the two-volume 1919 novel, *Christian Wahnschaffe*, by German author Jakob Wassermann (1873–1934); the protagonist rejects his family's wealth to dedicate himself to the service of humanity after a lifetime of pleasure. Kroch's International Book Store, established in 1907 by Austrian immigrant Adolph Kroch (1882–1978), was on North Michigan Avenue in Chicago.

To Kate Buss, 12 May 1922

Chalet Chamby
Chamby sur Montreux
Suisse
May 12, 1922.

Dear Miss Buss:—

Thanks ever so much for the letter and the book. Our concierge forwarded them both and I'll do the two reviews and send them to Johnson as soon as I've read the book, which I'm looking forward to doing tonight.[1]

It certainly looks corking.

Hope we will see you before you sail. I tried to get over to your hotel to get the wollume the day we left on such short notice but couldnVt make it so left instructions and postage with the fine, high-minded, conscientiously forwarding concierge.

If you go home by way of China will you let us know? I'd like you to know my uncle Bill if some of the embattled Wangs haven't killed him. They've been fighting in his province.[2]

Had a note from Pound giving his next address as Ravenna, Poste Restante[3] I suppose.

Thanks again for the book and good bye and very good luck.

Ernest M. Hemingway.

Brown, TLS

1 Buss, a friend of Stein and Pound, may have asked EH to review a book she had written, likely *Studies in the Chinese Drama* (Boston: Four Seasons, 1922). No EH review of a book by Buss has been located.
2 EH's uncle, Dr. Willoughby Hemingway, was a missionary in Shansi province, China. On 20 April 1922 the Associated Press reported that an anti-Christian movement organized at Peking University was spreading rapidly across China and that Christian leaders and U.S. consular authorities were alarmed at the extent of the movement, reportedly "backed by Communist agitators" ("Rival Chinese Armies Now Near Each Other / But Peking Does Not Expect Clash: Anti-Christian Movement Is Reported," *New York Times*, 21 April 1922, 12.)
3 *Poste Restante* indicates that the letter should be held at the post office until called for by the addressee.

To Clarence Hemingway, 24 May 1922

Chamby sur Montreux.
May 24 1922.

Dear Dad:—

Suppose by now you've a letter from me from Paris. The reason you didn't see anything of mine in the Star was because you get only the Star Weekly and my last 16 articles have been in the Daily running from the 24th of April til about the 8th of May. I'm getting some stuff off to the weekly from here now. They've been neglected because the Genoa assignment was a Daily assignment and Mr. Bone, the managing Editor, didn't turn anything over to them.

From the time I came back from Genoa until we came down here I was sick in bed nearly all the time and didn't turn out a thing.

It's great down here. My old pal Major Dorman-Smith has been spending his leave with us and we've been trout fishing and mountain climbing and next week are going to walk over the St. Bernard pass and then down into Italy and take the train back to Paris.[1] I've picked up all the weight I lost and am feeling fine again. My throat still bothers me, but for all Doctors seem able to do for it, I guess it will go on bothering the rest of my life.

Today we climbed Cape au Moine,[2] a very steep and dangerous climb of 7,000 feet and had a great time coasting down the snow fields coming down by simply sitting down and letting go. The fields in the lower valleys are full of narcissus and just below the snow line when we climbed the [D]ent du Jaman the other day we saw two big martens. They were about as large as a good big skunk but much longer and thinner. I've caught several trout in the strem called Canal du Rhone up the Rhone valley. It is all fly fishing and as the trout have been fished for over two thousand years or so they are fairly shy. I haven't been skunked on them yet though and have been out four times. The mountain streams are still too full of melted snow and roily to be able to fish, but there is one wonderful stream called the Stockalper over across the Rhone about twelve miles above where it flows into Lake Geneva that I am very keen to fish. It has [s]almon but is still too roily.

My credentials for Russia from the Star came today and also a good check, 465.00, expenses and three weeks salary at 75 dollars a week. It was quite welcome.

The summer camp sounds hectic. Who are the campers going to be? Hope you got away and got some fishing.

Hadley is very healthy and as red and brown as an Indian. She never looked better. It is nice here where we were in the winter and know the people. We have climbed all the high peaks near here and are about ready to start in on the best ones again.

Hope you are well and that everything is going along in good shape. Give ourlove to Mother and the kids and all sorts of greetings from Hash and me—

Your loving son,

Ernie

JFK, TLS; postmark: PARIS / R. MONGE, 16 30 / 2–5 / 22

1 The Great St. Bernard Pass is the oldest pass in the Western Alps, crossing the Valais Alps between Martigny, Switzerland, and Aosta, Italy, at an elevation of more than 8,000 feet. For an account of the journey see Baker *Life*, 91–94 and Reynolds *PY*, 53–54.
2 Peak in the Préalpes Freibourgeoises-Bernoises, to the northeast of Montreux.

To Gertrude Stein and Alice B. Toklas, 11 June 1922

Milan, Italy, June 11, 1922.

Dear Miss Stein and Miss Tocraz—

We've been here for about a week playing the races with tremendous success. I get up at dawn and study the dope-sheet and then after my brain has cracked under the strain Mrs. Hemingway, with about three cocktails and an indelible pencil to aid her, picks winners as easy as cracking peanut shucks. With the aid of her alcoholic clairavoyance and an old friend of mine that I think sleeps with the horses we've had 17 winners out of 21 starts.[1]

We walked down here from Suisse over the Grand St. Bernard. Made 57 kilometers in two days with Chink, the Captain, doing the Simon Legree[2] on us. We didn't walk all the way to Milan on account of Mrs. Hemingway's feet swelling on her at Aosta. It was a great treck because the pass wasn't open yet and no one had walked up it this year from the Suisse side. It took the combined efforts of the Captain and Mrs. H. and a shot of cognac every two hundred yards to get me up the last couple of kilometers of snow.

Going from here up to Recoaro and Schio in the Trentino and then down to the Piave and Venice and then back to Paris.[3] Want to be back by about the 18th. It is raining hard today and that will probably mean disaster at the track, I don't think Mrs. H's alcoholic genius could function on a muddy track and I know that once the going gets heavy I can't ever pick them at all. Still it's fun to see them run with their tails all plaited up and the mud scudding.

We had a fine time in Suisse. Climbed a couple of mountains with Chink and then he climbed one himself and nearly got himself killed on Ascension day[4] coming across a torrent that was too deep and fast for him and met us at the Bains des Alliaz[5] and we drank 11 bottles of beer apiece with Mrs. H. sleeping on the grass and walked home in the cool of the evening with our feet feeling very far off and unrelated and yet moving at terrific speed.

Hope to see you both soon.

Your friend,

Ernest M. Hemingway

Yale, TLS

1 After their trek across the Great St. Bernard Pass, EH and Hadley took the train to Milan and Chink Dorman-Smith returned to his military station on the Rhine (Baker *Life*, 92). Horse racing at San Siro, the track outside of Milan, would figure in EH's 1923 story "My Old Man" and *FTA*.

2 The cruel slave owner who flogged Tom to death in the influential best-selling novel *Uncle Tom's Cabin* (1852) by Harriet Beecher Stowe (1811–1896).

3 EH planned the trip to show Hadley many of his WWI haunts. For his account, see "A Veteran Visits the Old Front" (*Toronto Daily Star*, 22 July 1922; *DLT*, 176–80).

4 Christian feast day observed on the fortieth day after Easter, commemorating Christ's ascension into heaven. In 1922, Ascension Day (always a Thursday) was 25 May.

5 Bains-de-l'Alliaz, a Swiss spa with sulphur springs, about 4 miles north of Chamby sur Montreux, near Blonay.

To Howell G. Jenkins, 14 June 1922

June 14–22

Dear Carper—

New hotel at the old Dolomites. We went in a motor car from Schio to Rovereto. Valli dei Signori looks just the same. Santa Caterina rebuilt. Wish you were along.

Steen

phPUL, A Postcard S; verso: image of turreted four-story inn Albergo Dolomiti at foot of Mount Pasubio; postmark: Rovereto / 14 6.22 15 / Trento

Photocopied alongside this postcard on the same sheet of paper (Carlos Baker files, PUL) is a postcard of the same date from Hadley to Jenkins that begins, "Greetings to Il Carpatorio from scenes of his wartime exploits. Went out to the Schio country club yesterday and heard all about it all over again understanding why you all want to get back again." Before Italy entered WWI in May 1915, Rovereto (about 30 miles northwest of Schio) was in Austria-Hungary, a few miles from the border with Italy, which ran between the two towns. The area was heavily contested during the war; with the November 1918 armistice, Rovereto became part of Italy.

To Harriet Monroe, 16 July 1922

74 Rue du Cardinal
Lemoine.
Paris.
July 16, 1922.

Miss Harriet Monroe,
232 E.Erie Street,
Chicago, Illinois.

Dear Miss Monroe:—

I am very glad the poems are to appear in Poetry and am sorry not to have written before.[1]

Enclosed are some more you might be able to use.

With very best regards to Henry B. Fuller,[2] and, if you see him, Sherwood Anderson.

Very sincerely,
Ernest M. Hemingway

P.S. I met a boy, Ernest Walsh, here who says he is a friend of yours. He has been quite ill but is much better now.[3]

Autobiography—[4]

Born in Oak Park, Illinois.

Permanent address 74 Rue du Cardinal Lemoine

Paris V. e.m.

Occupation—At present in Russia as staff correspondent of the Toronto Star. (passport three weeks over-due now. However Max Eastman's came yesterday so I ought to get under way shortly.[5] Litvinoff promised me at Genoa there would be no trouble)

Published verse etc. in Double Dealer etc.[6]

UChicago, TLS

1 In the January 1923 issue of Monroe's *Poetry: A Magazine of Verse*, six of EH's poems appeared under the title "Wanderings": "Mitrailliatrice," "Oily Weather," "Roosevelt," "Riparto d'Assalto," "Champs d'Honneur," and "Chapter Heading" (193–95).

2 Henry Blake Fuller (1857–1929), Chicago novelist and outspoken member of the anti-imperialist movement. His works included *On the Stairs* (1918) and *Bertram Cope's Year* (1919), a novel that openly addressed homosexuality. A close friend of Monroe's, Fuller assisted in the editing of *Poetry*.

3 Ernest Walsh (1895–1926) initiated a correspondence with Monroe in August 1921 while he was hospitalized for lung damage sustained in a plane crash during U.S. Army training exercises. His injuries were exacerbated by tuberculosis, which he had contracted earlier and from which he never fully recovered. Monroe published four of Walsh's poems in the January 1922 issue of *Poetry*. After he was pronounced incurable and released from the hospital, she helped him secure a disabled veteran's pension and provided him with letters of introduction to Pound and other writers in Paris. With Ethel Moorhead (1869–1955), Walsh founded the little magazine *This Quarter* in 1925, which published EH's "Big Two-Hearted River" in its first issue. EH later wrote a cutting sketch about Walsh, "The Man Who Was Marked for Death" (*MF*).

4 EH typed this "Autobiography" on the verso of the letter. The page bears the stamped date, "JUL 29 1922," and the handwritten notation, "Biog," both presumably added by Monroe or a magazine staff member.

5 Max Forrester Eastman (1883–1969) was co-founder and editor of the socialist magazine *The Masses* from 1913 until it folded in 1917, when it was banned from the U.S. mails on the grounds that it undermined the war effort and therefore violated the recent Espionage Act. In 1918 he founded the pro-Soviet magazine *The Liberator* and in 1922 gave up its editorship to travel to the Soviet Union to observe the post-Revolutionary conditions there firsthand.

6 On the advice of Sherwood Anderson, EH had submitted work to the *Double Dealer* (1921–1926), a little magazine published in New Orleans by Julius Weis Friend with the stated mission of reversing the "artistic stagnation" that had plagued the South since the U.S. Civil War. EH's fable, "A Divine Gesture," appeared in the May 1922 issue, and his poem, "Ultimately," appeared a month later. As Hanneman notes in *Ernest Hemingway: A Comprehensive Bibliography*, the *Double Dealer* was the first American magazine to contain a contribution by EH, other than his high school literary magazine, *Tabula* (135).

To Howell G. Jenkins, 4 August [1922]

Aug 4—

Dear Carper—

Flew to Strasburg from Paris in 2 hrs 1/2—10 on the train! Flew over the Vosges and went over across the Rhine into Germany.[1] At 850 marks to the dollar two people can live all day for a dollar.[2] Beer 10 marks a stein. They have storks sitting on the roofs of the houses up here. Did you men go fishing? Shoot me all the dope—

always

Steen

Dick Baum was in town.[3] Very drunk!

phPUL, A Postcard S; postmark: [*place illegible*], 8 / 5–8 / 22

Although the postmark is partially illegible, the postage stamp indicates that this card was mailed in France.

1 EH described the journey in "A Paris-to-Strasbourg Flight Shows Living Cubist Picture," (*Toronto Daily Star*, 9 September 1922; *DLT*, 205–7).
2 The *Toronto Daily Star* published two pieces by EH about the post-WWI hyperinflation of the German mark: "Germans Are Doggedly Sullen or Desperate Over the Mark" (1 September 1922; *DLT*, 194–96) and "Crossing to Germany Is Way to Make Money" (19 September 1922; *DLT*, 208–10). By November 1923 the exchange rate was one trillion marks to one dollar.
3 Richard T. Baum, fellow member of ARC Ambulance Service Section 4.

To Ezra Pound, [12 August 1922]

[*William Bird writes:*]

Surprised to learn from this that Hem had been here before, during war.

WB

[*EH writes:*]

Denial registered. Suggest useing this as frontispiece to Hueffer's book.[1]

Hem

IndU, A Postcard S; verso: image of woman reclining on a park bench with one leg over a soldier who is reclining on the ground, with caption, "Repos du Soldat et d'un Ange Gardien" [Rest of Soldier and a Guardian Angel]; postmark: [*place illegible*], 12–8 / 22

Although the postmark is partially illegible, the postage stamp indicates that this postcard was mailed in France. William (Bill) Bird was an American correspondent and Director of the Continental branch of the Consolidated Press in Paris. He and EH met on the train en route to cover the Genoa Conference in the spring of 1922 and became good friends. That summer Bird purchased a hand press and installed it at 29 Quai d'Anjou on the Ile Saint Louis, founding the Three Mountains Press; EH put Bird in touch with Pound, and by 1 August Pound had agreed to edit a six-book series for the press, titled, "An Inquest into the State of Contemporary English Prose" (Hugh Ford, *Published in Paris: American and British Writers, Printers, and Publishers in Paris, 1920–1939* [New York: Macmillan Publishing Company, 1975], 95–100; Reynolds *PY*, 80).

Bill and Sally Bird, along with Lewis Galantière and his fiancée, Dorothy Butler, joined EH and Hadley in August 1922 for a fishing and hiking trip in the Black Forest of Germany. Bird figures by name in two of EH's accounts of the trip published in the *Toronto Daily Star*: "Once

Over Permit Obstacle, Fishing in Baden Perfect" (2 September 1922; *DLT*, 197–200) and "German Inn-Keepers Rough Dealing with 'Auslanders'" (5 September 1922; *DLT*, 201–4).
1 English novelist Ford Madox Ford (1873–1939) legally changed his name from Ford Hermann Hueffer in 1919. EH refers to Ford's *Women and Men*, published in 1923 as the second volume in Pound's "Inquest" series.

To Ezra Pound, [c. late August 1922]

Dear Ezra—

There's a little monkey maiden looking eastward toward the sea,
There's a new monkey soprano a'sobbing in the tree,
And Harold's looking very fit the papers all agree.[1]

L'ENVOI[2]
It was quite an operation,
But it may have saved the Nation,
And what's one amputation
To the tribe?

Yours very sincerely, my dear Pound,

Rudyard Kipling

Hotel Loewen National
Triberg,
Baden,
Germany.

IndU, TLS signed "Rudyard Kipling" in EH's hand

1 EH parodies the opening lines of Rudyard Kipling's poem "Mandalay" ("By the old Moulmein Pagoda, lookin' eastward to the sea, / There's a Burma girl a-settin', and I know she thinks o' me") to lampoon Harold F. McCormick (1872–1941), a wealthy Chicagoan who recently had undergone a widely publicized "rejuvenating operation" (see "McCormick's Surgeon Silent on Gland Story / Millionaire Is Recovering from Operation," *Chicago Daily Tribune*, 18 June 1922, 2; and "McCormick Silent on His Operation," *New York Times*, 19 June 1922, 13). Also in the news that summer were reports from Paris that Russian doctor Serge Voronoff (1866–1951) was experimenting with monkey gland transplants in humans ("Wizard Surgeon Plans Renewing All Vital Organs," *Chicago Daily Tribune*, 20 June 1922, 4; Reynolds *PY*, 65–66), as well as reports of a romance between Polish opera singer Ganna Walska and McCormick,

who divorced Edith Rockefeller in 1921. On 11 August 1922, McCormick wed Walska in Paris, becoming her fourth husband ("Ganna Walska and M'Cormick on Honeymoon," *Chicago Daily Tribune*, 12 August 1922, 5).

2 Envoi, concluding segment of a poem, often summarizing the moral of the whole or serving as a dedication. Pound and Kipling each wrote a poem by this title.

To Hemingway Family, 25 August 1922

Triberg in the Black Forest.

August 25, 1922.

Dear Folks—

Hash and I and Bill Bird of the Consolidated Press and his wife have been tramping through the Black Forest having a wonderful time. Because the mark keeps dropping we have more money than when we started two weeks ago and if we stayed long enough could doubtless live on nothing. Economics is a wonderful thing.

Thank you very much Dad and Mother for the birthday greetings and for the lovely handkerchiefs. I appreciated them very much.

We have been trout fishing several times here and Hash cought three nice big ones the first time she fished. We got ten one day and six another and I picked up five in the Elz river with the fly. I am still using my old McGintys and they seem to have a good international flavor.[1]

How did the summer camp go? And what sort of a summer did you all have? We haven't had any news for a long time. I'm enclosing some German money for Dad. Hope everything is going well. I'll shoot you a good letter as soon as I can get a lot of this work cleared up. We go off on a hike for two or three days over the mountains and through the forest and then get back to our typewriters and have our livings to earn.

Love to everybody, belated birthday greetings to Mother in June, Carol in July and Pop in September. Not to mention Nunbones coming on in Thanksgiving time.[2] Which reminds me that when we were down in Italy the last time we had a wonderful young turkey in a restaurant in Mestre for 20 cents apiece. But there wasn't any cranberry sauce.

Always

Ernie

Hash sends her love too. We're going to Frankfurt and take the boat trip down the Rhine to Cologne where Chink is with his regiment.[3]

The sixty two marks will buy 6 steins of beer. 10 newspapers. Five pounds of eating apples. or a seat at the theater. I'll try and send you some of the good looking money next time. They have some notes that are very beautiful. Saved some for you for a long time and then had to use them.

Ernie

JFK, TLS

1 Widely used in fly-fishing for trout, the McGinty fly resembles a bumblebee or wasp.
2 Grace's birthday was 15 June; Carol's, 19 July; Clarence's, 4 September; and Sunny's, 28 November.
3 Dorman-Smith was stationed at the British Occupation Garrison.

To Gertrude Stein, 28 August 1922

28/8/22—Triberg—Baden—

Suppose you all have gone back to Paris by now but maybe not.[1] We can't afford to leave this country. I'll never be able to spend a franc again without a heart burn when I think that it's worth 150 marks = 10 beers, or 5 fishing licenses, or a bottle of Wachenheimer.[2] We caught 10 trout one day but I'm homesick for Paris.

Best luck

Ernest Hemingway—

Yale, A Postcard S; verso: image of a man and four women in costume with caption, "Badische Volkstrachten. Glotterthäler aus Glotterthal" [Folk costumes of Baden. Natives of Glotterthal]; postmark: TRIBERG, 31.8.22.5–6N

Beneath the image and printed caption on the postcard, EH wrote, "Fall modes at the Local Yvonne Davidson's." The French-born Yvonne Davidson (d. 1934) and her husband, American sculptor Jo Davidson (1883–1952), were good friends of Stein and Toklas. (Among his most famous works is a Buddha-like sculpture of Stein, a photograph of which appeared in *Vanity Fair* in February 1923, along with Stein's word-portrait of him.) During WWI Yvonne ran a hospital for wounded officers near Perpignan; after the war she established innovative dressmaking shops in Paris and became a prominent name in fashion.

1 In August 1922, Stein and Toklas traveled to Provence for a vacation with sculptor Janet
   Scudder and her companion, Camille Lane Seygard. After their friends purchased a home in
   Aix-en-Provence, Stein and Toklas settled into a hotel in Saint-Rémy and did not return to
   Paris until March 1923.
2 A Riesling wine.

To Ezra Pound, 31 August 1922

Anonymous has always been my favourite author! Who is this impostor
"Strictly Anonymous"? Cut off the head and the legs of the wench on the
back of this and see if she doesnt remind you of Picasso's blue period.[1]

IndU, A Postcard; letterhead: J. BERNARD-MASSARD, SEKTKELLEREI / TRIER
a.d. MOSEL; verso: image of Greek goddess Hebe (cupbearer to the Gods), with three
angels holding oval labels bearing the names of specialities of the
J. Bernard-Massard wine cellar; with caption, "Göttin 'Hebe' ihre Lieblinge bezeich-
nend." [Goddess Hebe naming her favorites]; postmark: TRIBERG, 31.8.22.5–6N

1 Reference to Spanish painter Pablo Picasso (1881–1973) and the paintings of his "Blue
   Period" (c. 1901–1904).

To Gertrude Stein, [20 September 1922]

Had to go ~~back~~ down here to see Clemenceau[1]— Aren't you all ever
coming back to Paris? Might pretty near as well not— It's winter up here
now. Hope you come back soon.

Ernest Hemingway.

Yale, A Postcard S; verso: LES SABLES D'OLONNE. Le Pont d'Enfer; postmark:
[*illegible*], 20–9 / 22

1 French statesman Georges Clemenceau (1841–1929) served twice as prime minister, 1906–
   1909 and 1917–1920. After the war, he demanded harsh peace terms, insisting on German
   disarmament and strict reparations. EH joined Bill Bird on an excursion to Clemenceau's
   retreat near Les Sables d'Olonne, a French resort town on the Atlantic. In a letter to EH of 25
   September 1922 (JFK), John Bone acknowledged receipt of the Clemenceau interview,

enclosed in a 14 September letter from EH that remains unlocated. However, Bone took issue with Clemenceau's derisive comments about Canada's role in the war, and the *Star* did not publish the interview.

To John McClure, [c. September 1922]

Dear Mr. McClure:—

Mr. Lewis Galantiere, some months ago, suggested that when I write you I should tell you, for him, that you were a son of a bitch. I did so in jest.

I now send you the same message, not from M. Galantiere but from myself, and this time in earnest. You are a son of a bitch Mr. McClure, I repeat it.

For some time the title—Double-Dealer puzzled me. It is no longer a puzzle. Double Dealer means that your practice is to rook, gyp or kike both the subscriber and the contributor.

If you have enough money to buy the back cover of the New Republic why not pay for contributions[1]

JFK, AL

EH is responding to a letter from McClure, managing editor of the *Double Dealer*, turning down a group of EH's poems and encouraging him to send more work. McClure praised EH's "A Divine Gesture" and "Ultimately" (which appeared in the May and June 1922 issues) and encouraged him to send more work for consideration. He added that the magazine owed EH "several dollars on those" and said the check probably would arrive late in September, assuring EH that "there is no intention or likelihood of the Double Dealer's defaulting—it is merely in arrears" (JFK, [3(?) August 1922]). EH wrote this response, apparently unfinished and unsent, on the verso of handwritten notes documenting his September 1922 interview with Georges Clemenceau (the numbered pages of which continue in JFK, Item 773).

1 A full-page advertisement for the *Double Dealer* ran on the back cover of the 2 August 1922 *New Republic*. Whether EH ever received payment for his contributions to the *Double Dealer* is not known.

To Howell G. Jenkins, 26 September [1922]

Sept 26—

Dear Carper—

Passed through here going on the Simplon Orient en route to Constantinople for the Star.[1] Love to Dirty Dick and yourself—

Steen

phPUL, A Postcard S; postmark: MILANO / FERROVIA, 26 IX / 1922

1 The Simplon Orient Express, a deluxe train that ran between Paris and Constantinople via the Simplon Tunnel connecting Switzerland and Italy, began service in the spring of 1919 ("Paris-Orient Line To Be Opened May 1 / Part of the Train Service Through Non-Teuton Countries Starts April 15," *New York Times*, 28 March 1919, 13). EH was traveling to cover the final Turkish offensive of the Greco-Turkish War (1920–1922). The *Toronto Daily Star* published nineteen of his pieces between 30 September and 14 November 1922 (*DLT*, 216–52). His experiences there also figured in later works, including three chapters of *iot*, "Introduction by the Author" (*IOT*, 1930; later published as "On the Quai at Smyrna"), "A Natural History of the Dead" (*DIA*), and "The Snows of Kilimanjaro" (*FC*). (See Jeffrey Meyers, "Hemingway's Second War: The Greco-Turkish Conflict, 1920–1922," *Modern Fiction Studies* 30, no. 1 [Spring 1984]: 25–36.)

To Gertrude Stein, [c. 27 September 1922]

Going through here enroute to Constantinople etc.[1] Good hot weather. Train Six hours late now and rapidly getting later. You ought to make it some time in the Ford—[2]

Ernest Hemingway

Yale, A Postcard S; verso: image of street scene with caption, "Sophia. 'Boulevard Dondoukoff'"; postmark: [*illegible*]

1 EH briefly passed through Sofia, capital of Bulgaria, on his way to Constantinople.
2 In 1917 Stein acquired a Ford van, which she used to transport medical supplies for the American Fund for French Wounded; specially outfitted with a truck body, it was nicknamed "Auntie." In 1920, needing a "civilian" vehicle after the war, she bought a two-seater Ford; bare of amenities, it was dubbed "Godiva."

To John Bone, 27 October 1922

74 Rue du Cardinal Lemoine
Paris, France.
October 27, 1922.

John R. Bone Esq.
Managing Editor,
The Toronto Star,
Toronto, Canada.

Dear Mr. Bone:—

Enclosed is an expense account for the Constantinople trip. I hope there are no mistakes in it, but as I have no adding machine the auditor may find some.

The account is fairly self explanatory, however there are one or two items that perhaps should be explained. The charge of $30.00 for a visa to enter the Kingdom of the Serbs, Croats and Slovenes was a rank hold up. They refused to honor my return visa and it was a case of paying the triple rate at the border or forfeiting my birth etc. and going back to Sofia and getting another visa.

The cable, a carbon of which I enclose, is not charged for on the expense account as it was sent under rather unusual circumstances. I was in Adrianople with all the wires cut and no way to get a dispatch out and this, which looked like a great story, on my hands.[1] The only way was to get it in to Constantinople by some one and out from there. I did not have enough money to go back to Constantinople, pay for the cable and get home and as I was running a fever of around 102 I was rather keen on getting home. I finally found an Italian Carabiniere who promised to get his Colonel who was returning to Constantinople at 5 o'clock the next morning, it's twelve hours on the train, to file it for me.

To solve the problem of how to pay for it I had it sent Receiver To Pay to Frank Mason of the International News Service Paris with instructions to relay it to Mr. Somerville in London. The I.N.S. has an account with the Eastern Telegraph Company.[2]

Mason's office relayed it promptly but proceeded to steal and re-write as much of it as they could get away with. I had to take the chance of that when I sent it but had placed more confidence in Mason's honesty than it deserved.

At any rate I have had it out with Mason. It was a personal matter and a question of ethics. Naturally there was no question of our paying for something which was pirated from us. Mason would not allow me to pay for it since he had stolen it, in any case. Mason assures me that he made sure there were no papers with the I.N.S. service in Canada before he touched the dispatch. I was disgusted with the matter. Legally, of course, he had a full right to re-write the dispatch considering the way it came to him, but ethically, as our ethics run in the profession over here, it was a very sorry business.[3]

I have been very worried about the articles I mailed to you from Constantinople and hope they all got through all right. Mrs. Hemingway wrote me every day for two weeks and I only got three of the letters, although they were all addressed the same. Some of them were returned to her at once and some of them are beginning to come back now. When I was in Adrianople there had been no mail delivery for about eight days. It is very hard to figure on postal service as before Mrs. Hemingway's letters stopped coming I received six letters from her that came through perfectly.

As for salary, I was actually out of Paris from September 25 to October 21.

I hope the articles are satisfactory. After I picked up the fever I felt very depressed about my work and when I felt too bad to go on the destroyer to Mytilene everything looked very black. Thrace bucked me up though. However, if the stuff isn't any good adjust the salary accordingly

[*Cable carbon begins here:*]
PLEASE RELAY BONE TORONTO STAR EXPENSES
CONSTANTINOPLE TWO HUNDRED DOLLARS TRAVEL INCLUSIVE
AND NINE DOLLARS PER DAY LIVING STOP WONDERFUL
ASSIGNMENT BUT IF WAR HASTE NECESSARY STOP IF NO WAR
GREAT SERIES NEAR EAST ARTICLES ANYWAY
HEMINGWAY.

[*Expense account begins here:*]
EXPENSES CONSTANTINOPLE AND NEAR EAST TRIP.
ERNEST M. HEMINGWAY.
Rec'd from Star Francs 6,501.70 equivalent of $500.00 cabled to me at the Surete Generale.

		Francs.
Sept. 21	Passport visas	
	Greece—	65.70
	Bulgaria—	12.00
	Yugo-Slav—	120.00
	Italy—	135.00

	Taxis and tips——	35.00
Sept. 22	Tip for reserving wagon lit—	20.00
Sept 25	Ticket and Wagon lit Paris—	
	Constantinople	1187.75
	Taxi	10.00
	Dinner—lunch wagon	7.50
Sept 26	on train	
	breakfast	6.00
	lunch	18.00
	dinner	16.00
Sept 27	on train	
	breakfast	7.50
	lunch	17.00
	dinner	18.00
Sept 28	on train	
	breakfast	7.00
	lunch	18.00
	dinner	18.00
Sept 29	on train	
	breakfast	7.00
	lunch	17.00
	tip to sleeping car porter	25.00
	Francs	1767.45

Arrived Constantinople Sept 29 at noon. expenses from now on given in Turkish pounds which I purchased at an average cost of 7 francs per Turkish pound. 100 piasters equals 1 Turkish pound which is symboled thus Ltq.

	Ltq.
cab—	2.00
porters	1.00
bridge toll	.10
tips	.90

Expenses page 2

Sept 29 continued		Ltq.
	street car	.10
	papers	.90
Sept 30.	lunch	1.20
	postage	.20
	cabs	3.40
	airplane post	2.00
	courier	1.00
	dinner	3.50
Oct. 1	lunch	1.00
	dinner	2.75
	postage	.20
Oct. 2	coffee	.05
	lunch	2.50
	dinner	5.00
Oct. 3	lunch	2.00
	dinner	2.50
Oct. 4	paper	2.50
	carbon	1.00
	lunch	1.25
	dinner	2.00
	papers	.45
Oct. 5	lunch	1.25
	stamps	.55
	tip to airplane pilot	1.50
	car fare to airport	1.00
	St. Stefano	
	dinner	3.50
Oct. 6	breakfast	.40
	lunch	2.00
	dinner	1.60
	quinine	.75
Oct 7	lunch	1.60

	cab	2.00
	laundry	3.75
	dinner	1.65
Oct 8	lunch	1.55
	postage	.55
	papers	.40
	dinner	2.00
Oct 9	lunch	1.75
	cab	2.50
	dinner	3.00
	airplane post	3.00
	papers	.30
Expenses page 3		Ltq.
Oct 10	paper	.10
	lunch	1.50
	cab	2.00
	dinner	2.00
Oct 11	lunch	1.50
	papers	.40
	dinner	3.00
	laundry	1.50
Oct. 12	lunch	1.50
	dinner	3.00
	Inter-allied visa and courier	1.80
Oct 13	Lunch	1.80
	Doctor's bill	10.00
	dinner	2.00
Oct 14	blankets	13.00
	lunch	1.50
	dinner	2.00
	quinine	.80
	aspirin	.40
Oct 15	porter	.80

	cab	1.50
	porter	.80
	bridge toll	.10
	lunch	3.00
	dinner	3.00
	porter	1.50
Oct. 16	Fee for Italian carabiniere transporting dispatch	3.00
Oct 17	Madame Marie hotel bill	7.00

Oct 18 on train	breakfast	5.00 French francs
	Lunch	18.00
	Serb visa	360.00
	dinner	18.00
Oct 19	breakfast	4.00
	lunch	19.00
	dinner	19.00
Oct 20	lunch	18.50
	dinner	19.00
Oct 21	breakfast	3.50
	tip to pullam porter	25.00
	cab	6.50

expenses page 4

R.R. fare and wagon lit from Constantinople to Adrianople and Adrianople to Paris – – – –	Ltq. 28.75
French francs	1000.00

Rec't enclosed.

Hotel Bills enclosed	Ltq.
	57.85
	18.37

Total Ltq.	76.22

Cables – – –	Receipts enclosed	21.44
		49.27
		9.48
		21.64
		32.16
		3.29
		28.53

Total	Ltq.	165.81
Total French francs spent – – – – – – –		F. 3281.97
Total Ltq. or Turkish pounds spent – – – – –		416.88 equals
at 7 french francs to the		
pound. – – – – – –		F.2918.16
Grand Total		
French francs		6200.13

add expenses Constantinople—Thrace

		Ltq.
Oct. 14—	papers	.45
Oct. 15—	papers	.35
Oct. 16—	papers	.35
	cab	3.00
Oct. 17	cab	2.50
	tips	1.00
Expenses censorwards entertainment—		28.00
– – – – – – – – – – – – – –		
	Total	Ltq. 125.00

Ltq. cost me 62¢ each at Constantinople.

Ltq. 125.00 – – – – 77.50

JFK, TLcc with enclosures

1 The city of Adrianople, about 130 miles northwest of Constantinople at the confluence of the Tundzha and Maritsa rivers, was returned to Turkey along with the rest of Eastern Thrace in an agreement settled at Mudania on 11 October 1922. In reports to the *Toronto Daily Star* EH described the ensuing mass evacuation of civilian refugees and retreating Greek troops, who cut the telegraph wires behind them ("Betrayal Preceded Defeat, then Came Greek

Revolt," 3 November 1922, *DLT*, 244–45; and "Refugee Procession Is Scene of Horror," 14 November 1922, *DLT*, 249–52).

2 Frank Mason worked for the International News Service (INS) from 1920 to 1931, and was then manager of the Paris office. Part of the publishing empire of William Randolph Hearst (1863–1951), this wire service began in 1909 and supplied stories to Hearst's many newspapers.

3 Before leaving Paris and in violation of his exclusive contract with the *Star*, EH had made a secret agreement with Mason to cable spot news stories to the INS, which published them under the byline of "John Hadley, International News Service Staff Correspondent." EH's disingenuous explanation here is in response to John Bone's cable of 6 October (JFK) that other news agencies were printing the same stories EH had sent the *Star*. For details of EH's duplicitous arrangement (of which Hadley disapproved) and EH's trip to cover the Greco-Turkish war, see Baker *Life* (97–99, 578–79), Reynolds *PY* (71–78), and Donaldson, "*Star*" (263–81).

To Gertrude Stein, [3 November 1922]

Glad to get back from this place. Paris is rainy and cold.[1] You all have the right dope. Are you going to stay down there all winter? When is the book out? Why don't you come back and cheer up this town?[2] I've given up my other pursuits and sleep all day. Sleep is a great thing. I've just discovered it. It's a fine way to spend the winter.

Hemingway

Yale, T Postcard S; verso: Constantinople. Vue de Scutari au Bosphore; postmark: [PARIS / R. M]ONGE, [*illegible*]—22

The conjectured postcard date is based on an archivist's notation on the postcard at Yale.

1 EH had returned to Paris on 21 October after his journey of nearly four weeks to Constantinople and the Greco-Turkish war.

2 Stein's *Geography and Plays* (Boston: Four Seas, 1922) was released on 15 December 1922. She and Toklas remained in Saint-Rémy until March 1923.

To Ezra Pound, [8 November 1922]

Wednesday Night—

Dear Ezra—

I was tricked into a very childish position by being forced to defend my journalese, which I recognize *is* journalese, from the charge of being journalese. It was all silly.

I assed myself beautifully trying to save Steffen's feelings by standing up for the weaknesses in my stuff which Steff admires because they are what he has always been shooting at. There is little gained being snotty to sweet old men.[1] I'm quitting the sheet. [This is between us.] I know what I'm after in prose, now anyway, [meaning for the present] and hope to give you a couple of samples of it at the end of six months.[2] If it is no fucking good I'll know it and praise by Steffens, Mrs. Butler, George Horace Lorimer, Paul Rosenfeld,[3] Bill Bird, Warren G. Harding,[4] H. L. Menken,[5] Pussyfoot Johnson,[6] Dave O'Neil,[7] Eugene O'Neil,[8] Florence O'Neil,[9] Rose O'Neil,[10] Mother MacCree,[11] Rudyard Kipling, Clare Sheridan,[12] Max Eastman, John Quinn,[13] John Drew,[14] John Wanamaker,[15] Malcolm Cowley,[16] or Leticia Parker will cut no bloody ice.

Meantime I appreciate that you stuck me on the Three Mountains dodger out of friendship and think I ought to leave you know that I will not attempt to crab the act, bust up the show or detonate in any other way if you now regret having publicly backed some one who you realize has nothing worth printing and want to yank me out of the sextette.[17]

You have my blessing Missou.[18] I still think you are the only living poet altho. I am glad to read Herr Elliot's adventure away from impeccability. If Herr Elliot would strangle his sick wife, buggar the brain specialist and rob the bank he might write an even better poem.[19]

The above is facetious.

See you tonight—

Hem

Indu, ALS; postmark: PARIS / R. MONGE, 9–11 / 22

EH addressed the envelope to "Ezra Pound Esq. / 70 bis Rue Notre Dame / Des Champs / Paris E.V." (an abbreviation for *en ville*, or within the city). EH also wrote on the envelope, "Pneumatique," indicating that it be sent via Pneumatic Post, the pressurized tube system in operation 1866–1984 that quickly conveyed mail in canisters from one Paris post office to another. Printed on the back flap of the envelope is "WINDERMERE / WALLOON LAKE, MICHIGAN" (the name of the family cottage misspelled); a notation in French on the envelope front, presumably in the hand of a postal employee, translates, "Deposited to the Postal Service. Exceeds maximum dimensions under article 25."

1 EH met Joseph Lincoln Steffens (1866–1936), pioneering American muckraking journalist, at the Genoa Conference in April 1922. They stayed in touch and attended the fight between Carpentier and Battling Siki (né Louis M'Barick Fall, 1897–1925) on 24 September 1922, the

night before EH left Paris for Constantinople (Reynolds *PY*, 73). When Steffens expressed admiration for the vividness of EH's cables from the Greco-Turkish war, EH corrected him for merely "seeing the scene," rather than admiring the language of the "cablese" (*The Autobiography of Lincoln Steffens* [New York: Harcourt, Brace and World, 1931], 834; Baker *Life*, 102). After reading EH's "My Old Man," Steffens submitted the story with his recommendation to *Cosmopolitan*; the magazine rejected it in December 1922 (Smith, 10–11).

2 Although he complained that journalism was interfering with his serious writing, EH continued to write for the *Star* until December 1923. For some time, John Bone had been eager for him to return to the *Star* office in Toronto (as evidenced in his letters to EH of 20 February, 30 August, and 2 November 1922; JFK). In response to a letter from EH that remains unlocated, Bone wrote to EH on 13 December 1922 that he was sorry to learn that EH was unlikely to return to Toronto "before next fall," assuring him, "we are always anxious to get your material" (JFK). EH did, in fact, return the next fall to Toronto, where Hadley gave birth to their son, John Hadley Nicanor Hemingway, on 10 October 1923. Soon thereafter, EH quit the *Star* for good and returned to Paris in January 1924 to pursue his art. Square brackets in this letter are EH's.

3 Paul Leopold Rosenfeld (1890–1946) was a prolific journalist, essayist, and music critic who wrote a monthly column, "Musical Chronicles," for the *Dial*.

4 Harding (1865–1923) was the twenty-ninth president of the United States, in office 1921–1923.

5 H. L. Mencken (1880–1956) was one of the most influential social and literary critics of the time. He served as editor, columnist, and political correspondent for the Baltimore *Herald* (1899–1906) and *Sunpapers* (1906–1941), and as literary editor and then co-editor, with George Jean Nathan, of the *Smart Set* (1908–1923). He and Nathan later co-founded the *American Mercury* (1924–1933), which Mencken edited.

6 William E. "Pussyfoot" Johnson (1862–1945), a former law enforcement officer and Prohibition advocate who edited the Anti-Saloon League's weekly publication, *New Republic* (1913–1916)—not to be confused with the politically progressive *New Republic* magazine, founded in 1914 and first edited by Herbert Croly (1869–1930).

7 David N. O'Neil (1874–1947) and his family, wealthy friends of Hadley from St. Louis, recently had moved to Paris. In a letter to EH of [1 November 1922], Pound encouraged EH to "bring O'Neil round" for a visit (JFK). A businessman with a law degree and a passion for poetry, O'Neil had published a collection of his poems, *Cabinet of Jade* (Boston: Four Seasons Company, 1918). He later co-edited *Today's Poetry*, a paperback anthology in the Ten Cent Pocket Series of Little Blue Books (Girard, Kansas: Haldeman-Julius Company, 1923). The volume included works by Pound, Dos Passos, T. S. Eliot, Robert Frost, Marianne Moore, and an array of other modern poets, as well as O'Neil's own.

8 Eugene O'Neill (1888–1953), American playwright, was awarded the Pulitzer Prize for Drama in 1920 for *Beyond the Horizon* and in 1922 for *Anna Christie*.

9 Protagonist of *Florence O'Neill, the Rose of St. Germains; or, the Siege of Limerick*, a novel by Agnes M. Stewart (New York: Kenedy, 1871).

10 Rose Cecil O'Neill (1874–1944), American artist and writer best known for her illustrations of "Kewpies," cupid-like infants with wings, which first appeared in the *Ladies' Home Journal* in 1909. The popular figures inspired an array of commercial products, including Kewpie dolls. In 1922 she published an illustrated collection of new poems, *The Master-Mistress* (New York: Alfred A. Knopf).

11 A variation of "Mother mo chroí," an Irish phrase and term of endearment meaning "mother [of] my heart," or "my dear." The phrase was used in popular song, "Mother Machree," composed in 1910 by Ernest Ball (1878–1927) with lyrics by Rida Johnson Young (1869–1926).

12 Sheridan (née Clare Consuelo Frewen, 1885–1970), London-born sculptor whose works included likenesses of Lenin, Trotsky, and Sheridan's cousin, Winston Churchill. She also

worked as a journalist in the 1920s, interviewing Mussolini at the Lausanne Conference in November 1922, as EH would note in his account for the *Toronto Daily Star* (27 January 1923; *DLT*, 256).

13 John Quinn (1870–1924), American lawyer, art patron, and influential collector who provided financial support for Joyce and T. S. Eliot. He subsidized *The Egoist*, *Transatlantic Review*, and *Little Review*, and he defended the *Little Review*'s editors against obscenity charges in 1921.

14 John Drew, Jr. (1853–1927) was a prominent actor on the American stage; he was the son of actors John Drew (1827–1862) and Louisa Lane Drew (1820–1897).

15 John Wanamaker (1838–1922), prominent Philadelphia businessman and civic leader, actively promoted the YMCA, served as U.S. postmaster general (1889–1893), and developed his dry goods business into one of the nation's first major department stores.

16 Malcolm Cowley (1898–1989), American poet, editor, and literary critic. After serving in the American Field Service in France in WWI and graduating from Harvard in 1920, Cowley left Greenwich Village in 1921 for Paris, where he published in both little magazines and prominent newspapers.

17 Pound had asked EH to contribute work to the "Inquest" series he was editing for Bill Bird's Three Mountains Press, and Bird printed a notice for the series while EH was in Constantinople. Because Pound did not know what EH would submit, the title of EH's contribution to the series appeared on the circular as "Blank." The six-volume series would include books by Pound; Ford; American poet William Carlos Williams (1883–1963); B. Cyril Windeler, British wood merchant and Air Force colonel; B. M. G. Adams, an upper-class English woman and close friend of Pound; and EH (Reynolds *PY*, 80; Ford, *Published in Paris*, 103–4).

18 Likely EH's playful phonetic spelling of "Monsieur," French for "mister."

19 Eliot's landmark poem "The Waste Land" was published in New York in the November 1922 issue of the *Dial* and awarded the magazine's annual prize of $2,000. Eliot's wife, Vivienne Haigh-Wood (1888–1947), suffered from physical and mental illness throughout her life; they married in 1915 and separated in 1933. Eliot worked as a clerk in the Colonial and Foreign Department at Lloyd's Bank from 1917 to 1925. Suffering a nervous collapse in 1921, he took a three-month rest cure on his physician's advice; during that time he was able to overcome a long writer's block and complete "The Waste Land" under the mentorship of Pound, to whom the poem is dedicated.

To Harriet Monroe, 16 November 1922

74 Rue du Cardinal Lemoine,

Paris.

November 16, 1922.

Miss Harriet Monroe,
Chicago, Illinois.

Dear Miss Monroe:—

I have been wondering when you were going to use the poems, as the Three Mountains Press here, Ezra Pound editing, is bringing out a book of my stuff shortly and I want to use the poems you have if you will give me permission to republish them.[1]

Paris seems fairly quiet now. Dave O'Neil of St. Louis whom you know, I believe, is in town with his family and will probably stay over here a couple of years. He says indefinitely, but that usually means two years.[2]

Mr. Walsh was in Germany when last heard from. I am just back from Constantinople so I don't know the very latest about Mr. Walsh, ~~but~~ I saw Padraic Colum one night but didn't mention the matter to him.[3]

Gertrude Stein is down in St. Remy in Provence and says she won't come back to Paris till after Christmas. We had an enormous candied casaba melon from her in the mail yesterday. It was pretty nearly as big as a pumpkin. She is doing a new book.

I don't know whether you ever knew Lewis Galantiere when he lived in Chicago. He has just undergone a very trying love affair with a girl from Evanston Ill. who is over here getting cultured. She's just left town and we have all cheered up.[4]

Hueffer is coming to town tomorrow to stay a month. He's been living on his farm in England. Joyce is sick at Nice. He has a dreadfully hard time with his eyes. Frank Harris has been trying to get Sylvia Beach, who published Ulysses, to publish his autobiography. She doesn't want to although I tell her it will be the finest fiction ever written.[5]

T.S.Eliot's new quarterly The Criterion seems to have inspired the Dial and their last issue was pretty good.[6] But that's American gossip, not Paris.

They say that Gargoyle is going to cease publication. I don't know that gang so I don't know.[7]

The hot rum punch and checker season has come in. It looks like a good winter. Cafes much fuller in the day time now with people that have no heat in their hotel rooms.

This reads like the personal column of the Petoskey Evening Resorter.[8] Perhaps the gossip bores you anyway.

Yours sincerely,
Ernest M. Hemingway.

UChicago, TLS

1 All six of EH's poems that appeared in the January 1923 issue of *Poetry* were included in his first book, *Three Stories and Ten Poems*, published in Paris in the summer of 1923 by Robert McAlmon's Contact Publishing Company. EH's contribution to Pound's "Inquest" series was *in our time*, a collection of prose vignettes, published in 1924 by the Three Mountains Press.

2 Monroe had published a group of O'Neil's poems in the November 1917 issue of *Poetry*. Having made a fortune in the lumber business in St. Louis, O'Neil retired at age forty-eight and in August 1922 moved to Paris with his wife Barbara and children George, Horton, and Barbara. EH predicted correctly: the O'Neils would return to the United States in August 1924 (EH to George and Helen Breaker, 27 August 1924 [JFK]).

3 Padraic Colum (1881–1972), Irish poet and playwright and a friend of James Joyce.

4 Galantière's fiancée, Dorothy Butler.

5 Hueffer, Ford Madox Ford. Frank Harris (né James Thomas Harris, 1856–1931), Irish writer and editor, was best known for his four-volume autobiography, *My Life and Loves*. Because its sexually explicit content would have subjected a publisher to the risk of imprisonment under obscenity laws, Harris had it privately printed. The first volume was published in Paris in 1922; the remaining volumes appeared in 1925 and 1927, printed in Nice for subscribers only.

6 The *Criterion*, a quarterly literary review, was established in London by T. S. Eliot's patron, Lady Rothermere (née Mary Lilian Share, 1875–1937), and edited by Eliot throughout its entire run, October 1922–January 1939. The first number featured Eliot's "The Waste Land." The poem also appeared in the November 1922 number of the *Dial*, alongside the work of Pound, Anderson, and Picasso.

7 Paris-based little magazine (1921–1922) co-edited by Arthur Moss (1889–1969) and his longtime partner Florence Gilliam, who moved from Greenwich Village to Paris in 1921. *Gargoyle* was the first English-language review of arts and letters to appear in Continental Europe after WWI; its contributors included Malcolm Cowley, Edna St. Vincent Millay, Hart Crane, Sinclair Lewis, and H.D. (Hilda Doolittle). After a brief but remarkable existence, it folded for lack of financial support.

8 The *Petoskey Evening News and Daily Resorter* began publication in 1902; in 1915, the title was shortened to The *Petoskey Evening News*.

To Hadley Richardson Hemingway, 24 November 1922

= BEAURIVAGE OUCHY 24 11^{H}40
= POOR DEAR WICKEY STOP ANXIEST HAVE YOU COME STOP
SORRY BUM LETTER WASNT MEANT BE STOP WIRE WHEN ARRIVE
WEATHER GORGEOUS STEEE[1] SENDS LOVE STOP LOVE POO
WEELL STOP DIJON WAYHOME TOO = POO

JFK, Cable; destination receipt postmark: PARIS / V / CENTRAL, 24–11 / 22

Address on the flap of the French "TÉLÉGRAMME" form reads: "HANDLY HEMINGWAY 74 / RUE CARDINAL LEMOINE PARIS." On 21 November, EH again crossed into Switzerland to cover the Lausanne Peace Conference, convened to settle territorial disputes in the wake of the

Greco-Turkish war. He had been sent by Frank Mason of INS and Charles Bertelli at Universal News Service, another Hearst organization, to supply wire service stories about the conference.

1 Likely a telegraph operator's error for "STEFF," i.e., Lincoln Steffens.

To Hadley Richardson Hemingway, 25 November 1922

= PARIS BEAURIVAGEOUCHY (25/11–12,33)=
SORRIEST SICK HUSTLE DOWN HERE SOONS WELL ENOUGH FEEL
TRAVELLY LOVE WICKY LOTSA SUN GOOD CLIMATE STOP IF
REALLY SICK ADVISE INSTANTLY AS GLAD CHANCE COME HOME
= = POO =

JFK, Cable; destination receipt postmark: PARIS / V / CENTRAL, 25–11 / 22

To Miriam Hapgood, [c. 26 November 1922]

SUNDAY

Dear Miriam=

Enclosed are the pictures. You look jolly enough. Guy is sending the one of your father, himself and Steff.[1] Do you think I look enough like a serious international journalist? It's a hard pose to keep up.

How goes school anyway? It looked a fine gloomy place that night.[2] Your father came up with us to the press room and he and Guy sat around and talked and I sat at the bar and drank beer and wrote dispatches and we had a jolly time. I was trying to work out a powerful piece that would link up the connection between the arrival of Chicherin, the coming General strike the upbreaking of the conference and the Ottoman debt.[3] It couldn't be done. Then I thought of you going into this darned big, castle like school with the long drive way and the hedge and the moon and the door opening and shutting in that heavy gloomy manner and you not knowing anybody and thought you were the only brave one in the bunch.

I Hope you're not feeling blue or lonesome or homesick, but in case you are remember that the three of us are only a couple of blocks away and thinkingabout you and wishing you luck and so you're not reallyalone in Lausanne at all. Of course if you want to luxuriate in the feeling of being all alone and nobody within miles that's all right too. Anyway I hope it's all going finely and that you're having a dreadfully good time. Hope I'll see you soon. Steff is going away maybe Tuesday and we'll have to try and seeyou before then. Maybe Hadley will be here before then and the two of them can combine to get you out to eat with us. All sorts of luck anyhow and I hope you're having a good time,

Your friend
Ernest Hemingway

I think the pictures are sort of fun, don't you?

Stanford, TLS

This letter was not mailed until EH enclosed it in his letter to Miriam Hapgood of [10 December 1922]. He met her in Lausanne through Lincoln Steffens, a close friend of her parents.

1 Guy Hickok (1888–1951) was a seasoned newspaper reporter and head of the Paris bureau of the *Brooklyn Daily Eagle* since 1918, with whom EH struck up a close friendship soon after arriving in Paris. Miriam's parents, American writers Hutchins Hapgood and Neith Boyce, met in 1897 while working on Steffens's muckraking newspaper *Commercial Advertiser* and married two years later.

2 In 1922, the Hapgoods sold their home in Dobbs Ferry, New York, and went abroad to France and Switzerland, placing all three of their children in boarding schools.

3 The *Toronto Daily Star* would publish two stories by EH about the Lausanne conference, including one on Russian Foreign Minister Georgi Chicherin ("Gaudy Uniform Is Tchitcherin's Weakness: A 'Chocolate Soldier' of the Soviet Army," 10 February 1923; *DLT*, 257–59).

To Pier Vincenzo Bellia, [c. 26 November 1922]

Carrissimo Papa—

We are near here and having a good time

JFK, A Postcard; verso: Aigle. Le Château et les Alpes.

The conjectured postcard date is based on EH's reference in his letter to Hadley (postmarked 28 November 1922, a Tuesday) to a motor trip he had taken on Sunday (presumably 26 November) that included Aigle, Switzerland. The postcard image depicts Château d'Aigle, a medieval castle that looms above the town against a backdrop of mountains. The card is addressed to "Bellia Pier Vincenzo / Via Pietro Micca 6. / Torino / Piedmonte / Italia." Having been "adopted" by Bellia and his family during his 1918 convalescent leave in Stresa, EH referred to him as "My 'Italian father,' Papa Count Bellia" (EH to Clarence Hemingway, 14 November 1918). The card apparently was neither completed nor sent.

To Frank Mason, [27 November 1922]

~~Story Broke Eleven 23 Oclock If you want 24 hour service pay for it.~~
Story Broke 22.30 Oclock
Twenty four hour service costly

Hemingway

JFK, ACDS

EH drafted this response on the verso of a cable from Mason dated 27 November 1922 and sent to "hemmingway" at the Hôtel Beau-Séjour in Lausanne: "new york cables quote tell hadley we scooped curzons—open door announcement—mason." EH had written articles for INS under the name of John Hadley. As the 28 November 1922 *New York Times* reported in a front-page story datelined "Lausanne, Nov. 27," British Foreign Minister George Curzon (1859–1925) had announced support of an "open door policy" to guarantee all nations free access to the strategically important Dardanelles Straits. To this cable from EH, Mason wired back on 28 November, "ernest story was surely worth tolls dont understand whether costly refers tolls or what regards mason" (JFK).

To Hadley Richardson Hemingway, [28 November 1922]

Dearest Wicky— Poor dear little Wicky Poo, I'm so sorry you've felt so frightfully rotten and sick. I've had the same stuff, cough up green stuff with black specks from wwy down in my chest with a frightful coughing and pain and stuffed up head using millions of handkerchiefs and me with only four. Certainly has been bad for us little tinies. I'm glad Leticia[1] has taken care of you but I feel as though I ought to be doing it and Gee I wish I were with you. Poor dear Poo.

This is the first time I've had to write a letter for days it seems. I never eat till way after two and dinner always leftovers and the three places I have to go back and forth between are about 3 kilometers apart up and down hill and your always afraid you're missing something at one place or the other and they all talk French and the Russians are miles out of the way and I'm only a little tiny wax puppy. Mason has kiked me so on money that I can't afford taxi's and have to take the street car and walk. And they expect me to cover them until midnight every night starting at nine in the morning.[2]

Sunday I layed off and went on a mtor trip (free) to Chateau D'oeux or however it's spelle[d] and then from there to Aigle and past the Diablerets and the old Dent and then to Montreux and then I outgot from the car and took the funicular up the hill and had supper with Gangwisch's. They've heard from Mab and Janet coming the 23rd and Chink on the Sixteenth and Izzy the 2nd they are all reserving rooms for and spoke so lovingly of my Poo and it was dark and no snow yet except Rocher du Naye and the Dent but there was snow in the air and Sunday night it snowed.[3] Even Lausanne full of snow now turned slushwards full of gravel and mud here but smooth and lovely looking on all the hills and mountains. Gangwisches think the O'Neil's ought to go to the Grand Hotel at Les Avants because there is good food and people and music etc. and at the Narcissus is bum food and a funereal solemnity and nthing.[4] We'd be Les Avantsward everyday and they'd be down with us. That is undoubtedly the play. Advise Barbara and Dave. Semms like to me anyway.

I'm so sick of this—it is so hard. Everybody else has two men or an assistant, and they expect me to cover everything by myself—and all for one of Masons little baby kike salaries. It's almost impossible cause they happen at the same time and far apart and evrything.

I've been crazy for you to come and would love so still but if you say you are too miserable for the trip you know what. But please Wickey realise that I want you and wasn't trying to stall. Right now while I'm writing this letter I should be at the Russians. But something like that has happened every time I've started aletter and so hellwards with them. Unless Mason gives me a lot of money I'll upgive the job some time this week, and if he does give me money you've got to come here sick well or anything. You can fly you know. Had you thought of that? Why don't you do it? Then there'll be no Vallorbe or anything. Look up the planes. You can come by way of Bale too.[5] They say that's easy.

There's a Colonel Foster, I think, here from St. Louis, elderly man, knows your father and everybody, white mustache. Friend of J. Ham Lewis's.[6] Admiral Bristol's come and they want to meet Mummy.[7] Everybody sends you love. Steffens wrote you a letter. I love you dearest Wicky—you write the very best letters. Anyhow both being laid out with colds we haven't lost so much time on the time of the month because you've probably been too sick. I do so hate for you to miss what is the most comfortable and jolly time for mums. Won't we sleep together though? If I upgive the job this week can you meet me at Dijon on a couple days notice. I'll have to wire you to send me the pissport registered.[8] Deer sweet little feather kitty with the castorated oil and the thowing up, I think it is so pitiful I could just cry.

> I'm just your little wax puppy.
>
> Love Pups to mups ——

Dear sweet Mummy!
  Did you write the Steins?
  [*Ditto marks*: Did you write the] Ford Madox Fords

> 50 Rue Vavin

JFK, TL with typewritten signature and autograph postscript; postmark: OUCHY, 28.XI.22.19

1 Hadley's friend from St. Louis, Letitia Parker.
2 EH's initial pay from the INS of $60 a week for salary and expenses was less than the *Star*'s $75 a week plus all expenses covered, and he had underestimated both the effort and costs involved in the Lausanne assignment. EH's salary and expenses are a dominant topic of his surviving correspondence with Mason (JFK; see also Donaldson, "*Star*," 94–96, and Reynolds *PY*, 84–85).
3 Hadley's friends from St. Louis, Mrs. Percival Phelan and her daughter Janet, and EH's Oak Park neighbor Isabelle (Izzy) Simmons would join the Hemingways and Chink for a holiday at the Gangwisch pension in Chamby (*SL*, 74; Diliberto, 142; Reynolds *PY*, 94). The towns of Château d'Oex and Aigle and the peaks of Les Diablerets, Dent de Jaman, and Rochers de Naye lie to the east and southeast of Montreux, within about a 30-mile radius of the city.
4 The 105-bed Grand Hôtel was the largest and most expensive of the three hotels in Les Avants. The "Narcissus" is probably the 145-bed Grand Hôtel des Narcisses in Chamby, the only hotel in that village (Karl Baedeker, *Switzerland: Handbook for Travellers* [Leipzig: Baedecker, 1922], 285–86).

5 Vallorbe, Swiss border town in the Jura Mountains. Bâle (French): Basel, Swiss city on the Rhine bordering France and Germany.
6 James Hamilton Lewis (1863–1939), U.S. senator from Illinois, 1913–1919 and 1931–1939.
7 Rear Admiral Mark Lambert Bristol (1868–1939), high commissioner of the United States at Constantinople (1919–1927), served in the U.S. delegation at the Lausanne conference.
8 EH and Hadley held a joint U.S. passport.

To Isabelle Simmons, [c.1 December 1922]

[*Letter begins here:*] come yet. I've been hoping and looking for her every day. If she can't come I'll wire the I.N.S. to get somebody else and go on back to Paris. Poor kid, she's been feeling awfully bum, and it's no fun being sick in Paris.

There are two good trains you can get to go from London to Montreux. You only get a ticket to Montreux. We'll meet you there. The railway from there is a little jerkwater and doesn't sell tickets outside of the country. Both trains leave London at 11 o'clock. One is the Simplon Orient Express which is sleepers only and fairly expensive and the other is a first second and third class train with sleepers from Paris to Montreux. You should book your sleeper ahead if you want one[.] It gets into the Gare de Lyons[1] in Paris at 7.25 in the evening, that's 19.25 by the continental twenty four hour time, and leaves at 8.35 for Switzerland. You can register your trunk straight through to Montreux, if you are bringing one, and it won't have to be examined at the Swiss frontier. They'll do it at the station in Montreux and we know them there and they'll just pass it. The Simplon Orient gets into Montreux at 6.57 in the morning and the other train at 8.57. The only advantage of the Simplon Orient is that you don't have to get out with your passport and hand baggage at the Swiss frontier at Vallorbe, they do it all in the train. In either event the examination is absolutely perfunctory. They just ask you if you have any gold money, chocolate, tobacco, and you say "rien" and they say, "merci mademoiselle" and that's all.[2]

But as it's the first time you're crossing a frontier, and it happens darned early in the morning, it's easiest if you take the Simplon-Orient. I don't know how much extra it is. Not an awful lot. But the other is perfectly good. And when you can't get a birth we've often sat up all night and it isn't at all bad. Any way good luck to yez.

You can eat very well in the Gare des Lyons. The restaurant is upstairs.[3]

Wish we were going to be with you coming down. It's lots of fun when about four or three or so people travel together like that cause you dominate the compartment and sit up and talk and get out at Dijon for sandwitches and watch the moonlight on the country going past and open the window as fast as the French close it and one lies down and goes to sleep and the others say "shhh—Malade!"[4] and look very solemn when anybody tries to come in the compartment. It is an easy trip anyway. I've made it about twelve times this last year.

I suppose Hadley's written you about clothes. Mostly girls wear riding breeches for skii-ing and bobbing with a sweater and a tam. If you haven't got mountain shoes you can get very good ones in Montreux. Also skii-ing mitts of canvas with a string to them are cheap there. You know the sort of clothes, Hadley is taking an evening dress too I think for going to a dance or such. We don't dress for dinner in the chalet. It's half the fun eating in your tough clothes. Hadley wears riding breeches, puttees or golf stockings, usually the latter, a white flannel shirt and a sweater or the jacket of her riding habit with a belt. There's nothing formal about the clothes except that everybody wears riding breeks instead of knickers. Knickers are too full for skii-ing and spilling into the snow.

We'll have a wonderful time. I think it's the finest thing ever heard of, you're being in Europe and coming down to Switzerland. World is a funny place. The Seventh of January is the big bob races for the Canton of Vaud on the Col de Sonloup piste—you'll be an intelligent member of a bob crew by that time. Sonloup is a wonderful course when it's right.

Chink is coming the 16th. You'll like him any amount. And I know you'll love Chamby and Les Avants. I figure it's the finest place in the world. We'll have a lot of stuff to read and if you've any of the new American stuff bring it along. Chink does about a book a day when he's in his stride. I read the Roosians and Joe Conrad pretty near always in the country—because they're so long.[5]

Well this ought to be mailed. I don't know yet why or how you're in Yarrup, but that's a minor part. Point is you're here. That's a fine point.

This conference is very dull and very secretive and everybody follows everyone else around—the Turks today are just like wood chucks when you wanto find them their in their holes and then they pop out as soon as your gone. Well—So Long—

as Ever

Ernie

PUL, TL/ALSFrag

The beginning of the letter is missing. During a 1923 tour of Europe with friends, Simmons would visit EH and Hadley in Switzerland and Italy.

1 The Gare de Lyon, built over the period 1895–1902 on the Boulevard Diderot in the twelfth arrondissement, is the station in Paris that serves most trains en route to points south and east.
2 Nothing (French); thank you, Miss (French).
3 The Buffet de la Gare de Lyon, above the main entry of the station, opened in 1901. It was renamed Le Train Bleu Restaurant in 1963 and in 1972 was designated an historic monument for its Belle Époque interior.
4 Sick (French).
5 Presumably EH is referring to such Russian writers as Anton Chekhov (1860–1904); Fyodor Dostoevsky (1821–1881), whose work he later recalled reading in translations he borrowed from Sylvia Beach (*MF*); Nikolai Gogol (1809–1852); Leo Tolstoy (1828–1910); and Ivan Turgenev (1818–1883); and to Polish-born English novelist Joseph Conrad (1857–1924).

To Alice Langelier, 5 December 1922

Lausanne, Suisse.

December 5, 1922.

Dear Miss Langelier:—

In your note of December 4th you say that you sent me a check for 2/6 week salary and expenses at $60. a week and 4/6 week at $90. figured into francs at the rate of 14.40.

According to a wire I received from Mr. Mason dated the 29th of November the weekly increase was to be $35.00, not $30.00. I will ask you to add to my next check the difference between 4/6 week salary at $90. and the same length of time at $95. figured at 14.40 francs to the dollar.

Does the division of the week into sixths mean that employees of the I.N.S. Paris office are not paid for working on Sunday? I would like to have this point made clear.

Very sincerely,

Ernest M. Hemingway

JFK, TLS

The 4 December 1922 letter from Langelier to which EH is responding (written on letterhead of
the International News Service's Paris Bureau at 10, Place de la Bourse) survives at the JFK, as
does Mason's cable of 29 November.

To Miriam Hapgood, [10 December 1922]

The next Sunday—

Dear Miriam—

Enclosed are the pictures and the first letter.[1] Now I'd better mail this
without going any further or next Sunday I'll be writing "enclosed are the
pictures, the first and second letters—"

Guy and Steff left last Tuesday. Haven't heard from them yet. Hadley
came Sunday I think it was. She wants very much to meet you and were
going to come calling Some day this coming week. I've been working awfully
hard at the conference and she's been laid up. Think the conference is
quieting down now. Had a letter from your father this morning. I'm awfully
fond of him.

Hope school is going not too badly. Would they let you come and dine
with us some night this week[?] Let me know and if they will Hadley will
write a fine invitation that will pass the inspection of any school mistress.

Your friend

Ernest Hemingway

Stanford, ALS; postmark: LAUSANNE [*envelope torn*] / 10 [*envelope torn*]

The conjectured letter date is based on EH's mention of Hadley's arrival. She left Paris on
Saturday, 2 December, arriving in Lausanne the next day. What EH does not mention here is
the theft at the Gare de Lyon of the suitcase containing nearly all his past year's writing, which
Hadley was bringing to him as a surprise so that he could work on his stories during their
winter holiday. EH's letter to Pound of 23 January 1923 is his first surviving account of the
legendary loss (*SL*, 76–77), which he would describe decades later in *MF*.

1 Enclosed with this is EH's previous "Sunday" letter to Hapgood, most likely written two
weeks earlier [c. 26 November 1922].

To Frank Mason, [c. 14 December 1922]

INTERNEWS PARIS[1]

FRANK WIRE

RUSH EIGHT HUNDRED SWISS FRANCS NECESSARY PROHOTEL
EXPENSES UNNEED CLOSE ACCOUNT BEFORE DOING THAT AS
FAR AS EYE OR I CAN SEE SIMPLY WIRED YOU PROGET ACTION
DUE NECESSITY BANK WAITING SIGNATURE WILL GIVE YOU
BLANK CHECK COVERING ON GUARANTEE IF YOU WISH
FORWARDING YOU ACCOUNT HAVE UNREQUIRED TELEGRAPH
RECEIPTS PROPARIS BUT IF MY ACCOUNT UNSATISFACORY
WILLING BEAR LOSS IT WONT BE FIRST OR ONLY WORKING
SATURDAY MORNING NOON NIGHT IMPORTEST MEWARDS GET
EIGHT HUNDRED FRANCS PRECLOSING BANKS SATURDAY
REGARDS HEMINGWAY

JFK, TCD

The conjectured letter date is based on Mason's cabled response, dated 14 December 1922
(JFK): "ernest our books show approximately 500 swiss francs will be due you saturday but
must have your receipts for continental telegrams and accounting for 250 originally advance
you before can make final settlement stop sending you our statement by mail express stop
please rush your receipts and advise balance due us stop advise whether you working inclusive
saturday and sunday night kindest regards you both = mason"

1 Cable address for the International News Service.

To Frank Mason, [c. 15 December 1922]

INTERNEWS PARIS

SUGGEST YOU UPSTICK BOOKS ASSWARDS HEMINGWAY

JFK, TCD

EH apparently is responding to Mason's cable of 14 December, and perhaps also to Mason's
cable of 15 December 1922 (JFK), in which he advises EH, "instead sending me blank check
suggest simpler you telegraph directly your bank instructing them buy required swiss francs
telegraph them youward stop if youll simultaneously wire me copy message bankward ile
personally go bank upspeed them muchs possible."

To Frank Mason, 15 December 1922

Hotel Beau-Sejour
Lausanne, Suisse.
December 15, 1922.

Dear Frank—

Enclosed please find two receipts for wires prepaid by me. The one to N.Y. was prepaid by mistake by the concierge of the hotel here who did not know I, or you rather, had an account.

These vouchers amount to francs swiss 30.10. As you require receipts I am making no claim for the other numerous telegrams I sent you from here.

30.10 deducted from the 250.00 swiss francs which you advanced me leaves 219.90 swiss francs which I owe the I.N.S. according to your books.

You will please therefore deduct this sum from however many swiss franks you decide the I.N.S. owes me on Saturday at midnight and forward me the difference to Chalet Chamby, Chamby sur Montreux, Suisse.

Your refusal to wire me 800 swiss francs which I urgently needed has caused me a great deal of inconvenience, has smashed up all my plans and made me a great deal of extra expense. I can only regard it as an unfriendly and insulting action.

Of course it was asking you to do me a favor which you have a a perfect right to refuse. I did not expect you to refuse however since I had been doing a twenty four hour shift here for you at fifty dollars a week as a favour to you. The net result of my work here for the I.N.S. has been a net loss to me of $15.00. My salary has all gone into my expenses the 250 francs you have wired so much about were all spent on necessary expenses.

I wired you for money in the first place as that is the simplest easiest and most logical way for a newspaperman to get money; from his office. Banks are slow and there is supposed to be some benefits from an "organization". There seems no possible way to regard your refusal to forward the money to me except as a belief on your part that I was planning or t[r]ying to gyp you in some way. There may still be some way for you to change this view, which at present is the only possible one for me to hold. I hope there is.

Very sincerely,

JFK, TLcc

The recipients of letters included in this volume are identified here, rather than in endnotes, unless additional information is deemed necessary in the context of a particular letter. When a recipient cannot be identified by name, when the recipient's name has been conjectured by the editors, or when Hemingway's letter is directed to a publication, business, or other institutional recipient rather than a named individual, any editorial commentary will appear in an annotation to that letter. We provide birth and death dates for each recipient whenever possible. When we have been unable to confirm both dates, we have supplied whatever partial dating information we have been able to establish.

Sherwood Anderson (1876–1941). American novelist and short story writer who had written *Winesburg, Ohio* (1919) and *Poor White* (1920) when he and EH met in Chicago in 1921 through their mutual friend Y. K. Smith. Following his own first trip to Paris that year, Anderson suggested to EH that he move to Paris to pursue serious writing, providing letters of introduction to Sylvia Beach, Lewis Galantière, Ezra Pound, and Gertrude Stein.

Tennessee Claflin Mitchell Anderson (1874–1929). Piano tuner and music teacher of independent spirit when she and Sherwood Anderson met in Chicago in 1914. They married in 1916 and divorced in 1924.

Ruth Arnold (b. 1890). Grace Hall Hemingway's live-in music student from 1907 to 1919, who also assisted in the care of the Hemingway children and the upkeep of the family's Oak Park home. (In the 1910 U.S. Census record of the household, she is listed as a governess.) Although Clarence Hemingway banished her from the house under unclear circumstances in 1919, she remained Grace's lifelong friend.

Lawrence T. Barnett. A resident of the Chicago suburb of Winnetka, Illinois, Barnett served with EH in Italy in WWI in the American Red Cross Ambulance

Service Section 4. They maintained a friendship after the war, fishing together in northern Michigan. [Lawry, Lawrey, Barney, Marby]

Pier Vincenzo Bellia. A wealthy resident of Turin, Italy, who, along with his wife and three daughters, met and befriended EH when he was on convalescent leave in Stresa in September 1918.

Fannie Bernice Biggs (1884–1957). EH's high school English teacher, who taught courses in journalism and the short story and encouraged his passion for writing. She held A.B. and M.A. degrees from the University of Michigan and taught at Oak Park and River Forest High School 1912–1920.

John Rainsford Bone (1877–1928). A native of Ontario and an 1899 graduate in mathematics from Toronto University, Bone joined the staff of the *Toronto Daily Star* in 1900. He served as managing editor from 1907 until his death. Recognizing EH's talent as a freelance writer for the *Star*, Bone offered him regular employment on the paper in 1921.

Georgianna Bump (1903–1983). Younger sister of Marjorie Bump and a 1921 graduate of Petoskey High School, Georgianna was among the teenage girls with whom EH socialized in the fall of 1920. [Pudge, Useless]

Marjorie Bump (née Lucy Marjorie Bump, 1901–1987). A Petoskey native and one of EH's closest friends in northern Michigan. They met in 1915 in Horton Bay, where her uncle, Ernest L. Ohle, a professor at Washington University in St. Louis, had a summer home. Marjorie and Georgianna were daughters of Mate and Sidney Bump, founder of Bump and McCabe Hardware store in Petoskey. [Marge, Barge, Red]

Kate Buss (1884–1943). Poet and critic from Medford, Massachusetts, author of *Jevons Block: A Book of Sex Enmity* (1917) and *Studies in the Chinese Drama* (1922), and friend of the expatriate avant-garde in Paris. Buss avidly promoted Gertrude Stein's career, and her own publisher (Four Seasons Company of Boston) brought out Stein's *Geography and Plays* in 1922 at Stein's own expense. Stein's *Portraits and Prayers* (1934) included a piece devoted to her, titled "To Kitty or Kate Buss."

Miss Conger. An employee at the *Co-operative Commonwealth* in Chicago to whom EH wrote c. 1921 with layout instructions for an issue of the magazine.

Dorothy Connable (1893–1975). Daughter of Ralph Connable, Sr., and Harriet Gridley Connable of Toronto. Six years EH's senior, she had served with the Red Cross in France during WWI, establishing a YMCA for American soldiers, and aided the occupying army in Germany after the Armistice. She and EH became friends in early 1920, when he moved into the Connable home as a paid companion to her brother, Ralph, Jr.

Harriet Gridley Connable (b. circa 1871). While visiting her mother in Petoskey, she heard EH speak about his war experiences at a Ladies Aid Society meeting in December 1919. She was impressed and asked EH to move to Toronto for a few months to act as a live-in companion to her disabled nineteen-year-old son. EH accepted the offer and moved into the family's mansion in January 1920. Harriet's husband, Ralph Connable, Sr., a native of Chicago, headed the F. W. Woolworth Company in Canada.

Elizabeth Dilworth (née Elizabeth Jane Bewell, 1864–1936). She and her husband, James Dilworth (1856–1936), ran the blacksmith shop, chicken dinner restaurant, and Pinehurst Cottage guest house in Horton Bay. She and Grace Hall Hemingway were friends, sharing an interest in painting. As a teenager, EH frequently bunked at the Dilworth place and caught fish to be served to their dining room clientele. [Aunty Beth]

Lewis Galantière (1895–1977). Born in Chicago of French parents, he became one of EH's first friends among the American expatriates in Paris via an introductory letter from Sherwood Anderson. Galantière worked for the International Chamber of Commerce in Paris from 1920 to 1927. Under the name Lewis Gay, he wrote a column for the Paris *Tribune's* Sunday magazine called "Reviews and Reflections" beginning in 1924.

James Gamble (1882–1958). A captain in the American Red Cross, Gamble was Field Inspector for the ARC Rolling Canteen Service and EH's commanding officer at the time he was wounded in July 1918. In late December 1918, Gamble paid for EH to join him for a vacation in Taormina, Sicily. A 1906 Yale graduate who then studied at the Pennsylvania Academy of Fine Art, Gamble was living as a painter in Florence, Italy, at the outbreak of WWI. After the war, he returned home to Philadelphia and his career as a painter. [Jim]

Emily Goetzmann (b. 1898). Friend of EH and his sister Marcelline who moved from Oak Park to La Crosse, Wisconsin, sometime after 1912. EH wrote to her in 1916.

Irene Goldstein (1899–2004). Born in Chicago and a resident of Petoskey from infancy, Goldstein met EH at a party at nearby Bay View in late 1919. They spent time together both in Petoskey and in Chicago, where she attended a physical education program at Columbia College before taking a one-year teaching position in Grand Island, Nebraska. In later years she recalled that she had received dozens of letters from EH but kept very few of them. [Yrene]

Leicester Campbell Hall (1874–1950). EH's uncle; younger brother of Grace Hall Hemingway. A successful attorney in Bishop, California, he fought against discrimination on behalf of Japanese-Americans and Native Americans. After a long bachelorhood, he married Nevada Butler, and when the United States entered WWI, he enlisted in the U.S. Army despite his age, serving as a supply officer for the 617th Aero Corps. He went missing in action in France in September 1918, returning home in December to learn that his wife had died of influenza.

Nevada Butler Hall (d. 1918). Daughter of Belle and James Butler, who discovered the silver and gold fields of Tonopah, Nevada, in 1900. In 1916 she was elected chair of the Republican Central Committee of Inyo County, California. When her husband, Leicester, was serving in WWI, she visited the Hemingways in Oak Park, becoming a favorite of all; after returning to California, she died in the influenza pandemic.

Miriam Hapgood (1906–1990). Daughter of American journalist, poet, and fiction writer Neith Boyce (1872–1951) and journalist and social critic Hutchins Hapgood (1869–1944); niece of journalist, critic, and editor Norman Hapgood (1868–1937). EH and Hadley befriended Miriam in 1922 when she was in a boarding school at Lausanne.

Adelaide Edmonds Hemingway (1841–1923). EH's paternal grandmother, who was educated at Wheaton College, where she met Anson Hemingway. They married in 1867 and raised their six children in Oak Park, Illinois.

Anson Tyler Hemingway (1844–1926). EH's paternal grandfather, a veteran of the Civil War who fought under Ulysses S. Grant at the Battle of Vicksburg in 1863. In addition to running a successful Oak Park real estate business, he was a civic leader, active in the YMCA, First Congregational Church, and other community organizations.

Carol Hemingway (1911–2002). EH's sister and fifth of the six Hemingway children. [Dee, Deefish, Nubbins, Nubs]

Clarence Edmonds Hemingway (1871–1928). EH's father. A native of Oak Park, Illinois, he graduated from high school in 1890, attended Oberlin College in Ohio, and received his medical degree from Rush Medical College in Chicago in 1896. That year he married Grace Hall, an 1891 graduate of Oak Park and River Forest High School. In addition to practicing medicine, he was an avid hunter and naturalist and founded a local chapter of the Agassiz Club for youth in Oak Park. He suffered bouts of severe depression after 1903; he died of a self-inflicted gunshot wound at the age of fifty-seven.

Grace Adelaide Hemingway (1881–1959). EH's aunt; Clarence Hemingway's younger sister. She served as secretary of the Chicago branch of the National Story Teller's League and taught children's literature on the faculty of the National Kindergarten and Elementary College in Chicago. She lived with and cared for her parents, Adelaide and Anson Hemingway, until their deaths; in 1927 she married Chester Gilbert Livingston (1880–1961).

Grace Hall Hemingway (1872–1951). EH's mother. She and Clarence Hemingway met as high school students in Oak Park, and they married 1 October 1896. In her youth, Grace had aspired to be an opera singer and studied in New York City in 1895–1896. A well-known music teacher in Oak Park, she also directed the children's vested choir and orchestra of the Third Congregational Church. A strong-willed woman with progressive views on the role of women in society, she lobbied for women's suffrage and was active in civic organizations.

Hadley Richardson Hemingway (née Elizabeth Hadley Richardson, 1891–1979). EH's first wife. A native of St. Louis, Missouri, she attended Mary Institute, a private school for girls, graduating in 1910. She and EH met in Chicago in the fall of 1920 through their mutual friend Kate Smith, and were married at Horton Bay, Michigan, on 3 September 1921. They had one child, John Hadley Nicanor Hemingway (1923–2000). They divorced in 1927. [Binnes, Binney, Bones, Hash, Poo, Wickey, Wicky, Wicky Poo]

Leicester Hemingway (1915–1982). EH's brother and youngest of the six Hemingway children. [Bipe House, Bipehouse, Dessie, Lessie]

Madelaine Hemingway (1904–1995). EH's sister and fourth of the Hemingway children. [Nun Bones, Nunbones, Nunny, Sunny]

Marcelline Hemingway (1898–1963). EH's older sister and first of the Hemingway siblings. They graduated together in the Oak Park and River Forest High School class of 1917. [Ivory, Marc, Marce, Marse, Mash, Masween]

Ursula Hemingway (1902–1966). EH's sister and third of the Hemingway children. [Ted, Ura, Urra, Urs]

William D. Horne, Jr. (1892–1986). A 1913 graduate of Princeton University, Horne met EH in the American Red Cross Ambulance Service in WWI and the two became close friends. They were roommates in Chicago during 1920–1921, and Horne was a member of the wedding party when EH and Hadley married in 1921. [Bill, Horney Bill, Horney]

Howell G. Jenkins (1894–1971). A native of Evanston, Illinois, and a fellow member of American Red Cross Ambulance Service Section 4 in Italy in WWI, Jenkins was another of EH's closest friends. He was one of EH's fishing and camping companions in Michigan in the summer of 1919 and a member of his wedding party in 1921. [Carp, Carpative, Carper, Fever, Jenks, Lever]

Alice Langelier. An employee at the Paris office of the International News Service to whom EH wrote in 1922.

Kathryn Longwell. A 1919 graduate of Oak Park and River Forest High School, she was one of the young women EH dated in the spring of 1919 after his return from Italy following the war.

Susan Lowrey. A fellow member with EH of the Oak Park and River Forest High School class of 1917. They worked together on the school newspaper, the *Trapeze*, during their junior and senior years, first as staff members and then as associate editors.

Frank Earl Mason (1893–1979). A native of Milwaukee, Wisconsin, Mason served as a U.S. Army intelligence officer in WWI and as a military attaché at the U.S. Embassy at the Hague and in Berlin in 1919. In 1920 he joined William Randolph Hearst's International News Service as a Berlin correspondent, becoming London manager in 1921 and manager of the Paris office from 1922 to 1926. He later served as president and general manager of INS (1928–1931) before becoming an executive of the National Broadcasting Company (1931–1945). In 1922 EH sold him stories about the Greco-Turkish War that were published under the by-line John Hadley.

John McClure (1893–1956). Managing editor of the New Orleans literary magazine *Double Dealer*, to whom EH submitted work on the advice of Sherwood Anderson. EH's fable "A Divine Gesture" and poem "Ultimately" appeared in the May and June 1922 issues, respectively.

Harriet Monroe (1860–1936). Founder and publisher of *Poetry: A Magazine of Verse*, established in Chicago in 1912. Funded by subscription and wealthy patrons, the magazine aimed to elevate the status of poetry and promote new talent by paying for contributions and offering an annual prize. Among its contributors were such figures as Ezra Pound, T. S. Eliot, Marianne Moore, William Carlos Williams, and Robert Frost. Monroe accepted six of EH's poems for publication in the January 1923 issue of *Poetry*.

Edwin Pailthorp (1900–1972). The son of a local lawyer, he was one of EH's Petoskey friends. After withdrawing from the University of Michigan because of illness, Pailthorp moved to Toronto at about the same time as EH to work at one of the Connables' Woolworth stores. [Dutch]

Ezra Pound (1885–1972). American poet best known for *The Cantos* and for his role as a mentor and advisor to other modernist writers, including T. S. Eliot. Almost immediately after he and EH met in Paris via a letter of introduction from Sherwood Anderson, Pound became one of EH's earliest and strongest advocates. Pound helped him develop his writing and negotiate the politics of literary Paris, and their friendship lasted throughout EH's life.

Grace Edith Quinlan (1906–1964). A Petoskey native, Quinlan was one of the high school girls in EH's social circle when he lived there in the fall of 1919 to devote himself to writing after his return from the war. EH and Quinlan enjoyed a close "brother–sister" friendship and carried on a frequent and affectionate correspondence in 1920–1921 after he moved to Chicago. [G., Gee, Sister Luke]

Coles Van Brunt Seeley, Jr. A native of Newark, New Jersey, he served with EH in the American Red Cross Ambulance Service Section 4. According to fellow ARC veteran Henry Villard, Seeley had nearly blown his hands off and lost his eyesight in his quest for a battlefield souvenir, and he was hospitalized with EH and Villard in Milan in 1918 (Villard and Nagel, 13–14). Seeley was immortalized in chapter 17 of *A Farewell to Arms* as one of Frederic Henry's hospital mates, "a fine boy who had tried to unscrew the fuse-cap from a combination shrapnel shell for a souvenir."

Isabelle Simmons (1901–1964). A next-door neighbor of the Hemingway family on North Kenilworth Avenue, Simmons graduated from Oak Park and River Forest High School in 1920 and attended the University of Chicago 1920–1922. [Issy]

Katharine Foster Smith (1891–1947). Bill Smith's sister and one of EH's closest friends before his marriage to Hadley. A native of St. Louis, she was one of four children of William Benjamin Smith, a professor of mathematics, and Katharine Drake Merrill; after their mother died in 1899, the children were raised by their maternal aunt, spending summers in Horton Bay. Kate attended Mary Institute with Hadley and introduced her to EH in Chicago in the fall of 1920. She earned an A.B. degree in English and journalism from the University of Missouri in 1920 and pursued a writing career. She married American writer John Dos Passos in 1929. [Kate, Butstein, Stut]

William B. Smith, Jr. (1895–1972). Friend from Horton Bay, Michigan, where he and his sister, Kate, spent summers in a farmhouse renovated by their aunt and guardian, Mrs. Charles, and her husband, Joseph William Charles, a St. Louis physician. For several years Bill was one of EH's closest companions and con-fidants, and he served as best man at his wedding to Hadley. The relationship cooled after EH quarreled with Bill's brother, Y. K. Smith, in 1921; the men renewed their friendship in 1924, but it never fully regained its earlier vigor. [Bill, Bird, Boid, Avis, Honest Will]

Yeremya Kenley Smith (1887–1969). Older brother of Bill and Kate Smith, he worked in advertising in Chicago and introduced EH to Sherwood Anderson and Carl Sandburg. EH was among the bachelor boarders living in Smith's Chicago apartment from late 1920 through mid-1921. EH's vocal disapproval of the infidelity of Y. K.'s common-law wife, Doodles, led to the termination of the men's friendship. [Y. K., Yen, Yenlaw, Kenley]

Gertrude Stein (1874–1946). American expatriate writer of the Paris Left Bank whose best-known works include *Three Lives* (1909), *Tender Buttons* (1914), and *The Making of Americans: Being a History of a Family's Progress* (1925). Stein befriended EH soon after his arrival in Paris, and became an influential literary mentor and advisor. In turn, EH helped get her work published in 1924 in the *Transatlantic Review*. The relationship degenerated in 1925, culminating in EH's satire of Stein in his first novel, *The Torrents of Spring*.

F. Thessin. Coach at Culver Military Academy, a college preparatory boarding school in Culver, Indiana, to whom EH wrote in 1917.

Alice B. Toklas (1877–1967). Gertrude Stein's lifelong partner from 1907, she served as hostess at the literary and artistic gatherings at their residence, 27, rue de Fleurus, where EH was a frequent visitor. She and Stein were co-godmothers of EH and Hadley's son, John, born in 1923. She was immortalized in Stein's *The Autobiography of Alice B. Toklas* (1933).

Dale Wilson (1894–1987). A Missouri native and colleague of EH on the staff of the *Kansas City Star*, Wilson was drafted into the U.S. Navy during WWI. His nickname was "Woodrow," after U.S. President Woodrow Wilson.

CALENDAR OF LETTERS

Date of Correspondence	Recipient	Form	Location of Source Text	Previous Publication*
[c. early July 1907]	Clarence Hemingway	A Postcard S	Meeker	unpublished
28 September and 4 October 1908	Clarence Hemingway	ALS	Meeker	unpublished
[19 October 1908]	Clarence Hemingway	ALS	Stanford	*SL* (intro)
18 December 1908	Grace Hall Hemingway	ALS	Schnack	unpublished
9 June [1909]	Marcelline Hemingway	ALS	Cohen	Sanford; *SL* (intro)
9 June 1909	Grace Hall and Marcelline Hemingway	ALS	UT	unpublished
[c. 10 June 1909]	Grace Hall Hemingway	ALS	JFK	unpublished
[c. 17 June 1909]	Grace Hall and Marcelline Hemingway	ALS	JFK	*SL* (intro)
[23 July 1909]	Clarence Hemingway	AL	JFK	Griffin
[30 August 1910]	Ursula Hemingway and Ruth Arnold	A Postcard S	IndU	unpublished

*Listed are known full-text English-language publications of EH letters, excluding dealer or sale catalog listings and newspaper articles.

Date of Correspondence	Recipient	Form	Location of Source Text	Previous Publication
10 September 1910	Clarence Hemingway	ALS	IndU	unpublished
[11 September 1910]	Clarence Hemingway	A Postcard S	IndU	unpublished
13 September 1910	Marcelline Hemingway	ALS	UT	unpublished
[c. 1912]	Charles C. Spink and Son	ALS	JFK	unpublished
[c. second week of May 1912]	Clarence Hemingway	ALS	Sotheby's catalog	unpublished
22 October 1912	Leicester and Nevada Butler Hall	ALS	Private Collection	unpublished
11 May 1913	Clarence Hemingway	ANS	JFK	unpublished
[c. 30 August 1913]	Anson Hemingway	A Postcard S	JFK	unpublished
[c. late August 1913]	Clarence and Grace Hall Hemingway	A Postcard S	JFK	unpublished
[c. late August-1 September 1913]	Clarence Hemingway	A Postcard S	JFK	unpublished
[c. June 1914]	[Unknown]	Inscription	Sotheby's catalog	unpublished
2 September 1914	Grace Hall Hemingway	ALS	JFK	unpublished
8 September 1914	Grace Hall Hemingway	ALS	JFK	Griffin
10 April [1915 or 1916]	*Baseball Magazine*	TLScc	IndU	unpublished
[5 May 1915]	Marcelline Hemingway	ANS	phJFK	Sanford
17 July 1915	"Carissimus"	ALS	JFK	unpublished

Date of Correspondence	Recipient	Form	Location of Source Text	Previous Publication
31 July 1915	Grace Hall Hemingway	ALS	JFK	unpublished
[16 September 1915]	Clarence and Grace Hall Hemingway	A Postcard S	JFK	unpublished
[16 September 1915]	Ursula and Madelaine Hemingway	A Postcard S	PSU	unpublished
[c. 1916]	Susan Lowrey	ANS	OPPL	Morris Buske, *Hemingway's Education, A Re-Examination: Oak Park High School and the Legacy of Principal Hanna* (Lewiston, New York: Edwin Mellen Press, 2007)
[c. January 1916]	[Unknown]	AN	UTulsa	unpublished
[c. 18 March 1916]	Emily Goetzmann	ALS	Yale	unpublished
[c. Spring 1916 or 1917]	[Unknown]	AN	UTulsa	unpublished
[c. Spring 1916]	[Unknown]	AN	UTulsa	unpublished
[c. Spring 1916]	[Unknown]	AN	JFK	unpublished
[c. Spring 1916]	[Unknown]	AN	JFK	unpublished
20 June 1916	Marcelline Hemingway	ALS	phJFK	Sanford
13 July [1916]	Emily Goetzmann	ALS	JFK	unpublished
30 January 1917	F. Thessin	TLS	JFK	unpublished
[c. Spring 1917]	Al [Walker]	ALS	JFK	unpublished
[3 April 1917]	Clarence Hemingway	A Postcard S	IndU	unpublished

Date of Correspondence	Recipient	Form	Location of Source Text	Previous Publication
[5 April 1917]	Clarence Hemingway	A Postcard S	Swann Galleries catalog	unpublished
[c. late June 1917]	Fannie Biggs	ALS	JFK	Georgianna Main, *Pip-Pip to Hemingway in Something From Marge* (Bloomington, Indiana: iUniverse, Inc., 2010)
[3 August 1917]	Grace Hall Hemingway	ALS	JFK	unpublished
6 August [1917]	Anson Hemingway	ALS	JFK	*SL*
[c. 3 September 1917]	Clarence Hemingway	ALS	IndU	unpublished
6 September 1917	Hemingway Family	ALS	IndU	unpublished
[11 September 1917]	Clarence Hemingway	ALS	IndU	unpublished
12 September [1917]	Clarence Hemingway	ALS	IndU	unpublished
14 September [1917]	Clarence and Grace Hall Hemingway	ALS	JFK	unpublished
[15 September 1917]	Clarence Hemingway	A Postcard S	IndU	unpublished
[15 September 1917]	Marcelline Hemingway	A Postcard S	phJFK	Sanford
[16 September 1917]	Clarence Hemingway	A Postcard S	IndU	unpublished
19 September 1917	Anson Hemingway	ALS	JFK	unpublished
[19 September 1917]	Clarence Hemingway	ALS	JFK	*SL*

Date of Correspondence	Recipient	Form	Location of Source Text	Previous Publication
24 September 1917	Clarence Hemingway	ALS	PSU	unpublished
25 September 1917	Clarence Hemingway	ALS	IndU	unpublished
17 October [1917]	Hemingway Family	ALS	JFK	unpublished
25 October 1917	Clarence Hemingway	ALS	JFK	unpublished
[26 October 1917]	Marcelline Hemingway	ALS	phJFK	Sanford
[5 November 1917]	Madelaine, Ursula, Carol, and Leicester Hemingway	TL with typewritten signature	JFK	unpublished
[c. 30 October and 6 November 1917]	Marcelline Hemingway	ALS/TLS	phJFK	Sanford
15 November [1917]	Clarence and Grace Hall Hemingway	TL/ALS	JFK	unpublished
19 November [1917]	Hemingway Family	TL with typewritten signature	JFK	*SL*
21 [November 1917]	Grace Hall Hemingway	TLS	JFK	unpublished
[24 November 1917]	Hemingway Family	TL with typewritten signature	JFK	unpublished
[c. 28 November 1917]	Hemingway Family	TL with typewritten signature	JFK	unpublished
30 November [1917]	Clarence Hemingway	ALS	JFK	unpublished
[6 December 1917]	Clarence and Grace Hall Hemingway	TL with typewritten signature	IndU	unpublished

Date of Correspondence	Recipient	Form	Location of Source Text	Previous Publication
[17 December 1917]	Clarence and Grace Hall Hemingway	TL with typewritten signature	JFK	unpublished
2 January 1918	Hemingway Family	ALS	JFK	unpublished
[c. January 1918]	Madelaine Hemingway	TL with typewritten signature	PSU	unpublished
8 January [1918]	Marcelline Hemingway	TLS	James Sanford	unpublished
16 January 1918	Grace Hall Hemingway	ALS	JFK	*SL*
[c. 30 January 1918]	Hemingway Family	TLS	IndU	unpublished
[c. 30 January 1918]	Marcelline Hemingway	ALS	phJFK	Sanford
[12 February 1918]	Marcelline Hemingway	TLS with autograph postscript	PSU	unpublished
[12 February 1918]	Adelaide Hemingway	TLS	IndU	unpublished
[23 February 1918]	Grace Hall Hemingway	TLS	JFK	unpublished
[2 March 1918]	Grace Hall Hemingway	TLS	JFK	*SL*
[2 March 1918]	Marcelline Hemingway	TLS	James Sanford	Sanford
[8 March 1918]	Marcelline Hemingway	TL	phJFK	Sanford
14 March 1918	Clarence Hemingway	ALS	JFK	Griffin
23 March [1918]	Hemingway Family	ALS	JFK	unpublished

Date of Correspondence	Recipient	Form	Location of Source Text	Previous Publication
16 April 1918	Clarence Hemingway	TLS with autograph postscript	Zieman	unpublished
19 April [1918]	Clarence and Grace Hall Hemingway	TL/ALS	UMD	*SL*
[12 May 1918]	Anson and Adelaide Hemingway	A Postcard S	JFK	Griffin
[12 May 1918]	Hemingway Family	ALS	JFK	unpublished
[13 May 1918]	Anson, Adelaide, and Grace Adelaide Hemingway	A Postcard S	JFK	unpublished
[14 May 1918]	Hemingway Family	ALS	JFK	*SL*
[17–18 May 1918]	Hemingway Family	ALS	JFK	unpublished
19 May [1918]	Clarence Hemingway	Cable	JFK	unpublished
[19 May 1918]	Clarence Hemingway	ALS	JFK	Griffin
19 May [1918]	Dale Wilson	ALS	PUL	*SL*
[20 May 1918]	Hemingway Family	ALS	JFK	Griffin
[c. 31 May] and 2 June [1918]	Hemingway Family	TLS with autograph postscript	IndU	*SL*
[c. 3 June 1918]	Hemingway Family	ALSFrag	IndU	unpublished
[9 June 1918]	Clarence Hemingway	A Postcard S	PSU	unpublished

Date of Correspondence	Recipient	Form	Location of Source Text	Previous Publication
[c. 9 June 1918]	a friend at the *Kansas City Star*	Postcard [excerpt]	*KCStar*	unpublished
[c. 9 June 1918]	a friend at the *Kansas City Star*	Postcard [excerpt]	*KCStar*	unpublished
[c. late June–early July 1918]	Ruth [Morrison ?]	ALS	UMD	*SL*
14 July 1918	Clarence and Grace Hall Hemingway	ANS	PSU	Sanford
[16 July 1918]	Hemingway Family	Cable	JFK	unpublished
21 July [1918]	Hemingway Family	ALS	IndU	*SL*; Villard and Nagel
29 July [1918]	Grace Hall Hemingway	ALS	IndU	Villard and Nagel
31 July [1918]	James Gamble	TLS	phJFK	unpublished
4 August [1918]	Hemingway Family	ALS	PSU	unpublished
7 August [1918]	Clarence, Grace Hall, and Marcelline Hemingway	ALS	IndU	Villard and Nagel
[8 August 1918]	Marcelline Hemingway	ALS	phJFK	Sanford
[c. 14 August 1918]	Clarence Hemingway	Cable [transcription]	JFK	unpublished
14 August [1918]	Elizabeth Dilworth	A Postcard S	Metzger	unpublished

Date of Correspondence	Recipient	Form	Location of Source Text	Previous Publication
18 August [1918]	Hemingway Family	ALS	IndU	Sanford; *SL*; Robert W. Trogdon, ed., *Ernest Hemingway: A Literary Reference* (New York: Carroll and Graf, 2002); Villard and Nagel
29 August [1918]	Grace Hall Hemingway	ALS	IndU	Villard and Nagel
[c. August 1918]	Henry [S. Villard]	ALS	JFK	unpublished
11 September 1918	Clarence Hemingway	ALS	IndU	*SL*; Villard and Nagel
16 September [1918]	Ursula Hemingway	ALS	Schnack	unpublished
21 September 1918	Marcelline and Madelaine Hemingway	ALS	Cohen	Sanford
[26 September 1918]	Marcelline Hemingway	A Postcard S	JFK	Sanford
26 September [1918]	Clarence Hemingway	A Postcard S	IndU	Villard and Nagel
29 September 1918	Hemingway Family	ALS	IndU	Villard and Nagel
18 October [1918]	Hemingway Family	TLS	IndU	*SL*; Villard and Nagel
1 November [1918]	Hemingway Family	ALS	IndU	Villard and Nagel
11 November [1918]	Hemingway Family	ALS	IndU	Villard and Nagel
11 November [1918]	Marcelline Hemingway	ALS	James Sanford	Sanford
14 November [1918]	Clarence Hemingway	ALS	IndU	Villard and Nagel

Date of Correspondence	Recipient	Form	Location of Source Text	Previous Publication
23 November [1918]	Marcelline Hemingway	ALS	James Sanford	Sanford
[28 November 1918]	Hemingway Family	ALS	IndU	Villard and Nagel
11 December [1918]	Hemingway Family	ALS	IndU	Villard and Nagel
[13 December 1918]	William B. Smith, Jr.	ALS	PUL	*SL*
13 December [1918]	William D. Horne, Jr.	ALS	Newberry	unpublished
[3 February 1919]	William D. Horne, Jr.	ALS	Newberry	Griffin
3 March [1919]	James Gamble	TLS with autograph postscript	Knox	*SL*
[5 March 1919]	William D. Horne, Jr.	TLS with autograph postscript	Newberry	unpublished
30 March [1919]	William D. Horne, Jr.	TLS	Newberry	Griffin
9 April [1919]	Howell G. Jenkins	TL	JFK	unpublished
22 April 1919	Kathryn Longwell	A Postcard S	JFK	unpublished
18 and 27 April [1919]	James Gamble	TLS with autograph postscript	CMU	Griffin; Main
30 April [1919]	Lawrence T. Barnett	TLS with autograph postscript	JFK	*SL*

Date of Correspondence	Recipient	Form	Location of Source Text	Previous Publication
24 [May 1919]	Clarence Hemingway	A Postcard S	IndU	unpublished
[25 May 1919]	Clarence Hemingway	A Postcard S	PSU	unpublished
31 May [1919]	Clarence Hemingway	A Postcard S	IndU	unpublished
7 June [1919]	Clarence Hemingway	A Postcard S	PSU	unpublished
[9 June 1919]	Clarence Hemingway	ALS	CMU	unpublished
[c. mid-June 1919]	Clarence Hemingway	ALS	UT	unpublished
15 June [1919]	Howell G. Jenkins	ALS	PUL	*SL*
2 July 1919	William D. Horne, Jr.	TL with typewritten signature	Newberry	unpublished
[15 July 1919]	Howell G. Jenkins	TLS	phPUL	unpublished
26 [July 1919]	Howell G. Jenkins and Lawrence T. Barnett	ALS	phPUL	*SL*
7 August 1919	William D. Horne, Jr.	ALS	Newberry	unpublished
[16 August 1919]	Clarence Hemingway	A Postcard S	PSU	unpublished
27 August [1919]	Clarence Hemingway	A Postcard S	CMU	unpublished
[c. 31 August 1919]	Howell G. Jenkins	ALS	phPUL	*SL*
[3 September 1919]	Clarence Hemingway	T Postcard S	PSU	unpublished

Date of Correspondence	Recipient	Form	Location of Source Text	Previous Publication
[c. 17 September 1919]	Ursula Hemingway	TL/ALS	Mainland Collection at NCMC	unpublished
[18 September 1919]	Coles Van Brunt Seeley, Jr.	ALS [excerpt]	Christie's catalog	unpublished
[c. late September 1919]	[Unknown]	AL	NYPL	unpublished
28 October [1919]	Clarence Hemingway	TLS with autograph postscript	phPSU	unpublished
11 November [1919]	Grace Hall Hemingway	TLS	Mainland Collection at NCMC	unpublished
23 November 1919	[Georgianna Bump]	Inscription	Private Collection	Main
4 December [1919]	Grace Hall Hemingway	TLS	Mainland Collection at NCMC	unpublished
4 December [1919]	William B. Smith, Jr.	TLS	Stanford	unpublished
[c. mid-December 1919]	Ursula Hemingway	TL with typewritten signature	Mainland Collection at NCMC	unpublished
[20 December 1919]	Howell G. Jenkins	TLS	Stanford	*SL*
[c. 26 December 1919]	Grace Quinlan	ALS	Yale	unpublished
[1 January 1920]	Grace Quinlan	ALS	Yale	*SL*
[c. mid-January 1920]	Edwin Pailthorp	TCD with typewritten signature	UTulsa	unpublished
16 February 1920	Dorothy Connable	TLS	phPSU	*SL*

Date of Correspondence	Recipient	Form	Location of Source Text	Previous Publication
25 March 1920	William D. Horne, Jr.	TLS	Newberry	unpublished
6 April [1920]	Grace Hall Hemingway	TLS	PSU	unpublished
22 April 1920	Clarence and Grace Hall Hemingway	TLcc	JFK	unpublished
27 April [1920]	Clarence and Grace Hall Hemingway	ALS	PSU	unpublished
1 June [1920]	Harriet Gridley Connable	ALS	phPUL	*SL*
[24] June 1920	Grace Hall Hemingway	A Postcard S	JFK	unpublished
1 August [1920]	Grace Quinlan	ALS	Yale	unpublished
8 August 1920	Grace Quinlan	ALS	Yale	*SL*
[16 September 1920]	Howell G. Jenkins	TL with typewritten signature	phPUL	*SL*
30 September [1920]	Grace Quinlan	TLS	Yale	*SL*
9 October [1920]	Grace Hall Hemingway	TLS	PSU	unpublished
25 [October 1920]	William B. Smith, Jr.	TL with typewritten signature	PUL	unpublished
29 November [1920]	*Chicago Daily Tribune*	TL	UTulsa	unpublished
16 November and 1 December [1920]	Grace Quinlan	TLS with autograph postscript	Yale	unpublished
[2 December 1920]	*Chicago Daily Tribune*	TLcc	UTulsa	unpublished

Date of Correspondence	Recipient	Form	Location of Source Text	Previous Publication
[22 December 1920]	Grace Hall Hemingway	TLS	JFK	*SL*
23 December [1920]	Hadley Richardson	ALSFrag	JFK	unpublished
[c. 27 December 1920]	James Gamble	TCD	JFK	*SL*, Griffin
[29 December 1920]	Hadley Richardson	AL	JFK	unpublished
[c. 1921]	Miss Conger	TL with typewritten signature	JFK	unpublished
[10 January 1921]	Grace Hall Hemingway	TLS	JFK	*SL*
[before 26 January 1921]	William D. Horne, Jr.	TLS	Newberry	unpublished
[c. January 1921]	William B. Smith, Jr.	AL	JFK	unpublished
[15 February 1921]	William B. Smith, Jr.	TL with typewritten signature	PUL	unpublished
25 February [1921]	Grace Quinlan	TLS	phPDL	unpublished
2 March 1921	John Bone	ALDS	JFK	unpublished
4 March [1921]	William B. Smith, Jr.	AL	JFK	unpublished
16 March [1921]	Irene Goldstein	TLS	Stanford	unpublished
[after 7 April 1921]	Marjorie Bump	ALD	JFK	Main
15 April 1921	Clarence Hemingway	TLS	JFK	*SL*
[28 April 1921]	William B. Smith, Jr.	TLS	PUL	*SL*

Date of Correspondence	Recipient	Form	Location of Source Text	Previous Publication
[20 May 1921]	Marcelline Hemingway	TLS	phJFK	*SL*; Sanford
[25 May 1921]	Marcelline Hemingway	TLS	James Sanford	Sanford
[7 July 1921]	Hadley Richardson	ACDS	JFK	unpublished
[c. 21 July 1921]	Grace Quinlan and Georgianna Bump	TLS	Yale	unpublished
21 July 1921	Grace Quinlan	TLS	Yale	*SL*; Main
[c. late July 1921]	Grace Quinlan	TL	JFK	unpublished
[c. 3–5 August 1921]	William B. Smith, Jr.	TLS	PUL	unpublished
[7 August 1921]	Grace Quinlan	ALS	Yale	*SL*
[8 August 1921]	Grace Hall Hemingway	TLS	PSU	unpublished
[11 August 1921]	Marcelline Hemingway	TLS	JFK	Sanford
[19 August 1921]	Grace Quinlan	TLS	Yale	*SL*
[c. mid–late August 1921]	William B. Smith, Jr.	TLS with autograph postscript	Meeker	unpublished
[1 October 1921]	Y. K. Smith	TL	JFK	*SL*
29 October 1921	John Bone	TLD	JFK	unpublished
[8 December 1921]	Hemingway Family	ALS	JFK	*SL*
20 December 1921	Hemingway Family	ALS	JFK	*SL*
[c. 20 December 1921]	William B. Smith, Jr.	ALS	PUL	*SL*

Date of Correspondence	Recipient	Form	Location of Source Text	Previous Publication
[c. 23 December 1921]	Sherwood and Tennessee Anderson	TL/ALS	Newberry	*SL*
26 December [1921]	Howell G. Jenkins	ALS	Stanford	*SL*
8 January [1922]	Howell G. Jenkins	ALS	Stanford	*SL*
[c. late January 1922]	Hemingway Family	TLS	IndU	unpublished
[c. 25 January 1922]	Marcelline Hemingway	TLS	James Sanford	Sanford
[27 January 1922]	Katharine Foster Smith	TLS	UVA	unpublished
30 January [1922]	Lewis Galantière	A Postcard S	Columbia	unpublished
3 February 1922	Clarence Hemingway	ALS	PSU	unpublished
14 and 15 February 1922	Grace Hall Hemingway	AL/TLS	PSU	unpublished
[27 February 1922]	Lewis Galantière	A Postcard S	Columbia	unpublished
9 March [1922]	Sherwood Anderson	TLS with autograph postscript	Newberry	*SL*; Trogdon *Literary Reference*
20 March 1922	Howell G. Jenkins	TLS	UT	*SL*
20 April 1922	Howell G. Jenkins	A Postcard S	phPUL	unpublished
[c. late April 1922]	Marcelline Hemingway	T Postcard with typewritten signature	James Sanford	Sanford

Date of Correspondence	Recipient	Form	Location of Source Text	Previous Publication
[c. late April 1922]	Clarence Hemingway	T Postcard with typewritten signature	JFK	unpublished
[c. late April 1922]	Madelaine Hemingway	T Postcard with typewritten signature	PSU	unpublished
2 May 1922	Grace Hall Hemingway	TLS	PSU	unpublished
2 May 1922	Clarence Hemingway	TLS	JFK	*SL*
12 May 1922	Kate Buss	TLS	Brown	unpublished
24 May 1922	Clarence Hemingway	TLS	JFK	*SL*
11 June 1922	Gertrude Stein and Alice B. Toklas	TLS	Yale	*SL*
14 June 1922	Howell G. Jenkins	A Postcard S	phPUL	unpublished
16 July 1922	Harriet Monroe	TLS	UChicago	*SL*
4 August [1922]	Howell G. Jenkins	A Postcard S	phPUL	unpublished
[12 August 1922]	Ezra Pound	A Postcard S	IndU	unpublished
[c. late August 1922]	Ezra Pound	TLS	IndU	unpublished
25 August 1922	Hemingway Family	TLS	JFK	*SL*
28 August 1922	Gertrude Stein	A Postcard S	Yale	unpublished

Date of Correspondence	Recipient	Form	Location of Source Text	Previous Publication
31 August 1922	Ezra Pound	A Postcard	IndU	unpublished
[20 September 1922]	Gertrude Stein	A Postcard S	Yale	unpublished
[c. September 1922]	John McClure	AL	JFK	unpublished
26 September [1922]	Howell G. Jenkins	A Postcard S	phPUL	unpublished
[c. 27 September 1922]	Gertrude Stein	A Postcard S	Yale	unpublished
27 October 1922	John Bone	TLcc with enclosures	JFK	unpublished
[3 November 1922]	Gertrude Stein	T Postcard S	Yale	unpublished
[8 November 1922]	Ezra Pound	ALS	IndU	unpublished
16 November 1922	Harriet Monroe	TLS	UChicago	*SL*
24 November 1922	Hadley Richardson Hemingway	Cable	JFK	unpublished
25 November 1922	Hadley Richardson Hemingway	Cable	JFK	unpublished
[c. 26 November 1922]	Miriam Hapgood	TLS	Stanford	unpublished
[c. 26 November 1922]	Pier Vincenzo Bellia	A Postcard	JFK	unpublished
[27 November 1922]	Frank Mason	ACDS	JFK	unpublished
[28 November 1922]	Hadley Richardson Hemingway	TL with typewritten signature and autograph postscript	JFK	*SL*

Date of Correspondence	Recipient	Form	Location of Source Text	Previous Publication
[c. 1 December 1922]	Isabelle Simmons	TL/ALSFrag	PUL	*SL*
5 December 1922	Alice Langelier	TLS	JFK	unpublished
[10 December 1922]	Miriam Hapgood	ALS	Stanford	unpublished
[c. 14 December 1922]	Frank Mason	TCD	JFK	unpublished
[c. 15 December 1922]	Frank Mason	TCD	JFK	unpublished
15 December 1922	Frank Mason	TLcc	JFK	unpublished

INDEX OF RECIPIENTS

In this index of recipients, only the first page of each letter is cited. Letters to more than one person are indexed under each name and marked † (except in the case of letters directed to EH's family or another group in general).

GENERAL INDEX

References to works by Ernest Hemingway appear under his name. Names of baseball players, boxers, operas, plays and revues, ships, songs, and strikes are consolidated under those categorical headings. References to battles and other aspects of the First World War are consolidated under "World War I." All biblical references are gathered under "Bible." References to localities within a particular city (hotels, restaurants, bars, churches, schools, museums, monuments, and other sites) appear under the name of that city.

letter to EH, 279, 289
Bump, Sidney S., 45, 280, 381
Bumstead, Dale, Jr., 48, 62, 63
Bumstead, Frances, 158, 159
Bumstead, Mr. and Mrs. Dale, Sr., 47, 48
Burke, Mary, 21
Burns, Bill, 293, 297
Burns, Robert
  "Red, Red Rose, A," 174, 176
Burroughs, Edgar Rice, 167, 168
  Tarzan of the Apes, 167, 168
Buss, Kate, 343, 381
  Studies in the Chinese Drama, 343
Butler, Dorothy, lxxvii, 349, 368
Butler, James and Belle, 383
Butstein. *See* Smith, Katharine Foster
Byron, George Gordon, Lord
  "Prisoner of Chillon, The," 320

California Oil Burner Company, 54, 56
Camp Doniphan, Oklahoma, 55, 56
Camp Funston, Kansas, 62, 63, 65, 66
Camping and Camp Cooking (Bates),
  246, 247
Canary Islands, 162
Cannon, Lucelle, 26, 28, 113, 114
Cape au Moine (Switzerland), 344, 345
Capper, Governor Arthur, 65, 66, 79
Capracotta, Italy, 290
Capri, 290
Caracciolo, Domenico, xxiii, 173, 175, 193, 194
Cardinella, Salvatore "Sam," 280, 281, 307
Carp, Carpative, or Carper. *See* Jenkins,
  Howell G.
Caruso, Enrico, 231
Castiloni, Dr., 122
Castle, William R., Jr., 129
Castro, Fidel, xiii
Cavanaugh, Loretta, 137, 167, 168
Cézanne, Paul, lxviii
Chamby-sur-Montreux, Switzerland, lxxvi,
  lxxvii, 316, 322, 343–344, 346, 373, 375
  localities
    Chalet Chamby, 325, 373, 375, 379
    Grand Hôtel des Narcisses, 372, 373
Chandler (classmate), 5
Channahon, Illinois, 37, 38
Chantilly, France, 339, 340, 341, 342
Chaplin, Charlie, 31, 33

Charles Scribner's Sons. *See* Scribner's
Charles, Joseph, 66, 186, 209, 210, 236, 237,
  239, 244, 245, 325, 326
Charles, Mrs. Joseph, 65, 66, 185, 186, 189, 203,
  204, 206, 209, 210, 237, 241, 246, 270,
  294, 297, 306, 325, 326, 334, 387
Charlevoix County (Michigan), 14
Charlevoix, Lake. *See* Pine Lake (Michigan)
Charlevoix, Michigan, 16, 21, 42, 46, 183, 184,
  197, 198, 199, 200, 202, 236, 237, 239,
  240, 294, 297, 312, 324
  Cook's, 237, 240, 307
Chateau d'Oex, Switzerland, 372, 373
Chautauqua, Lake (New York), 6, 8
Chekhov, Anton, 376
Chénier, André-Marie, 255
Chicago, lxvii, 46, 77, 78, 93, 163, 182, 201, 206,
  227, 230, 232, 241, 246, 252, 277,
  290, 298
  localities
    19th Ward, 297, 298
    Auditorium Building, 65, 66, 222, 254
    Blackstone Hotel, 65, 66, 70
    Bush Temple, 6
    Chicago Beach Hotel, 144, 146, 325, 335
    Chicago Coliseum, 14
    Chicago Stockyards, 310
    Cohan's Grand Theatre, 265, 271
    College Inn, 248, 249
    Colonial Theatre, 219, 222, 254
    Congress Hotel, 197, 198
    Crerar Library, 287
    Ferretti Gymnasium, 301, 302
    Friar's Inn, 216, 217
    Gilmore's Gym, 36
    Kroch's International Book Store,
      341, 342
    LaSalle Hotel, 271, 272
    Lincoln Park Zoo, 329
    Marigold Gardens, 258, 260
    Municipal Pier (Navy Pier),
      196–197, 300
    Orchestra Hall, 263, 264
    Playhouse Theatre, 254
    Powers' Theatre, 254, 263, 265
    Royal Café, 287
    Rush Street, lix
    Venice Café, 218, 221, 227, 241
    Victor House, 248, 249

"Recessional" (Kipling), 39, 40
Recoaro, Italy, 345
Red. *See* Bump, Marjorie
"Red Gap and the Big League Stuff" (Wilson),
133, 134
"Red, Red Rose, A" (Burns), 174, 176
Reims, France, 339, 340
Reynolds, Jean, 238, 240
Reynolds, Michael S., xii, 279
Rhine River, 348, 352, 374
Rhône River, 326
Rhône Valley (Switzerland), 326, 327, 344
Rhône, Canal du (Switzerland), 344
Rice, Alfred, xix
Richardson, Hadley. *See* Hemingway, Hadley
Richardson
Riviera, 121, 126
Robben, John, xxi
Rochers de Naye (Switzerland), 372, 373
Rockefeller, Edith, 351
Rogers Park (Chicago), 125, 127
Rogovski, Florence, 62, 63
Rohrbach, Henri, 321, 323
Rohrbach, Marie, 319, 321, 323, 328
Rome, 126, 149, 156, 260, 261
Roosevelt, President Theodore, 80
Rosa, Monte, 145, 146
Rosenfeld, Paul Leopold, 364, 365
Rosenthal, Mrs., 276, 277
Ross, Lillian, xx, xxvi, xxx
Rothermere, Mary Lilian Share, Lady, 368
Rouse, Robert, 277, 282, 285, 309, 334
Rovereto, Italy, 346
Rowohlt, Ernst, xvii
Ruffo, Titta, 221, 222, 253, 254
Ruggles, Harold Lee, 245, 251, 254
Russia, 344, 347
Russian Revolution (October 1917), 48
Ryan's Point (Walloon Lake), 238

Salt Water Ballads (Masefield), 26, 27
Sam or Sammy. *See* Sampson, Harold
Sammarelli, Captain, 135, 139
Sampson, Harold, 15, 16, 17, 28, 31, 32, 33
Sampson, Mr. and Mrs. (Harold's parents), 15
San Francisco, California, 233
Sandburg, Carl, lxvii, 266, 267, 387
Sanford, John E., 19
Sanford, Marcelline Hemingway, xx, 103

see also Hemingway, Marcelline
Sangro River (Italy), 290
Sanibel Island, Florida, 281
Santa Caterina, Italy, 346
Santa Fe Railway (Atchison, Topeka, and Santa
Fe Railway), 93, 94
Sardinia, 159
Sassoon, Siegfried, 259, 260
Saturday Evening Post, lxv, lxxiv, 140, 169, 172,
174, 211
Savage, C. Bayley, Jr., 55, 56, 60, 61, 62
Schaefer, Jake, 272
Schio, Italy, lxiii, lxxiii, 112, 114, 170, 172, 187,
227, 345, 346
Schlitz Brewing Company, 154
Schoolcraft County (Michigan), 203
Schruns, Austria, xv
Scribner, Charles (II 1854-1930), xiii–xiv
Scribner, Charles (III 1890-1952), xiii–xiv,
xvi, xxx
Scribner, Charles, Jr. (IV 1921-1995), xiii–xiv,
xvi, xix
Scribner's (Charles Scribner's Sons), xvi, xx
Scudder, Janet, 353
Second Jungle Book, The (Kipling), 34
Seeger, Alan
"I Have a Rendezvous with Death," 59, 60
Seeley, Coles Van Brunt, Jr., 122, 123, 386
Seested, August, 104, 105
Seney, Michigan, lxxv, 198, 203, 204, 235, 295
Senior Tabula (OPRFHS), lxxii, 16, 28, 29, 42,
56, 77, 92, 307, 348
Senlis, France, 339, 340
Serbia, 126, 127
Sexton, Mr., 27
Seygard, Camille Lane, 353
Seymour Family, 265, 266
Shakespeare and Company, lxviii, lxxvi, 332
Shakespeare, William
Hamlet, 305, 307
Merchant of Venice, The, 47
Midsummer Night's Dream, A, 27, 28
Shanahan, Lisle, 294, 297
Shaw, Carleton, 182, 185, 186, 187, 188, 193,
194, 195, 197, 198, 200, 204, 227
Shay, Frank, 284
Shepard, Ernest Howard "Kipper," 161, 162
Sheridan, Clare, 364, 365–366
Sheridan, Philip Henry, 67